ECONOMIC
DEVELOPMENT

ECONOMIC DEVELOPMENT

The Underdeveloped World and the American Interest

WALTER KRAUSE

Professor of Economics
State University of Iowa

WADSWORTH PUBLISHING COMPANY, INC., BELMONT, CALIFORNIA

L.C. CAT. CARD NO.: 61-7374

PRINTED IN THE UNITED STATES OF AMERICA

MANUFACTURED BY
AMERICAN BOOK–STRATFORD PRESS, INC.

FIRST PRINTING, APRIL 1961
SECOND PRINTING, JUNE 1962

PREFACE

This book is about the world's underdeveloped countries. In scope, it treats the problem of economic development in these countries, *and* the significance of this problem for the United States—hence the full title selected for the volume: *Economic Development: The Underdeveloped World and the American Interest.*

The subject matter is arranged to help those seeking answers to six main questions. What is the nature of the problems that confront underdeveloped countries? What are these countries doing to improve their lot? What more (or different) might these countries reasonably be expected to do in this respect? What is the American interest in the plight of underdeveloped countries, and what is the United States doing as a consequence? What more (or different) might this country reasonably undertake to do? What are the implications for the world, and for this country, of success—or failure—in bettering the situation in underdeveloped countries?

The presentation is oriented toward public policy. The tone of the book is perhaps best grasped when it is noted that the final chapter is frankly titled: "What To Do?" Theory, description, history, and analysis all enter in varying amount, but they are viewed here primarily as means to an end, the end itself being *policy*.

I

Why did I undertake to write this book? There are two main reasons.

First, I felt dissatisfied with the body of literature as it stood. For example, I thought I detected a trend toward stressing the obstacles to development without sufficient emphasis on how action might then proceed. Again, a goodly portion of the literature seemed to me to be highly aggregative in treatment, so that one seeking guidance in how to proceed with specific action here and now was able to get only limited help. These features, particularly, seemed to me to comprise shortcomings in the existing body of literature, a conclusion to which I somewhat reluctantly was drawn during the course of my own professional endeavors both overseas in underdeveloped countries and in Washington.

My own conclusion, further, appeared to be underscored by complaints I heard especially among governmental personnel, both American and foreign, who frequently took a dim view of what looked to them to be a sharp cleavage between "theoreticians of the ivory tower" and "practitioners out on the firing line." It occurred to me that an attempt should be made to bring the two closer together.

Second, I felt a book was needed that would combine material pertaining to *both* the problem of underdevelopedness as seen by underdeveloped countries *and* the interest and activities of the United States in respect to this problem. Specifically, I felt that the present-day underdeveloped countries are not likely to become developed without outside help—not if democratic institutions are to survive or be fostered in the interim. And, if outside help is to be had, the finger seems to point straight at the United States—the country that is, above all others, the one with the means to do something "big" beyond its borders.

II

For whom has this book been written? I had three main categories of readers in mind: students, fellow economists, and public officials, both American and foreign.

Special comment may be in order concerning classroom use of the book. I have sought to provide broad coverage, largely because I believe a better understanding of the subject might thereby be had. I have sought to include various views on controversial matters, and have included sections devoted entirely to major issues. In general, however, I have made no attempt to conceal my own views on specific issues; to the contrary, I have sought to express my own ideas whenever I thought them worthy of print.

Notwithstanding the broadness of coverage, the length of the book should prove approximately right for a one-semester course. Persons who want to pursue additional reading may find useful the references cited at the end of each chapter or major section.

III

In the course of writing a book, one becomes indebted to many persons. Some acknowledgments are therefore due.

I want to express my appreciation to those who read the manuscript, all or in part, at various stages in its evolution, and who offered helpful comment on many scores. Particularly I want to thank Professor Paul R. Olson of the State University of Iowa, Professor Wilson E. Schmidt of The George Washington University, and two government officials who, I hope, will recognize this reference to them, even though I am abiding by their wish for anonymity. Also, I want to thank those of my graduate students who consented to pre-test the manuscript for readability and clarity, as seen from a student standpoint; special thanks are due Ethel Vatter and Robert A. Flammang. I alone, of course, am to be held accountable for what appears in the final version.

Walter Krause
June 1, 1960

CONTENTS

TABLES

FIGURES

ECONOMIC DEVELOPMENT

PART ONE

THE PROBLEM

For unto every one that hath shall be given, and he shall have abundance: but from him that hath not shall be taken away even that which he hath.

MATTHEW 25:39

Most of the world's people live in countries that are *underdeveloped*. The environment in these countries leaves much to be desired by their residents. Part One is devoted to a description of this environment, and to an explanation of how and why the prevailing environment is the basis of a world problem.

1

THE
UNDERDEVELOPED
WORLD

During a recent brief period, leading American news-papers carried news accounts and background com-mentaries from which readers could learn the following:

One-third of the world's people go to bed hungry, even under normal conditions; and when crop failures occur, death by starvation confronts tens of thousands in some countries.

A drought, accompanied by crop failures, had already cost many lives in Haiti; but, even if rain should come, it would be too late to save some people—partly because even the seeds needed for new crops had been eaten.

With no increase in the rate of growth, according to an Indian spokesman, 35 years would elapse before India's per-capita in-come would exceed $2 per week.

The USSR served notice that by the early 1970's, following completion of two projected Seven-Year Plans, the Communist World could be expected to have greater total output than the Free World.

Communist China's aggregate output was said to have grown, during the preceding decade, at a rate three times that of India.

The contrasting methods employed by India and Communist China in their attempts to improve economic conditions hold important implications for the whole world, according to the American Vice-President.

The Prime Minister of India said that his country needs and wants more external assistance, and means to get it—if not from the US, then from elsewhere.

US output, according to a Department of Commerce release, was at the highest level ever. Among other evidences of national well-being, the ratio of motor vehicles to people stood at 1:2.5.

4

According to a former President of the US, the Congress should not cut US foreign aid unless it finds the financial state of the country so poor that it is also ready to cut the salaries of its own members.

A critic of US foreign aid said that this country should concern itself more with its own problems and less with the problems of peoples living in farflung places of the world.

An American official was responsible, allegedly, for triggering civil disturbances in aid-receiving Bolivia with an off-the-cuff statement to the effect that the country's acute economic problems could be best solved by abolition of the country as a national entity.

The foregoing items, disassociated as they may seem at first glance, actually are closely related. Each in its own way is reflective of something central: wide economic disparities exist among countries.

It is obvious, of course, that the countries of the world are not equally well off. The world is a place of "rich lands and poor,"[1] with many shadings of opulence and poverty in between. The presence of such differences doubtless adds up to an interesting fact, under any circumstances. But something more than an interesting fact arises when people *choose* to concern themselves about the differences. Significantly, many people during our time are concerned about the presence of these differences— indeed, the inclination of growing numbers to question the necessity or inevitability of these differences indicates a change of far-reaching consequence. Unlike an earlier day, when the less affluent members of the world community were prone to accept their lot in silent resignation— while the richer members stood aloof—today's scene is one of dissatisfaction in the poorer countries, clamor for corrective action (fed somewhat by the richer countries), and considerable friction all around, despite no little effort to have it otherwise.

Involved are the ingredients of a major world problem—as the sample news reports cited earlier testify. The status-quo, with its wide economic disparities among countries, is being challenged. The poor countries no longer simply *accept,* and the rich countries—by force of circumstance— cannot *ignore,* even if so inclined. If all goes well in the immediate years ahead, the world may see a narrowing in the range of disparities among countries—presumably through gains by the present-day poor countries, rather than through retrogression by the rich. But such achievement perhaps is not likely without much pain and conflict, even under favorable circumstances (and these are by no means assured). Or, such achievement perhaps is not in store at all—as opportunity becomes a casualty of lethargy, misguided action, or destructive clashes of interest. Indeed, *whatever* the course of events, an important chapter in history

---

[1] To draw upon the descriptive title of a recent book: G. Myrdal, *Rich Lands and Poor* (New York: Harper and Brothers, 1957).

appears destined to be written about the poor countries, their status, aspirations, and achievements (or lack of such).

WHAT IS AN UNDERDEVELOPED COUNTRY?

Admittedly, the world consists of poor countries alongside rich. But how does one distinguish between the two? Economists make the distinction by resorting to a particular definitional framework. The labels *underdeveloped* and *developed* are substituted for *poor* and *rich,* and each of these is then defined solely in terms of economic performance. An underdeveloped country can be defined as one that, on the average, affords its inhabitants an end product of consumption and material well-being inferior to that being provided in developed countries;[2] conversely, a developed country becomes one that affords an economic end product superior to that of underdeveloped countries.

In attaching the labels *underdeveloped* and *developed* to particular countries, or in interpreting the meaning of these labels when applied to particular countries, one should bear two essential factors in mind. First, the term *underdeveloped* implies relative status. The term takes on meaning as comparisons are made among countries. An underdeveloped country is one that is economically poor *compared with* other countries (that is, with other countries regarded as developed[3]). Implicit, of course, is the notion that a country, even though labeled underdeveloped, is capable of something better eventually (i.e., is technically capable of undergoing development), given known resources and technology.

Second, the term *underdeveloped* is arbitrary in usage. There is no absolute rule as to the precise dividing line between underdeveloped and developed. General agreement on the designations applicable to countries at either extreme of the economic scale is readily had, but classification of countries in intermediate ranges almost always poses a problem. One rule of thumb is to regard as underdeveloped any country whose per-capita income is no greater than one-fourth that of the highest income country. Application of this rule seems to yield tenable results, *in general.* However, instances exist in which application of the rule offers little more than a rough first approximation, with subsequent modification warranted in the light of other considerations.[4]

Despite numerous conceptual and factual difficulties that result in differences among economists in the treatment they accord particular

---

2 The distinction made here between countries can also be made between regions of the same country. For example, Italy may rate classification as a developed country, but its South perhaps should be classed as underdeveloped.

3 Some countries regarded today as developed may become more developed in the future. In a sense, therefore, these countries are also underdeveloped, i.e., under-developed as compared with the development they *might* achieve.

4 However meritorious the income test may be *in general,* it yields doubtful results in particular instances. To illustrate, the test might lead one to conclude that Venezuela

countries in intermediate ranges, there is considerable agreement—as reflected in usage—as to the status of a wide range of countries. The general picture relative to countries customarily classed as underdeveloped is as follows. In number, there are approximately 50 underdeveloped countries (roughly one-half or more of the world's countries). With rare exception, these countries are found in Asia, Africa, and Latin America (Fig. 1). As for population, these countries are the home of some two-thirds of the world's people.

BASIC CHARACTERISTICS

What are some outstanding features of underdeveloped countries? Given the large number of countries concerned, it becomes difficult to make good generalizations. However, several features are sufficiently widespread and distinctive to warrant their being looked upon as earmarks of underdevelopedness.

LOW INCOME

The single fact most basic in a description of the environment in underdeveloped countries is that the prevailing level of income is low— as is the level of production from which this income stems, and which it reflects.[5] The general picture is that the two-thirds of the world's people who live in underdeveloped countries receive but one-third of the total world income being generated (while the one-third living in developed countries receives two thirds of the world's income);[6] thus, *per-capita* income in the underdeveloped world as a whole runs *very much below* that of the developed world.

While low income is general in the underdeveloped world, wide differences exist between major regions and individual countries (and similar differences also exist within the developed world). Examination of income estimates for major regions of the world reveals that, in 1955, per-capita GNP ranged from $2,300 down to $55, with the world norm

---

is developed and that Japan is underdeveloped. If this conclusion seems at variance with what observation leads one to suspect, one should presumably want to search for additional factors relevant for the classification process. For example, in the cited case, should not account be taken of the fact that the Venezuelan economy is characterized by a highly developed sector (in petroleum) alongside general underdevelopment? Again, should not account be taken of differing prospects for income growth? If prospects appear better in Venezuela than in Japan, should this serve as a basis for classifying Venezuela as *still* underdeveloped and Japan as *already* developed?

5 Besides low productivity, a factor technically capable of explaining low income is that of unfavorable export-import trading relationships—e.g., a decrease in the amount of imports that can be had on the basis of a given volume of exports serves, in and of itself, to diminish income within a country. The basic relationship is that income is dependent upon productivity, except insofar as modified by export-import trade.

6 For supporting data, see UN, *National Income and Its Distribution in Under-Developed Countries*, New York, 1951, Table 2, p. 3.

Fig. 1. The Distribution of Underdevelopment, 1955

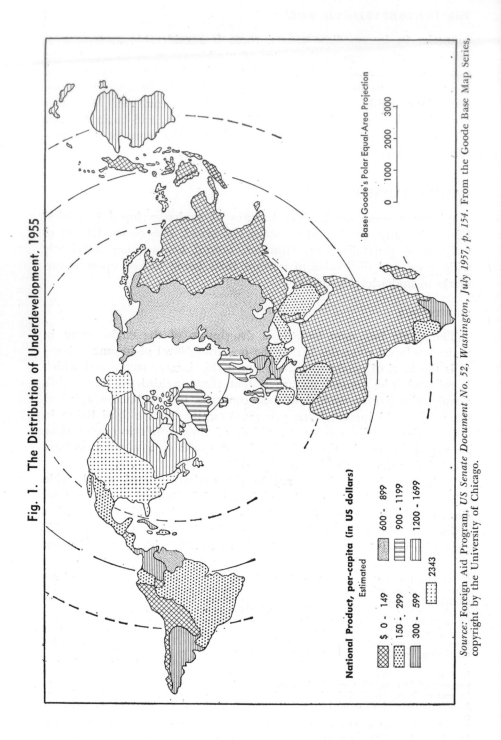

National Product, per-capita (in US dollars)
Estimated

$ 0 - 149   600 - 899
150 - 299   900 - 1199
300 - 599   1200 - 1699

2343

Base: Goode's Polar Equal-Area Projection

0   1000   2000   3000

Source: Foreign Aid Program, *US Senate Document No. 52, Washington, July 1957, p. 154.* From the Goode Base Map Series, copyright by the University of Chicago.

8

Table 1. Gross National Product, Per Capita, by Regions, 1955

REGION	AMOUNT (In US dollars)
United States and Canada	2,300
Occania	1,050
Western Europe[1]	750
USSR and European Satellites	600
Latin America	275
Near East	200
Africa	110
Far East and South Asia[2]	100
Communist China[3]	55
World Average	390

Source: Foreign Aid Program, US Senate Document No. 52, Washington, July 1957, pp. 161 and 241.

1 OEEC countries.
2 Excludes Communist (Mainland) China.
3 Mainland China.

placed at $390 (Table 1). Incomes in regions comprised entirely or very largely of underdeveloped countries ranged from $275 down to $55: Latin America, $275; Near East, $200; Africa, $110; Far East and South Asia, $100; and Communist (Mainland) China, $55. Concurrently, incomes in regions comprised entirely or very largely of developed countries ranged from $2,300 down to $600: US and Canada, $2,300; Oceania, $1,050; Western Europe, $750; and USSR and European Satellites, $600. Illustrative of the wide spread in incomes among regions, the richest region shown had an income roughly six times the world average, while the income of the poorest region was roughly one-seventh of the world average.

Examination of estimates for individual countries, both under-developed and developed, reveals that, in 1955, per-capita GNP ranged from above $2,300 to under $50 (Table 2). Most individual underdeveloped countries had per-capita incomes below $200 per year, less (and in some cases much less) than one-tenth that of the US. The lowest ranges on the income scale embraced, in fact, some of the world's most populous countries (e.g., India, Pakistan, and Communist China—all under $100 per capita per year).

While wide differences in per-capita income exist within the under-developed world (and also within the developed world), the essential central point is simply that low income and underdevelopedness tend to go together (as do higher income and developed status). As evidenced by Table 1, the major underdeveloped regions have incomes below the

Table 2. Gross National Product, Per Capita,
Selected Countries, 1955 (Amounts in US dollars)

PER-CAPITA INCOME RANGE	DEVELOPED[1]		UNDERDEVELOPED[1]	
	Country	Amount	Country	Amount
1,500 or over	United States	2,343		
	Canada	1,667		
800–1,499	New Zealand	1,249		
	Switzerland	1,229		
	Australia	1,215		
	Sweden	1,165		
	France	1,046		
	Belgium	1,015		
	United Kingdom	998		
	Norway	969		
	Denmark	913		
300–799	Germany (Western)	762	Venezuela	762
	Netherlands	708	Uruguay	569
	USSR	682	Argentina	374
	Ireland	509	Cuba	361
	Italy	442	Panama	350
	Union of S. Africa	381	Colombia	330
100–299	Spain	254	Yugoslavia	297
	Japan	240	Turkey	276
	Greece	239	Brazil	262
			Philippines	201
			Iraq	195
			Mexico	187
			Chile	180
			Saudi Arabia	166
			Peru	140
			Egypt	133
			Indonesia	127
			Thailand	100
			Iran	100
99 or under			Belgian Congo	98
			South Korea	80
			Haiti	75
			India	72
			Nigeria	70
			Bolivia	66
			Pakistan	56
			China (Communist)	56
			Afghanistan	54
			Ethiopia	54
			Burma	52
			Nepal	40

Source: Based on Foreign Aid Program, *US Senate Document No. 52, Washington, July 1957, Table 1, pp. 239–240.*

---

[1] As explained in the text, the classificatory treatment of borderline cases is necessarily arbitrary. Consequently, it is important to recognize that some countries, particularly in the $200–$600 income range, could creditably be classified as either developed or underdeveloped. The classification shown reflects an attempt (by the author) to resolve the status of doubtful cases by what seems to be the most common treatment accorded by economists.

world average, whereas the major developed regions have incomes above the world average. Similarly, as evidenced by Table 2, individual under-developed countries typically place in an income range below that char-acteristic of developed countries, although some overlap exists in inter-mediate income ranges.

LOW WELL-BEING

Evidence that underdeveloped countries fare badly, as compared with developed countries, is also found in various non-monetary measures of material well-being. These measures offer a more detailed picture of the poverty inherent in the environment of underdeveloped countries. Addi-tionally, these measures provide an alternative to data on money income in the course of an attempt to show relative status among countries— indeed, such measures possibly are technically superior to income data as a basis for inter-country comparisons.[7]

Of the various non-monetary measures available, the following most frequently capture attention: amounts and types of food intake, infant mortality rates, life expectancies, literacy rates, and extensiveness of public facilities (Table 3 and Fig. 2). In general, underdeveloped countries rate below developed countries on all scores. The picture portrayed is that people in underdeveloped countries tend, on the average, not to live so long as people in developed countries, and while they live, they tend to experience far more deprivation.

A composite index, as a substitute for tests of relative status along multiple lines, might be of some convenience. Such an index exists, rank-ing countries in terms of their national consumption levels (Table 4). The procedure employed in constructing this index was as follows. A total of 19 non-monetary indicators was singled out (covering food, medical and sanitary services, education and recreation, transportation

---

[7] Some economists question the advisability of using monetary data for inter-country comparisons. The central point is that they have doubts as to the quality of the end data available for making comparisons. Their skepticism stems largely from two con-siderations. First, each country has the initial responsibility for assembling the income data reflective of its economy, but differences exist among countries both in method-ology employed and in statistical competence. Despite great strides during recent years in the upgrading and standardization of fact-gathering processes, it is to be expected that both the meaning and caliber of the data reached vary somewhat among countries.

Second, added distortions are likely as reported income data, expressed initially in national currencies, come to be translated into a common monetary unit, say, the US dollar. Ordinarily, official exchange rates are the basis for these data conversions. Whatever its merits (e.g., convenience), this procedure poses serious statistical dilemmas. When official and free-market exchange rates coincide, the question arises as to whether an exchange rate, reflective of international transactions, can offer a meaning-ful guide in the valuation of all output, including that output not destined for inter-national channels. When official and free-market rates differ (as is common under exchange-control conditions), conversion at the official (and overvalued) rate serves to overstate income (for the country whose currency is overvalued). And, when multiple exchange rates prevail, a further complication arises as a consequence of the need to decide upon the rate or combination of rates to be used for purposes of conversion.

Table 3. Non-Monetary Measures of Material Welfare, Selected Countries, 1955

COUNTRY	Caloric intake per person per day (numbers)	Protein consumption per day (grams)	Infant mortality (number of deaths per 1,000 live births)	Literacy (percent of population 10 years and over)	Inhabitants per physician (number)
I. Annual per-capita income above $750					
United States	3,090	92	27	98	770
Canada	3,120	98	32	....	950
France	2,785	96	42	97	1,100
United Kingdom	3,230	86	26	98	1,200
Denmark	3,300	89	27	99	950
Germany (Western)	2,945	77	43	....	750
II. Annual per-capita income $300 to $750					
Uruguay	2,940	99	43	85	....
Israel	2,711	81	39	75	380
Austria	2,790	83	48	97	650
Italy	2,595	80	53	....	800
Argentina	2,800	96	62	86	1,300
Cuba	2,730	67	99	76	....
III. Annual per-capita income $150 to $299					
Turkey	2,678	86	....	35	3,100
Brazil	2,355	57	107	48	3,000
Japan	2,180	58	49	95	1,000
Greece	2,540	80	44	76	1,000
Philippines	2,280	....	109	62	12,000
Iraq	2,338	....	44	12	6,400
Mexico	2,210	....	81	55	2,400
IV. Annual per-capita income under $150					
Egypt	2,338	69	127	25	3,600
Indonesia	2,040	....	200	55	71,000
Ceylon	2,052	47	72	58	5,300
Syria	2,131	....	102	50	5,000
Thailand	2,080	....	65	54	6,800
India	2,004	50	119	18	5,700
Burma	1,612	....	102	31	4,700
Pakistan	2,124	53	125	14	13,000

Source: Based on Foreign Aid Program, *US Senate Document No. 52, Washington, July 1957, Table 3, p. 242. Monetary magnitudes in column 1 refer to US dollars.*

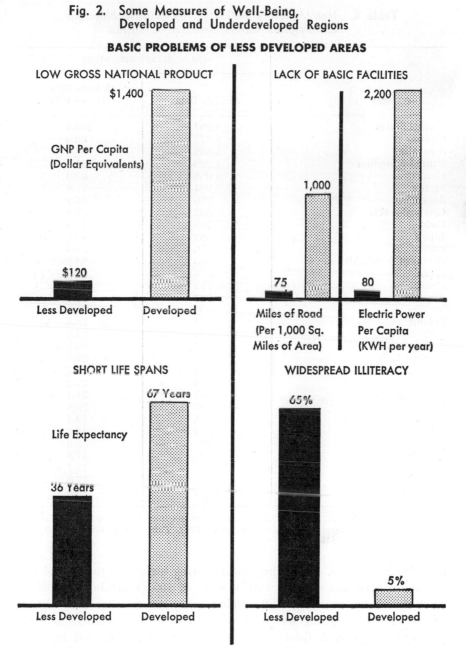

Fig. 2. Some Measures of Well-Being, Developed and Underdeveloped Regions

BASIC PROBLEMS OF LESS DEVELOPED AREAS

LOW GROSS NATIONAL PRODUCT

$1,400

GNP Per Capita
(Dollar Equivalents)

$120

Less Developed   Developed

LACK OF BASIC FACILITIES

2,200

1,000

75   80

Miles of Road   Electric Power
(Per 1,000 Sq.   Per Capita
Miles of Area)   (KWH per year)

SHORT LIFE SPANS

67 Years

Life Expectancy

36 Years

Less Developed   Developed

WIDESPREAD ILLITERACY

65%

5%

Less Developed   Developed

Source: Adapted from Department of State (and others), The Mutual Security Program, Washington, March 1959, p. 38.

Table 4. Non-Monetary Indicators of Relative National
Consumption Levels, Selected Countries

	NON-MONETARY INDICATORS	
COUNTRY	Absolute Data	Relative Data (US = 100)
United States	1,707	100.0
Canada	1,375	80.6
Australia	1,365	80.0
United Kingdom	1,290	75.6
Germany	1,058	62.0
France	984	57.6
Argentina	916	53.7
Czechoslovakia	803	47.0
Cuba	708	41.5
Japan	685	40.1
Italy	676	39.6
Union of South Africa	660	38.7
Spain	628	36.8
USSR	573	33.6
Brazil	540	31.6
Mexico	495	29.0
Poland	492	28.8
Yugoslavia	468	27.4
Philippines	439	25.7
Roumania	434	25.4
Turkey	413	24.2
Egypt	378	22.2
Thailand	365	21.4
India	355	20.8
Korea	331	19.4
Iran	310	18.2
China	307	18.0
Nigeria	306	17.9
Indochina States	302	17.7
Netherlands Indies	291	17.0
French West Africa	269	15.8

Source: M. K. Bennett, "International Disparities in Consumption Levels,"
American Economic Review, September 1951, Table III, p. 648. Primary data
typically 1934–38.

and communication, etc.[8]). The country rating highest in the case of any
given indicator was credited with a score of 100 (a maximum score of
1,900 thus being possible), while each country rating other than highest
for any given indicator was credited with a score computed as some
percentage of 100. A total absolute score was thus obtained for each
country, and from the array of absolute scores an array of relative scores

---

[8] Additionally, weight was given to needs being less in some climates and city-sizes
than in others.

was then derived. As high scorer on points, the US rated a relative score of 100; on this base, only 6 other countries of 31 surveyed rated above 50, and 16 rated below 30.

All the non-monetary measures cited—Tables 3 and 4, and Fig. 2— reveal wide variations among countries; but, significantly, the overall pattern revealed serves to supplement and reinforce, rather than to contradict, the general pattern previously referred to in the case of purely monetary data. Underdeveloped countries, previously categorized as low-income countries, are also deficient in terms of various non-monetary measures of material well-being.

RAW-MATERIALS PRODUCERS

The low income characteristic of underdeveloped countries derives from a pattern of production differing from that of developed countries. Underdeveloped countries are typically raw-materials producers, or primary-goods producers—to invoke alternate terminology of wide usage among economists. Output and employment tend to be heavily concentrated in agricultural or mineral fields (with an agricultural emphasis being the case in most countries), while manufacturing tends to account for very little, either in terms of output or of employment. In developed countries, in contrast, emphasis is typically on manufacturing, while raw-materials production plays a relatively lesser role.

Data indicating major productive sectors within which output arises in both underdeveloped and developed countries are shown in Table 5. In the low-income underdeveloped countries, the percentage of total output classed as having originated in raw-materials production invariably exceeds that regarded as having manufacturing origins, with ranges of 40%–60% and 10%–15%, respectively, being fairly depictive of the situation. In the high-income developed countries, in contrast, the percentage of output contributed by raw-materials production is invariably lower than that classed as stemming from manufacturing, the general ranges being 10%–20% and 30%–40%, respectively.

A similar picture prevails in the case of employment. In the low-income underdeveloped countries, upwards of 50% of the labor force is typically engaged in raw-materials production, and in some countries the figure exceeds 80% (Table 6). On the other hand, in the high-income developed countries, manufacturing employment characteristically exceeds employment in raw-materials production—in some cases, by a considerable margin.[9] Parallel with this emphasis upon raw-materials production, the populations of underdeveloped countries tend to be largely rural, especially in those countries in which production focuses on agriculture.

---

[9] Even in Denmark, noted for its proficiency in agriculture, employment in manufacturing exceeds that in primary production.

Table 5. Industrial Origin of Net Domestic Product, Selected Countries, 1957

	DEVELOPED[1]			UNDERDEVELOPED[1]		
		Percentage of product value originating in:			Percentage of product value originating in:	
	Country	Primary production[2]	Manufacturing	Country	Primary production[2]	Manufacturing
HIGH INCOME:	Belgium	12	36			
	Canada	12	28			
	Denmark	18	29			
	Norway	15	28			
	United Kingdom	8	38			
	United States	7	31			
MIDDLE INCOME:	Italy	21	32	Argentina	20	22
	Japan	21	26	Colombia	41	17
	Union of South Africa[3]	27	23[4]	Turkey	44	14
LOW INCOME:				Belgian Congo	43	12
				Bolivia[5]	52	16
				Burma	43	11
				Ecuador[3]	39	16
				Egypt[6]	36	11
				India[3]	51	16[4]
				Kenya	39	14
				Nigeria[3]	64	2
				Pakistan	56	11
				Peru[3]	39	16
				Philippines	40	14
				South Korea	46	8
				Thailand[5]	47	13

Source: UN, Statistical Yearbook 1958, New York, 1958, Table 162, pp. 432–436. Besides primary production and manufacturing, a category labeled Other could be set up (to embrace construction, commerce, transport and communications, public administration and defense, and all else). Income classifications in column 1 relate to general status as shown in Table 2.

[1] Division between developed and underdeveloped conforms with treatment accorded in Table 2.
[2] Includes agriculture, forestry, fishing, and mining.
[3] 1956.
[4] Includes construction.
[5] 1955.
[6] 1954.

Population classed as rural exceeds 80% in some underdeveloped countries and is over 50% in most of them (as compared with roughly 30% in the US, and less in some other developed countries, e.g., Great Britain).

The heavy concentration of the labor force in raw-materials production

Table 6. Occupational Distribution of Labor Force, Selected Countries

	DEVELOPED[1]			UNDERDEVELOPED[1]		
		Percentage of employment in:			Percentage of employment in:	
	Country	Primary production[2]	Manufacturing	Country	Primary production[2]	Manufacturing
HIGH INCOME:	Belgium	18	38			
	Canada	16	26			
	Denmark	24	29			
	Sweden	21	31			
	United Kingdom	9	37			
	United States	14	27			
MIDDLE INCOME:	Japan	41	18	Argentina	26	22
	Spain	50	18	Colombia	56	12
	Union of South Africa	44	11	Turkey	78	6
LOW INCOME:				Belgian Congo	86	3
				Bolivia	68	10
				Ceylon	53	10
				Ecuador	54	19
				Egypt	64	10
				Haiti	83	5
				India	71	9
				Nepal	93	2
				Nicaragua	69	11
				Pakistan	65	11
				Paraguay	54	16
				Peru	64	15
				Thailand	84	2

Source: ILO, Year Book of Labour Statistics 1958, Geneva, 1958, Table 4, pp. 14–57. Data typically cover the early 1950's. Besides primary production and manufacturing, a category labeled Other could be set up (to embrace construction, commerce, transport and communications, and services). Income classifications in column 1 relate to general status as shown in Table 2.

1 Division between developed and underdeveloped conforms with treatment accorded in Table 2.
2 Includes agriculture, forestry, fishing, and mining.

in underdeveloped countries can be attributed basically to three main factors. First, per-worker output in food production tends to be low in these countries, so that the services of relatively many persons are required to produce even the minimum of needed food supplies. Much agriculture, in fact, is on a subsistence or near-subsistence basis. Second, the pattern of production in many of these countries is geared toward the sale of raw materials in export markets. Clear-cut instances include those countries in which plantation agriculture has come to play a major role, and also those countries in which important mining operations exist. While the hope in the case of such countries is that the sale of raw materials in export markets can provide the means needed to finance the importation of other goods not produced at home, an automatic effect within the domestic environment is to make labor heavily dependent upon the dominant raw-materials production. Third, the general absence of alternate employment opportunities in many of the countries provides sufficient grounds for staying on the land, even if nothing better than mere subsistence is to be gained.

POOR MANPOWER UTILIZATION

Considerable data covering underdeveloped countries are available to show the occupational status of certain major categories of employed labor. When one seeks data on the quality of utilization of labor, however, one finds precious little available. Observation tells one that labor *as a whole* is used badly in underdeveloped countries (as compared with the caliber of usage in developed countries).[10] But, in trying to prove such, one is reduced simply to pointing out that the low real per-capita income which prevails reflects low per-worker productivity.

The low per-worker productivity of labor basically stems not so much from the presence of outright unemployment on a mass basis (with no contribution to output arising from totally idle workers) as from the existence of widespread and chronic *underemployment*. This is not to deny that there is unemployment in underdeveloped countries, for in some countries there may well be considerable. Just how much, or how little, actual unemployment exists, however, is difficult to say. Attempts to measure the extent of unemployment in underdeveloped countries typically give rise to results that leave much to be desired. Aside from the usual difficulties of definition, there is the difficulty of locating the unemployed. In the typical underdeveloped country, unlike the typical developed country, there is no official system for registering unemployed persons prior to the payment of unemployment benefits to them; no such services or benefits exist, and so no official record is kept. Unemployed persons in underdeveloped countries, when these persons are present, commonly tend simply to "disappear," in the sense that they come to mesh their lives with those in their respective family (or clan) groups, in which all members live off the earnings of the ones who are the bread-winners.[11]

---

[10] A bad use of labor is regarded here as one yielding low productivity.

[11] It is sometimes said that the strong emphasis upon the family unit, characteristic in the cultures of many underdeveloped countries, has been fostered or preserved by this element of "safety in numbers," which is valued as a protective measure by the various individuals identifying themselves as members of a given family organization.

More important, without doubt, is underemployment.[12] The under-employed are members of the labor force who are employed, in some sense of the word, but who have only a tenuous claim to this status (in that their efforts contribute very little to total output and certainly fall something short of what might reasonably be expected of them were a slightly improved combination of factors of production to prevail). The manner in which underemployment is generated in underdeveloped countries can be readily illustrated. In the apparent absence of better alternatives, persons in underdeveloped countries are likely to find themselves involved in one or another of the following situations. The farm plot of the family may already have enough, or more than enough, workers on it to handle the tasks involved, but when a younger member of the family reaches working age (i.e., becomes includable in the labor force) he may, since other avenues of employment are lacking or believed lacking, simply join others in the family in whatever they are doing—whether or not the presence of an additional person adds anything to total production. In the technical sense, no unemployment then shows up, but underemployment is induced (i.e., labor's relationship to comple-mentary factors of production is worsened, with the result that per-worker productivity is lowered). Or, persons may enter "make-work" types of service activities (e.g., as servants), that typically entail low productivity and low personal income. Or, again, persons may seek an outlet as sales-men, the stock in trade often being simply lottery tickets. Thus, what might under some circumstances result in outright unemployment evolves instead as disguised unemployment. Characteristically, much unemploy-ment of the disguised variety is to be found in underdeveloped countries, year after year.

The foregoing situation lends credence to the much-cited observation that underemployment is widespread and chronic in the underdeveloped world. In the underdeveloped world, it is more a case of many persons being caught in a lifetime of poor employment than it is one of complete idleness for a lesser number, now and again, as tends to be the case in developed countries.

CAUSE AND EFFECT

As outlined, underdeveloped countries have low per-capita income (and low material well-being), are raw-materials producers, and have consider-able underemployment. Up to a point, these factors are interrelated. Low

---

[12] Underemployment can exist for any factor of production (since the concept of underemployment hinges on relationships between the supplies of the various factors of production). However, the underemployment of particular significance in the under-developed world relates to labor. Significantly, underemployment (of labor) is not present only in the underdeveloped world; it exists also, in some degree, in developed countries.

per-capita income is reflective of low per-worker productivity. In turn, the low per-worker productivity occurs within an environment characterized by heavy emphasis upon raw-materials production (and within which environment there is, and long has been, widespread underemployment). Under the circumstances, it would be easy to conclude that low per-capita income prevails because of the emphasis upon raw-materials production—in which case the solution is also indicated by implication. Actually, such a conclusion may,[13] or may not, be valid. Certainly, prior to accepting or rejecting a conclusion in this vein, one needs to examine a number of other existing possibilities (as is done in a subsequent connection in this volume). What can be concluded at this point, however, is that the production which happens to prevail in underdeveloped countries is characterized in general by low productivity (per worker), and this situation then favors low per-capita income.

Whatever these relationships may be, an end objective relative to underdeveloped countries is presumably to see the evolution of a higher and rising level of per-capita income. Given such an objective, it is reasonable to expect that certain actions and policies will need to be invoked in order to facilitate the desired state of affairs. But, as a prelude to all this, it is essential to recognize that the environment prevailing in underdeveloped countries on some scores seems averse to change for the better. The status-quo may be deemed undesirable, but forces appear present and operative that tend to preserve (if not worsen) what is, rather than to lead from it to something considered more desirable. This situation, alluded to in the literature in terms of being "caught in a vicious circle," is regarded by some economists as central in a description of what ails underdeveloped countries.[14]

CONCEPT OF THE VICIOUS CIRCLE

The term *vicious circle,* as it applies to the environment in underdeveloped countries, refers to an inextricable interrelationship of cause-and-effect that operates so as to imprison an economy in its own shortcomings. The notion is that a given effect, as evidenced by whatever it is that happens to exist, acts as the cause leading to a substantially similar effect.[15] In essence, the status-quo tends to perpetuate itself—because of a process of circular causation.

This principle of the vicious circle is readily demonstrable. The central case involves poverty itself. Underdeveloped countries are poor in that

---

13 For strong presumptive argumentation, see *Studies in Income and Wealth,* Vol. 8 (New York: National Bureau of Economic Research, 1946), esp. p. 123.

14 Popularization of the term *vicious circle* in reference to underdeveloped countries is attributable in large degree to the writings of G. Myrdal. For example, see his *Rich Lands and Poor* (New York: Harper and Brothers, 1957), esp. Ch. II.

15 A possibility, of course, is that worsening may occur over time. Some economists, however, choose to limit their description simply to that of a general absence of change.

the level of real per-capita income prevailing is low, the result, in the first instance, of low productivity. Because per-capita income is low, per-capita consumption is also low. Despite low per-capita consumption, little saving occurs. So much of what is produced is needed to sustain even the low level of per-capita consumption prevailing that little surplus is left over as saving.[16] (As shown in Table 7, saving in the underdeveloped world approximates 5% of income—a rate roughly one-third that of the US; similarly, data covering rates of capital formation show under-developed countries at generally lower levels than developed countries.[17])

Table 7. Net Domestic Saving as a Proportion of National Income, by Regions, 1949

REGION	PERCENT
Latin America	8
Middle East[1]	6
Africa	5
South Central Asia	5
Far East[2]	3
Total	5

Source: Computed from UN, Measures for the Economic Development of Under-Developed Countries, New York, 1951, Table 2, p. 76.

1 Includes Egypt, which is excluded from Africa.
2 Excludes Japan, and includes Communist China.

Because the amount of saving (as an aggregate[18]) is low, the ability to undertake and sustain investment is also low. The low level of investment serves to leave largely unaltered the basic situation that gives rise to low productivity. The sequence thus is: low productivity, low saving (as well as low consumption), low investment, and low productivity. A vicious circle exists.

Instead of placing emphasis upon low saving and its consequences, as

16 Saving can be viewed in either monetary or real terms—i.e., the term is used in reference either to that portion of current *money income* not used to acquire consumer items, or to that portion of current *real output* (or real income) not devoted to con-sumption in the current period. In the final analysis, of course, the level (or rate) of *real* saving is of central importance; the basic end object of economic activity is goods and services, while the role of money to an important extent is to serve as a medium in facilitating the generation and channelization of these goods and services. (Additional references to this matter occur in Chs. 13 and 14.)

17 For the greater part, capital formation rates (as percentages of GNP) are sub-stantially lower in underdeveloped than in developed countries. Examination of 1954 data for a group of 38 countries (23 underdeveloped and 15 developed, classified to conform with treatment accorded in Table 2) reveals median rates of 12% and 18% for underdeveloped and developed countries, respectively. For supporting data, see *Foreign Aid Program,* US Senate Document No. 52, Washington, July 1957, Table 4, p. 243.

18 Combining absolute level of income and percentage of income saved.

in the foregoing sequence, emphasis might be placed with equal argumentative facility upon low consumption and its consequences. The vicious circle then is: low productivity, low real income, low consumption (and hence low demand), low investment (investment being discouraged by low demand), and low productivity. Or, emphasis might be placed upon low productivity, due to low consumption. The vicious circle then is: low productivity (due to poor consumption standards, which impair productivity), low real income, low consumption, and low productivity.

All of the foregoing sequences point to the same villain: poverty. The gist of the matter is that poor countries are poor because they are poor.

COMBATIVE TECHNIQUES

Underdeveloped countries, then, are victim to a central vicious circle, grounded in poverty itself. To this ordinarily can be added a series of subsidiary vicious circles of varying degrees of significance, all involving particular facets of the general environment of poverty.[19] In any event, presence of a vicious circle (or of vicious circles), consisting of a set of circumstances operating in circular fashion so as to perpetuate the status-quo, warrants consideration of the approaches that might be invoked for remedial action. Basically, two notions prevail on the subject.

The first notion regards a vicious circle as a complex of closely intertwined factors, with each factor bearing roughly equal weight within the complex. Based on this appraisal, the preferred combative technique is either through an across-the-board attack, through the use of economic and non-economic means aimed at all major factors within the complex, or through a selective attack upon some one or more factors within the total complex (the thought in this case, however, being that it is largely immaterial where special attention is focused, since all factors are regarded as closely interdependent in any event).

The second notion also regards a vicious circle as a complex of closely intertwined factors, but views some one factor as being pivotal, i.e., as holding the key within a complex of relationships. Based on this appraisal, the preferred combative technique necessitates identification of the pivotal factor and ascertainment of the measure(s) to be used in regard to it. This does not mean that other factors are regarded as unimportant, or that absolutely no action is ever to be recommended in their connection. Rather, the thought is that one factor—the *catalyst* or catalytic agent—can be used as the primary means to shake loose the whole complex (i.e., to produce catalytic action) and thereby invite motion in the direction desired.

---

[19] As aptly put by one economist, ". . . while all development circles are vicious, some are more vicious than others." See A. O. Hirschman, *The Strategy of Economic Development* (New Haven: Yale University Press, 1958), p. 11.

THE TASK

The world has many troublesome areas. Of these, a major one involves the status of the present-day underdeveloped countries. The situation in these countries, both absolutely and relative to the rest-of-the-world, forms the basis of a major world *problem*—particularly because of the reaction of large numbers of people toward it, and because of what is likely to be required of people in the course of altering it.

If the status-quo is to be altered, what is the *objective* sought through change? The objective is to create in underdeveloped countries an economic situation more akin to that already prevailing in so-called developed countries. Essentially, the hope is to replace general poverty and near stagnation with greater affluence and cumulative enrichment.

The *process* of change involved is development. The immediate and central task is to get things moving in a new direction or at a faster tempo. As seen by the economist or government official, this task, at its core, is one of discovering which vicious circles are the basic causes of the others, and of determining how these vicious circles can be dealt with so as to turn them into feedback mechanisms that might then induce sustained growth.

This book is concerned with the problem and implications of underdevelopedness, major earmarks of which are described in earlier paragraphs. The book is about underdeveloped countries, but it is also, of necessity—for reasons discernible later—about developed countries (with emphasis upon the US among these developed countries). Stripped of certain refinements, the subject matter treats *the problem of the underdeveloped world and the American interest in it.*

As a prelude to the pages that follow, several questions appear fundamental, as points of reference: Why are some countries underdeveloped when others are developed? What are underdeveloped countries doing to shake off their underdevelopedness? What are developed countries, particularly the US, doing relative to underdeveloped countries? What are the implications for the world, and for the US, of success—or failure—in the alleviation of the plight of underdeveloped countries?

SELECTED BIBLIOGRAPHY

A short bibliography, selective in content, is included at the end of each chapter or major section. The intent is to assist readers who wish to pursue particular topics somewhat further, or who wish to examine alternate treatments accorded particular topics.

References pertinent to matters treated in Chapter 1 include the following:

Peter T. Bauer and Basil S. Yamey, *The Economics of Under-Developed Countries.* Chicago: The University of Chicago Press, 1957.
Ch. 2, Examination of problems involved in measuring income and capital in underdeveloped countries.

Willem Brand, *The Struggle for a Higher Standard of Living.* Glencoe, Ill.: The Free Press, 1958.
Ch. 1, Views on the objectives and process of economic development.

S. Herbert Frankel, *The Economic Impact on Under-Developed Societies.* Oxford: Basil Blackwell, 1953.
Essay III, The problem of inter-country comparisons of national-income data.

Charles P. Kindleberger, *Economic Development.* New York: The McGraw-Hill Book Company, Inc., 1958.
Chs. 1–6, Basic characteristics of underdeveloped countries.

Harvey Leibenstein, *Economic Backwardness and Economic Growth.* New York: John Wiley and Sons, Inc., 1957.
Chs. 2–7, Basic characteristics of underdeveloped countries; Ch. 8, Concept of the vicious circle.

W. Arthur Lewis, *The Theory of Economic Growth.* Homewood, Ill.: Richard D. Irwin, Inc., 1955.
Broad coverage, with treatment organized in terms of the factors of production.

Gerald M. Meier and Robert E. Baldwin, *Economic Development.* New York: John Wiley and Sons, Inc., 1957.
Chs. 13–14, Basic characteristics of underdeveloped countries.

Gunnar Myrdal, *Rich Lands and Poor.* New York: Harper and Brothers, 1957.
Ch. 2, Concept of the vicious circle.

Lyle W. Shannon (ed.), *Underdeveloped Areas.* New York: Harper and Brothers, 1957.
Chs. 1–6, Basic characteristics of underdeveloped countries (sociological emphasis).

Henry H. Villard, *Economic Development.* New York: Rinehart & Company, Inc., 1959.
Part I, Measurement of, and differences in, living levels.

Major sources of statistical data on underdeveloped countries, and developed countries also, include the following:

Food and Agriculture Organization, *Yearbook of Food and Agricultural Statistics,* annual.

General Agreement on Tariffs and Trade, *International Trade,* annual.

International Labor Organization, *Year Book of Statistics,* annual.

International Monetary Fund, *International Financial Statistics,* monthly.

United Nations, *Demographic Yearbook,* annual.

_____, *Monthly Bulletin of Statistics,* monthly.

_____, *Report on the World Social Situation,* annual.

_____, *Statistical Yearbook,* annual.

_____, *World Economic Survey,* annual.

PART TWO

THE RESPONSE OF UNDERDEVELOPED COUNTRIES

Perhaps the most characteristic fact of our times is that economic development almost overnight has become the goal and ambition of millions of people. The needs which this desire creates are immense; they are urgent everywhere, and they cannot be postponed.

ANTONIO CARRILLO-FLORES, CHAIRMAN OF THE BOARDS OF GOVERNORS OF THE IBRD AND IMF, 1956.

The changes of the last few years have unleashed a giant. . . . Tremendous urges are coming up. . . . Who are we to criticize if people want better food, better clothing, or better living conditions?

JAWAHARLAL NEHRU, PRIME MINISTER OF INDIA, SPEAKING AT THE ANNUAL MEETING OF THE IBRD AND IMF, NEW DELHI, 1958.

Economic development is widely desired in the underdeveloped world, both at governmental and popular levels. Many obstacles confront attempts to achieve this development, although some favorable factors are also present. Accordingly, a major task in underdeveloped countries is to ascertain what can and should be aspired to in the way of development, and how progress in the intended direction might be fostered. Part Two is devoted to an examination of why development is desired, and to an exposition and analysis of obstacles to this development, and of possible courses by which it might nevertheless become reality.

2

DESIRE FOR DEVELOPMENT

As observed in Chapter 1, much of the world suffers from poverty. This situation is not new, for poverty is an old story in the world. But while the situation itself is not new, something new has arisen in recent times in the way large numbers of people *choose to react* to the situation.

People in poor countries seemed, in an earlier day, to be very largely resigned to their fate. Complacency and contentment were traits widely attributed to the societies of these countries by outsiders (who frequently viewed the traits as virtues). But, in recent times, large numbers of people in poor countries have obviously altered their outlook, in that they have come to be much less impervious to their surroundings. There has come to be a growing awareness of the poverty that prevails and an ever-growing readiness to challenge the status-quo in the interest of inviting the evolution of something better. For the greater part, the turning point in this connection came during and after World War II, marking a period for these countries sometimes labeled as "The Great Awakening."[1] Whatever else might be said of this period, complacency and contentment have been badly shaken in the course of it.

People in rich countries, too, have altered their outlook. These people, although commonly aware in general terms of the poverty prevalent elsewhere, long were inclined to view the plight of the less affluent countries and peoples as somehow inevitable. Individual members of rich societies seemed to find it rather easy to respond either with indifference, since the situation was not of

---

[1] G. Myrdal employs this term. See his *Rich Lands and Poor* (New York: Harper and Brothers, 1957), pp. 7–8.

their making and, anyway, incapable of cure by them personally, or with token assistance through charitable contributions, which were frequently given in the spirit of "conscience money." Recent decades, however, witnessed important changes. Unprecedented numbers in rich countries have become much more aware of, and concerned about, the basic situation that prevails in poor countries, and have come to ask themselves why general poverty should remain the lot of entire populations. In short, The Great Awakening in the underdeveloped world had its counterpart in the developed world.

For better or for worse, The Great Awakening has made its appearance, and in its wake a central formula has achieved prominence and now exists as a rallying point. The magic phrase, nowadays voiced over and over in country after country, is *economic development.*

MEANING OF ECONOMIC DEVELOPMENT

For the average person, the term *economic development* refers simply to achievement by poor countries of higher levels of real per-capita income and of improved conditions of living for their people, i.e., achievement of an environment more like that already prevailing in developed countries. However, the term also has a technical meaning, which differs in important respects from the foregoing popular impression of the matter. In this technical sense, economic development refers to a *process* of economic growth within an economy, the central objective of the process being higher and rising real per-capita income for that economy (with the benefits of this higher and rising income being widely diffused within the economy).

To elaborate, three essential tests are applicable in attempts to determine whether or not economic development is occurring. First, income must rise *cumulatively*[2] (i.e., year after year) for some considerable period.[3] A once-and-for-all increase in income is not enough.

Second, the increase in income must bestow income benefits upon the population as a whole, covering various occupational and income groups. It is essential to recall that per-capita income can rise either because added income accrues to a few persons within a highly inequitable income structure or because the same added income accrues to many people within a more equitable income structure. In the concept of economic

---

[2] The technical test imposes no specific magnitudes as to how high or how rapidly income must rise. As a consequence, it is possible for economic development to be occurring (as measured by the technical test of higher and rising income), even though some persons may choose to conclude otherwise, simply because their personal expectations as to income growth have not been met.

[3] One view holds the ultimate test to be that of rising income for a period of two generations. See B. Higgins, *Economic Development* (New York: W. W. Norton and Company, Inc., 1959), p. 199.

development, a rise in real per-capita income comes about as the result of more than just a few receiving higher income.

Third, as a modification of the general test that real per-capita income must rise cumulatively over time, instances *may* exist in which economic development can still be regarded as occurring even though real per-capita income does not rise. For example, an increase in population can serve to rule out a per-capita increase in income, notwithstanding a substantial addition to the aggregate level of income. If per-capita gains are insisted upon, even marked growth in aggregate income, over time, could conceivably be held as not reflective of economic development (e.g., as when aggregate income rises rapidly, but no more rapidly than population). In the light of this possibility, some economists choose to regard growth in aggregate income as indicative of economic development in any event—even when concurrent population growth results in per-capita levels of income being held constant, or even lowered. In defense of their view, these persons simply point to the fact that the alternative—in the absence of growth in aggregate income—is still lower per-capita income.[4] The popular hope, of course, is that aggregate income will rise faster than population, so that per-capita income can also rise.

Again, even if real per-capita income did not rise, the elimination or toning down of fluctuations in existent income might be considered an achievement. The fact that income levels in some underdeveloped countries are subject to wide fluctuations, both from year to year and over the longer period of a business cycle, tends to make any given level of aggregate income less desirable than would be the case if the same level of aggregate income were spread more evenly over a period of time. Viewed thus, progress toward the lessening of fluctuations in aggregate income—even in the absence of long-run growth in this income—might also be regarded as reflective of economic development.[5]

BASIC MOTIVATIONS

The Great Awakening in the underdeveloped world is, at root, a reaction—a reaction to various forces and factors. The particular forces and factors, or combinations thereof, responsible for having triggered it unquestionably differ somewhat among underdeveloped countries. Nevertheless, several forces and factors appear to have been basic for most countries, and hence merit characterization as paramount stimuli in the totality of the underdeveloped world.

---

[4] S. Kuznets, "Problems in Comparison of Economic Trends," in S. Kuznets, W. E. Moore, and J. J. Spengler (eds.), *Economic Growth: Brazil, India, Japan* (Durham, N. C.: Duke University Press, 1955), pp. 12–13.

[5] W. Krause, *The International Economy* (Boston: Houghton Mifflin Company, 1955), p. 277.

The following section is devoted to an examination of these paramount stimuli. As is readily apparent, not all are of equal caliber or sophistication. But, because of their role in The Great Awakening, they are important, and therefore merit emphasis here.

AWARENESS OF POVERTY

People in underdeveloped countries lived for a long time in relative isolation, largely unaware of the world beyond their immediate surroundings and largely ignorant of the mode and level of living in other, more developed, parts of the world. Recent decades have brought an important change in this respect. People have been brought in contact, as never before, with the world beyond the particular locales they happen to inhabit, and so have come to know much more about how life is lived elsewhere.

Two developments have been primarily responsible for bringing this greater contact and the increased awareness of conditions elsewhere that has sprung from it. The first of these developments has been technological advancement, centered in developed countries. Improvements in travel have served to bring people together, especially in the sense that people from developed countries have come to visit underdeveloped countries in increasing numbers, where they have been on display for the local populace to study and discuss. The evolution of motion pictures as a medium of mass entertainment, and education, followed by the spread of motion-picture exhibition to all parts of the world—including underdeveloped countries, where most people are very much starved for almost any entertainment—has served to acquaint many millions with life in developed countries, and especially with American life and living as depicted by Hollywood. Improved news media, including radio and magazines (especially pictorial magazines), have had a similar effect in creating greater familiarity with what exists elsewhere. Mechanical contrivances manufactured in developed countries, including those of a consumer-goods variety (e.g., sleek, chrome-splashed automobiles), have made their appearance to greater or lesser extent in underdeveloped countries, where their presence even in token amounts frequently serves to arouse interest and whet appetites among onlookers currently unable to avail themselves of them or anything of the type. And, of course, the occasional national of an underdeveloped country who has returned from a visit to a developed country generally has many stories to tell of the marvels he has seen, the telling and retelling of which stories naturally carries an educative impact.

In addition to technological advancement, a second development—war, and preparation for war (or, defense to prevent war)—has served to bring greater contact and increased awareness. The spectacular aspects of modern warfare and of the equipment of warfare have readily become topics of conversation, even among people far removed from actual or likely battle zones; and for people in zones of actual or potential conflict, awareness of military might, which today is a reflection of industrial might, has been largely inescapable. Thus it was during World War II, a period that figures importantly in The Great Awakening. In connection with warfare, too, large numbers of people from major participating countries found themselves in farflung places, where they served as an unconscious reminder of another country and culture. The classic case, of course, involved the American GI, the foremost American tourist and ambassador, whose impact in helping the world learn more about the US should not be minimized.

The effect of these major developments has been to make people in underdeveloped countries much more aware of the *differences* existing between underdeveloped and developed countries, and especially of the differences between them in terms of the mode and level of living of the typical inhabitant. The average person living in an underdeveloped country did not find out for the first time that he was poor; the hard reality of day-to-day life had impressed that fact upon him from virtually the day of his birth. What the average person did learn was just *how poor* he was, and he learned this when a set of circumstances arose that encouraged him to compare his material possessions with those enjoyed elsewhere.

Indeed, growing numbers have not merely become aware of the impoverished status of underdeveloped countries, but have also come to accept as fact the further proposition that underdeveloped countries are *growing relatively poorer*—a proposition that has also come to be widely accepted in developed countries. As pictured by the average person, untutored in the technicalities of the matter, the gap that separates the income levels of underdeveloped and developed countries has been growing wider (so that the poverty of underdeveloped countries tends to become more obvious over time, as comparisons come to be made).

Actually, while widely accepted as being true, the foregoing proposition is not given to ready proof. Those in professional circles who support the proposition generally place reliance upon two main contentions. The first contention is that aggregate income has, in fact, been rising more rapidly in developed countries during the past century than in underdeveloped countries. Unfortunately, absence of good, long-range income data for many countries seems to leave room for doubt—although available data covering the more recent years show average rates of increase in GNP to be 4.5% in developed countries, as compared with only 2.5% in underdeveloped countries.[6] The second contention is that differentials in

---

6 Rockefeller Brothers Fund (Special Studies Project, Report III), *Foreign Economic Policy for the Twentieth Century* (Garden City, N.Y.: Doubleday & Company, Inc., 1958), pp. 72–73.

rates of population growth have tended, further, to hold increases in per-capita income in underdeveloped countries below increases registered in developed countries (with the distinct possibility present that per-capita income has fallen, absolutely, in some underdeveloped countries[7]). The final conclusion these persons then reach is that differences in aggregate income and in per-capita income between underdeveloped and developed countries are at present absolutely greater, and probably also relatively greater, than they were in an earlier day.[8]

Whatever the precise factor(s) responsible, large numbers of people in underdeveloped countries have become aware of their poverty, and as a consequence are no longer content with their particular status. They have come to expect something better, and frequently are prepared to push for such. The course of action that has caught the imagination of many of them is economic development.

DESIRE FOR ECONOMIC INDEPENDENCE

Many people in underdeveloped countries have come to be concerned about the low economic independence that they feel characterizes the economies of their home countries. The problem, as they have been inclined to see it, is that the existing pattern of production serves to make the economies extremely dependent upon what transpires externally, and that in their case such dependence proves more harmful than beneficial.

What in the existing pattern of production evokes such a reaction? The usual reasoning proceeds as follows. Underdeveloped countries typically are raw-materials producers (Tables 5 and 6 in Ch. 1). In *some* of the countries, in addition, this raw-materials production is heavily concentrated in few products (Fig. 3), so that a considerable portion of income and employment normally stems from a very specialized economic base. The specialization, in turn, forces the countries to depend heavily upon sales abroad of exportable surpluses, and also upon purchases abroad of a variety of goods, including manufactures, not produced at home. The traditional notion is that specialization (and trade), if in conformity with the dictates of the law of comparative advantage, serves to maximize income. But if income can thereby be heightened, a basis for instability also comes into being, with the possibility that sufficient instability serves to jeopardize average income itself over the long-run. It is the matter of instability, particularly, that worries many people—and that is at issue here. In the view of many persons, the countries con-

---

[7] Because population rose more rapidly than did aggregate income.

[8] S. Kuznets, "Toward a Theory of Economic Growth," in R. Lekachman (ed.), *National Policy for Economic Welfare at Home and Abroad* (Garden City, N.Y.: Doubleday & Company, Inc., 1955), p. 27.

Fig. 3. Export Concentration in Few Products, Selected Countries, 1958

DEPENDENCE ON SINGLE COMMODITIES:

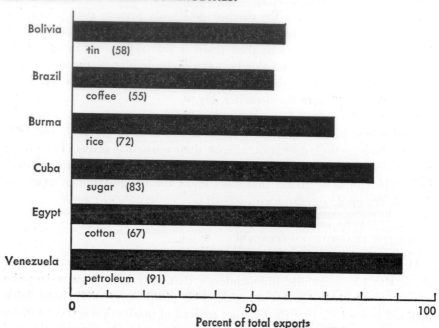

Percent of total exports

DEPENDENCE ON TWO COMMODITIES:

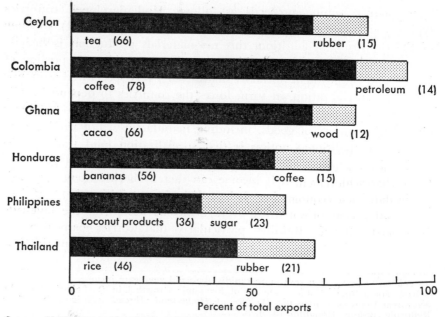

Percent of total exports

Source: IMF, International Financial Statistics, *Washington, February 1960, pp. 28–32.*

34

cerned cannot be regarded as independent, because the prevailing pattern of production serves to make them highly vulnerable to what transpires abroad. As they are quick to point out, if anything should go seriously wrong abroad, export markets and sources of import supply would readily come to be impaired, with devastating impact upon the domestic economies of the underdeveloped countries concerned.

The adverse external conditions that many persons in underdeveloped countries fear are associated, in the main, with two situations: depression and war. First, economic fluctuations arising in the major industrial countries hold important implications for underdeveloped countries. There is a widely accepted belief, of course, that a tendency toward instability of domestic origin is characteristic of the economies of major industrial countries. And, it is in these countries, and against this basic characteristic, that much of the specialized raw-materials output of underdeveloped countries finds its market. As levels of output and income fluctuate in industrial countries, their imports from underdeveloped countries also fluctuate—in fact, their imports have tended to fluctuate even more than have their incomes. As a consequence of these fluctuations in imports, economic fluctuations arising in industrial countries are transmitted to underdeveloped countries, frequently in intensified form—especially if export dependence in underdeveloped countries is particularly great. Serious as this situation can be in any phase of the business cycle, the recession or depression phase poses the major dilemma. Underdeveloped countries are then confronted by a dwindling foreign demand for their export products, but unfortunately find that they generally can do very little through price concessions to stimulate foreign sales (since the demand for raw-materials products typically is inelastic, i.e., reductions in price do not serve to increase sales volume sufficiently to boost total receipts). Under these conditions, when industrial countries experience a recession or depression, export markets for underdeveloped countries are depressed and in turn bring about adverse effects, to a greater or lesser degree, in the form of unemployment or added underemployment, foreign-exchange shortages, and impaired ability to import. On this account, a natural impulse within underdeveloped countries is to favor diversification—generally in the name of economic development—in the hope that achievement of a broader economic base will somehow serve to insulate these economies against foreign depressions.[9]

Second, periods of war similarly hold important implications for underdeveloped countries. Blockades and lack of shipping space serve to cut

---

[9] Not only are export proceeds vulnerable to foreign depression, but access to foreign capital is also impaired (as a depression environment makes it more difficult to generate surplus capital, and makes potential investors reluctant to commit themselves). For a brief account of how foreign countries were affected by the impact of the Great Depression upon the US (during 1929–33), see W. Krause, *The International Economy* (Boston: Houghton Mifflin Company, 1955), pp. 35–39.

off underdeveloped countries from customary export markets, toward which the production patterns of many of them are geared, and also from customary sources of supply, upon which they tend to be highly dependent in the absence of diversification at home. Aside from transport difficulties during wartime, additional difficulties arise in that major industrial countries concentrate on the production of the implements of war, so that those manufactures and other goods sought by underdeveloped countries become obtainable only in reduced volume, or only at substantially higher cost, or not at all.[10] Given the prospect of periodic repetition of such circumstances, many persons are ready to support economic development, which they believe will give rise to the safety inherent in a basic core of national self-sufficiency.

REACTION TO COLONIALISM

Numerous underdeveloped countries are ex-colonies, having once been parties to a colonialist relationship.[11] Though these countries have achieved *political* independence, some people feel the countries do not have *economic* independence (at least not to the extent thought desirable). These people feel, further, that unless a substantial amount of economic independence prevails, political independence becomes little better than an empty accolade.

The economic independence that many persons in these countries desire and deem a necessary counterpart of political independence involves more than a slight revamping of production to help insulate an economy against adverse economic repercussions arising abroad. A common belief in ex-colonies is that their economies were warped during the period of colonialism. A frequent allegation is that production was geared primarily to accommodate the colonial power, and was not geared to maximize per-capita income in the colony, then or ever. In the wake of these ideas, a conclusion that many persons in ex-colonies readily reach is that the prevailing production pattern, carried forward basically unaltered from the time the colonial power relinquished its political jurisdiction, is not appropriate for a supposedly independent country.

What many persons in these countries desire, and regard as necessary for economic independence, is achievement of substantial structural change, i.e., a fundamental reshaping of the pattern of production. Their objective is to see some fairly pronounced shift in emphasis from raw-

---

10 While foreign exchange earned during wartime could be retained for use in financing imports following the conclusion of hostilities, this possibility loses appeal in view of the lessening of purchasing power likely to result from a postwar inflation.

11 From the end of World War II through 1959, 22 "new" countries, all underdeveloped, came into being (each with a colonialist background). Together these countries embrace a population of over 700 million, or roughly one-fourth of the world's total. Further, the expectation is that the early 1960's will see a considerable number of additional new countries come into being, particularly in Africa.

materials production geared for export (e.g., plantation agriculture or mineral exploitation involving exportation of ore in unprocessed form) to greater diversification in production, preferably including industrial development. Nothing of a lesser order is regarded, in many quarters, as sufficient to shake off the alleged taints of colonialism. Indeed, structural change and economic development often tend to be regarded as synonymous.

TERMS OF TRADE

As intimated earlier, individual underdeveloped countries are prone to experience serious economic instability, with such instability transmitted *to them* as a consequence of fluctuations occurring abroad in countries in which their specialized raw-materials production seeks a market. Presence of this instability is readily verifiable—viewed either in terms of price paid per unit, volume of units traded, or total proceeds realized. Table 8 summarizes the extent of instability in the case of a group of important raw-materials commodities during a recent half-century period. Data shown there indicate that fluctuations in price per

Table 8. Instability of Raw Materials in World Trade, 1901–1951 (Percentage fluctuation per year)

	Year-to-year Fluctuations	
I PRICES		
Average (25 commodities[1])	± 13.7	
Range ⌠Upper	± 21.	
⌡Lower	± 5.	
II. VOLUME		
Average (18 commodities[2])	± 18.7	
Range ⌠Upper	± 33.	
⌡Lower	± 6.	
	Money value	**Real terms**
III. PROCEEDS		
Average (18 commodities[2])	± 22.6	± 22.0
Range ⌠Upper	± 36.	± 35.
⌡Lower	± 15.	± 12.

Source: UN, Instability in Export Markets of Under-Developed Countries, *New York, 1952, Tables 1, 2, and 3, pp. 4–6.*

[1] Includes bananas, cocoa, coffee, copper, copra, cotton, hemp, hides and skins, jute, linseed, manganese, nickel, petroleum, rice, rubber, shellac, silk, sisal, sodium nitrate, sugar, tea, tin, tobacco, wheat, and wool.

[2] Same commodities as (1) with exception of bananas, copra, hides and skins, manganese, nickel, shellac, and sisal. Data for volume and proceeds extend only to 1950.

unit averaged almost 14% per year, that fluctuations in export volume averaged almost 19% per year, and that fluctuations in export proceeds (linking price fluctuations and volume fluctuations) averaged nearly 23% per year.[12] According to any reasonable standard, the conclusion to be drawn is that the instability associated with specialized raw-materials production geared for export is great.

Some persons maintain that, in addition to being victims of domestic instability induced through fluctuations in foreign trade, underdeveloped countries have also been experiencing long-run deterioration in their export-import relationships. Such deterioration is evidenced, allegedly, in a tendency for the terms of trade for underdeveloped countries to worsen over time, i.e., in a tendency for a worsening to occur in the relationship between prices of exports (largely raw materials) and prices of imports (largely manufactures and semi-manufactures). Despite important short-run fluctuations (yielding temporary improvement on occasion, but followed always by retrogression), the long-run tendency is represented as one that requires an ever larger physical volume of raw materials to be exported in order to command a given physical volume of imports in return.[13] Relevant data on this score are shown in Table 9. Among facts discernible there are the following: the ratio of prices of raw-materials products to those of manufactured goods declined by roughly one-third between the 1870's and the post-World War II period; for the same amount of raw-materials products, only 69% of the manufactured goods available in the 1870's was available following World War II (or, put differently, some 50% more in raw-materials products was needed after World War II, as compared with the 1870's, to buy the same amount of manufactures).[14]

The combination of market instability and possible long-run deterioration in the terms of trade (which, when present, acts as an overall depressant) has served to arouse concern in numerous quarters, and to spur thinking as to what remedial measures might be invoked. Resultant

---

12 Viewed within the context of cyclical and long-term economic movements, substantially similar conclusions as to comparative instability are reached. For supporting data, see UN, *Instability in Export Markets of Under-Developed Countries,* New York, 1952, Tables 1, 2, and 3, pp. 4–6.

13 For a contrary view, which holds that the terms of trade for raw-materials-producing countries are destined to improve over the long-run (and which, hence, regards data indicating deterioration as reflective of a short-run situation, at best), see C. Clark, *The Economics of 1960* (London: Macmillan and Company, Ltd., 1942), esp. p. 54. Argumentation in support of the contrary view is generally based on the belief that the spread of economic development will cause a growing proportion of the world's productive effort to be devoted to non-raw-materials production, so that an altered supply-and-demand relationship will force the terms of trade eventually to move rather continuously in favor of raw-materials-producing countries.

14 An element ignored in these and similar computations concerns possible quality changes, an important consideration in the evaluation over time of manufactured goods especially.

Table 9. Ratio of Prices of Raw Materials to Those
of Manufactured Goods[1] (Base: 1876–80 = 100)

Periods	Amount of manufactured goods obtainable for a given quantity of raw materials
1876–80	100.0
1881–85	102.4
1886–90	96.3
1891–95	90.1
1896–1900	87.1
1901–05	84.6
1906–10	85.8
1911–13	85.8
. . . .	. . . .
1921–25	67.3
1926–30	73.3
1931–35	62.0
1936–38	64.1
. . . .	. . . .
1946–47	68.7

Source: UN, Post War Price Relations in Trade between Under-Developed and Industrialized Countries, *Lake Success, 1949; cited in UN,* The Economic Development of Latin America, *Lake Success, 1950, Table 1, p. 9.*

[1] Average import and export prices, according to Board of Trade data.

proposals that have been able to capture interest include those calling for shifts in production to types of output likely to fare better in external markets, or likely to diminish dependence upon high-cost imports. Significantly, proposals falling within either category have been lauded by proponents as comprising essential facets of economic development.

THE SPREAD OF BENEFITS

Classical economic theory holds that the operation of free-market forces at the international level tends to promote income maximization among countries. If each country concentrates its productive effort along lines of greatest comparative advantage (or, in the absence of this, along lines of least comparative disadvantage), and participates freely in the trading pattern that thereupon evolves of necessity, then total world income tends to be maximized, and the income of each participating country also tends to be maximized. All benefit in mutual fashion.

The foregoing theoretical proposition long enjoyed virtually universal acceptance and support. During recent periods, however, numerous persons (in both underdeveloped and developed countries) have had second thoughts. Included among the doubters have been some professional economists, who have raised questions on both theoretical and practical grounds. The starting point for them has been that the results that prevail in the world belie the promise inherent in the theory. Specifically, most present-day underdeveloped countries have practiced specialization (in fact, sometimes to a high degree), *but* some of them, despite their resort to specialization, appear to be poorer today than they were in an earlier day—at least in a *relative* sense.

The particular aspect that causes concern is the manner in which benefits arising from international specialization, and trade, are split among the world's countries. Benefits are not spread around evenly; rather, as some visualize it, benefits accrue largely to developed countries, which are generally industrialized, and only incidentally, if at all, to underdeveloped countries, which are raw-materials producers. Specifically, underdeveloped countries are pictured as receiving disproportionately small benefits from trade because of the way economic forces operate under conditions tailored to facilitate international specialization (and not because developed countries are parties to a diabolical plot to defraud underdeveloped countries—as an occasional person would have one believe). The plight of underdeveloped countries is held directly attributable to the poor bargaining position of raw materials in the process of exchange for manufactured goods—with explanations for this poor position of raw materials including, among others, the presence of an inelastic demand in foreign markets and the general inability to upgrade through product differentiation.

A leading critic of the proposition that specialization (and integration in an internationalist trading system) offers advantage for underdeveloped countries is Raúl Prebisch, who has stated that:[15]

> . . . reality is undermining the out-dated schema of the international division of labour. . . .
>
> . . . [While] the reasoning on the economic advantages of the international division of labour is theoretically sound . . . it is based upon an assumption which has been conclusively proved false by facts. According to this assumption, the benefits of technical progress tend to be distributed alike over the whole community. . . . If by "the community" only the great industrial countries are meant, it is indeed true that the benefits of technical progress are gradually distributed among all social groups and classes. If, however, the concept of the community is extended to include the periphery of the world economy, a serious error is implicit in the generalization. The enormous benefits that derive from increased productivity have not reached the periphery in a measure comparable to that obtained by the peoples of the great in-

---

15 UN, *The Economic Development of Latin America,* New York, 1950, pp. 1–2. (Prebisch is Argentinian.) It is to be noted that Prebisch refers to raw-materials-producing countries as comprising the *periphery* of the world economy—in distinction to the major industrial countries that he labels as the *centre.*

dustrial countries. Hence, the outstanding differences between the standards of living of the masses of the former and the latter and the manifest discrepancies between their respective abilities to accumulate capital. . . . Thus there exists an obvious disequilibrium, a fact which . . . destroys the basic premise underlying the schema of the international division of labour.

Hence, the fundamental significance of the industrialization of the new countries. Industrialization is not an end in itself, but the principal means at the disposal of those countries of obtaining a share of the benefits of technical progress and of progressively raising the standard of living of the masses.

Somewhat similarly, Gunnar Myrdal has written that:[16]

. . . [The theory of international trade] would, indeed, suggest that trade starts a movement toward income equalization, while instead a quite normal result of unhampered trade between the two countries, of which one is industrialized and the other underdeveloped, is the initiation of a cumulative process toward the impoverishment and stagnation of the latter.

. . . trade does not by itself necessarily work for equality. . . . A widening of markets often strengthens in the first instance the rich and progressive countries whose manufacturing industries have the lead and are already fortified by the surrounding external economies, while the underdeveloped countries are in continuous danger of seeing even what they have of industry . . . priced out by cheap imports from the industrial countries. . . . The main positive effect of international trade on the underdeveloped countries was in fact to promote the production of primary products; and such production, employing mostly unskilled labor, has come to constitute the bulk of their exports. In these lines, however, they often meet inelastic demands in the export markets, often also a demand trend which is not rising very rapidly, and excessive price fluctuations. When, furthermore, population is rising while the larger part of it lives at, or near, the subsistence level—which means that there is no scarcity of unskilled labor—any technological improvement in their export production tends to transfer the advantages from the cheapening of production to the importing countries. Since the demand is often inelastic, the market will not be greatly enlarged.

[Despite this, the] advice—and assistance—which the poorer countries receive from the richer is, even nowadays, often directed toward increasing their production of primary goods for export. . . . In a broader perspective and from a long-term point of view, what would be rational is above all to increase productivity, incomes and living standards in the larger agricultural subsistence sectors, so as to raise the supply price of labor, and in manufacturing industry. This would engender economic development. . . . But trade by itself does not lead to such a development; it rather tends to have backwash effects and to strengthen the forces maintaining stagnation or regression.

. . . [The free play of] market forces will tend cumulatively to accentuate international inequalities.

---

[16] *Rich Lands and Poor* (New York: Harper and Brothers, 1957), pp. 101, 51–53, 55. (Myrdal is Swedish.)

Other persons too are on record with statements embodying ideas along substantially similar lines. The basic notion common to these statements is that underdeveloped countries, given prevailing production-and-trade patterns, cannot hope to obtain just rewards for efforts expended, let alone realize their full potential. What comes to be suggested, by way of an alternative, is an *altered* production pattern,[17] one believed likely to prove more beneficial for these countries. An immediate consequence, of course, is that from the thinking which proceeds along these lines springs a motivation for economic development.

THE SOVIET EXAMPLE

The USSR was a poor country at the time of the Great Revolution, largely agricultural and little removed from feudalism. A scant 40 years later the USSR loomed as a powerful country, able to pair itself off against the US in a global struggle of coexistence. Obviously growth during the intervening years occurred at a remarkable pace, and the fact that this growth was engendered and sustained on the basis of the country's own internal efforts and through use of its own available resources—with remarkably little help from outside—makes the achievement all the more noteworthy. Harsh methods admittedly were the rule throughout, a fact that serves to dull the luster of the end result for many persons, but that nonetheless leaves unscathed its sheer realness in the world of today.

The record of growth in the USSR is common knowledge in all parts of the world, at least in its general outlines. It is widely known that the USSR has come a long way in a hurry and has done so, basically, under its own power. There is a realization that per-capita income in the USSR has risen sharply, and is now at a level considerably above most underdeveloped countries.[18] Moreover, there is a realization that the rapid rate of growth is continuing; and, since this rate is one of the world's greatest —if not *the* greatest—an aura of awe invariably is cast by implied speculations as to how far this growth will go.

The record of the USSR in the realm of accelerated growth has been sufficiently remarkable to attract attention on its own accord. Beyond

---

17 A further contention, however, is that once such countries are integrated members of an internationalist trading system, they tend to find themselves "frozen" into the prevailing production-and-trade set-up (so that it becomes difficult for them to break free, even when benefits believed derivable from continued adherence to the customary arrangement appear negligible as compared with those believed derivable under some alternate arrangement).

18 The relevant fact is that per-capita GNP in the USSR is currently estimated to be well above the world average, and far above the average prevailing in Africa, Asia, and Latin America (Table 1 in Ch. 1). Of course, a qualification of sorts needs to be introduced in view of the heavy "plough-back" in the USSR, which produces actual levels of living below what one might expect to find on the basis of data of per-capita income.

this, the USSR and outside proponents of its system of government have sought to call attention to the country's progress by means of propaganda techniques at their disposal. Significant in this connection, the USSR had attained a level of development by the mid-1950's that allowed it to embark upon a trade-and-aid offensive, involving economic and military assistance for numerous countries, especially in Africa and Asia. As was evidenced, the USSR, formerly a poor country, was no longer poor, but had become rich enough, in fact, to dispense assistance to other poor countries. Involved, in a sense, was an invitation for the other and still poor countries to emulate the USSR in goal and method.

In underdeveloped countries, reaction to the USSR's growth achievements is one of mixed emotions. Most persons unhesitatingly favor growth, but not all of these are prepared to condone forceful methods in attempts to achieve it. To say the least, much indecision prevails as to just how the countries should or might proceed to promote economic development, and experience minimum pain in the process. Significantly, thinking on the matter is taking place, and the fact that one major country, the USSR, has recorded considerable development in our time serves to spur on such thinking.

ECONOMICS AND POLITICS

It would be erroneous to conclude that *all* people in underdeveloped countries want economic development. Such simply is not the case. Some oppose development, outright or by subterfuge, mainly because they fear loss of relative status in the event of change. Others are neutral toward development—not opposed, but not aroused either as to its potential merits for them. However, a great many people in underdeveloped countries do want development. Relatively many are imbued with the idea that improved economic conditions are desirable, and are capable of realization. In fact, interest in and desire for development are so widespread in underdeveloped countries that the total situation has come to be labeled a *revolution:* a "revolution of rising expectations."[19]

Considerable popular sentiment thus exists on behalf of development. Alongside this popular sentiment, there is also a considerable outpouring of speeches and documents from officialdom subscribing to the desirability of development and detailing plans in this direction. Actually, as between the two—the populace and the officialdom—it may be, in fact, that popular sentiment on the matter of development has proceeded fully as rapidly as has official thinking, and perhaps even more rapidly. Significantly, a good deal of what officials of underdeveloped countries

---

[19] As nearly as this author has been able to determine, coinage of the label is attributable to Adlai Stevenson.

have to say *appears* intended not so much to whip up public sentiment in favor of development as it is to cater to interests and desires already known to exist among wide sections of the populace.[20]

Be this as it may, the expectations of large numbers of people as to developmental progress pose interesting questions. For example, do people realize what is involved in achieving development? It is necessary to note that it is one thing to fix one's eyes on the *benefits* of development and quite another thing to live through the *process,* and to withstand the *cost,* of achieving development. Undoubtedly the interest of most people who favor development is kindled and sustained by thoughts of the better life that is expected to be the result. What is frequently forgotten, or perhaps not understood, is that end-benefits tend not to accrue during a period of vigorous development. In fact, the price of development is likely to be certain added deprivations during some period, and certainly it is only "at the end of the line" that full end-benefits can legitimately be expected. Yet, what many people envisage is a better life all along the line (i.e., to "have their cake and eat it too"). For these, disillusionment may well be inevitable.

SELECTED BIBLIOGRAPHY

Wendell C. Gordon, *The Economy of Latin America.* New York: Columbia University Press, 1950.
> Contains considerable material relative to the colonialist background of countries within Latin America.

Seymour E. Harris, *International and Interregional Trade.* New York: The McGraw-Hill Book Company, Inc., 1957.
> Ch. 19, Economic development and the theory of international trade (critical of classical approach).

---

[20] It is interesting to note, in underdeveloped countries, the extent to which cognizance is given economic development in speeches and documents that emanate from officialdom and are expected to reach the ears and eyes of the populace. Some reference, be it by way of serious observation or mere platitudes, is nowadays almost always contained in top-level "state of the union" addresses in underdeveloped countries. Presentation of the annual fiscal budget or issuance of the latest policy directive on exchange control without inclusion of a prefatory statement tying the body of material to economic development in some fashion can scarcely be imagined in most underdeveloped countries. Virtually every underdeveloped country has a "National Economic Plan," avowedly designed to promote economic development. Whether or not anything different comes to be done because of a particular Plan is another story, but planning for development has caught on in underdeveloped countries to the extent that *a* Plan ordinarily is regarded as necessary by powers-that-be, and any underdeveloped country that happens not to have a Plan risks indictment by persons of other underdeveloped countries as being unprogressive. In fact, the need for top officialdom to "talk" economic development appears at the point at which heads-of-state in even those underdeveloped countries that are less than fully democratic (and where a free election does not have to be faced) find it good politics to include the "right" thoughts on economic development in their public utterances.

S. Kanesathasan, "Export Instability and Contracyclical Fiscal Policy in Underdeveloped Export Economies: A Case Study of Ceylon since 1948," in IMF, *Staff Papers,* Washington, April 1959.
> A case study of instability in a country specialized as a raw-materials exporter.

W. Arthur Lewis, *The Theory of Economic Growth.* Homewood, Ill.: Richard D. Irwin, Inc., 1955.
> Appendix (pp. 420–435), Analysis of the question: "Is Economic Growth Desirable?"

Gerald M. Meier and Robert E. Baldwin, *Economic Development.* New York: John Wiley and Sons, Inc., 1957.
> Pp. 2–10, Analysis of the meaning of the term economic development.

Gunnar Myrdal, *Rich Lands and Poor.* New York: Harper and Brothers, 1957.
> Chs. V and XI, Examination of the spread of benefits from international trade.

United Nations, *The Economic Development of Latin America,* New York, 1950.
> Parts I and II, Examination of the spread of benefits from international trade.

Jacob Viner, *International Trade and Economic Development.* Glencoe, Ill.: The Free Press, 1952.
> Chs. I–III and VI, Problems of international trade and economic development (treatment along lines of classical theory).

3

OBSTACLES TO DEVELOPMENT (I)

Despite widespread desire for economic development, progress frequently lags far behind expectation. A plain fact is that development is not easily induced or fostered. Rather, development is handicapped by the presence of various obstacles, economic, political, and social in nature.

It is easy to compose a long list of obstacles, but it is difficult to generalize about any such list as to its true bearing upon the course of development. In part, generalization is difficult because of wide variations among countries. Obstacles are more numerous, or of a more serious nature, in some countries than in others, and varying combinations of obstacles result in total impedimentary situations of widely differing severity. In part, also, generalization is difficult because, to a considerable extent, it is a matter of personal judgment as to just what comprises an obstacle, and when, and in what measure. Given identical situations, one person may conclude that development is quite impossible, while another person may conclude that considerable opportunity for development really exists.[1] In fact, because of the general overall

---

[1] Because of the great interest suddenly directed to the matter of economic development in only the relatively recent past, many contending hypotheses came to be advanced—and, by and large, these have continued to command attention alongside one another, basically because of insufficient opportunity thus far to *prove* the facts one way or the other (even as regards some of the larger issues). It seems reasonable to expect that important changes in points of view will occur as further research and observation add to existing knowledge. However, even though greater common ground may come to prevail in the future, particular specific problems and situations will doubtless always be subject to varying personal interpretations.

inclination, or bias, of some persons to conclude negatively and of others to conclude positively, it is common in some quarters to label those concerned with development matters (including professional economists) as being either *pessimists* or *optimists*.[2]

An assured fact, in any event, is that development does not proceed free of hindrances. Some factors, widely regarded as comprising important obstacles to development, bear mention here.

BLOCKAGE THROUGH VICIOUS CIRCLES

The core obstacle confronting underdeveloped countries in attempts to promote development involves vicious circles, as a consequence of which the status-quo poses resistance to alteration for the better. Accordingly, an initial task in attempts to promote development is to discover *which* vicious circles are the basic causes of the others, and to determine *how* these vicious circles can be dealt with so as to turn them into feedback mechanisms that might then induce sustained growth. All this follows from references made in Chapter 1.

The most essential attribute of a vicious circle is circular causation: "everything depends on everything." This may be fine by way of description, but it is much too nebulous, however, to offer a meaningful basis for action—or even for appraisal as to relative importance. More precise identification of component elements appears necessary. With this thought in mind, the examination of obstacles to development proceeds in succeeding paragraphs in terms somewhat more narrowly circumscribed than vicious circles, per se.

LACK OF NATURAL RESOURCES

The natural environment of a country is basic as a determinant of the type and amount of development that can likely occur. Obviously, some countries are much more favorably situated from the standpoint of climate, topography, and soil than are others. Also, known resources per person—including mineral and forest wealth—are far greater in some countries than in others. The situation can be summed up by saying that the blessings of nature are not evenly distributed throughout the world. Among underdeveloped countries, for example, the natural environment of Brazil or Venezuela appears to offer a potential far exceeding that of, say, regions of the Sahara. Despite wide variation, ranging from good to poor, it appears, however, that few underdeveloped countries, *if any*, are as favorably situated as the US in terms of natural ingredients for development (as gauged by known resources and present-day technology).

---

2 This simple characterization is resorted to, for example, in some US Government circles.

In measuring differences among countries on the basis of natural resources, three further observations appear particularly pertinent. First, most underdeveloped countries encompass relatively small geographic areas, so that the resource pattern of each readily tends to reflect shortcomings, especially as manifested in low diversity. Thus, an area in the underdeveloped world of comparable size with the US might be expected to compare at least somewhat more favorably in resources with the US than does any one of the individual countries embraced within such an area. Second, the degree of favorableness of a country's resource pattern and its present population bear no necessary relationship to one another. In fact, in some instances the most populous countries are the very ones that appear to have the least prospect for development, as measured by known resources. Third, countries having deficiencies in their resource patterns can conceivably draw upon the resources of other countries in support of their own development. Technically, trade offers a way for pooling resources. In practical terms, however, national borders in the real world are not invisible, and consequently do leave their imprint on resource utilization and on development itself. This is to say nothing of transport costs, which may prove considerable and thereby— as a minimum—serve to preclude entirely certain important categories of development.

All this is not to belittle the physical endowment of the underdeveloped world, or of large parts of it, or the potential inherent within this endowment. Whatever might be said of resource shortcomings, in general or specifically, the plain fact remains that present-day developed countries— and especially major industrial countries—have gone out of their way, time and again, to assure themselves of access to important resources found at many locales within the underdeveloped world. Certainly if developed countries find the resources of underdeveloped countries a sustaining force in their own economies, it seems incongruous to deny the *possibility* that underdeveloped countries on the spot *could* use these, and other, resources to further advantage in their own development.[3]

POLITICAL INSTABILITY

Political instability is a common ailment in the underdeveloped world. Whether rooted in a record of frequent changes of government[4] or based

---

[3] Indeed, not all countries that are today developed and prosperous are blessed with abundant resources of their own. For comment on this point, see P. T. Bauer and B. S. Yamey, *The Economics of Under-Developed Countries* (Chicago: The University of Chicago Press, 1957), pp. 46–47.

[4] An extreme case is that of Bolivia, which experienced an estimated 178 revolutions or violent, illegal changes of regime during the period 1825–1952. See "Bolivia in Trouble Again" (editorial), *The New York Times*, October 2, 1958, p. 36-C.

on anxiety fed by external threats of aggression or internal threats of subversion,[5] absence of political stability acts as a powerful deterrent to development.

Political instability deters development because it raises uncertainties as to the future that serve to affect adversely economic and other decisions made in the present. For example, rather than subject their capital to situations of high risk at home, moneyed nationals of underdeveloped countries often seek ways to shift their capital abroad to locales deemed safer, frequently to one or another of the developed countries. Such capital flights are fairly common, despite an acute shortage of capital within most underdeveloped countries. Or, moneyed nationals refrain from undertaking long term investment at home, other than in real estate, which in many underdeveloped countries is regarded as *the* investment outlet that offers both considerable scope and relative safety. The result is a less active interest in alternatives (e.g., for investment in industrial development), a bidding up of land prices, and widespread absentee ownership of lands characteristically assigned to uses of low productivity. Or, business talents turn to trading, in which rapid turnover of merchandise and near-liquidity of investment can be the rule, in preference to engagement in anything involving long-term commitments. Thus, entrepreneurial ability, which might have expressed itself as management in the course of industrial development, is prone to express itself instead in middleman services in export-import connections—a type of activity that characteristically comes to occupy relatively many persons in underdeveloped countries.[6] Or, needed foreign capital (e.g., private capital from developed countries) simply fails to enter. Instead, such capital comes to be invested at home—within the developed world—even when its anticipated productivity there appears considerably lower than in underdeveloped countries.

What a particular underdeveloped country can do—here and now—to achieve political stability, and thereby to invite development, is frequently somewhat limited. For many countries, political stability itself appears dependent to a high degree upon achievement *first* of some fuller measure of development. For other countries, given their weak positions relative to the disruptive influences confronting them, political stability appears dependent upon forces beyond what they themselves can bring

---

[5] This situation is said to comprise a familiar fact-of-life especially for some countries on the perimeter of the Communist Bloc.

[6] Investment in real estate and trade does not destroy the money capital involved, but capital so placed is tied up temporarily (while changing hands) and hence is not available *during that time* for use in industry. Additionally, the capital involved—once it has gotten into other hands—is subject to a series of individual decisions relating to consumption and saving, with the result that saving at a later point may not again comprise an equivalent block of money capital in the hands of persons readily able to place it in use in industry.

to bear.[7] But, be this as it may, the environment is not conducive to development when political instability—in any of its forms—continues to be present.

WEAK PUBLIC ADMINISTRATION

The process of development places certain positive responsibilities upon government and upon governmental personnel. As a maximum, government plays an active role as *leader,* either through the assumption of responsibility for developmental activity on its own accord or through the assumption of responsibility for inspiring activity within the private sector. As a minimum, government plays the tacit role of *partner,* providing certain supporting services necessary for developmental activity within the private sector. Unfortunately, however, the conduct of government, or of governmental personnel, leaves much to be desired in many underdeveloped countries, thereby tending to handicap development.

Public administration, generally, tends to be of low caliber. The fact that in the typical underdeveloped country a high proportion of governmental personnel, at all strata, is somewhat unskilled and unpracticed poses a handicap, whether government's role is that of an active leader or a tacit partner. If government chooses to undertake business operations on its own, the resultant management frequently is of distinctly poor quality, with inefficiency commonly running rampant. If government chooses merely to provide services to private entrepreneurs, these persons, too, are often left in a disadvantageous position. Private entrepreneurs need certain information by way of assistance from government, and they frequently are dependent upon certain arrangements in which government is directly involved. If they encounter difficulty in these respects (e.g., if fixed policies do not prevail, or if intended policies cannot be ascertained, or if arrangements cannot be worked out because of seemingly endless delays or because of seeming unwillingness or inability of personnel to assume responsibility in such a connection), the firm basis they need in order to initiate and conduct productive operations is absent. When, in addition, public morality is low, as is the case in some countries, the effort to initiate and conduct productive operations labors under a further handicap. While wide variations on these scores exist among countries, it is a certainty that any major shortcomings in the area of public administration tend to deter development.

Apart from various shortcomings in the ability or conduct of govern-

---

[7] To illustrate, an individual country on the perimeter of the Communist Bloc may find political stability beyond its grasp, in spite of anything it might undertake to do on its own accord. Since the instability to which such a country is subject is *area-wide* in scope, stabilization may be dependent upon *overall* assurances by a major outside power, e.g., by the US.

mental personnel generally, *some* top-level government officials may not even want development (even though they may insist publicly that they do, and may succeed very well in finding the "right" words to lend the impression that they do—as intimated earlier in Chapter 2). The course of "good politics" for top politicians, ever since the advent of The Great Awakening, appears to include occasional reference to economic development, the need for it, and what is being done or is about to be done to help speed it. However, what politicians say and what they do—and want—*sometimes* differ. Indeed, there is good reason why there might very well be such differences within the environment of the underdeveloped world. A first relevant fact is that the top political leaders, in many, if not most, underdeveloped countries, are also top economic figures.[8] A second relevant fact is that large scale development is likely to "rock the boat," in the sense of subjecting the status-quo to change. In the course of development, some people long "on top of the heap" are liable to find themselves no longer on top, or are liable to find themselves obliged to share their preferred status with others who are ascending within the new economic pattern (so that their power in the economy comes to be weakened, in a relative sense). It is reasonable to believe that top political figures are generally cognizant of this situation. Whether or not such awareness serves, in particular instances, to color decisions and actions is difficult to ascertain conclusively. However, *if* a given leader realizes this situation and is also determined to preserve his own preferred economic status at all costs, it is possible he may say what he thinks he is expected to say, in order to maintain political popularity, while doing what he thinks is best for himself (placing reliance, presumably, upon a policy of "go slow"). In that case, the very inspirational and policy leadership essential to accelerated development is hopelessly compromised. Significantly, an absence of genuine pro-development sentiment on the part of top leadership perhaps (*or* probably) poses an obstacle to development of far greater consequence than any combination of the varied failings frequently ascribed to the lesser bureaucrats situated further down in the official echelon.

MORES, TRADITIONS, AND CULTURE

Resistance to change is much cited as an alleged obstacle to development in underdeveloped countries. The mores, traditions, and cultural patterns that prevail, or particular aspects of them, are said to be responsible for this resistance.

---

[8] In fact, some top political figures appear to have ascended to eminent positions in part *because* they possessed an economic status that made political success attainable. (Beyond this, political power sometimes leads to enhanced economic status, corruption being one possible course toward greater personal wealth.)

Even casual observation serves to impress one with the fact that the mores, traditions, and cultural patterns of underdeveloped countries frequently are far different from those of advanced Western countries, and frequently work against the introduction of Western methods and against development itself. One might readily cite many examples to illustrate how development comes to be impeded, but a few are sufficient to indicate what is at issue. A caste system—formalized and rigid, or informal—exists in some countries and acts to impede occupational mobility and personal opportunity. Educated persons frequently are expected to engage only in certain lines of work (and, especially, to abstain from any activity that might involve the "dirtying of hands"); compliance with such dictates of public opinion serves to block the entry of qualified people into new and needed types of work. Landholding carries more prestige in some countries than does entrepreneurship in industry (manufacturing), with the result that moneyed elites tend to be deterred from entering into new industries. Frequently, there is resistance to new or different agricultural methods as time-honored ways are continued. Individualism and individual incentive often meet opposition since each individual is bound to a family or clan group to which he has established responsibilities. Ancestor worship is traditional in some countries, and is said to cause people to look back, but not ahead.

Historically, it is probably true that particular beliefs and practices arose and continued basically because they fitted the societies in question—or, at least they did not clash at later points with the societies in which they prevailed. But, if development comes to be desired at some juncture in history, the need for change becomes clear. Some modification in existent beliefs and practices comes to be required as a prelude. Once development is underway, many further modifications are likely to be induced (as a consequence of development). The difficulty at the time development comes to be desired, however, is how to bring about that change needed as a first step. This change is generally slow to be initiated, and afterwards sometimes evokes wide and long-continuing resistance, both conscious and unconscious.

Actually, resistance to change—viewed in terms of how it relates to economic development—is of two main types. First, there is resistance because "change would impinge on deeply held beliefs or status-determining relationships"; second, there is resistance because "change involves risk."[9] If change is to be facilitated, causes of the resistance to change must be dealt with. And, because causes of the resistance to change vary widely, as they are of two distinct types, what can or cannot be changed also varies widely.

---

[9] S. P. Hayes, Jr., "Personality and Culture Problems of Point IV," in B. F. Hoselitz (ed.), *The Progress of Underdeveloped Areas* (Chicago: The University of Chicago Press, 1952), p. 210. Copyright 1952 by the University of Chicago.

Devotion to "deeply held beliefs or status-determining relationships" tends to be difficult to alter. The will to see change come about in this connection is generally lacking to an important degree. The matter is akin to prejudice; people who grow up thinking a certain way generally never change their basic thinking (and frequently do not even want to). If the thinking pattern is to be altered, one is pretty much obliged to concentrate on the younger members of society (in order to catch people when their minds are still pliable[10]), in the hope that the stage can thereby be set for change in a subsequent generation.

Notwithstanding the elements of inflexibility cited, some real change is evident in the manner in which younger members of society in at least some underdeveloped countries are responding to the *idea* of change. There is little doubt but that, in some countries, a substantial proportion of the population in the younger age brackets, especially in urban centers, has "gone Western" and, indeed, wants to "go Western," while older members of the population for much the greater part continue in traditional ways—and, in fact, are frequently dismayed with what they observe in their juniors. The willingness, especially, of many younger people to copy almost anything that is Western is easy to observe in many underdeveloped countries (e.g., in the Orient, where cultural patterns traditionally differ widely from Western civilization). Some of this cultural adaptation is perhaps superficial, but certainly liberal borrowing is going on, and is proceeding at a pace set not so much by an unwillingness to absorb further as by the failure to have additional access. And, of course, any propensity to accept change now evident is likely to increase as development itself proceeds—and, also, as urbanization possibly increases with development.

Resistance to change because "change involves risk" is quite a different matter. Here there is no mental block to change—only a hesitancy to incur the risk associated with change. Such hesitancy has its base in what is considered eminently rational and reasonable, not in taboo. If change is then to occur, the logical stimulus is reduction in the risk that happens to comprise the impedimentary factor.

While it is easy to cite numerous cases, two will suffice to illustrate this second type of resistance to change. By way of a first example, agricultural technicians from developed countries sometimes complain that the explanations they give small-scale farmers in underdeveloped countries, about how to alter production methods in order to increase yield, go absolutely unheeded. The impression sometimes conveyed is that the typical farmer at issue lacks intelligence, or initiative, or both. One might point out, however, that the typical farmer is living at or very near

---

[10] The USSR reputedly is a prime exponent of this principle in the propagation of its theories.

absolute subsistence. There is no latitude in his total situation to allow for experimentation. To fail is not to survive (and this involves the fate of his family as well as of himself). He knows he is poor and that improvement is desirable, but he also feels that prevailing methods can likely assure him of survival in the future as they have in the past. Were he to change his ways, he might do better, but then he *might* also do worse. Given these alternatives, why should he choose to expose himself to added risk? The agricultural technician, in essence, gives the farmer a good technical lecture, but he fails to resolve away the farmer's risk—and it is this risk that is much at issue.

By way of a second example, people in underdeveloped countries tend to remain closely attached to their family or clan groups, seemingly unwilling to assume the mobility required to capitalize on opportunities in other locales within their respective countries. Such immobility, or attachment, is widely regarded as a deterrent to development. One might point out, however, that a person reaps a certain security as a member of a closely-knit group in that he probably will not starve should he fall victim to enforced idleness or other mishap. If the person should break away from the group and then fail to prosper at some point, his plight would be great. Underdeveloped countries typically have neither abundant job opportunities nor social welfare schemes with which to reassure the jobless; in the absence of better alternatives for workers, safety is attained or sought through close association within a family or clan group. Until the element of risk to which individuals are subject is minimized or can be dealt with outside a family or clan group, extensive mobility of labor cannot be expected.

In summary, one is obliged to conclude that the mores, traditions, and cultural patterns prevalent in underdeveloped countries do comprise impediments to development. To an important degree, however, something can be done about these impediments. Insofar as risk factors underlie the resistance to change, considerable scope for removal of impediments exists, here and now. In fact, much modification is already evident in this connection (and beyond it), and continues to occur. The final removal of a substantial portion of the impediments within this category appears dependent, however, upon the realization first of a greater amount of development.

INADEQUACIES IN LABOR

Deficiencies are apparent in the labor forces of underdeveloped countries, and act as an impediment to development. As a starter, virtually the entire labor force of the typical country is unskilled, all but completely lacking in training in modern production methods or in utilization of modern machinery. This situation is especially important when industrial development is at issue. Labor of particular types, absolutely essential to this form of development, is frequently entirely lacking (although labor in general may be super-abundant), and training of labor preparatory to the assumption of essential tasks ordinarily poses a costly procedure for any firm commencing new operations.[11]

Again, mobility of labor is generally low. Significantly, a general reluctance prevails on the part of individuals to break free of family associations in familiar locales and to venture forth to new occupations in sometimes distant parts of the country. Such reluctance is readily understandable, given prevailing circumstances, but its prevalence does pose an adverse factor in the developmental picture.

Additionally, general fluidity in society, in terms of which an individual can assume that "the best man can win," is lacking to an important degree in underdeveloped countries. For all practical purposes, there is no middle class; rather, the great mass of the population consists strictly of "have-nots," and at the top is a small strata of "haves." The haves characteristically take care of their own, and the have-nots rarely succeed in bridging the wide expanse that lies between them and the upper strata. The result is that opportunity for improvement through vertical progression in society is largely absent for the have-nots—even for persons of inherently high ability—while opportunity and money success tend almost automatically to be assured members born into the upper strata. Unfortunately, the general absence of social fluidity, upward or downward—but especially upward—serves to undermine individual incentive.[12]

These inadequacies in labor (and some others which might be cited, although probably of lesser importance) are widely regarded as important impediments to development. Nevertheless, the situation is not without some bright spots. As many a technician from an advanced country has noted, after exposure to the environment of one or another underdeveloped country, workmen often exhibit relatively high willingness and ability to learn about and adjust to new tasks when given a reasonable opportunity and motive to do so. Significantly, the plain fact is that in most underdeveloped countries there has traditionally been no good personal reason for large numbers of workers to master new skills, especially since no sizable demand for anything other than unskilled labor has prevailed. Consequently, the really important consideration seems to

---

[11] In advanced countries, the cost of preparing labor for frequently complex duties tends to be borne, entirely or largely, by the economy as a whole as a *social cost* (e.g., in terms of general or specialized education, provided at public expense). In underdeveloped countries, in contrast, outlays for comparable training tend to confront firms as a *business cost*, since those firms that are first to require particular labor are generally obliged to provide training on their own and at their own expense.

[12] To an important extent, the emergence of a middle class appears dependent upon further urbanization, which in turn is fostered by industrial development. Therefore, the situation may well be that some development is needed, as a first step, for evolution of a middle class.

relate not so much to the extent of current scarcity or abundance of skilled labor as it does to the ability or inability of labor to acquire skills when they are needed, and with reasonable dispatch. As intimated, ability along these lines appears to be present to at least a fair degree in numerous underdeveloped countries (as evidenced, for example, by the manner in which old machine and vehicular equipment is frequently kept in usable shape, even to the extent of hand manufacturing spare parts when foreign-exchange stringency prevents imports). And, in the light of evidence as to how individuals and groups among labor have responded to particular stimuli on previous occasions, it seems reasonable to believe that if employers were on hand to offer attractive outlets for skilled labor that provided workers with a particularized reason for acquiring new skills, at least some number of potential employees would attempt to qualify. Moreover, only *some* proportion of the labor force, not *all* the labor force, needs to be skilled, even under industrialization. Of course, even if one is convinced that skills in the necessary amount can be generated and that development itself tends to promote the acquisition of needed skills, the hard fact still remains that those employers on the scene in the early stages of development face a general shortage of skilled labor (which handicap they are obliged to overcome either by a training program or by hiring workers abroad, either of which is costly in the business sense).

Admittedly, it is difficult to overcome the immobility of labor and the lack of fluidity in the social structure, at least during the early stages of development. At root, remedial accomplishments in these connections appear to depend more upon economics than upon education. Marked improvement seems likely only as development itself serves to broaden the economic base and to create additional and varied economic opportunities for individual members of society. In comparison, efforts in the realm of education seem to carry potentially smaller immediate impact; admonitions as to what ought to be, even when heard and believed, are likely to make little real dent unless the economic structure can accommodate that which is desired. Of course, once some accomplishments are realized in these areas as a consequence of early developmental progress, the path is smoothed for further development. Significantly, however, whatever the situation becomes over time, the cited shortcomings do serve to hamper development during the early stages.

INADEQUACIES IN ENTREPRENEURSHIP AND MANAGEMENT

Entrepreneurial and managerial qualities are frequently cited as being at a low ebb in underdeveloped countries. Entrepreneurship—i.e., the willingness to take risks and to innovate—is said to be either generally scarce or poorly oriented, while managerial talent—i.e., competence as to the direction of enterprises—is similarly held to fall far short of what might reasonably be deemed desirable. Between them, some persons believe a situation is created that entails serious shortcomings in regard to the potential leadership necessary for initiating and promoting progress in development. The shortcomings involved are cited as comprising especially important barriers to progress whenever industrial development is contemplated.

Aside from the considerations pertaining directly to the overall supply of entrepreneurship in underdeveloped countries, a special complication from the standpoint of economic development arises from the manner in which prospective entrepreneurs on the scene tend to conduct themselves. The central point at issue is that the environment in these countries seemingly tends to endorse whatever is traditional and to work against that which is new or different. To illustrate, those persons of greater or lesser ability who might reasonably aspire to become entrepreneurs in new industrial undertakings frequently follow a path of least resistance and simply fall back on the customary types of outlets—real estate and trading. Both of these major outlets are time-honored, socially sanctioned as desirable, and generally adequate in terms of income yield. Additionally, these outlets commonly seem preferable (as compared with, say, entry into the realm of industry) because of the institutional rigidity typically associated with access to financing in underdeveloped countries. Specifically, bank credit facilities are commonly geared to provide financing for real estate and trade, but are not oriented toward the handling of industrial financing. Real estate, as a loan outlet, is regarded as safe, even if somewhat illiquid. Trade, especially export-import trade, is also regarded as a safe loan outlet, since merchandise capable of ready liquidation serves as backing. In contrast to these, a prospective entrepreneur who seeks to obtain financing for, say, a new industrial undertaking is likely to find that the banking community is less sure of the safety of loan funds so placed, and is therefore disinclined to venture into what it considers a new area of financing—and it is especially disinclined in view of the fact that all available funds might be placed in real estate and trade. The result is that a prospective entrepreneur may find financing unavailable if he desires entry into a new industry, but available if he is willing to enter real estate or trade. On the basis of the foregoing, the conclusion suggested is that entrepreneurial talent certainly is not absolutely lacking (as seems evidenced by the number of shrewd operators engaged in real estate and trading), but that much of the entrepreneurial talent is directed away from industry, in large part because the existing environment, with its institutional rigidities, tends to preclude anything else. A strong case seems present for supporting the contention that the real obstacle, in the immediate sense, to new forms of ventures is institutional rigidity, more than it is a shortage of entrepreneurial talent.

As for managerial talent, it seems significant that the numbers of people in underdeveloped countries who receive specialized training for assuming managerial responsibilities in new enterprises tend to be much smaller than in advanced countries. In important measure, these smaller numbers appear to be the result of two particular sets of circumstances. First, education is generally less widespread in these countries, and a low degree of sophistication is a general characteristic of the prevailing environment. Second, the overall environment, as previously intimated, is one within which there is little incentive for any substantial number to acquire special training, since the potential for the subsequent use of this training appears to be low.

Even if the numbers of persons recognized as possessing managerial talent were regarded as adequate, there still is the matter of these people's degree of competence. Significantly, there appears to be a basis for holding that, as a general rule, management in underdeveloped countries is not so competent as that found in advanced countries. And, of course, greater competence is desirable—on general principles, if for no better reason. There is some question, however, as to the *extent* to which any of the prevailing shortcomings in competence serve, here and now, to deter development. Clearly, when end-output is obliged to compete in foreign markets, it is a matter of considerable importance as to just how competent management happens to be. However, when end-output is destined for the domestic market, the market conditions prevailing therein are frequently such as to enable domestic production to prosper, notwithstanding major areas of inefficiency in the production process. This is the case in large measure because competitive imports are subject to various add-on costs prior to reaching end consumers,[13] thereby giving rise to a margin of protection for domestic producers of lesser efficiency. When, in addition, domestic authorities view new domestic output as a substitute for customary imports and proceed to bar competing imports,[14] domestic output is virtually assured of a market, even though efficiency may be at a low ebb. On the basis of the foregoing, the conclusion suggested is that high-level managerial talent is preferable to low, but that, up to a point, considerable developmental progress in underdeveloped countries appears possible even in the face of major shortcomings in managerial competency.

---

[13] End prices on imports embody transport costs, duty payments, and middleman profits at various levels (with all profit mark-ups typically at high percentage rates, the general business practice in underdeveloped countries being one of low volume, but high mark-up). The final price tends to be one that, in competitive terms, enables some domestic production to substitute for usual imports (and still yield returns above break-even, notwithstanding somewhat lesser efficiency).

[14] Through imposition of protective tariffs or exchange-control regulations.

One line of reasoning (frequently advanced in underdeveloped countries) is that some desired development—say, industrial development—is failing to come about, that this failure is attributable in part to a shortage of good entrepreneurial or managerial talent, and that an immediate approach ought therefore to be government's entry into production. This logic is then commonly buttressed further by the notion that government ought to "show the way" until such a time as the private sector is capable of assuming the task. At best, such a line of reasoning is only partially correct. To the extent that private entrepreneurs are unwilling to act in the light of risks or other adverse factors presumed to exist, a case can be made for government's taking the initiative to "show the way"; after all, government can proceed in the face of some risks that logically can be expected to deter private individuals. However, if a shortage of good managerial talent is the real reason why activity has lagged, the transfer of responsibility to government, as suggested, offers no solution. When good managerial talent is physically non-existent in a country, it obviously cannot be made available to either the private sector or the public sector.

Beyond what might be done by government to offset the hesitancy of private entrepreneurs, other avenues are open to countries to do something, in the short-run, about shortcomings in entrepreneurial or managerial talent—and thereby help alleviate a situation that otherwise serves to obstruct development. Relative to shortcomings in the entrepreneurial function, greater emphasis can be placed upon entry into the domestic economy of private foreign firms, presumably recruited from one or another advanced country. Relative to shortcomings in managerial talent, a country experiencing deficiencies can also place reliance upon entry by private foreign firms, which then provide talent as part of the investment process. Or, a country can attempt to foster the negotiation of management contracts under which foreign talent is hired for use in domestically-owned enterprises, either public or private. In the longer-run, of course, the only remedy for inadequacies in entrepreneurial or managerial talent is development of the requisite talent. This involves training, important particularly in the case of management, *plus* evolution of an economy in which entrepreneurship is lured into the desired types of outlets and in which the opportunity for managerial talent provides an incentive for its acquisition and refinement.

SELECTED BIBLIOGRAPHY

See the end of Chapter 4.

4

OBSTACLES TO DEVELOPMENT (II)

The series of obstacles cited and discussed in the preceding chapter can be supplemented with additional ones.

LOW VOLUME OF SAVING

A major impediment to economic development exists in the low volume of saving found in underdeveloped countries. Saving in the underdeveloped world is estimated to average only about 5% of national income, as compared with about 10% in the developed world as a whole[1] (and about 15% in the US[2]). A dilemma exists in that much capital is needed for developmental purposes, but the saving necessary for support of this development (i.e., for support of developmental investment) comprises only a low percentage of an also low level of income. Thus, attempts by individual countries to promote development, however favorably situated the countries may be on other scores (e.g., in terms of supplies of raw materials and qualified people), tend to encounter serious difficulties—simply because capital is lacking in an adequate amount to make substantial development possible.[3]

---

[1] Table 7 in Ch. 1; also UN, *Measures for the Economic Development of Under-Developed Countries,* New York, 1951, p. 35.

[2] For supporting data, 1949–59, see *Economic Indicators* (Prepared for the Joint Economic Committee by the Council of Economic Advisors), Washington, September 1959, p. 2.

[3] B. Ward, writing in *The New York Times,* November 8, 1959 (Section 6, p. 15), states: "Without capital, without massive saving, no program of modernization is even conceivable. Improved agriculture, power and transport, new industries, extended education—all are insatiable for capital; its availability . . . is the key to all development."

The basic explanation for the low volume of saving derives from the low level of income that prevails.[4] First a population must live, and it can save only that part of its income beyond the amount felt necessary to sustain certain consumption levels. This means that a greater volume of saving, barring an increase in income (which is not to be expected, in any event, in an immediate sense), can occur only at the expense of consumption (which happens characteristically to be low in underdeveloped countries).

Not only is the volume of saving low, but much of what is saved tends not to remain within the countries of origin. As intimated earlier, numerous moneyed nationals within underdeveloped countries are prone to move their capital to other countries, frequently to developed countries, in large part because they feel their holdings will be safer there. The apparent situation is that many underdeveloped countries lack the degree of political stability regarded by potential investors as essential for domestic investment; in addition, they lack organized capital markets, the presence of which might encourage domestic investment by making the investment process more convenient. It is somewhat ironical, of course, to find moneyed nationals of underdeveloped countries investing within the US and other developed countries[5] at a time when their own governments are attempting to promote development and are, in some instances, negotiating foreign loans or requesting foreign aid for this very purpose.

What can an underdeveloped country do to retain for use at home the capital otherwise likely to be shifted abroad? One possibility involves an improvement in the overall political and economic environment so that a national might regard investment in his own country as holding greater attractiveness. But, insofar as an improved environment is itself dependent upon further development, voluntary response on the part of private savers and investors is likely to prove small in any immediate sense. A second possibility, involving compulsion, is income taxation. If nationals insist upon moving their capital from a country, the government can eliminate much of the withdrawal through enactment and enforcement of a steeply progressive income tax. Private individuals cannot shift out of a country that which is no longer theirs. In essence, this procedure amounts to a socialization of the saving and investment func-

---

4 In addition to the overall level of income, the distribution of income is also of importance. Significantly, the distribution of income appears to be quite inequitable in numerous underdeveloped countries—with a relatively high proportion of total income accruing to, say, the upper 10% of income recipients. As a general rule, income inequality tends to favor greater saving on the basis of a given level of income. Thus the low savings-rate in underdeveloped countries is the result, fundamentally, of the low overall level of income prevailing, and the rate is low despite whatever pro-savings biases might spring from substantial income inequality.

5 Typically, they acquire foreign bank deposits or purchase stocks and bonds of foreign corporations.

tions. While it is possible to stop capital flights to a great extent through this approach, potential drawbacks are present in other connections. A question arises as to how total saving—and income—is likely then to be affected, since private incentive may be deterred. Also, a question arises as to whether channelization of funds through government is likely to produce overall results any better than those characterizing private utilization, since, after all, stories of gross mismanagement of public funds are quite common in the case of some underdeveloped countries. A third possibility, exchange control, also involves compulsion, but in a mild form as compared with taxation. Exchange control offers a means to block capital flights by giving power to a central governmental authority to deny access to foreign exchange for this purpose, but in so doing does not necessitate relinquishment of private ownership of the capital concerned.

On the other hand, capital that does remain within the countries of origin—whatever its magnitude—is frequently used in ways that leave much to be desired. Poor forms of utilization are widespread, whether capital comes to be employed in the private sector or in the public sector. Private individuals are prone to look upon the traditional outlets of real estate and trade as somehow preferable to new outlets, such as industry (manufacturing), and this is the case even when specific forms of industry appear to offer outstanding potential in terms of private profit, as well as in overall benefits for the economy.[6] And governments, when given power over utilization of capital, readily fall victim to political influences that result in the channelization of considerable funds into "monuments" of various sorts, in preference to investment in other and more productive categories. The overall fact that underdeveloped countries frequently put to seemingly poor uses the admittedly limited capital generated domestically constitutes grounds for concern in developed countries (e.g., in the US), especially when these countries are called upon by underdeveloped countries to make supplementary capital available. This normal concern in developed countries is sometimes reinforced by an element of irritation when particular underdeveloped countries choose to preface their requests with assertions to the effect that "all that can be done at home is *already* being done," and choose also to react as though their very sovereignties were impinged upon when questioned as to *how* currently available capital supplies are being utilized.

It is one thing for an underdeveloped country to attempt to do an effective job in the mobilization and placement of such capital as does arise domestically, but what if very little in the way of domestic capital proves forthcoming? If *voluntary saving* is low, the inflation method of financing—involving *forced saving*—is sometimes invoked. Under this ap-

---

[6] For an earlier reference to this matter, see Ch. 3, footnote 6.

proach, a country's total money supply is expanded (through bank credit creation to support loans to business or government), the effect of which is to alter the *relative* shares of purchasing power held by various major segments of the population. Recipients of loans so supported (i.e., holders of the additions to the money supply) are enabled to bid against consumers and voluntary savers for access to current output or to some of the productive ingredients of such output. The result is an immediate redistribution of purchasing power, with consumers and voluntary savers having relatively smaller claims within the new context, so that a shift in productive effort from meeting the desires of consumers and voluntary savers toward meeting the desires of holders of the additions to the money supply tends to be fostered. Indeed, as prices rise in the process of competitive bidding, consumers are put at a further disadvantage, since wages tend to lag behind prices. The overall impact is one of a reduction in total consumption, and of a shift in total productive effort as the orientation of production comes to be less toward consumer goods and more toward producer (investment) goods. In essence, recipients of current income who had not chosen voluntarily to save more are forced to save in the sense that their purchasing power is reduced and thus gives them access to a smaller volume of goods and services—hence the label of "forced saving" for the process as a whole.

The technique of forced saving is not new to underdeveloped countries, a number of which have invoked it, to a greater or lesser extent, in the interests of accelerating development.[7] Effective as the procedure is from certain standpoints, it is not free of criticism. First, the real income of consumers is cut, or is held below levels otherwise currently possible. It is the consumer on the scene who then "pays" for the development that results, and he does so involuntarily, not voluntarily. Second, resultant domestic price increases tend to impair the ability to export and hence affect foreign-trade balances adversely—thereby raising a question as to how needed imports can be financed. Third, the prospect of a rising price level tends to distort financing itself (e.g., as supplementary long-term financing in fixed-interest securities comes to be deterred). Fourth, domestic holders of funds, fearful of financial ruin as a consequence of rising prices, are encouraged to seek refuge in investment in real property or in capital flights (thereby accentuating particular tendencies already evident in numerous underdeveloped countries, and widely regarded as deleterious to the process of development).

If saving, voluntary or involuntary (forced), is not forthcoming in sufficient amount to allow support for a desired pace of development, and if such a developmental pace is deemed essential regardless, the remaining major recourse open to an underdeveloped country is that of

---

7 A classic case is that of Brazil.

access to capital originating abroad. Unfortunately, a number of obstacles are also likely to be encountered in this connection, either as to amount, terms, or form of capital obtainable—as is shown in detail at a later point in this volume.

SHORTAGE OF FOREIGN EXCHANGE

The term *saving* refers to amounts of money *or* to stocks of real items not consumed (i.e., to goods and services denied consumers and thus remaining eligible for possible use in investment). Actually, saving in the form of money has little value except for its buying power. In the final analysis, it is goods and services that count in development, and money and its manipulation merely offer a means by which access is gained to the desired goods and services. To illustrate, the monetary manipulation associated with the process of *forced* saving is undertaken with the hope of bringing about an increase in *real* saving (in the sense that goods and services will be reoriented from consumer ends to investment ends).

A sovereign government has the power to create any desired amount of national (local) currency.[8] This money can then be directed in its use so as to give particular persons or agencies claim to some portion of currently available goods and services (e.g., to enable channelization of such goods and services into investment purposes). While there is no limit to how much money a country can create, the amount of real saving a country is capable of *is* limited—limited, in the final analysis, to the difference between current real output and minimum subsistence (which sets a floor for consumption). This means that whenever the volume of domestic saving, in real terms, is insufficient to support desired amounts of real investment, one of three basic courses is at hand to close the gap: a reduction in consumption that makes possible greater real saving; a cut-back in the level of real investment initially envisaged; *or* access to external capital (i.e., access to externally-derived goods and services that can be channeled into the economy as a supplement to domestically-generated goods and services). In the absence of access to external capital, real domestic investment can increase no further at any given time than what proves possible on the basis of real domestic saving (present accruals plus unused accumulations from the past). Of course, in addition to this limitation, some goods and services required in development simply are not obtainable domestically, and can be had only from abroad (e.g., certain categories of machinery).

Access to external goods and services can be had, technically, on three

---

   8 In the final analysis, only the supply of paper and printer's ink constitutes a physical limitation.

bases: purchase, loan, or grant (gift). In each case, foreign exchange is ordinarily involved, not the local currency of the importing country. The act of purchase requires foreign exchange, which a country may have as a consequence of having earned it earlier or in the current period. Loans involve an extension of foreign exchange on credit, the repayment of which requires subsequent earnings of foreign exchange. Grants, like loans, involve an extension of foreign exchange on credit (typically), but differ in that no repayment requirement is attached. Significantly, then, local currency can be "manufactured" by a country, but foreign exchange has to be earned by it—past, present, or future (except in the case of grants)—through the achievement of an appropriate structuring of the balance of payments.

Clearly, foreign exchange is necessary in order to obtain some essential ingredients of development when these are not available domestically (e.g., machinery), or when these are desired in amounts greater than available domestically. In fact, not only is foreign exchange necessary, but there is need for the "right" kind of foreign exchange. When currency inconvertibility is widespread (e.g., as during the years following World War II), not every category of foreign exchange serves to give access to imports of the types desired. Most importantly, although foreign exchange is needed in connection with development, there tends to be an acute shortage of it in virtually every underdeveloped country. In the absence of loans and grants, countries are able to gain access to more foreign exchange only by earning it currently, and their capacities to earn it ordinarily are narrowly circumscribed—particularly in view of their prevailing state of underdevelopment. The dilemma faced can thus be summarized as one of scarce foreign-exchange supplies, great need for additional supplies, and rather low capacity to acquire these added supplies.

Reference is frequently made to one or another of several leading "avenues of escape" to help lessen the obstacle to development inherent in existent foreign-exchange shortages. A first suggestion is exchange control, which involves placement of foreign-exchange earnings accruing to a country—or to any of its residents—in an official pool, with subsequent allocations from the pool based on criteria intended to yield high overall benefit to the economy. Proponents are inclined to argue that official control along these lines is capable of yielding results superior to those likely to derive under free-market conditions, while their critics are prone to argue that official control results in market rigidities that act to jeopardize the total amount of foreign exchange potentially obtainable. In another vein, the existence of foreign-exchange shortages offers what many quarters regard as an excellent rationale for the launching of a campaign to obtain more foreign loans and grants. By way of final solution, of course, nothing appears quite so satisfactory as the achievement of economic improvement within the various underdeveloped countries to the degree that greater international trade under free-market conditions becomes possible. However, realization of this improvement is itself dependent upon the prior achievement of considerable development, which at present is hampered by the very shortage of foreign exchange.

LIMITED MARKETS

Even when all the difficulties previously cited are conquered and an increase in output becomes technically possible, the resultant capacity may not at all constitute a boon. Expansion of output in underdeveloped countries frequently proves difficult, or troublesome, simply because of insufficiencies in market demand. The obstacle at issue is readily demonstrable, as applied to attempts to expand either raw-materials output or industrial (manufacturing) output.

In the area of raw-materials production, heavy reliance within some economies upon subsistence agriculture tends to result in only a small domestic market outside the subsistence economy. With only a limited capacity to sell domestically for money, incentive is dulled for the production of additional food commodities for intended sale in the domestic market. In fact, producers frequently are deprived of even the stimulus that might stem from the sales potential in an integrated, though small, national market, since poor or costly transport facilities act to confine market exploitation mostly to areas where production occurs. Similarly, the sale abroad of raw materials—encompassing foodstuffs and other raw materials—is ordinarily hampered by time, cost, and some other considerations involved in reaching markets, as well as by conditions of inelastic demand that customarily confront the products. And, in the case of numerous raw-materials commodities that figure as highly specialized output for some countries (e.g., rubber, rice, coffee, and sugar—Fig. 3 in Ch. 2), only a distinctly limited amount of output is ordinarily capable of absorption domestically before saturation is approached, while an expansion of external sales is often handicapped by conditions of inelastic demand.

In industry (manufacturing), a similar deterrent to development is found in limitations in the size of the domestic market. Many underdeveloped countries are not populous to begin with, and all—whether they have a high or a low population—have low per-capita income. The result is a low *aggregate* domestic demand for industrial output, an important consideration for a country that might contemplate the establishment of new enterprises giving rise to this form of output.

By way of possible counter-argument, a proposition sometimes advanced holds that the process of industrialization is self-propelling. According to this proposition, industrialization gives rise to added income, which income then helps underwrite the market for the output of the production processes involved. In other words, "supply creates its own demand." The difficulty with this proposition, particularly when applied to underdeveloped countries, is that industrialization rarely, if ever, occurs simultaneously throughout the economy. Capital shortages in underdeveloped countries—at least in comparison with the immensity of the investment requirements of industrialization—tend to preclude across-the-board industrial development, so that development is forced to proceed selectively, pretty much one project at a time. A single industry or firm, however, cannot ordinarily create a demand for its own output. An industrial complex perhaps can create a total demand that goes far toward sustaining the total complex, but a single industry or firm cannot hope for a substantial market simply on the basis of the income it alone generates. In short, what may be true under general industrialization is not necessarily true under selective industrialization (but it is selective industrialization that underdeveloped countries are typically forced to accept, at least during the early stages of industrial development).

Even when the only developmental alternative is selective industrialization, however, hope nevertheless exists that the process of industrial growth can thereby be begun successfully, and perhaps progressively accelerated thereafter. Two major possibilities exist. First, special benefit might derive from a concentration of added investment in transportation and communication facilities. Investment of this type yields facilities that can help expand the domestic market by linking parts of the same country more closely. Additionally, the investment gives rise directly to expanded income that can bolster total demand. Second, and generally of much greater importance, *some* demand already exists, however small, and new domestic output, if it is of the right type, can capture it. Some domestic demand currently satisfied by importation could conceivably be catered to by domestic industry, were such industry to come into being and to turn out items capable of serving as substitutes for imports. Also, more value might be "built into" exports already occurring (e.g., as some raw-materials exports, currently exported in unprocessed form, come to some extent to be processed domestically prior to export).

Everything considered, one is obliged to conclude that development is handicapped when prevailing markets do not offer adequate outlets for production, and that market inadequacies of this type are common for underdeveloped countries. The exact extent to which market limitations pose a handicap for development, however, varies from country to country. Some consolation exists, of course, in that in many countries *something* appears readily possible to help ameliorate the handicap arising on this score.

PROBLEMS OF POPULATION

The central objective of economic development is to achieve a higher and rising level of real per-capita income. But if per-capita income shows a tendency to rise, might not these gains simply invite an increase in population that then results in the average person's status being largely unchanged? This is the problem posed by "Malthusians" as they observe the teeming, poverty-stricken millions of some of the world's under-developed countries.

First, as a prelude to an examination of the relationship of develop-ment to population, what is the current status of population, as to magnitude and growth, in the underdeveloped world? In terms of total numbers of people, the underdeveloped world is a populous place. Some two-thirds of the world's people live in underdeveloped countries, and two countries alone, India and Communist China, contain roughly one-third of the world's people. Apart from total numbers of people, density of population is quite high in many of the countries, although wide variation exists among them. Illustrative of the range that prevails are the high population densities in Communist China, Egypt (Nile belt), Haiti, India, and Indonesia (Java only), which stand in sharp contrast to the low densities in several countries of Latin America (e.g., Brazil, Paraguay, and Venezuela), the Indochina States, and parts of Africa (e.g., Kenya and the Belgian Congo).[9] Not only do high population densities already exist in numerous countries, but the situation in the under-developed world, as an entity, is that the current rate of population

---

[9] For data on population density, see UN, *Demographic Yearbook 1958*, New York, 1958, Table 1, pp. 86–103 (for country data), and Table 2, p. 104 (for regional data). Ascertainment of population density is commonly approached as a purely *statistical* matter of numbers of people per unit of area. Actually, however, the concept of population density acquires full economic meaning only when two *additional* con-siderations are taken into account, alongside the cited statistical data. First, areas differ in their capacities to sustain people because of differences in natural endowment. For example, viewed in terms of agricultural potential, fertile delta areas are superior to mountain terrain or desert wastes, and tropical areas tend to have at least one advantage over those areas in which a colder climate restricts the crop-growing period to a fraction of the year. Second, areas differ in their capacities to sustain people because of what man has done thus far in shaping the economic environment. For example, two countries, one developed and the other underdeveloped, may have identical numbers of people per unit of area, but the fact that the developed country is industrial or agro-industrial, while the underdeveloped country is exclusively or very largely reliant upon raw-materials production, constitutes a significant environ-mental difference that is important in evaluating capacities to support people, and hence in ascertaining population densities (in the economic sense). Application of these two considerations to underdeveloped countries reveals that, on the first score, great diversity exists among countries as to the degree of favorableness of natural endowment, and that, on the second score, concentration in raw-materials production is the typical situation. And, after taking the two additional considerations into account, the general conclusion that still seems warranted is that a considerable portion of the underdeveloped world has a high population density (*relative* to the developed world).

Table 10. Population, Birth and Death Rates, and Population Growth, by Regions

REGION	Population, 1957 (millions)	Rates per 1,000 population (annual average, 1953–57)			Annual percentage-rate of increase (1950–57)
		Birth rate	Death rate	Population growth rate[1]	
Africa	225	45	27	18	1.8
Northern Africa	74	45	26	19	1.9
Tropical & Southern Africa	151	45	27	18	1.8
America	381	32	12	20	2.1
Northern America	189	25	9	16	1.7
Middle America	61	41	15	26	2.6
South America	131	39	16	23	2.3
Asia	1,556	39	21	18	1.8
South West Asia	72	42	18	24	2.4
South Central Asia	513	42	28	14	1.4
South East Asia	193	42	25	17	1.7
East Asia	778	35	16	19	2.0
Europe	414	19	11	8	0.7
Northern & Western Europe	139	18	11	7	0.6
Central Europe	135	19	11	8	0.8
Southern Europe	140	21	11	10	0.8
Oceania	15	25	9	16	2.2
USSR	204	26	8	18	. . . .
World	2,795	34	18	16	1.6

Source: UN, Demographic Yearbook 1958, *New York, 1958, Table 2, p. 104.*

1 Birth rate minus death rate.

growth is also high. The general pattern in underdeveloped countries is high birth rates, high death rates, and—notwithstanding high death rates—high population growth rates (the growth rate being the birth rate minus the death rate). While significant variation exists among individual countries, the broad contrast between the underdeveloped world (Africa, Asia, and Latin America), on the one hand, and Europe and North America (which includes the US), on the other hand, is revealing (Table 10). In short, some parts of the underdeveloped world are already densely populated, and are currently subject, in addition, to a high rate of population growth.

In speculating about the likely effect of development upon population growth (and about their combined effect upon per-capita income), it is well to distinguish between those countries that are sparsely populated—relative to complementary resources—and those that are densely populated. In sparsely populated countries, a moderate increase in population is likely to raise few new economic problems. But in densely populated countries, the impact is likely to be quite different. There a real question arises as to whether aggregate income can be increased more rapidly than population, or even as rapidly. It is the case of the already densely populated countries that bears especially careful examination.

It is widely believed that an increase in the means of subsistence available within the densely populated countries—as a consequence of development—is likely to induce further growth in population (due largely to declining infant-mortality rates and to greater longevity, rather than to higher birth rates).[10] Involved is a widely-held notion to the effect that an increase in the means of subsistence is likely to be matched by "more mouths to feed" (some of which, in the absence of added means of subsistence, would have tended not to be around[11]). Some persons argue further that industrialization, if an ingredient of the process of development, is likely to reinforce the tendency toward marked population growth, since the urbanization that accompanies industrialization has the effect of removing people from direct dependence upon localized food supplies (and so tends not to force a declining birth rate). Moreover, considerable supporting evidence exists in the experiences of those countries that have gone through rapid development in past eras (e.g., the United Kingdom, Belgium, and Japan) to the effect that as the means of subsistence increase, population also tends to increase.

Implications of the foregoing for future levels of real per-capita income may well be enormous, especially considering that current population trends foreshadow the possibility, in any event, of a virtual *doubling* of the populations of some countries during an ensuing 30-year period (Table 11 and Fig. 4). However, despite the logic and evidence one can muster to paint a picture of gloom, it is possible also to cite some favorable aspects. For example, one is hard-pressed to discover even a single case in recent history in which development, per se, has been accompanied for any considerable duration by declining per-capita income. The usual situation, rather, appears to have been that development was accompanied by rising

---

10 Of some interest, a special problem currently exists in that the combination of high birth rates and short life expectancies gives rise to an age-distribution pattern that puts a high proportion of the population outside productive age brackets (i.e., the population pattern is one favoring youth), thereby imposing a special "drain" upon those who are within the productive age brackets, and upon the economy as a whole. For supporting data, see UN, *Demographic Yearbook 1956*, New York, 1956, Table B, p. 8.

11 As a consequence of "Malthusian checks" (i.e., famine, disease, and war), operative at subsistence levels of living, and all contributory to a higher death rate.

Table 11. Possible Population Magnitudes in 1980, by Continents

CONTINENT	Population 1950 (millions)	Estimated population, 1980 (millions)		
		"High" estimate	"Medium" estimate	"Low" estimate
Africa	198	327	289	255
North America[1]	168	240	223	207
Latin America	162	337	312	280
Asia	1,320	2,227	2,011	1,816
Europe	593	840	776	721
Oceania	13	19	17	16
World Total	2,454	3,990	3,628	3,295

Source: UN, Proceedings of the World Population Conference 1954, *New York, 1955, p. 77.*

[1] Excludes Mexico, Central America, and the Caribbean. These areas are included in Latin America.

Fig. 4. World Population: 1957 and 2000

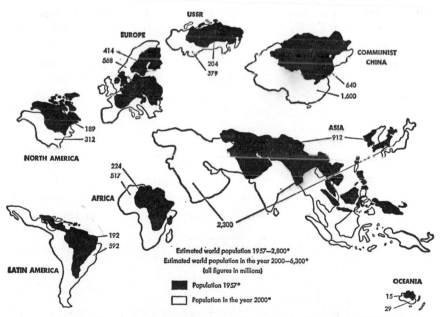

Source: Economic Assistance Programs and Administration (*Third Interim Report Submitted to the President of the United States by the President's Committee to Study the United States Military Assistance Program*), *Washington, July 13, 1959, Fig. 9, p. 43. Estimates for the year 2000 were based on UN "medium assumptions" for birth and death rates.*

population—at least for some period—and by rising per-capita income.[12]

Even if it is argued that potential gains in per-capita income, derivable from development, *need not necessarily* be obviated by an excessive growth in population, several troublesome situations nevertheless are apt to arise, at least in specific instances. For example, if the central measure in a developmental effort is directly aimed to achieve improvement in health conditions, and if this measure is unaccompanied by other supporting measures designed to increase the means of subsistence, there is a danger that population may increase without commensurate increases occurring in production; hence, per-capita income may decline. The particular points of emphasis in a program of development therefore assume great importance. Similarly, population may increase during early stages of development (as high birth rates continue but death rates decline), while marked increases in production may prove forthcoming only after some delay; hence, per-capita income may decline temporarily. Again, development can yield dividends only if there is scope for operation. Technically, it is possible for a country to reach a saturation point in its developmental efforts (given known resources and technology). In cases in which high population density is combined with few further avenues offering a potential for development, little improvement in per-capita income can result—even under the best of circumstances.

Beyond a certain point in the developmental process, a country must, of necessity, reconcile itself to one of three possible courses: emigration, birth control, or a lower and declining level of real per-capita income. Declining income cannot be regarded as an acceptable course. Actually, it is the consequence when all else fails. Nor can emigration necessarily be regarded as a desirable course. Even when possible, which is not always the case,[13] it offers nothing more than temporary help unless the birth rate is held down to approximately the death rate.[14] This then leaves birth control as the remaining course.

Some persons believe that the birth rate can be expected to fall, in the normal course of events (and without special governmental intervention), as people begin to realize that developmental progress offers a prospect for higher levels of living and become desirous of these higher

---

12 Perhaps the explanation in these cases was simply that the *particular* developmental efforts undertaken were sufficiently ambitious to produce income effects capable of more than offsetting population growth. On this point, see E. E. Hagen, "Population and Economic Growth," *American Economic Review,* June 1959, esp. p. 315.

13 Scope for a solution through emigration appears non-existent, for all practical purposes, in the present-day world—either because various countr s are economically incapable of accepting any truly sizable influx of immigrants, or because particular countries, even when economically capable of absorbing a sizable influx of immigrants, are unwilling on racial or other grounds to admit those categories of people whose plight is most acute.

14 Unless the birth rate is held to approximately the death rate, emigration of a mass of people merely creates a vacuum that others soon come to fill.

levels of living for themselves.[15] Other persons argue that an increase in aggregate income, given the environment of the already densely populated countries, can only result in approximately offsetting the increase in population, *unless* special governmental intervention is instituted to control population growth. Particular persons in the second category can claim responsibility for spearheading moves in several densely populated countries (e.g., Japan, India, and Haiti) for the promulgation, under official auspices, of programs of birth control.[16] Significantly, however, most countries confronted by acute population problems appear to be showing little receptivity thus far toward ideas along these lines. It is evident that the cultural patterns and religious beliefs of some populations now constitute powerful blocks to the spread of a birth-control movement. Unless modifications are accepted in these respects, only limited impact appears probable.

RIGIDITIES FROM INTERNATIONAL TIE-INS

Over the course of many decades, individual underdeveloped countries developed various links (or "tie-ins")—covering trade and other types of contact—with foreign countries, especially with developed countries. An effect of the inauguration and cultivation of these links was to help mould the economies of underdeveloped countries in particular ways. In essence, the economies of underdeveloped countries came to reflect in some degree, sometimes in a high degree, the countries' exposure to the general forces inherent in a process of international integration—a process of integration, however, in which the basic relationship was one of underdeveloped countries dealing with developed countries.

A problem for underdeveloped countries, as they attempt to promote development (which entails *alteration* of the course of economic evolution), is that the national actions that frequently come to appear necessary are *contrary* to those that might have appeared appropriate under previously prevailing concepts of international integration. As old links (and "tie-ins") are severed or modified, sometimes with difficulty, new and different links need to be fostered, but also frequently with difficulty. Importantly, the restructuring of an economy holds implications that go beyond the given country itself. The new scheme of things, as such emerges in a particular country, needs to become meshed with the

---

[15] K. Davis, "The World Demographic Transition," *Annals of the American Academy of Political and Social Science,* January 1945, esp. pp. 8–10.

[16] Japan's program generally is regarded as having proven successful. The programs of India and Haiti are of too short duration to permit clear-cut appraisal, although numerous persons have indicated skepticism as to the ultimate success. For interesting commentaries on India's problem and program, see: *Time* (Pacific ed.), October 3, 1955, p. 25; *The New York Times,* December 20, 1958, p. 12-C; *The Des Moines Register,* February 15, 1959, p. 3-G; and *Newsweek,* March 2, 1959, p. 40.

total world context; but this process tends to be far from easy or pain-less, due to the fact that considerable adaptation all around generally proves necessary.

A second problem for underdeveloped countries, as they attempt to promote development, is found in the fact that their developmental efforts follow those of developed countries. Specifically, underdeveloped countries find themselves obliged in their efforts, in many connections, to "buck the competition" posed by developed countries who "got there first." The problem for an underdeveloped country is more than that of breaking free of dependence upon developed countries by becoming more like them; rather, its problem is also one of how to survive in the face of competition posed by developed countries as it becomes more like them. To illustrate, new industrial development in underdeveloped countries, whatever its merits or demerits, frequently has to face intense competition from similar production in developed countries that is well past the introductory period during which high unit costs are common. This competition obviously represents a potent force, and tends to complicate the task of development.

ORDER OF IMPORTANCE

Which of the foregoing obstacles stand out as most important? As intimated earlier (in Ch. 3), generalization on this score is difficult—because many countries, reflecting widely different situations, are in-volved, and because individuals tend to interpret in different ways the situations that happen to prevail. Nevertheless, generalization *is* possible, and is undertaken time and again. Indeed, some generalization appears unavoidable, since such occurs—if for no other reason—as a legitimate by-product of serious efforts to gauge the overall plight of the under-developed world.

As an overall generalization, this author—after taking all the foregoing considerations into account—believes that the two foremost obstacles to economic development in the underdeveloped world, as an entity, em-brace the following.[17] First, there is political instability, which is viewed as the foremost *non-economic* block to development. The plain fact is that without some reasonable amount of political stability, development simply proves impossible, no matter how favorable the situation is on other scores (e.g., in terms of resource availability, labor and managerial ability, capital supplies, etc.)

---

[17] To state the obvious (but nevertheless to state it in the interests of avoiding misinterpretation), the generalization offered is not to be regarded as descriptive of each and every underdeveloped country. Also, the two obstacles isolated as paramount are from among the eleven cited in Chs. 3 and 4, pursuant to blockage through vicious circles, per se.

Second, there is scarcity of foreign exchange, which is viewed as the foremost *economic* block in the path of development.[18] To prove the foreign-exchange situation a greater deterrent than any other obstacles, direct comparison—item by item—appears necessary. In the interests of brevity, however, the comparison can be limited to two highly likely contenders. For example, scarcity of foreign exchange tends to be more crucial than a low volume of saving, per se, because only that portion of *any* saving (even a greater amount) which can be "translated" into a supply of foreign exchange can provide a basis for the importation of essential developmental ingredients (perhaps not otherwise to be had, e.g., machinery). Again, scarcity of foreign exchange appears more crucial than any inadequacies existing in entrepreneurship, because some persons possessing entrepreneurial talent of passable quality are seemingly present but are unable to proceed with new undertakings in consequence of a lack of foreign exchange with which to procure essential developmental ingredients from abroad.[19]

Apart from whether one elects to agree or disagree with this particular rating, it can creditably be argued, of course, that the basic approach involved really misses a vital point. Significantly, the obstacles referred to are represented as foremost in the underdeveloped world as a whole, whereas practical developmental policy is the responsibility of individual countries. Therefore, the essential consideration does not relate to what is generally true for a *grouping* of some 50 countries, but rather to what is specifically true for *each* of the countries encompassed. What holds true for individual countries varies widely, of course, and only in some instances is it likely to coincide with a characterization framed to cover numerous countries.

SOME ADVANTAGES

Although the obstacles one might cite are many and varied, one need not regard the prospect for development with unmitigated gloom. In fact, circumstances favorable to development show up in at least two major respects.

---

[18] In turn, there tends to be an interlocking relationship between political instability and scarcity of foreign exchange. Political stability is heavily dependent upon economic well-being, but economic well-being is difficult to achieve when there is political instability. However, those prone to argue along lines of economic determinism generally visualize the economic factor as the *lever* that can be used to cope with the non-economic factor. *Indeed,* a rationale of the US Government for providing economic aid (foreign exchange) to underdeveloped countries is that the resultant development helps promote political stability.

[19] To continue the line of reasoning, if more foreign exchange were available, unused entrepreneurship might soon be absorbed, after which—but not before—shortcomings in entrepreneurship might well come to represent an obstacle more serious than scarcity of foreign exchange.

On the one hand, individual obstacles to development are not necessarily insurmountable. Of particular significance, pro-development factors frequently exist alongside anti-development factors—and often largely serve to negate the dismal aspects, or at least comprise "levers" of possible help in the course of their negation. To illustrate: the resource patterns of some countries leave much to be desired, but considerable resources offering a potential for development are nevertheless present (in virtually all countries); existing cultural patterns tend not to favor development, but important segments of the populations of numerous countries are exhibiting a marked willingness to break with tradition; labor has its limitations, but it is generally plentiful and, according to various indications, appears also capable of some ready upgrading; domestic markets are typically limited in size, but some markets currently supplied by imports offer a possible opportunity for new domestic producers, to say nothing of additional markets that might be created as a consequence of development.

On the other hand, some clear-cut advantages are discernible. Three of these, especially, appear to hold considerable significance. First, underdeveloped countries are able to draw upon much technology and know-how already present in developed countries. While much of what is "borrowed" is likely to require adaptation, nevertheless underdeveloped countries are thereby spared some of the cost of trial and error involved in the course of evolving new processes and techniques in the first instance. Additionally, to the extent that underdeveloped countries can avail themselves of processes and techniques already evolved and tested, there is reason to hold that they can push their development more rapidly than had proven possible, historically, in the countries that preceded. Since underdeveloped countries frequently desire to telescope the process of development (in an attempt to accomplish in one generation, literally, what already-developed countries took half a century or more to do), the capacity to draw upon developed countries in the foregoing respect comprises a potential advantage of considerable importance. Second, emerging nationalism, characteristic of numerous underdeveloped countries, can act as an inspirational force, helpful in directing otherwise unharnessed energies toward the tasks of development. Some persons, particularly those in developed countries, appear fearful of the emerging nationalism (or appear fearful of what nationalism might become, or lead to), but without this nationalism the necessary drive to forge ahead in a developmental effort tends to be undermined and weakened. Third, potential profit margins in numerous likely lines of activity in underdeveloped countries appear sufficiently attractive to warrant interest on the part of new entrepreneurs. This consideration is vital, especially to the extent that prospective development is expected to occur within the private sector. After all, for private entrepreneurs, profit is the motivator.

In summary, a safe conclusion appears to be that *something* can be done about development in every underdeveloped country—the extent of achievement being dependent upon many and varied circumstances. The challenge is to ascertain what is reasonably possible, and how progress toward achievement can be fostered. And, of course, whatever action is initiated, it is desirable for effort to be in a direction that can result in lasting improvement rather than in a mere temporary amelioration of pressing ills.

SELECTED BIBLIOGRAPHY

Henry G. Aubrey, "Role of the State in Economic Development," *American Economic Review Papers and Proceedings,* May 1951.
Government as a factor in development.

J. Douglas Brown and Frederick Harbison, *High-Talent Manpower for Science and Industry* (Research Report Series No. 95, Industrial Relations Section, Princeton University), 1957.
Part III, The development of human resources in newly industrializing countries.

Norman S. Buchanan and Howard S. Ellis, *Approaches to Economic Development.* New York: The Twentieth Century Fund, 1955.
Chs. 2–5, Examination of problems related to resources, capital formation, social and cultural factors, and demographic factors.

Kingsley Davis, "The Amazing Decline of Mortality in Underdeveloped Areas," *American Economic Review Papers and Proceedings,* May 1956.
Examination of population trends; speculation as to their significance.

Walter Elkan, "Migrant Labor in Africa: An Economist's Approach," *American Economic Review Papers and Proceedings,* May 1959
An aspect of labor mobility, related to the problem of development.

Stephen Enke, "Speculations on Population Growth and Economic Development," *Quarterly Journal of Economics,* February 1957.
Examination of population growth, underemployment, and labor immobility in the underdeveloped world.

Walter Galenson and Harvey Leibenstein, "Investment Criteria, Productivity, and Economic Development," *Quarterly Journal of Economics,* August 1955.
The problem of labor productivity in underdeveloped countries.

Everett E. Hagen, "Population and Economic Growth," *American Economic Review,* June 1959.
Examination of the "Malthusian" idea that increases in income invite growth in population.

Frederick Harbison, "Entrepreneurial Organization as a Factor in Economic Development," *Quarterly Journal of Economics*, August 1956.
Appraisal of entrepreneurship as an impediment to development.

Bert F. Hoselitz (ed.), *The Progress of Underdeveloped Areas*. Chicago: The University of Chicago Press, 1952.
Part II, Cultural aspects of economic growth.

Charles P. Kindleberger, *Economic Development*. New York: The McGraw-Hill Book Company, Inc., 1958.
Chs. 1–6, Examination of problems related to land, capital, labor, technology and entrepreneurship, and scale of operation; Ch. 12, The population issue.

Harvey Leibenstein, *Economic Backwardness and Economic Growth*. New York: John Wiley and Sons, Inc., 1957.
Chs. 10 and 14, Population growth and progress in development.

W. Arthur Lewis, *The Theory of Economic Growth*. Homewood, Ill.: Richard D. Irwin, Inc., 1955.
Parts III–VII, Examination of problems related to economic institutions, knowledge, capital, population and resources, and government.

Gerald M. Meier and Robert E. Baldwin, *Economic Development*. New York: John Wiley and Sons, Inc., 1957.
Ch. 15, Analysis of obstacles to development with emphasis on vicious circles.

William H. Nicholls, "Accommodating Economic Change in Underdeveloped Countries," *American Economic Review Papers and Proceedings,* May 1959.
Consideration of institutional aspects pertinent for development in underdeveloped countries.

Ragnar Nurkse, *Problems of Capital Formation in Underdeveloped Countries*. New York: Oxford University Press, 1953.
Extensive treatment of the problems of capital formation in underdeveloped countries.

—————————, "Some International Aspects of the Problem of Economic Development," *American Economic Review Papers and Proceedings,* May 1952.
Relates Say's Law to "balanced" development, and to economic development generally.

Wilfred Owen, "Transportation and Economic Development," *American Economic Review Papers and Proceedings,* May 1959.
Transportation as a factor in development.

Lyle W. Shannon (ed.), *Underdeveloped Areas*. New York: Harper and Brothers, 1957.
Chs. XI and XII, Problems of cultural change.

Joseph J. Spengler, "The Population Problem: Dimensions, Potentialities, Limitations," *American Economic Review Papers and Proceedings,* May 1956.
Examination of population trends, and their implications for development.

Henry H. Villard, "Some Notes on Population and Living Levels," *Review of Economics and Statistics,* May 1955.
Views on population issues.

Harold F. Williamson and John A. Buttrick (eds.), *Economic Development.* Englewood Cliffs, N.J.: Prentice-Hall, Inc., 1954.
Chs. 2–10, Examination of problems related to natural resources, population and labor force, capital formation, entrepreneurship, cultural factors, and the role of government.

5

DIRECTIONS OF DEVELOPMENT (I)

It is fine to be *for* development, but what specifically is to be done about its promotion? A basic task, accordingly, is to discover *what* development is possible or desirable. Once this is ascertained, questions as to *how* to proceed are in order.

NO COMMON ANSWER

In approaching the matter of development and what to do about it, some persons quickly lump the world's countries into two broad categories, developed and underdeveloped, and then proceed to seek *"the* problem" of those classed as underdeveloped, hopeful that in the end they can proffer *"the* answer" applicable in their case. This line of attack presupposes that underdeveloped countries are all "in the same boat." It is true that underdeveloped countries have a great deal in common—so much, in fact, that it is possible to formulate a summarization, embodying considerable content, that is broadly descriptive of them all (Ch. 1). But it does not follow, as a matter of course, that one prescription is adequate for all the countries. Even though the symptomatic traits of underdevelopedness are broadly similar in all, potentials for development differ widely among them, presumably ranging from "good" to "poor" (Chs. 3 and 4). Since potentials differ, courses of action appropriate for their development can also be expected to differ. In this respect, therefore, underdeveloped countries are not "all in the same boat."

To anticipate a conclusion, two major types of empha-

ses figure by way of prescription: an underdeveloped country should continue along established lines as a raw-materials producer, but strive to do a
better job at this; or it should introduce structural change into the
economy—through promotion of industrial development (as a major supplement to, or partial replacement for, raw-materials production). In one
category of countries, developmental benefits appear more readily attainable through concerted effort along the first course; in another category
of countries, in contrast, the second course seems to offer better prospects.

Obviously, no responsible government is likely to want to devote its
entire attention to one facet of a developmental effort, to the absolute
exclusion of any other facet; however, a government may seek—advisedly
and deliberately—to single out one facet as being primary, and thereafter
view this facet as the focal point within its developmental effort. In the
selection of this focal point, upon which the course and pattern of
development then becomes fundamentally dependent, a government
needs to make a decision as to the type of emergent economy deemed
both attainable and "best" among the alternatives open to it.[1] This
decision is one that ought to be made only after consideration of various
relevant aspects—including, especially, consideration of the particular
supplies, and supply combinations, of factors of production[2] available
to the country at issue (along with consideration of the country's position
in this respect *relative to* other countries).

MAJOR FORMS OF DEVELOPMENT

The central objective in a program of development is to secure higher
and rising real per-capita income—although, in the event that the attainment of higher and rising income is not a possibility, prevention of decline or promotion of greater stability perhaps can reasonably be held to
reflect development, nonetheless. Significantly, if real per-capita income
is to rise, per-capita productivity must rise (except insofar as greater
returns can be had from that domestic output which enters foreign
markets). The key to the situation is productivity.

Theoretically, a country interested in promoting gains in per-capita
productivity has three major forms of developmental activity open to it.
The first involves "basic development," the provision of various services
and facilities customarily regarded as necessary as a foundation for sustained growth (e.g., improved health and education services, and strengthened transport, communications, and power facilities). The second in-

---

1 Thus, if a government of a raw-materials-producing country decides that structural change is both attainable and desirable, it can emphasize industrial development
through some "slanting" of its developmental efforts (but without forgetting that raw-
materials production *also* exists).

2 With attention paid to both quantitative and qualitative aspects.

volves improvements in production in existing fields of raw-materials output. The third involves shifts in the basic production pattern, either through diversification of raw-materials output or, perhaps more importantly, through promotion of industrial development.

Of these, basic development is in a class apart from the other two forms of developmental activity. Basically, the productivity gains upon which higher and rising income is dependent derive from what happens in either or both of the two forms of developmental activity beyond basic development. Essentially, the role of basic development is to *prepare the way for,* or *support,* the particular forms of developmental activity upon which productivity gains, and income benefits, are dependent.

In essence, therefore, basic development is a companion to either of the other two forms of developmental activity. This relationship is important because, on the strength of it, it follows that emphasis in a developmental effort ultimately involves a choice between only two alternatives: continuation (with improvement) in existing lines of production, or alteration in the basic production pattern prevailing.

BASIC DEVELOPMENT

Basic development, as it relates to the development of underdeveloped countries, is of three main types. Diverse as the three may seem, all have one thing in common: their essential importance, from a developmental standpoint, lies in the fact that they are concerned with *preconditions* for other and further development.

The first type of basic development involves creation or upgrading of *social capital.* The central objective in this connection is to improve the quality of a country's population, so that people can be more effective as productive agents. Prime examples include efforts in the fields of health and education, aimed at prevalent shortcomings. Low health standards typically invite low per-worker productivity for much of the labor force, a situation averse to high or rising per-capita income. Sick or disease-ridden people tend to be physically incapable of high work output, and tend also to lack drive.[3] The idea is that a health and sanitation program, by leading to improved health conditions, serves to raise the productive

---

[3] Additionally, short average life spans, an associated characteristic whenever low health standards prevail, serve to produce a population composition in which only a small proportion of the population falls within working-age brackets, whereas a high proportion is in a dependent position. Consequently, the burden upon those in working-age brackets tends to be great, particularly considering the low per-worker productivity prevalent there. Moreover, given the low income customarily prevailing, plus the heavy consumption overhead deriving from large numbers of dependent people, per-capita consumption tends, if anything, to worsen under pressure (not thereby abetting overall health standards, nor overall productivity), and saving tends to be all but precluded. See Ch. 4, section on "Problems of Population," for additional commentary on this subject.

capacities and personal drives of workers, and thereby provides a basis for greater output (and hence for the various subsidiary gains that can flow from greater output).[4] Similarly, a poorly-educated population is typically one of low per-worker productivity and of low per-capita income. People who are illiterate or who have had the benefit of only a little education are frequently handicapped in their customary productive efforts, and generally are curbed in their individual potentialities for advancement as both the imagination and training held essential for advancement are found wanting. Indeed, even access to and use of information regarding new ways of doing things tend to be held down when educational attainments are low. The idea is that better and more widespread education (with the virtual elimination of illiteracy frequently regarded as a minimum goal) can serve to prepare people to do a better job in existing types of work or to undertake new and better types of work, and can also serve to open their eyes to new and improved ways of doing things. The net effect is held conducive to higher per-worker productivity—and hence to gains in income also.

The second type of basic development involves the creation of *public overhead capital*. This category includes transport, communications, and power facilities. These facilities, in some amount and of some caliber, are necessary if other development is to follow, and especially so if industrialization is sought. To illustrate, transport facilities in an adequate amount need to exist, and need to function at least reasonably well, so as to provide necessary links between producers and markets. Again, an adequate power supply is essential if machinery is to operate. Significantly, many underdeveloped countries are sadly deficient in public overhead capital. In some countries, enough in the way of public overhead capital may be present to support some additional growth, but even there the requirement for more facilities at a fairly early date is certain if marked growth, which draws upon these facilities, gets underway. To the extent that facilities in this category are to arise, considerable effort through the public sector must be expected. Since these facilities only rarely give rise directly to marketable products, they are generally unsuited for private enterprise, and to this extent they must derive as a result of government action—or not at all.

A third type of basic development involves the removal or amelioration of those impediments to development that are grounded in the *legal situation*. To illustrate, existing legal provisions may favor the holding and utilization of considerable supplies of available land in a manner that gives rise to only low productivity (e.g., because of primogeniture,[5]

---

4 E.g., higher income, higher consumption, and higher saving.
5 C. P. Kindleberger, *Economic Development* (New York: The McGraw-Hill Book Company, Inc., 1958), p. 18.

or because of deficiencies in the system of property taxation[6]). Whenever this is so, it is possible that a change in the law, along with its enforcement, may invite or force better results (e.g., as landholders find it in their own interest, under the new circumstances, to alter their attitudes and approaches). Again, some cultural blocks to development, while deeply rooted in tradition, may also have actual or tacit sanction in law. Whenever this is so, it is possible that legal change may help in the process of reshaping the cultural pattern—and thereby serve to encourage development, instead of hindering it. A case in point relates to the caste system. A population may be used to the idea of caste, and not generally averse to it, but the public's notions as to caste may alter more readily if it knows that government is officially opposed to caste (i.e., may alter more readily than if government seems favorable toward caste, or simply is silent on the issue). The gist, in any event, is that some legal changes serve to create a situation in which development *might* occur, whereas absence of these changes serves, without a doubt, to endorse the status-quo.

SOME PROBLEMS

Introduction of basic development does not occur without raising problems. A few of these bear mention.

1. *Cost.* The creation of social capital tends to be a low-cost operation. In contrast, the creation of public overhead capital generally entails much cost. The possible cost involved for underdeveloped countries as they seek to acquire a needed complement of public overhead capital can be visualized by referring to the experience of countries already developed. In the US, for example, some 40% of all productive capital is invested in public transportation facilities and other public utilities alone.[7] Since, typically, underdeveloped countries are highly deficient in public overhead capital, the backlog in needed facilities to be dealt with is great, thereby posing impressive financial demands.

Underdeveloped countries, aware of their capital-poorness, are frequently prone to delay outlays on public overhead capital—indeed, are prone to grasp for reasons defensive of delay. In preference to outlays on public overhead capital, the limited supplies of capital on hand are frequently spread around on behalf of a series of industrial-type enterprises.[8] The end-products of industrial development are much sought

---

6 N. S. Buchanan and H. S. Ellis, *Approaches to Economic Development* (New York: The Twentieth Century Fund, 1955), pp. 253–254; B. Higgins, *Economic Development* (New York: W. W. Norton & Company, Inc., 1959), Ch. 22, esp. p. 521.

7 S. Fabricant, *Capital Consumption and Adjustment* (New York: National Bureau of Economic Research, 1938), pp. 248–249. The situation depicted relates to the years immediately preceding World War II.

8 For the greater part, preference for investment in operating enterprises over investment in public overhead capital is shown at two basic points of decision. First, taxation to raise funds for public overhead capital is frequently resisted, with the funds retained used privately instead, at least in part, for investment in operating

after, so that market forces tend to tip the balance in favor of investment in enterprises producing end-products (in preference to outlays on public overhead capital). Those responsible generally take refuge in the hope that enough public overhead capital is on hand to support the output of some added amount of end-products in the immediate future, conveniently shrugging off, at least for the time being, the worry as to what to do about public overhead capital itself. This practice, however understandable—and even meritorious in some respects—can prove short-sighted, since it gives rise to new enterprises that are small-scale, and thus incapable of reaping substantial benefits from economies of scale. Moreover, subsequent expansion on the part of the new enterprises comes to be handicapped by the external limitations posed by the status of public overhead capital (e.g., power shortages, or inadequacies in transport facilities that are essential for access to supplies and markets).

2. *Inflationary Effects.* The creation of public overhead capital is costly, but underdeveloped countries are characteristically short of the necessary means. Given the factor of limited means, those outlays that *are* made on public overhead capital tend to invite a special financial problem. This particular problem relates to inflationary impact.

The creation of public overhead capital typically links domestic goods and import goods, thus requiring financing both in local currency and in foreign exchange. On the one hand, some foreign-exchange demands are ordinarily incurred directly, as importation is relied upon for needed materials and equipment not obtainable domestically. On the other hand, heavy domestic outlays ordinarily occur, resulting in the placement of income with particular people (e.g., laborers, suppliers of materials, etc.), even while no marketable products arise as an accompaniment which can then move against the money income in existence.[9] If the amounts expended domestically represent sums derived through taxation or voluntary saving, the associated financial manipulations serve merely to reshuffle money income within the domestic economy.[10] But if the amounts expended domestically represent the first step in an intended process of forced saving, money income rises, and an imbalance between the money supply and the goods supply is fostered. In such an event, inflationary impact is registered. This inflationary situation, of course, holds varied implications. One of these involves added import demands,

---

enterprises. Second, funds already at government's disposal, instead of being used to create public overhead capital, may deliberately be routed to operating enterprises, either within the public sector or within the private sector (through recourse to some formalized loan procedure).

9 Most public overhead capital does not give rise, *directly*, to marketable goods— in the near-term future, or ever. However, a few exceptions exist, e.g., electric current supplied by new power installations.

10 Shifts of money income among people can affect average propensity to spend (and save), a consideration not to be ignored in measuring impact.

which arise indirectly because of the greater money income and rising prices. In the end, pressure, or further pressure, is placed upon foreign-exchange resources—which, significantly, are usually in short supply to begin with.

The particular dilemma associated with financing the creation of public overhead capital can be by-passed, at least to a major degree, if adequate external capital can be secured for the purpose at the outset. Failure to obtain access to external capital necessitates that the country concerned carefully appraise the maximum effort it can undertake and carry through safely on its own. In an appraisal of this sort, the country particularly needs to consider what adaptations in domestic policies (e.g., in monetary and fiscal policies) are possible and merited in the course of its attempts to divert resources from traditional channels to new outlets.

3. *Population.* One category of social capital relates to improvements in health and well-being through the provision of more and better health and sanitation services and facilities. Far from being unquestioningly accepted as "good," however, some persons are doubtful as to whether the creation of this form of social capital necessarily constitutes a gain. An element of controversy appears associated.

The creation of social capital finds its economic justification in an enhancement of the productive capacities of individuals. It is fine, of course, to favor a program that offers a way to increase the productive capacities of individuals, since such an achievement makes higher per-worker productivity possible for some people, and therefore offers a potential for favorable impact upon income. But are individuals automatically assured of a chance to exercise the enhanced productive capacities that become theirs? And what if a health and sanitation program serves to increase the total population—while death rates fall and birth rates remain high? Are not added numbers then likely to contribute simply to a general overall deterioration in the population-resources ratio?[11]

The essential sequence, by way of providing answers, appears to be as follows. Economic development calls for a higher and rising real per-capita income. The enhancement of per-worker productivity, in turn, is conducive to the realization of income effects generally compatible with the goal of development. Enhancement of per-worker productivity, however, is the product of two steps. First, the individual himself must be capable of enhanced productivity. Second, the individual must have an opportunity to use his enhanced capacity in production. From the ideas embodied in these two steps springs the contention that a health pro-

---

[11] See Ch. 4, the section on "Problems of Population," for earlier commentary.

gram, taken by itself, is not enough. Rather, it needs to be reinforced by developmental efforts in other directions, so that opportunities come to be generated which enable the utilization of people in a manner commensurate with their enhanced productive capacities. In fact, the major emphasis in the associated line of reasoning is upon opportunity, rather than on health. "More opportunity" is the crucial element, and "better health" enters the picture as an economic factor only because people are thereby helped to do something more with existent opportunities.

4. *Education and Training.* From the general proposition that knowledge is desirable flows the notion that more widespread and better education has merits for underdeveloped countries. Assertedly, education, both extensive and intensive, is useful as one part of a program of development in that it can enhance the productive capacities of the population, can help spark imagination and spur incentive, and can help dissolve impediments associated with cultural rigidity.

Education, if it is to contribute to development, needs to be geared to the unique demands of a program of development. In some underdeveloped countries, stress in education traditionally falls on classical studies, philosophy, or law. However, the process of development places a premium on other types of training, especially on training in engineering, business administration, and scientific agriculture. Accordingly, a strong case can be made for a reorientation of education. Not only is there a need for changed content, but also for a changed "tone." In general, education is needed of a type that helps divest intellectuals of the notion that it is undignified to get one's hands dirty, or that one automatically abdicates from all claim to prestige-status if one chooses to work with machinery or chooses to engage in managerial functions related to industrial production.

Ordinarily, underdeveloped countries are able with relative ease to widen the scope of elementary education, provided the will to proceed exists—which, however, is unquestionably not the case in all countries. Teachers at the elementary level are generally either available locally or can be trained locally without great difficulty, and minimum physical facilities can generally be provided, although dedicated effort and considerable improvisation may be necessary to bring about this end. At the upper levels of education, however, the situation is more complex. To offer more advanced forms of training, teachers are needed who themselves have had higher-level training. When adequate numbers thus qualified do not exist, as is usually the case, talent must be developed or imported. Talent development appears to be the only satisfactory long-run solution, and this entails the willingness and the ability to send some number of people abroad for preparatory training (and to leave them abroad long enough to assure more than a casual acquaintanceship with subject matter).[12]

5. *Unemployed Intellectuals.* A leading rationale for more and better education in underdeveloped countries is that the capacity of individuals, in terms of their productivity-potential, can thereby be enhanced. For this greater capacity to become truly meaningful, however, opportunities for the use of the capacity must exist—just as is the case in the increased productivity-potential stemming from improved health. And if adequate opportunities do not exist, their creation remains dependent—as it does in the case of health programs—upon developmental efforts in other directions.

One attribute frequently ascribed to the underdeveloped world is the general scarcity of well-trained people. However true this situation may be in many underdeveloped countries, *not all* countries fit the pattern. In some countries, considerable numbers of well-trained people can be found who are doing little or nothing, basically because the economies involved are so underdeveloped that inadequate opportunities exist for people to render services well within their capacity. People facing this plight are frequently referred to, formally, as *"unemployed intellectuals."* Their numbers are so great in some countries (e.g., in India) that they are regarded as comprising a national problem. In fact, special make-work arrangements under government auspices are sometimes proposed for the purpose of activating these people[13] (particularly because the combination of educational attainment and prolonged idleness tends to produce intense frustration and a state of mind apt to spawn made-to-order recruits for revolution-bent left-wing movements).

6. *Leadership.* Some persons, among them some of the most staunch advocates of greater education for people in underdeveloped countries, are inclined to stress the merits of mass education (i.e., "literacy for all" —which frequently means little more than mere literacy for most). This preference seems to spring, in large measure, from the belief that mass education is a key element in the promotion of the democratic ideal. Other persons point out that mass education is fine, *provided* this goal doesn't obscure the fact that "special" education is needed for at least a few people. The idea here is that some number needs to have a chance at better-than-average education, so that the qualities essential for leadership can be inculcated. Leadership is pictured as very important (since,

---

[12] It is impractical to send any really large number of advanced student-trainees abroad, year after year. Instead, a basic core of teaching talent needs to be developed so that it becomes possible thereafter to offer training domestically for the great bulk of qualified enrollees. In this way a leverage effect can derive from foreign-inspired training.

[13] A favorite proposal is for their utilization in social and welfare programs at the village level.

according to the associated line of reasoning, the masses *follow* the leaders —both in industry and in government[14]).

These two attitudes are sometimes represented as being in conflict: mass education (in keeping with the democratic notions of equality of treatment) *versus* special education for a few (who are frankly expected to acquire special status). Actually, of course, no conflict need exist if a core of training is made available for all, and is followed thereafter by further training, along specialized lines, for some lesser number selected from among the group in accordance with acceptable criteria. In any event, a significant factor, whatever the status of education generally, is that a country needs to have a core of leadership (and needs to pay heed to *how* adequate leadership can be fostered).

7. *Education and Cultural Blocks.* Cultural blocks to development are legion. A problem in development concerns how to eliminate or mitigate these blocks. In coping with the problem, some persons emphasize the need to change "how people think," and stress the role of education in this connection. A common line of reasoning proceeds as follows: attitudes need to be changed; education is helpful in this; but the process occurs gradually and is slow. An alternate approach—or perhaps really a supplementary approach—less frequently suggested, emphasizes the role of institutions (i.e., institutions in the sense of being creations of the state, designed to accomplish specific purposes). The reasoning here is that the imposition upon people of institutional change is likely to get them to alter their ways more rapidly, and more assuredly, than when the hope for change is based simply on its being a by-product of education. This is held to be the case because the imposition of institutional change forces people in a real sense to do things differently (and leaves them in the position of having to "rationalize" their thinking so as to catch up with the new order of things).

An example can be cited to illustrate this distinction. Assume the characteristic situation of low aggregate saving alongside conspicuous consumption by those who might well save. What can be done then to increase saving? The first approach would emphasize education as the means for altering attitudes regarding the merit of spending on conspicuous consumption. Saving, to the extent it did occur (probably after considerable delay), would be the residual left over because of a lessened desire to enjoy conspicuous consumption. The second approach would lead, conceivably, to an examination of whether the presence of a new type bank could not serve to encourage saving, and whether special

---

14 For example, most people simply want a job, and it is only a small number who in the end are instrumental in providing the jobs (in the sense of "meeting the payroll"). Again, the masses may vote and pass judgment, but it is only a small number who are "in" government and who have on-the-spot responsibility, day-by-day, for shaping policy.

legislation (e.g., in the tax field) could not "help make up the minds" of people that saving really is in their best interests. Saving, to the extent it then results, would occur largely because the persons concerned would see (if they took the trouble to look) that a personal penalty would be incurred, there and then, if saving was rejected.

The central notion behind institutional change, then, is to *force* change upon people, rather than simply to prepare them to *want* change (as is the idea in an educational approach). How much change can be forced upon people is related, of course, to their willingness to accept change (so that the role of education as a preparatory process cannot be ignored). The idea, however, is that some institutional change can precede popular clamor for such and, indeed, can help pull popular thinking along; institutional change need not lag forever behind popular thinking (or be limited to what people choose to ask for).

PRECONDITION OR PROPELLANT?

It is commonly accepted that some basic development has to be undergone before other and further development can occur, and that improvements in the realm of basic development are helpful in paving the way for this other and further development (which then might, or might not, occur). In short, basic development is viewed as a precondition. Some persons are inclined, however, to claim more for basic development. They view it as both a precondition for general development *and* a propellant directly responsible for some amount of this general development. Accordingly, the question raised here is: Is basic development a propellant in the growth process?

There are instances in which the creation of basic development serves to set in motion forces that give rise, rather directly, to other and further development. For example, the creation of transport facilities can serve to augment effective demand (as seen by a particular producer of marketable goods), so that the obstacle of "too limited" a market will be removed or eased for the particular producer, and hence encourage expansion in output. It does not follow, however, that basic development invariably sets in motion forces that give rise to other and further development. Rather, the usual situation is that basic development simply helps make further development possible, but leaves its actual realization dependent upon circumstances and actions in addition to the creation of basic development. For example, a particular case in India's developmental experience (arising during the course of the country's Second Five-Year Plan[15]) demonstrates that basic development, however necessary, may not prove sufficient to yield further development. According to planning authorities, India was not amiss in her aspirations to

---

15 1956–61.

achieve a build-up of steel-making capacity (e.g., enough basic development was believed present to handle at least the particular undertaking;
the prospect was believed present for ultimate production within the
limits of comparative cost; and the other ingredients necessary for successful production were also believed present). Despite the precautions
taken and the assurances given, however, the projected undertaking soon
met with severe difficulties. The country's supply of foreign exchange
proved insufficient to enable work to proceed as planned (i.e., equipment
imports in the necessary volume could not be financed). Thus, the primary obstacle proved to be a shortage of foreign exchange, not inadequate
basic development; indeed, basic development appeared fully adequate
for the immediate task at hand.

The conclusion suggested is that, fundamentally, basic development is
a precondition, not a propellant. Basic development sometimes serves to
evoke, directly, other and further development. For the greater part,
however, basic development simply helps make other and further development possible, which development then *may* (or may not) occur, depending upon whether or not the supporting factors are sufficiently strong.

Apart from the consideration of whether or not basic development is
merely a precondition or also a propellant, there is the consideration of
how much basic development is necessary if a program of general overall
development is to be fostered. The usual view is that a full complement
of basic development is not absolutely necessary for progress. All that is
essential in a current sense is the minimum needed to provide a workable
environment for the particular effort contemplated. But, as developmental progress is made, the process of continued expansion is circumscribed by the basic development that bears on the situation, so that
basic development and the development that goes beyond it need to go
hand-in-hand in a process of cumulative growth. Importantly, to wait
with any development of a follow-up sort until all the basic development
that could be regarded as desirable is actually present might literally
involve waiting forever.

COMMUNITY DEVELOPMENT

Closely related to basic development, though encompassing elements
that extend beyond, is community development. Community development
refers to a technique for the stimulation of local self-help through group
action at village and rural levels.[16] The objective is to set in motion a

16 As defined by the UN, community development is "a process designed to create
conditions for economic and social progress for the whole community with its active
participation and the fullest possible reliance upon the community's initiative." See
UN, *Social Progress Through Community Development*, New York, 1955, p. 6. A release
of the US Government's foreign-aid agency (ICA), in 1955, states that "Community
development is a technique for stimulating organized self-help undertakings through

systematic process that can get the "little people" in villages and rural areas (i.e., the masses in underdeveloped countries) to do more for themselves with means already at their disposal. The main resource in villages and rural areas often is simply that of plentiful underemployed labor. The aim in community development is to turn this labor upon whatever other resources happen to be available locally and thereby produce some objects, facilities, or other end-benefits of value to the people concerned (e.g., the construction of serviceable roads, school buildings, community buildings, wells, and irrigation ditches, or simply the stimulation of efforts to clean up normally unsightly and unsanitary surroundings). As phrased in one study:[17]

> In practically all the communities in question there are resources that can be tapped if the people want to and know how to, but not otherwise. There is underemployed manpower; in many less-developed rural areas the cultivator is idle during one-third or more of the year. There may be hoarded savings that can be put to productive uses, or contributions of land or building materials for community projects. There is an intimate knowledge of the local environment to complement technical information from outside. Last but not least is the great potential of local leadership which needs only encouragement, guidance and technical direction to take over most of the responsibility for local progress.

Since community development emphasizes self-help, it tends to be strictly a low-cost operation; little or no foreign exchange is required, and generally only little local currency. This means that even if low domestic saving and scarcity of foreign exchange serve to preclude all other efforts at development, community development is still a possible avenue of action. It is this attribute that gives community development special appeal in the eyes of many people. What community development is highly dependent upon, however, is organization. There needs to be organization in the sense that someone in each community assumes responsibility for leadership in initiating and directing action,[18] and it is desirable that this local leadership be coordinated nation-wide. Accordingly, programs of community development entail the recruitment and training of a corps of community-development workers. One source of workers is from among the unemployed intellectuals, whenever there are substantial numbers of these within a country.[19]

---

the democratic process. It aims to mobilize the principal resource of most underdeveloped areas—their manpower and their interest in improving their own lot—once they have become aware that improvement is possible. . . . The key to community development is group action at the local level."

17 UN, *Social Progress Through Community Development,* New York, 1955, p. 6.

18 Subject to approval by the people of the community, if democratic processes are to govern.

19 Community development entails much organization, but an issue almost invariably arises as to just *how much* organization is warranted. The issue does not pertain particularly to numbers of community-development workers, but rather to the

What is the contribution of community development to economic development? The basic economic rationale for community development, as intimated previously, is found in the bringing together—in better fashion than is otherwise the case—of idle or ill-used manpower and other resources, so that something useful (not otherwise had) can result. The idea is that if people with time on their hands can be induced to work with means at their disposal in the creation of objects, facilities, or other end-benefits of value to themselves, the economic effect upon these people, and upon a country as a whole, is necessarily all to the good.

Some persons thus are of the opinion that community development holds economic merit because it offers hope for "something more." Other persons, however, are prone to regard this viewpoint as having been arrived at too narrowly. Their belief, instead, is that the economic merit of community development depends, basically, on the nature of developmental courses open to particular countries. As a reference point for appraisal in the light of the developmental courses prevailing, these people assert that community development cannot yield greatly improved levels of living—since, after all, high income simply is not a likely outcome of self help efforts at the local level. Thereupon, three cases (or developmental courses) are distinguished. First, some countries, given known resources and technology, do not appear to have bright prospects for development in alternate directions. For them, community development represents an avenue that offers *some* added benefits, short-run and long-run. Second, some countries appear to have a reasonable prospect for development of a sort likely to yield benefits that far exceed anything potentially obtainable through community development. For these countries deliberately to select community development as *the* focal point of long-range developmental efforts is to pass by something better. Third,

---

organizational nature of the program—as to whether community development is to be a distinct program, separate and apart from already-existing programs concerned with rural improvement, or a new super-program superimposed upon these other programs (e.g., straddling programs in health, education, agriculture, and housing). The second, or super-program form, frequently is preferred by community-development proponents, generally on the grounds that greater coordination of effort thereby results, and that this has merit. For example, a release of the US Government's foreign-aid agency (ICA), in 1955, states (in reference to the agency's own program for stimulation of effort in community development): "Another aspect of importance . . . is the use of [community development] . . . as a tool for integrating program planning and execution, so that projects in the several fields of health, education, agriculture, housing, village and small scale industries, etc., can supplement each other and the work of the specialists in these fields can be coordinated."

Bureaucratic pyramiding has the potential merit of yielding greater coordination, but not all agree that greater coordination automatically yields greater end-benefits. If community development is limited to the coordination of existing program efforts, any final benefits that might then accrue from the community-development effort, per se, are the product entirely of greater effectiveness on the part of the other already-existing programs. And, if community development is limited to coordination, is greater effectiveness on the part of those programs being coordinated likely to result (considering that resentments readily arise as an existing organizational framework is subjected to the weight of another organizational framework placed upon it)?

some countries within the second category cited may nevertheless want
to invoke community development as a *transition* program. The reason
for this is that some benefits can be had from it during the short-run
period prior to the full accrual of those gains believed possible from a
more ambitious program upon which primary reliance is placed.[20] In
short, the potential role of community development, viewed in economic
terms, is dependent primarily upon the nature of developmental alternatives open to particular countries.

Aside from the foregoing, two further arguments—non-economic in
nature—can be cited, both on behalf of community development. First,
community development offers a means of getting more people into the
spirit of economic development. As many persons have noted, economic
development can "feed on" nationalism (i.e., on a nation-wide consensus
as to the desirability of the attainment of some central goal). Accordingly,
there is real merit in getting everyone "into the act" so that they can
feel they are part of a national effort. Through community development,
idle or partially-employed people in even outlying parts of a country can
be lured into a type of activity that accompanying national propaganda
can proceed to link to the theme of "a national effort for economic development."

Second, insofar as the strengthening of democratic processes is regarded an objective, community development can prove helpful. Participation by village and rural people in the determination of what is to be
done, even if decisions seemingly involve only small matters, exposes
them to a fundamental democratic process that runs counter to the
apartness and neglect previously experienced in their locales. When this
participation involves various efforts known to fit into an overall national
program, integration of the people into the stream of national life and
national political processes is fostered to a considerable extent.

SELECTED BIBLIOGRAPHY

See the end of Chapter 7.

---

[20] The appeal of community development as a transition program is heightened
by the fact that organized government is freed of some financial responsibilities as
local efforts along self-help lines give rise to particular new public facilities. To the
extent that self-help efforts operate in this manner, organized government is left with
added spendable resources then available for use in other connections, including
spending on other categories of development.

6

DIRECTIONS OF
DEVELOPMENT (II)

The first major form of developmental activity cited is that of basic development. A second major form of developmental activity involves improvement in existing lines of raw-materials production—meaning added effort aimed to increase output in prevailing types of raw-materials production, agricultural or mineral. As a prelude to or accompaniment of this category of effort, some improvement in basic development is ordinarily necessary, or at least helpful. As for offering a *basic choice* in developmental direction, however, improvement in raw-materials production (in existing lines) stands as *the* fundamental alternative to diversification (including industrial development as a supplement to, or partial replacement for, raw-materials production).

IMPROVEMENT IN RAW-MATERIALS PRODUCTION

The central argument for a developmental approach based on improvement in raw-materials production (in existing lines) is that, for some underdeveloped countries, it represents the "best alternative" for assuring an increase in per-worker productivity (and in real per-capita income), in the short-run and perhaps also in the long-run. This approach tends to recommend itself especially in the case of countries whose resource patterns are not favorable for either extensive diversification or widespread industrialization. In some instances, a shift of manpower and complementary factors into new fields of activity appears likely to entail a loss in productivity and income, short-run and perhaps also long-run, so that emphasis simply upon improvement in raw-materials production (in existing lines) remains as the hopeful way to proceed in an attempt to raise productivity. Even in instances where a resort to this approach appears to offer only a small potential for increased productivity, its appeal is frequently considerable. The approach is widely regarded as "safe," since it rules out the need to deviate from lines of production already established and familiar to the population.

Improvement in raw-materials production, as envisaged in the present connection, results from activity along two main courses. The first course involves the adoption of new and improved methods. In agriculture, for example, the practice of crop rotation offers a possible way to increase total yield (over, say, the continuation of a system of repeated tillage of the same crop or of leaving land fallow periodically). Again, the use of fertilizers and pest controls, the introduction of improved methods of irrigation, and the introduction of improved techniques of crop planting[1] all offer ways—on the whole, simple ways—to increase yield.

The second course involves the introduction of new and improved equipment. In agriculture, for example, equipment is frequently all but non-existent in some underdeveloped countries, or is of such poor quality or effectiveness that resultant crop yields are held down as a consequence of inferior tillage. More or better farm equipment frequently offers a potent way to increase productivity. In fact, substantially enhanced productivity commonly results even in instances in which introductions of new equipment are held to modest levels, such as steel plows instead of wooden plows or machine cultivators instead of hand hoes. Again, use of fencing provides a way to facilitate selective breeding of livestock, thereby resulting in better quality animals.

COSTS OF IMPLEMENTATION

The cost associated with the introduction of such methods and equipment can be expected to vary greatly, depending upon precisely what is undertaken, and how. New and improved methods in agriculture tend to entail little or no cost, in the sense of direct cash outlay. The challenge here, more particularly, is one of how to acquaint people with the methods thought preferable, so that revised practices can follow. The technique commonly found useful in this connection involves demonstra-

---

[1] Revised systems of rice planting are said to have resulted in increased yields in rice-growing areas of the Far East. For example, increased rice yields are being sought in the Philippines through wider use of the so-called Margate and Masagana systems ("masagana" is Tagalog for "bountiful harvest"), under which rice seedlings are spaced in transplanting in accordance with a "scientific" pattern. It is said that there has been an "upward trend in rice yields in recent years, probably due in large part to the emphasis placed on better cultural practices, including spacing." (Quoted from a letter by Paul E. Johnson of the ICA's Office of Food and Agriculture; letter dated May 23, 1958.)

tion projects, which give people a chance to observe the results of alternative methods. If sufficiently impressed, people are presumably tempted to follow suit.

New and improved equipment for agriculture ordinarily entails somewhat more cost, the exact cost being dependent upon the amount and complexity of the equipment concerned. If agriculture via small production units is at issue, total equipment costs ordinarily need to be held at a low level. Small-scale farmers rarely possess financial means adequate for anything more than limited outlays. For the greater part, this means that equipment has to be restricted to elementary types. To some extent, of course, it may prove possible to pool equipment among several users, thereby making possible some procurement of equipment beyond the simplest types—even while per-farmer outlays remain at low levels. If agriculture via large production units is at issue, more complex equipment tends to prove necessary in order to reap pronounced productivity gains. Aside from the imposition of heavy outlays upon ultimate users, procurement of the associated equipment ordinarily is only from abroad, thereby posing a foreign-exchange demand for the country concerned. If foreign-exchange stringency already prevails, any added import requirements contribute further to a serious problem (unless, of course, offsetting foreign-exchange benefits can be promptly realized as a consequence of the utilization of whatever it is that is imported). Significantly, the foreign-exchange requirements posed by equipment demands associated with large-scale agriculture stand in sharp contrast to the situation involving small scale farmers. In the case of these farmers, simpler equipment is made to serve, and it is frequently of a type that can be manufactured domestically with the minimum of preliminary difficulties (so that, in any event, immediate foreign-exchange demands tend to be of a considerably lesser order).

In mineral exploitation, factors involving areal concentration of deposits and technical conditions of production result in output by few production units. New and improved equipment, when required by these production units, is usually secured through importation. The complexity of the equipment ordinarily rules out its manufacture domestically, *but* access to it through importation is certain to prove costly of foreign exchange. However, since mineral exploitation is typically carried on in the anticipation of ore export (e.g., as in countries committed to raw-materials production, per se), foreign-exchange earnings on potential sales abroad can be viewed as an offset to the initial foreign-exchange drain associated with the procurement of the equipment. And, when foreign firms are responsible for the exploitation, the investment embodied in the associated equipment in essence comprises a "loan" to the economy, with foreign-exchange demands arising subsequently as repatriation is undertaken.

SELF-SUFFICIENCY OR COMMERCIAL PRODUCTION?

Assume that a government makes the decision, relative to its developmental efforts, to gear its activities and moral support primarily toward the attainment of augmented raw-materials output. The government is thereupon confronted by a further decision, relating to the size of production units to prevail. Is small-scale enterprise to be favored, or are fewer but rather large production units to be preferred?

Mineral exploitation is not likely to fall to numerous small-scale operators under any circumstances. Technical conditions of production tend here to favor concentration of activity within few production units, or even under a single production unit within a given country. In agriculture, however, there is considerable latitude for choice. Arguments in support of having numerous small-scale units include the following. First, beneficial impact, if it is to be had in any event, is likely to result more rapidly, for more people, and in more readily identifiable fashion if initial emphasis is placed upon small-scale operators. Second, because this approach tends to be economical in its demand for new and improved equipment, money costs are held down (and, of special significance, direct foreign-exchange outlays tend to be held down). Third, if government desires to be labeled democratic, special merit attaches to the placement of emphasis upon numerous small-scale operators (as compared with the placement of emphasis upon activity at the "top" in the hope that the benefits initiated there will seep down to the "common people" through the operation of the "trickle-down theory"). But in opposition to these arguments, emphasis upon small-scale operators in agriculture is tantamount to the sanctioning of self-sufficiency as a goal. If large production units are not practicable (because of terrain, popular resistance, etc.), there may be no alternative to small units. However, whether or not there is an alternative to small units, once production *is* dependent upon numerous small units, output geared toward localized use tends to be favored (e.g., as producers invoke their bias for output of a type usable in on-the-spot consumption—with the result that added output to a great extent comes simply to be consumed locally by persons concerned in its production). A conclusion to be drawn is that, with production dependent upon numerous small units, generation of an export surplus tends to prove difficult.[2] In such an event, foreign-exchange

---

[2] An interesting case in point is that of Haiti. While it was a colony under French rule, large production units prevailed in agriculture, and an export surplus also prevailed. Following independence, fragmentation of holdings occurred and persisted, and no comparable export surplus was experienced thereafter.

By way of possible qualification of the general conclusion drawn, it should be borne in mind that the agricultural surpluses of a colonial plantation economy may be *only partly* the product of superior productivity. The point is that the form in which production is then organized allows a "surplus" to be "wrung from" the diets of the colonial population (which "surplus" might not otherwise exist—say, if indigenous control existed over the production system).

stringencies continue largely unabated, despite an increase in domestic production. The foreign-exchange bottleneck then, in turn, continues to block added importation, either of developmental ingredients (needed for added development) or of consumption goods (needed for greater variety in domestic consumption patterns).

For the greater part, arguments in the case of large production units are roughly the reverse of the foregoing. Thus, emphasis upon large-scale operations in the course of improvement in raw-materials production tends to entail heavy initial costs (including heavy initial foreign-exchange outlays), and focuses initial attention upon *few* people rather than *many* people. Again, plantation agriculture and large-scale mineral exploitation represent potent avenues for generation of an export surplus, thereby giving rise to added supplies of foreign exchange, the receipt of which can then lend substance to thoughts of additional development— whenever such can be contemplated only if more foreign exchange is available. Importantly, however, both plantation agriculture and large-scale mineral exploitation are vulnerable on two major counts. First, plantations and mines tend not to create an economic environment conducive to the growth or endurance of a democratic political structure—not if observable situations in various locales suffice as a guide. For a country that chooses to look upon developmental progress as a force conducive to greater democracy, this possible shortcoming is a serious one, since it casts doubt upon the wisdom of a whole approach to development. Second, because plantations and mines are favorite investment outlets for foreign owner-operators, they readily become the target of anti-foreign sentiment. Operations having a foreign link, whatever their pure economic merit may be for the countries in which they are situated, are frequently resented in terms of being a manifestation of colonialism, and especially so when growing nationalism is present. Additionally, since such operations are frequently regarded as mere "economic extensions" of the country having an investment claim, their actual or potential contribution to the overall national development of individual underdeveloped countries comes readily to be questioned.[3]

LAND REFORM

Whenever attention in the developmental program of an under-developed country is focused upon agriculture, proposals almost invariably arise relative to land reform.[4] The populations of underdeveloped

---

[3] For example, G. Myrdal, refers to ". . . economic enclaves, controlled from abroad and mainly devoted to the production of primary products for export." See his *Rich Lands and Poor* (New York: Harper and Brothers, 1957), Ch. V, esp. p. 53.

[4] Land reform, as a procedure, commonly is classed under "new and improved methods" in agriculture—although it should be recognized that land reform may *not always* represent an "improvement." Alternatively, for those who so prefer, land reform can also be classed as basic development—on the grounds that the expected reform rests on legal change.

countries are largely rural, and most persons are directly dependent upon agriculture for their livelihood. Yet, the typical farmer in numerous countries is a landless peasant in the sense that he does not own the plot of ground he cultivates. Ordinarily, he leases from an absentee landlord, paying as rent a share of his output—the rental share commonly ranging from one-third to one-half, but sometimes higher.[5] Somewhat ironically, in locales not far distant, in some countries, are lands of potentially equivalent or near-equivalent productivity, but currently characterized by absolute or comparative non-use.

Three main proposals, or types of proposals, are associated with land reform. The first pertains to enactment of legal provisions concerning landlord-tenant relationships, and establishment of procedures for the settlement of conflicts that might arise between them. The second pertains to the opening up of new and previously unsettled areas, with resettlement there of farmers from old and overcrowded areas of settlement. The third pertains to the breaking up of large estates, with the sale of the land in small tracts to previous tenants and others. Proposals, of whatever major type, invariably emphasize—by way of an avowed central objective— achievement of a better deal for the small farm operator. Proponents almost without fail claim potential benefits on both economic and non-economic grounds.

Economic benefits, insofar as they accrue, are pictured as stemming from increases in productivity. The first form of land reform—legislation concerning landlord-tenant relationships—typically places its emphasis upon the establishment of rental ceilings, clarification of minimum allowable standards of landlord conduct, and the creation of a legal framework for settlement of landlord-tenant disputes. Efforts in this vein, however well intended, result primarily in a redistribution of income (toward the tenant), rather than in greater overall income. Only to the extent that the applicable legislation serves as a morale-booster for tenants is there any real basis to expect that worker effort might alter so as to yield increased productivity.

The second form of land reform—the opening up of new and previously unsettled areas—places its emphasis upon the shifting of people from overcrowded areas. A shift offers a real prospect for yielding an immediate increase in total production, since additional lands come under cultivation. Also, per-worker productivity can be expected to rise, since similar numbers of people become responsible for a greater total output.

The third form of land reform—the breaking up of large estates, with the sale of the land in small tracts to previous tenants and others—is probably the most complex of the group, for legal and financial reasons.

---

[5] A law of economics appears to operate, in practice, so as to correlate level of rent and pressure of population against land, i.e., rentals increase as population pressure increases.

Like resettlement, however, the method holds potential for increased productivity. If an upgrading in land utilization is a consequence of the break-up process, an increase in total productivity is to be expected. Probable increases in total productivity appear great when the break-up process involves estates previously subject to generally low forms of utilization (and upon which added numbers come to be settled, and who come to practice a different type of agriculture, capable of yielding higher output per area). However, when the break-up process merely involves the acquisition of title to small tracts by resident persons who formerly were tenants, probable increases in total productivity appear small, especially if methods of production remain basically unaltered.

In addition to the economic benefits related to potential increases in productivity, proponents of land reform generally claim for it certain non-economic contributions. For example, the preservation or promotion of the democratic ideal, assuming this to be an objective, requires the responsiveness of government to the needs and desires of all the people. In this respect, action especially toward landlord-tenant relationships offers a quick and inexpensive form of expression by government. Again, the democratic ideal and political stability itself tend to be fostered as added numbers come to have a more direct stake in the established economic order by achieving property ownership, either through resettlement or through the break-up and resale in small parcels of once-large estates.

Along with the cited benefits, land reform also has its limitations and problems. These are political and economic in nature. From a political standpoint, action along the lines of any one of the foregoing forms of land reform is dependent upon the passage of legislation. A dilemma of sorts arises at this juncture in that the legislation itself stems from a group that, in the typical underdeveloped country, is heavily weighted with important landowners, not with tenants. In any event, the legislation that emerges is frequently somewhat lacking in boldness or force. Even when the legislation reads well, half-hearted application often serves to reduce the impact to token levels.

The political problem can be illustrated through a reference to land resettlement. Here the problem would appear to be fairly minimal—in view of seemingly small overall obstacles, at least as compared with a program for breaking up large estates. In land resettlement, an initial task involves selection of the areas of potential settlement. A fairly common situation is that high-quality land in broad valleys is held privately in estate form and is placed in uses of generally low productivity (e.g., used for cattle ranches), while land of poorer quality in remote and narrow mountain valleys remains governmentally-owned and entirely unsettled. In selecting the area of potential settlement, the government of many an underdeveloped country—given the foregoing situation—ends by resettling masses of people on small tracts of the poorer-quality land, while leaving the choice estates intact and unaffected. Why? The explanation is usually found in politics, to a very important degree. The governments of some underdeveloped countries simply are not strong enough to take action relative to landed estates in general, especially not when legislation authorizing resettlement arises, exists, and functions only insofar as sanctioned by legislators who, to a great part, are important landowners themselves. The result is that government parcels out its own available land instead, good or bad, and thereby avoids a head-on clash with vested interests.

The economic problem relates especially to financing. Enactment and enforcement of legislation concerning landlord-tenant relationships involve no heavy financial burden for government. Nor does resettlement of people upon previously unoccupied land entail particularly heavy cost for government. Some outlays, ordinarily handled on a loan basis, are usually necessary in order to grubstake settlers, but total cost rarely approaches anything unmanageable.[6] When the break-up of estates and the resale in small parcels to former tenants and others are the objectives, however, financial problems become legion.

The process of breaking up estates requires that government purchase the land, and then resell it on easy terms to numerous small purchasers. If expropriation without compensation were possible, no direct financial problem would arise for government; however, satisfactory compensation has to be provided (under any other than totalitarian conditions). Assuming payment in cash, the immediate additions to the money supply readily prove troublesome in an inflationary sense, especially given the proneness to inflation characteristic of most underdeveloped countries.[7] Assuming payment in government bonds, the privilege of conversion invites rapid movement to a cash position, again augmenting the basis for inflationary pressure. On the other hand, denial of conversion privileges until a much later date appears tantamount to partial confiscation, in view of the presumed long-term upward movements in price levels. Thus, the purchase by government of estates prior to their break-up and resale (on credit) entails financial transactions that either generate inflationary pressure for the country or force sellers to bear the cost of some "disguised confiscation." With the realization of the financial problems involved, governmental activity in the acquisition and break-up of

---

6 The single cost that tends to be most sizable is that associated with the provision of shelter. In typical cases, however, the per-family cost in this connection is relatively low—with facilities held to very simple levels, and with heavy reliance placed upon the "free" labor of occupants-to-be and upon inexpensive on-the-scene raw materials.

7 Reliance upon current governmental revenues is not regarded as a hopeful course. Sufficient revenues to sustain a large-scale effort are not derivable in the typical underdeveloped country, so that financing out of current revenues automatically limits effort to minor undertakings.

estates tends quickly to degenerate into a mere token effort.[8] Significantly, there is no easy way to by-pass the inherent financial problem; a reputable government cannot simply order landlords to be shot in order to "solve" the financial problem of compensation following dispossession!

SPECIAL PROBLEMS

Among the problems commonly associated with efforts to increase raw-materials output, two loom very importantly. First, does mechanization create an adverse employment effect? Second, does added output find a market outlet?

1. *Employment Effects.* An important matter, particularly as it relates to agriculture, concerns the effect of the introduction of equipment upon employment. New and improved equipment offers a possible way to increase output, but some equipment, as it is added, is likely also to prove labor-saving. Importantly, a common situation among underdeveloped countries is that of already widespread underemployment. Given this situation, a likely effect of an introduction of labor-saving equipment—at least in the short-run—is either greater underemployment (for the labor force as an aggregate, including self-employed farmers), or the creation of outright unemployment (among workers in large-scale agriculture, as some hired employees come to be displaced by labor-saving equipment). Since the acquisition of equipment entails financial outlays, possibly including substantial foreign-exchange outlays (especially when the mechanization of large-scale agriculture is at issue), and since greater underemployment or unemployment constitutes no gain, an issue of some importance is raised. Resolution of the issue obviously requires, as a minimum, a balancing of the merits of possible added output, on a sustained basis, against the possible drawbacks inherent in added underemployment or unemployment.

If it is assumed that an initial effect of mechanization—say, of large-scale agriculture—is added underemployment or possible unemployment, it can be argued nevertheless that the mechanization can prove helpful in the developmental process if some other things *also* occur. To illustrate, if other employment outlets are opened up *concurrently* with the mechanization of existing large-scale agriculture—as, for example, by bringing previously unused acreage into cultivation or through new industrial development—the possible drawback inherent in the likelihood of added underemployment or unemployment is negated, or at least lessened. In fact, the process of freeing-up of some workers within the labor force can conceivably prove helpful to the extension of production into new

---

[8] In countries somewhat more developed, added latitude for possible action ordinarily exists. A good example is that of Japan, whose extensive program of land reform following World War II is generally conceded to have met tests of financial soundness. See UN, *Progress in Land Reform*, New York, 1954, pp. 24–25 and Ch. 3.

areas and activities, at least in some instances. However, the plain failure to assure added employment outlets, if this proves to be the case, ordinarily suffices to lessen considerably the potential merit of major agricultural mechanization.

2. *Market Outlets.* A second important matter, which arises as improvement in raw-materials production results in added output in existing lines, involves salability of the *additions* to total output. No special problem ordinarily arises in the case of small-scale agriculture. Production there tends to be largely of the subsistence type, with any added output going largely toward an increase in the consumption of persons immediately concerned. In the case of large-scale agriculture, however, production is predominantly for the market, and frequently for an export market. Market attributes then typically include the existence of overall rigidities deleterious to total sales potential and, more particularly, the presence of inelastic demand conditions. Added output is fine *if* it can be disposed of to good advantage. Significantly, however, for many an underdeveloped country, the real obstacle to expansion in output is found in inadequacies of the market, and not in the technical aspects of production, per se. And, if goods can't be sold advantageously and aren't consumable by their producers, why produce them?

EXPORT MARKETS

Raw-materials production on an individual self-sufficiency basis is not conducive to the generation of markedly higher income. Raw-materials production, with a substantial portion of output entering the money economy, offers greater hope for higher income; and when, in addition, a movement toward product specialization characterizes the output entering the market, a further force prevails that is favorable to generation of higher income. But, marked specialization in raw-materials production makes imperative a country's integration into the international economy, in the sense that the specialized output found in "surplus" supply requires an export market, while particular goods required (or merely desired) in the domestic economy, and not produced domestically, are left to be imported. Unfortunately, export dependence creates problems. Two major points of concern arise to confront the raw-materials-producing countries concerned. First, what is the *size* of the potential market? Second, how *stable,* or unstable, is the potential market? Or, in fact, how stable, or unstable, is the entire export-import relationship?

A developmental approach that emphasizes raw-materials production is obviously less than complete if it does not concern itself with market considerations. Problems do not end with the physical aspects of production. Commodities, once produced, also need to be disposed of satisfactorily. Not to anyone's great surprise, countries at present in the category of specialized raw-materials producers (including, also, countries charting a developmental course in which emphasis is placed on specialized raw-materials production) are exhibiting great interest in the matter of "what can be done" to generate and (or) stabilize export sales, and hence foreign earnings.

The size of the export market to which a given country can aspire is dependent upon demand in potential market areas, *and* upon the portion of the total demand that the given country can hope to capture for itself. The market areas—for underdeveloped countries generally—are found, very importantly, in developed countries, and especially involve the US, Great Britain, and some other countries of Western Europe. The demand for raw-materials imports on the part of these countries is fundamentally dependent upon their prevailing levels of economic activity and income. The demand for raw materials destined for use in industry is basically dependent upon the level of economic activity, with the upper limit to the demand set—at any given time—by certain technological capabilities on the physical-side of production. The demand for raw materials destined for consumption (e.g., foodstuffs) is basically dependent upon the level of consumer income. A given supply of raw materials viewed, in each instance, as the aggregate put forth by all supplier countries—can be disposed of through exportation only within the limits set by external market conditions so determined.[9] The fundamental relationship is that total demand establishes total markets, which then comprise a limiting factor for total production. Within this context, supplier countries are obliged—at any given time—to *share* an existent market. The attempt of any one country to expand its own exports can yield success, in the short-run, only at the expense of other countries.

Apart from the matter of the absolute size of export markets for raw materials, there is the matter of stability, or instability, in these markets. A consequence of export dependence in raw materials is a vulnerability in domestic production and income to fluctuations and trends in the terms of trade (Ch. 2, especially Tables 8 and 9). Recent proposals relative to stabilization are numerous and varied, but the actual solution of the problem remains a task for the future.

STABILIZATION

The problem of instability in the export earnings of raw-materials-producing countries is an old one, and has been grappled with in the past. Of the numerous approaches tried, two stand out in importance: buffer-stock schemes and international commodity agreements.

The buffer-stock approach, as commonly practiced to date, involves *unilateral* action by a given producer country. The approach is char-

---

9 Aside from possible, but likely limited, substitutions as among products.

acterized by additions of a primary commodity to a governmentally-maintained pool whenever export markets are regarded as weak, followed by withdrawals from the pool for export purposes whenever export markets are regarded as strong. By holding supply-and-demand relationships relatively unvaried by means of recourse to periodic additions to and withdrawals from buffer stocks, greater stability in export prices and proceeds can be achieved, or so it is hoped.

The buffer-stock idea has a sound economic basis, but practical difficulties are invariably encountered in its application. First, storage costs can prove considerable, to say nothing of the impracticality of an attempt at prolonged storage of perishable commodities. Second, persons responsible for administration frequently are unable to stand up against domestic pressures to "peg" average prices at high levels, so that additions to buffer stocks come over time to exceed withdrawals by wide margins, thereby entailing a substantial tie-up of public funds in non-liquidable stocks. Third, unilateral action proves self-defeating as an approach whenever competing supplier countries stand ready to augment their own exports, even as a country committed to a buffer-stock arrangement undertakes to withhold some of its output from international sale in the hopes of thereby promoting market stabilization.[10]

In view of these and other weaknesses, greater faith for successful stabilization generally comes to be placed on another approach, involving international commodity agreements. International commodity agreements are *intergovernmental* agreements between leading producer countries of particular raw materials, or between them and leading importer countries as well, and are concerned with matters related to the production and marketing of the particular raw materials (including the establishment of export and import quotas relative to the particular raw materials, and the fixing of upper and lower limits on prices). Major commodities covered by such agreements during recent years include coffee, sugar, and wheat.

Moderate success, at least as a short-run stabilization device, can be claimed for the technique involved in international commodity agreements. International coverage serves to lend strength to control efforts, and this strength is heightened when importer countries are included along with exporter countries. Nevertheless, two major shortcomings are inherent in the technique, at least insofar as underdeveloped countries are concerned. First, while the inclusion of both importer and exporter countries in agreements helps to make the arrangements more palatable and

---

10 Indeed, the mere possibility that competing countries may expand production *in anticipation* of added exportation ordinarily provides grounds enough for hesitancy on the part of individual countries otherwise receptive to a buffer-stock arrangement. In short, the fear is ever present that action aimed to withhold goods from international sale may not result in greater market stability, but rather in a *shift* in business *among* competing supplier countries.

durable, it also serves to limit action to whatever can be resolved out of a consumer-producer conflict of interest. The most that can be reasonably hoped for over time is some rather modest action at the margin, aimed to preclude merely the greater of the extremes otherwise believed likely.[11] Second, while a lessening in the amplitude of fluctuations in prices and proceeds constitutes an achievement, the future economic health of underdeveloped countries requires something more than stability in the export earnings accruing from basically unaltered production levels. Underdeveloped countries need to experience growth in output. The technique involved in international commodity agreements, of course, cannot assure advantageous disposal abroad of substantially increased output of existing types. Consequently, underdeveloped countries need to think in terms of disposal techniques other than international commodity agreements, or of added output in new lines of production (which again comprises a matter quite outside the scope of international commodity agreements).

In view of a widespread awareness of the shortcomings of the foregoing major approaches, much thought in raw-materials-producing countries is being given to alternate approaches that might be invoked to cope with the export problem confronting these countries. A favorite alternate proposal involves *international buffer stocks,* under which the responsibility for satisfactory disposal of "surplus" commodities is shared by a group of countries.[12] According to one version, the financial assistance needed to underwrite the scheme would be provided by the various exporter countries who choose to use the arrangement. According to a second version (one receiving considerable support, especially in some quarters in Latin America), financing would be supplied by the major industrial countries, especially by the US.[13] The rationale for financial participation by industrial countries proceeds in terms of their status as the major importers of raw materials, and in terms of their alleged "responsibility" for the instability experienced by raw-materials-producing countries (the idea being that the industrial countries fail to main-

---

[11] In fact, if truly substantial downward price movements are considered a distinct possibility, some importer countries are inclined to want to remain outside an agreement in order to take advantage of the lower prices, should they materialize, rather than to come into the agreement and help stabilize prices. The decision of Great Britain to remain outside the International Wheat Agreement of 1953, for example, is commonly regarded as the product of that country's appraisal of expected price movements in the free market. For comment on this point, see L. Soth, *Farm Trouble* (Princeton, N.J.: Princeton University Press, 1957), p. 191.

[12] For a concise discussion of international buffer stocks, see UN, *Measures for International Economic Stability,* New York, 1951, Ch. II, esp. pp. 22–25.

[13] To some extent, the US program for stockpiling strategic raw materials has the effect of underwriting a market for raw-materials-producing countries. However, this country's program falls short on two counts (when viewed in terms of the needs of raw-materials-producing countries). First, the program is limited to *strategic* raw materials—i.e., mostly minerals, *not* foodstuffs. Second, the program is geared fundamentally to this country's *defense* needs, and not primarily to the requirements of raw-materials-producing countries for assured export earnings.

tain economic stability at home, and thereby *cause* instability in the export earnings of raw-materials-producing countries). A modification of this second version suggests that the International Bank, a lending institution of multi-country membership (with the US as its largest single subscriber of capital), should provide or underwrite financing for the scheme.[14]

Some of the problems associated with unilateral buffer-stock arrangements are likely also to be present in the case of international buffer-stock arrangements. In at least one important respect, however, an international approach appears to offer a clear advantage: in financing. When financing is derived internationally, and especially when the source extends to major industrial countries or to international institutions (which institutions embrace major industrial countries within their memberships), finances potentially available tend to be greatly enhanced. While added financial potential can provide a needed source of strength, it can also serve to spur on grandiose thinking, culminating in large-scale and long-sustained stockpiling operations—with the possibility or likelihood present of an accumulation of surplus stocks not capable of orderly disposal. Significantly, when major industrial countries admit to an obligation to provide financing, the "door is opened" to pressures for added stabilization efforts (eventually focusing upon, conceivably, nothing short of *guaranteed* export markets at "high" average prices).

Some persons are of the opinion that international buffer-stock arrangements are limited, in effective operation, to the removal of some of the more objectionable surface features (e.g., marked instability of prices and volume) evident in the trade of raw-materials-producing countries with industrial countries. However, according to many of these persons, what is needed is not just an institutional "gimmick" aimed to make obvious symptoms seem more palatable, but rather some more basic course of action that can get at the root of the trouble. In this vein, two additional proposals are advanced.

The first of these additional proposals suggests that major industrial countries be impressed in some manner of the *absolute need* for them to maintain prosperity, so that healthy markets can exist for the raw-materials exports of underdeveloped countries. A common complaint in underdeveloped countries, as intimated earlier, is that the industrial countries (meaning, especially, the US) are given to marked economic instability,[15] and that this instability is transmitted—indeed, in ac-

---

14 UN, *Measures for International Economic Stability*, New York, 1951, p. 25.

15 As the late Lord Keynes put the matter (albeit in reference particularly to secular stagnation at that time): "Moreover the richer the community, the wider will tend to be the gap between its actual and its potential production; and therefore the more obvious and outrageous the defects of the economic system." See J. M. Keynes, *The General Theory of Employment, Interest and Money* (New York: Harcourt, Brace and Company, Inc., 1936), p. 31.

centuated form—to underdeveloped countries (as sales proceeds realized from raw-materials exports to the industrial countries tend to contract even more markedly,[16] during a recession or depression, than does aggregate income in these countries). The impact upon underdeveloped countries of such a contraction in foreign-exchange receipts can be devastating, especially in that the latitude within the economy upon which developmental progress is heavily dependent comes to be an early casualty of the contraction. Illustrative of what is at issue, the loss of export earnings to underdeveloped countries during 1957–58, paralleling a recession in the US, is estimated to have amounted to roughly *twice* the level of economic aid provided the underdeveloped world by the US during the same period.[17] It appears reasonable to contend that *if* the major industrial countries can achieve a high degree of economic stability within a framework of overall growth (with a reasonably high rate of growth prevailing), the beneficial effect upon underdeveloped countries—all raw-materials producers—is likely to prove very great, *possibly* far greater than anything potentially derivable from commodity stabilization, per se. In short, the basic notion behind the proposal at issue is that international economic stabilization be regarded as dependent upon stabilization first in the major industrial countries.[18]

Unfortunately, however, there is no evidence, in the view of many persons, that the major industrial countries are depression-proof, or are on the verge of becoming so. And, if the danger of occasional economic breakdown in the major industrial countries continues (with raw-materials-producing countries compelled to live in the shadow of this uncertainty), *what* is to be done? It is in this context that the second of the additional proposals referred to acquires special relevance. This additional possibility in the field of stabilization involves *greater diversification* within the economies of underdeveloped countries. Diversification—so as not to have "all the eggs in one basket"—stands in contrast to specialization with its inevitable high degree of international interdependence. To a great extent, diversification entails a course of action in which an underdeveloped country itself can take the initiative. This is espe-

---

16 In percentage terms.

17 Apropos to the impact upon underdeveloped countries of a recession in the US, the following statement regarding the situation in Latin America (in 1958) is illuminating: "So great is the dependence on the exporting of commodities that no domestic measures can make a serious dent in the crisis. Most of the governments are looking to Washington for some form of aid so that economic crises do not deteriorate into social and political troubles." See *The New York Times*, April 27, 1958, p. 4-E.

18 A recent suggestion (1958), offered in view of the shrinkage in foreign-exchange earnings experienced by raw-materials-producing countries when recession strikes the major industrial countries, would have capital supplied to underdeveloped countries, on a loan or grant basis, as an *offset* to such foreign exchange as is "normally" earned, but not earned during periods of recession in the major industrial countries. See "Letters to the Editor" (letter by H. C. Wallich), *The New York Times*, May 6, 1958, p. 34-C.

cially true when diversification emphasizes greater variety in raw-materials production, as apart from diversification through the promotion of industrialization (as a major supplement to, or partial replacement of, existing raw-materials production). But, diversification—as a developmental approach—constitutes a basic line of effort that goes beyond the improvement of raw-materials production (in existing lines) at issue in the present chapter.

SELECTED BIBLIOGRAPHY

See the end of Chapter 7.

7

DIRECTIONS OF DEVELOPMENT (III)

With basic development viewed as essentially a supporting force in any event (Ch. 5), the possible approaches to developmental activity then remaining are two in number: improvement in raw-materials production in existing lines of output (Ch. 6), and the fundamental alternative to it, *diversification*. The present chapter deals with diversification, an approach that seeks improvement in the economic situation through alteration of the pattern of production (as distinct from an attempt to obtain improvement within the confines of existing lines of output).

DIVERSIFICATION: TWO TYPES

Diversification can be of two basic types, proceeding in either of two directions. The first type entails continued dependence upon raw-materials production, but places the emphasis upon achievement of greater diversity in the commodity composition of this raw-materials production. The hope is that greater output and overall improvement will occur even as there is a lessening in the relative importance—and perhaps the absolute importance also—of the one or few commodities that traditionally dominated the production pattern. Although still entailing dependence upon raw-materials production, this approach is in sharp contrast to the previously-cited approach in the raw-materials field (Ch. 6). To recall, in that approach the emphasis is upon achievement of more output, but with this output falling within the existing pattern of production (frequently a non-diversified pattern, heavily geared toward exportation of a single or few major commodities).

The second type of diversification entails the promotion of industrial development as a supplement to, or partial replacement for, production of raw materials. This approach places the emphasis upon achievement of an economic base that, ordinarily, is broader and more varied than anything contemplated under diversification simply within the raw-materials field. The hope is that greater output and overall improvement will result from this altered economic base, particularly because of a lessened dependence upon the international market or, notwithstanding the extent of continued international dependence, a lessened vulnerability to repercussions that potentially stem from this market.

THE CASE FOR DIVERSIFICATION

Potential contributions to developmental progress, stemming from diversification, arise as gains either in income stabilization or in income generation, or in some combination of the two.

Diversification has much to recommend it as a stabilization procedure. In fact, the most common rationale for diversification derives from the greater safety allegedly possible when production is spread over fairly numerous commodities or lines of endeavor. Then "all one's eggs are not in the same basket," so to speak. There is always a possibility under diversification that should adverse conditions in production or marketing befall one sector of an economy, they might be softened or counterbalanced by what prevails elsewhere within the economy. Any reduction in the export-import dependence of a country, or any hedging of a country against the potential effects of export-import dependence, tends to make its economy less vulnerable or sensitive to external occurrences clearly beyond its control.

As a procedure to assure income generation, diversification has merit or not, depending upon particular circumstances. In order for real per-capita income to rise as a consequence of diversification, per-capita productivity must be brought to a higher plane (and preferably must average higher over time, not just momentarily). Either one of two sets of circumstances can assure the needed increase in productivity. First, if diversification leads to new production that constitutes an "add-on" to previous total production, per-capita productivity automatically increases, unless offsetting population growth occurs at the same time. Such added production is a distinct possibility in the typical underdeveloped country, since the existence of underemployed or unemployed manpower (and perhaps also of similarly situated complementary factors, e.g., raw materials) makes possible the channelization of some manpower (and complementary factors) into entirely new types of output without the need thereby to jeopardize the level of previous output—e.g., through the activation of idle manpower, fuller use of the partially idle, or upgrading in the use of some persons previously employed full-time.[1] Second, if diversification leads to lessened export-import dependence, with new domestic production providing some goods previously imported under a trading relationship characterized by decidedly unfavorable terms of trade, higher real per-capita income also becomes a possibility—in the sense that real-income benefit can then accrue in full to a country, instead of being partially "lost" to its trading partner.[2] In contrast to the foregoing, however, the possibility also exists that diversification can comprise a procedure that yields greater stability, but *at the price* of a loss in real per-capita income—whenever alterations occur in the production pattern that serve to lower per-capita productivity overall, and whenever this adverse effect is not compensated for by improvements in the essential external trading relationships prevailing or by the creation of a production-and-trade basis capable of yielding long-run gain once a short-run period of retrogression is weathered.

Apart from such generalizations, important variations appear when appraisal proceeds in terms of the *particular* direction diversification is to take. When diversification efforts are within the realm of raw-materials production, a common prospect is that of marked benefit in income stabilization, but only moderate benefit, at best, in income generation. Greater diversity in raw-materials production ordinarily tends to lessen proneness to economic instability. And, somewhat higher real per-capita income is often a reasonable expectation as a consequence of the new and added production associated with raw materials diversification with the new and added production encouraged, in fact, by the presence of underemployed or unemployed workers. However, there is reason to believe that while scope for income growth through diversification of raw-materials output exists, at least in some countries, this scope tends to be decidedly limited. Physical conditions of raw-materials production, coupled with limitations in market outlets for raw-materials products, appear to pose serious obstacles, likely in many instances and at some fairly early point to thwart attempts to raise overall productivity and real per-capita income, with the result that potential gains are held to fairly modest levels.

In the case of diversification through an emphasis upon industrial

---

[1] In its simplest form, the added output might come from garden plots, planted and maintained by rural families. Few products would likely enter the money economy; nevertheless, real income undoubtedly would be augmented, by however small an amount.

[2] In addition, both increases and shifts in output raise implications as to a country's foreign-exchange status. For example, if foreign-exchange stringency is characteristic to begin with, and if diversification helps ease the foreign-exchange situation, then a critical ingredient is made somewhat more abundant for possible use in further developmental activity (which, in turn, holds implications for both income stabilization and generation).

development (as a supplement to, or partial replacement for, raw-materials production), realization of some benefit in terms of income stabilization appears a reasonable prospect—as in the case of raw-materials diversification. But, in contrast to the emphasis upon simple raw-materials diversification, diversification through industrial development appears to rate a substantially different appraisal as to its potential for income generation. The essential point is that industrial development represents a whole new frontier, not just "more of the same" in some greater or lesser amount. If the basis exists for the successful launching of industrial development in the first place (which is not always the case), the potential for income generation frequently exceeds—and sometimes far exceeds—anything conceivably derivable from raw-materials diversification alone. In any event, it is this lure of markedly higher productivity and income that gives industrial development a special appeal in many underdeveloped countries.

THE CASE FOR INDUSTRIAL DEVELOPMENT

In underdeveloped countries, there is a widespread inclination to view industrialization with favor and longing. Industrialization frequently is regarded as a "must"—indeed, as a panacea for current economic ills, and also for varied non-economic ills. Growing numbers, as they contemplate the wealth of the industrial countries, seem prone to conclude that an increase in wealth is certain to follow from industrialization in their case too.[3] In developed countries, opinion seems sharply divided. Some persons appear convinced that only dreamers would dare campaign for industrialization in present-day underdeveloped countries, but others are prepared to argue that industrialization offers the "only way out"—at least for some underdeveloped countries. Actually, whether or not industrialization is likely to prove economically beneficial constitutes a question to which the safe initial answer is: "*It depends.*" A simple yes or no answer lacks meaning in the absence of certain points of reference. As one might expect, it is necessary to examine and appraise a number of factors in order to arrive at a reasonable answer relative to this whole matter. Fundamental to the matter—and alluded to in the section immediately preceding, but not approached there directly from the standpoint of industrialization—are two major considerations: Can industrialization help to stabilize income? Can industrialization help to generate income?

---

[3] F. Benham, in appraising the line of logic that frequently appears to prevail, put the matter as follows: "They think that because most rich countries are industrialized, their country will become rich if it industrializes. One might as well argue that because most wealthy men smoke cigars one has only to smoke cigars to become wealthy." See his "Full Employment and International Trade," *Economica,* August 1946, p. 167.

INCOME STABILIZATION

Industrial development—whether a supplement to, or a partial replacement for, raw-materials production—can contribute to economic stability in that it helps broaden a country's economic base. While diversification in raw-materials production can also be supported for its contributions to stabilization, industrial development carries diversification further, and into a new and important area of economic activity.

According to a widely-held notion, even if income rose no higher as a consequence of industrial development, realization of substantially greater stability in income can be regarded a significant achievement nevertheless. This notion survives and thrives, in important part, because countries very largely devoid of industrial development are prone, as evidenced by the record, to instability of a troublesome extent. The typical underdeveloped country is a raw-materials producer, a situation conducive to exportation in anticipation of importing other items, including manufactures. Production for exportation is fine, provided markets exist, and provided desired imports are obtainable on terms of mutual advantage. Over time, however, distinct shortcomings are reflected by the particular export-import relationship. In general, forces originating and motivated abroad end by leaving their imprint—sometimes in a highly adverse form—upon domestic income, employment, and levels of living. To illustrate, lulls in economic activity in the foreign countries in which markets are located give rise to repercussions, transmitted outward through fluctuations in trade. As exports decline as a consequence of a lull abroad, customary imports also decline (thereby eliminating some items from usage, even though they may well have come to be regarded as essential). The decline in exportation, while it has the general effect of inducing a contraction in income and employment for the economy as a whole, tends to hit particular parts of the economy with disproportionate severity; for example, the export sector feels the impact in sledge-hammer fashion, partly because it is on the "front line" in the essential relationship prevailing, and partly because it typically encompasses only a narrow and non-diverse economic base. All in all, the environment of the typical underdeveloped country is of such a nature that the achievement of greater economic stability is made to appear both attractive and worthwhile.

It seems only rational for a country to strive for the advantages associated with some reasonable amount of stability in its economy (or, in its export-import relationship—when this is crucial in terms of its impact upon the total economy). But, why should a country choose to view industrial development as a basic approach toward stabilization? Why not place emphasis on a less drastic approach? The central answer to these questions hinges on the idea that stabilization approaches short of industrial development are weak, as allegedly is evidenced in past experience, so that industrial development—which assertedly holds considerable merit in its own right—becomes, in a sense, the alternative of last resort.

The thought that other stabilization approaches, beyond industrial development, are typically found wanting is lent support when viewed at either of two levels. First, the record of stabilization-achievement through *unilateral* action is not generally regarded as a success story. For example, buffer-stock schemes of unilateral scope tend quickly to display their shortcomings (Ch. 6), especially so in the case of the smaller and weaker economies. Again, the placement of reliance upon foreign-exchange reserves sufficiently sizable to serve as an adequate buffer against possible fluctuations in the export-import relationship is also subject to important shortcomings. Significantly, a question always exists as to just how much foreign exchange a country should feel compelled to tie-up for reasons of stabilization; after all, when foreign exchange comprises an element that is both hard to obtain and needed for development, direct usage for developmental purposes of all beyond a moderate amount might well be regarded as preferable to tying it up as "buffer-stock" awaiting major fluctuations. Further, a raw-materials-producing country, when geared to export-import trade, tends—because of the nature of its economy—not to be well situated for invoking domestic fiscal-policy measures as a successful offset to "imported" economic fluctuations. To illustrate, assume a raw-materials-producing country, heavily dependent upon the sale abroad of raw-materials output and upon the importation of diverse commodities, and in possession of only sufficient foreign-exchange reserves to accommodate a relatively normal regimen of international transactions. Given this environment, assume a sharp deterioration in export markets. The initial impact is a decline in income, with additional adverse effects virtually certain to follow. In an attempt to bolster sagging income, the country may be tempted to introduce domestic fiscal-policy measures, e.g., may seek to initiate a governmental spending program based on deficit financing; after all, the technique is one widely employed by advanced industrial countries—to good advantage, in the opinion of many persons. Unfortunately, an attempt at offset in this manner can only fail in the case of the assumed raw-materials-producing country. If, on the one hand, the monetary injection is geared directly to a physical project, some demand is created for equipment and materials. But this demand is not easily satisfied; much of the demand cannot ordinarily be met from domestic sources, since the narrow economic base does not encompass the requisite production, and the prospect of meeting the demand through importation is poor, since foreign-exchange earnings are at low levels as a consequence of a reduction in exportation, the beginning of the immediate troubles. If, on the other hand, the monetary injection is geared to a purely "make-work" type of operation, one that poses no direct requirements for imported equipment and materials, the resultant situation merely poses a problem of a different order. The effect then is the creation of a commodity demand on the part of consumers who come into possession of money income, even while marketable goods in commensurate volume do not come into being. With foreign-exchange earnings at low levels (under the circumstances prevailing), this demand cannot readily be met through importation. Thus, pressure falls squarely upon the domestic economy and results in inflation, particularly since the narrow economic base precludes satisfactory domestic accommodation of the demand. The conclusion to be drawn is that an attempt to use domestic fiscal-policy measures to offset adverse repercussions arising abroad, under circumstances described above, is doomed to failure. A fairly broad economic base is necessary before any large-scale application of fiscal-policy measures can be regarded as offering reasonable prospect for success—unless, of course, extensive foreign-exchange reserves are on hand (not likely to be the case in a typical underdeveloped country, and perhaps not a reasonable expectation either—for reasons cited earlier).

Second, the record of stabilization-achievement through *international* action, while perhaps somewhat brighter than that under unilateral action, nevertheless also leaves much to be desired. International commodity agreements can be regarded as only partially successful, at best, in achieving stabilization, and alternative institutional arrangements of greater potency have not come into being—and perhaps have not for good reason (Ch. 6). Significantly, however, the failure of new and more effective international arrangements to materialize, despite continued international economic instability, has the effect of putting the stabilization problem squarely in the laps of the individual underdeveloped countries concerned.

Given the foregoing, what can the individual country reasonably do, on its own, in hopes of assuring itself of greater stability? Essentially, a country is reduced to diversification of its economy. This diversification can range in scope from incidental, involving only little change, to ambitious, involving national self-sufficiency as a goal. In terms of direction, however, diversification reduces to a choice, previously cited, between entry into supplementary lines of raw-materials production and development of an industrial sector as a supplement to, or partial replacement for, raw-materials production. Action in either direction offers some hope for greater stability by virtue of the wider and more varied economic base created. However, hope offered by industrial development appears to exceed anything offered simply by extensions in raw-materials production, since industrial development goes further toward making a wider and more varied economic base possible.

Aside from matters of stability, however, there are considerations related to levels of income. Significantly, diversification solely within the realm of raw-materials production appears capable of offering, at best, only small income benefit. *If* industrial development holds any considerable income-potential at all, it can readily outshine diversification in raw materials. In any event, selection of the course through which greater stability can reasonably be sought should occur, seemingly, only after relative income prospects have *also* been appraised.

INCOME GENERATION

Stability of income is a legitimate goal, but efforts to attain it can ill afford to proceed impervious to considerations related to the *level* of income. The important question is: Can industrial development yield a higher and rising level of income? The answer is that industrial development does not automatically assure added income benefits to every country attempting it. Such income benefits result only if certain circumstances prevail.

What industrial development can mean in terms of income varies with individual countries. Important considerations, in which relevant circumstances vary from country to country, include: the degree of population pressure against land resources (which factor favors or hampers additional effort in agriculture); the extent and quality of productive ingredients available for industrial development; the types of industrial development contemplated; the size of the potential market for industrial output; and the amount of industrial development contemplated (i.e., whether industrial development is to be incidental to raw-materials production, or is slated to equal or surpass it in importance). From among the maze of considerations, five major bases emerge to support the possibility of higher income through industrial development.

First, to the extent that industrial output is simply *in addition* to customary raw-materials output, an increase in per-capita productivity, and in real per-capita income, can be an automatic result. The physical possibility of industrial output being additional in the foregoing sense exists whenever prevailing raw-materials output occurs in an environment in which considerable slack remains among available factors of production—and the economic possibility of higher per-capita productivity and income is beyond dispute once it is established that factors of production drawn into industrial production do not detract from intended raw-materials output.

Second, to the extent that industrial output is characterized by per-capita productivity higher than the average prevailing in raw-materials production, an increase in the overall average results. Such higher levels of per-capita productivity are a distinct possibility in particular lines of industrial output in numerous countries—not simply because of the possibility of inherent superiority in the productivity-potential of some industrial output, but also because existing levels of per-capita productivity in raw-materials output, to which comparison is relevant, are frequently very low.

Third, to the extent that added production of raw materials is hampered by insufficiencies in market demand, slack in production can conceivably be absorbed by output of an industrial type, not similarly handicapped by market considerations. Some outlet for industrial output can likely be had through export routes—provided, of course, external competition can be met successfully. Perhaps more importantly, an added outlet can likely also be had domestically through displacement of particular items previously imported. Of significance, the substitution of new domestic production for particular imports need not lessen a country's *total* imports or exports; since import demand is strong in any event, the likely effect of a displacement of particular imports by new domestic production is simply to alter the *composition* of foreign trade, rather than to lessen its magnitude.

Fourth, industrial development opens a new frontier by making output possible in two separate lines, raw-materials production and industrial production, rather than just simply in one. Such an added frontier is especially important over the long-run whenever the factor of population pressure upon land resources appears likely to hamper expansion in raw-materials production. A report by the UN puts the matter as follows:[4]

> The main remedy for under-employment is to create new employment opportunities. Where more land can be brought into cultivation, this will afford some relief. But, in most countries where under-employment is acute, nearly all the cultivable land is already cultivated. Effort has then to be concentrated upon creating new industries off the land, of which manufacturing industries comprise the largest and usually the most promising category. Thus, the most urgent problem of these countries is industrialization.

In the absence of a new frontier in some countries, the likelihood exists of a worsened population-land ratio over time (as population growth continues), thus forcing a deterioration in per-capita productivity. A situation can be imagined in which further effort along lines of raw-materials production can only be accompanied by declining per-capita productivity, but in which equivalent effort expended upon industrial development can raise per-capita productivity, or at least hold the line against a decline.

Fifth, if one accepts the thesis that the "split" in the benefits of trade between raw-materials-producing countries and industrial countries tends to favor the industrial countries (Ch. 2), any diversification that gives

---

[4] *Measures for the Economic Development of Under-Developed Countries*, New York, 1951, p. 9.

some industrial development to a country otherwise confined to raw-materials output tends to assure that country of a more advantageous position in terms of end-benefits obtainable for its productive efforts. For example, according to a report by the UN:[5]

> . . . the advantages of technical progress have been mainly concentrated in the industrial centres and have not directly extended to the countries making up the periphery of the world's economic system. . . .
>
> [In the past, in fact,] while the centres kept the whole benefit of the technical development of their industries, the peripheral countries transferred to them a share of the fruits of their own technical progress.

The conclusion that follows from the foregoing points is that a case for industrial development exists whenever this development contributes toward the attainment or maintenance of levels of real per-capita income higher than would otherwise prevail. The strength, or weakness, of the case varies widely among underdeveloped countries. In a number of countries, however, the case appears to be a reasonably strong one—as, indeed, is borne out by experience already gained in some of them. For countries favorably situated, promotion of *some* industrial development at an early date recommends itself as a means to obtain income gains. For them to delay, or to have to delay, the introduction of industrial development is to pass up potential gains.

Over the longer-run, a question likely to arise relates to how much industrial production is needed in order that industrial production and raw-materials production together can assure rising real per-capita income. An associated question, of course, pertains to whether this aggregate of needed production is even possible (and, if not possible, declining real per-capita income results in any event). Significantly, precise answers to these questions are not crucial at the outset of industrial development (and, indeed, are likely to prove difficult, if not impossible, of formulation at that time anyway). What needs to be ascertained with some certainty at the outset is the potential economic merit of *some particular industrial development then at issue.* Whenever some industry can be introduced in economic fashion in the short-run, it is of economic advantage to the country concerned to get this industry started as soon as possible. After introductory phases are well passed, the question of "how much" industry and the question of "balance" between industrial production and raw-materials production can be taken up and resolved within the relevant context then prevailing.

The economic rationale for industrial development rests upon potential income benefits, related both to level and stability. The idea of autarchy, or economic self-sufficiency, is another matter, not defensible within the framework of this rationale. With autarchy thus set aside,

---

[5] *The Economic Development of Latin America,* New York, 1950, pp. 8, 10.

industrial development can be regarded as a process inextricably linked with continuation in raw-materials production. Rather than being competitive, the two tend to go hand-in-hand. Mutual benefit derives from joint exploitation: the industrial sector benefits from continued raw-materials production (especially through the access it gives to needed foreign exchange), and the raw-materials sector benefits from new industrial production (especially through added domestic markets). A report of the UN has the following to say on this matter:[6]

> [Industrialization] . . . is not incompatible with the efficient development of primary production. On the contrary, the availability of the best capital equipment and the prompt adoption of new techniques are essential if the development of industry is to fulfill the social objective of raising the standard of living. . . . Primary products must be exported to allow for the importation of the considerable quantity of capital goods needed. The more active . . . foreign trade, the greater the possibility of increasing productivity by means of intensive capital formation. The solution does not lie in growth at the expense of foreign trade, but in knowing how to extract, from continually growing foreign trade, the elements that will promote economic development.

Or, again:[7]

> . . . primary products must [not] be sacrificed to further industrial development. Exports . . . provide the foreign exchange with which to buy the imports necessary for economic development. . . . If productivity in agriculture can be increased by technical progress and if, at the same time, real wages can be raised by industrialization and adequate social legislation, the disequilibrium between incomes at the centres and the periphery can gradually be corrected. . . .

IS MORE RAW-MATERIALS PRODUCTION NECESSARY AS A PRELUDE?

A common argument is that raw-materials production has to be stepped up *before* industrial development can be undertaken with prospect of success. The line of reasoning, in its simplest form, can be summarized as follows. Embarkation upon industrial development involves a shift in emphasis in the economy from raw-materials production to industrial production, in consequence of which there is also a shift of workers (along with their families). The shift of workers entails a decrease in the production of raw materials, *but* consumption requirements are left undiminished. Thus, if raw-materials production has consisted of foodstuffs used in domestic consumption, a shift of workers into industry causes production of foodstuffs to decline; but people have to be fed just the same, no matter where they are located—in agriculture or in

---

6 *Ibid.,* p. 2.
7 *Ibid.,* p. 6.

new industry. Or, if raw-materials production has consisted of food-stuffs used in domestic consumption *and* of commodities produced for exportation (encompassing agricultural or mineral commodities, exported in the anticipation of importing other goods, including food-stuffs), a shift of workers into industry causes raw-materials production to decline, thereby resulting in some decline in exportation and also in importation; but the appetite for end goods, including foodstuffs, continues notwithstanding. A first requirement, therefore, is for an increase in output-capacity in raw-materials production, to the extent that domestic consumption needs can be met, either directly through production for domestic consumption or indirectly through production for foreign trade (i.e., for exportation, followed by importation). As put by some persons, "first an *extra* bowl of rice has to be provided" before a country can safely hazard the transitional phases of entirely new types of productive activity.

Whether or not the foregoing argument has merit depends upon the circumstances—a type of answer seemingly often warranted in the field of economics. First of all, behind the associated line of reasoning lies the assumption that the prevailing level of production is capable of sustaining only a low level of consumption (even when everything proceeds without a "hitch"), and that this level of consumption is incapable of any reduction without causing adverse effect in various connections—as, for example, upon output itself. At some magnitude of production, of course, consumption could be at a level at which some reduction could well be borne without a particularly adverse effect occurring automatically in other directions (and could be borne by consumers with no more than incidental personal inconvenience). However, the environment of underdeveloped countries is one in which both production and consumption are on the low side. And, the argument at issue is directed to these underdeveloped countries, not to the richer economies.

On the assumption that the overall level of consumption is low, a basic consideration centers on the degree of employment present. If full employment prevails, any shift of workers into new industry automatically invites some decline in raw-materials output, for—under circumstances then existing—these workers have to be withdrawn from their previous pursuits. Since the prevailing level of consumption is dependent upon the prevailing volume of raw-materials output, consumption then undergoes a decline (under the foregoing conditions)—unless sufficient foreign-exchange reserves exist or can be obtained, presumably through loan or grant, to offset the diminution in current raw-materials production. Significantly, because industrial output does not begin to accrue until installations are made operative, genuine production and consumption problems do arise—at least during the transitional period. The conclusion that follows then is that promotion of industrial development, under full-employment conditions, causes the level of consumption to suffer a decline during at least some period; and, if such a decline in consumption cannot be borne (a probable situation in a poor economy), it automatically follows that raw-materials output needs to be stepped-up prior to embarkation upon a program of industrial development.

However, a fundamentally different situation prevails when there is less than full employment—as, significantly, is common in underdeveloped countries. If acute underemployment or mass unemployment exists, workers—in some number—can move into new industry without raw-materials production having to diminish at all. Workers moving into industry can come from among the unemployed, or can come from jobs that are then taken over by others who were previously unemployed; or, workers can come from an environment of underemployment within which remaining workers then experience increases in per-worker productivity sufficiently great to offset whatever those who have shifted previously contributed.[8] In any of these cases, no decrease in total production needs to occur, despite the entry of workers into a new industry. Given this situation of undiminished production, the following line of reasoning *perhaps* becomes applicable (in support of the contention that an increase in raw-materials output is not necessary as a prelude to embarkation upon industrial development). Since the economy managed to support the population before, it can do so thereafter; after all, it has the same volume of production and the same number of people. Even though the level of consumption that has prevailed may not be the one desired, whatever has been its level, it need be no lower—at least not as a consequence of workers entering new industry.[9]

Significantly, however, the story does not end at this point. The problem of consumption associated with industrial development is not merely one of coping with existing demand. Entry of workers into new industry can result in an *increase* in demand. Thus, even though total raw-materials output may not decline, total consumer demand may rise. Workers entering industry have rising expectations as to their living standards, and receive money wages with which to do something about their expectations. Indeed, as the tempo of work comes to be upgraded in the course of the shift into industry, workers tend to require greater food intake, whatever forms their expectations might otherwise assume.

---

8 The relevance of underemployment can be illustrated through reference to a common situation in agriculture in underdeveloped countries. There it is frequently possible for, say, four workers within a family of six workers to produce the same amount as might all six; nevertheless, the extra two continue to work within the group, simply because there is nothing else, or better, for them to do. On this matter, see again Ch. 1, the section on "Poor Manpower Utilization."

9 Of course, a problem of distribution is involved. As workers shift location and status, channels of distribution must alter to accommodate the new situation. Within the total context, however, associated problems of distribution are ordinarily not of crucial significance, nor of unmanageable proportions.

Alongside this, new industrial facilities do not give rise to end products until after some lapse of time, the time interval between the beginning of the construction of a plant and the commencement of operations by the plant frequently spanning two or more years. Money wages are paid some workers throughout this period, so that—given the forms of financing customarily employed[10]—additional money is available for spending in the economy, but no additional domestic goods are immediately available for purchase. To some extent, the added money income can serve to bolster markets for domestic producers of raw materials (e.g., of foodstuffs), an effect that might be construed as beneficial in that an added incentive for expansion is given the raw-materials sector (Ch. 3)—although, here too, any added output can arise only following a lapse of some time.[11] To some extent, however, the added money income serves to create import demands, an effect that poses a serious problem, especially when foreign exchange is in short supply as is the common situation in underdeveloped countries.[12] If added importation is permitted in response to added money income, a drain on foreign exchange is set in motion in the course of procuring consumer goods, even while this foreign exchange is needed to obtain development goods for the program of economic expansion. If added importation is not permitted (e.g., by imposition of exchange-control regulations designed to curb imports), the full impact of greater personal income is felt domestically; price increases are to be expected unless a compensating expansion occurs in the domestic supply of desired goods, or unless other offsetting measures are instituted.[13] Thus, a potential problem of inflation is created during the transition period when new industry is getting under way. Significantly, if added raw-materials production can be achieved very promptly (or, better still, is already in the process of achievement when industrial development is initiated), the shift into industrial development can occur with less danger of inflationary impact—even in the absence of those other measures as are potentially invokable in an attempt to ameliorate inflationary impact.[14]

---

[10] Particularly deficit financing.

[11] Minimum required time is that interval needed to produce a new agricultural crop.

[12] The relationship between rising money income and rising import demands is reflected in the developmental experience of numerous countries. A major case in point is that of India during the course of its First (1951–56) and Second (1956–61) Five-Year Plans. For samples of news comments on this general situation, see *The New York Times*, November 17, 1955, p. 1-C, March 21, 1958, p. 4-C, September 14, 1958, p. 6-E, and *The Washington Post and Times Herald*, September 8, 1957, p. 13-A.

[13] For example, access to foreign loans or grants providing additional foreign exchange, or resort to specially-tailored fiscal and monetary policies able to reduce the effective demand below what would otherwise prevail.

[14] For additional comments on the relationships among investment, income, demand, and importation, see the FAO's report on the case of India: *Uses of Agricultural Surpluses to Finance Economic Development in Under-Developed Areas, a Pilot Study in India,* Rome, June 1955.

Once the cited transition period is over, the foregoing inflation problem—arising out of increased demand and reflected in price and foreign-
exchange pressures—ceases to exist; specifically, the problem fades away
as desired end products in substantial volume flow from the new industrial facilities. If industrial development is viewed as a continuing process
of growth, the problem is concentrated within the initial period during
which the first batch of industrial facilities is being installed. The matter
is much like that of filling a pipeline; one needs to draw upon a reservoir
at the outset to fill the pipeline, but thereafter the process is one of
feeding into the pipeline at one end and of catching the outflow at the
other. The problem focuses on the reservoir from which the pipeline is
filled in the first place. The reservoir, as applicable to the present case,
refers to a stock of consumer goods, which goods either are already
available to the economy, or—in the absence of this—have to be made
speedily available within the domestic economy, or have to be obtained
through importation. While various domestic policies, referred to
earlier, might be invoked in an attempt to lessen what is needed in this
connection, *some* addition is a probable requirement for the initial
period of industrial development in any event. But, whatever the scope
of the requirement posed by the initial period, no additional requirement
is posed by continuing development, provided the pace of industrial
development is not intensified.

Above all, beyond the added supply requirements arising as a consequence of rising income and consumption, some added supply requirements are also posed, directly, by industry itself. The process of creating
and operating industrial facilities entails a need for capital goods (e.g.,
machinery and equipment), followed by access to supporting raw materials. While some of these industrial ingredients may readily be had
domestically, some part of them—frequently a large part—is ordinarily
had by a newly-developing country only through importation. The
associated importation requires an outlay of foreign exchange, which a
country must earn for itself (in the absence of loans or grants—and even
loans are "earned," in the sense that eventual repayment requires foreign
exchange). In practical terms, foreign exchange is earned through exports
of goods and services. Over time, thus, the capacity to import developmental ingredients needed for industrial development comes to be
closely related to the ability to export;[15] the more that exports prove
possible, the more readily can developmental ingredients be imported.
Given the type of economy prevailing prior to embarkation upon industrial development, this means that raw-materials production, from which

---

[15] If importation is foregone and the ingredients are generated domestically (as in
the case of the developmental experience of the USSR), the problem of how these
ingredients can be "squeezed" from prevailing production nevertheless remains.

export goods arise, and industrial development are necessarily and closely linked. Under the circumstances, it is not enough to conclude simply that raw-materials production need not decrease when workers enter new industry (under non-full-employment conditions); what is needed, more particularly, is some *increase* in raw-materials production (including an increase in that production which can provide the capacity for added exportation). As stated in a report of the UN:[16]

> Primary products must be exported to allow for the importation of the considerable quantity of capital goods needed. The more active . . . foreign trade, the greater the possibility of increasing productivity by means of intensive capital formation.

Fortunately, when underemployment, or unemployment, is of substantial proportions, the choice—for a wide range of possible activity— need not be one of raw-materials production *or* industrial development; rather, to considerable extent, the environment admits to the possibility of raw-materials production *and* industrial development.

SELECTED BIBLIOGRAPHY

Norman S. Buchanan and Howard S. Ellis, *Approaches to Economic Development*. New York: The Twentieth Century Fund, 1955.
Ch. 12, Agricultural development; Ch. 13, Commerce and industry in economic development.

Richard B. Goode, "Adding to the Stock of Physical and Human Capital," *American Economic Review Papers and Proceedings*, May 1959.
Commentary on quantitative and qualitative aspects of factor ingredients basic to development.

Joseph A. Hasson, "Economic Stabilization in a Primary-Producing Country," *Journal of Political Economy*, June 1956.
Examination of the problem of economic instability; special reference to Australia.

Klaus Knorr, "Market Instability and U.S. Policy," *Journal of Political Economy*, October 1954.
The problem of market instability examined in a broad context.

John W. Mellor and Robert D. Stevens, "The Average and Marginal Product of Farm Labor in Underdeveloped Economies," *Journal of Farm Economics*, August 1956.
Examination of underemployment from the standpoint of the status of persons in agriculture.

---

16 *The Economic Development of Latin America*, New York, 1950, p. 2.

Gunnar Myrdal, *An International Economy*. New York: Harper and Brothers, 1956.
  Chs. XII and XIII, Wide and provocative coverage of developmental needs, problems, and policies.

William H. Nicholls, "Investment in Agriculture in Underdeveloped Countries," *American Economic Review Papers and Proceedings,* May 1955.
  Examination of the effects of mechanization, price supports, and expanded cultivation—using the experience of Turkey as a case study.

Ragnar Nurkse, "Reflections on India's Development Plan," *Quarterly Journal of Economics,* May 1957.
  Survey and critique of India's development under the First Five-Year Plan; some reference to the problem of shifting workers from agriculture to capital construction.

Hans W. Singer, "The Distribution of Gains Between Investing and Borrowing Countries," *American Economic Review Papers and Proceedings,* May 1950.
  A statement of Singer's views on the position of raw-materials countries relative to developed countries; includes views on terms of trade.

United Nations, *Formulation and Economic Appraisal of Development Projects,* Lahore, 1951, Book I.
  Lectures by Hans W. Singer, covering determination of the direction of development, and the problems associated with implementation of development plans; special applicability to Pakistan.

——————————, *Instability in Export Markets of Under-Developed Countries,* New York, 1952.
  Measurement of instability of raw-materials commodities in international trade.

——————————, *Measures for International Economic Stability,* New York, 1951.
  Examination of some possible methods of dealing with problems raised by instability of raw materials commodities in international trade.

——————————, *Progress in Land Reform,* New York, 1954.
  Description of programs of land reform, with some appraisal.

——————————, *Social Progress Through Community Development,* New York, 1955.
  Description of programs of community development, with some appraisal.

Charles Wolf, Jr., "Institutions and Economic Development," *American Economic Review,* December 1955.
  Examination of institutions as a factor in development.

8

ISSUES IN INDUSTRY (I)

Whenever an underdeveloped country chooses to pursue industrial development, a number of important issues peculiar to this category of development are likely or certain to arise, and then require attention by the country. The present chapter is devoted to one major issue, while the succeeding chapter treats major supplementary issues.

SELECTION OF INDUSTRIES: WHAT TESTS?

Once the developmental possibilities of a country have been appraised in general and a conclusion has been reached that embarkation upon or acceleration of industrial development should be sought, the question arises as to *what types* of industrial activity, specifically, should be given priority. The matter is an important one, for the future well-being of an economy comes to be dependent in large measure upon the nature of the "answers" provided, whether these answers arise through a formalized official procedure or through independent or chance actions by private individuals. Indeed, great interest exists in the matter, in part because of the attention focused upon it by the practice in some underdeveloped countries during recent years of relying upon official "screening committees" for decisions as to the merits of various proposed operations—a practice supported by the governments concerned in terms of improved utilization of available developmental means, but frequently criticized by persons within developed countries on the grounds that misguided action is a possible or likely result. Accordingly, the question raised here is: *What tests* might reasonably be applied in an attempt to ascertain the types of industrial activity likely to prove "best" for under-developed countries?

Two main ideas exist as to the procedure to be followed in the determination of the types of industrial activity to be preferred. The first relates to tests based on the *law of comparative advantage,* while the second relates to tests dealing with *foreign-exchange impact.* These ideas merit examination.

COMPARATIVE ADVANTAGE

The traditional view is that a country should aspire to pattern its production in accordance with the dictates of the law of comparative advantage, or law of comparative cost. The law of comparative advantage states that a country stands to gain economically if it concentrates its productive effort along those lines in which it has the greatest comparative advantage or the least comparative disadvantage, and then trades with other countries. The notion is that efficiency is thereby fostered (in that the factors of production then come to be allocated so as to yield the most output per given resource outlay), making it possible to maximize real income for the world as a whole, and for each country within the trading network.[1]

Many regard the law of comparative advantage as unassailable; these persons see it as one of a few fundamental laws of economics. But not all are so minded. Actually, as a basis for determination of the types of industrial activity to be preferred, the law of comparative advantage is the object of three major lines of criticism.[2]

1. *Assumes Full Employment.* A first criticism frequently offered is that the law of comparative advantage (cost) invites unsound conclusions and decisions because it rests on a central assumption that is faulty. Like classical economics in general, the law assumes "full employment"—an assumption widely regarded as not reflective of the real world or of a great part of it.

The importance of the distinction between a full-employment assumption and a non-full-employment assumption can be shown by reference to a simple hypothetical case. Assume an entrepreneur about to commence operations in an underdeveloped country who has per-unit costs of production[3] of $2.00 (with labor cost to the firm representing $1.00

---

1 For an elaboration of the definition of the law of comparative advantage, refer to any standard introductory book on international economics. For example, see W. Krause, *The International Economy* (Boston: Houghton Mifflin Company, 1955), Ch. 1.

2 The law of comparative advantage is rooted in classical economic theory. Outstanding statements critical of the classical version of international-trade theory include: S. E. Harris, *International and Interregional Economics* (New York: The McGraw-Hill Book Company, Inc., 1957), esp. Ch. 19; G. Myrdal, *An International Economy* (New York: Harper and Brothers, 1956), esp. Ch. 13; UN, *The Economic Development of Latin America,* New York, 1950, esp. pp. 1–7 (author: R. Prebisch).

3 All amounts are expressed here in US dollars in order to simplify comparisons.

of this amount). Assume, also, competitive firms in a developed country that have per-unit costs of production of $1.90. Assuming other factors as neutral to the situation,[4] is one to conclude that the planned production in the underdeveloped country is "uneconomic"? If both countries had full employment, one might well be tempted to so conclude (although, as a minimum, one might also want to examine what cost of production for the firm in the underdeveloped country is likely to be beyond early periods of operation). But if the underdeveloped country has an acute problem of underemployment, while the developed country enjoys full employment, a pertinent variable is introduced. While labor cost to the *firm* in the underdeveloped country is $1.00 per unit of output, the cost to the *economy* is zero (whenever the alternate use of labor is idleness), or is something under $1.00 (whenever the new production serves to upgrade labor, a likely prospect in the face of extensive underemployment). The crucial point is that cost to the firm (*business cost*) and cost to the economy (*social cost*) are two different things. The two may amount to roughly the same dollar-and-cents figure in some countries (e.g., when full employment prevails), but in countries having widespread underemployment or mass unemployment they differ, sometimes widely. In the light of this possible difference, the question raised earlier bears reiteration: Is one to conclude that the planned production in the underdeveloped country is uneconomic? (Or, should measures be contemplated that might help bring about the production?) Whatever specific answer might be warranted, the answer clearly should not be arrived at through comparison merely of per-unit costs of production as borne by firms or industries; the relevant comparison is not costs to business entities, but costs to the economies involved. Significantly, comparison of social costs as between the two countries cited requires reference to a framework other than the traditional law of comparative advantage, which is what is frequently applied in cases of this type; as a minimum, if the law of comparative advantage is to provide a meaningful guide in actual practice, it appears to require modification so as to give cognizance to the extent of underemployment or of unemployment prevailing.

The essential point illustrated by the foregoing hypothetical case is that the extent of underemployment or of unemployment that prevails among countries is an important consideration in arriving at conclusions and decisions as to what types of production are likely to prove economic. Since the traditional law of comparative advantage assumes full employment, its application serves to invite conclusions and decisions of doubtful merit (e.g., as unduly conservative appraisals of economic potential

---

[4] Simplifying assumptions here include: no transport costs, only two countries, only one commodity (thus permitting direct comparison without need for reference to other commodities), and an equilibrium rate of exchange.

are reached in the case of underdeveloped countries having widespread underemployment)—or so critics of the law of comparative advantage are inclined to argue. According to the argument, the law of comparative advantage provides an imperfect guide at best, given the environment of the real world—unless, of course, the law is treated, in practice, so as to take the extent of underemployment or of unemployment into account.

2. *Individual Interpretations.* A second criticism frequently offered is that the law of comparative advantage (cost) readily comes to be misapplied—presumably because those invoking it do not really understand the concept at issue; in essence, the law of comparative advantage is invoked in a mistaken form as "scholarly backing" for "wrong" decisions and actions. Perhaps the criticism offered is more one of people than of the law of comparative advantage itself, but a point of criticism is at issue in any event.

What people often proceed to do as they attempt to determine the types of industrial activity to be given preference is to compare directly the *absolute cost* of *an equivalent item* as between a firm in one country and firms in one or more other countries, impervious to all the comparative considerations arising from reference to arrays of items. Actually, this approach violates the spirit of the law of comparative advantage. Application of the law warrants consideration of an array of production possibilities in each of numerous countries, so as to enable the identification of those items of actual or potential output in each country that reflect high comparative advantage or low comparative disadvantage. The possibility exists, of course, that a country may have no comparative advantage in anything, whereupon it is obliged—according to the law— to concentrate its output along lines of low comparative disadvantage (and to produce some particular items even though another country, a country having a comparative advantage in numerous lines, is more favorably situated to produce the same items).

To illustrate, assume that a firm in an underdeveloped country is contemplating production when its per-unit cost is $2.00. Assume, also, that competitive firms in a developed country have per-unit costs of $1.90 for an equivalent item. Given this situation, direct comparison of absolute cost likely serves to rule out new production in the underdeveloped country because its costs appear to be "too high." While this depicts the manner in which some persons choose to pass judgment on the merits of contemplated production, no such approach is intended in the application of the law of comparative advantage. The crucial consideration relates to *comparative* advantage, not *absolute* advantage (comparative cost, not absolute cost). Determination of comparative advantage requires consideration of various items and their costs, and in various countries. The expectation thereafter, under the law of comparative advantage, is simply that each country will seek to specialize along lines in which it has the greatest comparative advantage or least comparative disadvantage.

In the final analysis, to argue that a country should produce nothing but what it can produce at an absolute cost below that of any other country is tantamount, conceivably, to a recommendation that some country or countries stop all production; after all, it is conceivable that some country exists that has no absolute cost advantage in the production of anything. For the sake of argument, assume that the underdeveloped country in the illustration is at an absolute cost disadvantage in every line of production. Should it then simply cease all efforts in all directions? Or, should it conclude that it ought to do the best it can with the population and resources it has, despite its admittedly poor situation? If this is what it concludes, it ought—according to the law of comparative advantage—to produce that in which comparative disadvantage is low (viewed within a world production-and-trade context), and then carry on trade with other countries, each of which in turn adheres to the idea of production along lines of greatest comparative advantage or least comparative disadvantage. Under these conditions, a cost in the underdeveloped country of $2.00 per unit might still reflect economic production, even though an equivalent item could be produced in another country for $1.90. However, reasonable as this prospect may seem within a world complex of production and trade, the essential idea is frequently missed by those entrusted with practical policy formulation.

3. *A Look at History*. A third criticism offered is that adherence to the dictates of the law of comparative advantage—even when the law is correctly understood and correctly applied—results in a situation likely to cause underdeveloped countries to remain raw-materials producers, but in that status the countries can expect to receive only disproportionately small rewards for their productive efforts as compared with the rewards going to industrial countries with which they carry on trade. If the criticism is valid, a potent argument exists in support of the acquisition of new industry by underdeveloped countries, even in instances in which the law of comparative advantage seems to suggest that this industry is uneconomic.

The criticism consists of two parts, the first of which involves the contention that strict compliance with the dictates of the law of comparative advantage serves to operate against a raw-materials-producing country's becoming anything else but that. The standard argument proceeds as follows. As the world currently stands, some countries are industrial while others continue as raw-materials producers. This pattern appears both natural and appropriate, approached from the standpoint of the law of comparative advantage. The notion is that specialization by countries, followed by trade among them, proves advantageous for all—

thereby offering a rationale for free trade. But given this trade pattern between industrial and non-industrial countries, the raw-materials producers are handicapped in any attempts they make to acquire new industry, since industry already existent elsewhere poses strong competition.[5] The problem associated with this competition is unique to the countries still remaining as raw-materials producers in the sense that, in an earlier day, those countries that first undertook to industrialize did not have to do so in the face of competition already existent elsewhere. It is in this situation, of course, that the infant-industry argument for temporary protection of the domestic market (ostensibly through tariffs) acquires strength.[6] To an important extent, however, the problem of competition simply forces raw-materials-producing countries to remain raw-materials producers, tied into a global specialization-and-trade framework on that basis. Thus, adherence to an international division of labor, instead of helping to lead a country from raw-materials dependence to further and "higher forms" of development, comes to be pictured as a course that acts to freeze the status-quo of a country—insofar as its pattern of production is concerned.

The second part of the criticism—extending beyond the criticism that adherence to the law of comparative advantage serves to prevent a raw-materials-producing country's becoming anything but that—involves the contention that a raw-materials-producing country cannot hope to get a "good break" in the allocation of rewards for participation in international specialization as contemplated under the law of comparative advantage. While various lines of argument, of differing degrees of sophistication, exist relative to the subject, each carries one toward the conclusion that a specialization-and-trade framework in which industrial and raw-materials-producing countries coexist operates—in the present-day world—so as to favor the industrial countries over the raw-materials producers. Further, with a conclusion that specialization and trade under these circumstances serves to work against underdeveloped (raw-materials-producing) countries in the division of income generated in the world, it follows that achievement of economic development, associated

---

[5] To say nothing of the obstacle posed by inadequate domestic means, a likely situation in view of the low real per-capita income characteristic of underdeveloped countries. As an offset, however, some advantages also exist—e.g., the ability to draw upon both the know-how and capital of countries already industrial (Ch. 4).

[6] For a full statement of the infant-industry argument, as applied to tariffs, see F. List, *The National System of Political Economy*, trans. S. S. Lloyd (London: Longmans Green & Company, 1922). While strong logic can be invoked to support the infant-industry argument, many difficulties ordinarily arise in efforts at implementation. To illustrate, new producers tend to be high-cost producers; only following initial phases of operation can representative cost conditions be said to prevail. Economists widely agree that infant-industry protection during these initial phases is defensible, provided a reasonable prospect exists that production can proceed later on its own, free of the support initially lent. But *how much* support should be given, and for *how long?* Clearly, reasonable answers are needed, but these are not easily come by (or easily defended).

with attainment of a higher and rising level of real per-capita income, requires consideration of how and to what extent new industries might be introduced into currently underdeveloped countries. Thus, strict compliance with the dictates of the law of comparative advantage, in its traditional version, does *not necessarily* result in development within an underdeveloped country, and it does *not automatically* assure such a country of its "just rewards" for contributions to development occurring elsewhere within the context of a global specialization-and-trade framework. As a consequence, an underdeveloped country finds itself in a position in which it may wish to seek new industry for itself, within *or beyond* the law of comparative advantage, in an attempt to assure itself of gains not otherwise to be had.

While numerous persons have reached this general conclusion, the precise reasoning they use varies somewhat. A version of major interest—referred to briefly earlier (in Ch. 2)—is associated with Raúl Prebisch,[7] who addressed himself particularly to the problems of Latin America, but whose comments have applicability in other underdeveloped regions also. In economics, according to Prebisch, "ideologies usually tend either to lag behind events or to outlive them,"[8] thereby providing logic at variance with facts. Applied to the law of comparative advantage, the theoretical framework in terms of which the law is grounded achieved prominence in the nineteenth century and carried over into the twentieth century, *but* the world environment changed very much in between—so that the results of the law of comparative advantage differ in practice between the two periods. Failure to recognize this basic situation, then, is to risk "wrong" conclusions because of faulty premises.

To continue with the Prebisch argument, while some few countries were well started on the industrial road even in the nineteenth century, the difference between them and those still strictly committed to raw-materials production was not particularly great, at least not as compared with the contrasts found in the twentieth century. Against this environment, the existent rationale was that raw-materials-producing countries had no compelling need to try to acquire industry for themselves, since they could share in the benefit of technological progress—wherever it occurred—through the simple expedient of international exchange; in fact, it was invariably emphasized that if any still non-industrial country attempted to "fall in line" and also industrialize, such action could well prove harmful for it as lower efficiency resulted from a loss of the conventional advantages of international exchange. And,

---

7 See the following for statements by Prebisch of his argument: UN, *The Economic Development of Latin America*, New York, 1950; R. Lekachman (ed.), *National Policy for Economic Welfare at Home and Abroad* (New York: Doubleday & Company, Inc., 1955), pp. 277–280; and "The Role of Commercial Policies in Underdeveloped Countries," *American Economic Review Papers and Proceedings*, May 1959.

8 UN, *The Economic Development of Latin America*, New York, 1950, p. 1.

given the prevailing environment, adherence to the law of comparative advantage seemed to work pretty well, by and large. In the twentieth century, however, industrial development in some countries had progressed far, so that the contrast between them and raw-materials-producing countries was great, as compared with the nineteenth century. The rationale behind the law of comparative advantage, to which many a country had faithfully subscribed, was that each country—simply through specialization and trade—could get its "just share" of income generated in the world. But, significantly, the "split in benefits" appeared to have shifted, over time, in favor of the industrial countries and against the raw-materials-producing countries.[9] In short, the "schema"[10] of the international division of labor no longer produced the same results it had in an earlier day.

Prebisch, referring to UN data on terms of trade between raw-materials-producing countries and industrial countries (Table 9 in Ch. 2), stated that "technical progress seems to have been greater in industry than in the primary production of peripheral countries."[11] However, if technical progress in industry had surpassed that in raw-materials production, prices of industrial products—according to performance normally expected under conditions of pure competition—*should* have fallen relative to those of raw-materials products. And if this had happened, "The countries of the periphery would have benefited from the fall in prices of finished industrial products to the same extent as the countries of the centre, [so that the] benefits of technical progress would thus have been distributed alike throughout the world, in accordance with the implicit premise of the schema of the international division of labor. . . ."[12] *But,* as seen (Table 9 in Ch. 2), this was not how prices responded; in reality, the terms of trade moved so that "in the centre the income of entrepreneurs and of productive factors increased relatively more than productivity, whereas in the periphery the increase in income was less than that in productivity,"[13] In short, "while the centres kept the whole benefit of the technical development of their industries, the peripheral countries transferred to them a share of the fruits of their own technical progress."[14] Why should this disparate movement in the relation of income to productivity have taken place? Prebisch attempted an answer by alluding to a difference in price flexibility (or rigidity) between industrial and non-industrial countries—specifically by referring to the differing status of trade-unions. As he pointed out, trade-union activity

---

9 See Ch. 2, the section on "The Spread of Benefits."
10 UN, *The Economic Development of Latin America,* New York, 1950, p. 1.
11 *Ibid.,* p. 8. (For definitions of basic terms used by Prebisch, see Ch. 2, footnote 15.)
12 *Ibid.*
13 *Ibid.,* p. 10.
14 *Ibid.*

in industrial countries has operated to push up prices in prosperity and to hold them up in recession (through resistance to wage cuts),[15] whereas in non-industrial countries "The characteristic lack of organization among the workers employed in primary production . . . [has prevented] them from obtaining wage increases comparable to those of the industrial countries and from maintaining the increases to the same extent."[16]

To summarize the Prebisch argument, technical progress seems, over time, to be greater in industry than in raw-materials production, and, in addition, industrial countries tend not only to reap the benefit of their own technical development, but also tend to attract a portion of the benefit of that technical development which happens to occur in raw-materials-producing countries. Thus the rewards to be had from economic growth within the world tend to accrue particularly to industrial countries, and only secondarily (or incidentally) to raw-materials-producing countries. The "policy message" which may seem to follow is that of industrial development for every raw-materials-producing country; however, Prebisch does not argue for industrial development in an all-out manner—e.g., he specifically rules out autarchy as a legitimate goal.[17] What Prebisch does maintain is that the traditional law of comparative advantage (in accordance with which some countries decided to specialize as raw-materials producers in the hope of securing benefits from world economic growth by means of trade) exerts a bias against raw-materials-producing countries that serves to throw doubt upon this law as a guide for determining what economic activity a country should or should not undertake. Specifically, according to Prebisch, the weakness of the theoretical framework—as propounded in the nineteenth century and then carried forward into the twentieth century—is that it makes no provision for the industrialization of some of the "newer countries"[18] (meaning those countries still situated as raw-materials producers in a world in which there is growing industrial development elsewhere). However, he adds the optimistic note that "Two world wars in a single generation and a great economic crisis between them have shown . . . [some underdeveloped countries] their opportunities, clearly pointing the way to industrial activity."[19]

---

[15] In accordance with the Keynesian principle, framed for advanced countries, of prices being flexible upward, but rigid downward.

[16] *Ibid.*, p. 13.

[17] *Ibid.*, p. 6. A case, of at least modest proportions, might be made at this point on behalf of a "common market" arrangement among "like" countries within a given region. This matter is treated in some detail in subsequent connections.

[18] *Ibid.*, p. 1.

[19] *Ibid.* H. Singer has advanced a somewhat similar line of argument; see his "The Distribution of Gains Between Investing and Borrowing Countries," *American Economic Review Papers and Proceedings,* May 1950.

The Prebisch-Singer thesis has been attacked in numerous quarters both on empirical and theoretical grounds. For example, alternate statistical computations undertaken by

Besides argumentation of the type used by Prebisch and his followers, there is a second major line of explanation. This second form of explanation, advanced by Gunnar Myrdal[20] and others, similarly holds that compliance with the dictates of the traditional version of the law of comparative advantage serves—in the present-day world—to operate against raw-materials-producing countries' getting new industry,[21] and against their getting a "good deal" on the basis of their current integration within a specialization-and-trade framework. Unlike the previous explanation, however, the argument here is that the fundamental reason why raw-materials-producing countries cannot hope to get a "good deal" is because of differences in *demand elasticities*, insofar as these pertain to the output of raw-materials-producing and industrial countries. Specifically, according to the argument, continued dependence upon raw-materials production serves, over time, to hamper income gains because some portion of raw-materials output comes to require export outlets, but is confronted there by an inelastic demand, in addition to market instability.[22] The need to sell against conditions of inelastic demand comprises a serious handicap, especially when raw-materials-producing countries have rapid population growth and are often already confronted by a high ratio of population to land. Significantly, no equivalent demand limitations tend to confront producers of industrial products, so that industrial countries experience strength while underdeveloped (raw-materials-producing) countries experience weakness.[23] Indeed, as Myrdal intimates: "[The classical theory of international trade suggests] that trade starts a movement toward income equalization, while *instead* a quite

---

C. Clark, W. A. Lewis, and H. G. Aubrey point to the conclusion that the *long-run* terms of trade need not necessarily move against raw-materials-producing countries. See C. Clark, *The Economics of 1960* (London: Macmillan and Company, Ltd., 1942); C. Clark, "Half-Way to 1960," *Lloyds Bank Review*, April 1952; W. A. Lewis, "World Production, Prices and Trade, 1870–1960," *The Manchester School of Economic and Social Studies*, Vol. XX, 1952; and H. G. Aubrey, "The Long-Term Future of United States Imports and Its Implications for Primary Producing Countries," *American Economic Review Papers and Proceedings*, May 1955. Again, the underlying theory is challenged; to illustrate, G. Haberler, who considers the approach as overly-aggregative, states: "Can anyone seriously maintain that the long-run change in the terms of trade is the same for (a) agricultural exporters (Argentina, Uruguay), (b) mining countries (Bolivia), (c) coffee exporters (Brazil), and (d) petroleum exporters (Venezuela)?" See G. Haberler, "Critical Observations on Some Current Notions in the Theory of Economic Development," *L'industria*, No. 2, 1957; the Haberler quotation appears on p. 8 of this source.

20 See his *An International Economy* (New York: Harper and Brothers, 1956), esp. Chs. III, V, and XIII, and his *Rich Lands and Poor* (New York: Harper and Brothers, 1957), esp. Chs. I, III, VII, IX, X, and XI.

21 E.g., because of the difficulties posed for new industry as it tries to gain a foothold in the face of competition from industry already entrenched in other countries; see G. Myrdal, *Rich Lands and Poor* (New York: Harper and Brothers, 1957), p. 52.

22 *Ibid.*

23 Prebisch later (in 1955) restated his argument along closely related lines. See R. Lekachman (ed.), *National Policy for Economic Welfare at Home and Abroad* (New York: Doubleday & Company, Inc., 1955), pp. 277–280.

normal result . . . [with trade between industrial and raw-materials-producing countries, undertaken pursuant to the classical theory (and to the law of comparative advantage)] is the initiation of a cumulative process toward the *impoverishment and stagnation of the latter.*"[24]

In short, a widely-held conclusion—arrived at by differing routes of reasoning—is that the "schema" of the international division of labor (and the guidance offered by the traditional law of comparative advantage) would relegate the raw-materials-producing countries to a generally inferior economic position. Thereupon, it follows that raw-materials-producing countries may have good reason for not wanting to comply with the dictates of the traditional law of comparative advantage. Rather, they may have good reason to *look beyond* the law of comparative advantage for guidance in determining "what next" to do in the evolution of their economies.

FOREIGN-EXCHANGE IMPACT

Apart from tests associated with the law of comparative advantage, there are tests related to foreign-exchange impact. These tests are relatively new in terms of direct usage (indeed, have been little used), but they are regarded in some quarters as superior to tests based on the law of comparative advantage, per se.

The primary rationale for placing foreign-exchange impact in a pivotal position is that the immediate bottleneck handicapping industrial development in the typical underdeveloped country is found in foreign-exchange stringency, and that, therefore, the effect of any new industrial enterprise upon total foreign-exchange supplies logically represents a core consideration.[25] The contention is that an enterprise has special merit if it helps ease the foreign-exchange situation, since added development then becomes easier, not harder; on the other hand, an enterprise loses in merit if its presence serves to impair the foreign-exchange situation further and thus automatically precludes additional development.[26]

Beyond this primary rationale, a major secondary rationale also exists: tests based on foreign-exchange impact are held to be practical, especially in the sense of being easy to apply. Some persons are convinced that tests rooted in comparative advantage are likely to prove impractical;

---

24 G. Myrdal, *Rich Lands and Poor* (New York: Harper and Brothers, 1957), p. 101. (Italics are mine.)

25 Other deterrents to industrial development are not thereby ignored; the point is simply that *the* shortcoming that forges to the forefront to inhibit the "very next step" in the course of industrial development tends, with almost uncanny regularity, to be foreign-exchange stringency. Relative to this point, the reader is urged to refer again to Ch. 4.

26 Typically, a major rationale for establishment of a screening committee proceeds in terms of the need for control over the evolving investment pattern so as to assure beneficial foreign-exchange impact from new investments (or to preclude adverse foreign-exchange effects).

attempts to judge new enterprises on this basis serve to raise a great many questions, both of theory and fact, so that over time the performance record is in danger of becoming one of "much talk and little new industry." These persons are inclined to regard action as much more probable when tests are based instead on foreign-exchange impact. They contend that greater action is fostered because only problems of immediate consequence are pivoted into a central position, with other issues left for later argument—presumably when industrial development is well underway and a country can afford the luxury of the debates likely to be associated with efforts toward the refinement of testing techniques. In essence, as these persons see the matter, what underdeveloped countries need is some new industry *now* whenever such can be had on a workable basis; absolute perfection is not necessary all along the line.

The key consideration, then, is foreign-exchange impact. Stated briefly, any enterprise that is *foreign-exchange-earning* or *foreign-exchange-saving* is regarded to have merit in terms of this approach (and the more foreign exchange earned or saved, per given amount of investment, the more meritorious an enterprise is presumed to be). But what, precisely, is a foreign-exchange-"earning" or "-saving" enterprise? A foreign-exchange earning enterprise is one whose output enters export markets, and whose presence has the net effect of adding to a country's foreign-exchange-earning capacity, so that the country's foreign-exchange reserves are increased by virtue of the new enterprise. Outstanding examples of foreign-exchange-earning enterprises include those devoted to the processing of raw materials prior to export. On the other hand, a foreign-exchange-saving enterprise is one whose output substitutes for previous imports. In order to "save" foreign exchange, new domestic production must cost less in associated foreign-exchange outlays than did imports displaced by it. Foreign exchange is not saved if the volume of domestic production is expanded to such an extent that associated foreign-exchange outlays exceed those previously made on imports of the product in question (or if any expansion in volume is not offset by substitutions in import composition such that total foreign-exchange outlays on the product and its substitutes are held below those previously made on the product and its substitutes). During early stages of industrial development, foreign-exchange-saving enterprises tend especially to be those concerned with articles of widespread domestic consumption, e.g., textiles, soap, and cigarettes.

Numerous advocates of industrial development are inclined to favor foreign-exchange-saving enterprises over those in the foreign-exchange-earning category—meaning that they prefer production for the domestic market to production for export. The explanation for this preference appears rooted, for the greater part, in a fear that reliance upon foreign-exchange-earning enterprises will give a country nothing better than some elementary processing of raw materials prior to exportation, which frequently is regarded as a "low" form of industrial development at best, and, at worst, just more colonialism in operation. Significantly, however, foreign-exchange-saving enterprises can save foreign exchange only insofar as imports occurred previously. Therefore, developmental potential in the foreign-exchange-saving category is limited by the size of the existent balance-of-payments configuration. On the other hand, foreign-exchange-earning enterprises are not limited in this manner; their earnings are not circumscribed within some previous or current balance-of-payments framework, but occur *outside* and beyond any such balance-of-payments framework. Therefore, developmental potential in the foreign-exchange-earning category is limited only by a country's capacity to produce and to secure foreign markets.

Always, however, an eased foreign-exchange situation—whether a result of foreign-exchange supplies being freed-up through the saving of foreign exchange or increased outright through the earning of foreign exchange—helps a country to sustain additional foreign-exchange commitments associated with further development, so that the process of growth is fostered. Foreign-exchange-earning and foreign-exchange-saving enterprises represent new development, in and of themselves, and, in addition, they "open the door" for further development in that they help ease the foreign-exchange situation. This is the essential appeal. As proponents, drawing upon the old adage that "the proof of the pudding is in the eating," like to put the matter (in support of basic tests related to foreign-exchange impact): industry ordinarily results thereby, and industry now is preferable to industry later (or maybe never).

POINT OF CONTROVERSY

As evidenced by the foregoing, a basis exists for controversy as between two distinct goals: maximization of *efficiency* versus *extrication* from a balance-of-payments straitjacket. Under terms of the first, the problem is seen as one of how to allocate resources and effort so as to maximize productive efficiency, i.e., of how to secure maximum output per given input. According to its proponents, pursuit of this goal requires each country to concentrate on activities in compliance with the law of comparative advantage, or some interpretation of it. Under terms of the second, the problem is seen as one of "how to get things moving"—or, "moving faster." According to its proponents, pursuit of this goal requires that special attention be given foreign-exchange impact. Given the differing points of emphasis, criticism and counter-criticism readily emerge. On the one hand, advocates of efficiency as the basic consideration fear that demotion of it as a test, in favor of tests related to foreign-exchange impact, is likely to result in the foisting upon an economy of enterprises that are destined to prove inefficient over the long-run, and hence prone to prove a drag upon the economy. On the other hand, advocates of foreign-exchange impact as a test question preoccupation with efficiency, particularly when underemployment is widespread (representing, perhaps, the greatest source of inefficiency of all); as they view the matter, even "inefficient" activity is defensible, if the only alternative is activity of even lesser caliber, or no activity at all.

The issue, as outlined, is a much-discussed one in certain quarters (e.g., within those US Government agencies concerned with the flow of official capital to underdeveloped countries), but discussion seems more often to lead merely to greater precision in the statement of divergent views than to a reconciliation of those views. In practice, no great conflict springs from the status of export-type enterprises. Foreign exchange-earning enterprises must be able to compete in an international market in order to survive; hence, tests of efficiency, stemming from some interpretation of the law of comparative advantage, are not entirely precluded. Clashes of viewpoint, insofar as they arise, tend to show up more particularly in reference to enterprises oriented to the domestic market. There individual positions tend typically to divide on whether, or how, to take the following three factors into account. First, does one allow for, or disregard, the presence of underemployment or of unemployment? Second, does one allow for, or disregard, implications attributable to the presence of exchange control and to the "artificial" exchange rates that typically exist and serve to distort international price relationships? Third, does one permit, or disallow, new enterprises catering to new domestic demands, i.e., demands of a type that place the new enterprises in the position of being neither foreign-exchange-earning nor foreign-exchange-saving? To say the least, the situation is made to order for disagreement. And disagreement there is!

A STATEMENT OF VIEW

Achievement of a world situation in which reasonably high real per-capita income and near-full employment are realized represents an "ideal" that many persons—including this author—are prepared to view as a worthy goal. But if the global environment thus envisaged as a goal is to be achieved, a transition period of some duration needs to be undergone. Seemingly, one should inquire what policies are appropriate when the ideal situation prevails, and what policies are appropriate during the transition period preceding its attainment; perhaps the two differ.

Significantly, the traditional law of comparative advantage assumes an environment that conforms more to the one pictured here as a goal than it does to the one actually prevailing or reasonably to be expected during the transition period preceding attainment of the goal. Accordingly, in the opinion of this author, the traditional law of comparative advantage is subject to important shortcomings as a guide in determining the types of industries a present-day underdeveloped country might reasonably contemplate in the course of its efforts to achieve development. Some deviation from, or modification of, the law of comparative advantage (in this form) seems warranted to help ease and speed the transition—as many persons have maintained in times past and as is much in evidence, for example, in infant-industry-type arguments. Yet, it seems inadequate simply to recognize a shortcoming in the law of comparative advantage and to condone deviation from it; some standards in terms of which basic decisions can be made still seem needed. Thus, the important question is what tests might prove workable during the transition. It is in this connection that "foreign-exchange impact" as a test acquires special relevance.

The central argument for foreign-exchange impact as a test—with which this author is in basic agreement—is that it "makes sense" in the here and now; it offers meaningful guidance for underdeveloped countries in the selection of the specific industries that can hope to survive and prosper, and that hence can help in the transition to that now-distant global environment in which conditions are reasonably akin to those assumed for the traditional law of comparative advantage—at which time the law of comparative advantage can well be looked to for the guidance its framers intended. In short, foreign-exchange impact is viewed as a meaningful test for the *short-run,* pending that time when evolution of an environment akin to that assumed by the law of comparative advantage serves to give meaning to its application as the *ultimate* test.

SELECTED BIBLIOGRAPHY

See the end of Chapter 9.

9

ISSUES IN INDUSTRY (II)

The preceding chapter dealt with one major issue peculiar to industrial development: the tests that might be applied in an attempt to ascertain the types of industrial activity likely to prove best for an underdeveloped country about to initiate or accelerate industrial development. The present chapter treats additional issues.

COTTAGE INDUSTRY

Some persons, while ostensibly in favor of industrial development, have difficulty visualizing anything but modest operations in present-day underdeveloped countries. These persons frequently come to be proponents of cottage industry. An essential aspect of cottage industry is that production is oriented to the home.

Support for cottage industry rests, for the greater part, on two main bases. First, employment comes to be created where people are, and with minimum "fuss or muss." With production centered in the home, various members of the family can readily turn idleness to some useful end and this can be the general situation throughout the economy, without there having to be a mass shift of people to new locales. In fact, such production often can be combined with whatever other pursuits the family is already concerned; for example, small-scale farmers conceivably can devote time to efforts of the cottage-industry variety in the weeks or months they are not occupied with farming tasks. Moreover, since production ordinarily stresses uncomplicated products, even the presence of a low order of technical skills tends to pose no serious handicap (so that some of the preliminaries associated with basic development—e.g., education—can be held to a minimum, at least for the time being). Second, only little capital is ordinarily required. Since production is based in the home, capital requirements for new buildings tend to be small, and the machinery required is ordinarily of a simple and low-cost type. As a method of creating employment with low capital outlay, development based on cottage industries tends to rate high.

Actually, three main types of cottage industry are discernible. The first is based on self-sufficiency production. In this case, people use their idle time to produce ordinary objects of direct use to themselves. The production process ordinarily is highly labor-intensive, with many hours of work typically involved in the creation of an end object. Illustrative of this type of cottage industry is the weaving of cloth in the home by means of a hand-loom process, e.g., along the lines suggested for the Indian populace by the late Mahatma Ghandi. By way of overall appraisal, it can be argued that when idleness is the only alternative, even time-consuming production methods have merit; however, production geared to self-sufficiency at the family level appears, at best, to offer only small prospect for a higher or rising level of living.

The second type of cottage industry emphasizes handicrafts. Many people in underdeveloped countries exhibit impressive ability as craftsmen, and some of the native arts are expressed in objects of considerable attractiveness. Notable examples of handicraft might include Puerto Rican laces, Middle East copper and bronze wares, Thai silks, Indonesian batiks, Chinese porcelains, and Haitian carvings. If people can be set to work in the production of these and similar objects, and if markets can then be found (of necessity, largely external markets), employment and income can accrue. However, all this is easier said than done. The problem involved, basically, is not one of the technical aspects of production, but one of organization: how to channel output toward market outlets, and how to procure the market outlets themselves. Significantly, the objects produced, while they may have appeal in specialty markets, tend not to be suited for sale on a mass basis. Standardization of end objects ordinarily is lacking (and cannot readily be achieved), and most prospective customers view the end objects as novelties or *objets d'art*. As a consequence, total markets tend to be limited, so that what can be hoped for in terms of total production—and in terms of employment and income—is also limited.

The third type of cottage industry involves a form of activity occurring at the fringes of an overall industrial complex in which large-scale industry sets the pace. Under the particular form of industrial organization at issue, some processes in the production sequence are "farmed out" by large industrial firms to various individuals, who undertake to handle the processes on a cottage-industry basis, frequently with the assistance of hired workers; upon completion, the output of the cottage industries moves to the large industrial firms, which then proceed to incorporate it into the final product. An historical example is that of the "putting-out system," widespread in England during the Industrial Revolution. A foremost example of the present day is that of Japan; the industrial economy of Japan makes much use of production along cottage-industry lines, the end output at this stage being linked to an important extent to a relatively few large enterprises at the core of an industrial complex—with the end output occurring, in fact, largely because the presence of large industrial enterprises provides a market outlet, and hence serves to underwrite the output in the first place. As is apparent, this type of cottage industry does not comprise a self-contained operation; rather, the production is sustained on the basis of the needs of large industrial production units that lie outside of it. Cottage industry within this category offers itself, therefore, as an *adjunct* to large-scale industry, not as an alternative to it.

For the greater part, cottage industry can be regarded as occupying a compromise position among the various possibilities in a hierarchy of industrial effort; this is essentially the case, apart from the third type cited—in which cottage industry comprises an adjunct to other and more ambitious forms of industrial effort. If large-scale industry is within grasp, cottage industry takes on the appearance of a poor substitute. But if large-scale industry seems not within reach, cottage industry represents a workable way of transforming additional effort into some gains. However, these gains that might be realized—measured particularly in terms of income benefits—appear to be of modest proportions, even under generally favorable circumstances.

ASSEMBLY OPERATIONS

Some persons are prone to conclude that if industrial development is "good" in the first place, then *any* type or amount of industrial development is automatically desirable for a country. Others believe such a conclusion a bit hasty, and often cite the case of assembly and packaging operations as evidence in support of their own reservations.

Assembly and packaging operations are ordinarily among the easier forms of industrial activity to introduce within a newly-developing country. The operations are generally not very complicated, representing merely one facet of the industrial process. Also, since finished products as a rule already enter the country in some amount, a market of some magnitude for new domestic output is known to exist. In short, neither technical nor market limitations tend to inhibit the new domestic production. Unfortunately, however, assembly and packaging operations can prove to be a curse—or so some persons maintain. The contention is that these operations—whatever benefits might derive from them in particular respects—quickly tend to cease being foreign-exchange-saving (under the guise of which they are commonly introduced), and come instead to be foreign-exchange-*"losing"* (as they "open the door" for a foreign-exchange drain).

The point at issue can be demonstrated by reference to an example. Assume a development-minded country, committed to the use of exchange control as a means for conserving scarce supplies of foreign exchange, which customarily imports 100 units of a product during the course of a year at a total foreign-exchange cost to itself of $100,000. Assume that an assembly operation is then introduced, whereupon the *same* 100 units come to be assembled domestically, but with a foreign-exchange outlay of, let us say, only $80,000 for the component imports occurring in knocked-down form. Clearly, the operation meets the test of being foreign-exchange-saving—provided, of course, the country uses its exchange-control system to preclude foreign-exchange outlays on additional like imports in assembled form[1] (since, in the absence of such exclusion, total foreign-exchange outlays on unassembled imports plus assembled imports could soon come to exceed $100,000). In short, some foreign exchange can be "saved" (and then become available for other uses), even while some additional employment and income are generated in the domestic economy.[2]

Assume, next, that the cited assembly operation is expanded, so that 150 units of the product are made available to the domestic market. Numerous persons are inclined, without further ado, to regard the new situation as reflective of progress; after all, more production means more employment (and probably more income also), and more end-users are served. But, since 150 units cost $120,000 in foreign exchange at the existing per-unit level on knocked-down imports, the assembly operation can be said to have become foreign-exchange-"losing"—by $20,000. The important question then is: Might not the extra foreign-exchange outlay have been used to a better end? Since assembly and packaging operations tend largely to be concerned with consumer-goods items, failure to preclude expansion beyond certain limits can lead to a foreign-exchange drain—all to the end of further gratification of consumer wants. Significantly, any foreign exchange used to satisfy consumer wants means that much less foreign exchange available for securing developmental ingredients, either of capital goods for new industry or of essential raw

---

[1] Significantly, stoppage of assembled imports (through no further foreign-exchange allocations for assembled imports) can help assure a domestic market for the enterprise handling assembly, even if the new domestic cost of the end product exceeds the previous import cost.

[2] While assembly operations serve to generate some domestic employment and income, impact in neither respect tends to be particularly great—not when measured against the impact of equivalent foreign-exchange and investment outlays in some alternate uses.

materials for already-existing industry. In short, assembly and packaging operations pose a potential threat in the sense that, instead of "saving" foreign exchange, they readily become devices for catering to growing consumer demand—thereby circumventing the very exchange-control regulations that are intended to curb consumer demand so that more foreign exchange might thus be made available for support of increased inflows of developmental ingredients. To say the least, many cases of abuse are citable, involving numerous countries and products; notable cases include firms that undertook to assemble industrial-type refrigeration equipment and later managed to add the assembly of household air-conditioners and refrigerators, and firms that undertook to package pharmaceuticals and later managed to add the packaging of cosmetic products.

Or, consider an assembly operation in which the owners come to think in terms of servicing foreign markets. Assume, by way of illustration, an American-owned assembly operation in Country A, an underdeveloped country, in which the following circumstances prevail: exchange control exists, the currency is "reasonably" high-grade (although not freely convertible), and there is a "fair degree" of political stability (enough, at least, to make it a "pretty good" country in which to locate for investment purposes). Assume, next, that at some point the owners of the assembly operation come to eye the potential market of Country B, an adjacent underdeveloped country, in which the following circumstances prevail: exchange control exists, the currency is low-grade (inconvertible, vastly overvalued, and not sought after), and political instability is clear-cut. Given this situation, investment in an assembly operation in B is not attractive, even though sales potential exists there. At the same time, A can gain added employment, and possibly some other benefits, if it allows an expansion of the assembly operation within its borders in order to permit servicing of demands in B. But, should A cooperate in the endeavor? If it does, a possible sequence in business transactions may well be as follows: payment for assembled imports by B in B currency, which is then converted in A for A currency, followed next by a remittance from A in payment for knocked-down imports of American origin (along with remission of profits). The effect is to impose a foreign-exchange drain—a US dollar drain—upon A, even though it is B's demands that are being serviced; as an offset, A ends by holding claim to B currency, but this currency has doubtful merit for uses to which A might want to put it. In short, the basing of an assembly operation in one country in the expectation of servicing a regional market poses currency problems (i.e., foreign-exchange problems) of a special nature for the country in which the assembly operation is situated. Unless precautions are taken, the country in which the assembly operation is based is likely to end up as a clearinghouse in the process of upgrading currencies on behalf of the owners of assembly operations.

Whatever else can be learned from an examination of assembly and packaging operations, an important point is demonstrated: just because some industrial development is found meritorious, it does not necessarily follow that more of the same is destined to prove equally meritorious.

SCALE OF OPERATIONS

An important question for countries interested in the initiation or acceleration of industrial development relates to the scale of operations. Specifically, of what magnitude must industrial effort be if economic, or business, success is to follow?

Underdeveloped countries are typically caught in a dilemma in determining what scale of operations is appropriate for them. On the production side, industrial activity is characterized by decreasing costs, i.e., per-unit costs decrease with increases in output, at least over a wide range of possible production. This means that the cost per unit for prospective output is dependent, in large measure, upon the scale of operations. But, on the outlet side, most underdeveloped countries have only small markets. Most of the countries have low total populations (e.g., roughly one-third of them have populations of under 5 million), and per-capita incomes average a mere fraction of the levels of developed countries. The countries are typically caught in a dilemma because their existing markets are too small to support operations of a size capable of yielding advantageous cost positions, but the attainment of favorable cost situations is essential to successful entry into and promotion of industrial development. Yet, such difficulties notwithstanding, virtually every underdeveloped country, including even the low-population countries, aspires for an industrial complex *of its own*.

Some persons tend to minimize the problem raised here. They are inclined to argue that the economies of a great many countries are really sufficiently sizable to support a scale of production at or near optimum levels. To illustrate, one writer summarized one facet of thinking on the subject in the following terms:[3]

> There is dispute concerning how many people and hence how many workers are essential to maximize returns per head from division of labor. For example, Jewkes estimates that a population of 20 million —i.e., a labor force of about 10 million—is sufficient to permit realization of "the full economies of large-scale production." P. K. Whelpton concludes that a population of 100–135 millions is sufficient to maximize

---

[3] J. J. Spengler, "Demographic Patterns," Ch. III in H. F. Williamson and J. A. Buttrick (eds.), *Economic Development* (Englewood Cliffs, N.J.: Prentice-Hall, Inc., 1954), pp. 67–68.

output per head in the United States. If these inferences are valid, it follows that populations of many countries of the world are in excess of the size required to extend the division of labor to the point where, under existing conditions, per capita income can be maximized. M. Gottlieb has suggested, furthermore, that technological change is no longer operating, as in the nineteenth century, to increase the size of the labor force required to maximize the economies associated with division of labor.

Other persons, however, do not feel so optimistic. These persons visualize a major problem as being at issue, one which individual countries can hope to cope with to a greater or lesser extent. At root, these persons visualize attainment of an optimum scale of operations in industry as dependent upon two main considerations: the type of industry in question, and the extensiveness of the market area.

First, then, the scale of operations that can prove itself as optimum is related to the type of industry in question. To illustrate, a larger population is needed to sustain a steel mill than, say, a soap factory. Thus, a particular country may reasonably aspire to some types of industry, but not to others. Interestingly enough, however, one country with a population of only roughly 7 million (Chile) is sustaining a steel mill.

Second, the scale of operations needs to be related to the extensiveness of the market area. In this respect, industrial production can be for a domestic market, or for an export market, or for both—as a consequence of which important variations exist. If production is for a domestic market, the size of that market—which is related, in part, to the country's own population size—essentially prescribes the possible maximum scale of operations. However, if production is for an export market, market considerations are obviously not tied to factors in the producing country; technical aspects of production remain important, but not in reference to the domestic population and the market associated with it.

Interjection of export-market considerations serves to raise many questions, one of which is the possibility of a *regional* approach to industrial development. Under it, two or more countries within a region undertake to pool both their industrial effort and their market potential. To illustrate, perhaps not one of the Central-American countries is large enough to support a plant in any one of a half dozen major lines of endeavor, but perhaps the region, *as a unit,* can support some or all of them—and can do so on an economic basis. In fact, a report of the UN, in treating the problem of independent national action within small political entities (in Latin America), hints at the possible merit of industrial development on a "shared" basis in the following terms:[4]

. . . one of the limits of industrialization which must be carefully considered in plans of development . . . concerns the optimum size of

---

4 *The Economic Development of Latin America,* New York, 1950, pp. 6–7.

industrial enterprises. It is generally found in Latin-American countries that the same industries are being attempted on both sides of the same frontier. This tends to diminish productive efficiency. . . . [It is possible to lose] a considerable proportion of the benefits of technical progress through an excessive division of markets. . . .

LOCATION OF INDUSTRY

With the introduction of new industrial enterprises in underdeveloped countries, a question arises as to where they ought to be located. The economics of the situation appears to favor location in or near major urban centers (which, in most underdeveloped countries, means in and around the capital city or the largest seaport), or near major sources of raw-materials supply. However, most of the population of underdeveloped countries is rural and oriented toward agriculture. Thus, placement of new enterprises in or near major urban centers or near major sources of raw-materials supply may well mean—indeed, is likely to mean—that the new enterprises are located at some distance from where the bulk of the population resides. How then can "the people" benefit from the new enterprises associated with industrial development?

The foregoing question is frequently posed by persons who favor a "grass-roots" approach to economic development in preference to industrial development, which happens not to meet their test of what comprises a grass-roots approach. According to these persons, the objective of economic development is to "help people"—and the more people helped, directly and in short order, the better. Industrial development, they seem to intimate, helps few people. Loan capital is placed in few hands for use in few enterprises; the enterprises employ few people (relative to the magnitude of underemployment prevailing); and benefits that do reach the masses do so through the "trickle-down" process, rather than directly. Viewed in this manner, a case is made for emphasis upon agriculture, or perhaps upon community development, but certainly not for emphasis upon industrial development.

Proponents of industrial development have three major answers by way of reply to the foregoing line of argument. First, even if industrial development is concentrated in few locales, the immobility of the population is not so great but that the workers who are needed shift to the new locations when they become aware of employment opportunities of sufficient attractiveness.

Second, while it undoubtedly is true that few new job opportunities are created *directly* within the new enterprises (in comparison with the number of persons desirous of improved employment status), *secondary* employment benefits ought not be ignored. A "multiplier principle" operates in conjunction with the introduction of the new enterprises. The enterprises have to be supplied with materials, new and additional services come to be supplied to the enterprises and their employees, and the added income generated by the enterprises circulates through the economy—all of which serve to boost employment outside the new enterprises themselves. An analogy, drawn from the American economy, appears pertinent: "The status of employment and income in Michigan also affects the economic situation in Mississippi."

Third, if long-run economic improvement and well-being depend upon the successful promotion of industrial development as an addition to raw-materials production, there is no reasonable alternative but to try to develop industry, as much and as soon as possible. To delay industrial development, under these circumstances, is tantamount to standing by while long-run economic stagnation, or even deterioration, proceeds and gradually takes its toll. As a concession, however, it is widely acknowledged that the potential benefits from industrial development do not accrue immediately in full force, so that a case remains for efforts in other connections that might create a beneficial effect over shorter-run periods (during which time industrial development is being initiated and accelerated, but before its impact is felt fully).

COMPETITIVE INDUSTRIALIZATION

Some persons in industrial countries feel that the promotion of industrial development in underdeveloped countries is certain to prove injurious to the economies of countries already industrialized. According to them, the effect of the new industry is to create competition that is liable to "kill off" some of the old-line industry in developed countries. Fear of competition, in fact, frequently provides the rationale for outright opposition—in various forms—to the introduction of new industry in underdeveloped countries.[5] Accordingly, the question might be raised here as to whether such a fear of "competitive industrialization" is warranted.

It is evident, of course, that the development of new industry in underdeveloped countries serves to create competition for *particular* firms or industries located in developed countries. Following commencement of operations by new firms, old-line firms face new competition in their sales, either in the markets of the particular underdeveloped country, or in the home markets of the particular developed country, or in "third-country" markets. This competition can restrict total sales of old-

---

[5] In some instances, the sentiments involved actually come to be embodied in legislation. For example, the Agricultural Trade Development and Assistance Act of 1954—one segment of the American farm program—states the following (in regard to use in loan form of local currencies acquired through sales abroad of American farm surpluses): ". . . no such loans shall be made for the manufacture of any products to be exported to the United States in competition with products produced in the United States or for the manufacture or production of any commodity to be marketed in competition with United States agricultural commodities or the products thereof."

line firms to levels below those otherwise likely to prevail, and conceivably serves, in some instances, to drive individual old-line firms out of business.

The really important economic consideration, however, concerns the effect of new industrial development, not upon a particular firm or industry, but upon an *economy as a whole*. As far as a particular country is concerned, new industrial development in underdeveloped countries does not hurt its economy, provided there is flexibility in the economy and a willingness to undergo adjustment. Short-run problems of adjustment are involved, and it is true that these sometimes can prove troublesome and difficult. Beyond transitional stages, however, a generally improved situation for the economy can logically be expected, since an improved foreign economic situation—when this results—is conducive, not harmful, to economic well-being at home.

DEVELOPMENT BANKS

In a conscious attempt to help economic development, especially industrial development, some underdeveloped countries resort to a new type of institution: a development bank. An institution of this type exists in numerous underdeveloped countries, and almost invariably those countries still without one are talking about establishing one. Indeed, sentiment in many quarters in the underdeveloped world appears near the point at which embarkation upon a concerted developmental effort without a development bank on the scene is regarded as virtually "unthinkable."

Development banks are institutions that almost always come into existence under government sponsorship, either by its creating its own bank or through its prodding to induce private action—avowedly for the purpose, as intimated earlier, of aiding development. To this end, development banks are invariably structured so as to place the emphasis in operations upon either of two main types of activity. Some development banks concentrate on providing assistance, and do not get involved themselves in actual ownership or management of developmental projects. Assistance then takes the form of financing (e.g., loans are made to cover domestic costs, or foreign-exchange costs, or both) or of technical services (e.g., engineering and managerial talent is provided). Other development banks concentrate on the actual establishment and operation of specific developmental projects.[6]

---

[6] Sometimes the label "development bank" is reserved for those institutions that provide assistance, while the label "development corporation" is applied to those institutions that emphasize the actual operation of projects. More commonly, however, the term "development bank" is used to cover both "banks" and "corporations." This second form of usage is generally adhered to by both US Government and international lending agencies. Illustrative of this form of usage, see IBRD, *Development Banks* (Baltimore: The Johns Hopkins Press, 1957).

Aside from such central unifying features, however, development banks differ very much among the various countries.[7] The wide differences can be readily grasped by referring to a few sample institutions. A first case is the Industrial Credit and Investment Corporation of India (ICICI), established in 1955, avowedly to provide long-term financing for private industry. The institution was established as a private undertaking, but had the full sanction of the Indian Government. Authorized capital, insofar as paid in, was met by private subscription (70% by private Indian, British, and American financial and commercial firms, and 30% by the Indian public). These resources were supplemented by an advance from the Indian Government, which used funds derived in the course of incorporating particular US foreign-aid goods into its economy. In addition, the institution was authorized to borrow up to three times the amount of unimpaired paid-in capital, Government advances, and surplus and reserves. Beyond the granting of loans from these resources, the institution was empowered to undertake the underwriting of capital issues. The institution has been active, in practice, both as a direct lender and in the underwriting field—and even during the initial years, a substantial profit was shown. Of a seemingly less favorable nature, the ICICI's loan volume has had to be held within the limits of a rather modest pool of resources (the equivalent of only roughly $100 million in 1959), and loans have been restricted to local currency (i.e., no foreign exchange has been provided directly, although a "stand-by" arrangement was negotiated with the International Bank).

A second case is the Industrial Development Center (IDC) in the Philippines, reconstituted in 1955, and given the responsibility for providing long-term financing for private industry (and also for providing some technical assistance for this industry). Although established as a government agency, the institution was limited in its activity to the promotion of industrial development in the private sector. Provision was made for financial resources, expressed in local currency, to accrue as a "flow" within the framework of the US foreign-aid program, although direct allocation from the country's own fiscal budget was regarded, in some quarters, as a likely source of financing at some future point. Significantly, the institution was not established as a bank in the sense of being empowered to lend directly to end-borrowers. Rather, the technique initiated was to have the institution make *time deposits* with existing private commercial banks, any such time deposit to run concurrently with a specific loan made by a private commercial bank to some end-borrower who had qualified for assistance. All loan risks were to be borne by the

---

7 See *Ibid.*, pp. 1–5, esp. p. 5. Important points of difference involve ownership of the institutions, sources of capital, types of financing undertaken, loan standards applied, and attitudes adhered to as to profit for the institutions.

commercial banks concerned, not by the central institution. An objective of the IDC procedure was to "lure" private commercial banks into industrial-type financing. Only in rare instances did commercial banks lend previously for industrial purposes; therefore, the hope was that the new "time-deposit-loan program" might provide an exposure likely to result eventually in a restructuring of commercial-bank loan policy. A second objective of the IDC procedure was to provide a sure-fire approach to the promotion of new industrial development. In fact, the tying of time deposits to the actual granting of loans by commercial banks represented an attempt to pinpoint results. After only two years' operation, an apparent consequence of the time-deposit-loan program had been a doubling in the rate of new industrial investment (as measured by an approximate doubling of industrial-type machinery imports into the country).

A third case is the Nacional Financiera of Mexico. Begun in 1934, but reorganized and enlarged in 1941, the Financiera has long comprised the main instrumentality at the disposal of the Mexican Government for the stimulation of industry and public utilities. Actually, the Financiera was set up to concern itself with functions and operations that go far beyond those ordinarily associated with a development bank. To cite a few of its activities, the Financiera has acted as a creator and financier of enterprises, a mobilizer of domestic capital, an intermediary for foreign borrowing (and a channel for subsequent placement of resources so obtained), a regulator of the stock exchange, and an agent for governmental units. Initially financed by direct allocations from the national budget, the Financiera has come to derive the great bulk of its funds from borrowings undertaken on its own, domestically and abroad. Some of the borrowings have been for various other governmental instrumentalities or quasi-government institutions, on whose behalf the Financiera has acted as agent. Importantly, financial resources of the Financiera have included both local currency and foreign exchange. Derivation of foreign resources has included borrowings from the US Export-Import Bank and the International Bank.

Whatever precise form the development bank assumes, its central objective invariably comes to be stated in terms of help for economic development—and especially for industrial development. But how successful are development banks proving in their support for this development? On the basis of the record thus far, two notable shortcomings are reflected in a great number, but not all, of the institutions. First, total resources available in the case of many of the institutions are not sufficiently great to permit more than mere marginal impact upon the economy. The standard approach of many countries, of course, is to try to "institutionalize" their problems away; each major problem, as it comes to be recognized, serves as the rationale for the creation of a new organizational framework (ostensibly to assure a framework within which it becomes possible to cope with the problem), after which, sad to say, the framework frequently is left pretty much alone to become the casualty of financial malnutrition. In the case at issue, economic impact depends upon much more than the presence of a development bank; it depends particularly upon what the institution possesses that it can bring to bear upon the situation. Perhaps adequate resources simply do not exist, so that it is not a mere case of lack of good faith. In this event, however, it is illusory to think that impact can be had through the simple creation of an institution, largely impervious to the resources placed at its disposal. Second, whatever the magnitude of available resources, the form resources take frequently poses a limitation. Many of the institutions have only local currency available for disposal. Yet, the number-one bottleneck to development is frequently a shortage of foreign exchange. In fact, unavailability of foreign exchange can sometimes render the availability of local currency on attractive terms largely meaningless, since local currency is typically linked with foreign exchange in developmental efforts.

On the other hand, some aspects of these institutions appear definitely of a favorable nature. First, in countries having a development bank, specific new projects or enterprises can be pointed to as a result of effort by the institution. Larger or smaller in number, these undertakings reflect that "things are on the move," presumably more so than would otherwise have been the case. Second, a development bank can help to mobilize domestic capital for productive uses. Even when total capital supplies are not increased, a reorientation of investment effort toward new types of activity can represent a big gain for development. Third, a development bank offers great potential in the sense that the typical organizational framework is ideally fitted for integration into the economy of foreign funds. To illustrate, most new enterprises in underdeveloped countries tend to be small—and especially so when they are in the private sector. Small-scale entrepreneurs are at a distinct disadvantage in direct attempts to negotiate loans abroad. However, a development bank can seek to negotiate a "package loan" of some substantial size, stating a general purpose by way of motive (e.g., "to provide loan capital to new small- and medium-size industries within the private sector"). The package loan, when received by the development bank, can then be parceled out by it, on-the-scene, among numerous qualifying applicants, all ordinarily small-scale in nature. Special appeal for the foreign lender exists in that much of the administrative responsibility then rests in the underdeveloped country; also, direct responsibility for repayment to the foreign lender rests with the development bank, as a consequence of which the lender is likely to anticipate less risk—and, hence, be inclined to offer more favorable loan terms.

SELECTED BIBLIOGRAPHY

Kenneth A. Bohr, "Investment Criteria for Manufacturing Industries in Underdeveloped Countries," *Review of Economics and Statistics,* May 1954.
> A study of capital requirements, skills requirements, location characteristics, and plant size of various manufacturing industries —all approached in terms of ascertaining what industries are likely to prove suitable for underdeveloped countries.

Hollis B. Chenery, "The Role of Industrialization in Development Programs," *American Economic Review Papers and Proceedings,* May 1955.
> An input-output model applied to economic development.

Seymour E. Harris, *International and Interregional Economics.* New York: The McGraw-Hill Book Company, Inc., 1957.
> Part IV, Analysis of the problems of international adjustment (esp. Ch. 19, Discussion of the theory of international trade as it relates to economic development).

International Bank for Reconstruction and Development, *Development Banks.* Baltimore: The Johns Hopkins Press, 1957.
> A survey of development banks—their nature, functions, and operations.

——————, *Problems and Practices of Development Banks.* Baltimore: The Johns Hopkins Press, 1959.
> Handbook on practices followed by existing development banks.

Harry G. Johnson, *International Trade and Economic Growth.* Cambridge: Harvard University Press, 1958.
> Theoretical; contains material significant for interpretation of the law of comparative advantage (see esp. pp. 28–29, 55).

Hla Myint, "The 'Classical Theory' of International Trade and the Underdeveloped Countries," *Economic Journal,* June 1958.
> Examination of "orthodox" international-trade theory relative to benefits gained by underdeveloped countries.

Gunnar Myrdal, *An International Economy.* New York: Harper and Brothers, 1956.
> Chs. XII and XIII, Presents a case for a "double standard" of morality in international economic affairs.

——————, *Rich Lands and Poor.* New York: Harper and Brothers, 1957.
> Esp. Ch. XI, Discussion of the theory of international trade and "inequality" among countries.

Raúl Prebisch, "Commercial Policy in the Underdeveloped Countries," *American Economic Review Papers and Proceedings,* May 1959.
> Views on how underdeveloped countries should interpret the law of comparative advantage in formulating their policies.

K. N. Raj, "Application of Investment Criteria in the Choice Between Projects," *The Indian Economic Review,* August 1956.
> Ideas on the determination of priorities.

Romney Robinson, "Factor Proportions and Comparative Advantage: Part II," *Quarterly Journal of Economics,* August 1956.
> Contains material relevant for criticism of the traditional version of the law of comparative advantage.

Hans W. Singer, "The Distribution of Gains Between Investing and Borrowing Countries," *American Economic Review Papers and Proceedings,* May 1950.
> Views on what the law of comparative advantage means to under-developed countries.

United Nations, *The Economic Development of Latin America,* New York, 1950.
> An attack on orthodox international-trade theory; presents a case for industrial development in underdeveloped countries. (Written by Raúl Prebisch.)

——————, *Processes and Problems of Industrialization in Under-Developed Countries,* New York, 1955.
> Summary of problems associated with industrial development; emphasizes potential benefits derivable from industrialization.

10

POLICIES FOR DEVELOPMENT (I)

As underdeveloped countries seek to promote economic development, they are obliged to make a number of crucial decisions concerning basic policies to govern during the period of development. As would appear likely, the attitudes of individual governments vary significantly as they face the task of policy decision-making. In broadest outline, some governments see their role as that of active leaders or partners in the developmental process, whereas others are inclined toward an essentially laissez-faire approach. In any case, decisions are made and policies result, thereby shaping the environmental framework within which specific programs and projects are expected to arise and thrive.

The present chapter and the one following are devoted to some of the more important areas of governmental policy decision-making, as these relate to the task of development.

THE CENTRAL OBJECTIVE

A first decision—and the most basic one—involves choice of the direction, or "end," of developmental effort. If this decision is tackled directly and deliberately, rather than left to chance in the absence of conscious direction, a government appropriately needs to assure itself of circumstances in at least two major connections. First, a government will want to know what is *the* basic economic problem that confronts the country. Isolation of the problem is necessary, since failure to identify the source of trouble correctly is to risk a course of action geared to treat mere "symptoms," rather than the "disease" itself. Second, a government will want to appraise—in the light of the basic economic problem previously identified—the relative merits of the *two* distinct developmental approaches open to the country: added raw-materials output in existing lines *or* diversification (including industrialization). This appraisal, in turn, requires, among other things, an evaluation both of production potentials[1] and of market potentials.

The task of decision-making in this realm is not an easy one. The nature of the issues, and their attendant perplexities, can perhaps best be grasped through reference to a likely case. Assume a country that is overwhelmingly agricultural, with output heavily concentrated among few commodities, and with these commodities destined largely for export. Assume, also, that the population per unit of currently cultivated area is already great (and that, say, chronic underemployment prevails), that population continues to grow at a rapid pace, and that little or no land is still idle. Assume, further, that per-worker productivity is low, as is real per-capita income, and that the various non-monetary measures of economic well-being all reflect a "poor" situation. Given this situation, what should a country try to do to improve its lot?

First, what is the basic economic problem? Is it found in the presence, say, of low health standards, or of low literacy standards, or, indeed, in the presence of general poverty? Or is each of these merely a surface manifestation of something bigger and deeper (i.e., a "symptom" of the "ailment" itself): low productivity, contributing to low real per-capita income and all that this entails in the mode of life of people? If it is concluded that the trouble, at root, rests with the level of production itself, what attitude then appears appropriate toward activities in the general area of basic development? A reasonable reaction might well run as follows: activities as regards basic development, generally, might *help* ease the sting of current shortcomings, and might well constitute necessary preconditions for meaningful overall improvement, but they are not likely to yield a "solution," in and of themselves. Rather, when all is said and done, overall improvement appears dependent upon success with *new* activity beyond basic development, for it is from this new activity that end-output stems.

Second, should this new and further production be sought primarily through added effort in existing lines of raw-materials output, or through acceptance of diversification (including industrialization) as the pattern for action? Added raw-materials production would appear to represent improvement; however, the question remains: To what extent could matters be helped thereby? Viewed from the standpoint of physical

---

[1] Evaluation of production potentials necessarily warrants that account be taken of resources actually at the disposal of the country, or conceivably accessible to it.

production-capabilities, inability to bring idle land into cultivation[2] automatically limits increases in total output to whatever additional can be wrested from existing acreage—which additional amount may prove to be small, given the technical characteristics of agricultural production.[3] If idle land were present, greater latitude for improvement would exist in this line of activity—but even then only for a while, until the population grew larger.[4]

Viewed from the standpoint of market-capabilities, the situation may be even less bright, since the problem of distribution is frequently more troublesome yet than is the problem of production. When production is geared toward exportation, a question arises as to whether added output can be disposed of abroad to good advantage. If added output cannot be exported to good advantage (as historic difficulties continue, even in aggravated form), the ability to sustain added imports is undermined from the outset—thereby impairing the prospect for an improvement in real per-capita income and overall living levels through the medium of foreign trade. As a minimum, balance-of-payments difficulties, well known to underdeveloped countries as a group, remain unresolved in the process. The conclusion, which then follows, is that an increase in the level of production is not sufficient unless satisfactory markets are obtainable for the output—whereupon, then, an eased balance-of-payments situation becomes possible within the context of a rising level of production.

Alternatively, of course, a country might look to its own internal market, and especially so when added production for an export market appears to offer a poor prospect for economy-wide improvement. Perhaps diversification in agriculture, with production for the domestic market in mind, offers a satisfactory way out. To the extent that production-capacity exists, some latitude for possible income expansion admittedly exists. However, taking into consideration both the technical aspects of production and likely market potentials for output, scope for income expansion along lines of this course appears limited to moderate levels. Indeed,

---

2 Whenever idle land is non-existent, or virtually so.

3 The fundamental technical consideration pertains to the law of diminishing returns, which has special pertinence for agriculture. To some extent, of course, the impact of diminishing returns may prove capable of being offset, or delayed, by a shift to other crops of higher return or by greater application of known technology, e.g., through introduction of improved equipment. However, crop shifts are not always physically possible, and scope for offsetting with technology tends to be more limited in agriculture than in industry.

Significantly, even a *doubling* of output, which would appear to be highly optimistic, would represent only limited gain, considering what is involved in any serious attempt to narrow the gap in income levels between underdeveloped and developed countries. After all, numerous underdeveloped countries currently have per-capita incomes of under $100 per year, as compared with well over $2,000 in the US (Table 2 in Ch. 1).

4 An ultimate prospect is stagnant or falling levels of real per-capita income, as population growth proceeds at a rate equal to or in excess of realizable productivity gains. See again Ch. 4, the section on "Problems of Population."

other limitations, too, are evident. Variety in the consumption pattern remains dependent upon importation, and—in the absence of domestic production of particular items—the extent of variety (through importation) continues to be linked to the ability to export. And, while diversification in agriculture can conceivably help ease a tight balance-of-payments situation, this can be the case—when emphasis for solution is upon the domestic market—only insofar as import-substitutes can be created.

There the matter rests if the country in question has no or only slight prospect in the area of diversification that includes industrialization. The country is then limited to do the best it can in the area of raw-materials production, and to reconcile itself to that which accrues. Before so dedicating its fate, however, it would appear only logical to consider the possibility of greater advantage through special effort extending *beyond* raw-materials production. Perhaps greater potential merit prevails in a course involving a basically altered structure of production—but which course then automatically raises matters in addition to those related strictly to *a* level of production, per se.

In weighing this further alternative, a country needs to appraise the supplies and quality of the factors of production available to it, both currently (in the sense of being on hand) and potentially (in the sense of becoming accessible under realistic circumstances). If the pattern of the factors of production appears to be such that productivity gains exceeding those otherwise obtainable are a reasonable prospect, deliberate action aimed at structural change is not amiss, and particularly not if the productivity gains can lead also to an easing in subsidiary problems, including the balance-of-payments situation.

Significantly, a complicating element likely to manifest itself in the course of considering this further alternative relates to the time period during which potential gains are to be measured and compared. Specifically, productivity gains during the *short-run* future may be less if structural change is preferred to a continued emphasis upon raw-materials production—but over the *longer-run*, productivity gains in the event of structural change may surpass anything realizable from a continued emphasis upon raw-materials production. When this is the case, what decision as to placement of emphasis in production is warranted? Needless to say, the decision is a difficult one for a government to have to make. However it may be resolved, the essential point here is that a hard look beyond the immediate can prove much in order.

Thus, many factors are involved in the choice of the direction, or "end," of developmental effort (of which those cited above comprise only some of the major ones). But even after a government has determined to its own satisfaction both the basic economic problem and the major developmental course to follow, the matter is not ended. The government will then want to ascertain the specific measures needed to implement the intended course of action. In the final analysis, it is action that counts, and action requires intent *plus* implementation. In short, a government needs to determine for itself what the basic economic problem is, what it should try to do (in general) about the problem, and how it should proceed (specifically) in the attempts it makes by way of solution or amelioration.

THE BASIC ATTACK

In deciding on the content of a developmental program, should a country attempt to push *general* development—in the sense of paying equal attention to the various sectors of the economy? Or, should it attempt instead to push *particularized* development—in the sense of focusing special attention upon a particular sector of the economy, or upon a particular problem or facet of a problem?

An attempt to "push ahead on all fronts at once" is fine, provided the requisite means are available. However, if only decidedly limited resources are to be had, as is typical of underdeveloped countries generally, allocation of effort across-the-board on an indiscriminate basis is to risk token effort on many fronts with little impact likely anywhere. The alternative is to devote a disproportionately great segment of available resources to a particular sector of the economy (whenever a particular sector is regarded as crucial to the entire developmental effort), or to a concerted effort aimed at the removal or lessening of a particular impediment (whenever a particular impediment is regarded as a fundamental obstacle to development generally). The outstanding feature of this second approach is that available resources are not spread equitably over many areas of activity. Rather, an "all-out" effort is made to insure definite impact in one or few connections, although other sectors or problems are not necessarily disregarded in the process. Certainly the likelihood of resources being dissipated tends to be lessened as the pitfalls of over-generalization in objectives or of excessive fragmentation of goals are circumvented. Indeed, more precise identification of the critical or strategic point or points under attack can also help to spur action along various supplementary lines.[5]

While pinpointing of effort offers potential advantages in a program of economic development, it also entails a potential danger. In practical terms, it is mandatory then that the strategic factor (or factors) be isolated with accuracy. This is necessary if appropriate remedial action is to follow, and is to lead to further development, preferably on an accelerated basis. Irreparable damage is the likely cost should effort be aimed in the wrong direction because of faulty diagnosis. Then, instead

---

[5] See again Ch. 1, the section on "Combative Techniques."

of the stage being set for progress, the day is delayed when progress can commence.[6]

In numerous countries, the avowed desire of economic planners—and, indeed, frequently of the general populace—is to see *"balanced growth"* come about within the economy. But when "balance" in growth is the objective, should developmental effort be aimed at general development or at particularized development? At first glance, balanced growth might seem to call for a general approach to development. However, an approach of this type is not necessarily the logical one to follow. Balanced growth—in the sense of growth within the framework of a diversified pattern of production—may well require substantial alteration in the prevailing pattern of production. General development, with application of effort across-the-board, is likely to endorse the current structure of production and to buttress the forces supporting its perpetuation. In order to modify the structure of production, developmental effort is likely to have to be focused upon a particular sector of the economy (e.g., upon development of industry) or upon particular problems (e.g., upon bottlenecks that obstruct deviation from the status-quo). In short, in order to achieve balanced growth, developmental effort may need to be applied in a manner quite different from across-the-board. Indeed, a particularized approach, aimed at removal of bottlenecks and at introduction of catalytic action is likely to constitute a necessary first step in the process of structural change, without which balanced growth—as understood here—is impossible.[7]

EMPLOYMENT VERSUS INCOME

Should a developmental effort be geared to attain maximum *employment* effect, or maximum *income* effect (i.e., maximum added output)? The issue is an important one since the typical underdeveloped country suffers from underemployment, so that employment-creation seems to represent a legitimate goal, and also suffers from low productivity and low real per-capita income, so that income-creation likewise seems to represent a legitimate goal. Yet, effort aimed at maximization of employment does not necessarily lead also to maximization of income, or vice versa.

---

6 Even if the strategic point (or points) is correctly identified, follow-up action can give rise to an additional problem of serious consequence. In event action is pursued to too great an extent or for too long, overall development can be thrown out of alignment to the disadvantage of the entire economy. The likelihood of this eventuality is small, however, if all action proceeds within a basic framework characterized by moderation, particularly as applicable to appraisals made of resource availability and developmental potential.

7 For interesting observations on the meaning and implications of "balanced" and "unbalanced" growth, see A. O. Hirschman, *The Strategy of Economic Development* (New Haven: Yale University Press, 1958), esp. Chs. 3 and 4.

If primary emphasis is placed upon employment-creation, with benefits realizable in the here and now, industrial development tends not to loom so hopefully as does further development along the lines of raw-materials production. The amount of investment needed to create a job in manufacturing tends to exceed, and generally far exceed, that needed to create a job in agriculture. Given the fact that the capacity to support investment is limited to start with, it follows that, typically, more employment is to be had when the emphasis in the placement of investment is upon agricultural development than when it is upon industrial development. Indeed, if the number of jobs realized in the near future is the paramount consideration, a case can readily be made for by-passing both agriculture and industry in favor of an entirely different orientation: public-works types of projects, e.g., road-building, slum clearance, or simple monument-building. There, effort can be geared to use all, or virtually all, spendable funds as wage payments, with no or only few "leakages" arising as a consequence of outlays for purposes other than the payment of workers.

The use of available resources in connection with public-works operations thus tends to hold a special appeal whenever a premium is placed upon rapidly realizable employment-impact. Jobs are created in short order, and purchasing power is placed directly in the hands of people who "need it" and who are most likely to use it promptly, thereby contributing to secondary income generation. Little financing tends to be diverted, of necessity, toward complementary materials, and only little demand for foreign exchange ordinarily arises conjunctively, in a direct sense. However, all is not pure gain. Given the nature of typical public-works projects, effort expended thereon does not ordinarily reflect itself in a wider production base. Specifically, the basis for added output of marketable goods and services tends not to be created thereby—in any direct sense, and frequently in no indirect sense either.

Failure in the course of sustaining public-works outlays to create a basis for added output of marketable goods and services holds important implications for underdeveloped countries. First, there is the matter of financial impact. In practice, purchasing power is activated (or created— if the technique of debt monetization is invoked), but the supply of marketable goods and services is not increased commensurately. In a developed country suffering from a cut-back in employment, such additions to purchasing power might well serve to activate previously-created productive capacity[8] that is currently idle. Not so, however, in an underdeveloped country. There the matter is typically not one of previously-created capacity being idle. Rather, the big question in their case is one of how to create more productive capacity in the first place, and public-works outlays are not geared to do this directly, and generally not

---

[8] Meaning "idle capacity" insofar as this capacity was man-made.

indirectly either. In an underdeveloped country, the result of added purchasing power in the face of basically unchanged supplies of marketable goods and services is the creation instead of an essentially inflationary situation.[9] Income, if it does rise, increases fundamentally because of higher prices on existing output, not because of what happens by virtue of possible new production. In essence, employment is created but at the possible price of inflation. Second, there is the matter of the duration of employment-impact. Quite in addition to possible inflationary impact, employment generated through public-works outlays tends to continue only so long as the sustaining outlays also continue. In essence, because no direct basis for production of marketable goods and services is created, no assured basis for *continuing* employment arises.

The general conclusion to be drawn is that public-works operations, in and of themselves, do not create added real income—not beyond possible minor incentive boosts given producers in existing lines; nor do they create lasting employment benefits, although employment gains are realized during the period public-works outlays are sustained. Viewed either in terms of employment-creation or income-creation, the role of public works is a somewhat limited one in underdeveloped countries. Essentially, merit is confined to two main instances (although merit is by no means automatic in either of the instances): as a purely short-run technique for creating some added employment, and—probably more importantly—as a means of support for undertakings in the area of basic development (Ch. 5).

With public-works outlays ruled out as a solution, the fundamental choice narrows to development in the raw-materials field versus development in the industrial field. As previously intimated, a given investment outlay in the raw-materials field *ordinarily* yields greater employment-impact during the near future than does an equivalent investment in industry—and a similar observation might also be made relative to income-impact. Given this situation, should a country determine to allocate scarce capital supplies so as to maximize employment-impact or income-impact during the near future—likely meaning continued emphasis upon raw-materials production? A plausible answer is that a country, before reaching any conclusive decision, may wish first to appraise the long-run implications of other possible courses in the placement of capital. In so doing, a complexity that possibly, or probably, arises to confront decision-makers relates to greater employment-impact and income-impact per unit of investment outlay in agriculture *during the near future,* as contrasted with greater employment-impact and income-impact in industry *over the longer-run.* Indeed, such an eventuality is

---

[9] It is possible, of course, to institute official measures designed to offset the attendant additions to purchasing power, e.g., through increased taxation.

likely whenever a country's long-run economic well-being is intimately tied to the achievement of structural change within the economy. In light of the cited alternatives, a country appears well advised to weigh short-run advantages against long-run advantages, or to reflect on how to allocate scarce capital resources so as to secure some satisfactory combination of short-run and long-run gains.

A further complexity that tends to confront decision-makers relates to the fact that gains potentially derivable from investment are certain to appear somewhat differently, depending upon whether measurement proceeds in terms of employment-impact or of income-impact. While it is true that investment in either raw-materials development or industrial development generally results in added output and real income alongside added employment (so that the inflation problem cited in connection with public-works operations tends not to arise beyond some possible transitional repercussions), impact is primarily in terms of either employment-creation or income-creation, depending upon the particular category of development given emphasis in the investment process. With a choice open in this connection, a strong case can be made to the effect that *employment needs to be regarded to an important extent as a by-product of added production*—i.e., if the goal is attainment of maximum long-run gains in real income with minimum risks of troublesome inflation. According to this view, essential relationships are as follows: added employment stems from increases in real income; creation of an added production base is needed to sustain added employment over time; and associated problems, such as inflation, tend to be eased in subsidiary fashion within the context of rising output. In any event, a paramount task for decision-makers in an underdeveloped country is to ascertain how income-impact can be maximized over time, given available resources; and, according to the essential relationships expressed above, if the income problem can be solved satisfactorily, the employment problem to a large degree can be expected to take care of itself within the framework of greater and growing output.

A CASE STUDY: INDIA

The foregoing issues of "employment versus income" and "short-run versus long-run" are certain to confront every country at some point during the process of economic development. Sometimes the issues are met head-on, resulting in deliberate decisions; in other instances, matters are simply allowed to take their course. But, in any event, the issues do arise. By way of concrete illustration, the developmental experience of India offers a classic case.[10]

---

[10] Various facets of the Indian experience are examined by N. A. Sarma, "Economic Development in India: The First and Second Five Year Plans," in IMF, *Staff Papers,* Vol. VI, No. 2, April 1958.

In its First Five-Year Plan (1951–56), India placed primary emphasis upon agricultural development (which developmental category, in India's planning, also embraced community development). Given the limited financial resources at the country's disposal, the extent of underemployment and unemployment, and the direness of the general economic situation, the desire was for rapid impact through a moderate-cost route; hence, a creditable rationale seemed to exist for emphasis upon agricultural development. As matters evolved, no insurmountable difficulties were encountered in carrying out the Plan, and some respectable gains were recorded (e.g., agricultural output increased by a creditable amount during the course of the Plan). Nevertheless, the country's fundamental economic plight persisted, whereupon the conclusion was reached at top-level—but not before much thought and debate—that long-run economic growth and markedly enhanced well-being were dependent upon achievement of structural change, i.e., upon accelerated activity within an industrial sector, projected as an important adjunct to agriculture. Specifically, since balance-of-payments difficulties were chronic, the introduction of varied foreign-exchange-earning (e.g., steel) and foreign-exchange-saving enterprises (e.g., textiles, metals, and metal products) was deemed highly important by way of overall remedial action. Moreover, the presence of a growing population and labor force appeared to dictate the opening up of a new frontier—believed inherent in augmented industrial development—as an important supplement to the raw-materials types of production already prevailing.

Accordingly, the Second Five-Year Plan (1956–61) was framed so as to place emphasis upon industrial development. While it was recognized that augmented financial demands would be involved, it was believed that effective attack upon the country's basic economic plight would require greater emphasis upon industrial development in any event. Therefore, thinking was in terms of industrial development, notwithstanding any foreseeable or unforeseen difficulties likely associated with this form of development. As matters evolved, foreign-exchange shortages soon appeared as *the* paramount bottleneck in implementation of the Plan. As a consequence of the foreign-exchange situation, the Plan was cut back to a core of indispensable projects, and intensified effort was launched to procure added external assistance that might allow continued progress on even the core of projects remaining. The investment pattern under the Plan was cut back initially to what would, as a minimum, still create employment outlets for *additions* to the labor force. In short, the backlog of underemployed and unemployed, placed at very substantial levels, was not dealt with under terms of the revised Plan; rather, maximum effort was restricted to merely preventing the employment situation from further deterioration. Foreign-exchange deficiencies continued nonetheless, although in diminished magnitude, and—in the absence of access to vastly augmented supplies of foreign exchange[11]—the employment situation (as viewed in 1959) appeared in grave danger of worsening. Under the circumstances, India faced the prospect of being in the unenviable position of "planning for unemployment."

The case of India illustrates how reasonably favorable employment-impact, short-run, may be found in investment-effort geared to agriculture, but how long-run gain may be held dependent upon large-scale investment-effort geared to industrial development—but for which type of effort adequate resources are lacking. As this case vividly illustrates, a country faces a major crisis when the realization dawns that the course of action it can afford can yield no solution, while the course of action that offers a solution costs more than it can afford.

PRIVATE VERSUS PUBLIC INITIATIVE

Should a government rely primarily upon private initiative for the intensification of developmental effort, or should government proceed to act directly on its own? Most underdeveloped countries have economies that are basically free enterprise, a feature bearing historical sanction. However, when contemplating a program of accelerated development, many of the countries are quick to conclude that substantial activity must fall to government directly, and that private enterprise, whatever its scope in the past, cannot be depended upon to assume primary responsibility.

From a physical standpoint, whatever production is possible under direct government auspices is also possible under private enterprise, and vice versa. Resource requirements for identical operations are the same, and the same "laws of economics" apply to the production and distribution processes themselves. Important differences exist, however, in methods of organization, in particular procedures as regards production and product-disposal, and in approaches to decision-making.

Each country has to decide for itself whether it wishes to de-emphasize government's role in favor of fuller reliance upon private initiative, or whether it wishes to de-emphasize reliance upon private enterprise in favor of direct action by government. In the course of arriving at this decision, a number of major considerations have special relevance. Those who are favorable to "more government," for example, have three main points of argument upon which to base their case. First, "government can do it better." Second, "private enterprise won't do it, so government has

---

[11] External assistance in increased volume proved forthcoming, particularly from the US and the USSR, following the revelation of the country's inability to carry out its projected developmental program on its own. In essence, the foreign-exchange dilemma was resolved, or partially resolved, through the combination of some added capital accessibility and some downward readjustments in the Plan itself.

got to do it." Third, "government can pave the way for private enterprise."

As for the argument that "government can do it better," it must be
recognized, at the outset, that some functions are properly those of government under any circumstances. Even the most staunch advocates of
laissez-faire, including no less than Adam Smith in his time, recognize
that some activities of necessity fall to government to deal with through
collective action—in preference to being left to the private sector, where
action in their case is likely to prove either impossible or improbable.
Little difference of opinion exists on the principle of this matter, but
wide differences of opinion exist as to the precise dividing line between
that which "properly" is in government's sphere of action and that
which "ought" to be left to the private sector.

Those who envisage government in an expanded role are inclined to
argue that certainty of action is a merit that can be claimed for government. When near-stagnation has long characterized an economy, the
possibility of positive and pronounced growth acquires special attractiveness, and forcefulness in the implementation process may well appear
to be a good way to assure the economy of the growth desired. If a
government is truly sovereign and is sufficiently entrenched and sufficiently powerful to enforce its decisions, it can literally inventory the
means currently at the economy's disposal, decide as to the extent to
which consumption can be restrained, and then plough back into the
economy as investment that surplus which has been squeezed out (with
this investment, in turn, being particularized in an attempt to promote
maximum progress toward planned objectives). What happens in an
economy is then the result of deliberate government decisions, made
according to plan, not the chance result stemming from a composite of
independent decisions by many people, motivated by diverse factors.
The classic case of "forced" development of the foregoing type involves
that of the USSR. The procedure has potential merit in that it tends to
make more rapid economic growth possible than otherwise likely; however, the very force that is involved tends to narrow the area of choice
remaining for individuals.

In addition to certainty of action, comprehensive decision-making
powers resting in the hands of government can lead to greater coordination among the various activities that comprise the totality of a developmental effort. The point is that when decision-making is centralized, a
similarity in intent and direction tends to characterize the various decisions made. This is in contrast to the situation that can be expected
under private-enterprise conditions, where decisions are made independently by numerous persons, resulting in a maze of decisions that may, or
may not, dovetail into a consistent whole.

Further, emphasis upon direct government action has merit in that access to resources generally, and to financial resources in particular, is ordinarily had on more favorable terms by government than by individual members of a private-enterprise community. The fact that both the fiscal budget and the foreign-exchange budget (under exchange control) are under the direct jurisdiction of government serves to give government an obvious advantage. A private entrepreneur typically needs to borrow national currency, with government sometimes being the lender, and—assuming exchange control—he is obliged to apply to government for access to foreign exchange. In contrast, a government can avail itself of national currency through taxation or debt monetization, both of which avenues can provide funds for it on an interest-free basis, and the foreign exchange available to an economy is directly in government's custody under exchange control. To a great extent, government has at its disposal the resources available in the first place, and it does not have to say "please" to others as a condition of getting these resources. And, whenever borrowing from the public or from external sources does become necessary, the borrowing power of government generally, but not always, exceeds that of a typical private entrepreneur. Since government's position as regards financing is advantageous, its position in terms of access to physical resources tends also to be advantageous—in the sense that, given sufficient financial means, most other things prove readily purchasable.

Finally, advocates of direct government action sometimes assert that government is obliged to undertake certain operations because absence of managerial talent of adequate caliber within the private sector rules out the operations there. However, as intimated in a previous connection,[12] an assertion along these lines cannot be supported with sound argument. If it is true that managerial talent is lacking in the private sector, and if the needed managerial talent does exist among government personnel, does not the possibility then exist for government to free-up this talent so that it can be utilized in the private sector? Or, is the case one of a general lack of managerial talent, leading to inefficient operation *throughout* the economy, but with this inefficiency showing up in the private sector where profit-and-loss tests have to be met, even while obscured in the public sector where similar profit-and-loss tests do not apply? Managerial ability of adequate caliber either exists in an economy, or it does not. If it does not exist, it is not available to *either* the private sector or the public sector. If it does exist, it is potentially available to either; and it can be channeled to either, depending upon the overall decisions made as to where given activity is to occur, in the public sector or in the private sector.

---

12 See again Ch. 3, the section on "Inadequacies in Entrepreneurship and Management."

The foregoing summarizes the central case made by those who hold that public-sector emphasis must characterize developmental effort because "government can do it better" than can the private sector. In opposition, two leading arguments can be advanced. First, there is a tendency for less efficiency to prevail in public-sector operations than in comparable operations undertaken in the private sector. While plenty of examples can be found that reflect both efficient and inefficient operation as regards the public sector and the private sector, the counter-argument is that the private sector has forces operative in it which tend, generally, to promote greater efficiency than ordinarily attainable in the public sector. The main force which operates toward this end is that of profit. A given private enterprise must show a profit if it is to continue in operation over time, but a government can ignore profit considerations if it so chooses, or it can so generalize the avowed purposes of its operations that a "true" price or profit is difficult, if not impossible, to determine. Points of vulnerability in government operations that invite inefficiency are frequently cited. All connected personnel is salaried, and returns to individuals do not vary directly with profits or losses;[13] hence, incentive for efficiency is allegedly lessened. Also, "padding the payroll" is a favorite pastime within some governments, with some underdeveloped countries being particularly easy victims in this connection; examples can readily be found in underdeveloped countries in which a government-operated factory lists, say, over 50% of its employees as administrative staff, while a roughly comparable factory in the private sector—frequently, indeed, a competitive factory— similarly lists only, say, 20% of its employees.

Second, there is a tendency for public-sector operations to branch out into the "monuments" variety of projects. Since public-sector projects normally are divorced from compliance with rigid price-and-profit tests, and since decision-making at governmental levels can readily be influenced by political considerations, it is not surprising to find projects arising and continuing that cannot be justified on standard economic grounds. However, it needs to be recognized that some projects, even when not justifiable on standard economic grounds, can nevertheless serve a useful purpose in the course of development—for example, if they capture the public fancy and thereby feed the spirit that helps carry forward a development program.

The argument that "private enterprise won't do it, so government has got to do it" has three main sources of strength. First, many projects in the area of basic development are not suitable for private enterprise, since they do not yield marketable goods and services, and hence do not

---

[13] For example, there is no direct dependence upon entrepreneurial profits or dividends, as in the case of at least some private-sector operations.

yield a profit, let alone enable capital-recovery. These tend automatically to fall to government. Other projects in basic development, including some forms of enterprise classed as public utilities, do give rise to market-able end-items; yet, if private enterprise for one reason or another lags in its entry into these projects, and the requirements of basic develop-ment—and of economic development generally—clearly endorse their support, government may well have little choice but to undertake the necessary investment on its own. The fact that government enters these operations, however, does not mean that government must necessarily continue in them indefinitely. The possibility of eventual sale to private owner-operators exists, although the terms of sale admittedly serve to raise practical problems.

Second, when risks are high (e.g., as when political instability exists as a consequence of threats of subversion from within or attack from without), private enterprise may choose not to act, irrespective of what-ever virtues might be cited on behalf of potential investment and activity. In contrast, a sovereign government, because it has an overall responsi-bility to the population as a whole,[14] has a rationale for action available to it which it can invoke at its convenience—e.g., as when desired activity proves not to be forthcoming from the private sector, and perhaps can-not be expected from it. Under circumstances readily imaginable, a strong case can be made for government action within the framework of this rationale. A potential difficulty, however, is that the basic rationale can easily be misconstrued, thereby serving as an opening wedge for abuse. The acid test tends to occur once a given crisis situation has passed; if government then voluntarily attempts to curb its direct efforts, it is difficult to contend that abuse has occurred.

Third, when profit expectations—in profit-motivated types of enterprise —are inadequate for encouraging investment by private enterprise, gov-ernment might step into the breach. Government can proceed, if it wishes, even in the absence of profit; indeed, no one seriously contends that government should regard profit as the sole guide for its activities. Nevertheless, one might still raise a question as to *why* profit expectations can be "too low" to bring forth activity within the private sector. A general argument rooted in classical economics holds that the presence of a profit level "too low" to bring forth profit-motivated investment constitutes evidence of inadvisability for the investment; or, conversely, if an investment is economically "warranted," profit return will be at a level sufficiently high to evoke the investment. According to this line of reasoning, government investment—regarded here as occurring because private investment fails to respond—can only reflect misallocation of in-

---

14 This responsibility can be construed to include the fending off of collapse of the government itself.

vestment effort, or subsidization of low-profit investment, or both. However, a possible situation in underdeveloped countries is that private individuals initiate capital flights, even in instances in which prospective returns abroad are lower than those possible at home,[15] or simply fail to save voluntarily in anticipation of investment. Since a sovereign government has an overall responsibility for the population as a whole, it may choose to invest on its own either in order to compensate for the capital flights the private sector engages in (reflective of the private sector's unwillingness to invest domestically) or to set in motion a forced-saving process (as a consequence of a low volume of voluntary saving and investment by the private sector). It can be contended, of course, that whenever tests related to profit are abandoned, the possibility of abuse readily creeps in; however, it should also be recognized that if the alternative is no or only very little investment, a case automatically comes into existence for the assumption of offsetting activity by government.

The argument that "government can pave the way for private enterprise" also has something to be said for it. Considerable governmental activity in the area of basic development, for example, falls within this category. Indeed, few people would be inclined to doubt the necessary role of government in the creation of the facilities of basic development, or the need for these facilities as an element of support for other development. Beyond basic development, however, a case can be made for governmental action to introduce "pilot projects." Whenever private entrepreneurs are fearful of launching into new and previously untried fields of activity, governmental action to establish a sample enterprise has the potential merit of fostering familiarization of would-be entrepreneurs with untapped opportunities and the processes involved in their exploitation. Some of the operations undertaken by development corporations are in this category, e.g., as in the case of several *fomentos* in Latin America. Once private enterprise shows a willingness and an ability to enter the field, government can decide whether or not it wishes to discontinue its own direct production efforts. In practice, some governments appear reluctant to withdraw from direct operations, even though activity was avowedly launched on a pilot-project basis. The rationale for continued operation by government is generally either that current production by the private sector is insufficiently great (so that supplementary production by government continues to be needed), or that governmental activity is needed to set standards for the private sector (this form of regulation being justified, assertedly, in the absence of effective alternate control procedures).

As the foregoing series of arguments reflects, government's "proper"

---

[15] This situation is in contrast to the classical position as regards movement of capital to points of greatest potential return.

role relative to an economy's productive effort is basically a matter of the particular circumstances that prevail and of the standards that are applied in the course of appraising these circumstances. Those who would minimize government's role as a direct producer typically assume, or believe, that expanded activity *can* occur in the private sector—indeed, that it can occur to better advantage in the absence of government's full-fledged entry into production. Ordinarily, these persons view the role of government primarily in terms of responsibility for creating an environment conducive to expanded activity within the private sector. If government creates the appropriate framework, the private sector is likely to respond with the actual productive effort, or so it is argued. Essential ingredients of the desired environment are generally believed to include the provision of adequate financing, the minimization of restrictive regulations, and the relative absence of government competition.

THE CASES OF INDIA AND CHINA

The matter of whether "more government" or "less government" is more likely to promote developmental progress holds important implications for the present-day world, both for underdeveloped countries and for developed countries. At root, the matter poses a major issue in the ideological struggle between the "isms." Indeed, the issue and the stakes involved can be illustrated by referring to the development plans and achievements of India and Communist China.[16]

India has an essentially private-enterprise economy. There is some evidence that the country's traditional devotion to private enterprise has weakened somewhat in the course of the new resort to centralized planning during recent years; nevertheless, the country's Plans continue to place heavy reliance upon income generation within the private sector, and upon new investment by the private sector—but all subject to somewhat greater control by government than known in pre-Plan days. As matters stand, under 10% of current GNP derives from the public sector (as compared with roughly 20% in the US)—with the expectation present, however, that the proportion of GNP originating in the public sector will rise at least moderately during future years (particularly in view of a shift toward greater governmental sponsorship of new investment).[17] While the picture thus is a "mixed" one (with a "socialist trend" in evidence), it appears not amiss—considering the extent of reliance upon

---

[16] For interesting views and informative documentation on this subject, see W. Malenbaum, "India and China: Contrasts in Development Performance," *American Economic Review,* June 1959.

[17] It can be argued, of course, that the sector-origin of GNP does not, *by itself,* provide a good test for determining the presence or absence of private enterprise (or of socialism). An important additional factor that merits consideration is the *extent of control* exercised by government over the private sector.

private enterprise—to regard India as having *essentially* a private-enterprise economy. Within this environment, developmental achievements under the First and Second Five-Year Plans appear to have been positive, but moderate. Significantly, the efforts undertaken to achieve even the moderate gains recorded encountered extraordinary difficulties—as evidenced, for example, by the country's balance-of-payments crisis of 1957–58.

Communist China, with a totalitarian-type government in power, has a closely controlled economy, one patterned substantially after the "model" of the USSR. Under its Plan, current income is being allocated so as to assure a plough-back as investment of a comparatively high percentage of GNP, while the rate of growth in income itself appears to be quite high. The likely result during the foreseeable future, given the forceful means being employed, appears to be one of continuing rapid growth.

India and China are the two most populous countries in the world. Each is referred to, from a historical standpoint, as a "sleeping giant." Each is cited by various persons as holding "the key to Asia." And now, at mid-century, a development *"race"* is in progress. In India, private enterprise continues to be relied upon, and continues to have official sanction; in China, the private-enterprise approach no longer remains in good standing. The "final score" in the "contest" obviously is to be an important one.[18]

SELECTED BIBLIOGRAPHY

See the end of Chapter 11.

---

[18] Some staunch advocates of the free-enterprise system, Americans as well as persons of other nationality, are inclined to decry the socialist trend held evident in India. Other persons, regarding themselves as equally devoted to the free-enterprise system, are inclined to believe that any censure of Indian policy should be tempered in the light of what is occurring outside India, e.g., in Communist China. Their view is that the development "race" between the two countries raises a fundamental issue that holds deep implications for US foreign economic policy (and for US policy generally). Specifically, the point is sometimes made that the US, despite its inclination to resist any marked deviation from the course of free enterprise anywhere, might nevertheless find it to its own advantage to provide augmented aid in support of a "semi-socialist" India—on the grounds that the *total* global situation conspires to make this course the one of lesser evil (as seen by the US).

11

POLICIES FOR DEVELOPMENT (II)

Once developmental policy is settled upon in broad outline (involving decisions as to the *direction* of development, the point or points of *emphasis* in development, and the source of *responsibility* for action), several subsidiary matters merit attention in the course of rounding out the policy framework. The present chapter treats some of the more important of these additional matters.

MARKET CONDITIONS: FREE OR CONTROLLED?

Should an underdeveloped country, as it contemplates development, seek to adhere to a system of free markets, or should it deliberately resort to market control? A decision on this matter is needed; indeed, the decision is very pertinent in the wake of a previous decision by a country to place primary reliance for economic activity upon the private sector.

The central argument for strict adherence to a free market is that resources then tend to be allocated in a manner likely to promote maximum efficiency and effectiveness, resulting in higher real income than otherwise possible. According to the argument, market control can only invite resource misallocation, and hence prove harmful to real income.

Many persons, including numerous economists, do not agree that strict adherence to a free-market system necessarily assures the best possible economic results. Doubt in this respect is expressed especially in the case of underdeveloped countries. Specifically, four main arguments commonly come to be advanced in support of deviation from a free-market system by underdeveloped countries. According to a first argument, free-market forces tend to preserve the status-quo in the production patterns of underdeveloped countries; yet, a common desire in underdeveloped countries is to promote change in the production patterns—indeed, hope for long-run improvement is frequently deemed dependent upon successful promotion of structural change. The crux of the matter is that a free-market system supplies a built-in rationale for international specialization along the lines of the law of comparative advantage (Ch. 8); however, once production patterns are attuned to the dictates of the law of comparative advantage, continued reliance upon free-market forces serves to reinforce production along the lines currently in effect,[1] and to operate against the evolution of some other pattern of production that, while different, might well prove economic—and, indeed, more hopeful as to potential real income. Thus, a case is made for deviation from a free-market system in order that a transition can occur from the status-quo to a new and potentially better pattern of production.[2]

According to a second argument, compliance with the dictates of free-market forces ideally calls for all parties concerned to be equals; but, it is obvious that not all countries are at the same stage of development or maturity, nor do they all possess similar bargaining strength. Compliance with the dictates of free-market forces in the realm of international trade requires allegiance to the law of comparative advantage, which carries with it the assumption that trading partners automatically derive mutual benefit. Actually, however, the situation is more complex than that blandly assumed to exist when analysis proceeds in terms of Country A, unnamed, trading with Country B, also unnamed. It is pertinent to know whether A and B represent, say, two industrial countries of roughly similar status, or whether they represent instead a large industrial country and a small raw-materials-producing country.[3] After all, if it is true that free-market trading conditions serve, over time, to disadvantage a raw-materials-producing country in its dealings with an industrial country (Ch. 8), a decision by a raw-materials-producing country to adhere to a free market is tantamount to the placement of its

---

[1] According to the argument, this effect is especially likely because the merit of any new enterprise comes to be appraised, in practice (under free-market conditions), in terms of a comparison between per-unit costs applicable to *specific* directly-competitive enterprises located among two or more countries. See again Ch. 8 for treatment of the matter of absolute cost versus comparative cost.

[2] Intervention in markets can take various forms, the main means being exchange control and tariff restriction.

[3] The importance of differing stages of development is clearly recognized in the infant-industry argument, a rationale developed during the nineteenth century for reliance upon tariff protection by lesser-developed countries. To insist, unqualifiedly, that free-market forces yield best results is tantamount to the rejection of possible merit in the infant-industry argument.

sanction upon receipt of a dwindling share in the international "split of benefits."

According to a third argument, the conclusion that free-market forces help assure a superior allocation of resources, and hence help yield higher real income than otherwise possible, is reached following the tacit assumption that full employment tends to prevail; but, full employment is not characteristic of underdeveloped countries (Ch. 1). Classical econo- mists traditionally hold that a free market serves to allocate resources at the margin in accordance with economic tests as to where productivity is greatest, the assumption all the while being that *all* resources will normally be utilized. A contrary notion is that full employment does not represent the normal situation; and, when underemployment is wide- spread, as is held to be common in the underdeveloped world, the main consideration is not viewed as one of allocation of scarce resources among alternate uses, but as one of *how to activate idle resources in the first place*.[4] The question arises, of course, as to why it is that some resources seem not to get activated. In the final analysis, an answer to this question must be framed either in terms of an inherent inability of free-market forces to assure full employment, or in terms of the presence of factors (including non-economic factors) that preclude effective operation of free- market forces. Whatever the case may be, it suffices to note here that the common situation among underdeveloped countries *is* one of under- employment. Given this situation, maximization of income comes really to be dependent upon development, which calls for a whole new tempo in productive activity, not just somewhat minor shifts among alternate uses at the margin in response to the dictates of free-market forces.

Finally, according to a fourth argument, it is unreasonable to expect underdeveloped countries to try to comply with the dictates of free- market forces when developed countries are unwilling to do so. Rightly or wrongly, developed countries do tamper with their production and price structures, and it is difficult to imagine a world in which they would not do so to a greater or lesser extent. Given this bit of reality, it appears inconsistent to advocate that underdeveloped countries follow another set of "economic morals." In fact, a free-market situation, pure and simple, may not even be possible for underdeveloped countries as long as developed countries, on their part, insist upon market inter- vention and thereby warp the international trading structure.

Actually, presentation of the issue as that of free markets versus con- trolled markets is largely academic. Rather than being capable of resolu-

---

4 The late Lord Keynes was instrumental in pointing out weaknesses inherent in a full-employment assumption. However, he concerned himself directly only with advanced industrial societies. Application to underdeveloped countries of the principles set forth by him remained a task for others. For a statement of the Keynesian position as initially set forth, see J. M. Keynes, *The General Theory of Employment, Interest and Money* (New York: Harcourt, Brace and Company, Inc., 1936), esp. Ch. 2.

tion in an absolute sense, one way or the other, the issue, in practice, comes to be posed more aptly in terms of the *degree* of control to be exercised. Resolution thereupon commonly occurs in terms of an admission of *some* control, handled on a *selective* basis in accordance with particular circumstances.

THE CASE OF EXCHANGE CONTROL

Market intervention takes many possible forms, including direct price fixing, subsidization of producers, tariff protection, and exchange control. Among the various possibilities, exchange control probably looms as *the* most important for the underdeveloped world during the post-World War II period. Accordingly, some attention to the pros and cons of exchange control appears pertinent as one surveys the general issue of free markets versus control.

Exchange control is a system designed to cover the mobilization and rationing of scarce foreign exchange. Under it, the foreign exchange accruing to an economy is turned over to a designated governmental authority, ordinarily the country's Central Bank, after which allocations from this accumulated supply are made in accordance with regulations and criteria established to govern operations. In short, intervention occurs on both the demand and supply sides of the foreign-exchange market. Importantly, because the exchange-control authority is a monopolist-monopsonist, or a near monopolist-monopsonist, it is automatically able to *influence* the types and directions of economic activity. In part, influence upon economic activity stems from the exercise of quantitative controls, as a consequence of which not all persons who desire foreign exchange are given access; in part, also, influence upon economic activity stems from the exercise of price controls, as a consequence of which the buying and selling rates for foreign exchange are fixed and thereby affect the movement of foreign exchange—quite aside from whatever direction is lent through quantitative controls.

The technique of exchange control first came into wide usage during the Great Depression. Exchange control continued to spread throughout the second half of the Thirties; indeed, considerable inter-country rivalry in foreign-exchange pricing arose during this period as individual countries sought to gain temporary competitive advantage. During World War II, exchange control was continued, and even extended, as a necessary wartime control device. However, many persons, and some governments, were never happy with the foreign-exchange practices that had arisen and persisted. Accordingly, much thought was given during the course of World War II as to what measures were needed to preclude a repetition during the postwar years of practices characteristic of the Thirties. Following the release of proposals and counterproposals, an international conference was held in 1944, the Bretton Woods Conference, attended by representatives of most Allied powers. A result of the Conference was the creation of the International Monetary Fund (IMF), an international body intended to concern itself with exchange-rate matters.

The crucial role of the IMF, according to its proponents, was to facilitate the transition to a new long-run period during which relative freedom in foreign-exchange markets might once again prevail in the world. Retention of exchange control during the immediate postwar years, when balance-of-payments difficulties were likely to be many and serious, was regarded as something to be expected, and even necessary; but, upon the restoration of "normalcy" in the world, exchange control was to be shed. The transition to a normal world was initially believed to require five years at the outside. Therefore, provision was made that following an introductory grace period, extending through 1951, the IMF would proceed each year to require explanations of those member countries still retaining controls.[5] But all this notwithstanding, exchange control continued. Despite periodic talk of convertibility being "just around the corner"—fairly common especially in some American business circles—progress in the shedding of controls was slow at best.

Numerous explanations have been offered as to why the IMF was unable to bring about a world free of direct exchange restrictions. Among these, two lines of explanation have stood out. First, the normal world necessary for freedom in exchange markets did not materialize as initially anticipated. Second, the IMF was not well set up organizationally to bring about the relinquishment of controls. The IMF was set up to cope with foreign-exchange difficulties in *particular countries,* occurring *on occasion,* but the foreign-exchange difficulties of the postwar world were both *general* and *persistent.* In retrospect, the IMF's initial resource-endowment was simply inadequate to permit the once-and-for-all "bail-out" operation that, if put into effect, might have succeeded in lifting more than half a world to convertibility-status.

Be this as it may, it is important that the IMF approach assumed exchange control to be undesirable, and as something a country should want to shed. Significantly, however, not every country having exchange control wants to shed it. In fact, a good economic case can be made as to why some countries, under some conditions, should want to retain, and strengthen, their exchange-control systems. The point is that the IMF simply assumed all countries to be "in the same boat" (in the sense that the early relinquishment of exchange control would contribute to the self-interest of each), when actually wide differences prevail among countries, economically-speaking. The existence of wide differences among countries, and the importance of these differences for the issue of ex-

---

[5] Consultations are called for under terms of the Articles of Agreement, Art. XIV, Sec. 4. Summary reports are published annually by the IMF under the title, *Annual Report on Exchange Restrictions.*

change control, can be illustrated with reference to the situation prevailing during the post-World War II period through 1957. During this period, three major and distinct categories of countries were discernible within the Free World alone. First, the US required no exchange control, since the dollar was, relatively, *the* scarce currency in the world[6] (thereby providing the central rationale for exchange control in some other countries).[7] Second, Western Europe, as a unit, experienced a dollar shortage of varying degrees of severity, whereupon exchange control readily came to be looked upon as a *protective* device (i.e., protective, in each instance, of a balance-of-payments structure). Third, many underdeveloped countries found themselves normally short of dollars and of some other major currencies,[8] and found this shortage a handicap in their developmental efforts; in these countries, exchange control readily came to be looked upon as a *developmental* device. Beginning with 1958, the dollar shortage vanished for Europe, as significantly also did exchange control (on current account).[9] However, for many countries of the underdeveloped world (e.g., most countries other than several petroleum-rich countries), foreign-exchange shortages remained a fact of life, and exchange control was also widely continued.

Thus, numerous underdeveloped countries have exchange-control systems.[10] Adherents employ various rationales to justify continued reliance upon the systems—just as various rationales were employed at the time the systems were instituted. Of course, it is probably true, as some persons are inclined to claim, that exchange control, however formally rationalized, serves no good purpose in some underdeveloped countries, considering the slipshod manner in which these countries choose to employ it.[11] Nevertheless, even if it is possible to cite instances in which exchange control has served no good purpose, a solid case—based on economic

---

[6] Canada, not classified separately here, is probably to be included in this category also.

[7] It is understandable, perhaps, why Americans have frequently looked askance at exchange control, considering that the US has not needed exchange control for itself but has found an obstruction to its exports in foreign-imposed exchange-control measures.

[8] British pounds sterling and Deutsche marks, to cite but two.

[9] According to one line of argument, the dollar shortage in Western Europe is of long standing (dating at least from World War I) and arose and persisted because of the area's long-run economic deterioration, relative to the rest-of-the-world. On this basis, a conceivable follow-up argument is that the recurrence of a dollar shortage at some future point is not to be ruled out. For interesting observations and analysis on the general subject of Europe's dollar shortage, see S. E. Harris, *International and Interregional Economics* (New York: The McGraw-Hill Book Company, Inc., 1957), Parts IV and V, esp. Ch. 20.

[10] For a listing of countries having exchange-control regulations on imports originating in the US, see Department of Commerce, *Foreign Commerce Weekly*, Washington, May 25, 1959, pp. 8–11. The information is as of May 1, 1959.

[11] Low-caliber administration is fairly common. Quite apart from the extent of honesty in administration, it is not always evident that administrators bear a central objective in mind as a guide to action.

grounds—can be made as to the potential merit of exchange control for the underdeveloped world.

The basic case for exchange control in underdeveloped countries rests on the aid derivable from it in support of a developmental effort. This potential aid has two main facets. First, reliance upon exchange control permits scarce supplies of foreign exchange to be channeled into those specific uses held likely to yield high developmental impact. The exchange-control authority can formulate a schedule itemizing various major categories of potential demand for foreign exchange, these categories being listed in the order of their likely contribution to a developmental effort; thereafter, allocations from scarce supplies of foreign exchange can be made in accordance with this scale of priority. For example, access to foreign exchange can be denied those wishing to finance capital flights, and the same foreign exchange can be held available for prospective entrepreneurs wishing to import, say, industrial machinery for new productive enterprises. Again, reliance upon free-market forces in the allocation of foreign exchange might result in the endorsement of nothing but consumer-goods imports, whereas a resort to exchange control permits consumer-goods imports to be curbed arbitrarily, so that some foreign exchange becomes available for capital-goods imports (which can then occur, even though a free foreign-exchange market would not have supported them).[12] To generalize, the availability of foreign exchange for certain purposes, along with its unavailability for other purposes, serves to favor certain activities over others. In turn, the forms of activity favored by exchange control, as they get underway, tend to draw additional resources toward them (e.g., manpower and raw materials), thereby leading to a gradual reshaping of the economy. Since a particular reshaping of the economy is frequently fundamental to a successful developmental effort, the potential aid to be had from exchange control in the course of development readily appears evident.

Second, reliance upon exchange control allows subsidization to occur for desired types of activity, and thereby has a potential for accelerating

---

[12] The US Government traditionally espouses the cause of multilateralism. Since exchange control comprises an impediment to multilateralism, the US is forced into a stand of opposition to exchange control, or of somewhat reluctant toleration of it. However, the US also offers economic aid to underdeveloped countries in order to assist them in their developmental efforts. The amount of external assistance needed by underdeveloped countries varies, in part, with the caliber of utilization by the recipient countries of their own available resources. Technically, exchange control can help to upgrade utilization of available foreign-exchange resources. Therefore, some persons are inclined to argue that exchange control—in fact, improved and strengthened exchange control—should be endorsed by the US as an appropriate policy for underdeveloped countries. Allegedly, the combination of the countries' own foreign-exchange resources plus whatever external assistance is provided can then serve to yield a total developmental-impact greater than otherwise likely or possible; or, alternatively, an upgrading in foreign-exchange utilization in underdeveloped countries can serve to reduce the requirements upon the US in the provision of external assistance.

development or giving it particular direction. Subsidization occurs in that those able to qualify for foreign exchange can be given access at an official rate of exchange, which rate can be arbitrarily fixed somewhat below what would prevail in a free market, thereby making imports less costly in terms of domestic currency. To illustrate, assume a country having an official (controlled) rate of exchange of ₱ 2 = $1, but with a likely free-market rate of ₱ 3 = $1. Machinery imports priced at $100,000 in, say, the US then cost a prospective entrepreneur ₱ 200,000 under terms of the controlled rate of exchange, not ₱ 300,000 as would be the case under the free-market situation assumed likely. The lesser cost to the investor tends to promote investment not otherwise likely, or not otherwise even possible (under particular cost-price relationships). Of course, exporters obtaining, say, $100,000 from sales abroad are able to convert and receive only ₱ 200,000 under the circumstances cited, not ₱ 300,000 as might have been possible under a free-market situation. Thus, the effect of exchange control is to *subsidize* individual importers and to *penalize* individual exporters (whenever the official rate of exchange overvalues the domestic currency).[13] The precise extent of the subsidization, or penalization, that comes to exist on this basis depends upon the disparity between controlled and free rates of exchange. Significantly, in some underdeveloped countries having exchange control, the disparity at issue is substantial.

In addition to the foregoing type of subsidization, the investor can be made the beneficiary of some follow-up subsidization. Assume a newly-established enterprise in the foreign-exchange-saving category. As the enterprise begins to pour end-products onto the domestic market, exchange control can be used to exclude competitive imports (in the sense that access to the foreign exchange needed to pay for competitive imports is denied prospective importers). A domestic market for the domestically-produced output tends thereby to be assured. In essence, then, exchange control subsidizes particular investment directly (by making importation of component elements less costly), and indirectly (by assuring a guaranteed market for the resulting output).

---

[13] It should not be assumed that exchange control merely supports a redistribution from exporters to importers. Importantly, the total of foreign-exchange earnings is also at issue. If conditions of inelastic supply, inelastic demand, or both, prevail as regards export products, a country's foreign-exchange earnings tend not to suffer even though individual exporters or export-producers are penalized in having to bear the cost of conversion at a disadvantageous (to them) official rate of exchange. However, conditions of elastic supply, elastic demand, or both, make production, sales, and foreign-exchange receipts closely dependent upon the extent of penalty imposed by forced conversion at an official rate of exchange that overvalues the domestic currency. In order to avoid loss in foreign sales volume, with accompanying declines in domestic production and in foreign-exchange receipts, systems of multiple rates of exchange are frequently evolved. A country's buying rates as to foreign exchange can then be tailored to support existing or expanded exportation of all or particular commodities, notwithstanding continued preferential treatment accorded select imports.

To conclude, the basic case for exchange control in underdeveloped countries rests on the aid derivable from it in support of a developmental effort. But, if exchange control is to serve as a major instrument in the promotion of development, it is inappropriate to think in terms of shedding control at an early date, or of weakening it bit by bit through the process of gradual decontrol. Rather, since development pertains to a process occurring over considerable time, exchange control—as a reinforcing technique—needs to be thought of on a long-range basis. Ideally, the technique of exchange control needs to be refined and strengthened, with the discontinuation of control occurring only at that later date when sought-after development is a *fait accompli*.

If exchange control is to be considered for retention for a considerable period, replies are necessary to those who lash out at the technique with two well-chosen lines of criticism. The first criticism is that exchange control leads to distortions in the economy. The answer to this criticism—if one supports exchange control—must show that exercise of control does tend to create distortions, but that these distortions are not necessarily bad. When official rates of exchange differ from free-market rates, import and export prices are affected, as are other prices through them;[14] in turn, modifications in the domestic price structure lead to modifications in production itself. Significantly, what looks like "harmful distortion" to some persons represents "needed change" for others. If change in the production pattern is to be assured and to occur rapidly, deliberate and forceful measures—which invite distortions (i.e., deviations from the previous normal course of things)—may well be absolutely necessary. Indeed, it is difficult to imagine marked movement from a status-quo situation without distortions arising in the process.

The second criticism is that exchange control invites abuse, e.g., corruption in administration. The answer to this criticism—if one supports exchange control—must show that the exercise of control may well reflect flaws in some instances, but is *nevertheless* worthy of retention. As intimated earlier, clear-cut cases of slipshod administration of exchange control can doubtless be cited in considerable number; however, granted that poor administration is fairly common, it does not make good sense to argue for complete rejection of exchange control simply because it is not 100% perfect—not if exchange control has something substantive to offer. If exchange control has strength as a technique in the promotion of development, and if development is the objective, then the appropriate attitude toward exchange control might well involve an attempt to improve it (including its administration), rather than to discard it.

[14] Import and export prices are particularly likely to affect the general price level when internationally-traded items loom importantly within the domestic economy, a situation characteristic of many underdeveloped countries.

SOURCES OF FINANCING

The major portion of the financial cost of economic development ordinarily falls upon the subject country.[15] An important question exists, however, as to how much supplementary financing a country should attempt to obtain externally in support of its developmental efforts. Persons in developed countries usually like to assume that underdeveloped countries are eager to receive any and all external capital that proves available. These persons tend to be quite disturbed when, on occasion, they discover that serious doubts exist in particular underdeveloped countries as to the wisdom of even allowing entry to select blocks of capital. Presence of this situation serves to indicate that there is a con-side, along with any possible pro-side, to reliance upon supplementary external capital in developmental efforts.

Fundamentally, the extent to which an underdeveloped country comes to rely upon supplementary external capital rests on its degree of availability, as well as on the terms governing access to it. If external capital is not to be had under any circumstances, it follows that a developmental effort needs to be sustained by domestic means, if it is to proceed at all. Assuming, however, that access to external capital can be had under some circumstances, the matter of potential advantage versus potential disadvantage becomes relevant; indeed, if exchange control is in effect, the weighing of pros and cons, in deliberate fashion, comes to be much in order. In this vein, the outstanding advantage, potentially, of access to external capital is that a developmental effort can then be larger-scale than otherwise possible, or can be pursued in a more accelerated manner than otherwise possible, or can be pursued at given levels of intensity with less need for current sacrifice on the part of the populace. On the other hand, outstanding disadvantages, potentially, of reliance upon external capital are two-fold. First, future financial demands upon the economy are created thereby, in the sense that the use of external capital in domestic investment poses subsequent payments requirements. Second, control frequently follows investment—as conceivable, for example, when investment involves the entry of foreign-owned enterprises.

The basic alternative as regards dependence upon external capital can be illustrated through reference to the developmental histories of the US and the USSR. The US, during early phases of its development, was the recipient of substantial external capital (derived particularly from Great Britain, which had experienced its Industrial Revolution earlier). The capital inflows took the form largely of loans, not of direct operations established by foreign firms, and in large part paralleled a movement of

---

[15] Rare exceptions exist, in which the preponderance of financing is supplied from abroad. Israel is a case in point.

people from Europe who were bent on permanent settlement in new locales. The added capital served to support accelerated development, and to make this development possible without the occurrence of an absolute decline in consumption levels. Significantly, in the American experience, sustained development at a reasonably rapid pace and long-run increases in consumption levels were coexistent, a situation not probable in the absence of substantive capital inflows.

The USSR, on the other hand, underwent rapid development also, but did so almost entirely on the basis of its own domestic means. At the time of the Revolution in 1917, the USSR was a country of quite low real per-capita income, and only little removed from feudalism. The new regime regarded a rapid increase in productive capacity as absolutely essential in order to assure the survival of the new state (which the new leadership envisaged as standing essentially alone in a generally hostile world), and in order to set an example of performance likely later to win support in some foreign quarters for the new form of economic system (which was avowedly dedicated to Marxian economic principles). Accordingly, a series of actions was initiated, aimed at the central objective of increased productive capacity. Since external capital proved generally not available, perhaps because the world at large was actually not sympathetic to the new regime, the developmental effort had to be one that could be sustained on the basis of whatever domestic means could be mustered. Rapid development on this self-contained basis was bound to prove difficult, of course, considering that the starting point was one of low current production. The technique adopted by the USSR involved "planned development," involving implementation measures of a generally forceful order. Since output (income) was at low levels, growth at an accelerated rate became dependent upon the denial of considerable currently-possible consumption, with the surplus (savings) thus squeezed out leading then to an augmented plough-back (investment)—the total process hopefully giving rise over time to progressively greater productive capacity. The procedure in essence involved more production in the interests of more investment (not more consumption, generally speaking), followed by a rise in production and still greater investment. In a sense, the worker was called upon to forego the possibility of more consumption for himself in order that his grandchildren might someday have more. The record of the USSR, after some four decades of controlled development, attests to the potential effectiveness of stern measures as a means for bringing about rapid growth; but, as numerous persons have pointed out in reference to the experience of the USSR, some of the most effective measures in terms of economic results are the very ones most destructive of individual liberty.

The moral that can be drawn is that access to external capital, as a supplement to available domestic capital, can help ease the pangs of a developmental effort; however, in the absence of access to external capital, development is still possible, although the road is a rougher one. Of course, even if external capital can be had, the form and conditions on which it can be had vary widely, so that reliance upon this source in a developmental effort automatically appears stronger or weaker—depending upon the particular circumstances prevailing.

THE ROLE OF IMITATION

Underdeveloped countries, as they seek to promote development, need to recognize that the environment confronting them includes numerous countries that are further along in their development. On the one hand, follow-up development in underdeveloped countries is handicapped by the competition presented by producers already established in the more mature countries; however, on the other hand, new development tends to be aided as underdeveloped countries draw upon the experience of the more mature countries. Many of the costly pitfalls that are otherwise strewn in the path of developmental effort can be avoided by the follower who can study and profit from the trial-and-error experience of the innovator. Specifically, the methods and processes already proven successful elsewhere can be borrowed, while the methods and processes previously tried elsewhere and found wanting can be by-passed. Of course, the act of copying is certain to place a premium upon adaptation, but adaptation is likely to prove easier and less costly than outright experimentation starting from scratch.

Even though underdeveloped countries are favored by virtue of their ability to borrow and adapt the methods and processes evolved earlier in the more advanced countries, they still need to exercise good judgment in their selection of what is appropriate for borrowing and in their procedures regarding the adaptation of whatever is borrowed. Easy as it is to state in general terms that an underdeveloped country needs to know *when* and *what* to borrow, and *how* to adapt to the local scene that which is borrowed, it is less easy to lend concrete substance to the generalized notions involved. However, good examples can readily be cited that, by indirection, shed considerable light on what it is that a country should guard against in the course of imitating others.

PUERTO RICO AS A MODEL

Some persons regard Puerto Rico as a pilot project in the realm of economic development. These persons feel that planning leaders in underdeveloped countries ought to study the case of Puerto Rico with a view toward the application in their countries of the methods and approaches found meritorious in the Puerto Rican developmental program.[16]

Puerto Rico long was definitely in the underdeveloped category, and in some quarters had the dubious reputation of being "America's poorhouse." During and after World War II, however, an intensified effort was made to promote the island's development—an effort known as "Operation Bootstrap." The central objective of the effort was to attract new industry, so that more income and employment might be generated. Accordingly, two main measures were initiated in order to encourage the growth of industry. First, provision was made to use the Commonwealth's borrowing power to create liberal financing for new private enterprises, and to construct plant facilities for occupancy by new private enterprises (on a low-rent or rent-free basis, or for sale on easy payments). Second, provision was made under the Commonwealth's tax system for generous treatment of new enterprises. With the passage of a decade, Puerto Rico was able to point to a substantial number of new industrial enterprises, and to considerably greater income and employment. In the opinion of many observers, the improvement was to be attributed directly to the measures that had been initiated earlier.[17]

Those who visualize Puerto Rico as a pilot project typically assume that the economic gain realized there is the result, basically, of the particular measures initiated: liberal financing and tax concessions, offered on behalf of private enterprise. Thereupon they are inclined to conclude that all an underdeveloped country has to do to assure itself of equivalent developmental-impact is to give private enterprise "a break"—meaning, mainly, access to generous financing and lower taxes. In all fairness, it is possible that the basic actions in the Puerto Rican approach are the crucial stimulants that make for accelerated development. But does the Puerto Rican experience *prove* this to be the case?

There are those who feel that the developmental success of Puerto Rico really proves nothing more than that "Puerto Rico hit upon what is good for Puerto Rico." The plain fact is that Puerto Rico occupies a unique position in the world. Perhaps, therefore, reference to Puerto Rico as an example has little meaning for underdeveloped countries generally, since none of them occupies a similar position and thus, presumably, cannot hope to duplicate the experience.

---

16 Sentiment within particular quarters of the US Government is of this type. For example, numerous student-trainees from underdeveloped countries, brought to the US under the auspices of this country's foreign-aid program, are sent to Puerto Rico on inspection trips as part of their training programs. Also, occasional news releases reflect this view. For example, see the following items: "A Pilgrimage to Puerto Rico . . . Underdeveloped World Finds Out How It's Done," *Newsweek*, May 6, 1957, p. 14; "Puerto Rico Gain Called Example," *The New York Times*, April 13, 1958, p. 70-L.

17 For example, see "'Bootstrap' Plan Is Surging Ahead," *The New York Times*, March 25, 1957, p. 33-L.

The uniqueness of Puerto Rico arises from the fact that the area is part of the US—e.g., tourist advertisements read: "Puerto Rico, U.S.A." Thus, Puerto Rico is part of the US customs area. Products manufactured in Puerto Rico can enter the American market duty-free and in unlimited quantity.[18] This means that American firms are able to establish operations in Puerto Rico, availing themselves of the plentiful labor and other advantages there, but the products produced remain unobstructed as to entry into the big American market. This differs from the situation in underdeveloped countries generally; their goods cannot enter the American market without first crossing the hurdle posed by tariffs, quotas, and any other existing restrictions.

Further, while an American firm establishing operations in Puerto Rico remains within the US customs area, it removes itself from the US tax area. Puerto Rico enjoys a special tax status relative to continental US. An American firm in Puerto Rico is subject only to Commonwealth taxes—indeed, it is these that were lessened under Operation Bootstrap. This differs from the situation wherein an American firm establishes operations in another underdeveloped country, entirely outside US jurisdiction. Liability under US income-tax laws then continues, with deduction from the US liability permitted only insofar as "equivalent" tax payments are made to the government of the underdeveloped country in question.[19]

Thus, the effort of Puerto Rico is one that has relied heavily upon the attraction of American firms, and Puerto Rico has been able to offer some potent bait with which to lure them. In a sense, an American firm establishing operations in Puerto Rico is able to get "the best of two worlds": continuing access to the US market and escape from US taxes. This set of circumstances is unique to Puerto Rico. Since circumstances elsewhere are different, the example of Puerto Rico, while interesting, seems not particularly illuminating in terms of providing a model capable of duplication.

THE US AS A MODEL

The real per-capita income of the US is the world's highest, a fact in which the typical American takes considerable pride. But, given this fact as a starting point, numerous Americans are ever ready to exhort poor, underdeveloped countries in terms such as: "Do it as we do it, and you too will be well off." Indeed, numerous persons in underdeveloped countries find these exhortations convincing. A question exists, however, as to whether or not the basic content of the exhortations is reasonable, given the circumstances prevailing.

---

[18] Significantly, also, the distance factor is not great.
[19] With one major exception, cited in a subsequent connection.

Economics looms as basic in the formulation of public policy. Applied to the case at hand, it is important to recognize that the same general body of economics holds different implications for underdeveloped countries, on various scores, than it does for the US or for other developed countries. Because of this, the public policy appropriate for underdeveloped countries is not necessarily identical with that deemed advantageous in the US. To illustrate, assume a situation of less than full employment, both in the US and in a hypothetical underdeveloped country. In the US, presence of a situation of less than full employment implies that there has been slippage away from full employment. The capacity to secure full employment exists, but the economy has faltered temporarily. Under the circumstances, government can invoke the Keynesian technique of deficit financing (through monetization of debt); a net injection of new money, if sufficiently great, can go far to activate the manpower and other resources found idle at the moment. Full employment, or something reasonably near to it, thereby comes to be restored. In the final analysis, only inaction by government precludes rather prompt restoration of fuller activity, following a lapse in the tempo of activity.

In underdeveloped countries, in contrast, a situation of less than full employment is usual, i.e., underemployment is widespread and chronic. Given this situation, currently-usable productive capacity that is capable of absorbing idle manpower does not exist; rather, the central problem is one of not enough capacity *at any time*. Under the circumstances, the Keynesian technique of deficit financing (through monetization of debt) is bound to yield results different from those that might be expected in the American environment. A net injection of new money then serves to create more demand for basically the same amount of goods and services; consequently (as intimated in Ch. 10), the primary result is rising prices and pressure upon foreign-exchange reserves as added import demands arise, rather than more employment.

It follows, on the basis of the foregoing illustration, that what is good policy for a developed country may not necessarily be good policy for an underdeveloped country. Unfortunately, however, remedies appropriate solely for developed countries sometimes come to be prescribed, inappropriately, for the ills of underdeveloped countries. A major reason for this state of affairs appears readily identifiable. In some instances, in which the "practitioners" are nationals of developed countries, prescriptions come to be offered largely impervious of the locale; for example, reference is sometimes made to foreign technicians who proceed simply to prescribe that which would seem appropriate in their home countries. In other instances, in which the "practitioners" are nationals of the underdeveloped countries in question, prescriptions come to be offered on the basis of ideas circulating in alien environments; for example, economic planners commonly receive professional training in developed countries, as a consequence of which some of them come to have an essentially American or European outlook on economic matters, and thereafter give vent to this in the recommendations they offer in their home locales.

Obviously, the problem of how to assure an approach to economic issues that can provide answers likely to meet the needs of individual countries is an important one. As a minimum, it would appear that professional economists should have impressed upon them, in the course of their preparatory training, that prescriptions can be expected to differ because economies differ. Prebisch, commenting on this matter (relative to Latin America), writes as follows:[20]

> . . . Considerable progress has been made [in the training of local individuals as economists] by sending them to the great European and American universities, but this is *not sufficient*. One of the most conspicuous deficiencies of general economic theory, from the point of view of the periphery, is its *false sense of universality*. [The unique environments of countries on the periphery need to be] . . . explained rationally and with scientific objectivity; [only then] can effective proposals for practical action be achieved.

REGIONAL DEVELOPMENT

National boundaries currently in existence are basically the result of political decisions, not of decisions reached in terms of economics. Given these boundaries, ultra-nationalists typically conceive of economic activity—including economic activity associated with development—as being almost exclusively, and by choice, a self-contained effort within each political entity. Opposed to them are persons who would de-emphasize the importance of national frontiers as a factor in the promotion of economic activity. Persons in this second category visualize advantages through greater linkage, in an economic sense, of currently separate national entities. However, these persons ordinarily admit to the impracticality of arguing for any wholesale re-drawing of national boundaries along economically-sanctioned lines. Instead, they commonly urge that attention be directed toward various less-ambitious approaches in an attempt thereby to lessen the economic obstruction posed by national frontiers. Important in this connection is the goal of greater economic activity along regional lines.

With greater emphasis upon economic activity along regional lines posed as a possibility, the question arises as to whether, or to what extent, an underdeveloped country desirous of development should rely on this particular approach. Desirable as it might be, a simple, all-embracive answer in this connection is not easy to come by, in part because regional

---

20 UN, *The Economic Development of Latin America,* New York, 1950, p. 7f. (Italics are mine.)

effort can take several widely differing forms. Given this factor of diversity, examination and appraisal can best proceed in terms of the three major categories of possible regional effort: projects, trade, and payments.

PROJECTS

Some projects are possible, in a *physical* sense, only if undertaken on a regional basis, as among two or more countries, or become possible on a more efficient basis, in an *economic* sense, if undertaken regionally, rather than nationally. This situation is observable in three distinct types of cases.

First, some forms of basic development can be handled better on a regional basis than separately by each country involved. To illustrate, assume that a river crosses or borders on several countries. Development of hydroelectric, irrigation, and transport facilities can probably then occur to better advantage if all countries concerned act together than if individual countries are left to act independently—in which case one country might choose not to act at all, and thereby block or greatly inconvenience the other countries. Future development of the Mekong River Valley is a conceivable case in point.[21]

Second, distribution of natural resources among countries frequently makes resource-pooling physically necessary, or economically helpful, in the promotion of development. To illustrate, assume a case in which one country has iron ore but no coal, while an adjacent country has coal but no iron ore. A steel mill might be possible if the iron ore and coal could be linked. While trade makes this linkage technically possible, a formal arrangement might well prove necessary in order to bring about the actual pooling of resources and establishment of milling facilities. A conceivable case in point involves Philippine iron ore and Taiwan coal.

Third, potential domestic markets may be too small, in the absence of a regional approach to production and distribution, to permit an economically-workable scale of operations. To illustrate, assume again the previous case involving iron ore in one country and coal in another. Admittedly, trade then makes a linkage of resources possible, resulting in a joint steel enterprise; however, it is possible that each country, when left on its own, will seek instead to install its own steel mill, with the resultant scale of operations in either country perhaps incapable of yielding efficiency in output. Therefore, a formal arrangement for the pooling of resources and a unified support for a single enterprise between the countries may well be a necessary prelude to action along potentially efficient lines.

Arrival at agreement on organization is necessary in the establishment

---

21 The Mekong River, which has its headwaters in Communist China, crosses or borders on Thailand, Laos, Cambodia, and South Viet-Nam.

of regional projects. However, the requisite agreement is frequently difficult to reach, and this fact poses a fundamental obstacle to progress on regional projects. Major impediments to the reaching of agreements involve cost-sharing aspects and location factors. Countries generally tend to underestimate the amount of the cost of a joint undertaking that would reflect their legitimate share. And, whenever an end facility has to be located in its entirety in only one country (e.g., as in the case of a steel mill erected in one country, but designed to serve the needs of two countries), it is a rare country that relishes participation in an arrangement that makes another participant the physical beneficiary of the facility in question.

Serious as organizational difficulties tend to be, they can ordinarily be lessened by the intervention of some outside motivating force. An illustration of this is found in the experience with the Asian Economic Development Fund. This Fund, established in 1956 within the terms of the US foreign-aid program, was endowed with $300 million to use in the support of qualifying regional-development projects in Asia. The record under it was one of numerous proposals, with the proposals stemming both from individual countries and groups of countries—presumably in response, in important measure, to the lure of assistance in financing. The record offers tangible evidence that considerable interest in regional projects does exist, and that this interest tends to lead to action when attendant circumstances seem right.[22]

TRADE

In the area of trade, the typical situation currently found is one of little trade among underdeveloped countries situated within the same general region; instead, individual underdeveloped countries tend to trade largely with industrial countries, generally located at some distance. Some persons hold that underdeveloped countries within the same general region ought to do more trading among themselves. It is argued that if more trade occurred regionally, added gain from greater specialization might accrue to individual trading partners. Accordingly, it is frequently suggested that particular barriers applicable to trade among countries within the same general region be eliminated or lessened, so that greater intra-regional trade can result. Generally, a customs-union arrangement of some sort is proposed, the usual term applied being that of *common market*.

Why do underdeveloped countries within the same general region currently tend not to trade with one another? Basically, the answer is

---

[22] Few projects actually received financing through the Fund. The explanation appears to rest more particularly in aid-program red tape than in any physical shortage of good projects.

found in the type of production prevailing within a given region in which all countries are underdeveloped. Briefly, production within a region of this type tends to be competitive, not complementary. As non-diversified raw-materials producers, underdeveloped countries tend largely to place their exports in industrial countries, in which demand ordinarily exists for raw-materials commodities of the type being produced, and from where imports of manufactures and semi-manufactures not otherwise available at home can be obtained. Neighboring underdeveloped countries tend not to desire the above-mentioned exports because they are producers of substantially similar raw-materials commodities, and face the same general need to seek raw-materials markets and industrial-type supplies in industrial countries. In short, little economic complementarity typically prevails within a region comprised entirely of underdeveloped countries; and, to the extent that economic complementarity does not prevail, the basis for mutually advantageous trade tends to be weak.

The situation in underdeveloped countries is far different in this respect than that in, say, Western Europe, where the Benelux arrangement existed for some years, and the "common market" idea has taken hold on a large-scale basis. While Western Europe is largely industrial, it also possesses—among the various countries—considerable diversity as to types of industrial output, so that the basis for intra-regional trade along mutually advantageous lines appears fairly strong. To illustrate, French iron ore, German coal, Swiss watches, and British textiles can be expected to fit reasonably well into the pattern of an intra-regional market arrangement—even while an equivalent number of leading raw-materials commodities within an equivalent-sized underdeveloped area would likely clash.[23]

Thus, the key to successful intra-regional trade is complementarity; if the pattern of production within a given region does not yield comple-

---

[23] Nevertheless, one finalized intra-regional trade arrangement and two far-advanced proposals for intra-regional trade arrangements pertain to sections of Latin America in which countries of varying degrees of underdevelopedness are situated. The arrangement already brought into effect involves movement to a free-trade area in Central America, involving Honduras, Guatemala, and El Salvador. Among the proposals, the first relates to a Gran Colombiana market arrangement, involving Venezuela, Colombia, and Ecuador. The second proposal, for a Free-Trade Zone (with emphasis on southern South America), applies to Argentina, Chile, Brazil, Mexico (as a replacement for Bolivia, which was initially proposed for membership), Paraguay, Peru, and Uruguay. For material on the movement for intra-regional trade arrangements in Latin America, see UN, *El Mercado Comun Latinoamericano,* Mexico City, 1959.

Among the foregoing, the major arrangement relates to the proposed Free-Trade Zone. This arrangement envisages gradual removal over a 12-year transitional period of impediments to trade occurring among the member countries, but trade barriers upon imports from non-member countries are to remain discretionary with the individual member countries. By way of contrast, the European Common Market envisages gradual removal of impediments to trade occurring among the member countries, but simultaneously calls for erection of a single uniform tariff structure then applicable to imports entering any member country from outside the Common Market area.

mentarity, little basis for intra-regional trade prevails. Even in the absence of current complementarity within a region, however, there may still be a case for arrangements likely to prove conducive to intra-regional trade, thereby to encourage *creation* of the complementarity in production that can then give rise to the greater intra-regional trade desired. For example, the output of new industrial-type enterprises would likely prove complementary to other already-existing production in underdeveloped countries. But, introduction of these enterprises tends to be discouraged in the absence of an opportunity to "get at" a sufficiently wide trade area to permit realization of the economies of scale necessary for successful operation. A common-market development, in making intra-regional trade possible, thus may help to bring about the introduction of some new enterprises.

PAYMENTS

Some persons regard regional currency-clearing arrangements as being of help in the promotion of regional trade. Since many underdeveloped countries currently employ currency restrictions, and since only little trade currently occurs among countries in underdeveloped regions, an arrangement aimed at the removal of foreign-exchange restrictions within any given region comes readily to be viewed by some persons as a means likely to assure greater trade within that region. In addition, they view the arrangement as one comprising a first easy step in a general sequence presumed to culminate in the restoration of world-wide multilateralism, the objective frequently regarded as paramount by these persons.

The drive for limited currency-convertibility arrangements at the regional level has taken its cue largely from the European Payments Union (EPU). The EPU came into being as a device intended to help free-up and promote intra-European trade, previously impeded by general inconvertibility within Western Europe.[24] Significantly, the EPU proved successful, to a point, in the promotion of intra-European trade. In view of the general success achieved, various proponents of greater intra-regional trade have urged adoption in other regions, including underdeveloped regions, of EPU-type arrangements.

Significantly, a currency arrangement can be expected merely to *accommodate* a trading arrangement economically justifiable on grounds other than pure currency considerations. In this regard, trade within a region in which all countries are underdeveloped is hampered by a general lack of complementarity, given the production patterns prevailing in the countries concerned. Since trade is not favored on real grounds,[25]

---

24 Formally introduced in 1950, the EPU replaced an earlier regional payments scheme, introduced in 1948 but found wanting.
25 Meaning, on grounds other than currency considerations.

there is a distinct limit as to what can be expected as a consequence of a currency arrangement. In short, a rationale exists for an EPU-type arrangement in Western Europe, where considerable complementarity among countries is an established fact, but a similar rationale does not exist within underdeveloped regions, since complementarity at present is essentially absent there.

At a later date, if and when the production patterns of countries within any given underdeveloped region have altered as a consequence of development (i.e., when greater complementarity has come to prevail), a currency arrangement can offer greater hope for trade promotion along intra-regional lines. Short of that time, the case that might creditably be advanced appears largely limited to that associated with a "stand-by" currency arrangement, employed in anticipation of physical alterations in production and trade. In short, actual growth in intra-regional trade remains dependent upon the evolution of *both* an appropriate production pattern and an appropriate currency mechanism, and in this sequence *the production pattern is basic.*

THE TIMING OF END-BENEFIT

Whenever a government undertakes to direct the path and pace of economic development, it is obliged to make important decisions as to the *timing* and *amount* of possible end-benefit to be made accessible to consumers. Specifically, as developmental progress occurs, a government needs periodically to take stock of the sort of "split" to be condoned, or forced, in the use of the added income (output) arising. To the extent that added end-benefit is permitted to go to consumers, potential investment (and the attendant capacity to evoke growth) is curbed; conversely, to the extent that end-benefit comes to be denied consumers, and can be done so without dulling incentive, potential investment and attendant growth are fostered.

The essential point is that when rapid and marked growth is the objective, deprivation of consumers becomes virtually imperative. To some extent, of course, access to external assistance can help lessen the pinch upon consumers. In any event, however, concessions to consumers occur at the cost of investment that "might have been."

Since developmental progress occurs over considerable time, the growth process leaves little latitude *ever* for improved consumption levels for those persons already adult at the time of the launching of an accelerated developmental program. Much of the population, while perhaps all for the idea of development, is probably quite unaware that the ultimate pay-off in end-benefit for consumers is rather far in the future. Obviously, a government bent upon carrying through a successful developmental program must be prepared to instill enthusiasm for continued undiminished effort in the face of lagging consumption, or be prepared to preside over a diminishing effort as concessions are made under pressure to a demanding populace.

SELECTED BIBLIOGRAPHY

Werner Baer, "Puerto Rico: An Evaluation of a Successful Development Program," *Quarterly Journal of Economics,* November 1959.
> Examination of Operation Bootstrap; generally sympathetic treatment.

Government of India, *The First Five Year Plan,* New Delhi, 1952; also *The Second Five Year Plan,* 1956.
> An outstanding example of one underdeveloped country's attempt to tackle governmental policy decision-making.

Seymour E. Harris, *International and Interregional Economics,* New York: The McGraw-Hill Book Company, Inc., 1957.
> Esp. Ch. 19, Presents material in support of the case for market intervention during the course of development.

Albert O. Hirschman, *The Strategy of Economic Development.* New Haven: Yale University Press, 1958.
> Presents a theory as to the type of developmental action needed to achieve balanced growth; see esp. Chs. 3 and 4.

Wilfred Malenbaum, "India and China: Contrasts in Development Performance," *American Economic Review,* June 1959.
> Examination of the basically differing developmental approaches employed by two major underdeveloped countries, along with an appraisal of resultant progress.

Rockefeller Brothers Fund (Special Studies Project, Report III), *Foreign Economic Policy for the Twentieth Century.* Garden City, N.Y.: Doubleday & Company, Inc., 1958.
> The "Rockefeller Report" on US foreign economic policy; advances a pro-regional approach to major world economic problems, using the Western Hemisphere for illustrative purposes.

N. A. Sarma, "Economic Development in India: The First and Second Five Year Plans," in IMF, *Staff Papers,* Vol. VI, No. 2, April 1958.
> Examination of, and commentary on, India's developmental experience.

Harry Schwartz, *Russia's Soviet Economy.* Englewood Cliffs, N.J.: Prentice-Hall, Inc., 1954 (Second ed.).
> Esp. Chs. III-V, Examination of the USSR's approach to forced development.

C. N. Vakil and P. R. Brahmanand, *Planning for an Expanding Economy.* Bombay: Vora & Co., Publishers, 1956.
> Analysis and commentary on Indian economic planning; the presentation is generally critical of what has been done.

Henry H. Villard, *Economic Development*. New York: Rinehart & Company, Inc., 1959.
    Part III, Examination of development under Communism.

Harold F. Williamson and John A. Buttrick (eds.), *Economic Development*. Englewood Cliffs, N.J.: Prentice-Hall, Inc., 1954.
    Ch. II (esp. pp. 42–43), The balanced versus the bottleneck approach to development; author: Joseph L. Fisher.

12

PLANNING FOR DEVELOPMENT[1]

National economic planning is not new to the world. What is new, as evidenced by developments of more recent years, is the particular manner in which numerous governments have chosen to exercise the function of national economic planning. Specifically, in country after country the matter of economic destiny has come to be approached by the governments concerned in terms of *formal national economic plans.* This movement toward wider reliance upon formal plans in the course of national economic planning can be explained largely in terms of three main factors.

First, socialist-type economies, in substantial number, made their appearance on the world scene. Devotion to a socialist philosophy induced receptivity to the expansion of governmental intervention in the economic realm. In general, adherence to the tenets of a socialist philosophy was paralleled by a willingness on the part of government to undertake overall and all embracive planning in the economic sphere—and also in the social and other related spheres insofar, especially, as these impinge upon the economic.

Second, with the introduction by the US of Marshall Plan aid to Western Europe following World War II, individual countries found themselves, of necessity, charting aid requirements and aid utilization. This development, superimposed upon the countries' general recep-

---

1 An earlier version of this chapter appeared in the *Proceedings of the Thirty-third Annual Conference of the Western Economic Association,* 1958, under the title "National Planning in Underdeveloped Countries."

tivity to governmental intervention in economic activity,[2] logically led them to embark upon fairly comprehensive economic planning—encompassing resource assessment and utilization *in toto,* not merely insofar as related to Marhall Plan aid. The US, which never deemed it necessary or important to have a formal national economic plan for itself, found itself, under the particular circumstances, in the role of actively supporting the formulation of national economic plans by individual countries within Western Europe. Such a role, the US felt, was fully warranted in the light of its assuming the responsibility for providing assistance for reconstruction of the individual (then) non-viable economies involved. At a later date, as the US shifted the emphasis in its foreign-aid program from Western Europe, in which the problem was one of *reconstruction,* to the underdeveloped world (and especially to Asia), in which the problem was one of *development,* similar encouragement for economic planning that might result in formal national economic plans was extended to encompass the new locales.

Third, the underdeveloped countries, on their part, awakened—in the sense that economic development, and the better life it presages, came to comprise a significant goal in country after country. The desire to speed development, and to minimize the pain in its attainment, spurred thinking as to the nature of appropriate policies, programs, and implementation measures. The culmination of this thinking, reinforced by some essentially external forces (e.g., moral encouragement and technical assistance under foreign-aid auspices), has been the formulation by a host of countries of comprehensive national economic plans.

Given the large number of countries within the underdeveloped category, and the formidable nature of the task involved in development, it is not amiss to reflect upon the role of formalized planning as an element in the developmental process. It is generally agreed that a formal national economic plan *can* prove valuable as a guide in a developmental effort. The precise plan frequently envisaged, however, assumes the form of a rather standardized document, basically unvarying among countries as to essential outline and approach. Indeed, the high degree of uniformity disturbs some students of the subject. These persons, while convinced of the potential merits of a national economic plan in a developmental effort, strongly feel that any plan, in order to prove truly effective, must be carefully tailored to fit the specific environment for which it is intended—and, significantly, environments vary widely and importantly among underdeveloped countries.

Accordingly, what should a particular country strive for in terms of formalized planning? In ascertaining what comprises effective planning

---

2 Significantly, a number of the countries had labor governments in power at the time.

in an underdeveloped country, two major considerations logically present themselves:

    (1) What is the fundamental purpose of a national economic plan?

    (2) Given this purpose, what should be the essential nature of a plan?

PURPOSE OF A PLAN

The fundamental reason why an underdeveloped country should perhaps want a national economic plan is that a good plan, by virtue of its existence, might help that country attain, more readily than otherwise likely or possible, the particular or general improvement[3] it desires.

Improvement involves a process of moving from a less desirable situation to a more desirable one. Accordingly, if a national economic plan is to yield improvement, it must, by definition, contain in it the ingredients necessary to make this possible. The process of formulating a national economic plan is not something to be viewed as an end in itself; rather, a good plan is one that has something substantial to offer as the *means to an end*. Specifically, the means offered should be appropriate in terms of the end sought.

Thus, a good plan needs to reckon with the actual environment that prevails, and needs to chart in realistic terms the course of action prescribed. Because environments vary among countries, it follows that national economic plans themselves should of necessity vary in form and content among countries.[4]

ELEMENTS OF A PLAN

In framing a plan that can offer a reasonable prospect of being deemed a success by the above criterion, a number of basic factors loom importantly. A few of the more crucial of these merit citation and analysis.

NATURE OF THE ECONOMIC ORDER

Economies differ from one another in terms of the extent to which the respective governments exert influence, direct or indirect, over economic

---

3 *Improvement* has been variously defined, but in the lexicon of the typical economic planner the term connotes higher and rising real per-capita income, but with this perhaps modified by—or accompanied by—greater income stability, more equitable income distribution, and any one or more of a variety of other economic and noneconomic considerations.

4 Thus, it is important to exercise considerable care and good judgment when using the plans of other countries as reference models in the formulation of a particular country's plan. "Be eclectic" and "know your own country" are sound bits of advice in this connection.

activity. Some economies can be characterized as *controlled,* whereas others are more properly classed as *free-enterprise.* While the exact dividing line between the two categories is anything but hard and fast, depending as it does upon the particular criteria applied in its ascertainment, the distinction is real and needs to be recognized for its relevance in economic planning.

In a controlled economy, the sphere within which government can exercise direct control over the utilization of resources tends to be great; in addition, fairly strong governmental powers typically exist that can be employed to affect the utilization of those other resources nominally held by private persons. In a free-enterprise economy, in contrast, a somewhat greater portion of resources is held by private persons who, by historic inclination and popular acceptance, determine within rather wide limits the form and timing of utilization of these resources.

Planning, as viewed by the economic planner, is a relatively easy matter in a closely controlled economy. The formulation of a national economic plan can then proceed, essentially, in terms of assessing aggregate resources available and of fitting these resources into some pattern intended to govern their utilization. All the while, the economic planner can assume that responsibility for and control over implementation of the plan, once initiated, will fall entirely or very largely within the sphere of governmental action—and, the assumption is that in a closely controlled economy governmental action will be forthcoming.

The task of formalized economic planning is relatively more difficult, if anything, in a predominantly free-enterprise economy. This is the case because much greater latitude exists for independent action (i.e., action beyond clear-cut control by government, and hence more or less unpredictable—as seen by government). Unlike government in a controlled economy, in which there is a high degree of direct control over resource utilization, government in a free-enterprise economy is so situated that its control over resource utilization, other than over those somewhat incidental resources it holds directly, must come indirectly through measures designed to influence persons in the private sector in their actions relative to the economic means to which they have claim. Instead of having to suggest simply how government should utilize resources, the task of the economic planner essentially becomes that of having to suggest how government should proceed in order to induce private persons to utilize resources in desired ways.

Under the circumstances, a national economic plan for a free-enterprise economy can properly be formulated in terms of either of two basic approaches. First, central attention can be focused upon the segment of the economy that is positively controlled by government, i.e., upon the public sector. A plan of this type would in reality consist of a scheduled program of public investment. The merit of the approach is that it is realistic in terms of the situation: it is particularly in respect to control over public investment, involving governmental outlays of local currency and foreign exchange, that government typically has strong and fairly inclusive power. The possible demerit of the approach is its treatment in direct fashion of only a portion of the economy—indeed, only a small portion in the typical free-enterprise economy; but, of course, it can be creditably maintained, by way of counter-argument, that the public sector offers itself for use as an impulse sector, triggering repercussions that affect the whole economy.[5]

Second, central attention can be focused upon overall public policies. A plan of this type would in reality consist of a series of basic governmental policies (e.g., a tax and budget policy, a foreign-exchange policy, a monetary and banking policy, an investment policy, an agricultural policy, a labor policy, etc.)—each with appropriate and necessary measures of implementation, and all integrated to form a cohesive environmental framework. The rationale is that government should try particularly to affect what occurs in the private sector, since it is this sector that is crucial in a free-enterprise economy. The way to affect the private sector, so the argument runs, is for government to shape the "rules of the game" so that private individuals will end doing what in essence government desires them to do.

The difference between the two approaches, basically, is one of *where* initial and primary emphasis is placed. Either approach has merit in a free-enterprise economy, and the decision as to which to use should properly depend, in the final analysis, upon an appraisal of the relative degrees of receptivity likely to be shown by the government and populace in question to the type of end document involved.

TARGET SETTING

The fundamental purpose of a national economic plan, as stated earlier, is to help a country in its efforts to achieve improvement. While on some scores there may be merit in portraying in graphic fashion what the environment will be like when sought-after improvement has become a fact, it is unfortunate that national economic plans frequently set forth the desired end results as specific targets, often in glowing terms—even while failing to show how these end results might be made a reality. In essence, some plans treat "what is" and "what ought to be," but fail to treat adequately how "what is" can be improved upon. These plans are then open to possible criticism as being long on promises, implied or otherwise, but short on implementation.

Since it is improvement that is desired, it is implementation—meaning-

---

[5] Preferably, actions in the public sector would be of a type that results in selective impact upon the general economy.

ful provisions relating to what is to be done, how, and by whom—that really counts. Crucial to the economic planner's task, *the measures and means of implementation incorporated in a national economic plan should prove compatible with the nature of the economic order.*

In a closely controlled economy, the economic planner can well proceed on the assumption that he should incorporate an array of specific targets into an economic plan. He can reasonably and safely expect to state that a particular plan—if adopted and followed—will result in, say, an increase in GNP of 6% per year, an increase of 20% in steel-making capacity, an increase of 10% in number of housing units, etc.; specific targets of this type are not then amiss, *provided* they are within the country's technical and economic capabilities, and provided these capabilities can be brought to bear upon the situation so that the projected results can become a reality in due course. A vital point is that government, in a closely controlled economy, has a high degree of direct control over the manner of utilization of resources available to the economy, and hence stands a good chance of making good (if it is so minded) on the promises implied in statements on specific targets.

In a fundamentally free-enterprise economy, however, the situation that confronts the economic planner is materially different. The economic planner, if he is at all realistic, must then recognize that scope for direct governmental action in the economic sphere is narrowly circumscribed. Thereupon, the meaningful course left open automatically dictates heavy concentration upon ways designed simply to influence activities within the private sector. Significantly, the certainty that a specific pinpointed result will take place, when such is dependent upon its being induced within the private sector as a consequence of something having occurred outside the private sector, is undoubtedly less than when government takes it upon itself directly to see to it that the specific desired result comes about. The wide latitude left for individual and independent action—with consequent uncertainty as to just what is to evolve—makes it important for the economic planner to formulate a plan that promises no more, through reference to specific targets, than can reasonably be expected when all available means likely to be used are brought to bear upon the situation; to do otherwise is to put in print what later might well become a record of "targets unattained." What a plan should emphasize, instead, is promotion of improvement (and a somewhat general understanding of what would constitute improvement is sufficient for the purpose at hand). Importantly, any intended emphasis should be buttressed with specific measures of implementation that can appropriately help promote this improvement (leaving unstated, in at least major part, specific narrowly-construed targets).[6]

---

6 The difficulty faced in attempts to set precise targets on an overall basis under fundamentally free-enterprise conditions can readily be illustrated through reference

It is not enough, however, simply to observe that, in a free-enterprise economy, a national economic plan should de-emphasize specific targets, and instead should stress promotion of improvement and appropriate measures of implementation conducive to this improvement. Reflection upon the general principle points to the fact that application will necessarily take two somewhat distinct forms, depending upon whether it is the impulse-sector approach or the public-policies approach that is followed in presenting the implementation framework.

In the impulse-sector approach, specific targets are not at all inappropriate insofar as their attainment is clearly possible as a consequence of what can evolve from resource utilization in the public sector. Thus, it would be realistic to set forth specific targets relating to *particular* government projects (e.g., amount of increase in generating capacity in government-operated power plants, amount of increase in new public housing units, etc.); in these cases, government has a means to control the resources crucial to the attainment of the targets in question. But, it would not be realistic to set forth specific targets relating to purely private-sector or *overall* aspects of the economy (e.g., amount of increase in private industrial output, amount of increase in overall job creation, etc.); in these cases, all or part of the responsibility upon which the final result depends lies within the private sector, the activities of which government can influence but not positively control, and hence should not attempt to pre-judge with precision.

In the public-policies approach, controversial questions relating to the setting of specific targets are not likely ever to arise, for these targets are in no way vital to the solidity of the presentation. Emphasis is squarely placed upon the development of a body of public policies, along with appropriate measures of implementation. In the case of activities in the private sector, specific targets are not regarded as meaningful in this approach; and, while specific targets could be set for activities in the public sector, they remain strictly optional in this approach.

STRUCTURE OF THE ECONOMY

Even if specific targets hold only limited relevance for the planning documents of some countries, economic planners in these countries must still be aware of general goals (as distinct from specific targets) toward

---

to particular underdeveloped countries. For example, India is much involved in national economic planning, but the great bulk of economic effort in that country occurs strictly outside the public sector and beyond any direct control by government. By way of comparison, Galbraith states that ". . . [the American economy] is both much the more manageable and the more managed economy. India has, in fact, superimposed a smallish socialized sector atop what, no doubt, is the world's greatest example of functioning anarchy." Given this environment, the true meaning of many *overall* targets that might be set seemingly becomes a matter of conjecture. See J. K. Galbraith, "Rival Economic Theories in India." *Foreign Affairs,* July 1958, esp. pp. 589–590 (where the cited quote appears).

which they would ha/e effort directed. In fact, whatever the nature of
the economic order of an underdeveloped country, the economic planner
must logically think in terms of some general goals, so that measures can
be formulated with a view toward moving the economy in a *direction*
deemed desirable.

Before deciding upon the direction toward which the economy is
consciously to be pushed, it is important that the economic planner
comprehend the nature and implications of the basic economic problem
(or problems) that warrants remedial action. A central matter in this
connection is the structure of the economy. The economic planner ought
to be aware, at least in general terms, of the capabilities and limitations
over time of the prevailing economic structure (be it agricultural or
balanced agro-industrial, diversified or undiversified), as well as of the
potentialities of alternate structures that might reasonably be fostered
over time.

The importance of understanding the structure of the economy, and
what to try to do about it, can be demonstrated by reference to a likely
case. Assume an underdeveloped economy with the following major
attributes: current production heavily concentrated in agriculture—with
more agricultural output physically possible, and with potential also
existing for new industrial development; relatively low real per-capita
income, with only slight increases over time; a rapidly rising population,
coupled with widespread and even growing unemployment or underemployment; and chronic balance-of-payments difficulties, involving a
lag in export expansion and persistent heavy import dependence under
the prevailing production pattern. Given facts of this general character,
the economic planner needs to make an initial decision as to whether to
plan in terms of doing the best that is possible within the present production pattern, or of trying to do better through conscious effort to
induce an altered production pattern. In most underdeveloped countries,
a decision is involved as to the relative merits of more agriculture as
compared with industrialization (with this industrialization presumably
a supplement to agriculture). Since resource supplies in practice do not
allow successful all-out support for both, the decision as to where to
place emphasis cannot be dodged.

In deciding, the economic planner may find the logical course to be
clear-cut, with action requirements pointing unmistakably either in one
direction or the other. However, the economic planner may find—indeed,
is likely to find—that emphasis upon more agriculture, with incremental
applications of effort going very largely to agricultural development, will
yield greater benefits[7] per resource outlay during the ensuing short-run

---

[7] Benefits in terms, primarily, of income, employment, and balance-of-payments
improvements.

(say, up to 5 or 10 years) than will emphasis upon industrialization, but that emphasis in this direction, whatever its merit in terms of the short-run, is inappropriate—either short-run or long-run—for solution of the country's basic economic problems, which characteristically are deep-seated. Put differently, the economic planner may find that emphasis upon industrial growth will not in the short-run yield benefits per resource outlay equivalent to that of a frankly agricultural-type approach, but is likely, on the other hand, to yield relatively favorable results over the long-run in the sense of getting at and ameliorating, once and for all, the fundamental structural shortcomings that otherwise act to impede consistent material progress. The economic planner is obliged to weigh carefully the alternatives at issue. As intimated, the general direction development should take is readily evident in some cases; but, in borderline cases, the answer is certainly far from clear.[8]

In the final analysis, the decision as to whether or not to plan for structural change rests not only upon economics, but also upon non-economic considerations. Involved are such factors as national aspirations, the political climate, etc.—which, if observation serves one correctly, characteristically do have a profound bearing, in conjunction with the purely economic, upon the direction and tone given national planning documents. The economic planner, of course, can decide on purely economic grounds as to what results he believes possible or likely with *and* without structural change, but the extent to which further, non-economic considerations actually come to be taken into account—or, indeed, have to be taken into account—depends upon the total environment. Realistically, the economic planner has to reckon with the various non-economic considerations, which for him represent part of the facts of life, and it is quite evident that his task is not thereby made easier.

USE OF STATISTICS

It is a common impression that "good" statistics (particularly good GNP data) are needed to formulate a good national economic plan. But in many underdeveloped countries comprehensive economic statistics are either largely lacking or, when present, are for the greater part not very reliable. What is the economic planner then to do? Wait until such time as the desired statistics become available before commencing work on a plan? Use the statistics currently available—good, bad, or indifferent—and incorporate them in a plan for better or worse? Or, is there another course open?

Good statistics, both as to coverage and reliability, are useful to the

---

[8] The concept of the incremental capital-output ratio (ICOR) could still be used by the economic planner for purposes of information and as a guide, but the mathematical results obtained would not be regarded as binding in policy decisions—in fact, might be deliberately ignored.

economic planner, whether or not he actually writes them into a plan. There is no denying this fact. But, in their absence, it does not make good sense to delay action on grounds that "one *cannot* plan without good statistics." If good statistics are regarded as an absolute prerequisite, the day when serious planning will commence in numerous countries is not yet in sight. Good statistics simply do not now exist in many countries; moreover, in some of these countries nothing basic is occurring to evolve better statistics. Meanwhile, time is passing and the benefits that theoretically could accrue to these countries as a consequence of serious planning are passed by, all because of an ill-conceived notion on the role of statistics in planning.

The basic point of relevance here is that the sought-after improvement depends fundamentally upon the formulation of appropriate overall policies, and upon the activation of these overall policies through appropriate measures of implementation. Good statistics, were they available, would admittedly aid the economic planner, but if necessary the economic planner can act without formal reliance upon extensive statistics. General comprehension of the economic scene (including an understanding of major deficiencies, of desired general directions of improvement, etc.) suffices for the purpose of formulating an appropriate policy-and-implementation framework. The foregoing, of course, does not constitute an argument to justify the failure to evolve good statistics; rather, the argument is simply that when good statistics are absent, effective planning can nevertheless occur, provided there is a will to act and an understanding of how to proceed.

As corollaries to the above, two additional observations are pertinent. First, "bad" statistics are probably worse than no statistics, when viewed in terms of the role statistics can play in planning. It would be a grave error to formulate a plan that is heavily dependent upon statistical series when these statistics admittedly are of poor quality. For example, if existing series show GNP as already rising at, say, 8% per year, the economic planner who places basic reliance (as a point of reference) upon this series in his planning document is likely to find himself under compulsion to "plan for something better," say, a whopping 10% or 12% annual increase in GNP. If the economic planner proceeds to incorporate the data, and goes along with what evolves out of this statistical situation, he runs the risk of ending up with an unrealistic plan (and risks ridicule at some later date when more adequate statistics reveal that growth is really proceeding at only, say, 3% per year). Under the circumstances, it would appear far better—more realistic for planning purposes, and safer for the economic planner—to formulate a plan that simply emphasizes improvement (with stress upon movement in the desired direction, supported by appropriate policy-and-implementation measures), and that de-emphasizes statistical precision.

Second, the need to de-emphasize formal use of statistics involves no great sacrifice when precise target setting is not resorted to. Significantly, as observed earlier, target setting is not crucial to planning in a free-enterprise economy, and should be avoided or minimized anyway. General goals, related to the direction of improvement, can be adequately expressed with minimum resort to statistical precision. In short, in a free-enterprise economy, the economic planner can hope to circumvent satisfactorily the statistical dilemma dependent upon insufficient or unreliable statistical data. In a closely controlled economy, however, target setting can be justified as a valid and meaningful core element in planning; and, if consistently followed as an approach, there is no effective or simple way for the economic planner to circumvent major statistical shortcomings (other than to move to a policy-and-implementation approach also, or to concentrate during an interim period on very rapid development of adequate statistical data).

THE BASIC PHILOSOPHY

The fundamental purpose of a national economic plan is to point the way in an economy toward desired improvement, and to make easier or more certain the attainment of this improvement. The success or failure of a national economic plan properly hinges upon whether, and how much, improvement results *from* the existence of the plan.

With the foregoing as the basic criterion, a national economic plan— if impact-potential is to be relatively great—needs to be realistic in the sense of giving due recognition to the subject country's total existing environment (including the limitations and potentialities inherent therein). Important above all else is strength in implementation. Accordingly, it is crucial to the economic planner's task that the tone given implementation aspects of a national economic plan be honestly reflective of the basic nature of the economic order characteristic of the particular country in question.

SELECTED BIBLIOGRAPHY

John K. Galbraith, "Rival Economic Theories in India," *Foreign Affairs,* July 1958.
    Exposition of salient characteristics of the Indian economy, with heavy overtones on the problems of planning.

Government of India, *The First Five Year Plan,* New Delhi, 1952; also *The Second Five Year Plan,* 1956.
    Interesting samples of national economic planning in a major underdeveloped country.

Seymour E. Harris, *Economic Planning*. New York: Alfred A. Knopf, 1949.
> Examination of the national economic plans of 14 countries (generally developed countries).

Benjamin Higgins, *Economic Development*. New York: W. W. Norton & Company, Inc., 1959.
> Pp. 642–653, The nature and role of the incremental capital-output ratio (ICOR).

Albert O. Hirschman, *The Strategy of Economic Development*. New Haven: Yale University Press, 1958.
> Presents new and significant views on priorities in a developmental program.

Wilfred Malenbaum, "India and China: Contrasts in Development Performance," *American Economic Review*, June 1959.
> Interesting contrasts between two major underdeveloped countries, reliant upon basically different economic approaches.

Edward S. Mason, *Economic Planning in Underdeveloped Areas*. New York: Fordham University Press, 1958.
> A small volume based on four lectures on economic planning in underdeveloped countries.

Ragnar Nurkse, "Reflections on India's Development Plan," *Quarterly Journal of Economics*, May 1957.
> Analysis of, and commentary on, India's economic problems and approach in planning.

C. N. Vakil and P. R. Brahmanand, *Planning for an Expanding Economy*, Bombay: Vora & Co., Publishers, 1956.
> Analysis and commentary on Indian economic planning; the presentation is generally critical of what has been done.

13

INTERNAL
READJUSTMENTS (I)

As observed in Chapter 12, when attainment of economic development is the objective, it is action along lines of implementation that counts. Theorizing has its place, but unless action occurs (and is of the right type), desired development remains an elusive quantity in an uncertain future.

The action deemed essential for the speeding of developmental progress fundamentally pertains to the utilization of resources. The resources at issue are materials (including raw materials, machinery, and equipment generally) and manpower (encompassing all labor, and including managerial capacity and technical know-how generally), both non-monetary in nature. It is upon the direction and caliber of usage of available resources of these types that the prospect for physical change within an economy is dependent; and, in the final analysis, it is only through physical change that development can reflect itself.

But, the typical situation is that the physical side of development has a monetary mantle[1] thrown over it. In simplest terms, goods and services move against money (and in response to market dictates, whether the market structure is free or partially controlled). Indeed, the movement or non-movement of money operates, funda-

---

[1] This is true to the extent that economic activity occurs within the monetary economy. While not all economic activity occurs within the monetary economy (and especially not in underdeveloped countries), it is significant—for purposes here at issue—that the monetary economy encompasses a very substantial segment of economic activity in even the most underdeveloped of countries.

mentally,[2] as a steering apparatus in respect to the utilization of resources.

In essence, monetary means provide a powerful lever with which to affect the physical side of development. A logical starting point, then, in an attempt to influence the direction and caliber of usage of available resources, and hence the direction and pace of development, centers on monetary matters. The monetary sphere, in turn, has two facets: domestic currency and foreign exchange. The two encompass the monetary ingredients crucial to investment (and to spending generally)—thereby representing potential claim to resources, the exercise of which influences the utilization of resources and the direction and pace of development.

From the foregoing it follows that two policy areas[3] certain to prove of central concern to a government interested in the promotion of development are those relating to, first, the *fiscal budget* (involving utilization of fiscal resources: domestic currency) and, second, the *foreign-exchange budget* (involving utilization of foreign exchange).[4] The present chapter is devoted to matters related to the fiscal budget, while the following chapter deals with matters related to the foreign-exchange budget.

THE FISCAL PICTURE

Fiscal policy—the use by government, in some coordinated manner, of the power to tax, spend, and borrow—provides a potentially forceful means to affect the level and pattern of production, income, and employment. Both taxation and spending offer ways to influence the utilization of resources; further, the use of public credit enables taxation and spending to proceed somewhat independently of one another, thereby giving wide scope for discretionary power in the pursuit of various possible overall goals, e.g., growth or stabilization.

While fiscal policy provides a potentially forceful instrumentality for use in a developmental program, even cursory inspection reveals that numerous underdeveloped countries are currently not committed to the pursuit of a type of fiscal policy geared to promote development. In many countries, fiscal affairs are handled in a vein designed for the minimal task of keeping the governmental structure alive from day to day, not for the more ambitious task of accelerating change in the economy.

---

2 A notable exception is found in the case of particular self-help projects. Whenever otherwise idle labor is coupled with readily accessible land and raw materials on a strictly self-help basis, a product is potentially derivable that then constitutes a form of investment (e.g., a road, a bridge, or a building)—and it occurs without the necessity of money as an intermediary, and without commensurate prior saving, monetary or real.

3 Or policy-and-implementation areas.

4 This is not to say that nothing matters beyond the fiscal and foreign-exchange budgets. The point is simply that the two comprise core elements in what is crucial in development. While the monetary magnitudes embraced by them ordinarily comprise only a small part of GNP, their importance in terms of actual or potential impact upon investment is relatively great.

When development is the objective, potential advantages derivable from an appropriate fiscal-policy framework would seemingly not be long ignored. But even when good intent is present, the type of action needed may not always appear clear. After all, what comprises an appropriate fiscal-policy framework? A quick answer is that the precise manner in which fiscal-policy measures need to be used to promote development depends upon circumstances prevailing, and these vary among the numerous countries at issue. However, despite important variations, some general principles are fairly easy to deduce.

TAX POLICY

The populations of underdeveloped countries typically are rural; most people live on the land or in small villages closely tied to the land. Much of the labor force is engaged in self-sufficiency agriculture or in the production of raw materials destined largely for export, and, ordinarily, a considerable proportion of GNP is directly attributable to these efforts. Given the nature and magnitude of prevailing production, a low level of real per-capita income becomes characteristic.

The foregoing summarizes the basic situation found in underdeveloped countries (described more fully in Ch. 1). Given the foregoing situation, two outstanding facts are discernible, each of major importance for tax policy and for fiscal policy generally. First, the capacity of government to raise revenue through taxation is severely limited. The main explanation for this is found in the low level of income that characteristically prevails, while an important contributory factor relates to shortcomings commonly experienced in attempts to collect even that revenue rightfully owing under prevailing tax laws.[5] In some underdeveloped countries, government is able only with the greatest of difficulty to raise sufficient revenue to finance even the most basic of current outlays, leaving little or no scope for the financing through tax means of developmental outlays.[6] However, despite the fact that government may suffer from a shortage of tax revenue, the tax burden upon the population ordinarily tends to be heavy; when an economy is poor, even a seemingly inconsequential tax payment readily looms as a burden.

Second, a great proportion of prevailing output typically arises under essentially free-enterprise conditions.[7] Under the basic environment

---

[5] Shortcomings in the tax-collection process are rooted, to an important extent, in underdevelopedness itself. See again Ch. 3, section on "Weak Public Administration."

[6] Apparent inability to raise in current tax revenue amounts sufficient to cover current operating costs of government, let alone to support any substantial magnitude of capital-type outlays, has provided the rationale in the US foreign-aid program for budgetary assistance to particular countries. Underdeveloped countries that have received assistance of this type include Pakistan, South Viet-Nam, Laos, and Jordan.

[7] Some exceptions exist, involving countries deeply committed to a collectivization of effort, e.g., Communist China. Significantly, too, some countries are frequently re-

carried forward from the past, the great bulk of output stems from rural areas, in which people live and activity proceeds very largely out-of-touch with whatever is going on in the capital city. This situation, whatever else might be said of it, reflects a high degree of free enterprise. To the extent that government chooses to push for an acceleration of development, however, the degree of purity of free enterprise may be lessened (notwithstanding any concerned country's avowed dedication to the concept of free enterprise). When accelerated development becomes a national goal, the central government ordinarily embarks upon planning, which is generally a prelude to augmented public investment. One result of greater public investment ordinarily is the evolution of a new socialized sector, superimposed upon a basically free-enterprise structure already in existence.[8] Nevertheless, it is significant that the new socialized sector is likely to be small in comparison with the established free-enterprise structure.[9]

Given the foregoing facts, a two-fold conclusion follows as regards formulation of a tax policy for development. First, to the extent that an acceleration in development is expected to occur through augmented public-sector outlays, government requires access to additional financial means. Accordingly, the matter of whether additional sources of funds exist, or whether currently-used sources can be worked harder, merits examination. Second, to the extent that additional financial means are not likely to prove forthcoming, or that it appears undesirable to attempt to obtain them, government is obliged to think in terms of greater incentive for desired action within the private sector. Accordingly, the matter of how tax policy can be used to induce greater private activity pushes to the forefront. Actually, the two potential courses need not be considered as mutually exclusive; to an important extent, complementarity between them offers a plausible public-policy goal.

REVENUE SOURCES

An increase in investment is a means to higher income and employment. If the inclination of government is to handle this investment entirely or very largely on a public-sector basis, added governmental revenue quickly comes to be needed. While the possibility, or even

---

ferred to as socialist, or as socialist-tinged, when what prevails is a relatively small, but growing, portion of GNP emanating from the public sector—as seems to be the case, for example, in India. For interesting comment on the ideological status of India, see J. K. Galbraith, "Rival Economic Theories in India," *Foreign Affairs*, July 1958, esp. pp. 589–590; also, see again Ch. 10, section on "The Cases of India and China."

8 This emergent relationship between free-enterprise activity and public-sector activity is evident in numerous underdeveloped countries engaged in developmental promotion. For a discussion of this relationship, as applied to Indian developmental experience, see *Ibid*.

9 However, while likely to be small, the new socialized sector ordinarily embraces activity at the all-important margin (upon which change in an economy is heavily dependent).

desirability (under particular circumstances), of budget imbalance—involving deficit financing—can serve to obviate somewhat the need for added revenue, any substantial increase in public investment, if it is to occur without provoking inflation, is almost certain to require collection of added revenue.[10] If the inclination of government, instead, is to place stress upon private investment, some added public investment nevertheless is likely to prove necessary in order to create the preconditions essential for the desired private investment. Ideally, public investment should then supplement and reinforce private investment, not compete with it, and whatever added revenue is needed to support the public investment should be raised in ways not likely to dull incentive for private investment.

Thus, whether government places primary reliance upon public investment or upon private investment, the need for some added public investment is in prospect; and, given the total environment, an increase in public investment poses the need for some added revenue. Accordingly, the question arises as to what might be done to augment revenue. Essentially, added revenue through taxation during the short-run future (i.e., prior to the evolution of a markedly higher GNP or wider economic base) appears dependent upon what can be accomplished in either or both of two connections. The first involves improved administration of existing tax laws (i.e., improved tax collections). The second involves formulation of a revised tax structure (i.e., adoption of new tax laws, along with their enforcement).

It is a rare underdeveloped country in which better administration of the existing tax structure will not result in some increase in total tax yield. The poor tax-collection record of the typical underdeveloped country is symptomatic of overall weaknesses generally evident in public administration. Administrative machinery frequently is poorly devised and poorly manned; especially, enforcement of tax laws tends to be weakened by the usual absence of an effective system of legal penalties.[11]

---

10 A budget deficit can be financed domestically through sale of government bonds, either to the public or to the banking system. The first method involves *transfer* of purchasing power from the public to the government, while the second method usually involves monetary *expansion* (through monetization of debt). In practice, few government bonds prove salable to the public in underdeveloped countries. Generally, prospective returns in alternative outlets appear more attractive, or fear of possible inflation or of possible political shake-ups dulls public enthusiasm for bond acquisitions. Therefore, sale of government bonds usually is very largely to the banking system, and generally almost entirely to a given country's own Central Bank. However, an unrestrained process of monetization of debt automatically invites inflation. Accordingly, the need to hold inflationary pressure in check requires that at some point some added revenue be acquired in lieu of continued monetization of debt.

11 Imprisonment for failure to meet, say, income-tax obligations borders on the unthinkable in many, if not most, underdeveloped countries. Aside from lax public sentiment, the governments frequently are either unwilling or unable to stand up against particular powerful and moneyed individuals or firms. In the absence of willingness and ability to apply effective penalties, of course, taxpayers appear encouraged to treat their tax obligations lightly.

Clearly, considerable room for improvement exists. However, given the environment generally found in underdeveloped countries, a marked upgrading in the tax-collection process is far from an assured prospect during the short-run future. And, even with improved administration, it is highly doubtful whether revenue potentially derivable under existing laws can prove adequate for the needs of development. In fact, the process of development is likely, at least in some countries, to call for a different type of tax structure from what currently exists; considerations are then involved that go far beyond those related solely to potential tax yield under the currently-existing tax structure.

Despite difficulties associated with any attempt to increase total tax yield within an environment of low GNP, some increase, even if perhaps only marginal, is a possibility for the typical underdeveloped country, even during the near-term future. This possibility is strengthened greatly, of course, if—quite aside from administrative improvements—there is a willingness to undergo modifications in the overall tax structure. The potential for some increase in total revenue becomes apparent as one surveys individual sources.

1. *Sales Taxation.* The backbone of the revenue structure in numerous underdeveloped countries is sales taxation. While frequently levied at some point prior to final sale, and sometimes not directly on any sale, the levies are properly classed as sales taxes nevertheless, since the expectation clearly is that incidence will rest entirely or largely with the end purchaser.

Sales taxation commonly finds few economist friends in developed countries; major criticism centers on an alleged lack of equity. Whatever the case in developed countries, however, sales taxation has much to recommend it in underdeveloped countries. To start, sales taxes ordinarily are fairly easy to administer, being collectible bit by bit at easy-to-detect points in the course of production or distribution. In an environment in which administrative weaknesses are legion, ease of administration constitutes an important merit. Additionally, because sales taxation is regressive, it helps curb consumption. While regressivity can be construed as economically bad in developed countries,[12] in which insufficient effective demand can jeopardize high-level output, regressivity is not necessarily bad in underdeveloped countries, in which a fundamental problem is concerned with how to augment the investible surplus that arises as a residual after consumption demands are met.[13]

---

[12] According to a contrary view, added sales taxation has much to offer a rich society. Particularly, it can provide government with the finances needed to support socially useful public investment (or public consumption). See J. K. Galbraith, *The Affluent Society* (Boston: Houghton Mifflin Company, 1958).

[13] The case for sales taxation in underdeveloped countries is strengthened if actual retardation of consumption is held to limits likely to preclude inducement of distinctly unfavorable side-effects. Ideally, therefore, attempts to step-up sales taxation incorporate the feature of selectivity in treatment.

A potential appears to exist in at least some underdeveloped countries for derivation of some added revenue from sales taxation. This appears to be the case as a consequence of either or both of two courses of action that might reasonably be followed: resort to added or heavier coverage, and continued denial to consumers of improved end-benefit, notwithstanding the generation of higher income in the course of development.

2. *Import and Export Taxes.* In a special category are two variations of sales taxation, import duties and export duties. Most underdeveloped countries currently have an elaborate system of import duties, the rationale largely being that of revenue for government. When developmental progress is the goal, however, a strong case arises for the restructuring of systems of import duties in order to shift emphasis from revenue to protection, thereby to assure shelter from outside competition to those infant industries arising internally.[14] As the rationale shifts to protection, it is presumed that some revenue potential is automatically sacrificed. Accordingly, grounds exist for believing that import duties may not (or, should not be expected to) offer a basis for increased governmental revenue during at least the early phases of development.

Export duties appear to loom somewhat more hopefully as a potential source of added revenue. These duties are ordinarily levied upon raw-materials exports in the belief that incidence rests with foreign purchasers, entirely or in large part, and that revenue is had thereby at the expense of foreigners.[15] A number of countries in Latin America and Asia, especially, are currently quite dependent upon export duties, and in some of them revenue from this source exceeds that from import duties.[16] To an important extent, export duties offer an alternative to systems of multiple rates of exchange, under which the exchange-control authority buys and sells foreign exchange at various levels of price—a procedure capable of yielding profit for government, along with any other possible purposes thereby served. Whichever procedure is favored, either represents a potential source of governmental revenue; indeed, a considerably expanded role frequently appears a reasonable possibility in

---

[14] Because consumption patterns in upper income brackets ordinarily are heavily biased toward import items, import duties are of considerable potential usefulness in attempts to discourage this type of consumption. In this respect, import duties provide an important form of reinforcement for whatever exchange-control measures may have been adopted, ostensibly to upgrade usage of scarce foreign exchange.

[15] Incidence tends to fall primarily upon foreign purchasers whenever the exporter country has a monopoly or near-monopoly in the particular commodity, and whenever the commodity is confronted by an inelastic demand in foreign markets.

[16] Illustrative of the heavy dependence of some countries upon export duties, El Salvador currently derives roughly 30% of its governmental revenue from a duty on coffee exports. This is to be compared with magnitudes of 7% in 1940 and 20% in 1950, which reflect the country's willingness (and ability) to rely upon this source to increasing extent. In fact, the current duty is one incorporating rate-progression, the applicable rate depending upon the prevailing level of price on coffee sales.

either case, particularly insofar as the volume of raw-materials exports may be increased in the course of promoting development.[17]

3. *Property Taxes.* Real estate is a favorite outlet for personal invest-ment in most underdeveloped countries. However, only little govern-mental revenue is currently derived from this source in most countries. For the greater part, tax payments on real estate occur only in token amount. As a first step toward increased tax yield, there is general need for an improved system of assessment of taxable values, providing a basis for greater uniformity in treatment. As a follow-up step, higher property-tax rates appear feasible for most countries, and even meritorious. Especially in those countries in which ownership of substantial areas is concentrated in few hands, with much acreage either withheld from cultivation or cultivated ineffectively, a strong case can be made for somewhat higher taxation as a means to compel better utilization (as well as to derive added revenue).[18]

As an accompaniment of higher tax rates on land values in general, a good case can also be made—on sociological, political, and economic grounds—for enactment of a system of homestead exemptions, under which absolute or virtual tax freedom is granted small peasant-scale holdings when they are owner-occupied.

4. *Income Taxes.* Virtually all underdeveloped countries have income-tax laws in effect in some form, although in many countries these laws are recent. Some countries tax personal income and corporate income separately, similar to the method employed in the US, but others rely solely on a personal-income tax, leaving business income taxable through income taxation only insofar as the income involved actually accrues to individuals.[19] Typically, rate structures are progressive, although not highly so. This fact, plus the fact that minimum exemption levels are ordinarily high, tends to produce a "class" tax rather than a "mass" tax. As for administrative aspects, compliance ordinarily is not particularly good, in large part because enforcement techniques are weak. Scope for derivation of additional revenue appears to exist in terms of improved enforcement, a somewhat more steeply progressive rate structure, a

---

17 In addition to use as a revenue source, export duties have potential use as a protective device for domestic industries. Protection is achievable if the tax is upon a raw material in heavy demand in industries located abroad, and if the raw material is one in which the supplier country holds a sizable fraction of the world's supply. The duty then tends to raise foreign costs above domestic costs, and thereby tends to encourage activity domestically. Examples are found in the export duties levied by Norway and Sweden upon unprocessed timber as part of an effort to encourage the location of woodworking and pulp industries within their borders.

18 To illustrate, several countries in Latin America (e.g., Brazil and Panama) employ land taxes geared to reflect potential output, rather than actual output. The rationale is that of encouragement for improved land utilization.

19 The corporate form of enterprise is fairly rare in many underdeveloped coun-tries. More common is family enterprise. Unquestionably, however, the corporate form of enterprise is growing in popularity, especially in particular countries.

modest lowering of exemption levels, and perhaps adoption of a somewhat broader definition of income, particularly by those countries that currently tax income from business only as personal income.

Aside from revenue considerations, stepped-up personal-income taxation holds potential merit in underdeveloped countries in that this can help curb consumption, and thereby help reorient productive effort from consumption to investment.[20] Additionally, the presence of a system of corporate-income taxation offers potential merit in that government is then put in the position of being able to invoke techniques related to "tax-forgiveness" (e.g., schemes of accelerated depreciation allowance[21]), in the hope thereby to encourage particular forms of investment and enterprise in preference to others not given similarly favorable treatment.

5. *Inheritance Taxes.* Somewhat less widespread in usage than income taxes are inheritance and estate taxes. Taxes of this type currently in effect in underdeveloped countries are typically characterized by rate progression in a mild form, generous exemption features, and a poor record as regards compliance.[22] A reasonable conclusion is that countries still without these taxes have a potential source of revenue open to them, while countries already having these taxes on the books appear capable, ordinarily with only little added effort, of increasing their receipts to some extent.

Aside from revenue considerations, taxation of this type has the merit of helping to tone down gross inequalities in wealth and income, a result ordinarily held compatible with greater equality of opportunity as a social goal. Given the rate structures in effect, it is difficult to contend creditably that collections seriously jeopardize needed capital accumulation; in fact, it appears reasonable to contend that the siphoning off of some assets by government in this fashion enhances overall developmental prospects. The important question to be resolved, of course, is one of what government *does* with the proceeds, as compared with what private persons *would have done* had they retained the amounts involved.

6. *Social Security.* Systems of social security are in effect in numerous underdeveloped countries. From a legal standpoint, coverage and benefits of the programs are generally more modest than what typically prevails in developed countries, although even seemingly limited effort can well be construed as comprising an ambitious undertaking when general poverty is characteristic. From a practical standpoint, however, few

---

20 A possible contrary argument is that consumption would not necessarily be curbed, since tax-payments *could* be made from private saving. The effect in that event, of course, would be a simple shift of investible funds from the private sector to government, with the possibility present that total investment (and total consumption) would be left unaltered.

21 Treated in detail under "Incentive Taxation" later in the present chapter.

22 Tax collection is generally geared to occur at the time an estate is probated. Significantly, this legal procedure is often long delayed. A common situation is that of a sizable backlog of property titles awaiting court action.

countries comply with the full content of their adopted programs, so that actually the programs tend to appear more substantive on paper than they are in fact.

Importantly, because substantial amounts ordinarily prove collectible in the name of social security, the temptation often arises to accumulate a fund for use in connections other than merely the provision of end social-security benefits. One idea that has been broached (e.g., in the Philippines[23]) is to use reserves amassed through social-security contributions as financial backing for a development fund. In essence, it is proposed that forced contributions from labor and management be used, at the discretion of government, to help finance specific development projects. Unfortunately, investment on this basis is likely to prove illiquid, whereas near-liquidity is essential for a substantial portion of the assets held by a social-security agency in view of contingent claims for benefit payments. The argument appears relevant that investment of the type cited is appropriate only if a large pool of idle funds exists. In this event, however, a contrary case can be made that the rate of contributions ought to be lowered, or that benefits ought to be increased (in keeping with the initial rationale for the program), or that investment ought to be by the route of government-bond purchases (thereby assuring near-liquidity).[24]

7. *Other.* Apart from taxation, revenue can also derive, possibly, from direct governmental participation in business operations. The importance of public-sector business operations varies widely among countries, depending upon the attitude prevailing relative to a socialist as against a free-enterprise approach. However, whether little or much involved in public-sector business operations, countries commonly do not show a profit on their undertakings in this connection. Indeed, most governments find themselves in the position of having to rationalize the absence of profit on the business operations they do undertake.[25]

---

[23] A proposal under consideration in the Philippines during 1956–57 suggested that reserve funds be used for loans for private-sector industrial projects.

[24] A relevant point, too, is that if social-security funds are held idle, deficit spending by government to a roughly equivalent extent then becomes possible without inflationary impact being a necessary consequence.

[25] Four main reasons can be cited for failure to make profit. First, outright loss is frequently invited when government feels obliged to pioneer new fields of operation as a prelude to entry into them by private enterprise, which can then, hopefully, make profit for itself. Second, private enterprise is motivated by profit, but some operations are not likely to yield profit, either in the short-run or in the long-run. Therefore, if these operations are deemed important, government is obliged to assume responsibility. Third, government can legitimately view itself as having numerous objectives, profit being only one of several conceivable objectives. Consequently, a case can be made for deliberate subordination of profit as an objective, as emphasis is given some other objective or objectives considered more important. Fourth, whatever offsetting merits might be cited, government frequently shows itself to be inefficient when cast in the role of entrepreneur. Consequently, what might have been a thin margin of profit can quickly give way to outright loss. Relative to this matter, see again Ch. 10, the section on "Private versus Public Initiative."

A few notable exceptions to the foregoing general situation can be found. One important exception involves the case in which government establishes itself in a monopoly position as regards an essential product or service, and then invokes a pricing policy intended to take advantage of its preferred market position. Examples include monopoly practices in the domestic processing and merchandising of tobacco and liquor products, or monopoly practices in the handling of crucial imports and exports. Select instances can be found in which considerable governmental revenue is derived in these ways. Indeed, somewhat more revenue than currently had can likely be garnered along these lines; however, as additional revenue comes consciously to be sought, a problem likely to be associated is how to balance the merits of added revenue against the possible demerits of consumer exploitation (as when monopoly pricing is vigorously pushed).

INCENTIVE TAXATION

To some extent, then, added revenue is a possibility in underdeveloped countries, despite the general handicap posed by the low level of GNP currently prevailing. Important as added revenue may be, however, it is important also that the tax structure under which the revenue accrues be of a type likely to foster economic incentive, rather than needlessly deter it.[26]

Incentive taxation refers to an exercise of tax powers so as to *stimulate economic activity*, either overall or selective. As intimated earlier, achievement of heightened economic activity is associated with an improved allocation and utilization of resources. Significantly, the manner in which resources are allocated and utilized can be influenced to an important extent through tax means. Specifically, three major tax approaches exist that might be used in an effort to influence resource allocation and utilization.

1.   *Tax Concessions.* In a first major category are tax concessions. The process of development calls for greater investment, with much of this investment generally devoted to entirely new forms of activity. Private entrepreneurs, even when financially well able to do so, are frequently reluctant to undertake the needed investment, in large part because of the risks presumed associated. Consequently, if government desires augmented private investment, tax concessions tailored to offset deterring risks offer one possible way to encourage investment. These

---

26 Incentive aspects of taxation are important, especially, when economic activity is heavily weighted toward a private sector. And, important as incentive aspects of taxation are in developed countries, their importance undoubtedly is even greater in underdeveloped countries; after all, as widely contended, it is easier to sustain a process of steady growth than to initiate it.

concessions are particularly relevant for income taxation, but are applicable in some other instances also, e.g., property taxation.

One form of concession involves tax-rate reduction. Notwithstanding some possible encouragement it lends to investment, this form of concession presents difficulties in application. If lower rates are made applicable only to new investment, or only to particular categories of new investment, other investors not given similar treatment can allege discrimination; and, if lower rates are granted on an across-the-board basis, beneficiaries are likely to include investors who merit no special encouragement, but who reap a windfall at the expense of total tax yield.

A second form of concession involves tax exemption for new enterprises over a period of time. This form of concession is of dubious merit. If a firm proves profitable, no tax exemption is needed; on the other hand, if a firm proves unprofitable, tax exemption is pointless (since, for example, no income tax is owing when no profit accrues).

A third form of concession involves a system of tax allowances based on accelerated depreciation (i.e., accelerated amortization). The procedure entails permissibility, under particular circumstances, for a rapid write-off of investment as against current earnings, in effect yielding lower tax liability during some short-run period than otherwise applicable. This procedure appears to embody attributes that fit it admirably for use in a developmental effort. High-priority projects can be accorded the privilege of accelerated depreciation, while low-priority projects can be required to extend depreciation over a longer period of time. In essence, favored investors are helped to a rapid recovery of their capital, which thereby lends encouragement to investment—in the sense that the tax concession offered helps to offset the impediment to investment arising from uncertainty as to the future.[27] Seemingly, this form of concession has much to commend it in the conceptual sense. In a practical sense, however, the procedure offers a serious challenge to administrators, as is evidenced even in developed countries. For successful application, a government must be able to withstand the strong pressure likely to be exerted as virtually every investor, irrespective of the nature of his investment, seeks the privilege of accelerated depreciation.

A fourth form of tax concession involves tax-forgiveness on current income whenever this income is committed for reinvestment within the firm. The rationale is that internal capital accumulation should not be handicapped through the subjection of firms to tax drains, and that reinvestment of earnings by firms should be encouraged in the interests

---

[27] The higher the profit return and the more quickly an investment is written off, the sooner a firm assumes liability for regular full tax payment (since resort to the privilege of accelerated depreciation is limited in time simply to that period required for recapturing the initial investment). Thus, what essentially occurs is that the taxpayer is able to shift tax payments from early years to later years.

of more rapid growth generally. Some sentiment for tax freedom for earnings committed to reinvestment also exists in developed countries; however, the case to be made there is rather weak, since capital sources external to individual firms, upon which these firms can draw for financing, are fairly abundant. In underdeveloped countries, in contrast, the usual absence of a well-organized capital market, or of accessible capital supplies generally, tends to give special appeal and pertinence to a tax procedure that allows for retention of earnings as a prelude to reinvestment.

2. *Taxes to Be Avoided.* In a second major category are taxes designed to be avoided. These taxes are imposed, not with the expectation that revenue will be collected, but in the hope that presence of the taxes will induce people to take particular action in order to avoid incurrence of tax liability. Included in this category are taxes on hoarding, whether of goods or of money. In underdeveloped countries, the speculative hoarding of goods is likely to comprise the more serious problem. A problem in this connection tends to arise, especially, when large-scale deficit financing in conjunction with a developmental program results in upward price pressure. In this case, imposition of a special tax upon excessive inventories[28] can serve to make the speculative holding of large stocks of goods unprofitable, thereby forcing goods onto the market where their presence can then help reduce existent inflationary pressure.

Actually, taxes in this category tend not to play a major role in any overall sense. They are important, rather, in terms of some special purpose on a particular occasion.

3. *Taxes to Compel Output.* In a third major category are taxes designed to compel increased output. The notion here is that imposition of particular tax levies can serve to compel increases in output on the part of prospective taxpayers as they are obliged to earn the means with which to meet the assessment. Included in this category are land taxes and head taxes.

To illustrate, an increase in land taxation allegedly tends to induce gains in output as landowners seek to compensate for added tax liability with heightened value of production—through more units of output, or upgraded output, or both.[29] Successful inducement of better land utilization represents a boon, of course, and especially so whenever large areas have been held in idleness or have been used ineffectively.

Again, a head tax—levied as a fixed amount per person (or per male

---

28 Meaning inventories larger than some stipulated norm.

29 If a landlord-tenant relationship is characteristic, the possibility exists that an initial impact of increased land taxation is stepped-up rentals and worsened living levels for tenants. However, to the extent that tenants already are at or near subsistence levels of living, the end effect of increased land taxation is likely to be either absorption by landlords of tax costs, or action by tenants to introduce more productive practices, or some combination of the two.

adult), and ordinarily payable annually in cash—allegedly has the effect of inducing added output in underdeveloped countries.[30] Thus, when production and income are at or near the subsistence level, added obligation tends to force greater work effort on the part of individuals who have no alternate way open to them for meeting the levy.[31] Beyond this, when a rising level of income is already an achievement, merit of another sort can be claimed. A head tax then helps drain away some of the added income accruing to the populace, and thereby helps to curb the added demand for consumer goods, or for leisure, which might otherwise arise to thwart the overall developmental effort.

CONCLUSIONS

Conclusions to be drawn from the foregoing are two-fold. First, an increase in tax revenue is not likely to be easily come by, although some marginal increase is generally a possibility. Second, whether or not total tax revenue is increased, it is desirable that the tax structure in existence has in it ingredients likely to provide an incentive for growth.

EXPENDITURE POLICY

When the annual level of expenditure is held strictly to the annual level of realized revenue, the ability of government to affect the pattern of saving and investment and of resource utilization is automatically somewhat limited, and especially so when taxable capacity is low, as typically is the case in underdeveloped countries. In the opinion of some persons, an approach to governmental finance along these lines is not compatible with the promotion of rapid development. These persons argue that when achievement of developmental progress is a national goal, a somewhat more positive and forceful role for government is in order. In keeping with this view, reference is frequently made to the essential merit of a fiscal-policy or *functional-finance* approach to governmental finance, under which *planned budgetary imbalance* is regarded as permissible, and even desirable. A truly active role for government is held dependent upon its capacity to undertake a level of expenditure

---

[30] In practice, use of a head tax to induce greater output ordinarily is limited to very poor and very underdeveloped regions, e.g., regions in Africa in which much of the populace hovers in indecision between continuation of tribal life and full-fledged entry into the market economy.

[31] Of course, the possibility exists that a head tax can be so high that it impairs incentive and output. For example, if presence of a head tax serves to lower the level of living below a certain minimum, incentive may be impaired, as may be also the capacity of individuals to continue in their work functions. Again, imposition of a head tax above a certain level may compel mass migration, with costly disruptions a possible consequence. Some persons contend that this has been the case in parts of Africa; imposition of a relatively steep head tax is said to have been followed by mass migration to cities, disruption of tribal life and established production, and creation of costly unemployment and related social problems.

that deviates (during an annual period) from the level of revenue accruing. Particularly, unless annual deficits are held permissible, the possibility of using a net monetary injection to accelerate investment[32] is denied government, and with this denial a major means through which development might be stimulated is ruled out.[33]

Of course, potential benefit derived from an approach of planned budget imbalance is linked to *how* fiscal management proceeds. More precisely, the extent to which an underdeveloped country can safely contemplate adherence to a system of planned budgetary imbalance, involving budgetary deficits of possible multi-year duration, is dependent upon two main considerations: the nature and purpose of governmental expenditure generally, and the magnitude and manner of financing any deficit.

PURPOSE OF EXPENDITURE

Viewed from the standpoint of the immediacy of the outlay, government expenditure falls into two major categories. First, government is obliged to support certain core functions, no matter what its view on development might be. Aside from defense, government is responsible for general administration and for the provision, in some amount, of basic public services. Typically, total current outlay in these connections in underdeveloped countries is low. Greater outlay would doubtless improve the overall environment, as seen by the average citizen. However, any added outlay would involve utilization of that much in the way of means that might have been devoted to, say, the promotion of development.[34]

Second, government can place emphasis, if it so chooses, upon promotion of development, and can do so in lieu of added support for core functions of the type cited. Emphasis upon development has the potential merit of giving rise to greater income capacity (on a sustained basis); and, significantly, it is upon the level of income itself that government's capacity to perform core functions on a consistent basis is ultimately dependent. Governmental outlay for purposes of development, in turn,

---

[32] Either directly *by* government, or indirectly *through* government (as loan capital comes to be offered by government in support of private investment).

[33] Historically, the approach of planned budget imbalance had its origins in developed countries, basically in response to business-cycle phenomena experienced there. For developed countries, the merit of the approach was associated with its usefulness as a stabilization device—unlike present-day underdeveloped countries, in which merit is associated more particularly with usage in the promotion of development.

Viewed from particular standpoints, of course, the approach of planned budget imbalance (annually) can only be regarded as unorthodox. Nevertheless, the idea involved appears to have enjoyed growing acceptance in many underdeveloped countries.

[34] Actually, normal population growth automatically requires application of some additional means for the handling of core functions, even though services rendered are made no more abundant per person.

is of three main types. In a first category is outlay for basic development, e.g., roads, schools, and irrigation systems. For the greater part, no marketable end-items arise directly; nevertheless, it is hoped that increased output will result, indirectly. In a second category is outlay for the creation of government-owned production facilities (e.g., factories) that can give rise directly to marketable end-items. In a third category is outlay for the endowment of loan facilities, with the loan funds at issue projected for use in the establishment of either public-sector or private-sector productive capacity that is capable of giving rise, directly, to marketable end-items. An illustration is capitalization of a development bank designed to provide financing for, say, factories.[35]

As government undertakes to augment its outlay as part of an effort to improve the lot of the people, a choice becomes necessary between added increments of outlay for immediate end-benefit and equivalent outlay for purposes at least one step removed from the provision of end-benefit. The choice is inescapable at some juncture, for the financial means that government might employ are not without limit. In making the choice, two basic points of reference are helpful to government. First, governmental outlay that creates a basis for *continuing* end-benefit, extending beyond the period of outlay by government, is to be preferred on that account to outlay that yields end-benefit only while new increments of outlay are put forth. According to this test, added expenditure for expanded social services or for make-work types of operations tends to be less meritorious than added expenditure for the installation of productive facilities that are capable later of sustained output of a marketable nature.[36]

Second, because underdeveloped countries are inclined to be inflation-prone, the merit of governmental outlay tends to vary, on that account, with the extent to which troublesome inflationary pressure can be avoided. According to this test,[37] outlay likely to give rise to marketable output that can move against added supplies of money appears generally preferable to outlay for purposes that do not yield marketable output.[38]

The conclusion which follows is that a government contemplating increased outlay for developmental purposes needs to take into account, as a minimum, both the potential developmental contribution and the potential inflationary impact of each major type of outlay. Significantly, some categories of outlay clearly rate better in terms of these factors than

---

[35] This procedure is notable because it offers a practical method by means of which public funds can be used to encourage private-sector growth.

[36] See again Ch. 10, the section on "Employment versus Income."

[37] Assuming deficit financing to be in operation.

[38] Because of the cited relationship, a strong case exists for budget balance (annual) as regards *current* operating costs of government, covering general administration and provision of core services. For further material on the matter of vulnerability to inflation, see again Ch. 10, the section on "Employment versus Income."

do others. An orderly appraisal of the relative merits of various categories of outlay, in terms of these and frequently additional factors, gives rise to a scale of priorities. Some underdeveloped countries view priority ratings as capable of being measured with mathematical precision, and proceed to develop formulae to assist in scoring.[39] Other underdeveloped countries do not employ a formalized approach of this type, but seek instead to apportion outlay in accordance with more generalized notions as to what comprises a reasonable array of priorities.[40]

FINANCING OF DEFICITS

A resort to deficit financing is often regarded purely and simply as an invitation to inflation. Actually, however, deficit financing need not necessarily prove any more inflationary than financing based on taxation. Sale of government bonds to the public involves a transfer of purchasing power from the public to the government, just as does collection of tax revenue; the central difference is that in the case of bonds members of the public receive an IOU, whereas in the case of taxes they simply receive a receipt indicating settlement of an obligation. If it can be assumed that the public would normally spend, either for consumption or for investment, that which is transferred to the government as a consequence of bond sales, subsequent spending of these funds by government involves no greater *aggregate* claim upon goods and services than if the spending privilege were exercised by the public. In practice, however, few government bonds are ordinarily sold to the public in underdeveloped countries;[41] rather, government bonds are characteristically sold to the Central Bank, in which they become backing for currency issues placed at the disposal of government. Under this procedure, deficit financing involves not a transfer of purchasing power from the public to the government, but an increase in the total money supply. Because the money supply is increased, potential for inflation comes into being. The extent of this potential for inflation is dependent, in turn, upon the magnitude of deficit financing, and the use to which borrowed funds are put in the course of being spent. The most important single consideration in the case of magnitude relates to the extent of slack in an

---

39 B. Higgins, *Economic Development* (New York: W. W. Norton & Company, Inc., 1959), pp. 653–686; see esp. pp. 654–668 and 682–686 for material on a formula developed in the Philippines.

40 The usual argument against use of formulae is that a precise mathematical approach is not particularly meaningful, considering that the variables involved can only be assigned specific values on an arbitrary basis in the first place. The premium is not upon mathematical precision, but upon good judgment—or so it can be argued. Only if good judgment prevails in the assignment of values to variables, and the formulae themselves are properly constructed, can results derived from formulae be trusted for public-policy purposes. But, if talent capable of exercising good judgment is on hand, the necessary public-policy decisions can be made anyway, short of dependence upon formulae—or so it can be argued.

41 See footnote 10 in the present chapter.

economy that is capable of being activated with a monetary injection,[42] while the most important single consideration in the case of use relates to the extent of added marketable output that arises as slack is taken up.

While deficit financing need not necessarily prove inflationary, under-developed countries typically do experience some price-level increases shortly after resort to it, and especially so when the means employed centers on injections of new money. According to the traditional concept of sound finance, inflation is economically bad. Indeed, considering sub-sidiary problems commonly raised in the wake of inflation, this view is not devoid of some claim to merit. Nevertheless, inflation is not *always* bad, nor in all respects. If what is referred to as inflation is a situation of moderately rising prices, with government continuously in control of the situation, at least one major benefit is potentially derivable: the stimulation of economic activity. Greater activity is a potential result largely because profits come to be augmented as costs lag behind prices in the cost-price relationship.[43]

Thus, the conclusion is invited that some inflation can yield benefit; but it also seems reasonable to hold that "too much" inflation jeopardizes the chance for economic improvement. Pronounced price increases, especially if erratic over time, are virtually certain to hamper growth in production—an expected consequence as values become highly distorted and unpredictable, and as personal motivation in effort comes to shift

---

[42] A basic fiscal principle, widely referred to, is that net injections of new money at points far short of full employment tend primarily to increase output and tend only incidentally to increase price, and that similar injections at points near full employment tend primarily to increase price and tend only incidentally to increase output. First propounded with the situation of developed countries in mind, the generalization appears less applicable to underdeveloped countries. The crux of the matter, alluded to earlier, is that the *chronic* underemployment of underdeveloped countries serves to produce different economic results than does the *occasional* un-employment of some developed countries. In developed countries, idle manpower and raw materials on occasion exist alongside idle production facilities (say, factories), so that an injection of new money can well help to activate idle factors in the existing but for the time being incompletely-used production facilities. In essence, new money can be used to help to bring existing means of production together, resulting in added output in rather short order—and with this output then able to move against the added money, thereby dampening possible price increases. In underdeveloped countries, however, production facilities through which underemployed manpower and ill-used raw materials might be better activated are largely non-existent. In these countries, the problem is one of how to create, in the first instance, the production facilities that, by their presence and operation, can create a demand for manpower and raw materials. An injection of new money, at best, can help create these production facilities; but, until these facilities are created and are capable of turning out products, there is an absence of more goods to match the added money. The result is that underdeveloped countries tend to be inflation-prone, *even when mass underemployment exists.*

[43] The late Lord Keynes, in weighing the relative merits of inflation and deflation (although against the environment of developed countries), favored moderate inflation. According to him, the tendency in the past toward a secular rise in prices has been good because ". . . depreciated money assisted the new men and emancipated them from the dead hand; benefited new wealth at the expense of the old, and armed enterprise against accumulation. . . . It has been a loosening influence against the rigid distribution of old-won wealth." See J. M. Keynes, *Monetary Reform* (New York: Harcourt, Brace & Company, Inc., 1924), pp. 12–13.

from new production to pure speculation. It is important, therefore, that government has at its disposal the means to check unwanted price movements, should these arise or threaten. In this respect, fiscal-policy techniques—tax and expenditure policies, and their interrelationships—readily lend themselves as potent instruments of control over the monetary and price structure. However, actions of the commercial-banking system also have an important bearing upon monetary and price matters, so that reasonable certainty of result in the application of fiscal-policy techniques is dependent in part upon the integration into fiscal policy of prevailing monetary policy (i.e., central-bank policy needs to be correlated with treasury policy).

DEBT BURDEN

If deficit financing is used in the course of promoting development, it is to be expected that national debt will rise over time, since the process of development itself is spread over time. Accordingly, some major questions arise as to the meaning of a rising level of debt within the environment of a developing country. How great a debt can be borne? Is not the debt a burden upon the population? Will not the debt bankrupt a country? The answer to these questions is that "it all depends." Basically, it depends upon how the debt arises and is handled, and upon how the funds generated are utilized.

An important initial consideration involves the distinction between a domestically-held debt and a foreign-held debt. If bonds are held domestically, servicing of debt proceeds in terms of domestic currency, and with payments made within the economy. In contrast, if bonds are held abroad, servicing proceeds in terms of foreign exchange, and with payments made outside the economy. As a consequence of this distinction, servicing and amortization ordinarily pose much more of a problem when debt is foreign-held than when domestically-held.

Assuming that borrowing proceeds domestically, the amount of debt a country can bear depends on two major considerations: income and interest. Relative to the first consideration, the ability of a country to service debt is closely tied to its level of output (real income) or, more importantly, to its capacity for output. Specifically, if a country's output or capacity for output come to be increased as a consequence of outlays based on borrowed funds, greater capacity to service the associated debt also comes to be present. In contrast, if the expenditure of borrowings occurs without a country's output or capacity for output reflecting beneficial impact, no offset against greater debt comes to exist; in this case, serious question may well arise as to how the added debt burden is to be handled. Thus, while incurrence of debt can serve to raise economic difficulties, it can also, under favorable circumstances, help to enrich an economy. Indeed, from this possibility of beneficial impact upon the economy springs the rationale for the use of debt as an instrumentality in the acceleration of development.

Beyond the cited relationship to income, the amount of bearable debt is also related to the applicable interest charge. Whether or not principal ultimately comes to be retired, interest payments on principal outstanding fall due periodically. These interest payments, on a domestically-held debt, comprise transfer payments within the economy; involved is some amount of redistribution of income and wealth within the economy, but the aggregates of these for the economy as a whole are left unaffected, at least in an initial sense. And, if borrowing proceeds through bond sales to the Central Bank, government in essence pays interest to itself—which then makes interest essentially a bookkeeping matter. For the greater part, therefore, liability for interest poses no stumbling block.

The general conclusion that seems warranted is that debt, far from being economically bad of necessity, offers itself as a medium of considerable potential usefulness in the acceleration of development. Whether or not this potential for usefulness comes to be realized depends, of course, upon particular practices and circumstances, some of the major of which are cited above.

SELECTED BIBLIOGRAPHY

Dragoslav Avramovic, *Debt Servicing Capacity and Postwar Growth in International Indebtedness*. Baltimore: The Johns Hopkins Press, 1958.
    Global survey of debt status; content includes statistical data and economic analysis.

Seymour E. Harris, *National Debt and the New Economics*. New York: The McGraw-Hill Book Company, Inc., 1947.
    Exposition of arguments pertinent to the national-debt question (emphasis on the US). For some views contrary to those of Harris, see James M. Buchanan, *Public Principles of Public Debt*. Homewood, Ill.: Richard D. Irwin, Inc., 1958.

Ragnar Nurkse, *Problems of Capital Formation in Underdeveloped Countries*. New York: Oxford University Press, 1953.
    Examination of various facets of the issue of capital formation in underdeveloped countries.

Sayre P. Schatz, "Underutilized Resources, 'Directed Demand,' and Deficit Financing," *Quarterly Journal of Economics*, November 1959.
    Demand and deficit financing in an environment of underdevelopedness; illustrated by references to Nigeria.

Henry C. Wallich and John H. Adler, *Public Finance in a Developing Country: El Salvador, a Case Study*. Cambridge: Harvard University Press, 1951.

Detailed examination of problems of public finance in an under-developed country.

14

INTERNAL READJUSTMENTS (II)

The companion of domestic currency is foreign exchange. Even if a satisfactory situation is achieved in the handling of domestic-currency matters, absence of a satisfactory situation as respects foreign exchange goes far to undermine the potential success of a developmental effort. Accordingly, given the particular environment and aspirations commonly found in underdeveloped countries, what policy or policies should prevail in the foreign-exchange area?

FOREIGN EXCHANGE AND DEVELOPMENT

An underdeveloped country is dependent upon access to some amount of foreign exchange.[1] Characteristically, this foreign exchange is hard to come by, and comprises

---

[1] Access to foreign exchange, in some amount, is important to an underdeveloped country for any one or more of three main reasons. First, given the low economic diversity typical of an underdeveloped country, some foreign exchange is needed for procurement abroad of particular consumer goods held essential to the pattern of life, no matter what view prevails as to developmental pace. Second, some foreign exchange is needed for procurement abroad of certain ingredients basic to development, e.g., machinery. Third, some foreign exchange may prove necessary for procurement externally of added supplies of goods in order to help vent internal market and price pressures arising in the course of an intensification of developmental effort.

Useful as some amount of foreign exchange is, it is possible, of course, for development to proceed on the basis of next to no foreign exchange. For example, the experience of the USSR demonstrates that development can proceed with the help of only little importation, but the experience also demonstrates that development is then confronted by extraordinary obstacles, involving extreme hardship and self-denial for the population.

a scarce item. Therefore, whatever foreign exchange does accrue ought to be used to good advantage. Basically, the foregoing describes what confronts the typical underdeveloped country as it sets out to formulate a foreign-exchange policy for itself.

Given this situation, a case exists for reliance upon exchange control. As pointed out in Chapter 11, the basic case for exchange control in underdeveloped countries rests on the possible aid that can be derived from it on behalf of a developmental effort. As pointed out there, this possible aid is of two main types. First, exchange control permits scarce supplies of foreign exchange to be directed to those specific uses most likely to yield high developmental impact. Second, exchange control allows subsidization of particular types of activity, and thereby holds potential as a means for accelerating development along preferred lines.

FOREIGN-EXCHANGE BUDGETING

Given the decision to use exchange control, it is imperative that the procedure be handled with a high degree of effectiveness. Minimum requirements are two-fold. First, on the supply side, all foreign exchange actually earned by an economy should fall within the purview of its exchange-control authority. Second, on the demand side, the foreign exchange deemed spendable should be used in accordance with a rational plan designed to give maximum advantage to the economy as a whole. What do these requirements call for, in practical terms?

On the first score, obvious leakages, such as those associated with deliberate undervaluation of exports and overvaluation of imports, should be guarded against. Only careful administration can prevent leakages of this type. On the second score, foreign-exchange allocations should occur in terms of a framework designed to promote development. This means that a country needs to formulate and adhere to a foreign-exchange budget, the counterpart in the foreign-exchange field of a fiscal budget in the domestic-currency field; in fact, the two budgets ought to be correlated to a considerable degree, especially since possession of domestic currency is a preliminary requisite for access to foreign exchange.

Some general principles can be cited as to the nature of a foreign-exchange budget. The budget should be prepared in annual terms, extending one or more years into the future, but for ease of administration the annual amounts can be subdivided to apply to shorter periods, say, quarter-year periods. The budget list should be limited to relatively few major categories of foreign-exchange demand (say, industrial-type machinery, other capital goods, raw materials, high-priority consumer goods, other consumer goods, and invisibles), and a clear understanding should exist as to what each category includes. Once the decision is reached as to the amount of foreign exchange available for allocations during the following year, this amount should be apportioned among the major categories listed.[2] The overall objective should be to allot as much of the available foreign exchange as is practical to the category or categories regarded as of high priority in the development scheme, and the category or categories deemed of lower priority in the development scheme should be treated less generously, i.e., as residuals.

Once a given foreign-exchange budget is deemed appropriate and is accepted, a determined effort should be made to adhere to it. Particularly, when the amount available for allocations in a category of low priority becomes depleted, there should be no quick replenishing of it through the simple expedient of dipping into the amount allotted to a category standing above it in the scale of values. Nor should the process of upgrading individual items by shifting them from a lower to a higher category be readily condoned, since this practice would undermine the entire allocation procedure.

The basic merit of a foreign-exchange budget of the type described is that it offers the best procedural framework yet devised for correlating available foreign exchange with the needs of a developmental program. It offers a way of assuring that the impasse will not likely arise in which a prospective importer of, say, high-priority industrial-type machinery has to be told that no foreign exchange is available for him because the necessary foreign exchange has been used to take care of importers of, say, low-priority consumer goods.

TECHNIQUES FOR INCREASING EXPORT EARNINGS

Foreign exchange is needed in the course of development, but it characteristically is in short supply in the countries seeking development.[3] If some amount of development could be realized, the foreign-exchange situation presumably would ease—as a consequence of the greater or more varied production then existent. The problem in underdeveloped countries, however, is one of how to get the desired development underway in the first instance, and to do so in the face of a short supply of foreign exchange.

Obviously, insofar as it is possible to increase the supply of foreign exchange at any given time, the push that can be given to development can be intensified. Therefore, are there policies or practices that an under-

---

2 In event the country is the recipient of external assistance, either through loans or grants, an amount stemming therefrom can be integrated within the total framework, along with the amount held available on the basis of current exchange earnings or accumulated reserves.

3 The petroleum-rich countries are possible exceptions to the general rule of foreign-exchange scarcity.

developed country might employ—currently, without further ado—in order to earn *some* additional amount of foreign exchange for itself? The following surveys some much-cited methods that, according to their proponents, hold potential for improving the foreign-exchange situation in *individual* underdeveloped countries, particularly as seen from the supply side.

MULTIPLE EXCHANGE RATES

Some exchange-control countries employ a system of multiple exchange rates, instead of a single-rate system. Under a multiple-rate system, purchases of foreign exchange occur at two or more rates, or sales occur at two or more rates, or both purchases and sales occur at two or more rates.[4]

Proponents of a system of multiple exchange rates can point to two possible advantages. First, governmental revenue can be derived through its use. If foreign exchange accruing to residents is purchased (converted) by exchange-control authorities at a rate lower than that at which subsequent sales to residents demanding foreign exchange occur, the difference constitutes a profit for government, arising in terms of domestic currency.[5]

Second, and ordinarily far more important for development, the direction and pace of economic activity can be affected through a system of multiple exchange rates. On the buying side, a favorable (high) conversion rate gives greater incentive for acquiring foreign exchange than does an adverse (low) rate. Thus, domestic output destined to enter export channels under any conditions can be accorded a low conversion rate without the danger that export volume, or total foreign-exchange proceeds, will be impaired by it; but, domestic output not likely to enter export channels unless given special inducement can be accorded a high conversion rate, as a consequence of which some added exportation may occur, and thereby help to increase the country's total foreign-exchange proceeds.[6] The important point is that a system of multiple rates on the buying side raises the possibility that some added exportation will be made possible, and that total foreign-exchange receipts will thereby be

---

[4] To illustrate, Brazil (as of January 1, 1958) had in effect thirteen distinct categories of buying rates, ranging (in cruzeiros per US dollar) between Cr$18.36 and Cr$103.00 per US$1.00, and eight distinct categories of selling rates, ranging between Cr$18.82 and Cr$246.82 per US$1.00.

[5] As a "tax" device, the exchange-rate differential has an effect somewhat similar to an import duty, or an export tax, or a combination of the two (both of which were treated in Ch. 13). Apart from the tax angle, of course, likely effect upon the supply of foreign exchange is of importance also. This aspect is examined under the second major advantage claimed for a system of multiple exchange rates: influence on the direction and pace of economic activity.

[6] When added exportation occurs because exporters reduce prices, an increase in total foreign-exchange proceeds can result only if the physical volume of exportation increases more than enough to offset the lower price obtained per unit.

increased somewhat; meanwhile, any concessions granted to induce the added exportation are confined to particular "sensitive" items, and are not extended across-the-board to all items, irrespective of whether or not these need special encouragement in order actually to enter export trade. Again, on the selling side, a favorable (low) conversion rate acts as a subsidy for importers, while an adverse (high) conversion rate acts as a tax. Thus, those imports especially desired, such as the machinery and equipment needed in a developmental effort, can be accorded a low rate by way of encouragement; but "non-essential" categories of foreign-exchange demand can be held to a high rate in the hope that requests by prospective purchasers will thereby be lessened. Involved is a channelization of foreign exchange away from low-priority uses and toward high-priority uses; low-priority uses are penalized, while high-priority uses are subsidized.

Seemingly, advantages inherent in multiple-rate systems are sufficiently great to make underdeveloped countries want to move to them. Yet, many underdeveloped countries do not have multiple-rate systems, a fact explainable in large part by wide acceptance of the idea that a major drawback is associated: complexities of administration. A multiple-rate system tends to be considerably more difficult to administer than a single-rate system. Under a multiple-rate system, exchange-control authorities typically come to experience pressure from both buyers and sellers of foreign exchange as these seek favorable classifications for themselves within the scale of rates prevailing. As a minimum, definitions—meaningful and enforceable—have to be arrived at as to what each rate bracket embraces, and this is no easy matter at best.

PRICE SUPPORTS

An alternate approach to indirect subsidies for exporters, or producer-exporters, through conversion of exchange proceeds at preferential rates is that of direct subsidies under a domestic program geared to guarantee minimum prices for producers.

While price-support schemes can take many forms, the central idea is assurance by government of certain minimum prices for particular categories of production, in order to stimulate output likely to eventuate in added exportation—even if (or because) foreign-exchange proceeds yield lower returns in the regular conversion process. To illustrate, assume the following circumstances: domestic cost of production of a commodity is ₱ 2.50; external selling price is $1.00; the official rate of exchange is ₱ 2.00 = $1.00; no transport costs or trade barriers are involved. Sale abroad of one unit of the commodity then yields the producer no more than ₱ 2.00, but his cost of production is ₱ 2.50. Obviously, the producer cannot continue export sales for long under these circumstances. But, if government subsidizes the producer by ₱ 0.50 per unit of export sales, production and exportation are possible, and foreign exchange can accrue to the country. Considering that added foreign exchange is needed by the country, and considering that the added exports are likely to embody what would otherwise be idle land and manpower, entirely or partially, the case for payment of a subsidy appears to be fairly strong.

There is another side to the story, however, which has made many a country reluctant to introduce a price-support program at any point. First, price-support programs tend to be costly in terms of the domestic currency a country's treasury is called upon to pay out. While foreign exchange comprises a more precious item for an underdeveloped country than does the domestic currency it uses in making subsidy payments, nevertheless the possibility always exists that an equivalent amount of public outlay in domestic currency might yield greater advantage if made in some other connection.

Second, price-support programs frequently come, over time, to encompass production going far beyond that initially intended to receive coverage, and far beyond what has even remote economic claim to subsidization. In essence, a subsidy for one person tends to constitute an invitation for others to try also to obtain subsidies. Pressures arise, and it is not always possible to resist them successfully. In the process, a possible result is that some inefficient producers can avail themselves of the helping hand of subsidization, which then obviates the need for them to strive for greater efficiency.

Further, legitimate questions arise as to what constitutes equity in application and administration. For example, if the export portion of the production of a particular commodity is subsidized, should not the domestically-used portion also be subsidized (since the items, as seen by producers, are identical)? And, if domestically-used output of one type is subsidized, should not other producers also have access to subsidization, even when their output is consumed domestically in its entirety? Given the prospect of these difficulties and pitfalls, a common reaction is that, desirable as the objective of price-support programs may be, it is better to seek attainment of this objective through other means.

TARIFFS, PLUS SUBSIDIES

A variation of the foregoing approach links revenue tariffs with subsidization of select exports. Under this method, proceeds from revenue tariffs are earmarked for subsequent allocation as subsidy to particular items of domestic production entering export markets, provided these items are not likely to enter export markets without a subsidy.

An advantage of this method over the immediately preceding one is that funds used here in subsidization come from specific sources, not from general treasury funds. The link to specific sources tends to lessen potential abuse, both as to the total magnitude of subsidization and the likely duration of subsidization. Significantly, removal at some point of the revenue tariffs automatically removes the basis for subsidization.

BARTER

When an expansion in exports and imports is sought, but the prevailing currency situation poses an obstacle, barter offers a possible way to by-pass important currency difficulties, thus helping to bring about an expansion in trade nonetheless. As proponents of barter arrangements point out, customary exports and imports continue to be handled through usual channels, with payments effected in terms of foreign exchange, but an attempt is made beyond this to arrange for specific additional exports in direct exchange for specific additional imports, with these transactions occurring outside the usual foreign-exchange channels. Since numerous countries have potential for forms of added output not currently disposable abroad on a cash basis, some scope for barter appears to exist. And, if added exportation as a consequence of barter arrangements can give access to added imports that are of overall value in a developmental effort, a clear gain is capable of being registered.

While a strong case can be made for barter as an addition to regular trade, a major weakness is found in the tendency for barter trade to cut into regular trade. This tendency shows up in the following manner. Export proceeds obtained from regular trade are converted at the official rate of exchange. If this official rate overvalues the domestic currency, as is common under exchange-control conditions, the conversion process yields exporters less in domestic currency than is rightfully theirs when measured by free-market tests. At the same time, importers who are able to obtain foreign exchange at the official rate, assuming again that this rate overvalues the domestic currency, are really being given low-cost access to foreign goods. Considering the further fact that imported goods are likely to be curtailed in supply under exchange-control conditions, and hence able to command premium prices in the domestic market, importers characteristically become beneficiaries of monopoly-type profits. Exporters are not unaware of this set of facts. As they see it, they are penalized in order to subsidize importers. Given no alternative, they are obliged to grin and bear what becomes their lot under the exchange-control procedure.

But, barter offers exporters an alternative. No longer are they necessarily obliged to convert foreign-exchange proceeds at comparatively unfavorable rates. Rather, the possibility opens for them to obtain imports in exchange for their exports, and these imports, if of the right types, then command premium prices in the domestic market, so that the effective return to them from given exports, in terms of domestic currency, can be augmented. The letter and spirit of exchange-control legislation and decrees, of course, may clearly hold that only additional exports are eligible for barter transactions. But, what are *additional* exports when items are standardized? Typically, once the door to barter is opened, pressure from exporters tends to grow as they clamor for barter rights. Given the administrative complexities involved, it is no surprise to find later that exports giving rise to foreign-exchange receipts undergo a decline, and that foreign-exchange proceeds fail to hold their own. The core explanation is simply that some exports previously sold outright, giving rise to foreign exchange subject to conversion under the exchange-control process, come to be used instead in barter trade.[7] Of some significance, the alleged inconvenience of barter—that it makes an importer of every exporter—is no meaningful deterrent to the tendency described; as barter trade comes to flourish, exporters acquire import rights, which they may well have no intention of using themselves, but which are salable in the open market to prospective importers. The result is that the monopoly-type profits arising from the sale of scarce items come to be transferred from importers to exporters.

Thus, a good theoretical case can be made for barter; barter offers a basis for additional exportation, and hence for additional importation. But, in practice, barter can be the instrument that pulls the props from under exchange control. This is the situation when barter trade comes to cover not only additional exports, but also considerable exports of types that previously yielded foreign exchange. In short, the key to a successful barter system is strong administration; exchange-control authorities need to have the power, and the willingness to act, to prevent the shifting of regular export trade into the barter category.

Additionally, successful administration of a barter system requires that the process of granting barter privileges be correlated with the formulation of the foreign-exchange budget. Added imports under barter tend, by and large, to be of those types most likely to command premium prices in the domestic market—which generally means non-essentials, i.e., low-priority items in the foreign-exchange budget and in the overall scheme for development. To the extent that added imports of this type occur, exchange-control authorities appear justified in taking action aimed to curtail regular allocations to the categories of import demand rated low in the priority scale. The potential merit of barter, in the final analysis, is that it offers an inducement for added exportation, and even

---

[7] A good case in point, which demonstrates some of the foregoing problems, is the No-Dollar Import Law, enacted in the Philippines in 1955. For comments on this law, see IMF, *International Financial News Survey*, Washington, June 1, 1957, p. 378.

though resulting importation is likely to be of types rated low in the priority scale, pressure is lessened upon exchange-control authorities for outright allocations of foreign exchange for similar imports; hence, the foreign exchange that exchange-control authorities do have under their control can be upgraded in use—as less is used for low-priority imports and more is used for high-priority imports. In this way, barter can prove helpful in a developmental effort. Indeed, the situation then is far different from that in which barter is used as a means to circumvent exchange control, thereby serving to undermine it.

RETENTION QUOTAS

A system of retention quotas is another possibility. Under this system, exporters of hard-to-export items are required to surrender to exchange-control authorities only a portion of their foreign-exchange receipts; the remaining foreign-exchange receipts either can be used directly by the exporters to acquire imports of the type likely to yield profit in the domestic market, or can be sold by the exporters to others demanding foreign exchange, some of whom can be presumed willing to pay premium prices when access through official exchange-control channels is severely restricted. The economic rationale for retention quotas is that particular exporters are thereby given an inducement to sell some items abroad that are not otherwise likely to prove salable; any profit made by the exporter from use or sale of the foreign exchange retained by him can help to augment returns realized on the sale of the export item itself, as a consequence of which export sales at prices equivalent to, or even below, domestic cost of production become possible. The expected effect is to enable some exports to occur *in addition to* those regularly occurring, and hence to add some amount to a country's total foreign-exchange receipts.

Meritorious as is the idea behind retention quotas, the system is not an easy one to administer. Once retention rights are to be had, more and more potential exporters clamor for inclusion. Indeed, a major difficulty is ordinarily encountered in reaching decisions as to where to draw the line. Each category of production has its marginal producer, who seems to have a valid claim to retention rights, given the basic rationale at issue. But, if retention rights are extended to a high-cost producer, should not similar rights be extended to all producers of the item, including low-cost producers? If these rights are denied low-cost producers, the system is open to criticism on the grounds of rewarding inefficiency with special privilege; and, if these rights are given low-cost producers, a question exists as to what gain the economy as a whole receives from the indirect subsidy granted.

If a system of retention quotas is introduced, the foreign exchange retained by exporters for disposal at their discretion tends to be used in ways accorded low status in the foreign-exchange budget; after all, it is the categories of foreign-exchange demand rating low in the scale of priorities that tend to be most deprived of foreign exchange by exchange-control authorities, and hence the potential profit realizable from foreign exchange diverted to them by exporters coming into possession of foreign exchange tends to be greatest there. Accordingly, simultaneously with the sanctioning of retention quotas, exchange-control authorities ought to curtail formal allocations to those categories of foreign-exchange demand rating low in the scale of priorities. As a consequence, a greater proportion of available foreign exchange can be allotted to those categories of foreign-exchange demand rating higher in the scale of priorities. The possible result, then, is an overall upgrading in the usage of foreign exchange. Assurance of this result, however, is dependent upon adept administration.

MULTIPLE CURRENCY RESERVES

A special case involves those countries that hold their international currency reserves in few currencies, rather than in many—i.e., in one currency, or possibly in two or three currencies, but certainly not in five or more currencies. It is contended on occasion that these countries would probably stand a better chance of expanding their total exports, and hence of improving their import potentials, if they were only willing to conduct international transactions in terms of additional currencies.[8]

The argument for a broader international currency reserve proceeds as follows. Viewed from the export side, the holding of reserves in one currency, or in few currencies, obliges exporters to sell for the particular currency or currencies. Significantly, the currency or currencies involved may be internationally scarce, in the sense that numerous countries have exchange-control restrictions in effect as regards usage, so that an attempt to sell exclusively in terms of the particular currency or currencies tends to limit potential export sales. Viewed from the import side, the holding of reserves in one currency, or in few currencies, results in payment for

---

[8] The holding of an international currency reserve in terms of one or few currencies is frequently the result of peculiar historical circumstances, more particularly than of unique economic characteristics. For example, the Philippines holds its reserve exclusively in terms of US dollars, an obvious consequence of its long and close relationship with the US.

Dissatisfaction in certain quarters in the Philippines with the volume of export trade possible in terms of US dollar payment (in a world in which the US dollar for some years had clearly been *the* scarce currency) invited examination during the mid-1950's of a proposal that the country move to a multiple currency reserve. Proponents argued that total export volume would rise if payment were accepted in, say, sterling, marks, and yen, in addition to the US dollar. Critics retaliated with the argument that legalization of sales on a multi-currency basis would lead to a weakening of the country's entire foreign-exchange structure. Specifically, it was feared that receipts in the new currencies would arise largely from sales that *might have been made* for US dollars, not from *additional* sales.

imports in the available currency, even though the imports might have been obtained with other, easier-to-acquire currencies not a part of the reserve. As opposed to this situation, the possibility exists that if a country is willing to sell for additional currencies, export sales might be increased; and, if the additional currencies are selected with some care, the possibility exists that the further foreign-exchange receipts derived can then give a country access to greater imports of types compatible with its developmental aspirations.

When a country seeks to broaden its international currency reserve, so as to enable transactions to occur in a wider trade area, two important precautions are ordinarily necessary. First, exchange-control authorities need to guard against the diversion of prevailing exports from current market channels, yielding currency or currencies commonly regarded to be of wide usage, to such new channels as are likely to yield forms of currency of less wide usage—although these further currencies ordinarily are worth having, especially if the acquisitions are actually in addition to previous earnings. In essence, acceptance of additional forms of currency needs to be limited to additional exports, at least during initial phases, and perhaps much longer. Furtherance of this prospect requires careful administration, in which connection a system of export permits is ordinarily regarded an indispensable aid.

Second, a higher total international currency reserve needs to be maintained when many currencies, rather than few, are involved. The basic purpose of a reserve is to act as a buffer to absorb the repercussions of fluctuations in trade. Since latitude for a cushioning effect is needed in the case of each currency, the greater the number of currencies, the greater, ordinarily, is the total amount required to be tied up in reserve. Admittedly, this factor constitutes a drawback of some consequence; certainly, a country needs to have a substantial reserve, or a rising reserve, if it is to venture safely into an expansion in the composition of its currency reserve. If this is a drawback, however, it is so only at the time a country shifts to the new reserve status; thereafter, the crucial basis for evaluation is simply the effect upon foreign-exchange earnings *in toto*.

STATE TRADING

Another possibility in the attempt to improve a country's foreign-exchange status involves state trading. State trading refers to the direct entry of government into trading activity, either to the exclusion of private traders or alongside them. In some underdeveloped countries, government limits its direct participation to the foreign-trade function, buying goods from private producers prior to export, and (or) selling imports to private distributors who then handle domestic sales; in other underdeveloped countries, however, the foreign-trade function is linked with a network of domestic government-operated enterprises engaged in the purchase and (or) sale of goods, encompassing both foreign-trade and purely domestic items.

Despite its fairly short history as a technique, numerous under-developed countries currently practice state trading, and the volume of trade carried on under these auspices continues to grow in some countries. Three major factors can be cited to explain this growth of state trading. First, channelization of trade through government automatically yields an element of control, which is frequently desired on particular scores. Control is maximized when government is a monopolist-monopsonist, but control can also exist when private trade coexists, since governmental activity can serve to set standards that private traders may not be able to ignore.[9]

Second, through participation in trading activities, government gains access to a potential source of revenue. Profit (in terms of domestic currency) accrues to government whenever sales occur at prices above costs, whether sales involve import items or export items. Few questions are raised by that profit derived from export items; but, a domestic-currency profit derived from sale of import items is not necessarily a clear gain. For example, it would be ironical if foreign-exchange outlays were intensified to give government access to more imports in order that these goods might then be sold domestically to realize a domestic-currency profit. In essence, maximization of revenue is inconsistent with conservation of foreign exchange; therefore, given the usual scarcity of foreign exchange, revenue from the import side of transactions ought to be regarded as secondary to some other functions performed by state trading. Actually, of course, not all state-trading operations result in profit. While potential profit is sometimes cited at the outset as one justification for state trading, reference to it as a goal is frequently found absent soon thereafter, presumably because profit fails to materialize (or is deliberately by-passed as other goals are given primary attention).

Third, and perhaps most important, conduct of trade under govern-mental auspices enables subsidization to occur pretty much when and as government sees fit. Thus, if certain domestically-produced items cannot be profitably sold abroad under the prevailing exchange rate, one method open to government is to purchase these items at prices at least sufficient to cover cost of production, and then to market the items abroad at going world prices. The loss in domestic currency incurred can be rationalized

---

[9] In some countries, governmental participation in import-export trade, and also in domestic trade, has been rationalized in terms of getting trade out from under the domination of foreigners, or of particular national minorities (e.g., as in the case of some countries of Southeast Asia that purportedly sought to curb the economic influence of their "overseas Chinese" minorities).

by government on the grounds that added foreign exchange—to say nothing of employment and other possible gains—accrues to the economy as a consequence of the particular sales. Again, if certain imports required in conjunction with a developmental effort prove too costly under the prevailing exchange rate to motivate private entrepreneurs, government can undertake the importation on its own, and thereafter sell the items to entrepreneurs at whatever price is required to promote purchase. The subsidy to end-users can be rationalized by government as an overhead cost in the stimulation of development.

FOREIGN-EXCHANGE AUCTIONS

An administrative problem that commonly confronts exchange-control authorities is how best to deal with persons determined to gain access to foreign exchange, but whose claim under the established priority schedule ranks them in the lower categories to which only little foreign exchange is ordinarily allotted. One procedure is simply to let exchange-control authorities make allocations insofar as quantity allows and in accordance with clearly prescribed criteria, saying "yes" to some applicants and "no" to others. Unfortunately, however, applicants whose needs can be met only from a pool that, for them, is seemingly forever undernourished—undernourished of necessity, if higher-priority categories are to be serviced in more generous fashion—are almost certain to resent the alleged arbitrariness of the exchange-control procedure, and become likely recruits for any concerted movement aimed at abolition of the system of exchange control. To overcome this point of potential difficulty, an alternate procedure is frequently recommended: foreign-exchange auctioning.

Under a system of foreign-exchange auctioning, exchange-control authorities continue to earmark foreign exchange for each major category of foreign-exchange demand. Allocations continue to be made on the basis of individual applicants being able to qualify within each of these major categories, *except* that categories low on the priority scale are treated differently. Instead of considering the relative merits of each individual application within these low categories, exchange-control authorities simply put up for auction, in a series of blocks periodically over time, the foreign exchange held eligible for disposal for the prescribed general purpose.

A first major advantage of auctioning is that anyone who wants foreign exchange can get it simply by out-bidding others. Exchange-control authorities are spared the unenviable task of having to say "no" to persons who are determined to gain access to foreign exchange even though they have only low-priority claim. A second major advantage involves revenue for government. In the absence of auctioning, those importers who qualify for foreign exchange frequently reap a windfall profit, since import items are in short supply and hence sell at premium prices. Under auctioning, as prospective importers vie with one another for import rights, they bid up the price of the particular block of foreign exchange put up for sale. As a consequence, the monopoly-type profit, which otherwise would accrue to private importers, tends to accrue to government.[10]

Auction systems are known, in one form or another, to several countries, with the classic case being that of Brazil.[11] Experience seems to indicate that auction systems can help exchange-control authorities in their public-relations problems, and can divert to government some moneys that would otherwise accrue as private profit. But no basis for access to additional foreign exchange is involved in the approach; the most that can be claimed is smoother operation for the exchange-control system, with a better overall job in allocation as a prospect.

WHAT RATE OF EXCHANGE?

The practice of exchange control makes possible, and even invites, maintenance of a discrepancy between the official and likely free-market rates of exchange. Specifically, domestic currency is likely to be or become overvalued relative to foreign currency. The question thereupon arises as to how great a discrepancy between official and free-market rates should be tolerated, or sought. Involved is an issue of deep implication, since the manner in which it is resolved affects both the path and pace of development and, in a collective sense, the status of the international payments framework.

In the opinion of some persons, any deviation from a free market in foreign exchange is bad, prima facie. However, for those who believe that market intervention can offer advantages, at least under particular circumstances, the matter becomes one, more particularly, of what price-tag to place on foreign exchange. Unfortunately, once a free market is abandoned, there is no one price figure that emerges clearly as most appropriate. Rather, the pricing of foreign exchange becomes a matter of plain government fiat. The best to be hoped for then is that the authorities responsible will exercise reasonable judgment as they pro-

---

10 In addition to the demand for foreign exchange to finance importation of low-priority commodities, the demand for foreign exchange to finance foreign travel and some categories of capital transfers typically also rates low in the priority scale, and hence is ideally suited for coverage under an auction system.

11 For information on the Brazilian procedure, see IMF, *Ninth Annual Report on Exchange Restrictions*, Washington, 1958, esp. pp. 61–62. For news comment on the introduction of the procedure in Brazil, see *Newsweek*, October 26, 1953, p. 64.

ceed to weigh the pros and cons of either a higher or lower rate of exchange.[12]

Whatever the rate or rates[13] of exchange selected, an important consideration is that relative stability then prevails in the exchange market. Business transactions involve commitments over time; hence, quite apart from the particular exchange-rate level, exchange-rate instability constitutes an added business hazard that should be avoided, or kept at a minimum.[14]

THE REINFORCING ROLE OF TARIFFS

If it is granted that government should give conscious direction to development, why not use a system of tariffs by way of implementation, instead of exchange control?[15] This is a question numerous economists ask, and some answer in favor of tariffs.

Tariffs have two main purposes: revenue or protection. Given the usual revenue situation in underdeveloped countries, it is quite legitimate for these countries to think in terms of a system of revenue-producing

---

[12] On the one hand, a vastly overvalued domestic currency (in terms of the official exchange rate) tends to increase the attractiveness of imports, since all those allotted foreign exchange then receive a form of subsidization, and tends to disappoint exporters or producer-exporters, since the treatment accorded them amounts to penalization. Between the dual pressures thereby fostered, the administrative difficulties that confront exchange-control authorities are likely to be great. In addition, the wider the discrepancy between official and free-market rates, the more the domestic price structure tends to deviate from external price structures. This situation needs not necessarily hamper development (indeed, it may even aid it), but it does raise questions as to the feasibility of reverting to a free-exchange system at some future date when the initial reasons for having exchange control no longer exist.

On the other hand, devaluation (i.e., moving the official exchange rate nearer the free-market rate) also has its drawbacks. For example, devaluation raises the domestic-currency cost of imports, and does so without regard to their essentiality or to the income status of their consumers. At the same time, external prices of exports produced under conditions of inelastic supply (a typical export situation in underdeveloped countries) decline only slightly or not at all, given the fact that little increase in output tends to follow devaluation; hence prices of these exports (in terms of domestic currency) tend to rise considerably, thereby yielding windfall gains for producers or exporters—which gains are theirs for no apparent good reason, and without a country's realization of any appreciable balance-of-payments improvement. Again, devaluation is inflationary, on balance, in its initial impact. Domestic-currency costs of imports rise, and come to exert an upward bias within the domestic price structure; concurrently, exporters gain access to additional domestic currency in the conversion process, and do so without any added output having necessarily occurred. While it can be argued that some amount of inflation may be a price a country has to pay to achieve accelerated development, this argument offers no support for the generation of inflationary pressures through action yielding sheer windfalls for producers or exporters.

[13] In a frank attempt to steer a "happy" course in this matter, some countries have resorted to multiple rates of exchange.

[14] Purchase and sale of forward exchange offers a way to hedge against the hazards of exchange-rate instability. There is ample evidence, however, that business tends to be psychologically distressed by exchange-rate instability, even when forward exchange is available as a hedge.

[15] This question might be raised, too, as respects the use of import quotas.

tariffs. When revenue is the objective, duty rates ideally should be moderate; rates above certain levels tend to discourage importation,[16] and duty is collectible only on items actually entering. A moderate rate structure has the possible additional advantage of not producing major price distortions that might act to warp economic activity. Besides the desirability of a generally low overall rate structure, some imports should ideally remain entirely free of duty, e.g., the machinery imports regarded as vital in a developmental effort. There is little point in penalizing development through deliberate action that makes key ingredients more costly to users.

Aside from revenue, tariffs can be used to provide protection, in which case duty rates tend to exceed by wide margins those ordinarily held justifiable on grounds of revenue. A foremost argument advanced for tariff protection is that of provision of shelter for infant industries, an argument of special pertinence for underdeveloped countries. The argument is that *temporary* protection is needed to help enterprises become established, after which the special protection can be removed, leaving the enterprises to compete on their own. Unfortunately, however fine the logic, much abuse is possible under the guise of such a rationale. For example, tariffs are frequently continued, sometimes in stepped-up form, as other arguments are used to replace the infant-industry argument initially relied upon. In short, the infant-industry doctrine holds economic merit; but, much abuse can occur in its name, unless a government is prepared to withstand the special pleas of vested interests.

In comparison with the foregoing, exchange control yields no revenue to government (other than in special instances), but protection automatically accrues from it, the precise amount depending upon the extent to which foreign exchange is denied would-be importers of items competitive with domestic output. If no foreign exchange is allocated for particular imports, the domestic market is reserved, absolutely, for domestic producers. In short, a country that wishes to protect domestic production has an option: protection through tariffs or through exchange control.[17]

Since either tariffs or exchange control can be used to provide protection, are there advantages that clearly favor one over the other? Three unique advantages can be cited on behalf of exchange control. First, exchange control is positive in its impact upon import levels. If no foreign exchange is made available, there is no competitive importation

---

16 Imposition of a tax upon competitive domestic production to offset an import duty can help nullify the protective tendencies of a tariff.

17 The infant-industry argument, as a rationale for protective tariffs, arose before exchange control gained popularity. Significantly, however, the infant-industry argument can be applied to exchange control just as readily as to tariffs, assuming the use of exchange control for purposes of protection.

at any price. In contrast, some doubt always remains in the case of protective tariffs, since what constitutes a protective rate under one level of price may yield no protection at another level. Second, exchange control has potential merit for underdeveloped countries on grounds besides protection. Specifically, exchange control involves the allocation, *on a basis other than price alone,* of scarce supplies of foreign exchange in order to achieve certain desired ends. Since exchange control holds this potential merit, in addition to its capacity to yield protective benefit, it has at least one clear-cut advantage over protective tariffs. Third, exchange control is administratively flexible. For example, as foreign-exchange supplies eventually become more abundant, exchange control can be administered so as to move toward a free-market situation in foreign exchange, and this can be done without new laws having to be passed. In contrast, protective tariffs are fixed in law, and tend to prove difficult to remove or even to lower, as the course of history attests.[18]

Actually, discussion of the matter in terms of tariffs versus exchange control is somewhat amiss, since the techniques are not entirely interchangeable, and hence ought not to be viewed as necessarily competitive. Even if it is admitted that exchange control has certain advantages, this is not to imply that tariffs do not have something to add on their own accord. To illustrate, it is possible to use simultaneously a system of tariffs for revenue and a system of exchange control for purposes of foreign-exchange allocation. Indeed, to the extent that tariffs for revenue discourage importation, pressure upon authorities responsible for administering exchange control is lessened. Instead of being competitive, then, tariffs and exchange control are capable of being used concurrently, and with considerable complementarity between them.

SELECTED BIBLIOGRAPHY

John H. Adler, "The Fiscal and Monetary Implementation of Development Programs," *American Economic Review Papers and Proceedings,* May 1952.
    Survey of implementation facets, covering fiscal and monetary matters.

International Monetary Fund, *Tenth Annual Report on Exchange Restrictions,* Washington, 1959. (Issued annually.)
    Survey of the status of exchange restrictions in member countries of the IMF.

---

[18] Two important counter-arguments against exchange control can be cited. First, exchange control may be administratively flexible, but the administrative process also opens the door to possible corruption. Second, when exchange control leads to a wide difference between the official and the free-market rates of exchange, resulting price distortions can be great, so that tariffs are not alone in being censurable on this score.

Alexandre Kafka, "The Brazilian Exchange Auction System," *Review of Economics and Statistics,* August 1956.
    Examination of the case for multiple rates of exchange, with particular attention given Brazil's auction system.

Raúl Prebisch, *Memoria de la Primera Reunión de Técnicos sobre Problemas de Banca Central del Continente Americano.* Mexico City: Banco de Mexico, 1946.
    Survey of major problems of monetary management in under-developed countries (as applicable to Latin America); heavy emphasis on relation of foreign trade to monetary matters.

Henry C. Wallich, *Monetary Problems of an Export Economy: The Cuban Experience, 1914–1947.* Cambridge: Harvard University Press, 1950.
    Examination of the monetary problems peculiar to a raw-materials-producing country.

15

EXTERNAL ASSISTANCE

Economic development involves a costly process. However, the magnitude of current GNP devoted to development by the typical underdeveloped country is small. Undoubtedly, if a more determined effort were made, this magnitude could be raised. But, even in the event of considerable added effort, although short of imposing severe totalitarian-type methods, the magnitude of current GNP going to development would *still* leave much to be desired. The essential point is that it is difficult to divert much of current GNP to development when real per-capita income is low. Yet, if the pace of development is prescribed by the means that can reasonably be generated domestically, growth rates are likely to remain at low levels.

One way to accelerate development is to draw upon external means in order to supplement and reinforce available domestic means. It is common knowledge that external assistance figured significantly in the development of some of the present-day developed countries, e.g., the US. In similar fashion, most present-day underdeveloped countries look to external assistance as an avenue of help toward attainment of the development they desire.

The external assistance under consideration takes the form, in the final analysis, of a transfer of goods and services.[1] In essence, the goods and services received stand

---

[1] External assistance commonly is expressed, in an initial sense, in terms of credits. In the course of drawing upon credits extended it, however, the beneficiary country acquires goods and services. The end result, therefore, is a transfer of goods and services. For a more detailed treatment of the mechanics involved, see W. Krause, *The International Economy* (Boston: Houghton Mifflin Company, 1955), esp. pp. 257–258.

in addition to whatever the recipient country can generate on its own. Ordinarily, external assistance is geared to supplement domestic capacity for undertaking investment, but sometimes it is aimed as a supplement for domestic consumption, e.g., foodstuffs.[2] In any event, the essential point is that external assistance accrues to a recipient country in terms of an inflow of goods and services, a situation not to be misconstrued in light of the term *capital inflow* commonly applied to the process.

If the environment in underdeveloped countries gave rise to abundant foreign exchange, these countries could procure abroad on their own the supplementary means they feel they need. A foremost problem in the underdeveloped world, however, relates to foreign-exchange stringency. Indeed, the need to circumvent in some way the obstacle posed by foreign-exchange stringency becomes, in industrialization phases of a developmental effort, the rationale for special emphasis upon foreign-exchange-earning and foreign-exchange-saving enterprises (Ch. 8). Since external assistance comes to be called for because of the inability of countries to procure equivalent imports on their own, it follows that whatever added imports are had should be used in ways likely to alleviate, directly or indirectly, the prevailing foreign-exchange stringency.

It is apparent that major questions are raised by the matter of access to external assistance. Of crucial importance, how much of a capital inflow do underdeveloped countries *need*? And, what *terms* are appropriate for the movement of this capital?

MAGNITUDE OF CAPITAL MOVEMENT

While some capital moves from underdeveloped countries to developed countries, as well as among underdeveloped countries, the *net* movement of capital is from developed countries to underdeveloped countries. What is the magnitude of this movement?

One much-cited study, undertaken under UN auspices, has placed the magnitude of capital inflows into the underdeveloped world at no more than $0.5 billion per year during the period of the 1920's, and at no more than $1.5 billion per year during the post-World War II period prior to 1951. The study implies that this amount has been too low in the aggregate to offer more than token assistance in any attempt to raise per-capita income; in addition, the geographical distribution in placement was held inadequate by virtue of an acute unevenness among countries.[3]

---

[2] It is possible for foodstuffs to increase capacity for investment, e.g., as when added food supplies facilitate the transition to new types of production. On this matter, see again Ch. 7, the section treating the question "Is More Raw-Materials Production Necessary as a Prelude?"

[3] UN, *Measures for the Economic Development of Under-Developed Countries*, New York, 1951, p. 79.

A second study, undertaken by M.I.T.'s Center for International Studies, has placed the magnitude of capital inflows into the underdeveloped world at roughly $3 billion for the year 1953. According to the study, this capital was had through the following routes: US direct investment (net), including undistributed earnings of subsidiaries, $570 million;[4] US Government foreign economic grants, $623 million; Export-Import Bank disbursements, $433 million (but with repayments totaling $65 million); International Bank disbursements, $112 million; and European foreign private and public investment, $1,275 million.[5]

An attempt by this author to ascertain the net capital movement from the developed world to the underdeveloped world during more recent years produced data shown in Table 12. According to this data, the net flow averaged approximately $3 billion per year during the 4-year period, 1955–58. This figure, built up from information obtained from multiple sources, admittedly represents a rough approximation. Nevertheless, it

Table 12. Movement of Capital (Net) from Developed Countries to Underdeveloped Countries[1] (In millions of US dollars)

	Annual Average 1955–58
US private direct investment[2]	$ 540
US foreign aid[3]	1,200
Export-Import Bank[4]	75
International Bank[5]	300
European foreign private and public investment	1,000
Total (rounded)	$3.1 billion

Source: Estimates based on information secured from Department of Commerce, International Cooperation Administration, Export-Import Bank, and International Bank.

---

1 All estimates refer to the US and other developed countries vis-à-vis underdeveloped countries (with the dividing line conforming generally with the treatment accorded in Table 2, Ch. 1). All amounts are net. The estimates are rough, and some gaps exist in data coverage; accordingly, the aggregate estimate reflects, at best, only general magnitude.

2 Change in total investment minus undistributed subsidiary earnings. Data referring to "net capital outflow" yield an average $200 million greater.

3 Expenditures under the MSP (including the DLF in 1958).

4 Disbursements minus repayments.

5 Disbursements minus repayments; includes the IFC.

---

4 Claim acquired by the US on the basis of its accumulation of direct investment outstanding was estimated at $1,007 million.

5 M. F. Millikan and W. W. Rostow, A Proposal: Key to an Effective Foreign Policy (New York: Harper and Brothers, 1957), Appendix, esp. Table 2, p. 159.

appears to hold some significance as an indication of the *general* magnitude of the net capital movement during recent years.[6]

THE DEMAND FUNCTION

Whatever the precise magnitude of the current movement, a common complaint in the underdeveloped world—and one with which many persons in developed countries are in sympathy—is that not enough capital is becoming available to them. While many persons share the view that the magnitude of capital moving to underdeveloped countries has been insufficient, there is wide disagreement as to how much capital would be adequate. In fact, there is even little agreement as to just how one should proceed to ascertain the amount that might legitimately be so regarded.

Actually, there are two basic approaches that might be employed in an attempt to determine the extent of capital shortage in underdeveloped countries. First, one can attempt to estimate how much capital could be used to good economic advantage. This approach raises the question of the capacity to absorb capital. Second, one can attempt to estimate how much capital would be needed to pursue certain courses of action. This approach raises the question of the financial requirements inherent in the attainment of designated goals, quite aside from any considerations as to whether or not the particular goals are consistent with economic advantage.

CAPACITY TO ABSORB CAPITAL

It is erroneous to hold that a country can absorb capital without limit and at any pace. Every country is limited in its capital absorptive capacity, and especially so if the country is poor. This capacity is circumscribed in the main by two factors: the availability of complementary factors of production with which capital can be matched, and the requirements of financial order, i.e., avoidance of excessive inflation and of pronounced balance-of-payments disequilibrium.

A poor country's capacity to absorb capital—i.e., its capacity to place capital in productive use—is hampered by important limitations in cooperant elements in the production process. Included among the limitations are low levels of technology, shortages of skilled personnel, and relative immobility of labor. While these and similar limitations may

---

6 According to an alternate estimate, covering 1957–58, the capital *flow* from industrialized countries to the underdeveloped world stood at roughly $4 billion per year, some $2.4 billion occurring under governmental auspices and some $1.6 billion under private auspices. For purposes of this estimate, retained earnings of private foreign investors in underdeveloped countries were included in current capital flow (unlike the procedure followed in Table 12). See P. G. Hoffman, *One Hundred Countries, One and One Quarter Billion People* (Washington: Albert D. and Mary Lasker Foundation, February 1960), Part III.

well come to be all but entirely eliminated as development proceeds, they readily rise to the fore to create bottlenecks in production in the here and now. Given the prevailing situation, an attempt to increase sharply the pace of investment is almost certain to meet with frustration at some point, frequently an early point, as the marginal productivity of capital begins to register a decline, and even becomes negative—basically because bottlenecks arise in production, and serve to rule out economic efficiency. The moral is that a developing country needs to pay heed to the supplies of productive elements available domestically with which injections of external capital can be linked. Important too, while there may be a general awareness of numerous projects that are both needed and likely to prove economically productive, the well-defined plans that comprise a necessary prelude to immediate action on specific undertakings are likely to be entirely or largely lacking. Sometimes the situation is one of existing opportunity, but with qualified entrepreneurs far from prepared to take speedy advantage of the opportunity—even when capital becomes available for their use.

Again, a poor country's capacity to absorb capital is limited by the need to restrain the tempo of development to what can be handled without inducing excessive inflation and pronounced balance-of-payments disequilibrium. An attempt to accelerate development beyond certain levels is likely to induce sharp price-level increases, largely because the prevailing economic structure cannot make goods and services available in sufficient amount, or in sufficient time, to sop up the added monetary injections.[7] To be sure, not every price increase is necessarily a deterrent to further development; in fact, as intimated earlier, a moderate price increase often offers added incentive for heightened economic activity. At some point, however, price increases tend, on balance, to become economically harmful. This point, one can creditably argue, is reached when the altered domestic price structure serves to throw the balance-of-payments structure into clear-cut jeopardy. Domestic price increases give rise to pressure for added imports (including, especially, consumer goods items), and at the same time give rise to a weakened position in the pricing of exports. It is in this way that inflation leads to balance-of-payments difficulties. In addition, capital inflows obtained on other than a grant basis have to be serviced, thereby adding to demands for foreign exchange.[8] And, because the balance-of-payments situation is crucial, the pace of development needs to be tempered, or moulded, so as not to induce disequilibrium, which—if pronounced—can bring all development to a grinding halt.

---

[7] Capital inflows are virtually always reinforced by injections of domestic currency, frequently provided through the country's credit structure.

[8] With the exception that no demand for foreign exchange arises if servicing is handled in the currency of the borrowing country.

Few persons would dispute the general proposition that a country's capacity to absorb capital is related to its supply of complementary factors and to its ability to weather price and balance-of-payments pressures successfully. But when it comes to assigning a specific magnitude to this capacity to absorb, even general agreement tends quickly to be left far behind.

Agreement on the magnitude of the capacity to absorb is hard to reach because standards of evaluation differ widely. The importance of standards, and their bearing upon the specific magnitude of the capacity to absorb, can be illustrated through reference to particular lending practices. For example, the International Bank, a lending institution commonly regarded as conservative, has done much to reinforce the impression of low capital absorptive capacity in underdeveloped countries. On this score, the Bank has said that.[9]

> Perhaps the most striking single lesson which the Bank has learned in the course of its operations is how limited is the capacity of the underdeveloped countries to absorb capital quickly for really productive uses.

The Bank has stated, further, that it has found a scarcity of investment outlets in underdeveloped countries:[10]

> . . . the principal limitation upon Bank financing in the development field has not been lack of money but lack of well-prepared and well-planned projects ready for immediate execution.

But, as intimated, the Bank has a reputation for conservative lending practices. In general, it lends only for projects, not for programs. Ordinarily, its loans cover only the foreign-exchange portion of the cost of a project. And, it doesn't want to touch risky loans. Loan standards of this type automatically and severely delimit the area within which loans can occur. It follows that an appraisal of the capacity to absorb made with these standards in mind invites a lower figure than one that might prevail were more generous standards used. Thus, the capacity to absorb becomes a *relative* matter, depending upon the standards applied.

Essentially, five major considerations loom importantly in the matter of standards, and provide a guide to the magnitude of the capacity to absorb. First, there is the question of the degree of risk to be assumed by the lender. It is understandable why particular lenders in the international field desire to make only safe, or bankable, loans. However, if one is determined to make only loans that are riskless, it is obvious that some borderline loans, which might either prove bankable or end in default, cannot be undertaken. Unfortunately, in underdeveloped countries many lines of endeavor are untried, and hence there is no past

---

9 IBRD, *Fourth Annual Report, 1948–1949,* Washington, 1949, p. 8.
10 *Ibid.,* p. 9.

record by which to judge likely outcome. Avoidance of risk, then, dictates virtual refusal to support new types of undertakings. But development requires that new things be begun. It is for this reason that some persons argue that an international loan policy that places stress on bankable loans is fundamentally incompatible with an avowed policy of promotion of development. If one is determined to test capital absorptive capacity, one must be willing to take a chance to the extent of pushing toward the margin. When a loan record shows that no losses have arisen, it is fairly obvious that marginal cases have not really been put to the acid test. In short, in lending for the promotion of development, the measure of success is not how much in the way of losses has been prevented, but how much capital has been placed productively.

Second, there is the question of loan terms. It is more difficult for a borrower to "absorb" capital when loan terms, for example, prescribe interest at 6% rather than 4%, repayment over 3 years rather than 10 years, and utilization of loan proceeds in a particular high-cost country rather than left open on a multi-country basis. When loan terms are stringent or restrictive, fewer potential borrowers are likely to be interested or are likely to be able to utilize the capital successfully, in a business sense, than would otherwise be the case. Failure of potential borrowers to apply for loans under the cited circumstances can readily be misconstrued as evidence of "few good projects" or "absence of entrepreneurs," all of which then seems to add up to limited capital absorptive capacity. Actually, the essential point is that the amount of capital which can be absorbed can be expected to vary with the type of terms attached to the capital in question.

Third, there is a question of the routines through which a borrower must go to gain access to capital. Some persons in underdeveloped countries, in relating their experience in attempts to obtain capital from foreign-based agencies, tell of involvement in a seemingly endless sequence of red tape, subjecting them to frustration and disillusionment. In fact, it is held in some quarters that the "run-around" said to have been experienced by others in the past is acting to discourage some prospective applicants from even having a try in the present.[11] Even if it were found true that some case histories are recounted in an exaggerated manner, it seems reasonable to conclude that the formal routines asso-

---

[11] Recognition of this complaint has given rise to one of the major arguments for the disbursement of externally-derived funds through domestically-operated development banks. Through "package loans" to the local institution, followed by local processing of end-user applications, a means is offered to decrease paper work and time loss for the ultimate users of capital. Whether potential entrepreneurs are more likely to devise plans, preparatory to the initiation of actual operations, when the capital to which they require access is already within the country than when the capital is still held afar is, of course, a moot question. Many persons are convinced, however, that the act of bringing capital "closer" to the potential end-user is likely to stimulate action on his part in order to qualify.

ciated with the lending process that stands between an applicant and capital have a bearing upon the amount of capital likely to be demanded, quite aside from the form and caliber of usage which follows upon the receipt of capital.

Fourth, there is the question of "projects versus programs."[12] It is significant that some lending which foreign-based agencies stand prepared to handle is geared to meet the needs of projects, but not of programs. One argument advanced in support of this approach (e.g., by the International Bank[13]) holds that linkage of loan capital with a specific project is more likely to assure utilization of funds for productive purposes. This appraisal may well be correct, but the inability to secure external financing for an overall program forces a country either to proceed in piecemeal fashion on a project-by-project approach, or to attempt to finance an overall program primarily from its own resources, supplemented only insofar as funds can be gotten from external sources for those specific projects that qualify within the overall program.[14] Unfortunately, individual projects frequently appear to hold less economic justification when viewed in isolation than when viewed as one segment of a larger developmental effort.[15] Thus, there is reason to believe that appraisal in isolation is likely to hold down the number of projects able to qualify for external financing. Again, adaptation of the tempo of an overall program to what an underdeveloped country can finance on its own is tantamount to reconcilement to a developmental effort of modest proportions, given the limited domestic means at the disposal of the typical country. And, when the overall pace of development is restricted, the environment is not one likely to bring forth an abundance of proposals for specific projects. Clearly, willingness to lend only for projects is likely to subject lenders to a lesser demand for funds than would be the case if lending for programs were also entertained. Hence, the ques-

---

[12] The term *program* is more inclusive than is that of *project;* in fact, the typical project can be fitted into some larger program, e.g., a particular industrial project can be viewed as being part of a broader industrial-development program.

[13] The Articles of Agreement of the International Bank requires that "loans made or guaranteed by the Bank shall, except in special circumstances, be for the purpose of specific projects of reconstruction or development." The Bank has said: "The objective of this provision is simply to assure that Bank loans will be used for productive purposes." See IBRD, *Fifth Annual Report, 1949–1950,* Washington, 1950, p. 7.

[14] The second alternative appears to conform with the International Bank's view of the matter. The Bank has said: "In the long run, international capital in any form can provide only a minor part of the capital needed for development. The larger share must come from domestic sources through the increase and productive investment of local savings. The Bank hopes, however, that it can make a substantial contribution to this end by helping to finance projects which will raise the level of production and thereby augment the available resources of the borrowing countries." See IBRD, *Fourth Annual Report, 1948–1949,* Washington, 1949, p. 14.

[15] The International Bank maintains that, even though it adheres to the specific-project approach, it does not view individual projects apart from the broader context within which they later have to operate. See IBRD, *Fifth Annual Report, 1949–1950,* Washington, 1950, p. 7.

tion of projects versus programs is an important one to consider in evaluating the capacity of underdeveloped countries to absorb capital.

Fifth, there is a question as to the portion of total cost of an undertaking held eligible for financing from external sources. A common practice of foreign-based agencies is to finance only foreign-exchange costs directly related to an undertaking, leaving all other costs to be financed from internal sources. True, a sovereign government has avenues of internal finance open to it that it stands free to invoke in an attempt to divert available domestic means to uses alongside whatever means come to be derived externally (Ch. 13). However, the magnitude of domestic means that actually can be channeled into investment is restricted; specifically, the need to avoid excessive inflation and pronounced balance-of-payments disequilibrium compels investment, and developmental effort generally, to be held to moderate levels. But, significantly, when domestic effort is held to these moderate levels (for internal reasons), the demand for the externally-derived means with which the domestic means come to be linked also tends to be restricted. Were access to external assistance permitted beyond whatever magnitude is needed to handle merely the foreign-exchange portion of the cost of any undertaking, a country could seek, with safety, to undertake added investment in conjunction with a greater developmental effort.[16] In short, capital absorptive capacity tends to vary with the extent to which the use of externally-derived capital is permitted in undertakings.

To summarize, it is valid to argue that every country is limited in its capacity to absorb capital. But whether the relevant figure is low or high depends importantly upon the standards one applies in appraising capital absorptive capacity. Beyond this, an additional major conclusion can be drawn. Whatever one holds to be the limit of capital absorptive capacity in the current period, the figure at some future date is certain to be different—if development occurs in the interim. With development comes an improvement in the complement of factors of production with which capital is linked, and also a broadening and strengthening of the total economic base upon which the price and balance-of-payments structures

---

16 For example, if external capital were made available for the financing of costs beyond those related to immediate foreign-exchange requirements, a greater volume of investment could be borne by an economy without price and balance-of-payments pressures coming into play. External capital in sufficient amount to cover total direct costs of investment, encompassing both foreign-exchange costs and domestic-currency costs, would eliminate the need on that account for a domestic monetary expansion in excess of a commensurate availability of goods and services; as a consequence, the point at which price and balance-of-payments pressures would likely arise could be postponed. Again, if external capital were made available to cover indirect foreign-exchange costs also, such as for the procurement of consumer-goods imports (which can then be used to curb inflationary pressure), the amount of external capital an economy would be capable of utilizing becomes virtually limitless. Of course, capital has to be used productively if it is to be regarded as "absorbed," and in the second instance—involving capital consumption—productive use is unproven.

are dependent, so that the capacity to absorb capital, quickly and efficiently, can be expected to rise over time.

REQUIREMENTS IN VIEW OF GOALS

A second approach to ascertainment of the capital deficiency in underdeveloped countries is to assess financial requirements for attainment of particular goals, and to compare these requirements with amounts of capital currently available. The results of several major studies, each of which proceeded in this vein, are available. The general conclusion reached, as evidenced below through reference to particular studies, is that the requirements for capital are not currently being adequately serviced; however, the specific amounts settled upon as constituting the deficiency vary widely.

1. *Food and Agriculture Organization.*[17] A report of the FAO, issued in 1949, placed the need in underdeveloped countries for external capital at roughly $8.5 billion per year (for each of the following 4 years). Assuming a net annual inflow of capital during this period of approximately $3 billion (Table 12), the annual deficiency held to exist was near $5.5 billion.

The estimate of $8.5 billion per year was arrived at by totaling projected capital outlays as depicted in the national economic plans of underdeveloped countries, followed by subtraction from this total of the amount regarded as reasonably obtainable within the countries on the basis of their own domestic saving.

2. *United Nations.*[18] A report by a study group working under UN auspices, issued in 1951 (but based primarily on 1949 data), concluded that a developmental effort adequate to increase real per-capita income in underdeveloped countries by 2% per year would require *annual* outlays in excess of $19 billion (Table 13). With net saving in the countries surveyed estimated at $5.2 billion, the annual domestic capital deficiency was placed near $14 billion. Assuming a net annual movement of capital from developed to underdeveloped countries of approximately $3 billion (Table 12), the annual deficiency still remaining appeared to be in excess of $10 billion.[19]

Methodology employed in arriving at the annual-outlay figure of

---

[17] FAO report on "International Investment and Financial Facilities"; see UN, *Methods of Financing Economic Development in Under-Developed Countries,* Lake Success, 1949, pp. 43–88.

[18] UN, *Measures for the Economic Development of Under-Developed Countries,* New York, 1951, Ch. XI.

[19] According to the study, the current level of capital movement, as a supplement to current domestic saving, is sufficient to increase real per-capita income by only about 3/4 of 1% per year. Barring an increase in the magnitude of capital inflow, the domestic savings-rate would need to *triple,* roughly, in order to eliminate the cited capital deficiency. Given the general poverty of the economies, however, an increase in the savings-rate by this magnitude is difficult to visualize, at least during the near-term future.

Table 13. Capital Required by Underdeveloped Areas Annually in Industry and Agriculture to Raise Their National Income Per Capita by 2 Per Cent Annually (In millions of US dollars)

AREA	National Income, 1949	Net Domestic Savings, 1949	NEEDED FOR Industrialization	NEEDED FOR Agriculture	NEEDED FOR Total Needed	Deficit ("Total Needed" minus "Net Domestic Savings")
Latin America	24,000	1,990	1,580	960	2,540	550
Africa, excluding Egypt	13,200	720	1,780	528	2,308	1,588
Middle East, including Egypt	9,000	540	940	360	1,300	760
South-Central Asia	24,000	1,200	4,360	960	5,320	4,120
Far East, excluding Japan	26,400	790	6,610	1,056	7,666	6,876
Total	96,600	5,240	15,270	3,864	19,134	13,894

Source: UN, Measures for the Economic Development of Under-Developed Countries, New York, 1951, Table 2, p. 76.

roughly $19 billion was as follows. Capital requirements were estimated in terms of two distinct tasks: transference of population out of agriculture and into non-farm occupations (so as to increase per-worker productivity, and thereby raise per-capita income), and enhancement of agricultural output. The annual rate of transfer of population out of agriculture, and into what is included under industrialization, was assumed at 1% of total working population.[20] The further assumption was made that $2,500 in capital would be required to create each new position in non-agricultural employment.[21] As regards agricultural development, the assumption was made of an expenditure on agricultural extension services and research of 1% of current national income, and further, of an investment in agricultural capital on and off farms of 3% of current national income.

[20] In one sense, this represents a high rate of transfer, since in most countries an annual increase of 10% or more in industrial output could be expected therefrom. In another sense, the rate of transfer is not high, since in most areas the exodus would still fail to prevent an absolute increase in the numbers of persons engaged in agriculture. See Ibid., p. 77.

[21] This amount was assumed to be a reasonable average that takes into account both the lower requirements associated with light industry and the higher requirements associated with heavy industry and public utilities. The amount was also taken to include expenditure on industrial research and on training.

The transfer of labor from agriculture to industry, taking into account both labor-surplus countries and non-labor-surplus countries, was assumed capable of yielding an annual increase in national income of $1\frac{1}{2}\%$, while investment in agricultural development was assumed capable of yielding an annual income increase of 1%. Together, then, national income in the underdeveloped world as a whole was held capable of being raised by $2\frac{1}{2}\%$ per year. Further adjustment of this figure for population growth, assumed at $1\frac{1}{4}\%$ per year, yielded a rate of increase in per-capita income of 2% per year.

3. *M.I.T.'s Center for International Studies.*[22] Millikan and Rostow, in a study prepared under the auspices of M.I.T.'s Center for International Studies and issued in 1957, estimated the amount of additional external capital capable of productive use in underdeveloped countries at a maximum of $3.5 billion per year. Assuming a net inflow rate of $3 billion (Table 12), the total requirement for external capital in underdeveloped countries was thereby placed at about $6.5 billion per year.

Methodology employed in arriving at the deficiency of $3.5 billion per year was as follows. Underdeveloped countries were classed in two groups: those that have not yet entered into the transition stage of growing income, and those that have begun to show income growth. In the case of the first group, the assumption was made that the average maximum expansion in the level of capital formation (during the first 3 or 5 years following the initiation of a developmental program) might reasonably be expected to run from 30% to 50%. Given the poverty of these countries, it was assumed that virtually all the additional capital needed to launch the growth process would have to be derived externally. In the case of the second group, the assumption was made that the average maximum expansion in the level of capital formation might be expected to run at lower percentages (partly because the capital base itself is larger), with the smallest percentages prevailing in those countries furthest along in the growth process. Also, it was assumed that a greater proportion of the capital requirements in these countries could be supplied from domestic sources. Combining the two groups of countries, annual external capital requirements were placed at from $2.5 billion to $3.5 billion. Since the objective of the study was to estimate the maximum amount of additional foreign capital that underdeveloped countries could use productively, the higher figure of $3.5 billion per year was selected as relevant for planning purposes.

It was felt, however, that the actual demand for additional external capital (when use is held to productive purposes) might run somewhat lower than the planned maximum—probably not over $2 billion per

22 M. F. Millikan and W. W. Rostow, *A Proposal: Key to an Effective Foreign Policy* (New York: Harper and Brothers, 1957), Ch. 10 and Appendix.

year. A basis for this view was believed to exist in the fact that countries are at various stages of development, so that the maximum demand for external capital in conjunction with developmental programs does not arise at the same time in all of them. In the most underdeveloped of countries, the introduction of stepped-up developmental plans was held likely to be followed during the immediately succeeding years by a rising capacity to absorb external capital; the important point in their case is that the maximum amounts of external capital likely to be required tend not to occur at the very outset. In the more progressive of underdeveloped countries, on the other hand, substantial growth has already been recorded; the important point in their case is that current capacity to absorb capital is fairly high, but a rising level of output and income also raises the prospect of progressively greater amounts of domestic capital formation, thereby serving to lessen somewhat the need for dependence upon external capital.

Proceeding with the planning figure of $3.5 billion per year, it was estimated that incorporation of this additional amount of external capital in underdeveloped countries might increase per-capita output by at least 1% to 2% per year. Reference was then made to the fact that this growth in per-capita output would make possible a substantially greater volume of domestic saving, and that this added saving might then be used to satisfy, entirely or in very large part, the heightened demand for capital associated with continued developmental progress. Emphasis was given the fact that the fraction of an increase in income that a country can save, and then invest, is much larger than the fraction of *total* income that can be saved. The study at this juncture made reference to the concept of the "take-off into self-sustained growth," a concept that assumes particular relevance as an underdeveloped country begins to experience pronounced and consistent growth in income, which is the essence of developmental progress. To quote the study:[23]

> . . . once the take-off occurs—that is, once a regular rate of growth in national income has begun—the requirement for a net inflow of foreign capital on a substantial scale is unlikely to last for more than ten or fifteen years. After that period of time the country can put itself in a position to supply all of its own requirements out of its own resources. It may still attract foreign capital, but it can do so on terms attractive to private international investors.

THE SUPPLY FUNCTION

If the current movement of capital to the underdeveloped world is inadequate, from where, specifically, might more come? As seen within

---

[23] *Ibid.,* p. 98.

the underdeveloped world, the finger obviously points first and foremost to the US, no matter wherever else it might also point. To underdeveloped countries, the US appears as *the* rich country, and is regarded as able to afford the desired capital. Of course, a question arises as to what the US really *can* afford to provide, and also as to what the US *ought* to provide (quite apart from what it can afford). At this juncture, however, it suffices to observe that the US is looked to for supplementary capital—indeed, is frequently looked to in the critical vein of, allegedly, "not doing its share" in making capital available, a view held also in some quarters in the US. As seen by many persons, the US is "able, but laggard."

Those concerned with the magnitude of US capital supplied externally, alongside the need of underdeveloped countries for additional capital, frequently dwell on the point that the US contribution is far less generous than was that of Great Britain during her great period as a world capital supplier. The conclusion, implied or stated, then is that the US should do more. A relatively greater effort on the part of Great Britain is, of course, a statistical fact. As pointed out in a study prepared under UN auspices, capital exports by Great Britain during the period 1905–13 amounted to roughly 7% of current income, while the post-World War II (prior to 1951) capital exports of the US, including both loans and grants (private and public), were in the vicinity of only 3% of current income.[24]

Comparison of British and American experience on this score may be

---

[24] UN, *Measures for the Economic Development of Under-Developed Countries*, New York, 1951, pp. 79–80. Elaborating upon the American effort, as compared with that of Great Britain in an earlier day, Harris has pointed out that: "Over a period of eight years (1946–1953), private capital exports from the United States were only $7.1 billion, or but 37/100 of 1 per cent of the national income of close to $2 trillion during this period. . . . Had these exports been equal to the 7 per cent of income sent abroad by the British in the years of her great capital exportation, the total amount would have been $136 billion, or nineteen times the actual figures. (Even in the postwar period British private exports of capital are four times, relative to income, those of the United States.) . . . Even the sum of all unilateral transfers (private and public) and loans (private and public) was only $52 billion in the years 1946 to 1953, or less than 3 per cent of United States national income during this period." See S. E. Harris, *International and Interregional Economics* (New York: The McGraw-Hill Book Company, Inc., Copyright, 1957), pp. 419–420. Reprinted by permission of the publisher. In a similar vein, Schelling has pointed out that: ". . . [Britain] invested the equivalent of nearly three-quarters of a billion dollars abroad per year on the average (over and above repayments received from previous loans) during the decade or so following 1900. This figure may not seem large to Americans in the present era, accustomed to a gross national product approaching half a trillion dollars per year. But the earlier figure has to be seen in the perspective of the times. If we were to revalue the British foreign investment of that time in today's prices, the figure might be doubled. If we compute what the *equivalent amount per capita* (at today's prices) would be for the United States today, the total might be ten times as much. Finally, if we compare the figure with a rough estimate of Britain's gross national product of the time, a comparable proportion of gross national product in the United States today might be around the magnitude of $30 billion annually!" See T. C. Schelling, *International Economics* (Boston: Allyn and Bacon, Inc., Copyright 1958), p. 393. Reprinted by permission of the publisher.

interesting, but it is questionable how much can be proven thereby. The essential point is that Britain's position in an earlier day differed widely from that of the US in the current period, so that direct comparison—without important qualification—is apt to prove misleading. A few of the major differences are worth noting.

First, the British economy of pre-World War I was geared much more to an internationalist environment than is the present-day American economy. In part, this difference can be explained in terms of geography and resource patterns. Britain, a small and insular country, stood to gain more from the development abroad of agricultural and mineral resources, which could lead to abundant and inexpensive food and raw-materials imports, than is probable in the case of the US, a large and diverse country. In part, also, the difference can be explained in terms of the attitude of business and government. Britain was firmly committed to free trade, while the US appears not quite prepared to shed itself of protectionist sentiment. A protectionist attitude is not conducive to foreign investment, since rising imports are an eventual consequence of this investment (as interest, profits, and amortization payments come to be transmitted to the lending country). Under free trade, import trade is not similarly resisted; in fact, investment then readily comes to be viewed as the means for development of sources of supply of desired imports.

Second, the movement of British capital was paralleled by a migration of peoples, whereas American capital is unaccompanied by a like migration. British exports of capital were largely to countries of low population density, located within the temperate zone, e.g., the US, Canada, and Australia. Alongside the movement of capital was a migration of European peoples who settled permanently in the new locales—so that, in essence, people and capital moved together. This is in sharp contrast to current American lending, in which case recipient underdeveloped countries are frequently already of high population density and thus not in need of a mass influx of common labor, and are situated largely in the tropics in locales not likely to attract a mass influx from the temperate zone in any event. Thus, the movement of capital, insofar as it occurs, is very largely unaccompanied by any migration of population; indeed, the limited numbers in technical or entrepreneurial categories that do accompany capital ordinarily look forward to returning home upon completion of a fairly short tour-of-duty.

Third, the international investment climate has changed substantially since the days in which Britain was a major capital exporter. To illustrate, the transfer problem associated with widespread adherence to exchange control did not plague British investors in an earlier day, nor did British investors have to contend with strong and growing nationalization movements. Again, the era of heavy British investment preceded the Great

Depression and its wave of debt defaults, as a consequence of which many potential investors were made fearful of foreign investment, and which all but brought an end to portfolio investment as a form of capital outlet. Moreover, business prosperity within capital-rich countries during and after World War II provided abundant profitable investment outlets at home, thereby lessening an attraction otherwise found in foreign investment.

Finally, a capital-exportation rate of 7% of current income appears unrealistically high in the case of the US. Percentages alone can prove misleading, since the base against which a percentage is applied is also relevant. While Britain may well have made capital available at the 7% rate, her aggregate income at the time was a small fraction of present-day American income. If the US were to make capital available at this rate, the aggregate amount involved would be nothing short of enormous; indeed, the additional capital at issue would approximate $15 to $20 billion per year. Actually, there is real question as to whether the underdeveloped world could even absorb inflows of this magnitude.[25]

Thus, there are good reasons to hold that the capital-exportation rate of the US should not be expected to equal that reached by Great Britain during the height of her international lending. Nevertheless, a rate *somewhat* higher than the current one appears not unreasonable of expectation.[26] Additionally, in the opinion of some persons, developed countries other than the US should also be looked to in any attempt to increase external assistance to underdeveloped countries above current levels. The UN, for example, is fairly persistent in its endorsement of joint responsibility in the provision of capital, citing Western Europe, Canada, and Australasia—in addition to the US—as major potential capital sources.[27] The precise responsibility within a multi-country complex remains, however, a matter lacking in clarity.

---

[25] Harris has pointed out, in reference to a capital-exportation rate of 7% of income, that during a period of only 3 to 4 years total *new* US investments abroad would then equal *all* foreign investment outstanding in 1913 (assuming that allowance is made for price changes between 1913 and the current period). See S. E. Harris, *International and Interregional Economics* (New York: The McGraw-Hill Book Company, Inc., 1957), p. 420.

[26] To cite Harris on this matter: "For many reasons, we should not expect the United States to contribute in the proportions of the British before 1913, e.g., the greater gains from capital exports obtained by the British, the early saturation if the British ratio to United States gross national product were maintained, the chaotic conditions of today. But larger loans than in recent years might well be expected." See *Ibid.*, p. 328.

[27] UN, *Measures for the Economic Development of Under-Developed Countries*, New York, 1951, p. 79. Similar sentiment has been expressed in particular quarters within the US. For example, a changed balance-of-payments picture during 1958–59 served as a basis for suggestions, spearheaded by the US Treasury, that other developed countries undertake to share responsibility with the US for provision of capital to underdeveloped countries. Countries specifically cited as capable of cooperative action included Great Britain, West Germany, France, and Japan. For comment, see *Time*, November 23, 1959, pp. 23–24.

THE FORMS OF ASSISTANCE

Apart from the *source* and *magnitude* of external assistance, the *form* this assistance assumes is also of importance. Therefore, in what forms does capital move internationally? And, is some one form to be preferred over others (as seen by recipient underdeveloped countries)?

Capital movements are of several major types, and are examined below. While strong features attach to each, what looks good to capital suppliers does not always appear so to recipients.

1. *Direct Investment.* Under direct investment, the foreign investor not only provides capital, but also assumes control of the enterprise or participates in its management. Examples include foreign-owned and foreign-managed factories, mines, and plantations.

Direct investment tends to be regarded with favor especially in developed countries, from which locales international capital moves. Indeed, a number of distinct advantages are ordinarily claimed for it. It is pointed out that, along with needed capital, key personnel and vital know-how are also provided. Since managerial and technical talent move with the capital, its speedy integration and efficient utilization are allegedly fostered. Moreover, it is argued that presence on the scene of able foreign talent provides a training service, since exposure gives local personnel an opportunity to upgrade its own abilities in anticipation of eventual assumption of more responsible positions. Also, foreign investors commonly have connections in their home country or in other developed countries that then presumably enable them to complete advantageous marketing arrangements for prospective output, thereby by-passing to some extent the obstacle of narrow or underdeveloped markets that frequently confronts indigenous entrepreneurs.

In contrast, some persons, in both underdeveloped and developed countries, are inclined to see major drawbacks in reliance upon direct investment.[28] Foreign ownership and management are often regarded as tantamount to foreign control, and charges of economic imperialism and exploitation come quickly to be voiced.[29] The fact that large foreign-owned installations often take on the appearance of an economic enclave within the country of domicile serves further to buttress this charge. Also, the high profit returns generally expected, and frequently gotten, come to be viewed as evidence of exploitation, to say nothing of the more sophisticated arguments that proceed in terms of the balance-of-payments drains associated with heavy remittances. Finally, the argument is some-

---

[28] For critical comment, see S. G. Hanson, *Economic Development in Latin America* (Washington: Inter-American Affairs Press, 1951), Ch. 12; G. Myrdal, *Rich Lands and Poor* (New York: Harper and Brothers, 1957), Ch. V, esp. pp. 51–54.

[29] For example, see "Canada: Vassal or Beneficiary?", *Time*, September 7, 1959, p. 33. The article quotes a leading Canadian newspaper as having written: "Canadians wonder whether they can call their country their own when outsiders own so much of it."

times made that a small local business elite is all too ready to join forces with the new foreign investors, and that together they act to preserve the status-quo in domestic income inequality in a manner regarded by them as compatible with their own mutual self-interest.[30] Rather than being a stimulant to progress (economic, social, and political), direct investment is then pictured as a force contributing to general stagnation.

2. *Portfolio Investment.* A portfolio investment involves a loan of money that occurs through the purchase of foreign securities (stocks or bonds, private or government).[31] Once a major form of international investment, the flow of funds on this basis dwindled to a mere trickle during and after the Great Depression. At first, a weakening record on the part of debtors in the servicing of obligations, accompanied by losses in capital values, served to dampen enthusiasm for this form of investment. Thereafter, continuing unpleasant memories, plus generally unsettled international financial conditions, forestalled any marked renewal of interest, so that portfolio investment continues at a low ebb.

Though currently not particularly important, the appeal of portfolio investment remains high in underdeveloped countries. This popularity is attributable to two main reasons. First, portfolio investment does not easily result in foreign control, or in direct foreign interference. In the case of loans to the private sector, no direct rights of control spring from bonds, and even the voting rights ordinarily attached to stocks do not usually give rise to outright control, since the typical investor holds an insufficient proportion of the total issue to exert certain control. In the case of government bonds, similarly, the possibility of outside pressure is largely precluded when sales of bonds are widely scattered among a foreign public; however, the sale of bonds in a large block to, say, a foreign financial institution can create the basis for subsequent pressure, as particular historical instances attest.

Second, portfolio investment ordinarily provides capital at a lesser direct cost to the borrower. Investors on a direct basis frequently get an annual return on their investment of anything from 10% to 40%, or even more; as a minimum, the common attitude is that investors can legitimately expect a return *above* that obtainable at home, where their expectations may well run 10% to 20%. In contrast, bond yields ordinarily run 4% to 8%, while stock yields are based on whatever dividends are declared, so that capital cost can be made to vary with capital profitableness.

Thus, the desire for cheap money with few strings attached is, at root,

---

30 H. Myint, "The Gains from International Trade and the Backward Countries," *Review of Economic Studies*, 1954–1955, No. 58, pp. 129–142.

31 Investment proceeds can then be used, in turn, to acquire imports of goods and services.

the appeal of portfolio investment in underdeveloped countries. True, portfolio investment does not carry managerial or technical talent with it in the way that direct investment does. Numerous persons point out, however, that this talent, when not obtainable in adequate quantity or quality at home, can be purchased from abroad, e.g., through the technique employed in management contracts. In fact, the added costliness of funds gotten as direct investment may more than equal, at least in instances, the cost of the various "extras" when these are purchased separately, rather than obtained in an overall direct-investment "package."

Accordingly, preferences and convictions being what they are in underdeveloped countries, there is strong sentiment—apparent in a number of countries—in favor of an effort to market government bonds in the capital markets of developed countries, especially in the US. However, experience with government bonds in the past, along with continuation of generally unsettled political and financial conditions in the world, contributes toward an environment likely to rule out any large-scale sale of government bonds to private investors in developed countries[32]—unless, of course, the bonds are especially underwritten (say, by the US Government).

3. *Loans by International Agencies.* International institutions for the transmission of capital from capital-rich to capital-poor countries are of fairly recent vintage, dating only from the period of World War II. The major of these institutions is the International Bank, which evolved from the Bretton Woods Conference, held in 1944; in addition, there are several other institutions of lesser loan potential or of narrower function, all of which arose subsequent to the International Bank.[33]

The rationale for these international lending agencies rested, on the one hand, upon a desire in capital-deficit countries for greater access to external capital and, on the other hand, upon a general unresponsiveness in capital-rich countries to the support of a capital flow of the desired magnitude through existing channels (as evidenced, in part, by the failure of a private securities market to revive). The overall intent was to create new formal arrangements to link prospective borrowers (largely governments, but private borrowers to some extent also) and potential lenders (including governments, and also prospective private suppliers of capital), and thereby encourage the movement of additional supplies of capital.

4. *Governmental Loans and Grants.* In contrast to channelization of funds through an international agency, governments sometimes prefer to lend on a *unilateral* basis. Unilateral action, as regards all or part of the funds destined for foreign areas, is preferred by a government espe-

---

[32] Government of Israel bonds are an exception, but they admittedly comprise a special case.

[33] These various institutions are treated in detail in Ch. 19.

cially whenever it views the extension of foreign assistance as part of its overall foreign policy. Retention by the lending country of the right to provide or withhold its funds at will enables it to pattern its lending policy so as to reinforce its general foreign policy. When identical funds are placed through the intermediary of an international institution, multi-country decisions dictate their placement, rather than the decisions of the individual capital supplier alone.

Unilateral assistance is employed by a number of countries and in a number of forms. The US Government offers loans through the Export-Import Bank and the Development Loan Fund, and offers grants, and also some loans, through the International Cooperation Administration (in the Department of State). Elsewhere, the United Kingdom and France both offer loan and grant assistance to overseas territories, while the USSR offers loans to select underdeveloped countries, repayable largely in raw materials.

5. *Agricultural Surpluses.* According to one line of reasoning, provision—on a grant or domestic-currency-repayment basis—of surplus agricultural commodities to an underdeveloped but developing country comprises a form of capital transfer meaningful for economic development. The major ingredient in this line of reasoning is that agricultural imports (on this basis) can help service the increases in domestic demand that accompany development, and thereby prevent growth from being choked off on that account. It is argued that if the particular added commodities were not forthcoming, the subject country would need either to proceed more slowly in its developmental effort (in order to dampen price and balance-of-payments pressures), to increase like imports through normal channels (which would require outlays of scarce foreign exchange), or to accept forced privation in the domestic economy in lieu of cut-backs in the tempo of development.[34]

The US attempts, under terms of the Agricultural Trade Development and Assistance Act of 1954, to link the disposal of surplus agricultural commodities with economic development. Agricultural commodities are sold, with most of the proceeds, collectible in the domestic currency of the recipient country, then lent or granted to the country in question.

6. *Other.* Beyond capital, per se, a special form of assistance, not previously given separate mention, is technical assistance. Technical assistance involves the provision of know-how to recipient countries through access to them of the services of foreign technicians, or through the training in foreign locales of persons from the countries being assisted.[35]

---

[34] See again Ch. 7, the section treating the question "Is More Raw-Materials Production Necessary as a Prelude?"

[35] Actually, technical assistance occurs in conjunction with operations falling within several of the previously-cited categories, e.g., categories 1, 3, and 4 above.

BALANCE-OF-PAYMENTS IMPACT

Through willingness and ability to draw upon external capital, a country has available to it the means to increase its rate of capital formation.[36] Since the rate of capital formation is a fundamental element in establishing the tempo of development, it might seem that every under-developed country aspiring for accelerated development would auto-matically welcome any and all external capital available. But, not every country is eager to draw upon external capital. Or, even when avowedly desirous of external capital, there nevertheless frequently continues to be much choosiness regarding which blocks of capital to accept and which to reject. Is there a logical explanation for this state of affairs?

Basically, there are two main reasons for hesitancy on the part of some underdeveloped countries toward the admittance of external capital. First, there is fear that an undue amount of foreign control is likely to accompany capital. Most frequently expressed relative to direct invest-ment, the fear undoubtedly has some basis in fact, as particular historical occurrences would seem to attest. It is often difficult to determine, how-ever, just how much of the expression of opposition to entry of capital is really motivated by fear of control; significantly, the possibility exists that the bogey of control can be invoked as a convenient "red herring" by means of which emotional and political sentiment can be turned against foreign investment, when all the while other reasons may be paramount in the decision to resist entry of external capital (e.g., fear by domestic business interests of new competition, or fear by the prevailing power elite of a loss in relative position in the event development shakes the economic status-quo). However, real, imagined, or contrived, there is no doubt but that fear of foreign control serves as a barrier to the entry of external capital, especially of direct investment.

Second, and probably of much greater importance, there is concern about the cost of foreign capital. When a country receives foreign capital, it becomes obliged—except in the case of a grant (gift)—to pay a return on the capital and, eventually, to repay the principal. The capital outflow involved in the servicing of debt requires exports of goods and services, and hence represents a drain upon the economy.[37] While a capital inflow gives a country more goods and services than it might otherwise have, a capital outflow leaves a country with fewer goods and services than

---

36 Since the actual transference of capital occurs in terms of goods and services, capital formation can be defined as the *excess* of domestic production plus importation of goods and services *over* domestic consumption plus exportation of goods and services. Or, stated otherwise, a country's level of capital formation depends upon its level of national saving *plus* the magnitude of its import surplus.

37 An exception to the cited drain bears mention: special arrangements to permit payment in domestic currency, e.g., as in the case of particular transactions under the US program for the disposal of surplus agricultural commodities.

would be the case otherwise. Ordinarily, of course, the movement of goods and services, in or out, is accomplished by recourse to the medium of foreign exchange, so that a country's balance-of-payments structure is brought into question, both in terms of its impact upon foreign-exchange reserves and upon the supplies of goods and services available within the economy. In any event, the impact of a capital outflow upon a country's balance-of-payments structure and upon its supplies of goods and services depends upon the cost of foreign exchange, and this varies widely.

Foreign investment in loan form generally claims a rather moderate annual return.[38] Bond yields rarely exceed 8%, and generally range between 4% and 8%, while returns on stocks vary according to dividends declared, but usually do not exceed 10% of investment. In contrast, foreign investors who have undertaken direct investment commonly expect a substantially larger return; in fact, 25% to 40% of the recognized foreign-investment base is the range of *allowable* annual outflow under the established exchange-control regulations of a number of underdeveloped countries. While some firms earn and remit a lesser amount, others go to the limit in the exercise of remittance privileges; indeed, some firms are known to have registered complaints about their "blocked profits," even under circumstances allowing them to remit, annually, at the rate of 40% of their foreign-investment base. Of course, not all profits need be remitted; reinvestment in the country in which they are earned is always a possibility. Then, however, an additional question arises: Should the reinvested earnings be counted as part of the investment base? If so, the reinvested earnings, a plough-back of domestic currency, become a basis for additional remittances in the future, with further consequences in terms of foreign exchange.

In short, the sequence of events that follows in the wake of an acceptance of external capital poses serious balance-of-payments implications for the recipient country. Economists have dealt extensively with the need of capital-exporting countries (e.g., the US) to prove willing acceptors of an import surplus.[39] Much less has been said directly on the subject of the export surplus that borrowing countries need to generate in order to carry capital, or to repay it. Yet, this export surplus is for a debtor country part and parcel of the same balance-of-payments problem that an import surplus is for a creditor country.

The long and short of the matter is that not all external capital capable of being had is automatically to a country's economic advantage. Quite apart from profitableness in the business sense, there is the matter of

---

[38] Loans are taken here to encompass, broadly, non-direct investment.

[39] See, for example, E. D. Domar, "The Effect of Foreign Investment on the Balance of Payments," *American Economic Review*, December 1950, pp. 805–826, and W. S. Salant, "The Domestic Effects of Capital Export under the Point Four Program," *American Economic Review Papers and Proceedings*, May 1950, p. 504.

how much foreign exchange an investment can earn or save for a country, directly or indirectly, as compared with the foreign-exchange cost of the investment.[40] The essential point is that the lower is the carrying cost of external capital, the less is the balance-of-payments drain incurred; or, conversely, the higher is the carrying cost of external capital, the greater is the balance-of-payments drain.[41]

Because the typical underdeveloped country already has a tight balance-of-payments situation, there tends to be little latitude within which to accept foreign investment of a type incapable of earning or saving foreign exchange.[42] Indeed, given this situation, it generally proves easier for a country to handle loan capital than direct investment, since loan capital is ordinarily less costly in terms of direct foreign-exchange outlay. Also, since a capital inflow does not earn or save foreign exchange immediately upon entry (e.g., several years may elapse before beneficial impact is felt), a country in difficult balance-of-payments straits simply cannot afford to accept any amount of capital. When carrying costs fall due before foreign exchange is likely to be earned or saved, and existing foreign-exchange reserves do not provide more than a minimal buffer for absorption of the carrying costs of capital, a country is obliged to pay special heed to balance-of-payments limitations and accept capital at a pace no faster than what available foreign-exchange resources will allow to be carried.[43]

General principles that evolve from the foregoing can be summarized as follows. First, the lower the carrying cost of capital, the more capital a country can afford to accept (in terms of balance-of-payments considerations). Second, the slower the repayment rate on principal, the more capital a country can afford to accept (in terms of balance-of-payments considerations). Third, it is possible for a capital inflow to worsen a country's balance-of-payments situation (especially if the carrying costs are high, the repayment schedule is rapid, and the past capital inflow

---

40 An investment can, at one and the same time, be both highly profitable business-wise and foreign-exchange-losing. A possible example is that of a gambling casino which, though foreign-financed, caters to the domestic populace only. While the enterprise may show a high rate of profit for its operators, it earns no foreign exchange for the country, but does give rise to a demand for foreign exchange in the servicing of the capital import.

41 As indicated in Ch. 8, the practice of some countries has been to establish a special governmental body, or screening committee, with responsibility for the appraisal of proposed foreign-financed projects, especially in terms of probable balance-of-payments impact.

42 In emergency situations, when there appears to be no acceptable alternative, capital inflows might prove to be a boon anyway. Frequently, however, capital inflows then occur on a grant basis (as under the US foreign-aid program) or under special arrangements as to repayment (as under the procedures of the International Monetary Fund).

43 It can be argued, of course, that a continuing inflow of capital automatically gives a country greater balance-of-payments latitude. The argument is that new capital inflows help to ease the entire balance-of-payments situation, and thereby enable previous capital inflows to be serviced more readily.

has been large); a worsening of the type at issue becomes fact whenever a capital inflow initiates a balance-of-payments drain that exceeds beneficial foreign-exchange impact to be had from use of the capital.

Viewed in terms of these principles, loan capital rates better, generally speaking, than does direct investment. It is interesting to note that sentiment in underdeveloped countries frequently is much more favorable toward the entry of loan capital than of direct investment. It is not easy to ascertain whether the primary basis for the more favorable sentiment toward loan capital rests upon the presumed lesser control attached, or upon the generally lower carrying cost, or upon other possible reasons. But, whatever the true reason may be, a basis for sentiment of the type commonly held can be found in balance-of-payments considerations, apart from any others.

LONG-RUN IMPLICATIONS

If economic development is to occur at a rapid pace, considerable capital is certain to be needed. Underdeveloped countries, as a unit, do not currently have what can be regarded, from a developmental standpoint, as considerable capital. Access to substantial external capital as a supplement to available domestic capital would help to make more rapid development possible, and would do so, generally, without extreme control measures having to be relied upon domestically. But, if external capital is unobtainable in volume, or is unobtainable in volume on acceptable terms, hope for rapid development is either ruled out or becomes dependent upon acceptance of extreme control measures domestically. The foregoing sequence points to a dilemma confronting the underdeveloped world—a dilemma that holds major implications, economic and political, for the world at large.

Most underdeveloped countries want to experience accelerated economic development, and want to "get going" without delay.[44] In fact, numerous persons, both in underdeveloped countries and in developed countries, are convinced that if truly substantial development is not an achieved result prior to the year 2000 (by which time world population will be, perhaps, more than double the current level—Fig. 4 in Ch. 4), the very chance for development will have been foregone; the breathing spell during which there is still time to act on development grows shorter with each decade—as population continues to rise, and to press ever harder against the means that might be used on behalf of development.

The crux of the matter is that the underdeveloped world is forced, in the present day, to think of a developmental process compressed into a 40- or 50-year period at most, even though it is well known that a com-

---

[44] Exceptions to the rule doubtless exist (see Ch. 2).

parable developmental effort in the already-developed countries that managed to retain democratic institutions occurred over the course of a century or longer. *But,* an intensified developmental effort of the type envisaged is dependent upon the use of much capital. Failure to obtain needed supplementary capital on workable terms from the already-developed countries can only serve either to rule out development at the necessary rate and level, or to compel dependence upon extreme domestic measures as regards capital formation (akin to the method used by the USSR in its developmental history).[45]

In *either* case (i.e., failure to develop, or extreme domestic action in order to develop), a big unanswered question arises as to whether it will be possible for underdeveloped countries to keep alive or foster, over the long-run, the basic ingredients of what goes under the general heading of "democratic institutions and processes." Suffice it to say, there are those who regard the matter of *access to external capital* as holding the key to the situation.

SELECTED BIBLIOGRAPHY

Howard S. Ellis, "Accelerated Investment as a Force in Economic Development," *Quarterly Journal of Economics,* November 1958.
Criticism of the "big-push" theory of investment for economic development.

Arnold C. Harberger, "Using the Resources at Hand More Effectively," *American Economic Review Papers and Proceedings,* May 1959.
Examination of domestic effort in underdeveloped countries; implications for amounts of external assistance required.

Seymour E. Harris, *International and Interregional Economics.* New York: The McGraw-Hill Book Company, Inc., 1957.
Ch. 24, Examination of the contribution of foreign loans and grants.

Charles P. Kindleberger, *Economic Development.* New York: The McGraw-Hill Book Company, Inc., 1958.
Ch. 3, The role of capital in development; Ch. 15, various aspects of the economics of foreign borrowing (esp. pp. 262–265, capacity to absorb capital).

Gerald M. Meier and Robert E. Baldwin, *Economic Development.* New York: John Wiley and Sons, Inc., 1957.

---

45 According to Allen Dulles, head of the US' Central Intelligence Agency: "Soviet propaganda charges that it took the West 150 years to achieve industrially what the Soviets have built in a generation. In the newly developing countries the drive for economic betterment has become a crusade, not always based on reason. . . . [The underdeveloped countries] feel that the democratic process of economic development may be too slow." (Quoted from an address before the 46th annual meeting of the United States Chamber of Commerce, May 6, 1958.)

Ch. 16, Capital accumulation, investment criteria, and capacity to absorb capital; Ch. 20, Foreign investment.

Max F. Millikan and W. W. Rostow, *A Proposal: Key to an Effective Foreign Policy.* New York: Harper and Brothers, 1957.
Ch. 10 and Appendix, Capital requirements of underdeveloped countries.

Gunnar Myrdal, *An International Economy.* New York: Harper and Brothers, 1956.
Chs. VIII and IX, Historical treatment of international capital movements and of particular problems related to the movements; pp. 212–215, Capacity to absorb capital.

Ragnar Nurkse, "International Investment Today in the Light of the Nineteenth-Century Experience," *Economic Journal,* 1954.
International investment in historical perspective.

W. W. Rostow, *The Stages of Economic Growth: A Non-Communist Manifesto.* Cambridge: Cambridge University Press, 1960.
Presentation of the Rostow theory relative to the growth process encompassing five stages.

United Nations, *Measures for the Economic Development of Under-Developed Countries,* New York, May 1951.
Ch. XI, Financial requirements for economic development.

——————, *Methods of Financing Economic Development in Under-Developed Countries,* Lake Success, 1949.
Part II-A, Financial requirements for economic development.

PART THREE

THE ROLE
OF THE
UNITED STATES

We could be the wealthiest and the most mighty nation and still lose the battle of the world if we do not help our world neighbors protect their freedom and advance their social and economic progress. It is not the goal of the American people that the United States should be the richest nation in the graveyard of history.

PRESIDENT DWIGHT D. EISENHOWER, 1959.

. . . our contribution to the contemporary revolution will be measured by our concern: by our ability to embody universal values, by the degree to which we can relate ourselves to the hopes of people beyond our borders.

THE "ROCKEFELLER REPORT" ON FOREIGN ECONOMIC POLICY FOR THE TWENTIETH CENTURY, 1958.

The US Government is a proponent, in word and deed, of development in underdeveloped countries. Part Three is devoted to an examination of the interest of the US in this development, and of some major efforts by this country to assist these underdeveloped countries.

16

INTEREST IN DEVELOPMENT

The US is committed to assist underdeveloped countries in their efforts to accelerate development. At the national level, this decision to assist is bi-partisan in nature. While influential members can be found within each of the two major political parties who are strictly isolationist in attitude, the two parties currently are in substantial agreement, officially, as to the need for the US to pursue an active role in world economic development. At the popular level, further, widespread support for a policy of assistance for underdeveloped countries is found to exist, as evidenced in numerous public-opinion polls taken, as well as in expressions through votes cast for particular candidates for public office. While considerable isolationist sentiment can be found at the popular level, and while many persons of whatever conviction remain ill-informed on the whole matter, the predominant attitude appears to be that the US *should,* for one reason or another, concern itself with the status of the underdeveloped world.

Quite apart from political or popular sentiment, the US Government itself is deeply committed to the course of promotion of development in underdeveloped countries. As successive reports by official investigating groups and as a sequence of official policy statements and directives all attest, interest in economic development comprises an integral part of US foreign economic policy. Therefore, what is the nature of US foreign economic policy? And, how—specifically—does the matter of development in underdeveloped countries fit into the overall foreign economic policy of the US?

US FOREIGN ECONOMIC POLICY: A RESUME

The broad objective of US foreign economic policy is identical with that of the overall foreign policy of the US (and with that of US Government policy generally): to protect and advance the national interest, i.e., to improve, or maintain, the well-being and security of the US and the American people.

The identity of objective—as between foreign economic policy and overall governmental policy—appears entirely realistic, given the fact that foreign economic policy is merely one facet of the country's overall policy. To learn, however, that the central theme of US foreign economic policy is national self-interest proves a disconcerting experience for some persons. While much might be said at this juncture in an attempt to justify the particular policy position, it perhaps suffices to point out that adherence by a country to a policy intended to foster its national self-interest does *not of necessity* rule out subsequent acts and arrangements based thereon that are capable of yielding mutual benefit for the particular country and a series of other countries.

More important, unquestionably, than a statement of general policy is the *particular meaning* given to the policy (as a prelude to action). In the case of the US, the central policy objective has three main components. First, the US is interested in the promotion of its own economic strength. To this end, there is an interest in large and growing markets abroad, capable of absorption of substantial exports from the US; in an assured supply of needed raw-materials imports; in more international trade generally, thereby to assure receipt of whatever benefits are obtainable from international specialization; and in greater and more attractive investment outlets abroad for domestic capital, particularly of private capital.

Second, the US is interested in the promotion of the economic strength of other Free-World countries, i.e., countries outside the Communist Bloc. To this end, there is desire for prosperity (with peace) within the Free World generally, including an accelerated rate of development in those countries currently in the underdeveloped category.

Third, the US is interested in the creation and maintenance of a united Free World. To this end, the hope is to eliminate or minimize disputes among other Free-World countries, so as to prevent any weakening of the Free World on that account, and—more importantly—to keep the countries concerned outside the Communist Bloc.[1]

---

[1] Admittedly, the US would prefer that countries be actively pro-Free World; but in the absence of this, the hope is that countries at least be neutral, rather than pro-Communist Bloc.

Vice-President Richard M. Nixon, in speaking of Free-World underdeveloped countries, put the matter as follows (in 1958): "[It is in] our self-interest to provide

The component elements of the central policy goal thus point to an amalgamation of economic and political considerations. The US is aware that its own prosperity is important for, and also considerably dependent upon, prosperity elsewhere in the world. But, prosperity *without peace* offers little consolation. For this and other reasons, the US, confronted by an ideological struggle in the world (reflected in the "cold war"), regards itself as obliged to pursue policies geared to assure a strong position for the Free-World "power bloc" relative to the opposing Communist Bloc. The hope is to preserve peace (even if it is only a precarious peace, as some believe is the case), and an *economically* strong Free World is regarded as a positive deterrent to all-out inter-bloc strife. Economics and power politics thereby find themselves closely intertwined.

In efforts to promote achievement of the central objective of national self-interest (as conceived above), the US has three main courses of implementary action at its disposal. First, expansion of foreign trade offers an avenue of implementation. The avowed policy of the US in this connection is to strive for an all-around expansion in trade. By way of action, the US has assumed a leadership role in a multi-country movement to lower governmentally-imposed barriers to trade, particularly through support of the Reciprocal Trade Agreements Program,[2] and has placed itself on record as also opposed to private barriers to trade.[3]

Second, promotion of foreign investment offers an avenue of implementation. The avowed policy of the US in this connection is to encourage greater American private investment abroad. By way of action, the US has sought means to eliminate or lessen deterrents to the movement overseas of private capital.

Third, provision of mutual assistance offers an avenue of implementation. The avowed policy of the US in this connection is to provide assistance, economic and military, whenever usable in ways regarded as of mutual benefit. By way of action, the US Government has financed a

---

help economically, so that they can be strong enough to be economically independent and thereby politically independent of foreign domination, even of the United States." Committee for International Economic Growth, *Foreign Aspects of U.S. National Security*, Washington, April 1958, p. 81.

2 The Reciprocal Trade Agreements Program, in effect since 1934, has as its avowed purpose the lowering of tariffs, gradually and on a reciprocal basis. Besides this measure, other specific actions of the US geared to yield a lowering in trade barriers include the following: participation in the General Agreement on Tariffs and Trade (an international arrangement, instituted in 1947, to help multilateralize tariff reductions); participation in the International Monetary Fund (an international institution, begun in 1945, to help speed withdrawal of payments restrictions); and support of the European Payments Union (begun in 1950, with financial help from the US, to facilitate intra-European trade, and thereby also, indirectly, trade between the US and Europe).

3 For example, the US is officially opposed, in principle, to cartel practices and other restrictive business practices; however, in practice, at least one notable exception is made: continued adherence to the Webb-Pomerene Act of 1918, which allows American firms to combine for purposes of greater competitive strength in exportation.

program of economic aid, dispensed both as loans and grants, to assist particular foreign areas in efforts of reconstruction (e.g., aid under the Marshall Plan) or of development (e.g., post-Marshall Plan economic aid). Also, the US Government has provided military aid to buttress the military strength of those countries allied with the US in what is regarded as a common defense effort (thereby, ostensibly, to lessen somewhat the magnitude and cost of the total military effort this country would find itself obliged to support, were it to proceed unilaterally).

Implementation of US foreign economic policy thus proceeds in terms of trade, investment, and aid.

THE US IN A GLOBAL CONTEXT

The foreign economic policy of a country constitutes a guide to conduct for that country in an important area of its relationships with the rest of the world. Formulation of this policy framework appropriately proceeds in the light of a seasoned appraisal by the country of its economic position, viewed both in an absolute sense and relative to the rest of the world. Additionally, attention needs to be directed to a country's political-military position—alongside its economic status, with which political-military status ordinarily is closely associated. And, other sets of factors presumably enter also, although these then are likely to be of a lesser order.

In the case of the US, what are the major overall economic and political-military factors that have a direct bearing upon the country's foreign economic policy?

ECONOMIC POSITION

The US is an economic giant. The country's aggregate GNP is by far the greatest of any country (Table 14); it is roughly three times the GNP of the USSR, the second ranking country, and is greater than the *combined* GNP's of 80 countries (in a tabulation of 84 countries covered in Table 14). In summary terms, the value of US output accounts for roughly 40% of the world's total.

In addition to being large, the American economy is also highly self-contained. Exports typically run about 5%, and imports about 4%, of national income. These percentages are lower than those applicable to other major countries (except the USSR), and are lower than those characteristic of underdeveloped countries, in which exports and imports each typically range from 10% to 40% of national income.[4] The high measure of self-containedness of the US is the result, in part, of the

---

[4] For supporting data, see IMF, *International Financial Statistics*, Washington, (monthly), or UN, *Statistical Yearbook*, New York, (annual).

Table 14.   Gross National Product, Major Countries, 1955

COUNTRIES	AMOUNT
(In order of absolute magnitude of GNP)	(In billions of US dollars)
United States	387.2
USSR	150.0
United Kingdom	51.1
France	45.2
Germany	38.1
China (Communist)	35.0
India	27.4
Canada	26.0
Japan	21.3
Italy	21.2
Next 14 countries (combined)	109.7
Next 30 countries[1] (combined)	70.2
Next 30 countries[2] (combined)	14.6

Source: Foreign Aid Program, *US Senate Document No. 52, Washington, July 1957, pp. 239–240.*

[1] All underdeveloped (with the exception of Portugal).
[2] All underdeveloped (with the possible exception of Iceland and Israel).

country's own barriers to trade, e.g., as found in its historic structure of protective tariffs. However, even in the absence of man-made barriers to trade, the US could still be expected to have a highly self-contained economy. This would be the expected case because within its geographic confines is found a resource pattern perhaps unequaled in any other country in abundance and diversity.[5]

Despite the low ratios exports and imports bear to total output, foreign trade is nevertheless important to the American economy. For example, an expression of dependence in overall percentage-terms readily obscures the fact that *particular* items traded are of *special* meaningfulness to the economy, or to segments of it. Thus, the exports that do occur are vital to the economy on at least two major grounds. First, exports make it possible to obtain imports. In essence, exports are the price paid for imports—and some imports are crucial. Second, access to foreign markets is essential to the economic well-being of particular producers, or of particular localities. In some industries, domestic production far exceeds

[5] The resource pattern of the USSR also appears to be rich, and some persons rate it a close second to that of the US. Published estimates on this score vary widely, and—in any event—overall comparisons in this connection are ordinarily difficult to make, considering the number and differing combinations of resources that typically characterize any two countries.

Table 15. United States Exports as a Percentage of Production,
Selected Commodities, 1957

INDUSTRY		AGRICULTURE	
Construction and mining			
equipment	31	Rice	81
Textile machinery	25	Cotton	58
Lubricants	24	Wheat	55
Anthracite coal	17	Soybeans	36
Bituminous coal	16	Dried fruits	31
Agricultural machinery	15	Leaf tobacco	26

Source: Department of Commerce, Statistical Reports (World Trade Information Service), Washington, Part 3, No. 59 31.

domestic consumption (at prevailing prices). Exportation then offers an avenue for disposal of surplus output. Cases in point are numerous, and exist both in industry and in agriculture (Table 15). In these cases the importance of foreign trade is not necessarily a mere 5%, but is likely to be a much higher percentage: 20%, 30%, or even more. Or, when a particular locality is heavily dependent upon the well-being of one industry, which industry in turn is strongly oriented toward exportation, the importance of foreign trade for that locality is obvious.

Similarly, imports are vital to the economy on at least two major grounds. First, the US is dependent upon particular raw-materials imports essential to national defense, and also to the smooth operation of its peacetime economy. The country is entirely lacking in a number of strategic minerals, and is only partially self-sufficient in others (Fig. 5).[6] Second, the American standard of living owes much to imports not ordinarily obtainable otherwise. An elementary category is that of foodstuffs (e.g., tropical and semi-tropical products), to say nothing of such imports as quebracho (used in tanning) and crude rubber (used for automobile tires and many other purposes). Clearly, the diet and mode of life of the typical American would undergo rather sharp changes were imports suddenly cut off.

Again, an expression of foreign-trade dependence in overall percentage terms tends to obscure the fact that total trade, viewed in an absolute sense, is substantial nonetheless. Given the sheer size of the American economy, even a seemingly low percentage-magnitude embraces quantities

---

[6] Included are minerals needed in the manufacture of equipment crucial to defense industries, e.g., chromite, cobalt, and manganese ores. Some of the same strategic imports essential to defense industries are also needed for the successful operation of a peacetime economy. Additional raw-materials imports provide the basis for further processing within domestic industries, e.g., raw wool and silk, timber products, and various metal semi-manufactures. Many of these, or substitutes for them, could conceivably be derived domestically, but generally only at much higher cost and frequently only at considerable inconvenience.

Fig. 5. Some Vital Imports of the United States

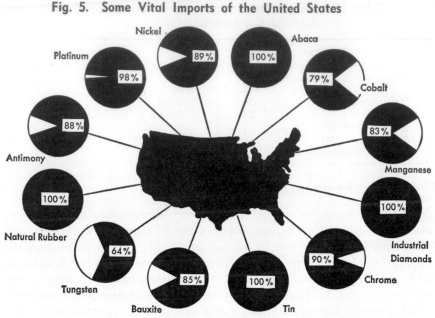

Source: *Department of State (and others)*, The Mutual Security Program, *Washington, March 1960, p. 41.*

capable of consequential impact—as can be demonstrated in terms of employment, and in terms of income also. In terms of employment, for example, it has been estimated that some 4.4 million Americans owed their jobs (in 1952) to this country's participation in foreign trade (Table 16). This number represents 7% of the country's labor force.[7] The 7% figure is economy-wide; it follows, of course, that both higher and lower percentages would apply to *particular* industries or localities.

The conclusion, then, is that foreign trade is important, *directly,* to the US. Beyond this, however, the foreign-trade relationship also is important to the US *indirectly,* because of the way in which trade affects other countries. While wide differences exist among these other countries, most of them are relatively more dependent upon foreign trade than is the US, e.g., foreign trade as a percentage of GNP tends to average higher for them than for the US. Thus, these countries find themselves quite dependent upon foreign trade, but outside their borders they face an environment in which a dominant factor is the sheer size of the

---

[7] It would be erroneous to conclude that cessation of foreign trade would necessarily entail a decrease in the country's employment in the amount cited. The possibility exists that persons previously employed in foreign-trade activities could be re-employed along other domestically-oriented lines as necessary readjustments were effected (although a loss in real income for the country would remain a distinct possibility).

Table 16. United States Employment Attributable
to Foreign Trade, 1952

	Number of employees (In thousands)	
On the basis of exports:		
Total	3,126	
Nonagricultural		2,150
Agricultural		976
On the basis of imports:		
Total	1,250	
Manufacturing		800
Transportation and distribution		450
A. *Total employment in foreign trade*	4,376	
B. Total United States employment[1]	61,293	
Percentage of United States employment in foreign trade (A as per centage of B)	7	

Source: Foreign Aid Program, *US Senate Document No. 52, Washington, July 1957, p. 819.*

1 Monthly average, 1952.

American market, and of the American economy generally.[8] Significantly, this American market is automatically of concern to the other countries.

The size of the American market, of course, comprises a first factor of concern to other countries. Their employment and income are much dependent upon the extent of access to the big American market (either directly, or indirectly by means of the route of third-country trade). Additionally, the stability (or lack of it) of this market is of concern to other countries. On this score, the US has the reputation—on historic grounds—of being given to considerable economic instability.[9] Significantly, fluctuations in domestic economic activity, when these occur within the US, characteristically lead to *disproportionately* great fluctuations in the country's imports.[10] And, since the imports of the US are the exports of other countries, instability in the American economy is quickly transmitted to other countries. Specifically, the effect of a dip in US

8 US exports and imports, *as aggregates,* exceed those of any other country. For supporting data, see IMF, *International Financial Statistics,* Washington (monthly), and UN, *Statistical Yearbook,* New York (annual).

9 As indicated in Ch. 6 (footnote 15), the late Lord Keynes linked the tendency toward instability with the degree of richness in the economy.

10 For example, whatever the percentage of decline registered in aggregate income during a downswing, the percentage of decline in the aggregate value of imports tends to be greater.

economic activity is reduced sales (for foreigners) in the American market, accompanied by curtailed foreign-exchange earnings, impaired import capacity, and a lowered level of employment and income generally. Thus, given the high foreign-trade dependence of the countries whose economies are geared toward production and sale in the American market, any contraction in the American economy tends to induce still greater contraction in the economies of its trading partners.[11] The foregoing situation provides the basis for the much-repeated statement: "When the US sneezes, the rest of the world catches pneumonia."

The immediate and direct rationale for sales in the US, as seen by other countries, is found in the foreign exchange (dollars) thereby earned. This foreign exchange provides a basis for added imports in the countries making the sales (with the added import capacity usable for either greater investment or greater consumption), and hence the foreign exchange is of value to them. A prime fact, however, is that the US characteristically has an export surplus.[12] As some persons assert, frequently with a tinge of moral indignation, the US is an "eager exporter, but a reluctant importer." Their view perhaps suffers from oversimplification, for basic differences in the economies at issue—as between the US and other countries—would appear particularly relevant to an explanation of why the trade pattern is what it is. In any event, however, accepting the rationale for trade with the US as that of a need to earn foreign exchange, it is significant that the rest-of-the-world, as a unit, typically is a net loser to the US as far as merchandise trade, or merchandise trade plus services, is concerned.

However, a country's balance of payments must balance, no matter what the situation may be relative to the trade balance alone. In the American case, the essential picture is that of an export surplus in trade

---

[11] In short, economic fluctuations originating in the US are not merely transmitted to other and economically-smaller countries, in both their contraction and expansion phases, but are transmitted in magnified fashion—because foreign trade looms bigger in the economies of these countries than it does in the economy of the US.

The period of the Great Depression (1929–33) is frequently cited to illustrate the manner in which economic repercussions are transmitted internationally, and the extent to which particular countries experience contraction as a consequence of "imported" repercussions. See, for example, W. Krause, *The International Economy* (Boston: Houghton Mifflin Company, 1955), pp. 35–39. By way of possible modification, a popular contention of recent vintage holds that impact upon underdeveloped raw-materials-exporting countries as a consequence of recessions in the American economy has proven far different during the post-World War II era than in earlier periods. It is true, of course, that impact has been much less adverse during the postwar recessions than, say, during the Great Depression—as is statistically verifiable. Of significance in this connection, seemingly, is the fact that these recessions were relatively mild and of fairly short duration (as compared with, say, the Great Depression); nevertheless, adverse impact was experienced and served to create considerable alarm (see, for example, Ch. 6, esp. footnote 17).

[12] The annual value of merchandise exports typically exceeds that of like imports; or, exports of goods and services typically exceed like imports. For relevant historical data, see Department of Commerce, *Statistical Abstract of the United States,* Washington, 1959, p. 870.

being offset by a net outflow of investment capital plus the granting of aid (Table 17).[13] Always it is a matter of the interrelationship of *trade, investment,* and *aid,* the basic triad within a balance-of-payments framework.

The US has sought to resolve the matter of "trade, investment, and aid" for itself by "giving in" to some extent on all scores. Essentially, the total approach has been one characterized by considerable compromise, perhaps so of necessity. In the interests of a balance of payments in which export trade is at a reasonably high volume, the US has supported—as a starting point—liberalized trade. Beginning in 1934 with the initiation of the Reciprocal Trade Agreements Program, the avowed policy has called for a gradual reduction in the country's tariff barriers, with negotiations proceeding on a reciprocal basis. A basic motivation behind the movement has been the realization that more imports provide a basis for more exports. But, since tariff reductions under the program have been possible only on a reciprocal basis, the central impact in all probability has been that of an increase in total trade, not an alteration in the fundamental structure of the balance of payments itself. Significantly, the world dollar shortage, which assumed major proportions during the post-World War II period (and which has continued in its relevancy for particular regions, e.g., for numerous underdeveloped countries[14]), appeared to call for a restructuring of trade, not simply for a mutual (reciprocal) increase in trade. Accordingly, some persons have maintained that reasonable question exists as to the very appropriateness of the country's trade-and-tariff program, given the overall economic situation in the world.[15]

Quite apart from its merit, real or imagined, continued life for the Reciprocal Trade Agreements Program was dependent upon periodic renewal by the Congress, and this did not always come easily in the face of considerable protectionist sentiment—as demonstrated particularly in 1953. Because of difficulties associated with renewal in that year (but for other reasons also), the Commission on Foreign Economic Policy[16] was established to re-examine the country's foreign economic policy. The theme of the report[17] that emerged in 1954 was "Trade, not Aid." The

---

13 A balance of payments for the rest-of-the-world would picture the inverse of the US balance of payments.

14 Gold outflows from the US during 1958–59 are cited in some quarters as proof that the dollar shortage is ended in the world. As one counter-argument, it can be maintained that despite unquestioned improvement in the positions of numerous countries during the postwar years (especially in Western Europe), the position of the great majority of underdeveloped countries relative to unmet demands for foreign exchange has undergone little change. For comments on the matter of gold outflows, see "The Softening Dollar" (editorial), *The Wall Street Journal,* September 14, 1959, p. 12.

15 For an elaboration of this point, see W. Krause, *The International Economy* (Boston: Houghton Mifflin Company, 1955), esp. pp. 241–242.

16 Commonly referred to as the "Randall Commission."

17 Commission on Foreign Economic Policy, *Report to the President and the Congress,* Washington, 1954; see also *Minority Report,* 1954, and *Staff Papers,* 1954.

Table 17. Balance of Payments of the United States, 1952–1959
(In billions of US dollars)

	1952–1956 (annual average)		1957		1958		1959[1]	
	Debit	Credit	Debit	Credit	Debit	Credit	Debit	Credit
TRADE								
Merchandise	11.3	14.0[2]	13.3	19.3[2]	12.9	16.2[2]	15.3	16.2[2]
Services[3]	6.5	5.3	8.1	7.2	8.7	7.0	9.0	7.2
INVESTMENT								
US private capital (net)	1.5	....	3.2	....	2.8	....	2.3	....
Foreign long-term investment in US (net)	....	.3	....	.3	....	.0	....	.5
AID								
Government grants and capital (net)[2]	2.3	....	2.6	....	2.6	....	1.9[4]	....
OTHER								
Increase in foreign gold and liquid dollar assets through transactions with US	....	1.4	....	....	....	3.4	....	3.7[4]
Transactions unaccounted for (net)	....	.6	....	.9	....	.4	....	.9
	21.6	21.6	27.7	27.7	27.0	27.0	28.5	28.5

Source: Department of Commerce, Survey of Current Business, Washington, February 1959, Table 11, p. 22 (for data 1952–57), and February 1960, p. 19 (for data 1958–59).

(1) Preliminary.
(2) Excludes military supplies and services transferred under aid programs.
(3) Includes military purchases (and sales), as well as private remittances and pensions.
(4) Excludes $1,375 million in increased subscription to the IMF.

288

notion was that aid to offset a world dollar shortage could be ended if the US were to push for some more trade liberalization and for much more foreign investment (meaning private foreign investment).

Despite encouraging signs, at least momentarily, the Reciprocal Trade Agreements Program again experienced rough sledding in 1955.[18] Although renewal proved forthcoming, this occurred only over intense protectionist opposition and following concessions that materially tempered the punch of the program. In the face of this development, the need for continued aid seemed apparent—especially since US private investment abroad, despite some concerted efforts to stimulate it, did not attain the proportions needed to allow termination of aid without thereby also cutting back, absolutely, the volume of exports previously existent. Indeed, it was not long thereafter that the need for continued aid was given top-level recognition. This recognition was highlighted by a Presidential statement, offered in 1955, to the effect that foreign aid is a permanent part of US foreign policy.[19] During the span of two years, therefore, the US had moved from "Trade, *not Aid*" to "*permanent* foreign aid." Essentially, the revamped position continued operative throughout the second half of the 1950's.

In summary terms, then, the descriptive slogan most nearly applicable to US policy is "Trade, Investment, *and* Aid."[20] The US is interested in a large and growing volume of exports, and it is willing to undertake some reductions in the barriers to imports it has inherited from earlier days in order to help bring about this large and growing volume of exports. In addition, an accelerated flow of US capital to overseas areas is desired (especially of private capital), and means to facilitate attainment of this end are sought. But, in the final analysis, the US remains ready to make economic aid available—whenever this aid can be regarded as justified in terms of the country's overall foreign economic policy.

POLITICAL-MILITARY POSITION

Linked as allies in a common military effort during World War II, the US and the USSR parted company shortly after victory had been achieved. Thereupon began what has been aptly called the "cold war," a situation lying somewhere between all-out war and full-fledged peace. At the basis of the misunderstanding has been an ideological conflict not given to ready conciliation. In the course of the following power play, each of the two key countries has sought support for itself in external quarters. The USSR succeeded in linking itself with its satellites, giving rise to the

---

[18] Similarly, difficulties were again encountered in 1958.

[19] The policy statement was offered in June 1955 in conjunction with legislative renewal of the foreign-aid program (as the International Cooperation Administration became the successor agency of the Foreign Operations Administration).

[20] As seen during the second half of the 1950's.

so-called Communist Bloc. The US, on its part, succeeded in concluding a series of pacts and other arrangements intended to strengthen the Free-World position. From this situation emerged a stalemate of sorts, commonly referred to as "coexistence." Apart from the two major power camps, there continued to stand uncommitted certain countries (neutrals), regarded in both quarters as prizes worthy of being wooed (and if not won, at least withheld from the other). Basically, such has come to be the environment within which the US and the USSR confront one another, each avowedly desirous of peace but also always prepared for war.

The US, interested in the maintenance or promotion of its own total security position, has sought to strengthen itself, relative to the Communist Bloc, through externally-directed action of two major types, either of which holds impact-potential in the political-military realm. First, the US has become party to a series of military-type arrangements with other countries, the arrangements being intended to help "contain Communism." Included are arrangements under which the US is enabled to construct and operate its own military installations in foreign territory, thereby placing this country's armed strength at strategic locations in farflung corners of the globe.[21] Included, too, are pacts under which, typically, each member agrees to come to the defense of any other member in the event of aggression[22] against it (Fig. 6). These pacts in effect assure other members that the US guarantees to help in event of aggression (with Communist force being the main potential aggressor in mind). Presumably the moral encouragement lent tends to strengthen the member countries' own will to resist, or to prepare to resist. Included, additionally, are arrangements under which the US supplies military aid (e.g., equipment, materials, and training)[23] in order to buttress the defense forces of countries that have expressed a willingness to stand up against aggression or subversion. In essence, countries that share with the US a common determination to resist aggression or subversion are helped by this country in their performance of the task (which task, as some people see the situation, would otherwise have to be performed by the US alone, and perhaps under much less advantageous circumstances and surroundings).[24]

Second, the US has undertaken to advance the economic welfare of the other countries outside the Communist Bloc. The rationale for this

---

[21] The US has over 250 major active military installations abroad. For a map indicating major locations, as of 1958, see Department of State (and others), *The Mutual Security Program*, Washington, February 1958, p. 15.

[22] Some questions arise in the identification of aggression. For example, a prime point of controversy involves internal subversion supported from outside, sometimes referred to as indirect aggression. Does this comprise aggression in terms of existent pacts? Or, are the pacts binding only in event of overt aggression?

[23] Virtually always on a grant basis.

[24] The military strength of the non-Communist world increased substantially in response to efforts along lines of a collective defense build-up. For general data relative to the build-up of US and Allied strength, see Department of State (and others), *The Mutual Security Program*, Washington, March 1960, p. 26.

Fig. 6.   United States Collective Defense Arrangements, 1960

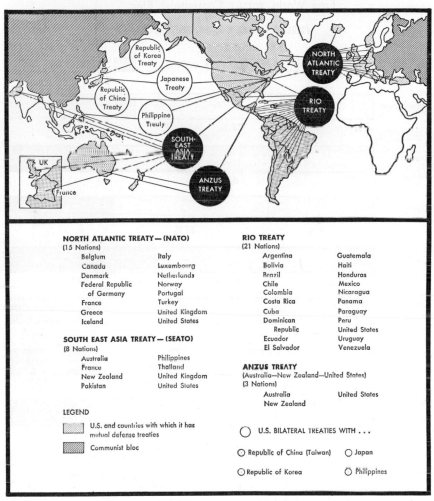

NORTH ATLANTIC TREATY — (NATO)
(15 Nations)

Belgium	Italy
Canada	Luxembourg
Denmark	Netherlands
Federal Republic	Norway
of Germany	Portugal
France	Turkey
Greece	United Kingdom
Iceland	United States

SOUTH EAST ASIA TREATY — (SEATO)
(8 Nations)

Australia	Philippines
France	Thailand
New Zealand	United Kingdom
Pakistan	United States

LEGEND

U.S. and countries with which it has mutual defense treaties

Communist bloc

RIO TREATY
(21 Nations)

Argentina	Guatemala
Bolivia	Haiti
Brazil	Honduras
Chile	Mexico
Colombia	Nicaragua
Costa Rica	Panama
Cuba	Paraguay
Dominican	Peru
Republic	United States
Ecuador	Uruguay
El Salvador	Venezuela

ANZUS TREATY
(Australia—New Zealand—United States)
(3 Nations)

Australia	United States
New Zealand	

U.S. BILATERAL TREATIES WITH . . .

Republic of China (Taiwan)   Japan

Republic of Korea   Philippines

Source: Department of State (and others), The Mutual Security Program, *Washington, March 1960, p. 86.*

interest rests, importantly, on the advancement of the US security position, although other grounds for interest also exist. Many persons, both in official and popular circles, adhere to the view that a healthy economy, or one undergoing marked improvement, offers a poor target for Communist inroads. Whether correct or erroneous, the view is a widely-entertained one, and it serves as a major motivating force in the case of the US. Also, there is widespread conviction that the outcome of the coexistence struggle over the long-run—whether resolved peaceably or other-

Fig. 7.   Measures of Productive Strength:
          Free World versus Communist Bloc

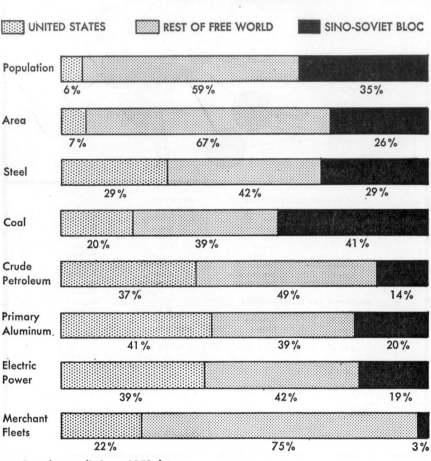

FREE WORLD VS. SOVIET BLOC

Based on preliminary 1958 data.

Source: Department of State (and others), The Mutual Security Program,
Washington, March 1959, p. 18.

wise—is likely to hinge on productive capacity: the capacity of the US
and those countries oriented toward it versus the capacity of the Communist Bloc (Fig. 7). In accordance with this and similar reasoning, the
US is regarded as having a stake in the economic well-being of its allies (in
fact, in the economic well-being of all those countries, ally or neutral, not
clearly within the Communist orbit). To this end, US policy calls for an
expanding volume of trade with these other countries and for a greater

flow of capital to them, as well as for provision of economic aid for the basic purpose of initiating or speeding economic progress in the particular recipient countries—all on the grounds that such action helps strengthen the economies in question. To an important extent, an economic solution is being sought for a political-military problem.

HUMANITARIANISM

In addition to the economic and political-military factors cited, the factor of humanitarianism[25] also has a direct bearing on what evolves as foreign economic policy. Americans have the reputation in the world of being a generous people. The typical American is not comfortable when he sees others in distress. His cultural background and economic environment both operate to make him want to help those he regards as less fortunate than himself. Also, Americans want to be loved (in the sense of being accepted and liked by others). The typical American regards himself as a friendly person, and he wants the friendship of others. He is disturbed when he senses criticism instead of the friendship he craves. These outstanding aspects of the typical American's attitude, when viewed in a collective national sense, are bound to leave their imprint upon what occurs in public policy. No matter how hard headed and devoid of emotion some formalized presentations of US foreign economic policy may appear to be, the plain fact is that among the myriad influences that figure in the evolution of the country's position are the humanitarian inclinations of the American people.[26]

A SUMMARY VIEW

In shaping its foreign economic policy, the US is compelled—above all else (but not exclusively)—to think in political-military terms, i.e., in terms of its overall *security* position. The results of historical evolution make this orientation inevitable at this juncture. But, given the primacy of political-military considerations, the basic means through which policy is given substance are economic in nature. This, however, is not to imply that all economic actions occur only or solely as a consequence of a political-military motivation.

Such appears to be the basic interrelationship between economic and

---

25 Defined here as regard for the interests of mankind.

26 Aside from its role as an environmental factor, some persons regard the humanitarian motive to be also important in that it offers a rationale in terms of which particular policies can be "sold" to particular persons. Some policies, though perhaps perfectly defensible on one or another non-humanitarian basis, are not likely to hold appeal for particular persons unless presented within the context of a humanitarian framework. Therefore, in the interest of "making a go of things" in the world of practical politics, an expedient course for government may involve resorting, on occasion, to the tailoring of actions so as to make them generally palatable on humanitarian grounds, even when they are really initiated on other bases.

political-military considerations, as relevant for the formulation and application of American foreign economic policy.

RELATIONSHIP TO THE UNDERDEVELOPED WORLD

The foreign economic policy of the US applicable to the underdeveloped world is just one portion of the country's overall foreign economic policy, and it is intended to fit smoothly into the total picture. In keeping with its overall policy, the US has both political-military and economic objectives in mind in its dealings with the underdeveloped world.

The central political-military objective is to keep outside the Communist orbit those underdeveloped countries not already aligned with the Communist Bloc. Three main means are employed to help achieve this objective. First, some underdeveloped countries are allied with the US through collective defense arrangements (Fig. 6). Second, some underdeveloped countries (27 in number, including 15 also covered by collective defense arrangements[27]) are beneficiaries of military aid. This military aid is intended to increase the military strength deemed vital for the task of mutual defense. Third, some underdeveloped countries (50 countries and 9 territories,[28] including 25 countries also covered by military aid[29]) are beneficiaries of US economic aid. This economic aid is intended to strengthen the economies of the countries, thereby helping to make them—whether allies of the US or neutrals—less vulnerable to unsolicited pressures (e.g., Communist appeals), as well as helping to give those who are allies greater potential for the mutual-defense effort to which they are committed.

The central economic objective is to promote the economic well-being of underdeveloped countries. The main means relied upon to help achieve this objective are trade expansion between the US and these countries, more US (private) investment in the countries, and the provision by the US to the countries of economic aid. Given the difficulties characteristically involved in an attempt to expand trade when one set of trading partners is economically underdeveloped, and given the obstacles in the path of the movement to underdeveloped countries of a truly enhanced volume of private capital, the key means remaining at the disposal of the US—at least at this juncture in history—is economic aid. As a consequence, the US, whatever it is likely to succeed in doing in terms of the promotion of trade and investment, finds itself heavily reliant upon the rendering of economic aid. The major channel through which the US

---

27 As of 1960.
28 As of 1960.
29 All except Uruguay and Saudi Arabia.

Government provides economic aid is that of the Mutual Security Program (under which, as previously cited, 50 underdeveloped countries and 9 territories, including both allies and neutrals, are recipients). Additionally, economic aid is provided in lesser magnitudes through other US Government lending facilities, and through international lending institutions in which the US has membership.

Above all else in the economic area, the hope of the US is that progress in economic development may be achieved in the underdeveloped world. Statements abound as to the American interest on this score, and these varied expressions of interest have been backed by a flow of multi-billions in funds and the movement of thousands of technicians. But why, specifically, should the US choose to go out of its way to assist in the economic development of underdeveloped countries? By way of an answer, several major reasons can be cited—reflecting a mixture of economic, political-military, and humanitarian motivations.

First, the US has an interest in strengthening the economies of underdeveloped countries so that the peoples residing in these countries will be less likely to succumb to the appeals of political extremists, e.g., Communists. The notion is that the prospect of a "brighter tomorrow" will cause people to be more receptive to the idea of progress under the present order (but perhaps with important modifications, on a peaceable basis, occurring within that order)—this in preference to sympathy for a drastic change-over to another order, presumably a totalitarian regime of extremist leanings. If the effect of economic progress is as pictured,[30] the assistance the US provides for development is really the price paid for the orderly progress that contributes to this country's overall security. In addition to what are essentially short-run political considerations, the development (or preservation) of democratic processes *over the long-run* is held dependent, in large measure, upon the achievement of economic progress (so that the common man can hope for, and get, a better deal over time). Not all underdeveloped countries are democratic; importantly, a number have essentially fascist regimes. If totalitarian regimes of the

---

[30] Not all are convinced that economic well-being or progress necessarily assure resistance to Communism. While most persons agree that aid to Western Europe under the Marshall Plan once helped halt the march of Communism in that area, some are inclined to doubt that developmental aid to underdeveloped countries can be expected to have the same effect. The argument is advanced that stagnation and complacency go together, but that once prospects for economic progress are raised (and, with this, prospects for personal advancement in a changing economic and social framework), discontent with the status-quo quickly comes to replace complacency. Any concerted effort to speed change, according to this argument, really serves as an invitation for even more rapid change, i.e., it gives people their cue to speed the demise of the prevailing order—very possibly through revolution, rather than evolution. Carried to its logical conclusion, however, this argument appears very "hard"; the conclusion pointed to appears to be that the course of wisdom is to halt progress: keep people ignorant, in poverty, and devoid of hope, or they will "run away with things."

right-wing variety are to give way in time to democratic regimes, and not to left-wing totalitarian regimes thrust upon them in some sudden "blow up," the economic basis for the successful operation of a democratic regime has to be cultivated. It is in this connection that developmental progress is held to play an important role.

Second, the US has an interest in strengthening the economies of under-developed countries so that these countries can put forth a better defense effort, either to protect themselves against aggression or subversion, or to assist, as needed, those other countries (including the US) with which they may have entered into mutual-defense commitments. Economic capacity and defense potential are closely related, of course, and the importance of this fact for the US in a global political-military context is fairly obvious (Fig. 7). Provision of economic assistance for developmental purposes thus can prove justifiable, from the US standpoint, in terms of overall defensive alignments.

Third, the US has an interest in strengthening the economies of under-developed countries on the grounds of the aid to trade likely to result therefrom. As the matter is frequently put: "Everyone knows that one cannot sell merchandise to parties who do not possess the wherewithal to make payment." Underdeveloped countries are poor, and they do not buy much, per-capita, from the US (or from any country); the presumption is that if they were richer, an expected consequence of development, they would be able to buy more, per-capita—in the way developed countries already do (Fig. 8). Provision of economic aid for the promotion of development can thus prove justifiable, from the US standpoint, in terms of making better customers of present-day underdeveloped countries.[31]

Fourth, the US has an interest in strengthening the economies of underdeveloped countries on the grounds of humanitarianism. Americans, as a people, are willing to help others in need. Even those Americans who regard other reasons as basic in the provision of economic assistance, and who would rate humanitarianism as last on any list, are not absolutely devoid of those human emotions upon which humanitarianism is nourished. And, for many Americans, no other reason than humanitarianism need be present. While humanitarianism is a factor in determining US action, recipients of American assistance are doubtless fully aware that humanitarianism alone is not enough, given the nature of practical conduct in world affairs, to sustain a large-scale effort over extended time. Significantly, however, humanitarianism need not be viewed in opposition to other possible motivations; to an important ex-

---

31 By way of appraisal, however, it should be noted that an outlay within the US equivalent to that provided as developmental assistance for underdeveloped countries might just as readily create additional markets for domestic output. Presentation of the argument in terms of development aimed to achieve a better world-wide utilization of resources (including manpower), rather than simply to promote more business, would appear to give it greater credence.

Fig. 8.   United States Exports Per Inhabitant of Importing Countries: Underdeveloped versus Developed Countries, 1959

ECONOMIC DEVELOPMENT BROADENS U.S. MARKETS

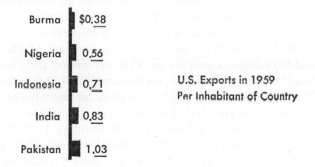

Underdeveloped Countries Buy Little from U.S.

Burma	$0.38
Nigeria	0.56
Indonesia	0.71
India	0.83
Pakistan	1.03

U.S. Exports in 1959
Per Inhabitant of Country

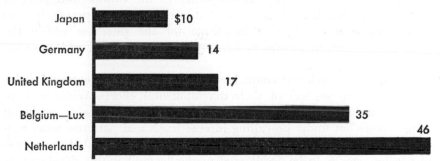

Developed Countries Buy More from U.S.

Japan	$10
Germany	14
United Kingdom	17
Belgium—Lux	35
Netherlands	46

Source: Based on Department of State (and others), The Mutual Security Program, *Washington, March 1960, p. 123.*

tent, the aims of humanitarianism are convergent, not divergent, with those expressed in the rationales offered on economic and political-military grounds.

METHODS OF HELP

In its support of development in underdeveloped countries, the US can offer help, potentially, along three major lines. First, underdeveloped countries need peace if they are to develop. Underdeveloped countries need the political stability, the freedom from distraction, and the access externally to supplementary developmental means that can exist only if there is a reasonable absence of friction internationally. The US is a potent force in the world on this score, and—as underdeveloped countries tend to see it—this country has an obligation to the world to do its utmost to assure peace.

Second, underdeveloped countries need improved market outlets externally for some of their output. Notwithstanding serious shortcomings in prevailing production levels and patterns, current economic well-being and rising capacity to sustain the investment crucial to development are both dependent, to a greater or lesser extent, upon an assurance of reasonable access to foreign markets. Since the American market is the largest single market, what occurs there is especially important to underdeveloped countries. Accordingly, some courses on the part of the US, likely to affect underdeveloped countries in whatever efforts they undertake to "do the best they can, market-wise, on the basis of what they have," include the following: maintenance of high-level prosperity in the domestic economy (since this country's level of prosperity affects its level of imports, and hence the level of exports of underdeveloped countries); liberalization of trade restrictions beyond accomplishments thus far[32] (thereby facilitating access to this country's domestic market); some added willingness to deal in buffer stocks as applicable to particular raw-materials imports (thereby lessening instability in the volume and price of particular traded items); and added resort, insofar as practicable, to "offshore procurement" as a substitute for the purchase within the domestic economy of equivalent items (thereby, in essence, adding to US "imports").[33]

Third, underdeveloped countries need access to more external assistance for use in support of their developmental efforts. While savings-rates in underdeveloped countries undoubtedly are capable of being upped somewhat under prevailing income levels and patterns, more generous access to external capital nevertheless appears needed if the tempo of development is to be accelerated markedly (and if this development is to occur without resorting to extreme control measures). Along with capital, access to technical assistance in particular subject-matter areas also continues in importance. Accordingly, questions as to the role of the US are raised in the following major respects: the amount of American private capital accessible to underdeveloped countries, and the basis upon which it is to be had; the amount, types, and terms of American capital to be had through official (governmental) channels; and the placement of emphasis as between commodity assistance and technical assistance in the course of offering a helping hand.

Assuming conditions of peace, the major contributions the US might make toward development in underdeveloped countries are then two-fold:

---

32 Involving, preferably, tariff reductions on a unilateral basis.

33 Offshore procurement figures importantly in the case of various items intended for US military use overseas. For information on this subject, see "Defense Expenditures Abroad" in Department of Commerce, *Survey of Current Business,* Washington, November 1959, esp. Tables 1 and 3.

first, assurance of an opportunity for the countries to earn for themselves, through expanded external sales, more of the developmental ingredients they need; second, insofar as efforts to expand external sales yield insufficient supplies of developmental ingredients, provision for these countries of supplementary means, either as investment or as aid. Significantly, to the extent that underdeveloped countries can earn their own way with resort to trade, dependence upon the second course can be lessened.

A basic question, then, is: What more can be expected through trade in giving underdeveloped countries access to developmental ingredients? Unquestionably somewhat more can be accomplished than has been realized thus far. In terms of the big American market, favorable factors include the prospect of long-run income growth within the economy (thereby giving rise to the likelihood of growing importation), plus the possibility, under favorable circumstances, of some added liberalization in the country's commercial policy (thereby giving rise to at least marginal increases in importation at any given level of domestic income). While some added earnings through further trade with the American economy would appear a reasonable prospect, caution needs to be exercised so as not to exaggerate the potentials inherent in the situation. Indeed, three major reasons seem to add up to the likely conclusion that only *small* additional earnings through further trade with the American economy are in store during the near-term future. First, despite an impressive record of trade liberalization on the part of the US during a period of a decade or longer,[34] the pace of liberalization has slowed to a virtual standstill during more recent years—and nothing currently observable on the horizon appears destined to make matters otherwise. Greater hope for added export earnings for underdeveloped countries may well be offered by trade prospects in third-country markets.[35] Second, even if the US were serious as to further trade liberalization, there is a real question as to whether any conceivable further liberalization, coming at this juncture when the tariff barriers that still remain are at reduced levels, could serve to alter aggregate import magnitude in truly substantial amount.[36] Third, it can be argued

---

[34] Duties collected as a percentage of the value of dutiable imports fell from a high of 52.8% during 1930–33 to 15.3% in 1947. See Tariff Commission, *Operations of the Trade Agreements Program,* Part 1, Washington, 1948, p. 19. Some slight lowering continued thereafter, with the applicable percentage in 1952 placed at 13.3%. See Tariff Commission, *Operations of the Trade Agreements Program,* Fifth Report, Washington, 1953, p. 20.

[35] In fact, some persons argue that the US should relinquish trade expansion in third-country markets to dollar-short countries—this in lieu of a continuation in the drive for lower trade barriers on the part of the US. For example, see S. E. Harris, *International and Interregional Economics* (New York: The McGraw-Hill Book Company, Inc., 1957), Ch. 20, esp. p. 325.

[36] According to one economist, elimination by the US of all tariffs and quotas would likely increase aggregate American imports (under conditions prevailing in 1951) by an annual amount of only $1.2 billion to $2.6 billion. See H. S. Piquet, *Aid, Trade, and the Tariff* (New York: Thomas Y. Crowell Company, 1953), p. 23.

that neither of the foregoing considerations merits more than passing attention in the present connection, since underdeveloped countries are in no position to do much about enhanced export opportunities in any event. Given their current developmental status, aggregate production in underdeveloped countries is low, as is overall export capacity. Moreover, that export capacity which does exist tends to involve particular commodities confronted in export markets by inelastic-demand conditions, which situation operates to impede exportation even though foreign incomes rise and trade barriers diminish.[37]

Significantly, whatever cannot be accomplished through trade is left for possible treatment through investment and aid. In the light of the foregoing analysis, therefore, attention is directed primarily to investment and aid. Accordingly, succeeding chapters in Part III are devoted to an examination of what the US has been doing during recent periods in the realms of investment and aid, and to the consideration of what more might be done in these connections to help underdeveloped countries in efforts they may choose to make in order to promote their own development.

SELECTED BIBLIOGRAPHY

Commission on Foreign Economic Policy, *Report to the President and the Congress,* Washington, 1954. (See also *Minority Report,* 1954, and *Staff Papers,* 1954.)
    Views of a special US Government commission and staff on what American foreign economic policy ought to be.

William Y. Elliott (and others), *The Political Economy of American Foreign Policy.* New York: Henry Holt and Company, 1955.
    US foreign policy (including foreign economic policy): diagnosis and prescription.

Seymour E. Harris (ed.), *Foreign Economic Policy for the United States.* Cambridge: Harvard University Press, 1948.
    Views of 25 experts on selected aspects of US foreign economic policy.

---

[37] However, even if the export earnings of underdeveloped countries can be expected to rise only little as a consequence of anything the US can do, directly, to facilitate added sales in the American market, reasons can be advanced as to why the US should still make the effort involved in further trade liberalization. First, a sincere show of effort would likely serve to remove or lessen an important psychological block to added productive and sales effort currently evident in underdeveloped countries. These countries frequently appear inclined to rationalize lack of better performance within their economies in terms of an alleged inability to sell abroad. If formal barriers to trade were lessened, a potential excuse for inaction or haphazard action would be undercut, with the possible result that the countries might try harder on their own. Second, even some seemingly small amount of added exports, giving rise to some added foreign earnings, is meaningful, particularly when capital-poor countries are at issue.

Don D. Humphrey, *American Imports*. New York: The Twentieth Century Fund, 1955.
Analysis of the role of imports in the American economy.

Raymond F. Mikesell, *United States Economic Policy and International Relations*. New York: The McGraw-Hill Book Company, Inc., 1952.
Examination of some major aspects of US foreign economic policy, pre- and post-World War II.

Howard S. Piquet, *The Trade Agreements Act and The National Interest*. Washington: The Brookings Institution, 1958.
Survey of recent tariff history in the US, and examination of the role of tariffs in American foreign economic policy.

William Reitzel, Morton A. Kaplan, and Constance G. Coblenz, *United States Foreign Policy, 1945–1955*. Washington: The Brookings Institution, 1956.
Largely factual treatment, in chronological sequence, of major occurrences during 1945–55 which had a bearing on US foreign economic policy.

Rockefeller Brothers Fund (Special Studies Project, Report III), *Foreign Economic Policy for the Twentieth Century*. Garden City, N.Y.: Doubleday & Company, Inc., 1958.
The "Rockefeller Report," containing views of a private group on what American foreign economic policy ought to be.

W. W. Rostow, *The United States in the World Arena*. New York: Harper and Brothers, 1960.
Survey and examination of the US position in world affairs during recent times.

Eugene Staley, *The Future of Underdeveloped Countries*. New York: Harper and Brothers, 1954.
Examination of the political implications of economic development.

Willard L. Thorp, *Trade, Aid, or What?* Baltimore: The Johns Hopkins Press, 1954.
Survey of some major questions pertinent to US foreign economic policy.

17

PRIVATE FOREIGN INVESTMENT

Much of the American populace is aware of the need and desire of underdeveloped countries for access to external capital in connection with their developmental efforts. While there is widespread willingness to see domestic capital made available for this purpose, the usual preference is for investment over aid, and for *private* investment over investment in any other form.

The present chapter is devoted to an examination of US private foreign investment as it relates to development in underdeveloped countries. Included is an examination of the record of US private foreign investment, and of the prospect for investment on this basis in the foreseeable future.

MOVEMENT OF PRIVATE CAPITAL: THE THEORY

When one views international capital movements within the framework of a "classical" model, one can argue that capital tends to move toward areas and uses of relatively high productivity (and returns), and that this movement tends to continue until a general equality in productivity (and returns) prevails. Applied to the real world, the expectation then is for a net capital movement from capital-rich advanced countries to capital-deficit underdeveloped countries, with the movement continuing until returns per unit of capital are everywhere roughly equivalent (at which point equilibrium is said to be approximated). From a public-policy standpoint, capital-deficit countries are supposed to conclude that they will be assured of a net capital inflow as long as capital's returns within their borders exceed levels prevailing elsewhere.

Thus, the argument is that private capital *can* do the job—in the sense of being available whenever the "price is right," and then in any amount up to the finite limits of total world capital supplies. And, of course, this line of argument builds no case for the diversion of available capital from normal free-market channels into governmentally-administered programs of capital assistance, let alone into governmentally-administered-and-subsidized programs.

This thesis has its proponents, but it also has its critics.[1] There are those who feel it is a good theory, but that it will not work out in practice. And, there are those who feel it will work in practice, but who fear the way in which it would likely work.

Those in the first category point out that the free international movement of capital envisaged by classical theory is impossible in view of various legal, institutional, and other impediments. The theory and the practice are two different things because the requisite conditions presumed for the translation of theory into practice do not prevail, and cannot be readily achieved.

Those in the second category point out that the theory is sound, and that it could be applied, but that the steps necessary in the application process are too costly. On the one hand, countries would need to relinquish various regulatory practices in the interests of facilitating the international adjustment process, even though some of these practices may well have merit that offsets them on other grounds.[2] On the other hand, the peculiar situations of some countries, economically or politically, would serve to put the price of capital for them within a range likely to give rise to decidedly adverse side-effects, either economic or political in nature.

It follows, according to the critics, that a dilemma of major proportions exists. The world is characterized by wide discrepancies in savings-rates and capital stocks. But an attempt to lessen the existing discrepancies under a system of strict adherence to free-market processes (i.e., by placing reliance upon an allocation of private capital in accordance with the dictates of a free competitive market) is bound either to leave the discrepancies largely intact or to remove them at a cost regarded as unduly high. Either way, then, the conclusion comes to be drawn that private capital moving in response to, and *only* in response to, free-market forces cannot do the job.

Of course, capital movements do not occur today in a free-market en-

---

[1] For a fuller exposition of the central thesis, see J. E. Meade, *The Theory of International Economic Policy* (London: Oxford University Press, 1955), Vol. II (Trade and Welfare), Part III.

[2] Exchange control is a possible case in point (see Chs. 8 and 11).

vironment, and this has not been the case in many a day—if ever really so. Deliberate actions of many types affect the market environment. A discussion of capital movements in terms of free-market processes, thus, appears to be more academic than practical under prevailing circumstances.

ATTITUDE OF THE UNITED STATES

The official attitude of the US Government is that the American interest is served by placement abroad of domestic capital (whatever may also be the resulting benefit for recipient foreign countries). The hope, however, is that primary reliance in the movement can be placed on private capital. To be precise, the hope is for achievement of a greater flow of capital from the US to foreign countries, *but* occurring primarily in response to private action. This hope is in keeping with the general philosophy long held in the US, both in official and private quarters, that responsibility for economic action should rest in private hands whenever reasonably possible.

As matters stand, reference to placement of primary emphasis on private capital comprises more a statement of principle than a description of practice. Despite an expression of hope that the great bulk of the country's capital exports might occur under private auspices, and despite moral and real encouragement to this end, actual performance—during recent decades—has consistently failed to reflect the desired emphasis on private capital. In fact, the discrepancy between hope and realization has served to provide the US with a rationale for a two-fold interim effort in the foreign-investment field. On the one hand, the US has continued to seek *the* magic formula that might serve to unleash a flow of private capital of unprecedented magnitude toward foreign investment outlets. On the other hand, the US has found itself in the business—in some ways ever more so—of providing supplementary capital through governmental channels, i.e., supplementary to private capital, as a consequence of the failure of private capital movements to reach the volume desired. All the while, of course, the US has been obliged to recognize that, in any event, not all investment requirements are capable of being serviced with private capital; some foreign investment, including some investment in high-priority categories, frankly calls for non-private capital, e.g., investment associated with particular projects in the realm of basic development.

Thus, the US is desirous of an enlarged flow of private capital from it to foreign countries, but private capital has not proven forthcoming in the volume hoped for, so that governmentally-supplied capital has continued to comprise a larger proportion of total capital flows than desired.

In the course of consideration of the dilemma confronting the country in this connection, a number of special Presidential investigating commissions were established, resulting in reports containing recommendations for specific measures regarded as likely to promote private foreign investment. Included among these reports are the Gray Report[3] (1950), the Rockefeller Report[4] (1951), the Paley Report[5] (1952), the Randall Report[6] (1954), and the Straus-Dillon Report[7] (1959). Some of the recommendations (but by no means all) were followed by passage of legislation by the Congress. Beyond this, some additional legislation designed to promote private foreign investment was enacted by the Congress, e.g., specific provisions contained in the Marshall Plan legislation and in subsequent foreign aid legislation, and several acts devoted exclusively to the matter of investment promotion. Of further significance, statements at Presidential level during the post-World War II period directed attention to the American interest in the promotion of greater private foreign investment, e.g., President Truman's statements in conjunction with the initiation of the Point Four Program in 1949,[8] and President Eisenhower's statements in messages to the Congress, especially during 1954 and 1955.[9]

In short, the US has exhibited concern over the level of capital exports, and has tried to discover ways through which greater investment activity by the private sector might serve to raise total capital flows.

---

[3] *Report to the President on Foreign Economic Policies,* Washington, November 1950.

[4] International Development Advisory Board, *Partners in Progress,* Washington, March 1951.

[5] *Resources for Freedom* (Report to the President by the Materials Policy Commission), Washington, June 1952, Vol. I (Foundations for Growth and Security), Ch. 12.

[6] Commission on Foreign Economic Policy, *Report to the President and the Congress,* Washington, January 1954.

[7] *Expanding Private Investment for Free World Economic Growth* (Prepared under the direction of Ralph I. Straus, Special Consultant to Under Secretary of State for Economic Affairs, C. Douglas Dillon), Washington, April 1959.

[8] In his Inaugural Address, January 20, 1949, President Truman stated as follows: "I believe that we should make available to peace-loving peoples the benefits of our store of technical knowledge in order to help them realize their aspirations for a better life. And, in cooperation with other nations, we should *foster capital investment* in areas needing development. . . . Our aim should be to help the free peoples of the world, through their own efforts, to produce more . . . [and with the] cooperation of business, *private capital,* agriculture, and labor in this country . . . increase . . . industrial activity in other nations. . . ." (Italics are mine.)

[9] For example, in his message of January 10, 1955, President Eisenhower stated as follows: "The whole free world needs capital; America is its largest source. In that light, the *flow of capital* abroad from our country must be stimulated and in such a manner that it results in investment largely by individuals or private enterprises rather than by government. . . . An increased flow of United States *private investment* funds abroad, especially to the underdeveloped areas, could contribute much to the expansion of two-way international trade. The underdeveloped countries would thus be enabled more easily to acquire the capital equipment so badly needed by them to achieve sound economic growth and higher living standards. This would do much to offset the false but alluring promises of the Communists." (Italics are mine.)

THE PATTERN OF PRIVATE INVESTMENT

US investment abroad reached a total of $59.2 billion in 1958, of which total $40.8 billion represented private investment and the remainder US Government investment (Table 18). At the same time, foreign investment in the US totaled $34.8 billion, thereby making this country a net creditor by a margin of almost $25 billion.

Table 18. International Investment Position of the United States, Selected Years (In billions of US dollars)

	1914	1939	1946	1953	1958[1]
United States					
Investments Abroad:	3.5	11.4	18.7	39.5	59.2
Private	3.5	11.4	13.5	23.7	40.8
Long-term	3.5	10.8	12.3	22.1	37.3
Direct	2.6	7.0	7.2	16.2	27.1
Portfolio	.9	3.8	5.1	5.9	10.3
Short-term	. . . .	.6	1.3	1.6	3.5
Government[2]	. . . .	. . . .	5.2	15.7	18.3
Foreign Investments					
in the United States:	7.2	9.6	15.9	23.6	34.8
Long-term	6.7	6.3	7.0	9.1	15.2
Direct	1.3	2.0	2.5	3.7	4.9
Portfolio	5.4	4.3	4.5	5.4	10.3
Short-term assets[3]	.5	3.3	8.9	14.5	19.6
United States					
Net Creditor Position:	−3.7	1.8	2.8	15.8	24.3
Net long-term	−3.2	4.5	10.5	28.7	40.4
Net short-term	− .5	−2.7	−7.6	−12.9	−16.1

Source: *Department of Commerce, Survey of Current Business, Washington, May 1954, Table 1, p. 10 (for data through 1953), and August 1959, Table 1, p. 29 (for 1958 data). Components do not in all instances add to totals, because of rounding.*

1 Preliminary.
2 Excludes World War I loans; includes some short-term assets.
3 Includes US Government obligations, beginning with 1946.

Of the US private investment of $40.8 billion outstanding at the end of 1958, $27.1 billion had been placed as direct investment. This amount was slightly more than double the 1950 total, and indicated an average annual increase since 1950 of roughly $2 billion.[10] The remainder, amounting to $13.8 billion (or roughly one-half the magnitude of direct investment), represented all private investment other than direct investment. The increase in this private non-direct investment after 1950

10 For 1950 data, as needed for comparison with 1958 data in Table 18, see Department of Commerce, *Survey of Current Business,* Washington, September 1958, pp. 15–23.

averaged under $1 billion per year, with roughly two-thirds of the in-crease attributable to portfolio investment (including private participa-tion in loan activities by international agencies, e.g., the International Bank) and roughly one-third of the increase attributable to short-term investment (bank deposits, and other). In short, the US private investment that has been occurring has been primarily direct investment; private portfolio investment has remained low throughout the post-World War II period.

While US private direct investment has more than doubled since 1950, and is officially regarded as having undergone "record growth,"[11] it is characterized by an unevenness in its global distribution (Fig. 9). Roughly one-third of all the investment is in Canada, and roughly another one-third is in Latin America. Over 80% of all the investment is in Canada, Latin America, and Western Europe. Under 20% is in the rest-of-the-world, comprising Asia, Africa, and other remaining areas. An outstanding attribute of present-day US private direct investment abroad is its relatively small magnitude in the countries of Asia and Africa, which countries go to make up the core of the underdeveloped world.

The annual increases registered in total investment are attributable in part to the net movement of capital from the US and in part to the reinvestment of earnings from that investment already existing abroad. Thus, the increase of slightly over $1.8 billion in US private direct in-vestment abroad that occurred during 1958 was the product of two com-ponents: a net capital outflow from the US of roughly $1.1 billion, and the accumulation abroad by American investors of roughly $0.8 billion in the form of undistributed subsidiary earnings.[12] Of the net capital outflow from the US during the year, 81% went to Canada, Latin America, and Western Europe, while 19% went elsewhere (but with Asia and Africa, together, getting only 14%).

Not only is private direct investment abroad being concentrated in particular regions, to the relative exclusion of others, but it is also being concentrated particularly in one or two types of economic enterprise, rather than evenly across-the-board. Roughly one-third of outstanding US private direct foreign investment is concentrated in the petroleum

---

11 An appraisal in these terms, covering the period through 1956, appears in De-partment of Commerce, *Survey of Current Business,* Washington, August 1957, pp. 22–30.

12 For supporting data, see Department of Commerce, *Survey of Current Business,* Washington, August 1959, Tables 2 and 3, pp. 30–31. Some private estimates involve higher totals than shown by the Department of Commerce; for example, see E. G. Collado and J. F. Bennett, "Private Investment and Economic Development," *Foreign Affairs,* July 1957, pp. 631–645. These authors estimate US private direct investment abroad to have increased by $3.7 billion during 1956, as compared with a $2.9 billion magnitude shown by the Department of Commerce. Their higher total stems largely from the particular value assigned reinvested earnings.

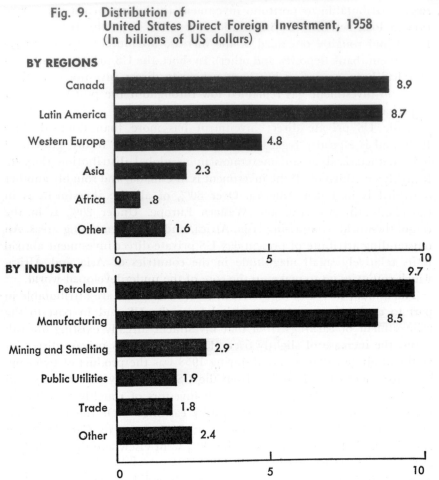

Fig. 9.   Distribution of
United States Direct Foreign Investment, 1958
(In billions of US dollars)

BY REGIONS

Canada	8.9
Latin America	8.7
Western Europe	4.8
Asia	2.3
Africa	.8
Other	1.6

BY INDUSTRY

Petroleum	9.7
Manufacturing	8.5
Mining and Smelting	2.9
Public Utilities	1.9
Trade	1.8
Other	2.4

Source: Based on data in Department of Commerce, Survey of Current Business, Washington, August 1959, Table 2, p. 30. Western Europe includes dependencies in Western Hemisphere; Asia encompasses Middle East and Far East; "other" encompasses Australia and New Zealand (with $0.7 billion) and "international" (involving largely American shipping under foreign registry).

field, and roughly another one-third is in manufacturing (Fig. 9). In fact, the record shows that during recent years some two-thirds of the net capital outflow from the US—on a direct-investment basis—has gone into the petroleum field alone.[13] Emphasis—growing emphasis, in fact—upon petroleum development is an outstanding attribute of US direct foreign

---

[13] For supporting data, see Department of Commerce, *Survey of Current Business*, Washington, August 1957, Table 3, p. 25 (for 1956 data), September 1958, Table 3, p. 19 (for 1957 data), and August 1959, Table 3, p. 31 (for 1958 data).

investment.[14] Indeed, two facts—the attraction of petroleum as an investment field, and the tendency for particularly large capital movements to occur toward certain countries (e.g., Canada and Venezuela)—are part and parcel of the same thing.[15]

SHORTCOMINGS IN THE PATTERN

It is widely felt that private direct investment offers some unique advantages. Private direct investment comprises, in a sense, a package that contains more than just so much capital. Aside from the quantitative contribution resulting from a capital inflow, a qualitative contribution can also result. The private investor can bring with him technology, managerial experience, and new business concepts that help revamp thinking and practices in the recipient country. Also, the private investor can carry with him special know-how as to the whereabouts of and the means of access to external markets. All in all, the qualitative contribution can prove highly important, and particularly so when the private investor is from an industrially-advanced country and is undertaking development in the industrial sector of an industrially-underdeveloped country.[16]

But, despite the various important advantages generally acknowledged as associated with private direct investment, the fact remains that such investment has major shortcomings too. These shortcomings relate especially to the magnitude and distribution of investment, and to its suitability or unsuitability for utilization in particular connections.

MAGNITUDE

The net capital outflow occurring from the US—averaging $1.4 billion per year during 1955–58—is a large or small amount, depending upon how one looks at it. Those inclined to regard the movement as small can cite, in support of their position, a number of studies undertaken to ascertain the amount of external capital likely to be needed to assure even a modest acceleration in development. To recall, according to a UN group that assumed as a goal an annual rate of growth of 2% in per-capita income in the underdeveloped world, the annual deficiency exceeds $10 billion (Table 13 in Ch. 15). Or, according to several groups investi-

---

14 The profitability of petroleum investment appears to exceed that of other major categories of investment. The earnings-rate during 1956, for example, *averaged* 14.2% for all direct foreign investment; rates, by types of industry, were as follows: 19.4% in petroleum, 14.6% in mining and smelting, and 12.1% in manufacturing. Computations based on data in Department of Commerce, *Survey of Current Business,* Washington, August 1957, Tables 2 and 4, pp. 24–25.

15 For supporting data, see Department of Commerce, *Survey of Current Business,* Washington, August 1957, Table 3, p. 24 (for 1956 data), September 1958, Table 3, p. 19 (for 1957 data), and August 1959, Table 3, p. 31 (for 1958 data).

16 Obviously, the extent of qualitative contribution is limited by how much quantitative contribution occurs in the first place.

gating the US foreign-aid program during 1956–57, the minimum annual deficiency (measured by the amount of added aid recommended, in the absence of more private investment) lies somewhere between $1 billion and $3 billion.

Apart from the foregoing consideration, there is the matter of stability or instability regarding whatever private capital movements do occur. One is obliged to cope with allegations like the following, which frequently are heard abroad (and sometimes also in the US): "During prosperity US private capital is invested at home, and during depression not much private capital is available for anyone"; or, "The ability and willingness of the American economy to sustain private capital exports are dependent upon its own well-being, and the American economy is given to instability."[17] The conclusion that such allegations invite is that private external capital is a dependable source only up to a point.

DISTRIBUTION

Even if one were satisfied that the aggregate movement of private capital from the US as direct investment is "adequate," there still looms the complicating fact that this capital has tended to concentrate in certain regions and types of economic activity, and to shy away from other regions and types of economic activity. Not all of the capital moves to regions of acute capital scarcity; much moves to regions already in the developed category. Significantly, under 20% of the current net private capital outflow from the US moves to Asia and Africa. And, the petroleum field alone accounts for roughly one-third of all US private direct investment abroad, and during recent years has been capturing almost two-thirds of the net private capital outflow. A conclusion which many persons reach is that a higher level of capital movement, given *unchanged* proportions as to destination and utilization, continues to leave much to be desired.

PUBLIC OVERHEAD

The whole category of investment associated with public overhead (i.e., basic development) is largely ignored as a legitimate outlet for private direct investment. Since a marketable product only rarely arises in direct fashion, the possibility of a "pay-off" in the private-enterprise profit sense is generally excluded, thereby largely ruling out this category of investment as one suitable for handling on the basis of private direct investment. Yet, investment (and development) of this type is necessary,

---

17 Of possible relevance, net capital outflows from the US as direct investment fell from $2.1 billion in 1957 to $1.1 billion in 1958, during which period the American economy experienced a recession. Department of Commerce, *Survey of Current Business,* Washington, August 1959, Table 3, p. 31.

and is frequently a prerequisite for other investment, either indigenous or foreign.

BALANCE-OF-PAYMENTS IMPACT

Some countries, particularly underdeveloped countries, suffer from a chronic inability to earn foreign exchange in amounts adequate to allow importation in volume of needed developmental ingredients. This situation, in fact, is the very basis for what undoubtedly is the number-one reason why these countries should seek the capital inflow that private direct investment offers. Admission of this capital, however, does not always serve to ease the recipient country's balance-of-payments position (as intimated in Ch. 15). Whenever an investment is foreign-exchange-earning or foreign-exchange saving, the balance-of-payments situation is eased; but whenever an investment on its own account causes a net foreign-exchange drain, it aggravates the balance-of-payments situation for the recipient country, whatever its merits may be on other scores.

In practice, some categories of investment, including that for public overhead (but not limited to such), do not directly earn or save foreign exchange, so that the utilization of external capital in their case on other than an outright grant or domestic-currency-repayment basis—results in the imposition, at least in the short-run, of a certain amount of dead weight upon the recipient country's balance-of-payments structure. The amount of dead weight of this type that can be borne by an economy is directly dependent upon the latitude the country's balance-of-payments structure allows for the servicing of remittances. This latitude, in turn, tends to be intimately related to the status of a country's development. Significantly, the typical underdeveloped country, while it has high capital requirements, also has limited balance-of-payments capacity to sustain servicing of capital—although if it can get over the initial hurdles in the developmental process, its capacity to sustain servicing of capital tends to improve.

The overall observation, pertinent at this point, is that the foreign-exchange cost incurred in servicing direct investment ordinarily far exceeds that incurred in servicing loan capital (portfolio investment). This comparison, and the relevance it holds in an explanation of what type and how much capital a country can absorb in the balance-of-payments sense, is frequently alluded to in capital-poor underdeveloped countries in their attempts to justify a preference for "loans" over "entry of foreign companies."

EXISTENT AIDS TO PRIVATE INVESTMENT

US private investment occurring abroad during recent years has not been the result, in its entirety, of purely unsupported private effort. Reinforcing governmental action has been forthcoming at various times and in various ways, and ideas continue to be advanced detailing ways in which government can supposedly do more to stimulate the flow of capital under private auspices.

Major types of governmental action instituted thus far for the purpose of promoting private foreign investment are summarized below.

FINANCIAL SUPPORT

Some US funds, channeled either through this country's own governmental agencies or through international institutions with which this country is affiliated, are utilized "in support of" American private investment abroad. The funds routed into American private investment through these channels are currently of substantial magnitude—indeed, account for a sizable proportion ot the current flow abroad of private capital. The major formalized facilities of relevance in the placement of the funds are two US Government agencies, the Export-Import Bank and the Development Loan Fund, and one of the international institutions in which the US Government participates, the International Bank. While the bulk of the lending through these facilities occurs on behalf of foreign borrowers, American investors are generally eligible to compete alongside foreign applicants.[18]

Thus, presence of these facilities, in the financing and operation of which the US Government is directly involved, helps make capital available for private American firms that wish to undertake investment abroad. The result is the materialization of *some* American private investment abroad that would not have occurred otherwise—or, indeed, that might not even have been possible under other conditions.

SUPPORT THROUGH FOREIGN AID

Some portion of the expenditures under the US foreign-aid program has the direct effect of improving the economic environment abroad (to say nothing of the political environment), thereby creating a situation more conducive for private investment than would be likely to prevail otherwise. Some expenditures on public overhead are especially beneficial in this respect. In a sense, foreign-aid expenditures thus pave the way for private investment.[19]

---

18 Indeed, some official funds are specifically earmarked for use by American private investors abroad, e.g., a portion of the foreign-currency proceeds from sales abroad of US surplus agricultural commodities, entrusted to the Export-Import Bank for administration. Additionally, access to private domestic capital markets is aided, in instances, as private borrowings are guaranteed by the agencies or institutions, e.g., as by the Export-Import Bank or the International Bank.

19 However, the argument has been advanced that foreign aid discourages private investment, in the sense that foreign countries come to shun private capital in the belief that they can obtain capital on better terms through official channels. For example, see The American Enterprise Association, Inc., "American Private Enterprise, Foreign Economic Development, and the Aid Programs," Study No. 7 in *Foreign Aid Program,* US Senate Document No. 52, Washington, July 1957, esp. p. 603.

INVESTMENT GUARANTIES

Through the Investment Guaranty Program, established within the framework of the US foreign-aid program, insurance is obtainable to cover specific risks ordinarily regarded as constituting impediments to the movement abroad of US private capital. The insurable risks are inconvertibility, expropriation, and war loss. While these risks are not thereby eliminated, they are rendered ineffectual as obstacles as far as the individual private investor needs to be concerned.

TREATIES

During roughly the past half century, the US Government has negotiated Treaties of Friendship, Commerce, and Navigation with a number of countries in an attempt to improve conditions for Americans doing business abroad. Since World War II, treaty provisions have been specifically geared toward the promotion of private capital exports from the US. The major objective of the treaty program has been the definition of general standards of treatment that investors might regard as their "right" in foreign areas.[20]

Beyond the formal treaty process, the fact that an investment is American, and has behind it the prestige and backing of the US Government, tends to yield—with notable exceptions—certain protective benefits.

TAX TREATMENT

The US Government has negotiated tax treaties with a number of countries, the major objective being the elimination of double taxation in the case of American foreign investment. Involved has been an effort to achieve legal clarification and clear-cut identification of specific areas of taxation available to each of the two countries concerned (i.e., the host country and the US). Mutual understanding on these matters has been held especially important because income derived from American private investment abroad is taxable under the US corporate-income tax, but with like taxes paid the host government eligible for deduction from the US tax liability (up to the point that the US tax liability exceeds the foreign tax liability).

Further, a recent innovation, first incorporated in a tax treaty with Pakistan (in 1957), relates to "tax sparing." Involved is the inclusion in a treaty of a provision that enables an American investor to receive as added tax-free profit the benefit of any reduction in income taxation granted by the host government—instead of requiring the investor to pay the US Government the difference between the foreign tax liability

---

[20] The treaty program has yielded a codification of accepted policies (important especially in event of legal actions), but only little appears to have been accomplished by way of alteration of policies.

and the regular US tax liability (which earlier procedure had the effect of leaving the total income-tax liability unaltered for the investor, irrespective of what action the host government initiated in order to lower taxes in the interests of stimulating an inflow of private capital).

Additionally, those American-owned corporations organized under US law as Western Hemisphere Trade Corporations are given special treatment by being allowed to claim, by virtue of their particular legal status, a 14 percentage point reduction in their effective income-tax liability in the US.

INFORMATION

The commercial sections of this country's Foreign Service are the source of considerable information on prospective private-investment outlets abroad. The Department of Commerce makes available to potential investors much of the information so obtained.

POSSIBLE FURTHER AIDS TO PRIVATE INVESTMENT

Despite the foregoing and other action taken in the hope of bringing about a substantially greater (and rising) level of American private investment abroad, the result—as reflected in the investment record cited earlier—leaves much to be desired. On the assumption that more encouragement is warranted, proposals for further or different action continue to be made. Among the numerous and varied proposals offered, several appear to merit particular attention.

INFORMATION

Some persons feel that the commercial sections of the Foreign Service need to be strengthened with a view toward making a fuller effort to seek out investment opportunities and to bring them to the attention of potential investors among the American populace. A common impression is that, as matters stand, information reaches potential investors in the form of an impersonalized brochure, containing merely a series of sketchy listings of rather obvious potential investment outlets (a sample entry reading something like "Country X needs a cement plant"). It is widely contended that even basic information *about* a given potential investment outlet, let alone detailed information, typically proves unobtainable from official sources, and that no real assistance is given interested parties in their efforts to unearth this information, or to act upon whatever information they do have. In essence, what information or help is available is held freely available to all, but of little value to any.

What, precisely, potential investors would like the US Government to do for them on this score is not entirely clear; while generalized criticism has been rampant, concrete proposals for reform have been singularly few. Certainly it is not reasonable to expect the US Government to enter into the business of investment counseling, providing clients with any and all vital information desired (including, conceivably, such information as the profit positions of firms later to be faced as competitors). And, it can be creditably contended that all a potential investor needs from his government anyway is a clue; if even remotely interested, the potential investor can then proceed to look into the matter on his own and in his own way (a reasonable procedure, in the view of many, since the investor will presumably want to check into matters personally at some point anyway before committing himself or his funds).

All in all, it can be argued that there is a distinct limit as to how far the government of a lending country should go to gather economic intelligence on behalf of its profit motivated businessmen (especially when overall foreign-policy issues are also at stake), and that there is a distinct limit as to how far a government should obligate itself in an attempt to convince a potential investor to take action, when such action might eventuate in business failure. On one point, however, room for reasonable speculation remains: the philosophy that guides the commercial sections of the American Foreign Service. Are the people involved as interested in promoting new US private investment abroad as they are in seeing that all goes well with the US investment already existing abroad? If the answer is "no," there would appear to be a case for additional or changed action, whatever else might be said, pro or con, on other grounds.

GUARANTY COVERAGE

Authority exists under the Investment Guaranty Program[21] to issue guaranties on new investment to the total extent of $1 billion.[22] Guaranties issued from inception in 1948 through mid-1959 total $449 million, with applications still pending approximating $1 billion.[23] Many persons

---

[21] Established under the Economic Cooperation Act of 1948, and expanded thereafter under the Mutual Security Program.

The International Cooperation Administration, the US Government's foreign-aid agency, administers the Investment Guaranty Program, but it is assisted by the Export-Import Bank, which acts as an agent of the ICA. The sequence of responsibility is as follows. The ICA develops the individual guaranty contract, but the contract is written as an agreement between the investor and the Export-Import Bank. Eligibility for a contract is subject to certification by the ICA (to the effect that the investment covered is one that, broadly construed, "furthers the purposes of the Mutual Security Act," under which legislation the ICA operates). The contract provides that payments to investors due thereunder are payable by the Export-Import Bank from funds authorized by the Mutual Security Act. The Program is operated on a fractional reserve basis.

[22] This capacity to issue guaranties was increased in 1959 from a previous maximum limit of $500 million.

[23] The distribution of guaranties issued through mid-1959 was as follows: convertibility, 55%; and expropriation, 45%. While no guaranties had been issued to cover war risk, some applications were received. To illustrate, 16% of all applications pending at the end of 1958 involved war risk, the remainder being distributed as follows: convertibility, 57%; and expropriation, 27%. Source of data: Investment Guaranties Staff, International Cooperation Administration.

regard the Program as a success. For some, the extent to which the Program's services have come to be drawn upon is proof enough. Others go further, holding that access to the Program's services unquestionably helped dispel uncertainty and indecision, and hence helped stimulate private foreign investment. However, many of these persons remain of the opinion that the Program could do more to stimulate private foreign investment if only it were modified or expanded. Three main points are cited by way of possible improvement.

First, not all major risks to which foreign investment is subject are currently insurable. Coverage is provided for risks involving inconvertibility, expropriation, and war loss. Some persons feel that coverage should be extended to include at least two additional deterrents to investment: risks associated with possible devaluation and with possible damage from civil disturbances short of war. Extended coverage doubtless could be expected to yield some beneficial effect in the stimulation of investment, but the process of applying the added coverage poses special problems. For example, the wide discrepancy between the official and the free-market exchange rates in some countries would likely make necessary a rather high insurance fee on devaluation risks, i.e., a fee substantially higher than that attached to other insurable risks cited. Again, extension of insurance to cover damage from civil disturbances raises problems of definition, e.g., the term probably would need to be construed rather narrowly in order to prevent the inclusion within this category of such things as labor strikes.

Second, insurance is not currently available to cover investment contemplated in particular countries. Intergovernmental agreement is a prerequisite to the issuance of guaranties covering investment in any country. Participating countries currently number 44.[24] Countries not participating include some in the underdeveloped category urgently in need of better access to external capital.[25] Extension of the Program to additional countries, especially to those capital-deficit countries in which the investment climate is highly deficient, would appear to offer hope as a meaningful avenue to stimulate investment.[26]

---

24 As of the end of 1959. Of the 44 countries, 28 might reasonably be regarded as underdeveloped.

25 Approximately two-thirds of total guaranties issued through mid-1959 applied to countries in Europe alone, with the remainder spread among countries in Latin America, Asia, and Africa.

26 Under an amendment to the Mutual Security Act, effective January 1, 1960, issuance of new guaranties was henceforth to be restricted "to investments that will further the development and productive capacities of less-developed areas. . . ." See ICA, *Digest,* January 19, 1960. The effect of the amendment, for all intents and purposes, was to exclude Europe from the Program. The action was taken as one move in response to "adverse" balance-of-payments repercussions experienced by the US during 1958–59; justification was believed to exist in the new prosperity that had come to Europe, and that had served to strengthen its competitive position vis-à-vis the US.

Third, the insurance obtainable is not without cost, and an occasional person is inclined to regard the rate charged as too high. The normal fee is ½ of 1% per year of the guaranty coverage for *each* type of guaranty (i.e., the investor can select the particular risk or risks against which he wishes to insure, and a separate charge is then computed for each type of coverage contracted for). Of course, the intent in selecting the prevailing rate had been to make the Program self-supporting. While the demands upon the Program to cover losses sustained have been all but non-existent thus far, it is not entirely clear as to just what volume of possible loss ought be borne in mind as a point of reference in the building up of an adequate reserve.

TAX INCENTIVES

Tax proposals unquestionably receive the greatest attention among the various methods suggested for the stimulation of American foreign investment. It is generally agreed that more generous tax treatment of foreign-earned investment income by the US would encourage greater investment.[27] The precise effect a tax liberalization measure would have upon the magnitude of new investment can, of course, only be estimated in the absence of an actual test on the matter. It appears significant, however, that even those who argue against tax liberalization are inclined to admit to the likely effectiveness of incentive aspects, but frame their opposition on other grounds.[28]

Current favorites among proposals in the tax-reform category are four in number. The first proposal is that foreign-earned investment income not be taxed by the US, provided the income is reinvested abroad rather than remitted to the US. The proposal has the advantage of offering encouragement for reinvestment (and for higher total foreign investment), but it has no effect, in and of itself, by way of providing new and additional capital inflows for the borrowing country.[29] A positive disadvantage involves the loss of potential revenue for the US Treasury.[30]

A second proposal urges wider acceptance of the principle of tax sparing. Under this approach (as illustrated by the precedent established in the US-Pakistan tax treaty, cited earlier), the tax treaty prevailing

---

27 See, for example, Joint Committee on the Economic Report, *Federal Tax Policy for Economic Growth and Stability* (Papers submitted by panelists appearing before the Subcommittee on Tax Policy), Washington, November 1955, esp. pp. 745–756.

28 One team of authors, for example, visualizes investment gains as a consequence of the acceptance of particular tax-incentive measures, but is dubious of probable losses in revenue for the US Treasury; see E. R. Barlow and I. T. Wender, *Foreign Investment and Taxation* (Englewood Cliffs, N.J.: Prentice-Hall, Inc., 1955), Ch. 17.

29 The procedure appears likely to lessen foreign-exchange demands arising as a consequence of remittances otherwise undertaken; also, it might encourage, indirectly, the movement of new capital.

30 Some persons might also regard inequity of treatment to be a disadvantage, i.e., *inequity* by virtue of a difference in the treatment of foreign and domestic reinvested earnings.

between the US and any given foreign country contains a provision to the effect that any reduction in the foreign country's income-tax rate as applicable to the earnings of American private investment within that country is automatically to be taken into account by the US Government so as to be reflected in a reduction in the effective US tax rate applicable to the income in question. The alleged advantage of a tax-sparing arrangement is that a given foreign country is thereby encouraged to cater to American private investors through tax reductions upon the income arising from investment undertaken within its borders, since any tax concession then offered represents an actual tax saving for the American investor, not simply more revenue for the US Treasury at the expense of the foreign country's own public finances. Or, viewed from another angle, any tax reduction undertaken by a given country then tends to encourage American private capital to move to the particular country, since total effective taxes at issue—US plus foreign—are thereby lessened for American investors, even though the US Treasury experiences no loss of revenue in the process. By way of possible disadvantage, the system could lead to foreign governments' being pushed into a competitive scramble to cut taxes in an attempt to lure American capital, thereby jeopardizing their own tax and revenue structures—even while they are frequently in the process of trying to develop more adequate revenue sources, in many instances with the help of technical assistance supplied by the US Government under its foreign-aid program.[31]

A third proposal seeks to make applicable on a world-wide basis the US tax concession currently available only to corporations qualifying as Western Hemisphere Trade Corporations.[32] Assuming that the WHTC tax concession has proven conducive to American private investment in the Western Hemisphere, the argument simply is that world-wide application would encourage greater private investment by Americans in additional regions. On the negative side, it can be argued that there is no good reason to grant the WHTC tax concession to US private operations in developed countries. The investment lag is especially evident in Asia and Africa, but not particularly so in Europe. To generalize the con-

---

[31] A counter-argument, in turn, is that a foreign country may be better off with more investment, coupled with lower tax rates than with less investment, coupled with higher tax rates.

[32] To be eligible for classification as a Western Hemisphere Trade Corporation, a US corporation must—with one exception—be located in the Western Hemisphere outside the US (i.e., in Latin America or Canada), and must do at least 95% of its business (e.g., produce 95% of its output) in that region. The exception involves those corporations located in the US that have at least 95% of their sales in the Western Hemisphere outside the US. This exception provides the basis in terms of which some producers in the US have organized sales corporations for the specific purpose of handling sales from the US to other countries in the Western Hemisphere, thereby qualifying them for the tax concession. Through resorting to this legal loophole, sales activity—indeed, involving any type of merchandise—can receive the benefit of a tax concession initially put through to help promote "private foreign investment."

cession would yield a windfall for investors in some regions, and would do so at the cost of revenue to the US Treasury.

A fourth proposal proceeds in terms of accelerated amortization for purposes of tax computation. Since the tax concession would apply only to new investment, US Treasury revenues from existing investment would not be jeopardized. Actually, tax revenues derivable from a new investment would merely be postponed from the early years to the later years of the investment's life. In this way the system would help allay the fears of investors that the time required to obtain a pay-back is too long to justify the risks involved.[33] On the negative side, however, a possible major criticism involves the discriminatory nature of the system—in the sense of giving a concession to new investment not granted to previous investment, even when in the same line of business.

GOVERNMENT LOANS TO PRIVATE INVESTORS

A view of some recent popularity—representing, actually, a new variation of an old theme—holds that foreign investment contemplated by private investors should be eligible, under certain conditions, for governmental loan support in ways and on terms going beyond whatever else has been offered previously. Applied to the US, the notion is that the governmental loan support to which American private entrepreneurs contemplating foreign investment have had access (e.g., the facilities of the Export-Import Bank and the Development Loan Fund) should be supplemented through the creation of additional loan facilities.

A tangible proposal along these lines, addressed to the task of promoting US private investment in underdeveloped countries, embodies the following principle elements:[34]

> The U.S. Government would make loans to private enterprise up to 75 percent of the value of approved foreign investment in less developed countries in which the U.S. Government has assistance programs.
>
> To the greatest extent feasible, financial assistance to private enterprise which undertakes approved foreign investment projects would be substituted for direct loans to foreign governments.
>
> Other types of U.S. Government and international public assistance to the less developed countries would be coordinated with the private investments promoted under this program.

Proponents of the proposal point to two major benefits (or alleged benefits) as being likely results in the event of adoption. First, the possibility

---

33 See Ch. 13, section on "Incentive Taxation," for a discussion of the approach as applied to tax systems in underdeveloped countries.

34 R. F. Mikesell, *Promoting United States Private Investment Abroad* (Washington: National Planning Association, October 1957), pp. 65–77, esp. pp. 66–67. The proposal outlined does not limit loan assistance to American private investors; as stated, the investor "could be British, or German, or even a local private firm," just as readily (p. 67). In the connection under discussion above, however, the proposal is cited and examined in terms only of American private foreign investment.

is raised that particular private entrepreneurs would be given the added incentive needed to induce them to embark upon foreign investment, and that this investment could then substitute, at least in part, for the capital assistance otherwise supplied of necessity through intergovernmental loans and official foreign aid in loan or grant form. Since the US Government would provide loan assistance only up to 75% of the amount of the investment undertaken by a private investor in an underdeveloped country in which the US currently offers foreign aid, the possibility would exist that the Government could reduce its own direct cost in supplying capital to the affected countries through the customary routes of intergovernmental loans and official foreign aid. In a sense, the 75% provided by the Government would be the "bait" used to attract the 25% put up by private investors, and the 75% would be a loan, never a grant. Second, the possibility is raised that capital invested abroad by American private enterprise "can be *more effective* in promoting economic growth and the efficient use of resources than capital which is lent or given to foreign governments."[35]

By way of appraisal, an assumption that private investment (as direct investment) is better than capital provided directly by government can be summed up as just that: an *assumption*. Hence, little further needs be said about this facet of the proposal—other than to allude to earlier analyses of the subject, including analyses covering the disinterest of private investors in particular types of investment outlets (e.g., much of basic development) and the high cost in terms of foreign-exchange requirements generally associated with the servicing of private direct investment. As for the contention, however, that the proposal helps private investment to substitute for direct capital assistance under governmental auspices, much more can and doubtless needs be said. Of significance, there appears to be implied in the proposal an admission that private investment, unaided by direct governmental support, really is not up to the job. The proposal thereupon suggests a procedure believed likely to help private investment do *more* of a job. The procedure is that of giving private enterprise added access to public funds (through loans), including added access through greater participation in the foreign-aid program (by "cutting in" private enterprise on what normally are aid funds). The proposal appears to imply that foreign aid is a legitimate tool with which directly to promote US private investment abroad. This is a far cry, indeed, from another current view which holds that US private investment could "do the job" if only official foreign aid were eliminated.[36] But, assuming for the moment that the use of foreign-aid

---

[35] *Ibid.*, p. 67. (Italics are mine.)
[36] See The American Enterprise Association, Inc., "American Private Enterprise, Foreign Economic Development, and the Aid Programs," Study No. 7 in *Foreign Aid Program,* US Senate Document No. 52, Washington, July 1957, pp. 548, 603.

funds on the basis outlined would help private investment do more of a job (and that some additional help for private investment, rendered in some fashion, is warranted), a highly significant question nevertheless remains and merits resolution on at least a workable basis: How is foreign aid to be rationalized abroad when what foreign peoples see as the very first impact of aid-program funds is the setting up in business of American entrepreneurs?

THE PROSPECT FOR PRIVATE INVESTMENT

Viewed from the standpoint of the US Government, it is logical to strive for an increased flow of American private capital into foreign investment—*whenever* mutual benefit is likely to derive from the capital movement. If additional means exist that might be used to stimulate the flow of American private capital into foreign investment on this basis, it is reasonable to contend that these means should be used. It appears indeed to be a rare person who would choose to quarrel with this position. However, considering the number and nature of the major additional means that might be invoked, *to what extent does it appear likely that private foreign investment is capable of increase?*

Certainly some increase in the flow of private capital can logically be expected in the wake of adoption of particular added incentive measures. Just how great the increase might be cannot be ascertained precisely, short of putting the matter to an actual test. What can be done, more readily, is to examine how great an increase would be necessary in order to meet certain designated goals. By means of this approach, one is put in a position of being able to judge, for one's self, as to whether it is reasonable to hold that the avenue of private investment offers the potential to "do the job."

One meaningful point of reference is the level of official economic aid[37] being supplied by the US Government (under the Mutual Security Program). Accordingly, by how much would US private foreign investment have to increase in order to equal the current level of this country's official economic aid? First, viewed as a world-wide aggregate, growth in private direct investment abroad—measured in terms of current net capital outflows plus reinvested earnings—would have to show an increase of *roughly 50%* in order to reach the level of current official economic aid (*current* referring to the situation prevailing in 1957[38]). Second, viewed as a world-wide aggregate, growth in private direct investment

---

37 Apart from any military aid.
38 Investment data are for CY 57, while foreign-aid data are for FY 57 (ICA economic-aid expenditures, inclusive of technical assistance). These data, though tied to one year, are not unrepresentative of the entire post-Marshall Plan period; if anything, they understate the case that might be made in the present connection.

abroad—measured in terms of current net capital outflows alone (exclusive of reinvested earnings)—would have to show an increase of *roughly 75%* in order to reach the level of current official economic aid. Third, growth in private direct investment in Asia and Africa—measured in terms of current net capital outflows plus reinvested earnings—would have to show an increase of *more than 300%* in order to reach the level of current official economic aid going to these regions. Fourth, growth in private direct investment in Asia and Africa—measured in terms of current net capital outflows alone (exclusive of reinvested earnings)—would have to show an increase of *almost 1,000%* in order to reach the level of current official economic aid going to these regions.[39]

Can US private foreign investment be reasonably expected to increase by these amounts (in the short-run, and following realistic incentive measures)? To say the least, it would appear that one would be expecting a great deal were one to conclude affirmatively *even* in the case of the *global* requirement. However, if one did conclude that an increase in the aggregate by the magnitude cited does not pose an impossible objective, what about the situation relative to particular areas, e.g., Asia and Africa? Clearly, when one views capital movements on an area basis rather than simply on a global basis, the task some persons would "cut out" for private investment appears simply staggering in its immensity.

Actually, the practical task at issue may be still more formidable than pictured thus far. For example, is the current level of capital movement from the US, private capital plus official economic aid, adequate?[40] If not adequate, as numerous economists appear prepared to argue, then the foregoing really understates what is at issue. Again, is private investment capable of handling all types of operations for which capital is needed? If not thus capable, as many persons contend (e.g., as respects much of basic development), then partial incapacity is added to the possible indictment of insufficient magnitude.

The overall conclusion that appears here as warranted is that it is not unreasonable to hope for some increase in the flow of private capital to foreign areas, but that it is unrealistic to expect private capital to do anything like the "full job" in meeting the demands of foreign areas for external capital. Private capital has a role to play, but it is important not to exaggerate this role to the point of giving rise to unreasonable expec-

---

[39] Growth in private direct investment in Asia and Africa—measured in terms of current net capital outflows (exclusive of reinvested earnings) less amounts returning as capital remittances and repatriation—would have to show an even greater percentage increase in order to reach the level of current official economic aid going to these regions.

[40] Adequate in terms, say, of the achievement of some particular rate of income growth. See materials included in Ch. 15; note especially comments made there relative to views set forth in UN, *Measures for the Economic Development of Under-Developed Countries,* New York, 1951.

tations. Significantly, the crucial issue—from the US standpoint—is not so much one of private capital versus government capital as it is one of how to achieve a satisfactory level of total capital movement. It appears important to realize the limitations to what can be expected in terms of private investment (along with the several merits to which potential claim can be laid). Once these limitations are better understood, it may prove possible to divert some of the energy customarily given to recurring debates on private capital versus government capital to a fuller effort aimed at provision of *more capital* for capital-deficit areas.

SELECTED BIBLIOGRAPHY

The American Enterprise Association, Inc., "American Private Enterprise, Foreign Economic Development, and the Aid Programs," Study No. 7 in *Foreign Aid Program,* US Senate Document No. 52, Washington, July 1957.
> Espouses the viewpoint that American private foreign investment can be hampered by an over-aggressive provision of funds under governmental auspices.

E. R. Barlow and Ira T. Wender, *Foreign Investment and Taxation.* Englewood Cliffs, N.J.: Prentice-Hall, Inc., 1955.
> Broad coverage of the problems of private foreign investment, and of the manner in which taxation can help or hinder this investment; considerable attention given legislative aspects.

Irving Brecher and S. S. Reisman, *Canada-United States Economic Relations.* Ottawa: Royal Commission on Canada's Economic Prospects, July 1957.
> Examination, from the Canadian standpoint, of Canadian-American economic relationships; the study raises serious questions regarding Canada's heavy dependence on US private capital.

Emilio G. Collado and Jack F. Bennett, "Private Investment and Economic Development," *Foreign Affairs,* July 1957.
> Examination of the statistical magnitude of American private foreign investment; Department of Commerce data challenged on grounds of understatement of magnitudes.

Commission on Foreign Economic Policy, *Report to the President and the Congress,* Washington, January 1954; also *Minority Report,* January 1954, and *Staff Papers,* February 1954.
> The "Randall Report," along with dissenting views and background materials; considerable material devoted to why and how American private foreign investment can do more.

Committee for Economic Development, *Economic Development Abroad and the Role of American Foreign Investment,* New York, February 1956.
> The CED's ideas on the role of American private investment in foreign economic development; written for a layman audience.

Department of Commerce, *Factors Limiting U.S. Investment Abroad*, Washington, 1953 (Part I) and 1954 (Part II).

Part I surveys limiting factors in various countries; Part II presents businessmen's views on the US Government's role in promoting private foreign investment.

——————————, *Investment in India,* Washington, 1953.

Sample publication in a series covering various countries; content of each devoted to a survey of conditions within the given country and the outlook there for US investment.

——————————, *Survey of Current Business,* Washington, August 1959.

Pp. 25–32, Examination of US foreign-investment data for 1958 and earlier years.

Expanding Private Investment for Free World Economic Growth (A special report prepared at the request of the Department of State), Washington, April 1959.

Examination of what is being done to promote US private foreign investment, and of what more might be done.

Raymond F. Mikesell, *Promoting United States Private Investment Abroad.* Washington: National Planning Association, October 1957.

Concise coverage of the pattern and problems of American private foreign investment; presents a proposal for promotion of private investment.

Daniel L. Spencer, "Dare We Renege?", *Business Horizons* (Indiana University, School of Business), Fall 1958.

Examination of the social responsibility of business in the world scene; generally critical of notions that US private foreign investment is "doing the job."

United Nations, *The International Flow of Private Capital, 1956–58,* New York, August 1959.

Examines changes, and causes for them, in the movement of private capital during a 3-year period. An appendix summarizes recent governmental measures relating to foreign investment.

——————————,*United States Income Taxation of Private United States Investment in Latin America,* New York, January 1953.

Detailed examination of particular points in US tax legislation, with illustrations of effects upon hypothetical private firms.

18

INSTITUTIONAL
ASSISTANCE (I)

If US private investment has not "done the job," and can be expected to do only *part* of the job, the question arises as to what the US Government might, or ought, do on its part to make assistance available through special institutional arrangements.

In terms of this purpose, a number of institutional arrangements, mostly of recent origin, are in existence. Included are three specialized agencies of the US Government: the Export-Import Bank, the International Cooperation Administration, and the Development Loan Fund; also included are six international institutions with which the US is affiliated: the International Bank, the International Finance Corporation, the International Monetary Fund, the United Nations (Technical Assistance Program and Special Projects Fund), the Colombo Plan, and the Inter-American Development Bank. In addition, some proposals, advanced with a view toward providing greater assistance to underdeveloped countries, are still in the study stage.

The present chapter is concerned with the agencies of the US Government. The chapter following is concerned with the international institutions, and with major proposals for added or revised institutional arrangements.

EXPORT-IMPORT BANK

The Export-Import Bank of Washington had its beginnings in February 1934. A first Export-Import Bank, of modest capitalization, was created at that time for the avowed purpose of financing trade with the USSR, with which country the US had just established formal diplomatic relations. Contrary to early expectations, the financing of trade along the lines proposed failed to materialize, basically because the US and the USSR were unable to reach agreement regarding the settlement of long-standing debts and claims. Even while these negotiations with the USSR were still in progress, however, a second but smaller Export-Import Bank was created to finance trade with countries other than the USSR. Subsequently (early in 1935), with the realization that negotiations with the USSR were going to end in failure, the two Export-Import Banks were reconstituted to form a single Bank. This institution, with some important modifications from time to time, has continued in existence through the years.

The avowed purpose of the emergent Export-Import Bank, as stated in its charter, was "to aid in financing and to facilitate exports and imports and the exchange of commodities between the United States . . . and any foreign country or the agencies or nationals thereof." More precisely, however, the Bank has been used over the years with two main objectives in mind. First, the Bank has been used as an instrumentality with which to stimulate US exports. It is significant that the Bank came into being during the Great Depression, when its mere presence served as an invitation to adapt it as a domestic anti-depression device, i.e., for the creation of employment through an expansion of lagging exports. Beyond this, continuing support for the Bank over the years, both in Congressional and business quarters, in large measure has been in terms of increasing this country's "share of the world's exports through the weight of America's lending power."[1] Second, the Bank has been used to implement US foreign policy. The Department of State has always been an active participant in directing the Bank's affairs.[2] Indeed, the incorporation of the Bank's operations into the country's overall foreign-policy activities has generally been regarded favorably in official circles.[3]

EVOLUTION

While support of exportation and reinforcement of foreign policy have constituted the two basic objectives of the Bank, significant shifts in emphasis have occurred during the course of operation. During initial years (prior to 1939 or thereabouts), the Bank's attention was directed primarily at export expansion. The situation of widespread unemployment within the American economy offered a ready rationale for governmental intervention in efforts to expand exports. The hope was that

[1] O. S. Pugh, *The Export-Import Bank of Washington* (Columbia, S.C.: University of South Carolina Bureau of Business and Economic Research, June 1957), p. 23.
[2] However, only a portion of the political requests for extension of credit have gotten Bank approval. *Ibid.*, p. 29.
[3] To illustrate, the Randall Commission referred to the Bank in terms of being *"essentially"* an instrument of United States foreign policy." (Italics are mine.) See Commission on Foreign Economic Policy, *Report to the President and the Congress,* Washington, January 1954, p. 24.

through the extension of liberal credit for exports, the volume of exports —and the magnitude of employment attributable to export activities— might be raised. Of considerable significance, the period of the Great Depression (and even during the years immediately prior to it) was one in which numerous governments had introduced protectionism in various guises, including programs of export subsidization, e.g., state measures such as export bounties, liberalized credit for foreign sales, and insurance against risks assumed in the granting of export credits.[4] Accordingly, action by the US Government to extend special help to exporters by means of the facilities of a new lending agency did not represent a novel approach, but constituted—in the opinion of many persons—a proper form of governmental counter-activity, taken in order to put American business and the American economy generally on a par with foreign producers and economies.

As World War II appeared ever more imminent, emphasis in Bank operation came to be dominated increasingly by political considerations. Most importantly, the Bank's power and capacity to render financial assistance to foreign governments were expanded, thereby putting the institution in a potent position to operate as an arm of the Department of State in the implementation of US foreign policy. Lending during the ensuing period was largely to China and Latin America, giving added life in the case of Latin America to the currently popular Good-Neighbor Policy. With the actual outbreak of hostilities, increasing emphasis was placed upon "hemispheric solidarity," which resulted in a marked expansion in Bank lending as part of an effort to cultivate closer economic ties between Latin America and the US. Latin America, normally heavily dependent upon sales in European markets, was offered access to American goods on terms designed to lessen the possibility of a build-up of pressure in the countries concerned that might eventuate in a temptation to run the blockade the Allies had thrown around Continental Europe. In fact, the Bank expanded its scope to the extent of offering credit, for the first time, for purposes of economic development.

With the ending of World War II, the Bank embarked upon a period of activity in which financing of the needs of reconstruction, especially in Europe, loomed importantly. During the war, Lend-Lease represented the major basis for provision of assistance to the Allies, but with the termination of Lend-Lease the Bank's resources were expanded with a view toward handling the financing of reconstruction requirements, among the Allied powers and others. Accordingly, the Bank's business came to be heavily slanted toward Europe and reconstruction—at least until 1948 and the advent of the Marshall Plan, a program instituted in part because the Bank, or any combination of already-existing facilities,

---

4 By 1934, for instance, no less than 14 countries had systems of government export-credit insurance in effect.

was considered inadequate for handling the enormous task at issue. Beginning in 1948, then, the Bank's activities were re-directed primarily toward financing general US exports—including among them, however, exports destined for reconstruction *and* for economic development.

No great change in the nature of the Bank's activity was evident between 1948 and 1953. In 1953, however, with the advent of a Republican Administration following 20 years of Democratic rule, questions were raised in higher echelons of the Government as to what the Bank should do—or, indeed, as to whether the Bank should even be continued. As a consequence, Congressional hearings were held on the matter, a virtual trial by fire for the Bank. The "verdict" arrived at gave the Bank a clean bill of health. Interestingly, two strategic developments had come into play during the crucial period that helped generate the support needed by the Bank to survive the critical re-evaluation then in progress. These developments were the recession experienced by the American economy in 1953–54 and the entry into foreign markets in enlarged volume of the output of rejuvenated European producers, both of which developments served to imperil American export volume to some extent (and hence to win considerable support for the Bank in both business and Congressional quarters). In fact, the Bank emerged from its ordeal not merely unscathed, but actually stronger than ever within the bureaucratic hierarchy. Because the Bank had successfully met inspection, whereas not all other agencies could claim the same for themselves, the Bank's voice took on more meaning. Moreover, the Bank's lending resources had been increased in the process, so that an expanded role became possible. Thereupon, the Bank engaged in operations with new vigor, rationalizing its loan conduct as circumstances warranted, or demanded—largely in terms of aid for American exports or for foreign economic development.

In 1958, the Bank's resources were again expanded, bringing its lending capacity, which had been increased over the years in easy stages, up to a total of $7 billion. In part, the latest increase was deemed necessary in the light of the Bank's unprecedentedly high volume of business. In part (and perhaps in major part), however, the increase was attributable to a deliberate governmental decision to route a greater portion of the financial assistance for foreign economic development through the Bank on a loan basis—in preference to channelizing it through other agencies on a generally "softer" basis, e.g., as with grant aid.

NATURE OF BUSINESS

As intimated earlier, the practical functions of the Bank are two-fold: to provide financing in a manner likely to increase American exports[5]

---

[5] The Bank was empowered to finance imports also, i.e., the institution was established as an Export-*Import* Bank. However, import financing by the Bank has

and to implement US foreign policy. Neither financing of exportation nor financing undertaken to implement foreign policy need be incompatible with assistance for promotion of development abroad. The added exports at issue can represent ingredients for development; similarly, implementation of foreign policy can proceed through assistance for development in underdeveloped countries. Unfortunately, the precise extent to which the Bank's activities actually constitute assistance for developmental effort is difficult to determine. Multiple purposes are generally at issue in individual transactions, with the result that clear-cut identification of what might properly be labeled developmental assistance is not ordinarily an easy matter.[6] One hopeful approach in an attempt to gauge the Bank's contribution to development, however, is to examine the essential nature of each of the Bank's major categories of lending activity.

Dollar loans by the Bank fall into three major categories. First, the Bank makes *exporter loans*. The objective of the Bank in these instances is to finance the movement of goods from the US to foreign countries, whenever this movement is regarded by the Bank as worthy and not likely to occur under arrangements accessible elsewhere to sellers or buyers. Under current procedure, the Bank is willing to finance, on a non-recourse basis, up to 68% of the invoice value of a shipment; beyond this, it is expected that the foreign importer will pay the exporter at least 20% of the invoice value prior to shipment, and that the exporter will carry on his own at least 12% of the invoice value.[7] In short, the foreign importer, acting under the Bank's arrangement, can be financed to the extent of 80% of the invoice value of his purchase; the exporter can receive immediate cash payment for his exports to the extent of 88% of their invoice value (and, in event of eventual failure of the purchaser to pay the 12% carried by the exporter, the exporter does not necessarily suffer an equivalent out-of-pocket loss, for anticipated profit is included in total invoice value); and while the Bank assumes an obligation to the extent of 68% of the invoice value, no funds of its own need necessarily

---

been virtually non-existent, and in its more recent releases the Bank has discontinued reference to the subject. Absence of emphasis upon import financing has been held justified on the grounds that adequate private capital is available for the purpose. Attention in this presentation, therefore, is directed to export financing only.

6 Moreover, the Bank itself has not always been consistent (or, perhaps, even logical) in its system of classifying credits. To illustrate, the Bank has classified its financing of US sales of cotton to Japan as *"development* credit"; see the Bank's annual *Report*, issued for the year ending June 30, 1956.

7 Financing of export credit under the 20–12–68 formula was inaugurated in September 1959. Prior to that time, a 20–20–60 formula governed, i.e., involving at least a 20% cash payment by the foreign buyer prior to delivery, with the US exporter carrying not less than 20% of the contract price of a sale, and with the Bank assuming credit responsibility for not more than 60%. The reason given for the change was to make exporter credit terms "consistent with terms generally available to suppliers of other countries under various export credit arrangements." See Export-Import Bank, *Press Release* (No. 608), September 22, 1959.

be used (short of subsequent default by the importer[8]), since the Bank's assumption of liability is sufficient to enable the IOU to be discounted at a commercial bank by the exporter. Significantly, added exports occur in the process, but economic development is also fostered—provided the goods shipped are of a type holding meaning in a developmental effort. Of some interest, the initiative for negotiation of an exporter loan ordinarily comes from the exporter, but a loan, once made, is typically listed by the Bank in the name of the foreign importer, i.e., the loan is treated as a "foreign" loan.

Second, the Bank makes *loans to private firms,* foreign or American, to finance investment abroad. The Bank's preference is to lend for specific projects, so that the usage of funds is clear-cut and readily identifiable. Moreover, the Bank's policy is to lend only that amount needed to cover the direct foreign-exchange cost of a given project, or something less than this amount. As a condition for lending, the Bank ordinarily requires that the borrower obtain the guarantee of the government of the recipient country. Thus, the sequence that characteristically applies is initiation of loan negotiations by the private firm, approval of the investment by the government of the recipient country in question, and arrangement of a loan contract between the private firm and the Bank. Of interest, also, is the fact that a loan in this category, even when made to an American firm operating abroad, comes to be classified by the Bank as a foreign loan (on behalf of the country in which the investment is located).

Third, the Bank makes *loans to foreign governments* or agencies thereof. As in the case of loans to private firms, the Bank's preference is to lend for specific projects, but on occasion the Bank has deviated from this position in its intergovernmental lending and has provided dollars for some general purpose or program (going beyond any specific project). In the case of intergovernmental loans for projects, the amount lent is customarily held to the direct foreign-exchange cost involved, or to some portion of this; but, in the case of general or program loans, similar clear-cut identification of funds lent with direct foreign-exchange cost ordinarily proves impossible—a situation commonly cited to explain the Bank's historic hesitancy toward involvement in non-project financing. An important form of non-project financing toward which the Bank has shown some receptivity, especially during recent periods, is that of loans offered as "balance-of-payments assistance." These loans, however, do not ordinarily constitute pure balance-of-payments assistance, for usage is customarily tied to particular categories of imports (i.e., a loan is generally premised on the assumption that *particular* imports, considered

---

8 The importer, in turn, is ordinarily required to have a guarantor, generally his bank or government.

important in some approved connections, would be early casualties in an impending balance-of-payments squeeze[9]).

In all instances, the Bank regards itself as being *non-competitive* with private capital. According to its charter, the Bank ". . . should supplement and encourage and not compete with private capital. . . ." In the area of loans to governments, of course, private capital is only rarely interested. In the areas of exporter credit and private investment, however, interest on the part of private lenders is potentially present. Accordingly (in reference to the second case), the Bank has resolved its position of "no competition" through adherence to two elementary working principles. First, the Bank has put into effect various procedures of possible help to private lenders and investors, e.g., supplementary credits and guarantees. Second, the Bank has cultivated for itself the posture of "lender of last resort" (in its relationship to the private capital market); the Bank expects prospective borrowers, at the time they open negotiations, to have already surveyed likely private sources of financing, and to have found adequate financing on reasonable terms unavailable.

Cumulative lending (dollar credits) by the Bank from its inception through mid-1959 totaled $10.2 billion, of which amount $6.9 billion was actually disbursed (Table 19). The tempo of activity varied widely, however, during the Bank's quarter century of operation. The great bulk of lending—roughly 90%—occurred after World War II, and annual variations during the postwar period ranged between $0.2 billion and $2.2 billion. During the 5-year period ending with mid-1959, new credits authorized averaged slightly over $0.6 billion per year, while disbursements averaged about $0.4 billion per year.

The geographic distribution of Bank loans has been characterized by considerable unevenness (Table 19). While over 60 countries have been direct beneficiaries of some amount of Bank credit, a substantial number managed to avail themselves of little more than token assistance. As of mid-1959, Europe and Latin America together had been allotted roughly 75% of all new credits authorized (cumulative), but the comparable statistic for Asia and Africa together was only 20%. If Asia, Africa, and Latin America are taken to comprise the underdeveloped world (in the classification shown in Table 19), under 60% of the Bank's lending has been to underdeveloped regions—and not all of this lending, by any means, has been for economic development.

In addition to its function of providing dollar credits, the Bank is engaged in three major subsidiary functions. First, the Bank acts as agent for the International Cooperation Administration (ICA) in the

---

[9] For example, in anticipation of balance-of-payments difficulties likely to arise in the wake of the Suez crisis of 1957, the Bank granted a line of credit of $500 million to the United Kingdom in that year to help it meet future dollar requirements for materials and equipment.

Table 19. Export-Import Bank Loans, 1934–1959
(In millions of US dollars)

AREA	Credits Author- ized	Cancel- lations & Partici- pations[1]	Undis- bursed Bal- ances	Dis- burse- ments	Re- pay- ments	Out- stand- ing Loans
Africa	243	12	32	199	67	132
Asia	2,028	444	399	1,186	722	464
Canada	376	193		183	183	. . . .[2]
Europe	3,745	681	282	2,782	1,358	1,424
Latin America	3,809	722	588	2,498	1,068	1,430
Oceania	24	5	. . . .	19	7	12
Other Countries	8	8	. . . .	. . . .	. . . .	. . . .
Miscellaneous	5	1	. . . .	4	4	. . . .
Total	10,238	2,066	1,301	6,871	3,409	3,462

Source: *Export-Import Bank,* Report to the Congress, June 30, 1959, *Part I, Washington, 1959, p. 193. Data cover February 1934–June 1959, inclusive.*

[1] Amounts expiring unused, or taken over by others.
[2] $8,000.

administration of the Investment Guaranty Program (treated in Ch. 17). Second, the Bank acts as agent for the ICA in the administration of local-currency loans undertaken abroad on the basis of those funds derived from foreign sale of US surplus agricultural commodities, and held by the ICA through completion of loan arrangements. Third, the Bank is empowered to lend, on its own (subject to certain limitations[10]), up to 25% of the local currencies derived in any country as a consequence of the sale of US surplus agricultural commodities.

SOURCE OF FUNDS

The lending authority of the Bank has been expanded eight times since commencement of operations, reaching $7 billion in 1958, follow-

[10] Sec. 104(e) of Title I of Public Law 480 (the Agricultural Trade Development and Assistance Act of 1954, as amended), adopted in 1957 and commonly referred to as the "Cooley Amendment," provides that up to 25% of the local currencies derived from the sale abroad of US surplus agricultural commodities can be earmarked for use, through the Export-Import Bank, either as loans to American business firms undertaking investment in the countries concerned, or as loans to American or foreign firms establishing facilities considered likely to increase markets for US agricultural commodities.

The first loan of this type, involving Mexican pesos, was announced in August 1958; see *The New York Times,* August 10, 1958, p. 1–F.

ing an increase by $2 billion in that year. Under terms of its charter, the magnitude of lending authority establishes the upper limit to total dollar credits, plus guarantees and insurance, the Bank can have outstanding at any one time. By way of comparison, applicable amounts outstanding in mid-1959 totaled slightly under $4 billion.

Of the $7 billion, $1 billion consists of capital stock subscribed by the US Government and $6 billion consists of rights given the Bank to borrow from the US Treasury. In the language of the authorizing legislation, the Bank[11]

> . . . is authorized to issue from time to time for purchase by the Secretary of the Treasury its notes, debentures, bonds, or other obligations; but the aggregate amount of such obligations outstanding at any one time shall not exceed $6,000,000,000. Such obligations shall be re deemable at the option of the Bank before maturity in such manner as may be stipulated in such obligations and shall have such maturity as may be determined by the Board of Directors of the Bank with the approval of the Secretary of the Treasury. Each such obligation shall bear interest at a rate determined by the Secretary of the Treasury, taking into consideration the current average rate on outstanding marketable obligations of the United States. . . .

Considerable significance attaches to the fact that the great bulk of the dollars the Bank has to lend are borrowed from the Treasury, rather than gotten through a Congressional appropriation. Indeed, many persons regard the foregoing fact as the basis for much of the popularity enjoyed by the Bank in particular quarters. To elaborate, if the Bank were obliged to get its funds from the Congress, the resulting appropriation (in the absence of cut-backs elsewhere) would register an impact either in increased taxes or in deficit financing (with the full amount in the second case being treated for accounting purposes as a budgetary outlay in the current fiscal year, and hence additive, immediately, to national debt). Thus, in 1958, had the Congress found it necessary to appropriate $2 billion to increase the Bank's lending authority by this amount, national debt would have been affected by the full $2 billion in the current fiscal year (in the absence of deliberate offsetting tax increases or outlay reductions elsewhere). However, the Bank is organized as an independent corporation, and is empowered to sell its obligations to the Treasury, within prescribed limits. This procedure has the effect of taking the immediate burden off the Congress; even though taxes are not increased or outlays elsewhere are not reduced, an addition to lending authority, in and of itself, need not create budgetary or national debt impact. Impact in these respects arises only insofar as the Bank actually exercises its privilege of offering obligations in increased amount to the Treasury.

---

[11] Export-Import Bank Act of 1945, as amended, Sec. 6.

Significantly, the impact then does not occur simultaneously with an increase in lending authority, but rather comes to be registered little by little over time as drawing rights are invoked (and probably never falls in its entirety within a single fiscal year). Thus, in 1958, the increase by $2 billion in the Bank's lending authority necessitated neither an increase in taxes nor a cut-back in other outlays, nor did it result in an immediate increase to this extent in national debt.

Interestingly enough, not all other agencies established to render dollar assistance for the conduct of activity abroad are similarly organized or similarly equipped to by-pass the need for periodic appeals to the Congress for funds, e.g., the ICA is not so situated. Hence, for those persons who are interested in having dollar credits made available for foreign activity, but who are also interested in seeing this availability occur without *direct* impact either upon taxes or upon debt, the Bank readily offers special attractiveness in any competition among alternatives.

It appears of some significance that the Administration in power after 1953 repeatedly stressed its interest in achieving a balanced budget, and in holding the line on taxes and the level of national debt.[12] Given this overall environment, the Bank's position of advantage in any popularity contest is not difficult to comprehend. In essence, an increase in the Bank's lending authority allows the US to cite added resources as being ready and available for the financing of foreign activity, and to do so without having to earmark in advance an equivalent amount of public funds (which action, if taken, would carry immediate consequences in the realm of public credit). An equivalent increase in the resources available to an alternate agency, one dependent upon direct Congressional appropriation for funds, would allow the US to claim no more in the way of contribution to increased foreign activity, but related consequences in the realm of public credit would be immediate.

In short, the Bank is obliged to draw upon the Treasury only insofar as funds actually come to be required by it. Moreover, the Bank economizes in the use of dollars theoretically available to it through the expedient of fostering participation by private capital. The Bank maintains close contact with private lending institutions in order to encourage their participation in its lending operations. This relationship finds expression in a number of ways, including use of commercial banks for the issuance of guaranteed letters of credit, advances by commercial banks to borrowers of the Bank on a guaranteed basis, and *pari passu* participation with the Bank in its credits without guarantee by the Bank. The procedure, of

---

12 During the period at issue, the national debt stood near the debt ceiling established by the Congress. While the ceiling could have been raised, as had been done numerous times in previous eras, there was a general reluctance by the Administration in power to request this action, at least for this purpose—perhaps, or probably, because of its earlier campaign promises to hold the line.

course, is in keeping with the Bank's avowed policy to supplement and encourage but not compete with private capital.[13]

EVALUATION

The Bank, the principal[14] international lending agency of the US Government, has long regarded its presence and activities as helpful in the promotion of development in the underdeveloped world. Officials of the Bank have stressed this role in public statements,[15] and various documents of the Executive Office have made reference in this vein.[16] On the other hand, some persons have been inclined to be critical of the Bank in regard to its position relative to the underdeveloped world. The question, therefore, is raised: How effective has the Bank been in the promotion of development?

Of the criticisms leveled at the Bank, five appear central. First, it is contended that the Bank's areal distribution of loans leaves much to be desired, if the development of underdeveloped countries is held to be a truly important objective. As indicated earlier, under 60% of the Bank's lending has been in regions that might be regarded as underdeveloped (Table 19). And, while Latin America has received approximately as much in loans as has Europe, Europe alone has received almost double the amount that has gone to Asia and Africa combined. In fact, particular countries of Asia and Africa have received no, or virtually no, assistance from the Bank. The existing situation has motivated some persons to comment that the Bank helps developed countries fully as much as it does underdeveloped countries—or, further, that the Bank is not even interested in

---

13 In addition to dollar credits supplied along lines outlined above, the Bank also is empowered to make loans in foreign currencies. As intimated previously (in footnote 10), a 1957 amendment to Public Law 480 makes the Bank responsible for lending certain foreign currencies to private enterprise. Specifically, the Bank is permitted to receive in foreign currencies up to 25% of the proceeds of sale, under Public Law 480, of US surplus agricultural commodities. Foreign-currency loans made from these proceeds are required to be mutually agreeable to the Bank and the foreign governments concerned; are prohibited for purposes giving rise either to manufactured goods likely to enter the US and compete with domestic output, or to any goods likely to be marketed anywhere in competition with US agricultural commodities or the products thereof; and are permissible for use either by American firms operating abroad, or by American or foreign firms offering a means to expand markets for US agricultural commodities abroad.

14 *Principal* in terms of dollar loan volume (to mid-1959). The Bank acknowledges its status as that of principal lender; see, for example, the Bank's *Report to the Congress for the Twelve Months ending June 30, 1958,* Part I, Washington, 1958, p. 4.

15 See statements by Samuel C. Waugh, President of the Bank, in *Hearing before the Committee on Banking and Currency, United States Senate* (on S.3149, concerning "Increased Export-Import Bank Lending Authority"), 1958, esp. p. 4.

16 For example, the President's Budget Message (January 1958) stated that the Bank has had an "increasing role in promoting United States exports and imports and in *financing economic development* projects abroad. . . ." Again, the Economic Report of the President (January 1958) stated that the Bank's activities "in financing exports are directly helpful in promoting production and employment in the United States economy as well as in *assisting the economic development* of foreign countries." (Italics are mine.)

promoting loan activity in some underdeveloped countries. Of course, the Bank has merely said that it *helps* in the development of underdeveloped countries (by financing certain transactions); it has never purported to *limit* its activities to underdeveloped countries. To be precise, the Bank was set up, basically, to help move US exports, whether going to developed *or* underdeveloped countries. And, the very fact that some of the more underdeveloped of countries are among the poorer of credit risks obviously has tended to operate against their availing themselves of assistance through the Bank, given the Bank's devotion to business-like standards in its loan policy.

Second, the Bank's loan terms are tough—to the point, as contended by some, that the credit is not suited for financing more than a small fraction of what comprises developmental needs. The Bank ordinarily extends dollar credit to cover no more than the direct foreign-exchange cost of a project, so that the borrower is typically obliged to seek additional financing elsewhere. The Bank requires dollar repayment on dollar credit, so that balance-of-payments considerations loom importantly in the problem of repayment (and serve entirely to preclude use of the Bank's credit in particular connections). The Bank is particularly interested in extending medium-term credit (3 to 5 years duration), but some potential borrowers need long-term credit (up to 10 years duration, or longer) if they are to embark successfully upon new operations.[17] The Bank's loans are "tied" (i.e., loan proceeds must be used directly in the American market[18]), so that, for example, equipment must be purchased in the US even though less-costly or better-suited equipment may be obtainable elsewhere.[19] The

---

[17] The Bank has granted some long-term credit (up to 20 years duration, in fact). The Bank's *primary* interest, however, is in medium-term credit—to the extent that a substantial sector of the public has come, in its thinking, to associate medium-term credit with the Bank.

[18] The Bank's charter does not specifically state that credits are to be tied to direct US usage, but the Bank's usual practice is to incorporate a tying clause in the loan contracts negotiated.

[19] The price of US equipment frequently runs considerably higher—roughly one-third more in many instances—than that of comparable equipment obtainable in other industrial countries, e.g., Germany or Japan. US suppliers, in defending their prices, frequently assert that the American equipment may well involve a higher initial cost, but that the equipment is well worth the added amount because it is better—generally meaning that it is more labor-saving and that, therefore, it can offer lower costs in operation. However, potential buyers in underdeveloped countries frequently reply that, better or not better, the initial cost is an important consideration for them as investors, and can make the difference between initiation or deferral of action. Or, potential buyers assert that even if American equipment is better in the sense of being more labor-saving, this attribute is of no great value in underdeveloped countries, given the surplus labor and low money wages characteristically prevailing there. To illustrate, some potential buyers of textile machinery for use in underdeveloped countries in, say, Asia assert that Japanese equipment is better suited for their purpose than is American equipment—precisely because Japanese equipment tends to be more labor-using and also somewhat cheaper in terms of initial outlay.

There is a possible counter-argument, however, to the effect that restriction to US supplies, despite a higher cost for these in terms of initial outlay, does not necessarily pose a deterrent to overall investment in developmental projects in underdeveloped countries. The argument is that US supplies, financed through the Bank, can be used

Bank's interest rates vary with the type of loan and degree of tightness of conditions in US money markets[20] (ranging, ordinarily, from $4\frac{1}{2}\%$ to 6%[21]), but tend to be at a level that must be regarded as on the high side, given the circumstances ordinarily prevailing in developmental efforts (especially as seen by an end-user who borrows from a foreign financial institution, and in the process is obliged to bear the Bank's charge upon the package loan made to the foreign institution plus the latter's own mark-up[22]). Bank credit is ordinarily obtained only after considerable delay, both because the Bank customarily expects potential borrowers to test their chances first in private capital markets and because the Bank's mode of loan processing takes time (said to require up to 18 months on occasion[23]). The very atmosphere in which operations occur is inimical to easy credit; the Bank takes pride in its adherence to "sound" and "business-like" practices. Perhaps the best indication of the Bank's toughness, however, is found in its record of repayments on credits granted. Losses through default thus far are negligible; in fact, a sizable net profit each year is typical—despite the fact that the Bank, as in the case of other government agencies, is not in business for profit. In view of its record of virtually no losses, it would appear important to examine not merely

---

in combination with other supplies obtained from non-US sources, and financed through other means. The arrangement then is a combination of financing, followed by a combination of the various physical ingredients of investment. In essence, this argument holds that sheer volume of financing for purchasing needed supplies constitutes a factor of greater relevance in economic development than does some marginal difference in cost as between alternate sources of financing.

20 Since the bulk of the Bank's funds are obtained through borrowing from the Treasury, the terms upon which the Treasury is able to obtain and make funds available come to be reflected in the Bank's own interest rates.

21 Actually, rates as low as $2\frac{1}{2}\%$ have been offered. These lower rates, however, have applied, by and large, to special categories of credits, e.g., reconstruction credits provided during the immediate post-World War II period.

22 When the Bank renders a firm line of balance-of-payments assistance to a country, the borrower—say, the country's Central Bank—assumes responsibility for the interest owing the Bank. In subsequent sales of foreign exchange, the Central Bank receives domestic currency in exchange for dollars, so that (in the absence of an interest charge in this transaction) the interest cost that the Central Bank is obliged to bear needs to be viewed, in actuality, as a charge upon the economy as a whole. When, however, the Bank's loan is to a development bank in the recipient country (either directly, or indirectly through balance-of-payments assistance to the Central Bank, with subsequent lending by the Central Bank to the development bank), the Bank's interest charge, plus the additional interest charged by the domestic lender, ordinarily comes to be passed on to the end-borrower. Since the end-borrower ordinarily settles his interest obligation in terms of domestic currency, the borrower named in the Bank's loan contract, be it the Central Bank or a development bank, is held responsible for settlement with the Bank in terms of dollars. In any event, because remission of interest charges requires foreign exchange, impact upon the country's balance of payments as a consequence of utilization of dollars lent becomes of basic importance.

23 In the process, private borrowers contemplating investment abroad are ordinarily obliged to obtain the guarantee of the government of the recipient country. Aside from the time sometimes involved in obtaining the assurance, private investors frequently react adversely to the requirement—on grounds that a guarantee by government invites future control by government, directly or indirectly.

what has been done by the Bank in the way of lending, but also what has *not been done* by the Bank, in the light of never having exposed itself to the type or magnitude of risks that might have raised its volume of losses.

Third, the Bank—by its presence, attitude, and action—inhibits loan activity by rival agencies, or so some persons believe. Whatever its comparative status may have been during earlier years, since 1953 the Bank has definitely enjoyed a strong bureaucratic position—to put the matter in the parlance of Washington. An effect of the investigation the Bank underwent in that year was to swing considerable Administration support behind it. From then on, the dominant governmental attitude has been that the Bank is to be regarded, in theory and fact, as the US Government's principal international lending agency. As a consequence, the Bank has found itself operating in an environment in which, for all practical purposes, it has been able not merely to assure itself of "first crack" at whatever international lending the Government has contemplated for itself, but also to bring its ideas regarding loan standards to focus upon other governmental agencies in the international lending field in such a way that the activities of these agencies have come to be circumscribed so as to lessen inter-agency competition. Thus, the right to make grants has remained within the orbit of the ICA, but the issue of lending by the ICA (for, say, private industrial development), alongside similar lending by the Bank, has been generally resolved in favor of the Bank. Again, the ICA has been put on the defensive, allegedly, in its attempts to allocate given sums of grant or loan aid to particular countries, on the grounds that full effort has not been made to use the Bank credit available. Further, interest rates charged on dollar-repayable loans extended by the Development Loan Fund were set at levels comparable with those of the Bank (and not comparable with those offered on loans by the USSR under its trade-and-aid offensive, even though a major argument used to support initiation of the DLF was to counter possible inroads by the USSR). As some persons see the situation, some of the potential effectiveness of those other agencies also engaged in supplying capital internationally has been deliberately foregone—and all, assertedly, to make life more convenient for the Bank. The criticism of the Bank, then, is that it has thrown its weight around too much; either this, or the criticism is an even greater one: that the Administration created a situation in which the Bank has been able to wield excessive power and influence. In either case, the conclusion suggested is that the Bank has not only provided less capital than warranted, but it has also prevented other agencies from providing more of the warranted capital in its place.

Fourth, the Bank's practice of tying utilization of loan proceeds directly to the American market is widely regarded as in blatant conflict with the principle of multilateralism, long espoused by the US Government as a cornerstone of its foreign economic policy.[24] Actually, experience under the Mutual Security Program indicates that a substantial portion of loan proceeds is used within the US even in the absence of any tying provisions;[25] specifically, prior to late 1959, up to which time the Program sanctioned procurement anywhere within the Free World, well over one-half of total expenditures normally occurred within this country. Thus, if the objective is to capture business for the American economy, the tying clause could well be dropped (with only moderate adverse effect likely upon the country's aggregate trade volume), thereby helping to strengthen the position of the US Government as a true advocate of multilateralism. However, as frequently pointed out, a tying clause also operates toward another end; it tends to assure *particular* exporters, or classes of exporters, of business as a consequence of particular loans.[26] But, if this is the objective of a tying clause, how is one to reconcile the Bank's reliance upon it and the Bank's status as an instrument of US foreign policy? In the opinion of many, adherence to a tying clause seriously compromises the Bank's position in administering US foreign economic policy.

Fifth, political considerations enter into the Bank's loan policy. Admittedly, the Bank is used to implement US foreign policy, and the Department of State has always been an active participant in directing the Bank's affairs. Some persons strongly feel that development is not a political matter, and that assistance for development should therefore be free of political taint. Others, however, view criticism in these terms as unduly harsh, pointing to the fact that receipt of external capital by an underdeveloped country need not be incompatible with support for development even if political considerations figure in the capital-supplying country's decision to provide the capital. In any event, if this is accepted as a legitimate criticism in the case of the Bank, other US Government agencies acting in the international lending field are also vulnerable to indictment. Indeed, similar criticism is sometimes offered in their case, and frequently comes to be used as the core argument for the transmission of capital through an institutional framework under international control.

As opposed to these and other possible criticisms, supporters of the Bank have two main arguments at their disposal. First, it is unfair to expect too much of the Bank. The Bank does not have sole responsibility for

---

24 For example, the *Economic Report of the President* (January 1957) stated: "A major objective of United States foreign economic policy continues to be to facilitate and increase the international flow of goods and capital on a *nondiscriminatory* basis." (Italics are mine.)

25 Beyond impact through direct utilization within the American economy, impact is also had indirectly through third-country trade channels. (Further comment on the status of tying provisions in the Mutual Security Program occurs at a later point in the present chapter.)

26 W. Krause, *The International Economy* (Boston: Houghton Mifflin Company, 1955), pp. 259–260.

supplying needed capital; therefore, it should not be held accountable for some unreasonable proportion of the shortcomings in the realm of international lending, within which context it is but one of a number of lenders. The Bank purports to service only particular credit needs; hence, its success or failure should be judged within this more limited frame of reference.

Second, whatever the Bank's shortcomings may be, it has done some good too—as evidenced by the volume of business handled. New credits authorized have averaged over $0.5 billion per year during recent years, with over one-half of all this amount involving underdeveloped countries as beneficiaries. In addition, action by the Bank has primed further investment, as supplementary funds have been induced to come forth from other quarters, e.g., US private capital and domestic capital in recipient countries.

INTERNATIONAL COOPERATION ADMINISTRATION

Second, the US Government renders assistance—grants, loans, and technical assistance, both as economic aid and as military aid—through its specialized foreign-aid agency, the International Cooperation Administration. This agency is currently authorized under the Mutual Security Act (first enacted in 1951), but its true beginnings date from the Marshall Plan (introduced in 1948). The chronology of evolution is as follows: administration of the Marshall Plan was made the responsibility of a new agency, the Economic Cooperation Administration (1948–51), and this agency was followed by a series of successor agencies, the sequence being the Mutual Security Agency (1951–53), the Foreign Operations Administration (1953–55), and finally the International Cooperation Administration (since 1955).

As indicated, the International Cooperation Administration is authorized under the Mutual Security Act. Alongside this agency, the Mutual Security legislation also covers a special loan agency, the Development Loan Fund. Together, the two agencies comprise the operating arms of the *Mutual Security Program*—and, together they comprise *the* US foreign-aid program. The Development Loan Fund, initially established as an operating unit entirely within the framework of the International Cooperation Administration, is currently a separate organizational entity (following its incorporation as a distinct agency subsequent to its initial establishment).[27]

---

27 Also, budgetary requests for the DLF were initially handled within the overall ICA request; however, with the incorporation of the DLF as a separate organizational entity, the DLF budgetary request came to be treated apart from that of the ICA (but with the two requests, together, comprising the request for the Mutual Security *Program*). Apart from the legal separateness, however, cooperation in varying degrees has characterized operations throughout.

Examination of the Mutual Security Program (other than special comments devoted to the Development Loan Fund)—its purposes, operations, and problems—is reserved for Chapters 20 and 21. However, the Development Loan Fund closely parallels the Export-Import Bank on a number of scores, and is therefore treated in the present chapter.

DEVELOPMENT LOAN FUND

Third, then, the US Government supplies capital assistance through the Development Loan Fund, an agency of recent origin. The DLF, in terms of the basis upon which it supplies capital assistance, stands somewhere between the Export-Import Bank and the International Cooperation Administration; the DLF, unlike the ICA, deals only in loans, but its loan terms characteristically are considerably easier than those of the Bank.

BACKGROUND FACTORS

By 1957, roughly a decade following the introduction of the Marshall Plan (which, for all practical purposes, marked the US Government's acceptance of responsibility for rendering foreign aid on a systematic basis), considerable sentiment had built up for a new approach in the provision of capital assistance. On the one hand, the ICA, the country's designated foreign-aid agency, was becoming the object of widespread criticism on a number of scores—particularly that its operations, heavily geared toward grant aid, added up to a gigantic "giveaway" inimical to the best interests of both the US and recipient countries. On the other hand, the Export-Import Bank, the country's principal international lending agency, dealt in loans (not grants or giveaways), but its lending policy was characterized by conservatism and toughness—to an extent, many felt, that barred servicing from this source of the great bulk of the external-capital requirements of the underdeveloped world. Accordingly, the notion arose and gained ground that the US Government needed a new approach to the provision of capital for underdeveloped countries, an approach standing somewhere between the ICA's emphasis upon grants and the Export-Import Bank's emphasis upon "tough" loans.

The precise approach that was suggested in 1957, involving a new lending framework, did not emerge as the end product of long and similar thinking on the part of various people or groups. Rather, it emerged pretty much as an isolated suggestion, standing in sharp contrast to another line of thought of widespread popularity in both official and nonofficial quarters, especially during and after 1953. The conclusion commonly reached was critical of grant aid, but the accompanying proposals for change were generally not in terms of governmental provision of capital under revamped arrangements, but in terms of the ending of grant aid,

along with placement of more hope upon increased private foreign investment. At the non-official level, those most vociferous in their denunciation
of "giveaways" typically sought solution through the dissolution of foreign
economic aid and rededication to the principle of "let private investment
do it." At the official level, several investigating groups indicated their
views on the matter, the gist of which in at least two outstanding instances
closely paralleled the attitude widely held in influential non-official quarters. For example, the Randall Commission recommended (early in 1954)
that "economic aid on a grant basis . . . be terminated as soon as possible," and urged greater reliance upon private foreign investment as the
alternative.[28] Again, the Fairless Committee recommended (early in 1957)
that "assistance in grant form . . . be given only in . . . exceptional
cases," and urged increased incentives for private foreign investment.[29] In
short, the common attitude that had evolved was a combination of "end
grant aid" and "let private foreign investment do the job." The basic
idea that a new lending framework should be instituted within the Government for international placement of capital did not forge to the front
until the appearance of the Johnston Report in early 1957.[30] Though
contemporary with the Fairless Report, contents of the Johnston Report
marked a departure from prevailing thought, not a reinforcement of it.

The Johnston Report started with the basic assumption that more
assistance for development in underdeveloped countries should be made
available than was previously the case (although not at the expense of
private foreign investment). It was felt, moreover, that some added portion of the assistance should be provided on a loan basis (as distinct from
grants), but on sufficiently generous terms to prove workable in the environment peculiar to underdeveloped countries. Therefore, the recommendation was made that a new organizational framework, referred to as
the International Development Fund, be created for the purpose of providing loan funds along proposed lines.

Actually, four main considerations helped shape the Report's recommendation for the creation of a new lending facility. First, it was felt that
the US should have a governmental lending facility geared to provide
loan capital to underdeveloped countries on the basis of the economic

[28] Commission on Foreign Economic Policy, *Report to the President and the Congress,* Washington, January 1954, esp. pp. 8, 16–27.
[29] *Report to the President (by the President's Citizen Advisers on the Mutual Security Program),* Washington, March 1, 1957, esp. pp. 8, 10–11. For a good summary of the Fairless Report, along with a comparison of its major content with other con-temporary views, see IMF, *International Financial News Survey,* Washington, March 22, 1957, p. 290.
[30] International Development Advisory Board, *A New Emphasis on Economic Development Abroad* (A Report to the President on Ways, Means and Reasons for US Assistance to International Economic Development), Washington, March 1957. Formally issued on March 7, 1957, the Report contained some recommendations that had been widely discussed elsewhere within the Government during immediately preceding months.

merits of the situation alone, unencumbered by other considerations, e.g., military considerations. The ICA program, as then organized, had come to be criticized in some quarters on the grounds that it treated economic and military aid too much as part and parcel of the same operation. The view had come to be widely held that economic aid should be clearly divorced from military aid, so as to lessen the likelihood of confusion of goals on the part of the US, or of misunderstanding as to US motivation on the part of recipient underdeveloped countries. The Report, accordingly, recommended a new lending facility, one in which economic assistance might be handled apart from the military-assistance portions of the Mutual Security Program.

Second, adoption of a long-run approach to developmental assistance was considered important. The argument had come to be advanced that the ICA's need to seek annual appropriations from the Congress made impossible effective long-range planning for the provision of capital assistance; after all, some developmental projects require a period of years for completion. The Report, accordingly, stressed that the new lending facility be given assurance of life spanning a period of years, with initial appropriations sufficient to cover operations for a minimum of 3 years.

Third, a shift in emphasis from grants to loans was considered important. The practice of providing capital assistance through grants was believed vulnerable in that it served to limit this country's willingness to sustain more than token assistance, and also served to lessen self-reliance and dignity in recipient underdeveloped countries. Moreover, it was felt that provision of a great portion of capital assistance on a loan basis was perfectly workable, provided applicable terms were sufficiently flexible to allow the accommodation of a wide range of likely needs in underdeveloped countries. The Report, accordingly, recommended that the new facility devote itself to provision of capital assistance on a loan basis, with terms tailored to fit the situation—meaning terms generally more liberal than characteristic of the Export-Import Bank.

Fourth, access by underdeveloped countries to a block of capital assistance not allocated beforehand on a country-by-country basis, but available rather on the basis of the merit of each individual application, was considered important. The customary procedure of the ICA had been to program (allocate) foreign aid, both economic and military, among countries in accordance with prevailing criteria. In contrast, the Report proposed that a block of financing intended for economic assistance be set aside in a fund, upon which any country might then seek to draw, theoretically up to the full amount of the financing available. Under this approach, no country was to be guaranteed an allocation; rather, each country was to be placed in the position of having to compete for economic assistance. It was felt that this procedure would induce countries to propose projects that might qualify for financing, and thereby encourage the type of thinking and planning in underdeveloped countries likely to spur development. As a minimum, it was felt that the procedure would undercut the attitude, then allegedly widespread among countries customarily receiving American aid, of viewing an aid inflow as a right, or as something to be had as a matter of course and in a substantially inflexible amount, irrespective of what was or was not done at home.

LEGISLATION

Establishment of the new lending procedure was proposed to the Congress, to be considered by them in conjunction with the pending Mutual Security Act of 1957. Following the usual course of investigation, deliberation, and give-and-take, the Congress passed legislation covering the proposal, although this legislation differed in some important respects from what had initially been proposed. Thereafter (during the second half of 1957), the new lending facility, labeled the Development Loan Fund, came into being.

In the course of making its plea for the enactment of legislation covering the DLF and its projected operations, the Administration maintained that the new approach being proposed was necessary if the US were to supply developmental assistance to underdeveloped countries on an effective basis. For example, according to one Administration spokesman:[31]

> . . . more emphasis should be placed on long-term development assistance.
>
> It is true that our economic aid cannot be more than a marginal addition to any country's development efforts. This addition can, however, be significant and even determining. It can break foreign exchange bottlenecks and it can be a key factor in stimulating a country to a more effective program of its own. If our development aid is to have this effect, however, we must do two things: (1) break away from the cycle of annual authorizations and appropriations, and (2) eliminate advance allocations by countries.
>
> Economic development is a continuing process, not an annual event. Present annual appropriations have resulted in procedures which do not allow either us or the receiving countries to make the most efficient use of the resources which we are providing.
>
> The best way to achieve this greater efficiency is . . . the establishment of an economic development fund to provide assistance through loans on terms more favorable than are possible through existing institutions. To be effective, such a fund would need continuing authority and a capital authorization sufficient for several years, to be renewed when needed.

---

[31] Statement by John Foster Dulles, then Secretary of State, before the Senate's Special Committee to Study the Foreign Aid Program, April 8, 1957. For the full text, see *The New York Times*, April 9, 1957, p. 10–C.

Such a fund could extend aid for specific programs or projects submitted by applicant countries. Each request for a loan from the fund should meet certain criteria, including a showing (1) that financing cannot be obtained from other sources; (2) that the project is technically feasible; (3) that it gives reasonable promise of direct or indirect contribution to a nation's increased productivity.

Three main provisions stood out in the legislation that authorized the DLF.[32] First, the Fund was to carry on loan activities in accordance with certain standards, described only in broad terms in the legislation —leaving specific rules and procedures to be worked out later under the general authority granted. The relevant section of the legislation read as follows:[33]

> . . . the President is hereby authorized to make loans, credits, or guaranties, or to engage in other financing operations or transactions (not to include grants or direct purchases of equity securities), to or with such nations, organizations, persons or other entities, and *on such terms and conditions as he may determine*, taking into account (1) whether financing could be obtained in whole or in part from other free world sources on reasonable terms, (2) the economic and technical soundness of the activity to be financed, and (3) whether the activity gives reasonable promise of contributing to the development of economic resources or to the increase of productive capacities in furtherance of the purpose of this title. Loans shall be made from the Fund only on the basis of firm commitments by the borrowers to make repayment and upon a finding that there are reasonable prospects of such repayment. The Fund shall be administered so as to support and encourage private investment and other private participation furthering the purposes of this title, and it shall be administered so as not to compete with private investment capital, the Export-Import Bank or the International Bank. . . .

Second, the Congress authorized an initial appropriation of up to $500 million for the Fund, without fiscal-year limitation (as to time of use), and authorized a second appropriation for the ensuing fiscal year of up to $625 million. The actual appropriation subsequently approved, however, set maximum funds for FY 1958, the first fiscal year of operation, at $300 million; as for FY 1959, the Congress simply authorized a possible appropriation of $625 million during the next session. Third, the Fund was placed, organizationally, within the ICA, itself situated as a semi-autonomous agency within the Department of State.

As matters stood at this point, the precise operating procedures of the DLF remained to be defined. What would evolve became dependent, significantly, upon the adeptness of various interested agencies and officials at bureaucratic maneuvering. In terms of principle, however,

---

[32] Mutual Security Act of 1957, Title II (Development Loan Fund).
[33] Title II, Sec. 202(b). (Italics are mine.)

some persons felt that the major battle had already been lost by virtue of certain basic ingredients in the enabling legislation approved by the Congress. Specifically, the Administration had sought to sell a new idea. It had sought approval for a new loan fund with a 3-year capitalization of $2 billion—on the grounds that development aid cannot be provided effectively when funds are had only on a year-to-year basis. The Congress, however, neither came through with the amount of funds requested, nor with a long-range commitment to provide funds. The Congress provided only $300 million on the Administration's request for $500 million for the first year, and the Administration's request for $750 million for each of the two succeeding years was met only with an authorization for a possible appropriation in the second year of $625 million (with no mention of a possible third year). Whatever could be said of the cut rendered the budget request for even the first year, the overall action taken plainly indicated that the plan to get the Congress to assume, in tangible form, a long-run commitment to provide funds for developmental loans had suffered a severe set-back.[34]

OPERATING PROCEDURES

In the course of formulating the precise rules to govern operations of the DLF, a series of conferences were held, attended by representatives of various interested agencies: the ICA, the Export-Import Bank, and the Departments of State and Commerce. Recommendations that evolved helped shape the basic framework subsequently put into effect by the Department of State (acting on authority delegated by the President[35]), thereafter to guide the newly-appointed staff of the DLF in its administration of the loan program. Major operating criteria adopted included the following.

1. *Location of loan recipients.* Ordinarily, access to Fund financing is limited to projects located in underdeveloped countries (and only within the Free World). Loans to developed countries are not specifically barred, but preference in the administrative process is normally expected to favor underdeveloped countries—especially since developed countries are generally in a preferred position in their access to most other sources of financing, e.g., the Export-Import Bank or private capital markets.

2. *Types of projects.* Eligible projects are held to those likely to contribute, directly or indirectly, to the economic growth of the country in

---

34 On this point, see "Aid Bill Ignores 'New Approach'," *The New York Times,* September 1, 1957, p. 10-E.

35 The Under Secretary of State for Economic Affairs was given overall responsibility for coordination of activities carried on by the DLF, the Export-Import Bank, and the ICA (aside from the Fund). For news comment on this matter, see *The New York Times,* November 15, 1957, p. 1-L.

which located, and adjudged both economically sound and technically feasible. Additionally, there must be reasonable prospect of loan repayment.

Industrial, agricultural, financial, commercial, extractive, power, transport, communications, and other undertakings are eligible for financing, provided the foregoing conditions (and some other pertinent tests) are met.

3. *Categories of borrowers.* The Fund is empowered to lend to foreign governments or to private entrepreneurs, either foreign or American, but use of loan proceeds in any event is restricted to investment abroad. In the case of much of basic development, there is no choice but to support government investment. However, insofar as there is choice (as generally is the case, for example, in the realm of industrial development), loans in support of private investment are preferred over loans for government investment.[36]

The Fund is empowered to lend to foreign development banks or like institutions, with these institutions then empowered to use the loan proceeds—within broad limits of discretion—for on-the-scene sub-loans to end-borrowers. As suggested earlier (in Ch. 9), this procedure offers a way to link a loan by the Fund to a governmental institution (e.g., many development banks are government-operated) with the provision of capital to local private entrepreneurs (assuming that the development bank's own activities are geared toward promotion of the private sector).

In its lending to private investors, a form of loan outlet expected to prove important over time involves assistance for joint-ventures. This form of business organization links private American investors and private foreign investors, including investors from third countries—e.g., support of a private undertaking in Thailand linking Thai capital with, say, German and American capital. Indeed, the Fund is especially interested in the promotion of investment arrangements of the joint-venture variety.[37]

In keeping with the legislation that established the Fund, loans to support investment of a type likely, in turn, to encourage added private investment generally, domestic or foreign, are considered particularly desirable. Similarly, applications for funds that propose joint-financing (i.e., the linkage of loan proceeds obtained from the Fund with loan proceeds obtained from other capital sources, such as the Export-Import Bank, the International Bank, or the private capital market) tend to be viewed with favor.

4. *Avoidance of competitiveness.* The Fund is supposed not to be competitive with other lending sources. The expressed intent, accordingly, is

---

36 The Fund has stated that private investors should give evidence that they are willing and able to augment funds from the Fund with a reasonable contribution from their own resources.

37 The Fund has stated that applications in which American participation is linked with foreign participation on a joint-venture basis will be looked upon with favor.

to limit financing to those projects not able to gain access to capital on reasonable terms in other US or Free-World quarters. The burden of proof of dependence upon the Fund's resources as a last resort falls upon the applicant.

5. *Loan terms.* Loan terms are handled on a negotiated, case-by-case basis—but in accordance with several major principles that serve as a general guide. Generally speaking, the loan terms of the Fund, in keeping with the intent expressed in proposals leading to its establishment, are liberal—or, at least substantially easier than those offered by the Export-Import Bank.

Loans of up to 40 years duration are within the scope of the Fund. The expectation, however, was that most loans would be of somewhat lesser duration, and early experience showed many loans in the range of 10 to 20 years. In terms both of permissibility and of practice, then, the Fund's loans are of longer duration than those of the Export-Import Bank.

Interest rates on loans for non-profit-making projects are normally at $3\frac{1}{2}\%$, while rates on loans made to profit-making enterprises generally parallel those applied by the Export-Import Bank to roughly similar undertakings, ranging ordinarily between $5\frac{1}{2}\%$ and $5\frac{3}{4}\%$ (but subject to change, depending upon the cost of money to the US Treasury).[38]

The Fund deals in loans, not grants, and thus repayment is required. The loan contract specifies the currency of repayment: US dollars, or local currency, or third-country currency, or some combination of these. The possibility of non-dollar repayment constitutes what is probably the major way in which the Fund's lending is more liberal than that of alternate lending sources (say, the Export-Import Bank, which always requires dollar repayment of its dollar loans). In general, dollar repayment is called for when the loan is used for investment purposes capable of earning or saving foreign exchange, while non-dollar repayment is held acceptable when the loan is used for investment purposes yielding no direct or concurrent balance-of-payments benefit, e.g., as with basic development.[39]

Governmental guaranty of repayment is not necessarily required by the Fund. However, the Fund adheres to a general rule that loans for private

---

[38] ICA, *Press Release* (No. 367), January 19, 1958.

[39] Provision for repayment in both dollar and non-dollar terms holds interesting implications for the Fund. During early phases of operation, loans occur only from dollars supplied directly by the Congress. Thereafter, as repayments occur, dollar receipts provide the basis for further dollar loans (quite apart from any further dollar appropriations by the Congress). But, insofar as repayments occur on a non-dollar basis, the Fund's resources shift, little by little, from dollars to other currencies. In short, the Fund is set up to have a revolving pool of loanable funds at its disposal, but the gradual transformation of dollars into other currencies can be expected to give rise periodically to a need for access to additional dollars (assuming that the volume of lending initially established is not cut back, and that the initial pattern of lending—as between dollar-repayable and non-dollar-repayable lending—remains unaltered).

investment will not be made if the investment is unacceptable to the government of the recipient country. This rule has special relevance in the case of loans intended to enable American private entrepreneurs to undertake investment abroad, and is in keeping with the notion that a sovereign government has the right to screen new investment, particularly in the light of possible attendant balance-of-payments implications. The Fund's procedure is in contrast to that of the Export-Import Bank, which ordinarily requires a guaranty by the government of the recipient country as a condition for lending.

As initially established, proceeds of dollar loans by the Fund were not tied to usage in the US; rather, procurement anywhere in the Free World was deemed permissible. This procedure stood in contrast to the practice of the Export-Import Bank, which customarily inserts a tying clause in its loan contracts. However, in October 1959, following "reversals" in the US balance of payments, the Fund's policy was abruptly altered, with tying clauses henceforth a usual ingredient of loan contracts. In the words of the Managing Director, the new policy was adopted[40]

> . . . in view of the growth in the economic strength of the industrialized countries of the free world and their steadily increasing ability to assist the less developed countries, and taking into account the changes which have taken place in the world payments situation.

6. *Ineligible uses.* Some operations are not eligible for Fund financing —on the grounds that the proposed activities either are incompatible with serious stimulation of long-range economic growth or are of low-priority among potential uses open to available funds. For example, financing is held unavailable for purposes of refunding or refinancing. Again, the financing of exports intended for resale abroad is held generally outside the scope of the Fund. Further, use of the Fund's resources to provide working-capital loans is generally ruled out.

7. *Origin of applications.* Individual persons or business entities, as well as governments, are eligible to submit proposals for Fund financing. Some proposals arise unsolicited, but others arise following active on-the-scene encouragement and assistance extended by US Government personnel (generally aid-program personnel). In some instances, considerable technical help is needed to lay the groundwork for a tangible proposal that might be seriously considered by the Fund.

8. *The role of programming.* According to initial intent, appraisal of proposals was to proceed solely in terms of merit under the Fund's loan criteria, not in terms of formal programming designed to assure some predetermined areal distribution of loans. It was felt that distinct advantages would accrue from an absence of formal programming in advance, country by country, of the Fund's resources. In essence, the US Government would

---

[40] *The New York Times,* October 20, 1959, p. 1-C.

be able to tell any country[41] that capital is technically available to it in large amount (say, in hundreds of millions of dollars) if it can come forth with qualifying proposals—an approach the very opposite of one under which a country can simply sit back and wait in the belief that an allocation is due it (or in the knowledge that an allocation will in all likelihood prove forthcoming in any event). As a consequence, action on the part of a potential recipient country was believed likely to be encouraged, thereby serving as a stimulus for development generally. Additionally, projects of better caliber were considered likely to fall subject to Fund financing under this procedure.

In the course of operations, however, the Fund soon came to deviate to a substantial extent from the procedure initially favored. While still looked to as an ideal, the pressure of specific situations of immediate consequence in due time "forced" a resort to special attention for particular areas. This development came as no surprise to some observers who regarded it as inevitable that the Fund, notwithstanding possible contrary good intentions, would need to face up to the immediacy of crisis situations as they arose.

RECORD OF BUSINESS

The Fund has done an active business. Loan applications in volume proved forthcoming in prompt fashion (with over $1 billion in applications being received in a matter of weeks following the commencement of actual operations). Indeed, the usual situation for the Fund has been that of many applications awaiting servicing, when and as the Congress would make additional funds available. Following the introductory appropriation of $300 million for FY 1958, the Congress appropriated the following amounts: $400 million (plus a special supplementary appropriation of $150 million) for FY 1959, and $550 million for FY 1960. The Fund's loan approvals, through mid-September 1959, totaled $815.5 million (Table 20)—leaving roughly $500 million in funds still uncommitted, but with some $1,400 million in applications also on hand. Types of loan outlets serviced, in order of dollar-magnitude, were as follows: transportation and communications, industry, power, general economic development, development banks, food and agriculture, health and sanitation, and mining.

Individual loans by the Fund have varied widely in amount and terms, as is readily observable through reference to several sample cases. India received a loan of $75 million to be used in the purchase of materials and equipment needed in connection with that country's developmental program. Loan terms included repayment in local currency (rupees), with interest at $3\frac{1}{2}\%$ on $40 million (involving a railway project in the public sector) and at $5\frac{1}{4}\%$ on $35 million (involving a road transportation

---

[41] That is, any country participating in the program.

Table 20.   Development Loan Fund Loans, 1959

REGION	AMOUNT (In millions of US dollars)
South Asia	310.0
Far East	166.3
Near East	166.2
Europe	77.1
Latin America	65.8
Africa	30.1
Total	815.5

Source: Development Loan Fund. Data are for loan approvals, cumulative, through September 15, 1959.

project, a cement industry project, and a jute industry project—all in the private sector), and with repayment spanning 20 years on $40 million of the loan (the portion involving the railway project) and 15 years on the remaining $35 million.[42] Honduras received a loan of $5 million, scheduled to be used in financing local-currency costs of a highway project. Loan terms included repayment in local currency (lempira), with interest at $3\frac{1}{2}\%$ and repayment spanning 20 years.[43] Pakistan was the beneficiary of a loan of $4.2 million made to the Pakistan Industrial Credit and Investment Corporation—a private development bank established with the help of Pakistani, American, British, and Japanese investors—in order to enable it to make sub-loans to private industrial enterprises, in amounts ranging from $20 thousand to $400 thousand, for use in the importation of capital goods. Loan terms included repayment in local currency (rupees), with interest at 5% and repayment spanning 5 years.[44] Iran received a loan of $40 million for use in financing select development

---

[42] Department of State, *Press Release* (No. 102), March 2, 1958. Concurrent with the Fund's loan, the Export-Import Bank agreed to extend $150 million in credit to help India finance equipment purchases in the US (for use in irrigation and reclamation, power development, coal and iron-ore mining, road transportation, communications, and industrial development). Loan terms included dollar repayment, with interest at $5\frac{1}{4}\%$, and repayment spanning 15 years—but with no payment, other than interest, scheduled during the initial 5 years of the loan. The loan actions of the Fund and the Export-Import Bank occurred subsequent to the offer of the US Government—announced January 16, 1958—to extend approximately $225 million in new loans to assist India in coping with bottlenecks encountered in current developmental effort.

The Fund's resources, besides being linked with the resources of the Export-Import Bank in the cited loan operation, became complementary to an earlier loan to India by the International Bank (to assist in the financing of the Indian railway project).

[43] Department of State, *Press Release* (No. 270), May 16, 1958. The loan was scheduled to be used in conjunction with a loan of $5.5 million secured from the International Bank (for financing the cost of imported equipment, materials, and services).

[44] Department of State, *Press Release* (No. 374), July 1, 1958.

projects; the direct beneficiary was the Plan Organization, Iran's official agency charged with planning, financing, and executing the country's Second Seven-Year Development Program. Loan terms included repayment in dollars, with interest at $3\frac{1}{2}\%$ and $5\frac{1}{4}\%$, depending upon usage, and with repayment spanning 12 years.[45] Malaya received a loan of $10 million for use in seaport improvement. Loan terms included repayment in dollars, with interest at $3\frac{1}{2}\%$ and repayment spanning 30 years.[46] The Paraguayan economy was the beneficiary of a loan of $2.6 million made to a private corporation (engaged in ranching, meat packing, and production of quebracho extract) to allow it to modernize and expand its operations. Loan terms included repayment in dollars, with interest at $5\frac{1}{4}\%$ and repayment spanning 6 years.[47]

EVALUATION

Two major advantages can be cited on behalf of the DLF. First, the Fund handles as loans some business that might otherwise have been handled through grants. According to one argument, loans are to be preferred over grants because the self-respect and dignity of capital-receiving countries are thereby better preserved. Beyond this, it can be argued that loans are perfectly workable in many connections (provided the loan terms are right), whereupon it is reasonable to question why equivalent capital should be provided in grant form. Also, it can be argued that there is reasonable likelihood that the Congress will, over time, see fit to support with more funds an assistance effort involving repayment than one involving straight unilateral transfers. Given the bottleneck posed for the developmental process in many underdeveloped countries by foreign-exchange shortages, any procedure favorable to a greater movement of capital to the affected countries, on a basis both acceptable and workable, appears worthy of serious consideration.

Second, the Fund's loan terms are easier than those of other major lending institutions, e.g., easier than those of the Export-Import Bank (and easier also than those of the International Bank and the International Finance Corporation). A formalized procedure exists for the tailoring of loan terms to fit basic environmental factors, so that loans can be used to advantage in more connections. A major feature is the possibility of soft-currency repayment, which permits, for all practical purposes, the circumvention of balance-of-payments obstacles to the acceptance of external capital.[48]

---

[45] Department of State, *Press Release* (No. 385), July 3, 1958.

[46] Department of State, *Press Release* (No. 433), July 30, 1958.

[47] Department of State, *Press Release* (No. 460), August 11, 1958. A feature of the loan, new to the Fund at this particular point, was acceptance for part of the loan of $500,000 in $5\frac{1}{4}\%$ convertible debentures.

[48] The record, through 1959, reveals that non-dollar repayment applies to roughly three-fourths of the Fund's loan business.

On the other hand, potent criticism of the Fund, in its current form, can also be offered. First, a common view is that the Fund suffers from financial malnutrition, in the sense of having resources that are insufficient in magnitude for the task at hand. Supporting evidence is found in a volume of applications so large that only the best applications can be assured of financing, leaving many good requests unprovided for. It is possible to seek solace, perhaps, in the knowledge that larger appropriations had been requested of the Congress, thus shifting blame for the failure to service more applications from the Fund to the Congress. The issue that remains unsettled, however, is: How are good applications, still pending, to be dealt with? Several major possibilities exist. One possibility is to do nothing, i.e., to limit the Fund to financing only those applications regarded as best among an array of many good applications. This possibility has the drawback, of course, of suggesting that the high hopes initially held for a new approach in the provision of developmental assistance must be deliberately foregone to an important extent. Another possibility is to induce, by some means, greater appropriations by the Congress. A major obstacle in this respect is not so much a feeling in the Congress that the Fund cannot do more as it is one of conservatism—or, more specifically, of reluctance to add to budgetary or debt pressure through the incurrence of further obligations for this purpose. Still another possibility is for the Fund to use its limited resources more particularly to promote joint-financing (i.e., to make financing available in conjunction with financing arising from other capital sources), or to stimulate American private foreign investment (e.g., by means of a guaranty system). The Fund is receptive to joint-financing, and has been from the outset, so that no drastic policy revisions impinge on this score. Beyond this, the provision of guarantees to cover private investment offers the initial advantage of helping to move private capital to foreign areas, which can be regarded as desirable *if* the private investment itself can be justified on various relevant scores (Ch. 17); however, for a leverage effect upon investment to result from a guaranty system, fractional reserves need to exist—but, significantly, legislation under which the Fund operates requires full reserves.[49]

---

[49] Mutual Security Act of 1957, Title II, Sec. 202(b).

One other possibility for greater financial impact exists: a system of financing akin to that of the Export-Import Bank. Under this procedure, the Fund—which also is separately incorporated (following an early period when it comprised an integral unit within the ICA)—would be given drawing rights at the Treasury, rather than held dependent upon outright Congressional appropriations. As intimated earlier in the case of the Bank, the Fund would then have lending capacity without there necessarily being commensurate impact upon the country's budgetary and debt structure. In the case of the Fund, however, the capacity to lend and the rate of disbursement might well roughly parallel each other (unlike the gap that has been characteristic of the Bank); loan applications awaiting servicing far exceed funds available, so that unused drawing rights would likely prove unimportant (unless drawing rights were of a magnitude vastly higher than prevailing appropriations). The only seeming advantage would derive if special emphasis were placed upon a guaranty program. Guarantees

Second, the Fund is supposed not to compete with other major capital suppliers, e.g., private capital, the Export-Import Bank, or the International Bank; but, some persons contend that the interpretation given the applicable stipulation obliges the Fund to stand "at the end of the line." Since the Fund's loan terms are typically somewhat easier than those characteristic of alternate lending sources, a no-competition stipulation is obviously necessary; otherwise, no matter what the nature of their proposals, potential borrowers would be encouraged to contact the Fund first, in preference to the "tougher" loan sources—which other sources would then stand the risk, literally, of being driven out of business. As put into effect, however, the no-competition stipulation operates to make a "lender of last resort" of the Fund. The Fund is expected to lend only when funds cannot be had from alternate sources on reasonable terms. The unfortunate aspect of this procedure is that precious time often comes to be lost in the course of testing whether or not alternate lending sources are interested. Some persons feel that particular categories of applications are not likely to prove acceptable to the alternate lending sources in any event, and should therefore be regarded as within the Fund's province without further ado. But, for administration to proceed in this vein, some predetermined standards are needed to offer guidance. Admittedly, meaningful standards in this connection are not easy to formulate. Basically, attack along either of two main lines is possible: a functional approach, or a geographic approach. Unfortunately, in the matter at hand, a functional approach—which, essentially, is the approach followed by the Fund (but strictly on a case-by-case basis)—does not readily lend itself to administration in accordance with clear-cut rules of a precise nature.[50] Greater hope for administrative success appears to lie in a geographic approach. Under it (by way of illustrating a possible method for the division of business between the Fund and the Export-Import Bank), the Fund might be given primary lending rights in Asia and Africa (in which the Export-Import Bank's record is one of low-volume lending), while the Export-Import Bank might be given primary lending rights in the rest-of-the-world (in which its lending record is more impressive). Adherence to the foregoing general rule would have one main advantage: it would

---

for private investment, for example, could then be offered, conceivably up to the limit of lending authority, but no Treasury impact would be registered beyond required reserves—and, if reserves were handled as a contingent liability, no Treasury impact would be registered at all in the absence of losses by private investors covered by guarantees.

50 For example, the Fund might, *as a minimum,* be regarded as having first chance on projects involving basic development (where non-dollar repayment is generally deemed a reasonable condition), leaving other projects open, i.e., eligible for financing from *any* source (but with the Fund being held accountable under the no-competition rule). But, even in the case of basic development, some projects are capable of being undertaken under loan terms regularly offered by the Export-Import Bank. Therefore, why should the Fund have an assured first chance on even this limited category of financing?

gear the Fund very much toward Asia and Africa, the core of the under-developed world (embracing individual countries receiving only relatively small amounts, heretofore, through either loans of the Export-Import Bank or inflows of American private capital—Table 19, and Fig. 9 in Ch. 17). Resort to a rule of this type would require its imposition "from above" (say, by the Department of State, or the National Security Council), so that *both* the Fund and the Export-Import Bank, the two main contenders directly involved, would be obliged to abide by its terms. In the absence of more precise standards as to lending jurisdiction, however, the current case-by-case approach (along with efforts at coordination, say, by the Department of State) appears to be the only course open.

Third, the Fund's loan terms are easier than those of, say, the Export-Import Bank, but some persons nevertheless feel they are not easy enough. According to the argument, the Fund's primary responsibility is that of the promotion of development in underdeveloped countries (with the basic rationale for the US being *political* in nature—Ch. 16). Thus, the success or failure of the Fund is to be judged in terms of developmental achievement abroad, and not, for example, in terms of avoidance of competitive conflicts among alternate US lending sources. To this end, therefore, some easing in loan terms may well be warranted, even if the loosening up should then serve to shift the interest of some potential applicants from other lending sources to the Fund. The following editorial comment, concerned especially with interest-rate policy, points up the issue:[51]

> . . . the Soviet Union is offering loans carrying interest rates of 2 or 2½ per cent or less, as against the 3½ to 5½ per cent or more charged by agencies of our Government.
>
> The core of the problem involved here is obviously that normal economic criteria governing interest rates do not apply in the case of foreign aid loans. In terms of supply and demand factors and taking account of the risks involved it may well be that from an economic point of view higher rates than the highest now charged by the United States would be required. But foreign aid loans are not purely economic in nature and they do not and should not have to meet the test of the market place in the same sense that a loan given by a bank to an individual or a corporation has to meet such tests.
>
> Basically, foreign aid loans, whether by the United States or the Soviet Union, are intended to serve political purposes. In our case these purposes are to help strengthen friendly nations, to promote their economic development and to increase their internal political and economic stability. To serve these ends the rate of interest should not be one which the borrowing nation feels is beyond its capabilities or feels is in any sense "unfair." In the absence of economic criteria for

---

[51] "Interest and Foreign Aid" (editorial), *The New York Times*, January 25, 1958, p. 18-L.

such interest rates it would seem sensible to give those who negotiate for the United States greater flexibility in setting such rates than they now have.

But, if a case could have been made during the Fund's early days for *easier* loan terms, it is then doubly significant to note that the course of events witnessed instead a movement to a *tougher* loan policy. Specifically, in October 1959, the Fund's policy was altered, as intimated earlier, to make tying clauses a usual ingredient of future loan contracts. In the official explanation offered, justification was claimed in terms of two new factors: first, a balance-of-payments reversal during 1958–59 that resulted in net gold outflows from the US, and second, an increased ability by some other countries (e.g., Germany and Japan) to "go it alone" without help from foreign sales made on the basis of non-tied US loans to under-developed countries.[52] Whether or not the US balance-of-payments position vis-à-vis the rest-of-the-world was in the jeopardy presumed (and, significantly, considerable sentiment existed to the effect that the action was ill-based[53]), adverse reaction in particular quarters in underdeveloped countries proved forthcoming almost immediately. For example, an Asian delegate at the 1959 Colombo Plan Conference, meeting in Indonesia, criticized the new "Buy American" policy as follows:[54]

> [Terms offered by the DLF] are too rigid and too difficult for . . . underdeveloped countries to meet. . . . If they lay down that loaned money can only be used in payment of goods and services purchased in the lending country, then the benefit of low interest rates may be more than canceled out. . . . In such cases, prices of goods and costs of services are not competitive and are higher than the world price.

Fourth, the trend has been for the Fund to become divorced, organizationally, from the ICA, but some persons feel that it is integration that should have been fostered.[55] At the outset, the Fund was an integral part of the ICA, but over time separateness has been emphasized: first, by movement of the Fund to its own building; then, by incorporation of the Fund as a distinct legal entity (but with both the ICA and the Fund embraced by the Mutual Security Program[56]). The major argument against separateness is that the ICA has the organizational framework and technical-assistance staff overseas needed to help formulate and process applications and, subsequently, to help implement the utilization of loan proceeds. Arrangements can still be made for use of these ICA services (as is

52 *The New York Times,* October 20, 1959, p. 1-C. Also see editorials in *The New York Times,* October 25, 1959, p. 2-E; November 21, 1959, p. 22-C; November 28, 1959, p. 20-C.
53 For example, see *The New York Times,* November 22, 1959, p. 1-E.
54 *The Des Moines Register,* November 13, 1959, p. 2.
55 *The New York Times,* November 15, 1957, p. 1-L.
56 The Director of the ICA serves on the Fund's Board of Directors.

done), but some persons question the degree of effectiveness that can be expected to prevail in the absence of formal union (just as some persons question how well the ICA's overseas staff pushes the loan program of the Export-Import Bank). In larger terms, the matter of separateness raises questions as to the future of the ICA, i.e., as the country's *central* foreign-aid agency. Is a policy of attrition under way, with the foreign-aid operation to be parceled out among various agencies (e.g., the loan function to the Fund, the policy-formulation function to the Department of State proper, the military-aid function to the Department of Defense, etc.)? If so, is the country thereby likely to be helped or hindered in the conduct of its foreign-economic-policy activities?

SELECTED BIBLIOGRAPHY

See the end of Chapter 19.

19

INSTITUTIONAL ASSISTANCE (II)

The preceding chapter dealt with the US Government's own agencies for the provision of developmental assistance to underdeveloped countries: the Export-Import Bank, the International Cooperation Administration (treated more fully in Chs. 20 and 21), and the Development Loan Fund. The US Government also participated in some international arrangements that supply assistance to underdeveloped countries: the International Bank, the International Finance Corporation, the International Monetary Fund, the United Nations Program, the Colombo Plan, and the Inter-American Development Bank. These arrangements are treated in the present chapter.

Additionally, the present chapter deals with some private American efforts in the provision of developmental assistance, involving forms of effort going beyond those explicitly treated in Chapter 17, and examines major proposals for the added provision of developmental assistance still pending.

INTERNATIONAL BANK

The major international institution through which loan capital, including American capital, moves to the underdeveloped world is the International Bank for Reconstruction and Development (generally referred to as the International Bank, the World Bank, the IBRD, or simply as the Bank).

ORIGINS

The Bank came into existence as a consequence of discussions held during World War II. Even while the global conflict was in full progress, thought was being given in official Allied quarters to the probable nature of the postwar world. Importantly, widespread hope was entertained that the postwar years might witness the emergence of a better world economic order, one able to measure up to the momentous tasks assumed certain to prevail, and able to remain free of major shortcomings of the type characteristic of the world economy of the 1930's. The pioneering in ideas proceeded furthest in Great Britain and the US, resulting in the preparation of two rival postwar plans, the Keynes Plan in England and the White Plan in the US.[1] Release of these documents served to evoke much public discussion and was followed, in mid-1944, by an international conference, the Bretton Woods Conference. This Conference, attended by delegates from most non-Axis countries, was concerned with the content of the rival plans, as well as with some additional subject matter introduced during the session. In due course, the conferees succeeded in drawing up a compromise document, the Bretton Woods Agreement. The central element of the Agreement involved the proposal that two new international institutions be established: an International Bank (to assist in the transmission, internationally, of loan capital) and an International Monetary Fund (to assist in the maintenance of exchange-rate stability). With approval of the Agreement by the US Congress in 1945, along with approval in the requisite number of other countries, the two new institutions came into formal being, both with headquarters in Washington.

As intimated by its full title, the new Bank was intended to serve as an additional source of international capital for use in two main connections: reconstruction (during the early postwar years) in countries devastated by war, and development (over the longer-run) in a whole array of countries, but especially in underdeveloped countries. In short, it was contemplated that once the early postwar years had become history, the basic function of the Bank would be limited to the provision of loan capital for the promotion of economic development.

Significantly, initiation of the Bank appealed, by and large, to both potential borrowing countries and potential lending countries. Prospective recipient countries were favorably inclined, especially because they saw the Bank as holding an assured supply of international capital to

---

[1] The Keynes Plan was named after Lord Keynes, while the White Plan was named after Harry D. White, an official of the US Treasury. Despite much similarity in content, including high coincidence in the identification of problems, some important differences existed, especially as to *where* responsibility in various connections was to rest and *how* it was to be met. A convenient reference source for the text of the two plans is J. H. Williams, *Postwar Monetary Plans* (New York: Alfred A. Knopf, 1945), Appendices 2 and 3, pp. 237–297.

which access might be had on generally advantageous terms. The major prospective capital-supplier country, the US, also saw advantages in the Bank; for example, the need for the American economy to supply capital appeared obvious, but provision of capital through an institution having multi-country membership could serve to shift encumbent risk from the US alone to the membership as a whole.[2]

ORGANIZATION

According to plans agreed upon, every country was held eligible for membership, provided it subscribed to the Charter, and provided it also joined the companion institution, the Fund. From an initial membership of 44 countries, the Bank has grown to encompass 68 countries.[3]

Authorized capital was set, at the outset, at $10 billion. Each member was given a quota based on its relative economic importance, which quota became the basis of the individual member's subscription. Total subscriptions of members, by mid-1959, exceeded $9.5 billion. The US subscription within this context was $3.175 billion, or roughly one-third of the total, while Great Britain, China (Taiwan), France, and India comprised other large subscribers.

The lending authority of the Bank was limited to total subscriptions plus reserves and surplus. Any member, irrespective of its quota, was held technically eligible for borrowings up to this total, except that the sum of all member borrowings was restricted to the limit set by the total lending authority. Actually, the organization agreed upon offered a clever framework for the transmission, internationally, of capital. While all members were eligible to borrow, some countries were, in fact, not likely to do so. For example, the US, the largest subscriber, was not likely to borrow, but the capital provided by it, or made available to the Bank because of its membership, became accessible to other members—in fact, became accessible to them in amounts far exceeding their individual quotas.

While the Bank's lending authority, under its initial terms of reference, was near $10 billion (subscriptions plus reserves and surplus), funds actually on hand for immediate disposal were but a fraction of this amount. Capacity to move capital rested, in the final analysis, upon what occurred in any of three connections. First, the Bank was empowered to lend from paid-in subscriptions. Funds derived in this manner, however, amounted to only 20% of each member's subscription (2% in gold or US dollars, and 18% in the member's own currency), providing a total of under $2 billion. The other 80%, while remaining subject to call

---

[2] For a fuller discussion of the special appeals the Bank is said to have held for both prospective borrowers and likely lenders, see W. Krause, *The International Economy* (Boston: Houghton Mifflin Company, 1955), pp. 300–301.

[3] As of 1959.

(though not likely to be called[4]), nevertheless offered itself as backing in the guarantee of whatever obligations the Bank might incur in the course of operations, e.g., as in the sale of its own bonds, or in the underwriting of private loans. Second, the Bank was empowered to lend from proceeds obtained through the sale of World Bank bonds. Such bonds, bearing interest at from 2% to 4¾%, were outstanding by mid-1959 in the amount of roughly $2 billion (47 issues having been marketed to obtain various needed currencies, including US dollars, Belgian francs, Canadian dollars, Deutsche marks, Netherlands guilders, British pounds sterling, and Swiss francs). Indeed, as practice evolved, this method of financing came to represent the main one relied upon by the Bank. Third, the Bank was empowered to guarantee loans negotiated by borrowers in private capital markets. However, this procedure, despite early hopeful expectations for it, came to be used very little (total guarantees, cumulative to mid-1959, amounting to under $0.1 billion).

The significant fact that shows up on the basis of the foregoing is that the Bank's organization qualified it, potentially, as an important instrumentality for moving capital from capital-rich countries to capital-deficit countries, and *especially from the US to the underdeveloped world*. The crucial nature of US membership in the Bank can readily be visualized. First, it is highly doubtful whether the Bank would ever have come into existence without the presence of general knowledge of the US's intention to participate; and, even had it come into existence without participation by the US, absence of US membership would have involved impaired capacity for it in any attempt to function as a large-scale intermediary in the transmission of capital. Second, the US is the largest single contributor of funds made available to the Bank on a *direct* basis. The large US dollar contribution is important especially in view of the disproportionately heavy demand among borrowers for loans providing US dollars.[5] Third, the high-grade backing offered by the contingent liability assumed by the US (in the commitment involved in its unpaid subscription) represents the major basis that makes the sale of World Bank bonds possible in private capital markets. *Indirect* access to funds along these lines is vital to the Bank's operation.[6] And, insofar as the

---

[4] A reasonable presumption is that numerous countries would have been deterred from membership had payment of the total subscription been required at the outset, or had there been widespread expectation that the unpaid portion of the subscription would be called for at a later date (except in the event of a need to offset wholesale losses). The rationale at the time was that a subscription, even if unpaid, would provide the backing that might allow the Bank to activate other capital.

[5] Not only was the initial US subscription roughly one-third of the total, but the payable-portion of the subscription represented a contribution in US dollars and gold—whereas other members paid mostly in terms of their national currencies (with payment in US dollars or gold being but 2% of subscription).

[6] Access on this basis to various currencies totaled $2.4 billion by mid-1959, including $2.1 billion in US dollars gotten through bond sales in the American private capital market alone.

Bank chooses to engage in guarantee operations, the contingent liability assumed by the US also offers special support.

Thus, because the Bank is engaged, to an important extent, in tapping American capital for use in other countries, especially in underdeveloped countries, consideration of the institution in the light of its actual and potential contribution to economic development acquires special relevance.

NATURE OF BUSINESS

The Bank deals in loans, not grants. While the Bank has a reputation for conservatism, its loan terms are easier, on the whole, than those of the Export-Import Bank (although tougher than those of the DLF).[7]

Eligible borrowers include member governments or agencies thereof, as well as private enterprises located within member countries. Private borrowers are required to have the guarantee of the member government concerned. In practice, lending to governments and their agencies exceeds lending to private enterprises, a distribution attributable in part to an especially heavy demand for assistance for public-sector investment, largely concerned with basic development, and in part to the deterrent posed for private investment by the guarantee provision.[8]

The Bank regards itself as a lender of last resort. Its stated practice is not to compete with private investors, and to lend, or to guarantee a loan obtained elsewhere, only if needed capital cannot be secured from other prior sources on reasonable terms.

The Bank sees itself as a lender on behalf of development;[9] purely commercial ventures (e.g., trading activities) are held not eligible for financing. Reports of the Bank and statements by its officials indicate, further, that the Bank visualizes its major role in the stimulation of development—at least at this juncture in history—as being in terms of provision of assistance for basic development, i.e., in support of the *prerequisites* for other development.

The Bank customarily lends only for specific projects (in fact, only for the "more useful" and "urgent" of projects), but some program-type loans do occur, e.g., package loans to developmental institutions, offered with the final disposition of funds unstipulated except in general terms,

---

[7] For a summary statement of the Bank's policies and operations, see "Policies and Operations of the World Bank," *Lloyds Bank Review*, July 1953; also, see the Bank's annual reports.

[8] Governments are frequently reluctant to provide guarantees for private investment (either because they are unwilling to assume the encumbent financial liability, or because they fear that indirect endorsement lays them open to possible charges of favoritism), while private investors are frequently hesitant to request guarantees (largely because they fear that acceptance of the helping hand of government comprises an invitation for future control—as suggested earlier in Ch. 18, esp. footnote 23).

[9] Ever since the early demands for reconstruction, following World War II, ceased to confront the Bank.

thereby providing a basis for sub-loans to end-borrowers for use in conjunction with particular projects undetermined at the time of the Bank's loan.

The Bank customarily lends only the amount needed to cover direct foreign-exchange outlays associated with an undertaking, or only some portion of this amount, leaving all other required funds to be gotten from other sources. The Bank proceeds on the assumption that domestic sources should be tapped for local-currency financing, and that foreign-exchange demands arising indirectly as a consequence of developmental investment should be met without the Bank's help, presumably through accommodation within a given country's total economic structure. Beyond the foregoing, the Bank is receptive to the use of its resources within a joint-financing context—i.e., the Bank is amenable to sharing with others the burden of providing required foreign exchange (e.g., with the Export-Import Bank, the DLF, or private investors).

Interest rates on loans vary, with recorded loans carrying rates of $3\frac{3}{4}\%$ to 6%, but with most loans in the range of $4\frac{1}{2}\%$ to 5%. Variation in rates is explainable largely in terms of differing categories of loan utilization, and in terms of changes in the cost to the Bank for obtaining its own borrowed funds. In addition to an interest charge, the Bank collects a small commission (or fee) on all amounts outstanding, whether direct loans or guarantees for loans, ostensibly as the basis for a reserve against possible losses (negligible thus far). The duration of loans also varies, but periods of 15 to 25 years are common.

The Bank's loans are not tied, so that procurement in a wide area is technically possible. The Bank's policy in this respect is in keeping with its avowed objective of promoting multilateral trade. In practice, however, most loan proceeds are used in connection with purchases spread among only a few countries: specifically, major developed countries. This result stems, basically, from the fact that select developmental ingredients (e.g., capital goods) are to be had in volume only in some countries. Significantly, given the situation of widespread currency inconvertibility, particular currencies come to be preferred over others because of their greater usefulness in the procurement of required developmental ingredients. The US dollar has been especially favored, since it is usable both in the US and elsewhere (and has been throughout the post-World War II period). Indeed, a major long-range concern of the Bank has been one of access to US dollars for use as loanable funds.[10]

---

[10] The overall preference for US dollars accounts, in important measure, for the sale for that currency of $2.1 billion of a total of $2.4 billion in World Bank bonds marketed by mid-1959. Of course, some currencies besides the US dollar are also widely usable for procurement of desired developmental ingredients, and this fact accounts for the Bank's effort, especially *during more recent years*, to sell bonds for particular currencies other than the US dollar, e.g., for Canadian dollars, Belgian francs, Deutsche marks, Netherlands guilders, British pounds sterling, and Swiss francs.

With rare exception, repayment is scheduled in terms of the currency borrowed. In an attempt to lessen possible difficulties associated with repayment, the Bank adheres to two major practices. First, the Bank screens loan applications in order to ascertain likely repayment prospects, thus to avoid lending in cases holding obvious trouble. As stated by the Bank's President, a major consideration in loan appraisal is the "willingness and *ability* of the country concerned to follow economic policies which will enable it to earn enough foreign exchange to pay its debts."[11] Second, flexibility in loan arrangements is permissible in the event repayment does prove exceedingly difficult—notwithstanding prior screening intended to prevent this eventuality. For example, a hard-pressed debtor country can request a relaxation in the terms of repayment (e.g., a shift to an eased amortization schedule), and the presumption is that Bank approval will follow if circumstances warrant special treatment. Or, in case general exchange-rate pressure comes to be experienced by the debtor country, the Bank is empowered to accede to repayment in terms of the member's own currency for periods of up to 3 years, provided the debtor country is willing to accept certain accompanying conditions.[12]

Loans by the Bank, cumulative through mid-1959, totaled $4.4 billion, of which $3.9 billion was regarded as for development (Table 21). Total disbursements stood at $3.4 billion. Individual loans numbered 234, with 50 member countries and territories as beneficiaries.[13]

Two significant trends appear evident in the Bank's lending activity. First, the tempo of lending has been stepped up during the more recent years. Loans for development, from the inception of the Bank through mid-1957, averaged roughly $240 million per year, but during each of the two succeeding fiscal years exceeded $700 million per year. Second, the direction of lending for development has been undergoing a moderate shift, with more emphasis upon development in underdeveloped countries and less upon development in already developed countries. From the inception of the Bank to mid-1957, roughly two-thirds of all developmental-loan volume was directed toward the underdeveloped world (as measured by amounts destined for Africa, Asia, and the Western Hemisphere outside the US and Canada), with the remainder destined for developmental purposes in developed countries (Europe and Australia); during the two succeeding fiscal years, however, roughly 80% of the

---

11 Statement by Eugene R. Black in *Ibid.*, p. 23. (Italics are mine.)

12 Repayment in domestic currency becomes possible provided the debtor country agrees to (a) allow use of its currency in Bank operations, (b) maintain the foreign-exchange value of its currency, and (c) repurchase its currency on appropriate terms when able to do so.

13 By March 31, 1960, cumulative loan commitments reached $5.1 billion, of which $3.7 billion had been disbursed. At that time, individual loans undertaken by the Bank numbered 256, with 52 countries and territories as beneficiaries. IBRD, *Press Release* (No. 632), May 6, 1960.

Table 21. International Bank Loans, by Purpose and Area, 1959 (In millions of US dollars)

PURPOSE	Total	AREA				
		Africa	Asia	Australia	Europe	Western Hemisphere
Development Loans	3,929	589	1,297	318	791	934
Electric Power	1,398	178	415	29	273	503
Transportation	1,297	332	458	132	69	306
Communications	24	2	....	....	....	22
Agriculture and Forestry	316	....	68	104	88	56
Industry	689	37	281	53	271	47
General Development	205	40	75	....	90	....
Reconstruction Loans	497	....	....	....	497	....
Total	4,426	589	1,297	318	1,288	934

Source: IBRD, Fourteenth Annual Report, 1958–1959, Washington, 1959, p. 11. Data are cumulative through June 30, 1959. Amounts are net of cancellations and refundings.

Bank's new loan volume was destined for the underdeveloped world, with roughly one-half of all new loans destined for use in Asia alone.

APPRAISAL

Many persons feel that the Bank's activities quickly gave it claim to a considerable measure of success. Capital moving through the Bank's channels unquestionably helped promote some development that otherwise would not likely have occurred. Along with the favorable factors, however, some potent criticisms came to be offered. Of these criticisms, two appeared to dominate during a period of several years—at least until 1959, in which year the Bank underwent reorganization.

First, the charge was made that the Bank is overly conservative in its approach to development. The standard line of the Bank during its first dozen years of operation was that underdeveloped countries have low capacity to absorb capital.[14] Admittedly, underdeveloped countries do not have an unlimited capacity to absorb capital productively (as pointed out in Ch. 15). But, in the opinion of some critics, the argument of low absorptive capacity, as used by the Bank, stemmed either from a decidedly conservative appraisal of the amount of development possible in underdeveloped countries, or from a belief that something plausible was needed

---

[14] For a clear-cut statement to this effect, see IBRD, Fourth Annual Report, 1948–1949, Washington, 1949, p. 8.

to get the Bank "off the hook" for its failure to do more. On the first score, capacity to absorb capital is a *relative* matter—dependent, among other things, upon the particular loan standards applied. If the Bank found absorptive capacity to be low (as it says it did), a possible explanation might then be sought in the Bank's own standards applied in judging absorptive capacity. Actually, the Bank's loan terms were never especially tough, e.g., as compared with those of the Export-Import Bank. Perhaps failure to lend in greater volume might be explained more particularly in terms of a reluctance by the Bank to parcel out more funds than in terms of prospective borrowers finding the Bank's loan terms unpalatable. Therefore, on the second score, *if* the Bank was reluctant to lend in greater volume (and, as implied, used the argument of low absorptive capacity to explain away its own failing), why was this so? Was it due to limited lending resources available to the Bank? Another criticism intimated as much.

Second, then, the charge was made that the Bank's lending resources were adequate to support no more than a moderate effort. While the Bank's legal capacity to lend and guarantee was equal to total subscriptions plus reserves and surplus, an amount approximating $10 billion, its economic capacity to proceed fell short of this amount. Funds on hand, and available for *actual* lending, were always at a lesser figure. Funds consisted of paid-in subscriptions (plus reserves and surplus) and the proceeds gained from the sale of World Bank bonds. Bonds offered for sale always sold well, with sales exceeding $2.4 billion having occurred by mid-1959. A significant fact, however, was that bond issues up to the total amount of $3.175 billion, the amount of the US subscription, were in essence guaranteed by the US Government (and, additionally, yielded the buyer an equivalent or better return than US Government bonds). The result was that bond sales up to the total US subscription, $3.175 billion, could be expected to sell well. The real question involved the prospect of sale beyond this amount, when the US Government would in essence no longer be *the* guarantor. The conclusion to which some persons came was that the Bank's effective lending capacity under prevailing arrangements was no more than roughly $5 billion, and probably no more than $4 billion—i.e., the amount of the US subscription, usable as backing for the sale of World Bank bonds, plus paid-in amounts on subscriptions in terms of gold, US dollars, or other desired currencies. Given this amount, the Bank itself was limited in what it could do; for example, assuming total available funds of $4 billion and 20-year duration on all loans, the long-run annual average of Bank lending would be held to $200 million (with greater lending in any one year forcing lesser lending in another year).

In short, critics of the Bank visualized the institution as being caught in a dilemma. Given prevailing resources, it had either to limit its activity (in which case, according to critics, its own incapacity to lend more could well, but mistakenly, be construed as an inability on the part of potential borrowers to qualify for more) or it had to attempt to expand its resources (using as its rationale the argument that there is a job to be done but prevailing resources are not adequate to do it).

REORGANIZATION

Traditionally, the Bank pictured itself as a provider of marginal amounts of capital[15] to a world in much of which capital absorptive capacity is distinctly limited. But, during 1958, the Bank's "tune" suddenly changed. No longer did Bank officials put primary emphasis on limited capital absorptive capacity. Rather, they saw big opportunities that the Bank should be prepared to meet. In essence, the Bank was making a bid for enlarged capitalization. Indeed, a case in these terms was formally presented by the Bank's President at the Annual Meeting, held in New Delhi in October 1958:[16]

> Up to now there has been no reason for me to suggest . . . that the financial resources available to the Bank were insufficient in amount for the task that the Bank is designed to perform. In our earlier experience, the most significant limitation on our operation was the lack of suitable projects; this is still the limitation in some member countries. Later, weakness in fiscal management and its effects on . . . "creditworthiness" emerged as another limitation on our lending; it is still a substantial limitation.

> But despite the persistence of these limitations, we are now confronted with a situation of another kind. We are approaching the day when the Bank may be getting . . . a larger number of meritorious applications than we shall be able to find money for on reasonable terms. As the increased tempo of our lending implies, many of our member countries are satisfying the tests of project preparation and fiscal management; moreover among our rapidly increasing membership, all our new members are capital hungry. For the first time in the Bank's existence, the quantity of financial resources available to the Bank may soon be seriously inadequate.

> And there is another—a qualitative—aspect of this situation. Some of our rapidly developing member countries . . . are approaching the limits of their present capacity to assume additional obligations, which . . . must be serviced on a fixed timetable and in scarce foreign exchange. To a considerable extent, this is a reflection of the widely observed phenomenon that rapid economic development brings heavy pressure on a country's balance of payments. . . . In some developing countries, this persistent pressure may be accentuated at times through

---

15 According to Eugene R. Black, President of the Bank, ". . . the Bank's lending can never be more than marginal. . . . [Emphasis] . . . is not on what the Bank itself can lend, but on ways in which it can stimulate the growth of investment nationally and internationally." See "Policies and Operations of the World Bank," *Lloyds Bank Review*, July 1953, pp. 19, 32.

16 IMF, *International Financial News Survey*, Washington, October 17, 1958.

adverse developments in their commodity trade, sometimes (though by no means always) beyond their effective control. In these circumstances, substantial periods of time may be required to carry out the adjustments necessary to convert rising productivity at home into an equally healthy foreign trade position. In the meantime, it may be imprudent for such countries to undertake additional foreign exchange obligations even for the execution of projects which, taken by themselves, would strengthen the economy and promise eventual beneficial effects. In member countries that find themselves in these situations, further Bank lending may be limited simply because there may be insufficient foreign exchange to service our loans.

These prospects have led us to look with increasing concern at the amount and character of the Bank's financial resources.

Stripped of certain refinements (including possibly some elements of logic introduced to help smooth the change-over from one outlook to another), two main factors appeared to motivate the Bank in its request. First, the tempo of loan activity by the Bank was showing acceleration, forcing the Bank to have more funds on hand. For example, the volume of lending rose sharply during 1957–58 (to $711 million for FY 1958, as compared to an annual average of $366 million during the preceding 4 years). Reasonable question remained, however, whether the acceleration was to be attributed primarily to altered conditions in recipient countries, as suggested by the Bank, or primarily to a changed attitude within the Bank.[17] Second, the Bank's ability to gain access to more funds for further lending appeared in jeopardy under the established mode of operation. Specifically, the day was drawing near when the Bank would be compelled to put to a test the matter of whether or not World Bank bonds would sell well when offered beyond the limit of the US subscription. Many persons felt that the Bank had no ready alternative but to seek an enlarged financial framework, which would then at least postpone any showdown on the matter of salability of bonds.

Official reaction to the Bank's proposal proved favorable in most countries. Accordingly, formal steps were instituted in an attempt to enlarge the capitalization of the Bank from $10 billion to $21 billion. This increase became effective September 15, 1959, following approval by the requisite number of member governments (including the US Government).[18] Under the new arrangement, the US subscription was raised from $3.175 billion to $5.715 billion.[19] As was the case earlier, only nominal

---

[17] Some persons have commented, in a cynical vein, that the advent in 1957 of the DLF as a rival of the Bank served to force the Bank to reappraise its role. For those so inclined, the greater activity of the Bank during FY 58 might, of course, be explained as having been motivated by competition.

[18] Approval had been obtained from 40 member countries. Most countries approved roughly a doubling of their earlier subscriptions. Some countries (17 in number), however, agreed to somewhat larger increases in their subscriptions in order thereby to reflect their relative economic importance better among countries in the current period.

[19] IBRD, *Press Release* (No. 601), September 16, 1959.

amounts were to be paid in on the basis of the enlarged subscriptions; rather, the major portion of the new subscriptions simply remained subject to call. The main effect of the increase in subscriptions was to give the Bank a better prospect for continuing the sale of its bonds, and hence to have ready funds at its disposal for the conduct of its operations; specifically, in this connection, the effective guarantee of World Bank bonds assumed by the US Government stood thereafter at roughly *double* the previous level.

INTERNATIONAL FINANCE CORPORATION

A second international lending institution in which the US holds membership is the International Finance Corporation. Basically, the IFC is *subsidiary* to the International Bank, engaging in business of a type not within the province of the Bank, but supplementary to it.

ORIGINS

In a report[20] issued in 1951, the International Development Advisory Board (attached to the Department of State) recommended that an International Finance Corporation be established as an affiliate of the International Bank, with authority to engage in certain activities related to capital provision not within the scope of the Bank as then constituted.

Specifically, the IFC was proposed for the services it might provide in two main connections, both regarded as important for private-enterprise development. First, the IFC was to have the authority to provide capital to private enterprise without government guarantee. While the Bank was empowered to lend directly to private borrowers, its Charter required the government of the country concerned, or an agency thereof, to act as guarantor. This guarantee procedure, as indicated earlier, has proven generally distasteful, both to governments and to private investors. Accordingly, the creation of an international facility able to accommodate private borrowers without their having to secure a government guarantee was considered essential—if a significant boost was to be given private-enterprise development in the underdeveloped world.

Second, the IFC was to have the authority to invest in equities (i.e., in the securities of private firms) in participation with private investors, something the Bank had no authority to do. Creation of an international facility able to engage in equity financing was considered important as an aid to private-enterprise development in view, assertedly, of the demonstrated inability of some private investors to proceed with plans in the absence of access to funds on this basis. Indeed, absence of an institution of the proposed type had resulted, allegedly, in the non-usage

---

[20] *Partners in Progress*, Washington, March 1951.

of accessible Bank funds in particular instances, simply because the "co-operative" financing represented by equity capital proved unobtainable.

It was proposed that the capital of the IFC be obtained by means of subscription by member governments, not by diversion of funds from the Bank. The amount of capital likely to be required was believed to be modest. The view was that the IFC could count on the occasional sale of securities from its portfolio (particularly once the private enterprises involved took hold and thrived, and their securities became generally marketable), thereby giving rise to a revolving fund for equity financing.

The proposal evoked mixed reactions. Proponents of development under private-enterprise auspices invariably saw merit in the proposal, probably in large part because of the supplementary source of financing thereby created. Some governments, however, were inclined toward skepticism, particularly because purchase by the new institution of equities of uncertain future value raised the possibility of dissipation of initial subscriptions. However, necessary action eventually proved forthcoming, and the IFC was inaugurated in July 1956.

ORGANIZATION

The IFC was established as an affiliate of the Bank. Although given separate legal status, with an officialdom and staff of its own, and with the authority to maintain and manage funds on its own account, the expectation was that the institution would work closely with the Bank. Indeed, membership was held open only to member countries of the Bank. Authorized capital was set at $100 million, with all payments on subscriptions to occur in US dollars.

The IFC stated its objective as that of furthering economic development through the encouragement of productive private enterprise in member countries, particularly in those members in the underdeveloped category. Implementation was to proceed through three courses of action (the first generally being regarded as paramount): (1) investment in select private enterprises, in association with private investors and without government guarantee, provided sufficient private capital was not available on reasonable terms; (2) service as a clearinghouse to bring together investment opportunities, private capital (both foreign and domestic), and experienced management; and (3) general efforts aimed at the stimulation of private investment, both domestic and foreign. The basic intention was to "invest" rather than to "lend"—i.e., the plan was to provide equity capital, entailing an interest charge, along with some right to participate in the profits and growth of the business (as distinct from the provision of capital on a straight loan basis, yielding merely a fixed interest return).

Capital needed by the IFC for its financing operations was considered obtainable on two bases. First, during the early phases of operation, it was expected that the IFC would limit provision of capital to amounts available on the basis of paid-in subscriptions. As indicated, a maximum subscription of $100 million was scheduled; the actual subscription reached $93.7 million by mid-1959 on the basis of a membership of 57 countries,[21] with the US subscription amounting to $35.2 million, or roughly one-third of the total. Second, at some later time, it was expected that the IFC would invoke its authority to borrow funds (through the sale of its own bonds or obligations).

NATURE OF BUSINESS

The IFC's investment record, although limited in duration and scope, provides a basis for some generalization as to the nature of the institution's business operations.

The IFC restricts itself to the support of private enterprise. Unlike the Bank, the IFC deals directly with private business people and finances only private enterprises, doing so without government guarantee.[22] Although no financing is provided undertakings owned or operated by government, this ineligibility does not extend to enterprises in which some public funds have been invested, provided the enterprises concerned are essentially private in character. Financing occurs in participation with private capital, with the IFC ordinarily providing no more than one-half the capital required, and no more in any event than the amount unavailable from private sources on reasonable terms.

While the IFC likes to draw a distinction to the effect that it invests rather than lends, capital is typically provided on a basis placing it somewhere between loan capital and share capital (pure equity financing)—i.e., involving some combination of an interest return on capital and a right to participate in the growth of the business. The precise form of the financial participation is subject to negotiation on a case-by-case basis, major possibilities being (1) a loan carrying rights of conversion, all or in part, to share capital at a later date (or rights to subscription to share capital, with freedom to exercise this option at a later date), or (2) a loan yielding interest plus some additional return related to earnings. The IFC is not primarily interested in exercising conversion or option rights on its own, but rather looks upon these rights as features likely to give its holdings greater marketability in private capital markets, thereby allowing it to exercise its intended role as initiator of new operations through the provision of needed marginal capital from its revolving

---

[21] Initial membership involved 31 countries.

[22] While no formal government guarantee is required, the IFC, before making an investment in a country having an inconvertible currency, is likely to seek an understanding with the government concerned regarding transferability of income and principal. The IFC says, however, that no such understanding is expected to reflect preferential treatment not generally available to private investors similarly situated.

fund. But, in the interim prior to the sale of its holdings in private capital markets, the IFC is interested in return upon investment—hence, the IFC's desire to obtain some participation in profits, in addition to any fixed interest rate.

While no flat rule exists to prevent the IFC from financing private enterprises in any field of activity or in any locale, the preference (at least during early years) is to finance enterprises that are predominantly industrial (manufacturing, processing, or mining), and that are located in underdeveloped countries. The IFC is especially interested in enterprises organized as joint-ventures or able and willing to resort to joint-financing.

The IFC prefers to deal with enterprises contemplating a total investment of no less than $500,000 and requiring assistance of no less than $100,000 (although the expectation is that the IFC's maximum assistance to any single enterprise will be held to $2 million). The IFC does not adhere to any uniform interest rate, the practice being to negotiate the rate in the light of likely risk and of rights obtainable relative to participation in profits or to conversion or subscription to stock. The period for which the IFC provides its capital varies, ranging generally from 5 to 15 years. The IFC is interested in maintaining its liquid funds as US dollars; therefore, assistance is provided as dollars, and repayment is normally also expected in dollars.

The general philosophy of the IFC, in accordance with which operations occur, was stated by its President in the following terms:[23]

> I conceive that a goal for IFC is to demonstrate in concrete form that soundly conducted investment in the less developed areas can be highly profitable, and by that demonstration to stimulate the flow of private management and capital into such investment. Our success or failure will be reflected not so much in the amount of our own operations as in the extent to which they encourage others to channel their resources into productive private enterprise in these areas.
>
> Such a concept requires, first, that we select projects which are well-conceived, well-executed, well-managed—with proper financial set-up and prospects of attractive profits related to the risks; and second, that our investments be made on terms which promise returns greater than those available from more familiar, and generally safer, opportunities in the more developed countries. Only by such terms, and by their producing satisfactory earnings to IFC, can we demonstrate that this type of investment is attractive.
>
> Thus it follows that IFC operates as an investment fund, taking the risks and seeking the rewards of enterprise, and plays the role of the investor rather than merely a lender of money.
>
> This role seems to me rather well set forth in the dictionary definition as "the acceleration of a reaction produced by a substance, called the *catalyst,* which may be recovered. . . ."

---

23 From an address by Robert L. Garner, delivered at the First Annual Meeting of the Board of Governors of the IFC, Washington, September 27, 1957.

By late 1959, the IFC had entered into 28 commitments, involving 13 countries and total capital of $25.2 million.[24] Reference to one commitment serves to illustrate the nature of the help available from the institution. A private Guatemalan corporation (Industria Harinera Guatemalteca, S.A.), organized in 1955, arranged in 1958 for assistance from the IFC in connection with the construction of a flour mill. Total cost of the project (local-currency plus foreign-exchange cost) was expected to run about $1 million, with the IFC investment amounting to $200,000 (in US dollars). In the transaction, the IFC acquired notes bearing interest at 5%, repayable in US dollars during the period 1963–66. In addition to fixed interest, the arrangement provided that the IFC was (1) to participate in profits (with returns payable in local currency), and (2) to have an option to subscribe to ordinary shares of the company at par for an amount equivalent to $37\frac{1}{2}$% of the IFC's investment.[25]

APPRAISAL

Despite the apparent plausibility of its rationale, the IFC is the object of some criticism. The major criticism made relates to the small amount of business handled. The institution, according to a common contention, does not do much (viewed in an aggregative sense)—indeed, is not in a position to do much.

Although the IFC's capitalization of $100 million is far from a large sum in terms of world capital requirements, this fact does not warrant one's writing off the institution as of no real importance—or so some persons are willing to argue. As they see the situation, the institution's paid-in capital is merely a starting point. To illustrate, the intent of the IFC is to use its capital as a catalyst, so that the total investment effect generally comes to be some multiple of the institution's own assistance. In the words of the institution's President:[26]

> . . . the primary significance of our operations is not the amount of our funds employed, but their multiplying effect in supplementing and attracting larger amounts of private capital. We estimate that the enterprises in which we have participated represent . . . [total new investment consisting of] . . . about $3.50 of other funds for each dollar invested by I.F.C.

Again, the intent of the IFC is to use its capital as the basis for a revolving fund. If rapid turnover in the institution's assets proves possible, impact upon investment over time automatically is greater than possible under an alternate procedure in which equivalent capital re-

---

24 As of September 30, 1959. Regional distribution of commitments was as follows: 2 in Australia, 6 in Asia, and 20 in Latin America.

25 IFC, *Press Release* (No. 19), October 2, 1958.

26 From an address by Robert L. Garner, delivered at the Second Annual Meeting of the Board of Governors of the IFC, New Delhi, October 8, 1958.

mains tied up in long-term loans. In addition to the foregoing, the intent of the IFC is to concentrate upon one particular type of investment, not upon investment across-the-board. The IFC is geared to support private development only (and then only in select instances), so that its potential ought properly to be judged in terms of this more limited context.

Actually, however, the IFC admits to a shortage of funds (which results in restricted activity). First, the institution is highly selective in its screening of projects—as evidenced, in part, by the fact that only 7% of the projects presented during the first two years of operation were held promising for near-term action.[27] As some persons have pointed out, when funds are short, standards governing access can afford to be high. Second, the institution is eager to expand its supply of available funds. One proposal, concerned with additions to capital in the form of soft currencies, served to evoke the following comment from the President of the institution:[28]

> I am convinced that the availability of usable amounts of various currencies would be the greatest single factor in expanding the corporation's activities.

INTERNATIONAL MONETARY FUND

As indicated previously, the Bretton Woods Conference, held in 1944, led to the inauguration of two new international institutions: the International Bank and the International Monetary Fund (the IMF, or simply the Fund). The Fund was expected to concern itself with monetary and exchange-rate matters. From an initial membership of 44 countries, the Fund has grown to encompass 68 countries.[29] Among this membership, the US is the largest subscriber, and underdeveloped countries account for over one-half of the total.

The key function of the Fund involves the promotion of *relative* exchange-rate stability; importantly, the rationale in terms of which the Fund came into being was prevention, during the post-World War II era, of a chaotic international payments situation of the type characteristic during the 1930's. The Fund is *not* supposed to serve as an instrument for the transmission, internationally, of developmental capital. However, presence of the Fund does have a bearing upon development—in two main ways. First, the Fund is instrumental in shaping the prevailing international payments framework, which then comprises part of the fundamental environment conditioning the pattern and

---

[27] *The New York Times,* October 9, 1958, p. 53-C. The information is attributed to Robert L. Garner, President of the IFC.
[28] *Ibid.*
[29] As of 1959.

tempo of development. Second, despite the fact that the Fund is not supposed to act as a supplier of capital for development, some persons feel
that Fund resources come to be used, at least on occasion, in a manner
basically akin to developmental finance. If this is true, the Fund in
essence gives rise to a *disguised* capital movement.

On either of the two scores, the role of the US in the Fund is of special
relevance—by virtue of this country's direct financial participation and
moral influence.

OBJECTIVE AND IMPLEMENTATION

The central function of the Fund, as indicated, was to be that of
promoting relative exchange-rate stability. Upon commencement of
operations, therefore, the Fund had to cope with a basic first task, that of
determining and approving the par values of currencies, which thereafter
were to be regarded as norms. The task involved was not easy, considering the various production and price distortions then evident as a consequence of the events of World War II. Once, however, the issue of
initial par values had been settled, the Fund was ready to tackle its main
task: the maintenance of stable rates of exchange (but with a change in
these rates, beyond a 10% deviation, remaining permissible if expressly
sanctioned by the Fund).

The approach to be followed, which has governed the Fund's activities
to date, was two-pronged in nature. First, the Fund was to help members
in the maintenance of their approved rates of exchange—hopefully in a
free exchange market, the global restoration of which at an early date
was sought as a matter of principle—by providing assistance (foreign
exchange) whenever required by them to withstand pressures arising from
balance-of-payments difficulties of a temporary (short-term) character.
The theory was that temporary balance-of-payments difficulties should
not be permitted to force a country into exchange-rate depreciation (involving movement to a new exchange rate perhaps not at all appropriate
in terms of long-run considerations), but rather should be dealt with
through the provision of supplementary foreign exchange that might then
enable the country to tide itself over its period of difficulty without need
for action as drastic as depreciation.

To put this theory into practice, the Fund needed a supply of currencies, i.e., a fund of foreign exchange. Accordingly, each country, upon
assuming membership, was assigned a quota intended to serve as a
reference point for contributions *to* and drawing rights *from* the Fund.
The initial range of quotas was from $2.75 billion for the US, roughly
one-third of the total of $9.2 billion assumed through mid-1959, to
various lesser amounts for other countries. Contributions on these quotas
were held payable as follows: (1) 25% of the quota in gold (or 10% of

the member's stock of gold and US dollars, if this amount was lower), and (2) 75% of the quota in the member's own currency. Drawing rights were held exercisable by any member when considered needed in order to prop up its balance of payments, access being held to (1) 25% of the member's quota in any given year, with (2) a 5-year limit applied to availability in the event maximum drawing rights were invoked. In the event a member needed supplementary foreign exchange, it was eligible to exercise its drawing rights (within prescribed limits)—meaning it could "purchase" needed foreign exchange through the process of pledging an equivalent value of its own currency (but with the expectation, not always realized, that the member would repurchase its currency at a later date when the short-term difficulty in its balance of payments had subsided).

In short, the Fund consists of a pool of foreign exchange (gold and various national currencies, with US dollars comprising the largest single block of currency), right of access to which yields a buffer-effect for a member country as it copes with the impact of a short-term difficulty in its balance of payments. But, because the US dollar is a "scarce" currency (in high demand), the activity of the Fund, very importantly, is one of exchange of dollars for various other currencies. Thus, since the US is the largest single subscriber (and the key provider of the currency most in demand), the American economy is actually on the paying end of an arrangement in which, so to speak, dollars melt into other currencies. Proponents of the approach, however, far from viewing it with misgiving, see more-than-offsetting gains for the American economy in terms, purportedly, of a more smoothly functioning international payments framework than otherwise likely to prevail.

Second, if balance-of-payments difficulties of members appeared to be chronic in nature (involving a fundamental disequilibrium[30]), rather than simply short-term, the Fund was to provide the machinery through which an orderly change in exchange rates might be undertaken without triggering a wave of competitive exchange-rate depreciation. Thus, the idea was to help members to weather short-term balance-of-payments difficulties without need for depreciation, but to allow, or even foster, depreciation when essential for the correction of deep-seated difficulties (but to confine this action to members actually in need of the particular corrective). Since exchange-rate changes require only permission (no disbursement of Fund resources being involved), the presumption from the outset was that a member subject to prolonged exercise of its drawing rights would, at some point short of actual exhaustion of its borrowing

---

[30] For a discussion of the meaning of this concept, cited in the Articles of Agreement, see R. Triffin, *National Central Banking and the International Economy*, Postwar Economic Studies, No. 7, Board of Governors of the Federal Reserve System, Washington, 1947, esp. p. 77.

privileges, seek to depreciate—or, indeed, be encouraged by the Fund to do so.

APPRAISAL

The Fund's operations, spanning more than a decade, offer a substantial basis for appraisal.

On the one hand, anything akin to what might be truly labeled chaotic currency conditions failed to arise. Unquestionably, a large share of the credit can be claimed by the Fund—as a consequence of the balance-of-payments assistance and the supervision of exchange rate adjustments it provided.[31] In appraising this aspect of the Fund's record, it should be noted that the period involved was anything but free of complexities. Problems of readjustment in the wake of World War 11 were enormous. In addition, the decision of numerous underdeveloped countries to push development did not lessen pressures upon the international payments structure.

The Fund's view toward development has been that stability (meaning price and exchange-rate stability) is a necessary precondition and co-feature. To this end, the admonition of the Fund to underdeveloped countries has been one of "get your financial house in order (and keep it so)." While some persons feel that the Fund has stressed stability to the point of discouraging particular underdeveloped countries from making serious efforts at development (for fear of thereby jeopardizing stability), others cite the fact that the Fund has found it necessary to come to the rescue with balance-of-payments assistance after some countries found themselves in trouble, their developmental programs often having been an important contributing factor. What some underdeveloped countries tend to do, allegedly, is to devote too much of their resources to development (or in the wrong manner); thereafter, when balance-of-payments difficulties arise, these likely as not come to be used as the rationale for access to supplementary balance-of-payments assistance from the Fund—so that, in essence, the particular assistance the Fund is called upon to render is tantamount to a disguised developmental loan.[32] In short, as some persons have appraised the matter, the Fund is looked upon in some quarters as a "stand-by" financial source, probably capable of being tapped in the event balance-of-payments difficulties are encountered, thereby encouraging underdeveloped countries to over-spend in their

---

[31] By April 30, 1959, the Fund had provided balance-of-payments assistance to 37 countries in a total amount of $3.3 billion, and had agreed to exchange-rate adjustments, under supervision, in roughly two-thirds of the member countries.

[32] In actuality, the Fund has then been placed in the position of assuming the burden of absorbing some of the financial shock arising from development, instead of each developing country's having to anticipate the full requirements of development and, having gauged them, making an allowance in developmental efforts for those amounts of resources likely to be required to combat various encumbent pressures.

developmental efforts—so that when, finally, the Fund's resources are drawn upon, the assistance provided is really a development loan, although *ex post*.

On the other hand (aside from whatever success it experienced in the promotion of international financial stability), the Fund did not succeed in ushering in a world free of currency restrictions—regarded a basic objective, as evidenced by the Articles of Agreement and subsequent statements by managing officials.[33] Because exchange restrictions have continued to be widely relied upon, two basic matters appear to merit attention. First, why have exchange restrictions continued to exist, despite the Fund's avowed intent to free-up foreign exchanges? Over the years, the Fund cited numerous impediments to explain why exchange restrictions remained in effect[34] (and to explain, presumably, why it had failed as an organization to assure the general convertibility it espoused). Some persons, however, rather quickly concluded that the Fund was omitting from its listings the most basic factor responsible for its inability to eliminate exchange restrictions: the *nature of the Fund itself*. According to this viewpoint, the Fund, as initially set up, was simply not prepared to cope with a world environment of the type that arose and persisted following World War II. The framers of the Articles of Agreement, meeting during the course of World War II, acted on the assumption that the postwar era was likely to pose problems in the realm of foreign exchange substantially similar to those of the prewar era. They visualized a world economy, once the immediate postwar years had been lived through, in which balance-of-payments equilibrium would be the normal situation for the great majority of countries. Disequilibrium was pictured as the exception to the rule—as something likely to confront only particular countries, and then only on occasion. Accordingly, the Fund was set up to render assistance from a fairly modest pool of resources to the occasional member experiencing short-term difficulty in its balance of payments; and, if the difficulty proved persistent, controlled depreciation was believed to offer a way out, since only one country, or only a few countries, might reasonably be expected to be directly involved at any one time. However, the environment of the postwar world proved far different from what had been anticipated. Disequilibrium was not confined to one country, or even to only a few countries, nor was it essentially short-term in nature. Rather, the disequilibria of the postwar world proved both general and persistent. Under the circumstances, no single country could hope, ordinarily, to move to convertibility as long as other coun-

---

[33] The Fund publishes an annual report on the status of exchange restrictions. For information on the situation in 1958, see IMF, *Tenth Annual Report on Exchange Restrictions*, Washington, 1959.

[34] For example, see IMF, *Second Annual Report on Exchange Restrictions*, Washington, 1951, pp. 8, 12; also *Fourth Annual Report on Exchange Restrictions*, 1953, pp. 7, 9.

tries failed to do likewise. But, the Fund was not equipped, in terms of the magnitude of its resources, to support a move to convertibility by all countries acting simultaneously. In short, the Fund did not have at its disposal resources adequate to allow it to undertake the once-and-for-all action that *might* have resulted in a general restoration of convertibility.

Second, is the Fund's urge for convertibility an admirable one? The Fund, of course, is committed to the merits of multilateralism, and thus is interested in speeding the liquidation of exchange restrictions everywhere. Some persons, however, feel that the Fund is misguided in this ambition. As these persons point out, not all countries are "in the same boat." Whatever may be said of particular countries, or of countries in general, underdeveloped countries are different (in regard to the role played by exchange restrictions). In their case, strong reasons can be cited for the continuation of exchange control—reasons associated with assistance for development (Ch. 11). The conclusion then arrived at is that insistence upon removal of exchange restrictions by all countries may well serve to promote multilateralism *in the current period,* but does so at the possible cost of development *over time.*

REORGANIZATION

Not only did the Bank's status come under review during 1958, but so also did that of the Fund. The basic factor that served to raise questions in the case of the Fund was the diminished supply of resources, especially of US dollars, still eligible for use by it.

A formal bid for increased resources for the Fund was made in October 1958, in the form of an address delivered by the Managing Director at the Annual Meeting in New Delhi.[35] In the case presented, three main points were emphasized. First, while trade volume had risen greatly since the commencement of operations, long-run inflation had lowered the real value of resources initially assigned the Fund. Therefore, it was argued, if the Fund is to do its job effectively in the present-day environment, it needs to have more resources at its disposal. As stated by the Managing Director:[36]

> It is pertinent to recall that the resources available to the Fund were determined at the Bretton Woods Conference in 1944, and that most of the data on international trade available at that time related to the period just before World War II. By 1957, the physical volume of world exports was 60 per cent higher than in 1937, and the prices of goods moving in international trade had increased by 140 per cent. The delegates at Bretton Woods may possibly have foreseen, and thus allowed for, a long-term rise in the volume of world trade, but it would seem

---

[35] Address by Per Jacobsson, reproduced in IMF, *International Financial News Survey,* Washington, October 17, 1958.
[36] *Ibid.*

from the records of the Conference that the delegates did not, in general, count on the considerable inflationary rise in prices which has taken place; rather, they feared a depression after the war. The result of the price rise has been that, in real terms, the Fund's resources are now considerably less than was envisaged when its original endowment was made.

Second, experience was held to have demonstrated that crises tend to hit a number of countries at the *same* time, not one at a time. Therefore, it was argued, the Fund needs to be prepared to help numerous countries simultaneously, which involves a need for considerable resources. In the words of the Managing Director:[37]

> . . . the ability of the Fund to make its resources available on a large scale at one time is also of importance, since experience shows that in a period of acute tension extensive drawings will occur, usually affecting several countries at the same time.

Third, the development push going on in the underdeveloped world was held to pose special requirements for the Fund. The Fund, as pictured, is interested in maintaining, or in enhancing, the creditworthiness of underdeveloped countries so that they can attract developmental capital. This creditworthiness is related to monetary and balance-of-payments solvency. While stressing the need for discipline on the part of underdeveloped countries (meaning the practice of sound, or restrained, monetary and fiscal management), the Fund sees itself as willing to bend over backwards on occasion in order to bail out countries that have gotten into difficulties in having pushed development too hard. The Fund's view is that development should be encouraged (within limits), and that a certain liberality in the use of Fund resources in bail-out operations is permissible at this stage of world economic affairs; the hope all the while, however, is that someday the countries concerned will have learned to exercise sufficient restraint to avoid excessive inflationary and balance-of-payments pressures—at which time, presumably, the Fund can afford to be harder in its attitudes. As put by the Managing Director:[38]

> It is the broad purpose of the Fund to combine assistance with the observance of that financial discipline without which no international monetary standard can function properly. . . . More monetary management is needed today. . . . [However,] *time is often required for corrective measures to take effect—and to gain that time financial assistance may be needed.* But without the corrective measures, assistance will be of little avail. . . . But even so, . . . access to the Fund's resources may make countries more confident in their attempts to restore balance, and may indeed induce them to take stricter and more constructive measures than if they had to rely on their own resources alone.

---

[37] *Ibid.*
[38] *Ibid.* (Italics are mine.)

Thereafter, formal steps were initiated to raise the Fund's total resources. A new schedule of quotas for member countries became effective September 15, 1959, following approval by the requisite number of governments (including the US Government). At the time, 40 member countries had consented to higher quotas, ranging from 50% to 100% above those initially applicable to individual members. The US, for example, consented to an increase in its quota from $2.75 billion to $4.125 billion. The previously-existing *total* quota-commitment of $9.2 billion was scheduled to rise by $5.8 billion to a new total of $14 billion.[39] Accordingly, the Fund's capacity to engage in operations was increased by a substantial margin.

In the course of negotiation for the increase, however, some persons indicated their misgivings about a straight unencumbered increase in resources for the Fund. The view of some was that expansion of the Fund's resources should be made conditional upon a revision in the Articles of Agreement. It was felt that the dictum regarding exchange restrictions under which the Fund operates is too all-embracive. The Articles of Agreement should be modified, it was felt, to allow exchange control to be continued, *with sanction,* in those cases in which its use is defensible in terms of promotion of development. It did not make good sense, according to critics, to have countries free to dissipate their available foreign-exchange resources in various low-priority uses (under a free exchange market), and then, with their resources depleted, to approach the Fund for assistance in order to buttress their deteriorated position. Rather, it was felt, countries should be encouraged to use their available foreign-exchange resources in accordance with some rational development scheme, and *then,* if need arose to seek supplementary help, the Fund at least would have the knowledge that it was coming to the rescue because of over-development, and not because of poor usage of available resources.[40]

UNITED NATIONS PROGRAM

The US Government also provides assistance through the United Nations. Traditionally, the UN has offered only technical assistance, but arrangements were finalized during late 1958 under which some capital assistance became possible thereafter. In terms of dollar magnitude, how-

---

39 IMF, *International Financial News Survey,* Washington, September 18, 1959.

40 In another vein, a proposal aimed at a fundamental recasting of the Fund was offered by Robert L. Triffin. According to this proposal, the Fund would be revamped to make it a true central bank for central banks, thereby ostensibly to reduce the vulnerability of the international currency structure to breakdown—feared to be a distinct possibility at the time in light of the practice of most countries to hold their monetary reserves in terms of *particular* (or key) currencies, such as US dollars or British pounds sterling, themselves allegedly vulnerable to potential deflation. For a summary of the Triffin view, see "Economists Get Storm Warning," *Business Week,* September 26, 1959.

ever, the US contribution, as well as the total UN effort, remains small.

The UN effort has two main facets. First, there is the Expanded Program of Technical Assistance. This program, begun in 1950, is concerned with the provision of technical assistance. Operations are carried on by 7 specialized agencies, all under the jurisdiction of a central Technical Assistance Administration that holds responsibility for coordination. The record of recent years reveals that technical assistance is being rendered by technicians of various nationalities in a great number of countries; for example, during 1959 technical assistance was received in some form and to some extent by 132 countries or territories. Financial support for the conduct of activities stems from voluntary contributions by member countries, but is of generally modest proportions; during 1959, for example, contributions were received from 81 countries.

Second, there is the Special Projects Fund. This phase of the UN effort stemmed from a proposal by the US to the UN General Assembly in 1958. The US proposed that a new program be undertaken, supplementary to the existing Program of Technical Assistance, and capable of service in two main connections: (1) provision of technical assistance in greater volume and over longer periods than theretofore possible solely under the Program of Technical Assistance, and (2) provision of some amount of capital assistance for special projects, e.g., for surveys, research and training, and demonstration projects. The General Assembly promptly approved the proposal in principle; thereafter, in late 1958, following a period of preparation, the Special Projects Fund came into formal existence. As in the case of the Program of Technical Assistance, financial resources are dependent upon voluntary contributions by member countries; total contributions have been modest thus far.[41]

Importantly, total financial resources available to the UN for use in the foregoing programs have been small to date. As a point of reference,

---

[41] Actually, the Special Projects Fund stems from an earlier proposal, the Special United Nations Fund for Economic Development (SUNFED), initially offered by a group of underdeveloped countries (and of considerable interest within the UN Organization during 1953 and immediately thereafter).

As proposed, SUNFED was to have an initial capitalization of $250 million, derived from among the membership of the UN (the US being the largest contributor in any event). Lending was to be exclusively for purposes of economic development, and was to be long-term and low-interest in nature. Some grant aid was also to be available. In general, capital assistance was to be offered on a basis somewhat more liberal than that characteristic of the International Bank.

The SUNFED proposal, as initially outlined, did not secure the backing of the US. This country was reluctant to throw itself open to the financial obligations associated, or likely to be invited over time. Allegedly as a sidetracking tactic, the US at one point offered to provide, instead, additional funds for a "beefed up" technical-assistance program—and, subsequently (in 1958), support was lent to the more "conservative" proposal for a Special Projects Fund. In any event, with the introduction of the Special Projects Fund, which offered hope for additional technical assistance and *some* capital assistance under UN auspices, interest in the SUNFED proposal largely ceased.

For a summary and discussion of the SUNFED proposal, see UN, *Report on a Special United Nations Fund for Economic Development,* New York, 1953.

the UN in late 1959 placed its goal for funds for the following year, for
the combined programs, at $100 million.[42] Whatever funds are available
are the result of voluntary contributions by member countries, and accrue
in various currencies. The largest single contributor to date has been the
US. In late 1959, the US pledged itself to supply $40 million for the
ensuing year, but with the understanding that any contribution by it was
not to exceed 40% of the total raised by other members.[43]

COLOMBO PLAN

The Colombo Plan for Cooperative Economic Development of South
and Southeast Asia came into being in 1950. Essentially, the Plan began
as a British endeavor, but was multilateralized shortly thereafter. Membership by 1959 totaled 18 countries, and included the US.[44] Membership
encompassed, basically, two types of countries: donor and recipient—the
common consideration linking them being location in or vital interest in
South and Southeast Asia.

The Plan itself provides no assistance directly. Rather, the function of
the Plan is that of *coordination*. The coordination sought refers to the
development plans being formulated by underdeveloped countries within
the Colombo Plan area (South and Southeast Asia); to the financial assistance provided on a bilateral basis to underdeveloped countries within the
Colombo Plan area by more highly developed countries outside the area,
or provided on a multilateral basis by international institutions; and to
the exchange of technical assistance among the member countries.

The principal machinery of the Colombo Plan is the Consultative Committee, which meets annually to review and assess what has been accomplished and to evaluate the task and problems in the period ahead. The
Consultative Committee publishes an annual report on its findings.

Assistance in all forms, and through all routes, provided recipient
members by donor members during the period 1950–59 totaled the equivalent of roughly $6 billion, the great bulk of this amount stemming from
the US on a bilateral basis.[45]

INTER-AMERICAN DEVELOPMENT BANK

In addition to participation in the foregoing international arrangements for the provision of assistance to underdeveloped countries, the US

---

42 *The New York Times,* October 9, 1959, p. 3-C.

43 *Ibid.* The US payment is derived from funds allotted under the Mutual Security
Program.

44 Besides the US, members include Australia, Burma, Cambodia, Canada, Ceylon,
India, Indonesia, Japan, Laos, Malaya, Nepal, New Zealand, Pakistan, the Philippines,
South Viet-Nam, Thailand, and the United Kingdom (together with Singapore and
British Borneo).

45 Sizable as this amount is, it represented only a small fraction of the magnitude
of domestic investment effort sustained by the recipient countries themselves.

during 1959 assumed membership in a new *regional* institution, the Inter-American Development Bank. The new institution, embracing two agencies, the Inter-American Development Bank and the Fund for Special Operations (commonly referred to together as the Inter-American Development Bank), is directly concerned only with the Western Hemisphere, i.e., with Latin America and the US.

ORIGINS

Throughout the 1950's, considerable sentiment existed on behalf of regional approaches to the solution of pressing problems affecting under-developed countries. Nowhere was this sentiment more pronounced than in Latin America. A common impression there was that existing institutional arrangements tended to favor other underdeveloped regions over Latin America; as proof, reference was frequently made to the small portion of total capital assistance being placed in Latin America. Accordingly, the notion took hold within Latin America that the region ought to have some new institutional arrangements of its own, thereby to assure itself of desired developmental assistance.

A formal resolution, calling for study of the matter of formation of an Inter-American Development Bank, was approved at a meeting of the Inter-American Economic and Social Council, held in Brazil in late 1954. The proposed study was made and was submitted in 1955 for the approval of member countries of the Organization of American States.[46] Following this early flurry, little further of a basic nature occurred for several years. Not until 1958, following a visit to Latin America by Vice-President Nixon (during the course of whose tour disturbances occurred in Peru and Venezuela), did serious attention again come to be directed to the matter. In August of that year the US Government announced that it would be willing to join in the formation of an Inter-American Development Institution.[47] The hopes of Latin America were thereby aroused, and considerable discussion promptly followed.[48] A major point that came under discussion, and that automatically involved the US, related to the type and scope of operations to be held appropriate for any projected institutional arrangements.[49]

---

[46] The study recommended that a Bank be established, with capital set at $200 million, one-third to be subscribed by the US and two-thirds to be subscribed by countries of Latin America. See IMF, *International Financial News Survey*, Washington, June 17, 1955.

[47] See "A New Hemispheric Policy" (editorial), *The New York Times*, August 15, 1958, p. 20-C.

[48] President Kubitschek of Brazil, for example, outlined a six-point plan for a broad attack on Latin America's economic problems. The Kubitschek plan had grown out of an exchange of letters between him and US Government officials. The plan ushered in what came to be known as *Operation Pan American*, and provided the basis for a conference of The Committee of Twenty-One, held in Washington commencing in November 1958. See *The New York Times*, November 17, 1958, p. 1-L.

[49] See, especially, *The New York Times*, November 19, 1958, p. 1-L, and January 11, 1959, p. 1-L.

By April of 1959, the 21 American republics (acting through the OAS) had completed a charter for a new Inter-American Development Bank of $1 billion capitalization, intended to assist Latin America in its developmental efforts.[50] Following formal ratification by the requisite number of governments, the new institution came into being in January 1960.[51] Specifically, the new institution gave rise to two separate but complementary agencies, an Inter-American Development Bank and a Fund for Special Operations, each with headquarters in Washington.

INTER-AMERICAN DEVELOPMENT BANK

The purpose of the Bank, according to its Charter, is "to contribute to the acceleration of the process of economic development of the member countries, individually and collectively." To this end, the Bank is empowered to engage in lending on its own, and also to guarantee loans made by governments and public or private lending institutions.

Capitalization of the Bank totals $850 million, with $400 million to be supplied in annual installments during the initial 3 years, and with $450 million remaining callable. The US contribution is $350 million, with $150 million to be supplied during the initial 3 years, and with $200 million remaining callable. The scheduled contributions of countries in Latin America are in accordance with relative weights assigned under the IMF procedure. The US contribution is payable in gold and dollars, while the contributions of other members are payable 50% in gold and US dollars and 50% in applicable local currencies. In addition to capital resources acquired through paid-in contributions, the Bank is authorized to offer its own bonds in the general capital market; the expectation, however, is that the sale of bonds will not be attempted during the early years.

The avowed intent is to restrict the Bank's lending very largely to "wealth-producing" projects, meaning those capable of being self-liquidating. Repayment is to occur in the currency medium lent, so that evolution of a revolving fund becomes a possibility. Loan terms are to be comparable, in general, with those applied by regular commercial banks. The hope is to use the Bank's resources to supplement other capital sources, and to avoid duplication and competition.

Viewed in an overall sense, the Bank—in its organization and intended operations—is roughly comparable, *on a regional basis,* with the International Bank.

FUND FOR SPECIAL OPERATIONS

The major purpose of the companion agency, the Fund, is to undertake loans for projects normally regarded as posing unacceptable bank risk.

---

[50] For press comment, see *The New York Times,* April 9, 1959, p. 1-C, and "A Bank for the Hemisphere" (editorial), April 10, 1959, p. 28-C.
[51] IMF, *International Financial News Survey,* Washington, January 8, 1960.

Such loans are expected to involve projects deemed "socially useful," but not necessarily self-liquidating. Associated loan terms are expected to be easier than those offered by the Bank, with local-currency repayment being usual. In addition to the provision of financing, the Fund is empowered to offer technical assistance.

Capitalization of the Fund totals $150 million. Of this amount, the US allotment is $100 million, with the remaining $50 million applicable to the aggregate of all other members. Of the total, 50% is held payable at the outset, and the remainder remains callable as needed. All contributions are to occur in gold and US dollars.

APPRAISAL

Not everyone was in sympathy with the proposal for a new lending institution for Latin America. Two main opposing arguments were to be heard amid the widespread clamor for action (but both limited largely to persons within the US). The first rested on the notion that regional approaches, in general, do not offer quite the potential for remedy of the world's ills that enthusiasts would frequently like to picture.[52] The second, and more important, involved the contention that a new institution of the type suggested could do nothing for Latin America but what already-existing institutions *could* do *if* means were placed in their possession and there were a will to act. The contention, further, was that the immediate rationale for the new institution, from the US standpoint, was based not so much on the economic merit of the situation as on political expediency—i.e., the US allegedly was ill-prepared, in global political terms, to meet the desire of Latin America for more attention with anything less than a show of special recognition.

As seen after the fact, however, the consideration perhaps most important is that the institution did come into being, and thereby offers a precedent for other regional banks that might be suggested. Indeed, proposals along these lines exist, e.g., an Arab Development Institution (for the Middle East) and a Far East Development Institution (for the Far East and Southeast Asia).[53]

PRIVATE EFFORTS

The US Government thus provides assistance directly through its own agencies, and indirectly through participation in international arrange-

---

[52] The basic outlines of this argument are cited in Ch. 11, section titled "Regional Development."

[53] A second consideration, regarded in some quarters as highly significant, involves US provision of assistance through the new institution *without* a military rationale being attached, thereby differentiating it from what has characterized US assistance supplied under the Mutual Security Program.

ments. Besides this assistance by government, assistance also occurs on a private basis. Private investment, treated in Chapter 17, consists largely of direct investment, but does encompass some portfolio investment. A particular category of private foreign investment, not previously identified separately, involves that supplied by private American business enterprises, operating on a loan basis, and by private American philanthropic organizations, operating on a grant basis.

LOANS

The American Overseas Finance Corporation provides an example of a private American loan agency geared to lend for development, and for other purposes, on a profit-making basis. The AOFC was formed in 1955 by a small group of large American commercial banks, and participation was later expanded to include several large American business enterprises as well.[54]

The larger part of the AOFC's business has involved financing of American exports through acceptance by the institution of the notes of foreign importers. These financial transactions generally have merited the rating of developmental loans, since funds provided in most instances have covered sales of machinery intended for use in developmental efforts. Typically, the AOFC has provided financing to cover up to 60% of the amount of the sale, leaving the foreign buyer and the American exporter responsible for financing the remainder (generally with the foreign buyer making a down payment of 20% and the American exporter carrying 20% on his own). A second and growing part of the AOFC's business has involved financing aimed at the initiation or expansion of foreign private enterprises. This financing has been either on a "loan" basis (involving the receipt of notes bearing fixed interest) or on an "investment" basis (involving the receipt of securities giving subsequent claim to profits).

Loans normally run up to 5 years in duration, with the minimum amount per loan held to around $20,000. Loans of considerably larger magnitude are generally approached by the AOFC through the formation of a syndicate, involving an invitation for other banks and investors to participate in financing.

GRANTS

A particular facet of the operations of the Ford Foundation provides an example of a private American effort geared to supply grant aid for development. The Foundation periodically provides funds to support

---

[54] For a good description of the AOFC and its operations, see *The New York Times*, January 8, 1958, p. 66-C. Business enterprises cited as being linked to the AOFC include the Rockefeller Brothers' International Basic Economy Corporation, CIT Financial Corporation, Trans-Oceanic Development Corporation, the General Tire and Rubber Company, and the Chesapeake and Ohio Railway Company.

technical assistance to foreign areas in fields such as education, health, agriculture, public administration, and community development. Funds are used largely for salaries of technicians, although some amounts are used for the procurement of demonstration equipment and absorption of administrative overhead.

APPRAISAL

Private assistance of the type under discussion here is worthy of commendation, insofar as it occurs. A pertinent fact, however, is that total outlay along these lines is small, so that total effort and impact following from it tend to be of only token scope when viewed against the task at hand. Technical assistance is less vulnerable on this score than is capital assistance, largely because it is less costly, thereby permitting more of a "dent" to be made with given limited outlays. Capital assistance provided on this basis, however, is of such an aggregate magnitude that overall impact tends to be only minimal, no matter how illustrious particular sample projects may appear to be.

Some persons see a danger in private approaches to organized developmental assistance. These persons fear that the American public, receptively inclined as it tends to be toward private approaches, is likely to be misled as to what is being accomplished when it hears accounts about a *few* successful private-assistance operations abroad. Specifically, the public might conclude that "things are being taken care of," thereby diminishing popular enthusiasm for the big (and costly) governmentally-sponsored programs called for if truly large-scale impact is to be registered abroad.

SOME PROPOSALS

Notwithstanding the diversity of institutions and programs through which the US currently is committed to provide assistance to the underdeveloped world, several proposals for institutional additions still remain unacted upon. Of these, the following appear most important.

INTERNATIONAL DEVELOPMENT ASSOCIATION

In addition to the IFC, a second international lending institution *subsidiary* to the International Bank has been proposed: the International Development Association. The intended objective of the IDA is to provide loan capital for development in underdeveloped countries, but to do so on easier terms and for additional purposes than those that currently characterize the business of the Bank. In essence, the IDA is expected to bear a relationship to the International Bank similar to that which the DLF bears to the Export-Import Bank.

Initial impetus for the establishment of the IDA stemmed from statements by Senator A. S. (Mike) Monroney early in 1958—as a result of which the proposal, in its earlier stages, was frequently referred to as the Monroney Plan.[55] While early reaction appeared mixed, a decision by the US Government, in late 1958, to offer its endorsement represented a turning point,[56] leading to a series of actions intended to culminate in the formal introduction at an early date of the proposed institution.

Two main considerations are generally regarded as responsible for the official support lent by the US. First, the proposed institution was viewed as offering a way by means of which additional resources held available in other developed countries could be channeled toward underdeveloped countries, thereby helping, possibly, to take some of the burden of foreign aid off the US. Specifically, it was felt that currencies supplied by countries of Western Europe and Japan might thereby be routed to potential borrowers, and that these might give borrowers access to developmental ingredients in some uses just as readily as might dollars supplied by the US.[57] Second, the proposed institution was viewed as an outlet for a portion of the foreign currencies derived by the US in its sale abroad of surplus agricultural commodities.[58]

Capitalization proposed for the IDA is the equivalent of $1 billion, with the projected US subscription placed at $330 million. Loan terms are expected to be generally easier than those provided by the Bank, e.g., longer maturities, lower interest rates, and some eligibility for local-currency repayment.

REGIONAL INSTITUTIONS

The year 1959 witnessed the process of formalization of the Inter-American Development Bank. Remaining unacted upon, however, were proposals for two additional regional institutions: an Arab Development Institution and a Far East Development Institution. Each proposal envisaged a financial institution financed jointly by the US and the countries within the particular region, and geared in its operations to the promotion of development within that region.

The special rationale for an Arab Development Institution rests on the hope for a better utilization within the Middle East of resources already present there. Of central importance, the hope is that a regional institution might provide the framework through which the petroleum earnings of a few countries can be made available for the support of development in any or all of the countries within the region.

---

[55] See *The New York Times,* February 23, 1958, p. 1-L.

[56] *The New York Times,* December 8, 1958, p. 1-C.

[57] See "Change in 'Foreign Aid'" (editorial), *The New York Times,* September 30, 1959, p. 34-M.

[58] *The Des Moines Register,* October 2, 1959, p. 25.

The special rationale for a Far East Development Institution rests on the hope for a fuller usage of Japanese capital, especially, in the developmental efforts of various capital-poor underdeveloped countries in the Far East and Southeast Asia. This possibility appears eminently reasonable, according to the rationale, since the economy of Japan is basically complementary to the economies of the other countries within the region.

In the case of either of the proposed regional institutions, a feature of possible appeal for the US involves the fact that any capital within the region that comes to be used *in lieu* of capital the US Government would otherwise have to supply means that much less burden upon the American economy (or increases total capital available to capital-deficient countries by that much).

SELECTED BIBLIOGRAPHY

Colombo Plan

Department of State, *The Colombo Plan,* Washington, 1958.
Handbook on what the Colombo Plan is and how it works.

Development Loan Fund

International Development Advisory Board, *A New Emphasis on Economic Development Abroad,* Washington, March 1957.
Presentation of the rationale for creation of the Development Loan Fund.

Legislation on Foreign Relations (Printed for the use of the Senate Committee on Foreign Relations), Washington, 1957.
Legislation relative to the Development Loan Fund (see esp. pp. 11, 95).

Export-Import Bank

Export-Import Bank of Washington, *Report to the Congress,* Washington, 1959. (Also issues covering other years.)
Summary information on policies and operations.

Hearing before the Committee on Banking and Currency, U.S. Senate (on S.3149), Washington, 1958.
Testimony relating to "Increased Export-Import Bank Lending Authority."

Olin S. Pugh, *The Export-Import Bank of Washington* (Columbia, S.C.: University of South Carolina, Bureau of Business and Economic Research), June 1957.
A history of the Export-Import Bank; includes analysis of operations.

International Bank

International Bank for Reconstruction and Development, *Fourteenth Annual Report, 1958–1959,* Washington, 1959. (Also issues covering other years.)
Summary information on policies and operations.

_____, *Summary Proceedings* (Annual Meeting of the Board of Governors), Washington, 1959. (Also Proceedings covering other years.)
Analysis of current problems confronting the Bank.

International Finance Corporation

International Finance Corporation, *Third Annual Report, 1958–1959*, Washington, 1959. (Also issues covering other years.)
Summary information on policies and operations.

International Monetary Fund

International Monetary Fund, *Annual Report, 1959*, Washington, 1959. (Also issues covering other years.)
Examination of world currency and exchange-rate problems.

_____, *Tenth Annual Report on Exchange Restrictions, 1959*, Washington, 1959. (Also issues covering other years.)
Summary of exchange restrictions in effect in various countries; contains comments by the Fund on the status of exchange restrictions.

United Nations

United Nations, *Report on a Special United Nations Fund for Economic Development*, New York, 1953.
Examination of the SUNFED proposal.

_____, *The United Nations Special Fund*, New York, 1959.
Handbook on what the Special Fund is and how it works.

20

FOREIGN AID (I)

As pointed out in Chapter 16, the contribution of the American economy toward the task of development in the underdeveloped world occurs through some combination of effort in the realms of *trade, investment,* and *aid.* Thereafter, in Chapters 16–19, attention was directed to the record of trade and investment, covering investment through both private and public channels. The conclusion suggested, in each instance, was that a somewhat bigger or better contribution is within the capabilities of the American economy. While under present-day conditions no one avenue alone appeared to offer scope for a solution to the problem of meeting the external-assistance needs associated with development in underdeveloped countries, the totality of these avenues appeared to offer substantial further opportunity—even if not the basis for what might reasonably be regarded a final answer.

In any event, the present-day contribution of the American economy in the realms of trade and investment is regarded by the US Government as inadequate, as measured by what is believed needed to facilitate the achievement of the country's foreign-policy objectives. This fact is evidenced by the country's willingness to provide *aid.* Viewed broadly, any contribution of the American economy on behalf of the economies of other countries could be labeled aid, so that even private direct investment might thereby be encompassed; however, the term is reserved here particularly for that assistance which occurs under the formal and specialized US foreign-aid program, the Mutual Security Program. As intimated earlier, this Program encompasses two operating agencies: the International Cooperation Administration and the Development Loan Fund (with special reference to the

DFL occurring in Ch. 18, along with the Export-Import Bank, for reasons cited there).

The present chapter and the one following (Chs. 20 and 21) treat the foreign-aid program of the US. The present chapter is devoted to a survey of the history of the program, to an examination of the immediate objectives of the program, and to a description of operations under the program (i.e., beyond the special reference relative to the DLF already offered in Ch. 18). The following chapter (Ch. 21) is devoted to major issues associated with the rendering of aid.

HISTORY OF AID

Foreign aid is not a new operation of the US Government. While the Mutual Security Program (MSP), under which foreign aid is dispensed to underdeveloped countries, dates only from 1951, the beginnings of foreign aid, *as a procedure,* are found in a much earlier period, and massive doses of foreign aid—supplied for various reasons—were characteristic of the earlier post-World War II years, prior to the introduction of the MSP.

The history of the US Government's involvement in foreign aid can be divided, basically, into two periods: an early period, covering the relevant years prior to the end of World War II, and a follow-up period, covering the years since World War II. The post-World War II era, in turn, can be divided into three stages, according to points of emphasis prevailing. One stage emphasized foreign aid for purposes of relief and rehabilitation, primarily in war-ravaged areas. A second stage emphasized foreign aid for purposes of long-term economic reconstruction, primarily in Western Europe. A third stage emphasized foreign aid for purposes of mutual security, farflung as to country-coverage, but with heavy attention paid underdeveloped regions.

Succeeding paragraphs survey the history of American foreign aid from its beginnings to 1960. An examination of this history appears to warrant two major conclusions. First, the aid program, as it has come to exist, is the product of an evolutionary process, during the course of which the applicable aid policy has taken various twists and turns. Second, the aid program, in the course of its evolution, has been oriented toward various pressing problems, of which poverty within foreign locales has been only one.

EARLY AID

It is often difficult to pinpoint exactly when a particular type of activity really had its beginnings. This is the case with the US Government's involvement in foreign aid. While room for disagreement as to timing certainly exists, isolated instances can be cited as evidence that the US accepted the idea of foreign aid, *in principle,* many years ago.

A first isolated instance, which might reasonably be selected as the starting point of US foreign aid, pertains to this country's decision relative to the utilization of indemnity payments arising from a settlement with China in 1901, following the Boxer Rebellion.[1] Payments owing the US under the arrangement agreed upon were earmarked for use in defraying educational costs for Chinese nationals. This program of educational assistance was similar, in important respects, to foreign-aid efforts in the education field during recent years, so that the label of aid appears not to be farfetched in the particular instance.

While further efforts, all relatively minor, can be cited as having been initiated during immediately succeeding years, the next major occurrence in the evolution of foreign aid developed in 1933. In that year the US inaugurated the Good-Neighbor Policy relative to Latin America, ostensibly in order to foster hemispheric solidarity. An essential aspect of this Policy pertained to the provision of technical assistance. Two important international conferences followed shortly thereafter,[2] at each of which the 21 American republics formally declared their desire to exchange scientific, technical, cultural, and educational knowledge. Acting in response to these expressions of interest, the Congress in 1939 approved legislation empowering the President to carry out reciprocal undertakings and cooperative agreements within the hemisphere, insofar as these might serve to implement the intents of the Good-Neighbor Policy. Adoption of this legislation was followed by a series of organizational steps, eventuating in 1942 in the formation of the Institute of Inter-American Affairs, organized as a governmental corporation. The basic objectives of the Institute, according to its charter, related to the furtherance of the general welfare of the peoples of the American republics and to the strengthening of friendship and understanding among them. Achievement of these objectives was sought through close collaboration among the governments and governmental agencies of the American republics in the planning and implementation of technical programs and projects, especially in the fields of public health, sanitation, education, and agriculture. As for procedure, any activity supported by the Institute was to proceed under terms of a bilateral agreement, known as a "basic country agreement," entered into by the US Government and the government of each participating country with which it was paired.[3]

---

[1] See W. Krause and M. C. Paxton, *The Point Four Program* (Salt Lake City: University of Utah Press, 1951), p. 10.

[2] The Inter-American Conference for the Maintenance of Peace (Buenos Aires, 1936) and the International Conference of American States (Lima, 1938).

[3] Under the program of the Institute, health and sanitation projects—totaling 1,940 by June 1948—were introduced in all countries of Latin America except Argentina and Cuba. Education projects were introduced in 14 countries, with emphasis placed on the training of teachers later usable at elementary and secondary levels. Agricultural projects were introduced in 10 countries, with effort geared to increase or improve the production of basic foodstuffs. See the Institute of Inter-American Affairs, *The Program of the Institute of Inter-American Affairs*, Washington, 1949, p. 12.

It can be argued that the early foreign-aid operations cited, despite the varied objectives present, did make a contribution toward economic development, although it can also be argued that any such contribution was small, at best. Emphasis in the earlier programs was upon technical assistance, or something akin to technical assistance. They were not big-money programs, since attention was directed to something other than the provision of capital assistance (although, beginning in 1933, the Export-Import Bank was on hand to provide some capital assistance). And, quite apart from the purpose or magnitude of the US contribution, a particular procedural arrangement for the channelization of aid was established as use was made of formalized bilateral agreements.

On the basis of the foregoing, it can be concluded that by the time of World War II the US Government had gotten its "feet wet in the waters of foreign aid." It had shown itself willing, in principle, to extend foreign aid, and it had accepted some procedures as being appropriate in the provision of this aid. It remained for events associated with World War II, however, to turn US foreign aid into a big-money operation. This occurred in short order once this country saw fit to embark upon its program of lend-lease aid.

The Lend-Lease Act, approved by the Congress in March 1941, was intended to place the material support of the American economy behind the countries fighting the Axis powers. The Act authorized the President to "sell, transfer, exchange, lease, lend, or otherwise dispose of" any defense article to any country whose defense he (the President) deemed vital to the interests of the US. Put into effect prior to this country's formal entry into World War II, the lend-lease program was heralded as offering aid "short of war" to "those on our side." Following this country's formal entry into the war, the only major alteration in the program was a stepping-up in the flow of aid. During the period to the end of World War II, the US extended lend-lease aid in excess of $47 billion, 69% of the total going to Great Britain and 25% to the USSR.[4]

At the end of World War II, then, the US had behind it a record of small-scale peacetime aid and large-scale wartime aid. Although assistance for economic development had been a trifling consideration within the total context of what had occurred to that point, the idea that the US

---

[4] A small additional amount was extended between the end of the war and the close of FY 50, bringing total lend-lease aid, wartime and postwar, to $49.1 billion. See Department of Commerce, *Foreign Aid by the United States Government, 1940–1951*, Washington, 1952, for foreign-aid data covering the period immediately before, during, and immediately after World War II.

The Lend-Lease Act provided that final settlement was to be postponed until after the termination of hostilities, and a stipulation was embodied calling for settlement in a manner not likely to impair the international payments structure. Return receipts on the lend-lease extended, through 1959, totaled under $10 billion, including an offset of over $8 billion for so-called reverse lend-lease received by the US. The history of repayment, in general, was that Great Britain appeared "unable" to undertake fuller payment, while the USSR appeared "unwilling" to pay.

could, if it saw fit, offer foreign aid—*for one purpose or another*—had come to be anything but new or likely to shock. And, significantly, before the US loomed the postwar era, a period certain to be fraught with many troubles and problems, but which the US was obliged to face in its strengthened, although perhaps unsought, role as a world economic, political, and military leader.

AID AFTER WORLD WAR II

Foreign aid during the post-World War II era, as intimated earlier, underwent three main phases: aid for relief and rehabilitation; aid for economic reconstruction; and aid for mutual security.

1. *Relief and Rehabilitation.* World War II had wrought havoc in numerous countries, disrupting production and subjecting literally whole populations to privation. The US, long viewed by many people as "a country with a heart," was widely expected to come to the rescue, and these expectations did not prove amiss. The US committed itself very early to help the unfortunate victims of war. It was widely anticipated in the US at the time, however, that the efforts of this country were "special" and would need to cover only a rather short interim period. Actually, this interim period lasted until 1948, after which—somewhat to the surprise of many Americans—another phase of aid operations, supported by another rationale, was regarded as necessary.

During the period of relief and rehabilitation, the US engaged in several major programs. The first involved support lent the United Nations Relief and Rehabilitation Administration (UNRRA). Sponsored by 44 anti-Axis powers, this organization was begun during World War II to provide assistance in countries that were war-damaged in the course of resisting the Axis. Approximately $3.7 billion in assistance, largely in the form of food and medical supplies, was provided between November 1943 and June 1947, some 73% of the total cost being borne by the US. In May 1947, the US initiated a Post-UNRRA Aid Program, providing for additional assistance of $350 million for Austria, Greece, Italy, Trieste, and China.

Alongside the UNRRA Program, the armed forces of the US also rendered foreign aid. Acting through an organizational structure of its own, called Government and Relief in Occupied Areas (GARIOA), it provided roughly $3.2 billion in relief between mid-1945 and late 1948, $1.9 billion for Europe and the remainder for Asia. In an attempt to preclude the possibility of ever-continuing relief at an undiminished level, program emphasis was shifted, beginning with FY 1949, from relief to relief and recovery. The budget for that year embraced $1.2 billion for GARIOA and $150 million for a new and supplemental program, Economic Rehabilitation in Occupied Areas (ERIOA). The succeeding year saw a shift of these activities, as they applied to Europe, to other programs or agencies, and while both GARIOA and ERIOA continued in operation in Asia, a curtailed budget prevailed.

Although the initial postwar rationale for foreign aid was that of relief and rehabilitation for war-devastated and occupied areas, it was not long before additional, but somewhat different, situations arose to present a bid for aid. Importantly, Great Britain, a victor in the recent conflict and situated in a crucial position within the international complex, faced serious postwar economic problems, which problems already appeared to be coming to a head in 1946. In essence, a series of factors had contributed toward an end situation in which the country appeared simply unable to earn its way internationally—as evidenced by a persistent, and even growing, dollar shortage. In the absence of counter-action, devaluation seemed imminent. There appeared, however, to be compelling reasons why the country should not be forced to undergo devaluation. Given the alternatives at hand, the US Government decided to offer assistance in an attempt to bolster Britain's sagging balance-of-payments position, and thereby to rule out the need for devaluation. The assistance was offered in the form of a loan arrangement, the Anglo-American Financial Agreement, negotiated by American and British treasury officials, and ratified by the Congress in July 1946.

Terms of the loan arrangement included (a) agreement by the US to advance $3,750 million to Great Britain over a 4-year period, (b) acceptance by Great Britain of a liability of $650 million by way of settlement for past lend-lease, (c) agreement by Great Britain to repay both amounts, totaling $4,400 million, over a 50-year period, beginning in 1952, with interest at 2%, and (d) agreement by Great Britain to plan for the restoration of full convertibility no later than July 15, 1947. Rising prices on Britain's foreign purchases (accentuated by the repercussions of price decontrol in the US in mid-1946), along with heavy withdrawals by countries having a surplus in their British accounts, caused the loan proceeds to vanish at a pace much more rapid than initially anticipated. This situation, plus a seeming absence of genuine improvement in Britain's international-earnings position, resulted in a new, and even more severe, dollar crisis in 1947. As a consequence, the idea of convertibility by 1947—accepted only with reluctance by the British as a condition of the 1946 loan—was abandoned, and thoughts turned instead to the longer-term assistance needs of an ailing British (and European) economy.

As Britain's international-earnings position failed to improve, her capacity to bear indefinitely the financial burdens associated with carrying out various international commitments assumed in an earlier and happier day began to appear ever more doubtful. The political-military situation in the eastern Mediterranean, an area in which British influence had been great, was a matter of immediate consequence. A decision by the British to retrench in that area threatened to create a power vacuum likely to result in Communist inroads. Accordingly, as the conviction spread in Britain that there was no alternative but to cut back, the US saw fit to take over. Pronouncement of the so-called Truman Doctrine, a policy aimed at containment of Soviet influence, was followed by the Congress' passing the Greek-Turkish Aid Act in May 1947, providing $300 million in military and economic aid for Greece and $100 million in military aid for Turkey.

But as each day passed, economic deterioration—rather than economic improvement—seemed ever more pronounced and widespread, extending throughout and even beyond Western Europe. The view came to be widely held in the US, and elsewhere, that unless this country came through with further assistance in substantial amount and in rapid fashion, the political and economic breakdown of much of the so-called western community was a virtual certainty. As a hasty stopgap measure, pending the formulation of a more deliberate and larger-scale program, the Congress approved the Interim-Aid Program in December 1947, providing $597 million for use in Austria, France, and Italy, all of which were then regarded as on the brink of falling victim to Communist influence.

Thus, the early post-World War II foreign-aid efforts of the US were geared initially toward relief and rehabilitation in war-devastated and occupied areas, but came soon—as previously unforeseen circumstances evolved—to be directed also toward other pressing problems. And, in view of the magnitude and gravity of these other problems that had arisen, a new type of program, supported by a new rationale, appeared necessary.

2. *Economic Reconstruction.* Gross foreign aid rendered by the US between the end of World War II and early 1948 totaled $16.8 billion, $8.1 billion in grants and $8.7 billion in loans.[5] Despite this aid, 1957 was a year of crisis in that the economic recovery of Western Europe especially, which had appeared to progress satisfactorily in earlier postwar days, then gave acute evidence of faltering. Essentially, the economy of Western Europe was geared to earn its way along internationalist lines, but the combination of production shortcomings and payments impediments conspired to make difficult, if not entirely impossible, the smooth and healthy functioning of the system. The key surface manifestation of Western Europe's troubles was its perennial dollar shortage.

Because the economic well-being of Western Europe was regarded as highly important to the US (indeed, to the trading world as a whole), and because adverse economic conditions threatened to provoke major political repercussions inimical to the interests of the US, this country undertook to consider the merits of a larger-scale and longer-run program of aid geared specifically for economic reconstruction, with immediate and primary attention directed to the plight of Western Europe. An

---

5 Department of Commerce, *Survey of Current Business*, Washington, May 1952, Table 1, p. 15. Data are for the period July 1, 1945, to April 3, 1958, and are exclusive of "offsets" to grants.

official "feeler" on the matter was put out in mid-1957 by the then Secretary of State, George C. Marshall, in the course of a commencement address delivered at Harvard University. According to his views expressed there, assistance to Europe should not be "on a piecemeal basis as various crises develop," but should offer potential as "a cure rather than a mere palliative."[6] Public reaction to the views expressed was generally favorable, and steps were promptly initiated by the US, and also by various countries of Western Europe working in close cooperation with the US, to lay the groundwork for a new aid program. This program, the European Recovery Program (or Marshall Plan), was authorized by the Congress under the Economic Cooperation Act, and operations officially commenced April 3, 1948.

The immediate and central objective of the US Government in inaugurating the Marshall Plan was to forestall the spread of Communism in Europe. It was felt that if economic deterioration could be halted and the process of economic recovery renewed, receptivity to Communism would fade. A reversal of economic trends was held dependent upon increased production in the cooperating countries,[7] along with a solution of their external-payments problems. Achievement of these ends, it was realized, would prove costly, and would require concerted effort over at least several years. It was felt, however, that if all went well the need for further "extraordinary" outside assistance might be ended by 1952. In short, proponents of the Marshall Plan regarded the new program as one providing *"aid to end aid."*

Through 1951, the US provided aid totaling $11.4 billion under the Marshall Plan, about 90% as grants and the remainder as loans. Major recipient countries included the United Kingdom (24%), France (20%), Western Germany (11%), and Italy (10%). Exclusive of amounts used to cover freight costs incurred in transmitting goods (amounting to almost 10%), the remainder was used to procure the following major categories of goods: food, feed, and fertilizer (36%), raw materials and semi-manufactured goods (33%), fuel (15%), machinery and vehicles (14%), and miscellaneous items (2%).

The aid was offered, basically, as balance-of-payments assistance. Each recipient country was encouraged to formulate a well-thought-out plan to serve as a guide in its recovery efforts, and an attempt was made to coordinate these individual plans within an overall framework likely to produce recovery for Western Europe as a whole. Insofar as the potential resources of any country were believed clearly inadequate to meet agreed-

---

6 Department of State, *Department of State Bulletin*, Washington, June 15, 1947, p. 1159.
    7 Sixteen in number: Austria, Belgium, Denmark, France, Greece, Iceland, Ireland, Italy, Luxembourg, the Netherlands, Norway, Portugal, Sweden, Switzerland, Turkey, and the United Kingdom.

upon objectives, supplementary resources were to be provided under the Marshall Plan. These supplementary means involved imports, requiring the availability of foreign exchange—hence, the emphasis upon balance-of-payments assistance under the Marshall Plan.

In order to facilitate the incorporation of external assistance, a new technique was devised: the generation of *counterpart funds*. Under this procedure, each recipient country agreed to set aside an amount in its own currency equivalent to the value of the imports received as aid. Aside from a small amount held usable solely for US purposes (e.g., for defraying particular administrative costs), sums accruing as counterpart were used, subject to specific approval by both the US and the aid-receiving country concerned, for purposes deemed compatible with the overall operations and objectives of the Marshall Plan, e.g., to defray local-currency costs of particular projects or operations, or to retire governmental debt.

Viewed in retrospect, the Marshall Plan, if not an unqualified success, appears at least to have been a limited success. The major objective of containing Communism in Europe was realized, although other factors may also have contributed significantly toward this result.[8] Substantial economic improvement occurred during the period of the Marshall Plan, and did so, presumably, in large part because of the assistance received. Production in Western Europe, which during early postwar years stood well below prewar (1938), had risen by 1951 to levels considerably above prewar—roughly 40% above prewar in industry, and roughly 10% above prewar in agriculture.[9] Similarly, Western Europe's dollar shortage, which had stood at an unprecedented $7.6 billion in 1947,[10] appeared well on its way to extinction by 1950.[11] Prospects for an absolute ending of the dollar shortage in the near future were shattered, however, with the advent of new and complicating developments, particularly the outbreak in 1950 of the Korean conflict.

Whatever success can be claimed for the Marshall Plan, the expectation that it would serve as a program of "aid to end aid" was not met. It can be argued, of course, that the expectation might have been met by 1952 had the international scene remained reasonably serene. Be this as it may, the outbreak anew of armed conflict in 1950, even though comprising only a "limited" war, served to create a basically new situation in the

---

8 For example, the North Atlantic Treaty Organization (NATO), which came into being in 1949, linked the US, Canada, and 10 countries of Western Europe in a 20-year mutual-defense alliance.

9 UN, *Economic Survey of Europe in 1951*, Geneva, 1952, p. 21.

10 UN, *Economic Survey of Europe in 1948*, Geneva, 1949, Table 71, p. 112.

11 An accompanying factor of importance was the general devaluation occurring in September 1949. Great Britain devalued the pound sterling by 30.5%, which action was rapidly followed by devaluations of roughly equivalent amounts by 28 additional countries, both in Europe and elsewhere.

light of which previously-held expectations as to the duration of aid merited reappraisal. As a consequence, well before the Marshall Plan's scheduled termination date, the US initiated steps to ensure a continued flow of aid of some magnitude. The immediate rationale for this further aid derived from the extra defense burdens placed upon the economies of a number of countries because of their decision to team up with the US in a joint defense program. The end result was the passage by the Congress, in 1951, of the Mutual Security Act,[12] which authorized further dollar assistance, both as military aid and as economic aid, for various participating countries, located both in Europe and in other areas.

3. *Mutual Security*. The passage of the Mutual Security Act, in 1951, marked the beginning of the third phase of US foreign-aid operations during the post World War II era. The new legislation represented a departure in two major respects. First, emphasis in the regional distribution of aid was shifted from developed countries (Western Europe) to underdeveloped countries. Second, the type of aid offered underwent substantial alteration.

The shift in aid emphasis from developed countries to underdeveloped countries occurred in stages, and in response, basically, to a changing political-military situation in the world. The Marshall Plan had taken form during a period in which the political future of Western Europe appeared in jeopardy. By 1950 or thereabouts, the containment of Communism in Europe appeared to have been achieved. Meanwhile, however, the political situation had become destabilized in Asia. First, Mainland China had fallen (and the Nationalist Government had withdrawn to Taiwan); then, Indochina had been ravaged by conflict (ending in the loss to the Communists of North Viet-Nam, and in the division of the remainder of Indochina into three states: South Viet-Nam, Cambodia, and Laos); and, finally, the Korean crisis arose (bringing forth military counter-action under United Nations auspices in an attempt to draw a halt to further Communist inroads). Many persons reached the conclusion that the Communist movement, blocked in Europe, had turned its primary attention to other regions, and especially to Asia at this juncture in history.

All indications appeared to be that the underdeveloped regions, whose economic shortcomings were numerous and notorious (and which, consequently, seemed to be especially vulnerable in a political sense), would comprise the new battleground in the "cold war." The considerable political disintegration already a matter of record in the Far East was widely regarded as a forewarning of what might also happen elsewhere, con-

---

[12] The Mutual Security Act established the Mutual Security Agency (MSA), the first of the successor agencies of the Economic Cooperation Administration (ECA). In 1953, the work of the MSA was assumed by the Foreign Operations Administration (FOA), which was succeeded, in turn, by the International Cooperation Administration (ICA) in 1955.

ceivably on an even larger scale, if new and grave crises were allowed to develop or to run their course unimpeded by counter-action. Accordingly, faced by this possibility, the US undertook to reorient its foreign-aid program. The initial shift of emphasis from Western Europe was to the Far East (occurring in response to the exigencies of the immediate situation prevailing in that region), but gradually—in the course of adapting to a sequence of situations or anticipated situations—the foreign-aid program came to be more and more a global program, encompassing relatively numerous countries throughout Asia, Africa, and Latin America, as well as some countries in Europe. While Western Europe did not come to be totally excluded from further aid, the great bulk of assistance was henceforth rendered countries in the underdeveloped category.

Apart from the regional shift in emphasis, the foreign-aid program also underwent important changes in content. As the focal point shifted from Western Europe to underdeveloped countries, the basic problem at issue called for attack along different lines. As a consequence, given the need to tailor operations to fit the new locales, a fundamentally new type of aid program was evolved during the early 1950's. Appropriate or inappropriate, the revamped aid program arising during this period placed in existence an overall pattern that, with some modifications,[13] continued in effect for the remainder of the decade.

The aid program, as it had come to be constituted, incorporated both military aid *and* economic aid, with qualifying countries able to receive either or both (Fig. 10). Actual aid outlays during the period 1951–59 averaged slightly under $4 billion per year, divided roughly equally between military and economic. To be sure, provision of aid on a dual military-economic basis represented no basic change for the US; but, the economic portion of the revamped program did reflect important departures, occasioned by the shift in emphasis to new locales characterized by different environmental factors.

Important new elements that came to figure in the economic portion of the program were four in number. First, the shift in emphasis from Western Europe to the underdeveloped world involved a parallel shift in emphasis from *reconstruction* to *development*. Because development called for a course of action substantially different from that followed when reconstruction was the task, the aid program was placed under pressure to unearth and introduce numerous subsidiary adaptations relative to its operations. Moreover, the overall task cut out for the aid program appeared considerably enlarged, for development unquestionably posed a far greater challenge than had reconstruction.

Second, the shift in emphasis to development evoked an attempt to

---

13 One major modification, occurring in 1957, involved the inauguration of the Development Loan Fund as an integral part of the MSP (see Ch. 18).

achieve *centralization* under aid-program auspices of various means available to this country in its effort to cope with the task of development.
Specifically, the aid program was organized to allow the provision of both
capital assistance and technical assistance, with some countries receiving
thereafter both capital assistance and technical assistance, but with others
receiving only technical assistance. The technical-assistance portion of the
program was carried forward from the so-called Point Four Program,
proposed by President Truman in 1949[14] and enacted into law by the
Congress with passage of the Foreign Economic Assistance Act of 1950.[15]
The case for the provision of technical assistance under auspices of *the*
foreign-aid program was largely non-existent when emphasis had been
upon reconstruction (involving developed countries), but with the shift
in emphasis to development (involving underdeveloped countries), a
much stronger case for the provision of technical assistance, especially
as an accompaniment of capital assistance, came into being.

Third, the shift in emphasis from reconstruction to development raised
the specter of *long-continuing* foreign aid. Reconstruction could be
thought of as an essentially *short-run* task (likely to require no more than
several years), but development posed a *long-run* task (conceivably requiring 20 or 40 or more years). While appropriations by the Congress
following the shift in emphasis continued to be made available on an
annual basis, with no official guarantee that the program would not face
sudden termination, programming operations conducted by those responsible for administration proceeded on the assumption of a continuing program.[16] Not until 1955, when President Eisenhower had occa-

---

14 "Point Four," dealing with the role of technical assistance in the development
of underdeveloped countries, was the last of four ingredients cited by President Truman
in his Inaugural Address of January 20, 1949, as being essential in the formulation of
a foreign economic policy for the US. The President stated in part: "We must embark
on a bold new program for making the benefits of our scientific advances and industrial progress available for the improvement and growth of underdeveloped areas.
Greater production is the key to prosperity and peace. And the key to greater
production is a wider and more vigorous application of modern scientific and technical
knowledge." See Department of State, *Department of State Bulletin,* Washington,
January 30, 1949, p. 125.

15 Title IV of this law, labeled an "Act for International Development," contained
the following policy statement: ". . . it is declared to be the policy of the United
States to aid the efforts of the peoples of economically underdeveloped areas to
develop their resources and improve their working and living conditions by encouraging the exchange of technical knowledge and skills and the flow of investment capital
to countries which provide conditions under which such technical assistance and
capital can effectively and constructively contribute to raising standards of living,
creating new sources of wealth, increasing productivity, and expanding purchasing
power."

16 Projects of multi-year duration were undertaken (following bilateral agreement
to proceed) in the expectation that those portions of total cost falling within future
years could be met from appropriations made available in the future years. Because
there was less than complete certainty as to these future appropriations, however, a
clause was inserted in each project agreement stating clearly that continuation of the
project was dependent upon availability of funds.

Fig. 10.   The Mutual Security Program, FY 1961

Source: Department of State (and others), The Mutual Security Program, *Washington, March 1960, pp. 10–11. Country coverage shown refers to the FY 61 program proposed to the Congress (which coverage conforms with country programs in effect during the first half of CY 60).*

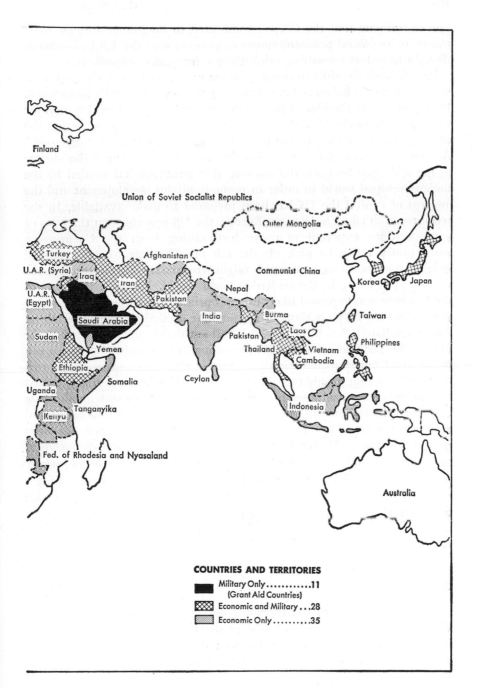

Finland

Union of Soviet Socialist Republics

Outer Mongolia

Turkey
U.A.R. (Syria)
Iraq
U.A.R. (Egypt)
Saudi Arabia
Sudan
Yemen
Ethiopia
Uganda
Kenya
Tanganyika
Fed. of Rhodesia and Nyasaland

Afghanistan
Iran
Pakistan
Nepal
India
Pakistan
Ceylon

Communist China

Korea
Japan

Burma
Laos
Thailand
Vietnam
Cambodia

Taiwan
Philippines

Indonesia

Somalia

Australia

COUNTRIES AND TERRITORIES

Military Only 11
(Grant Aid Countries)
Economic and Military . . . 28
Economic Only 35

sion to intimate that the US was committed to long-range foreign aid,[17] was there an official pronouncement to indicate that the US Government thought of aid as something other than a temporary expedient.

Fourth, with the shift in emphasis from reconstruction to development, the idea of aid as balance-of-payments assistance was generally abandoned. In its place arose the idea of *project assistance*. No formal explanation for the change was offered, although various statements made following the change appeared to imply that project assistance is somehow "very good." A common non-official explanation, however, has attributed the change to the wide gap between the amount of external capital needed by the underdeveloped world in order to promote all-out development and the amount of capital the US has been prepared to make available. In the reconstruction effort in Western Europe, the US was able—on the basis of appropriations expected to prove forthcoming from the Congress—to agree pretty much to pick up the tab on whatever foreign-exchange deficits the countries concerned might reasonably encounter. In the development effort in the underdeveloped world, however, the amount the Congress was expected likely to appropriate under the best of circumstances seemed *very* far short of the amount needed to cover the tab on foreign-exchange deficits arising, *were* all-out development pushed in the face of the peculiar environment prevailing. The conclusion, which can be derived from an explanation presented in the foregoing terms, appears to have been that an aid-providing country, whenever it is not prepared to bear the cost as computed on one basis, should simply seek an alternate basis for calculation—in the hope that a lower liability might result and also prove acceptable. The alternate basis in this instance has been project assistance. Under it, aid—either capital assistance or technical assistance, or both—has been tied to some variable number of specific projects, each initiated and justified[18] on the basis of a particular ill it is expected to remedy. But one ill not faced directly under the approach has been that of an *overall* and persistent foreign-exchange shortage, which may well comprise *the* major block to successful stepped-up development.[19]

OBJECTIVES OF AID

As is apparent from the foregoing survey of foreign-aid history, the US gave only little attention to the promotion of economic development in underdeveloped countries prior to the introduction of the Mutual Security Program. But, even the MSP did not direct its undivided atten-

---

[17] See Ch. 16, esp. footnote 19.

[18] *Justified* in terms of a rationale regarded as compatible with the covering Mutual Security legislation.

[19] See again Chs. 3 and 4, "Obstacles to Development."

tion to this task. Rather, the MSP represented a "mixed" program, with developmental facets existing alongside other program facets. Given this situation, a question arises as to the precise nature of the US Government's rationale for foreign aid under the MSP. Unless this rationale is understood, a misdirected appraisal of the program, very possibly followed by erroneous conclusions, is an ever-present danger.

The rationale underlying the MSP is that of promotion of *mutual* security (as between the US and the various aid-receiving countries), involving an objective that is *political-military* in nature.[20] Under the operational approach employed, this country renders both military aid (to those countries willing to join with this country in a common, or similarly-oriented, military-defense effort) and economic aid (to help poor countries undertake or accelerate programs of economic development or growth, thereby to build a bulwark against political or military deterioration in these countries[21]). With the major overall objective one that is expressed in political-military terms, the primary justification for economic aid comes to be cast in terms of its merit as an implementary device in the course of striving toward attainment of the political-military objective. While the economic aid being rendered under the program may well provide a powerful stimulus for economic development in underdeveloped countries, the official justification for this economic aid nevertheless *is not that of promotion of economic development for the sake of economic development,* but rather it is that of promotion of economic development for the sake of facilitating attainment of another and paramount objective, expressible in political-military terms.[22]

Thus, for the US, attainment of mutual security is *the* objective, and provision of economic aid for the promotion of economic development represents simply *one* means relied upon to help achieve this objective. But, it can also be argued that for the country receiving economic aid, the economic development accruing therefrom, whatever the rationale invoked by the giver, appears nonetheless real.

STATISTICAL RESUME: 1945–1958

Data appearing in Tables 22, 23, and 24 show the magnitude, purpose, and distribution of US foreign-aid expenditures during the period from mid-1945 through March 31, 1958.

---

[20] The opening statement of the Mutual Security Act reads as follows: "An Act to promote the security and *foreign policy of the United States* by furnishing assistance to friendly nations, and for other purposes." (Italics are mine.)

[21] Economic aid is available to neutrals as well as to countries allied with the US. Aid for neutrals is held justified, in terms of the overall rationale, in that promotion of a stronger economy helps a country to ward off unwanted political influences.

[22] See again Ch. 16 for other comment on the role of the foreign-aid program within the total context of US foreign economic policy.

MAGNITUDE

During the period covered, foreign-aid expenditures (net) totaled $63.3 billion (Table 22). Of this amount, $52 billion (82%) was in grants and $11.3 billion (18%) was in credits (loans). The annual rate of expenditure approximated $4.9 billion during the period, with the expenditure for CY 1957, the most recent full year encompassed, totaling $4.5 billion.

Table 22.   United States Foreign Aid, Grants and Credits, 1945–1958 (In millions of US dollars)

	July 1, 1945 through March 31, 1958	CY 1957
Grants[1]	52,029	4,122
Credits[2]	11,314	346
Total	63,343	4,468

Source: Department of Commerce, Foreign Grants and Credits by the United States Government, Washington, June 1958, Table 2, p. S-5. The grants and credits shown represent transfers of goods and services or cash payments to foreign account, but do not include the accumulation of foreign claims from the sale of surplus agricultural commodities for foreign currencies. All amounts are net.

[1] Gross grants totaled $56.1 billion from mid-1945 through March 31, 1958; deduction of $2.3 billion for prior grants converted into credits and $1.8 billion for reverse grants and returns yields the net total of $52 billion.

[2] New credits (loans) totaled $14 billion from mid-1945 through March 31, 1958; addition of $2.3 billion for prior grants converted into credits and deduction of $5 billion for principal collections yields the net total of $11.3 billion. New credits totaled $981 million during CY 57; deduction of $635 million for principal collections yields the net total of $346 million.

PURPOSE

Of the expenditures (net) during the period, $21.7 billion (34%) was for military purposes, all in grants, and $41.6 billion (66%) was for non-military purposes, 72% in grants and 28% in credits (Table 23). During CY 1957, military aid accounted for 56% of the total, and non-military aid for 44%.

DISTRIBUTION

While Western Europe was the major recipient of aid during the full period under discussion (largely because of emphasis lent by the Marshall Plan), underdeveloped countries have been the major beneficiaries during the more recent years, as typified in the distribution prevailing during CY 1957 (Table 24). Western Europe's share, amounting to 59% for the full period, was but 31% during CY 1957; on the other hand, the

Table 23. United States Foreign Aid, Military and Non-Military,
1945–1958 (In millions of US dollars)

	July 1, 1945 through March 31, 1958	CY 1957
Military:		
Grants	21,705	2,508
Non-military:[1]		
Grants[2]	30,324	1,614
Credits[3]	11,314	346
Total	63,343	4,468

Source: Department of Commerce, Foreign Grants and Credits by the United States Government, Washington, June 1958, Table 2, p. S-5. All amounts are net.

[1] Non-military grants and credits include all defense support, relief, development, and technical-cooperation assistance, encompassing all cash transfers to foreign governments except the contributions to the multilateral-construction program of the North Atlantic Treaty Organization and for mutual weapons development.
[2] Less conversions.
[3] Including conversions.

portion going to Asia-Africa-Latin America was 37% for the full period, but amounted to 65% during CY 1957.

AID OPERATIONS UNDER THE MUTUAL SECURITY PROGRAM

As intimated earlier, events occurring during the early 1950's were responsible for a marked shift in the allocation of foreign aid toward the underdeveloped world, where emphasis in the program remained thereafter. The following section is devoted to a description of some major operational aspects of the foreign-aid program as it came to prevail during this most recent period (focusing upon FY's 1952–60).

BASIC OUTLINES

The foreign-aid program—referring here exclusively to that segment of US foreign-aid activities conducted under the MSP—embraces assistance, as of 1960, to 65 countries and 9 territories (Fig. 10). Among the countries covered, 52 can be classified as underdeveloped (as measured by standards applied in Table 2 in Ch. 1). Among these, 25 receive both military aid and economic aid, 25 receive only economic aid, and 2 receive only military aid.

Table 24. United States Foreign Aid, by Area, 1945–1958
(In millions of US dollars)

AREA	Total Grants and Credits[1]		Military Grants		Non-military Grants and Credits[1]	
	July 1, 1945, through March 31, 1958	CY 1957	July 1, 1945, through March 31, 1958	CY 1957	July 1, 1945, through March 31, 1958	CY 1957
Western Europe[2]	37,475	1,399	12,543	1,072	24,932	327
Eastern Europe	1,113	14	....	....	1,113	14
Near East, Africa and South Asia[3]	7,355	866	3,113	523	4,241	343
Other Asia and Pacific	14,158	1,720	5,448	822	8,710	898
American Republics	1,839	338	383	66	1,457	272
Canada	−7	−1	....	....	−7	−1
Other[4]	1,408	131	217	25	1,191	106
Total	63,343	4,468	21,705	2,508	41,638	1,960

Source: Department of Commerce, Foreign Grants and Credits by the United States Government, Washington, June 1958, Table 2, pp. S-5-S-19. Components do not add to totals in all instances, because of rounding.

1 Net grants are minus conversions; net credits include conversions.
2 Excludes Greece and Turkey; includes dependent areas.
3 Includes Greece and Turkey.
4 Includes international organizations and unspecified areas.

410

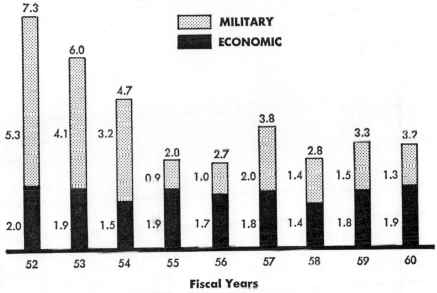

Fig. 11. Foreign-Aid Appropriations under the Mutual Security Program, Military and Economic, FY's 1952–1960 (In billions of US dollars)

Fiscal Years

Source. International Cooperation Administration. Funds earmarked as defense support are included under economic aid.

Total aid appropriated by the Congress for use under the MSP, FY's 1952–60, ranged from $2.7 billion to $7.3 billion per year (Fig. 11), averaging roughly $4 billion per year. The military-economic ratio has altered substantially during the period, revealing a shift from military aid to economic aid; during FY's 1952–54, only one-third of the total appropriated consisted of economic aid, but during more recent years the split has been roughly 50–50.

The shift in the economic portion of assistance during this period was generally toward underdeveloped countries, with only a token amount during the later years going to countries not in the underdeveloped category (Fig. 12). The shift in the economic portion of assistance was most pronounced toward Asia. Since FY 1954, the Far East has been the major recipient region, with South Korea, South Viet-Nam, and Nationalist China (Taiwan) being the three countries most important (in the order named) in terms of the amount of aid received. While Asia has loomed foremost during recent years in terms of the absolute magnitude of aid, amounts destined for Africa and Latin America have shown the greatest increase on a percentage basis during the latest years shown.

Fig. 12. Regional Distribution of Economic Assistance under the
Mutual Security Program, FY's 1952–1959

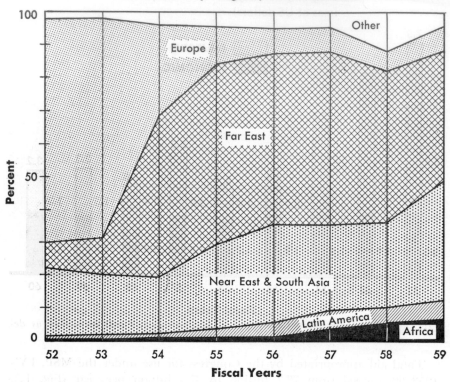

Source: International Cooperation Administration. Basic data cover amounts
obligated, inclusive of commitments by the DLF.

BILATERAL APPROACH

Assistance under the MSP, either military aid or economic aid, is provided on a *bilateral* basis. Assistance is provided any country only after
the satisfactory negotiation of an aid agreement between the US Government and the government of the particular recipient country. Thus, aid
is not "forced on" an unwilling recipient (or at least before aid is
granted, a prospective recipient must indicate in writing a willingness
to accept aid and to comply with certain prescribed practices in its
utilization).[23]

---

[23] Some assistance, particularly in the military-aid category, is provided following
the negotiation of an arrangement of regional scope, e.g., the North Atlantic Treaty
Organization (NATO) and the Southeast Asia Treaty Organization (SEATO); see Fig.
6 in Ch. 16. In these cases, however, particular aid continues to accrue to particular
countries, although the process of allocating some aid then occurs in the light of
considerations going well beyond any particular recipient country.

PROGRAM CONTENT

Assistance under the MSP consists of several major categories of aid. In broadest outline, of course, there is the division between military aid and economic aid. Each of these two major divisions, however, embraces several distinct subdivisions.

1. *Military.* Military aid has two components: direct military assistance and defense support.

Military assistance, per se, consists of military equipment, training in the use of this equipment, and other supplies and services for use by foreign military forces, all furnished directly to particular foreign countries in order to help strengthen their military establishments (and thus help the countries concerned in their participation with the US in a similarly-oriented military-defense effort).

Defense support consists of economic resources (not military resources) supplied to particular countries in order to help strengthen their economies so that support of the existing or a larger military-defense effort can prove possible.[24] In short, defense support is indirect military assistance—but it can also properly be viewed as economic assistance, at least in some instances. To illustrate, capital assistance for an industrial development program can be justified as defense support—e.g., as in the Philippine program—on the grounds that introduction of new productive capacity helps strengthen the economy, and hence makes possible a greater military-defense effort. For the greater part, however, defense support involves provision of various consumer-goods and producer-goods imports (as part of a commodity-import program), undertaken to prop up an economy unable because of its military-defense commitments or plans (or for other reasons) to achieve or maintain viability on its own; country examples include South Korea, South Viet-Nam, and Nationalist China, the three largest aid recipients under the MSP.[25]

2. *Economic.* While the precise composition of economic aid has undergone some changes over the years, five main categories have prevailed during the most recent years: the Development Loan Fund, special assistance, technical cooperation, a contingency fund, and a classification labeled "other."

---

24 In the absence of external economic assistance, these countries presumably would need either to (1) reduce their defense forces to a level they can afford on their own, or (2) accept the economic and political consequences of supporting military forces beyond their capabilities. In many (if not all) instances, the second alternative is not a possible or reasonable course. In any event, either choice would tend to weaken Free-World defenses.

25 In addition to the countries cited, defense support has been received during recent years by Cambodia, Greece, Iran, Laos, Pakistan, Spain, Thailand, and Turkey. Defense support is supplied only when all of three conditions are met: (1) the country must be one receiving military assistance from the US; (2) the military assistance so received must be in support of significant military forces; and (3) the purpose of defense support must be to secure a specific contribution by the recipient to the common defense.

The *Development Loan Fund,* treated in Chapter 18, provides loan capital for developmental purposes. Organized as a distinct corporate entity (since 1959), funds for the DLF are had through the overall MSP appropriation. Requests for financing for specific undertakings are entertained by the DLF from any country with which the US has a bilateral agreement (and in any number, and theoretically for any amount).[26]

Special assistance involves economic aid in cases in which defense-support considerations do not apply (e.g., as in the financing of undertakings in countries in which no agreements concerning military aid exist, or in which the support of significant military forces is not an important objective of US policy), or in cases in which aid cannot be provided through the DLF or other means (e.g., because repayment prospects are negligible). Thus, when no alternate means exist for providing economic aid, but provision of economic aid for promoting economic stability or growth is nevertheless held desirable (from the standpoint of the US interest), special assistance is the category from which financing is obtained.

Technical cooperation involves the transmission of know-how to aid-recipient countries in the hope that they will then be more able to fill the gaps that exist in the basic technical skills needed to plan and implement sound developmental programs. As such, technical cooperation involves, basically, the movement and maintenance of people, not the movement of commodities.[27] During 1959, for example, over 3,000 American technicians were located in aid-receiving countries,[28] and over 8,000 nationals of cooperating countries were provided an opportunity to study or observe in foreign locales.[29]

---

[26] Prior to initiation of the DLF in 1957, a special category of assistance, labeled *economic-development assistance,* existed. This category was discontinued shortly after the DLF was introduced, and undertakings of the type formerly financed under it (largely on a grant basis) came to be handled under the DLF (on a loan basis). In addition, some undertakings formerly financed under defense support came to be handled under the DLF.

[27] Commodities and equipment are involved directly only insofar as they are required to demonstrate new techniques or to assist in the build-up of local institutions needed for the continuing application of newly-acquired know-how.

[28] As of June 30, 1959, American technicians were distributed as follows: Far East, 964; Near East and South Asia, 959; Africa, 390; Latin America, 841; and Europe, 67. ICA, *Operations Report,* Washington, FY 1959 issue No. 4, p. 75.

[29] Nationals from the following locales embarked upon foreign training during FY 59: Far East, 3,203; Near East and South Asia, 1,731; Africa, 367; Latin America, 1,636; and Europe, 1,544. *Ibid.,* p. 74.

Training is not limited to locales within the US. Technically, training anywhere within the Free World is permissible; for example, roughly one-fourth of all persons commencing training during FY 59 did so in locales outside the US. "Third-country training" is regarded, in some instances, to hold distinct advantages. To illustrate, exposure to machine techniques employed in, say, Japan may prove of more value to a trainee from, say, Southeast Asia than would alternate training in the US, in that Japanese techniques place a smaller premium upon labor-saving aspects of production than do American techniques, and hence tend better to acquaint the trainee with practical approaches readily applicable in his underdeveloped homeland.

The *contingency fund,* as its designation implies, is for use in event of contingencies. Contingencies at issue are of two main kinds: (1) those that can be foreseen, but not with certainty as to the amount of funds needed, and (2) those that are unforeseen, but that merit prompt attention when they do arise. By holding some funds in reserve (and unallocated as to specific use), administrators of the MSP are placed in a stronger position to act efficiently and effectively in meeting particular situations, especially crises.[30]

In addition to these categories of assistance, there is a residual grouping, labeled here as *other.* The associated appropriation provides for the US contribution to the United Nations Children's Fund (UNICEF), certain refugee programs, the Atoms-for-Peace program, and for the cost of administering the MSP.

3. *Program for FY 1960.* For illustrative purposes, the composition of the MSP during FY 1960 is shown in Fig. 13. If defense support is classified as military assistance, the division between military and economic was 61% and 39%, respectively. If defense support is classified as economic assistance, however, the division between military and economic was 40% and 60%, respectively.

Among the components of economic aid (excluding defense support), the largest segment was that appropriated on behalf of the DLF (45% of total economic aid). In comparison, for example, technical cooperation appears as a distinctly low-cost operation (15% of total economic aid).[31]

THE APPROPRIATION PROCESS

Congressional appropriations for operation of the MSP are handled on an annual basis. Despite attempts by some proponents of foreign aid to get the Congress to move to multi-year appropriations, ostensibly to put the aid program on an assured long-range basis, an annual budgetary approach persists. Even the less ambitious attempt that was aimed at securing a multi-year appropriation for the DLF alone ended unsuccessfully.

Accordingly, the MSP comes before the Congress each year as a bid is made for fresh funds. The general procedure adhered to in securing financing is as follows. First, a tentative budget, designed to sustain intended operations during the forthcoming fiscal year, is prepared within

---

30 Prior to FY 59, the amount set aside for contingencies had been included within the *special assistance* category. This practice, however, was believed subject to the disadvantage of confusing rather than clarifying the specific purpose of the particular appropriation.

31 Interestingly enough, if news coverage devoted to each of the two—the DLF and technical cooperation—were measured in numbers of inches, it is possible that technical cooperation would win. The essential point is that technical assistance, whatever its other merits, claims much newsworthiness per dollar outlay. Since public support is vital to ensure a substantial aid program, a strong public-relations argument can be advanced on behalf of continued farflung technical-assistance efforts.

Fig. 13.   Composition of the Mutual Security Program, FY 1960
(Appropriations, in millions of US dollars)

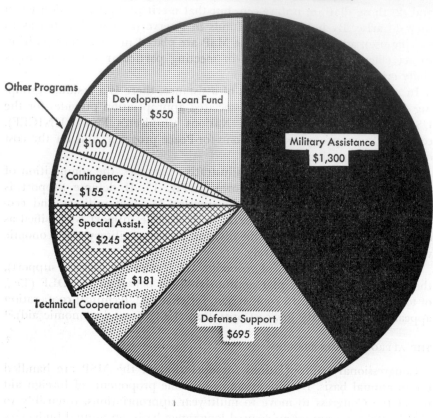

Other Programs

Development Loan Fund
$550

Military Assistance
$1,300

$100

Contingency
$155

Special Assist.
$245

$181

Technical Cooperation

Defense Support
$695

Total .｡｡. $3,226 Million

Source: International Cooperation Administration.

the aid agency.[32] Second, this budget is submitted to the Bureau of the
Budget for appraisal along with budget proposals submitted by other
agencies, all of which, in essence, are competing for funds within the
framework of a limited economy-wide budget. Third, once the aid agency
receives the "go ahead" from the Bureau of the Budget (which may be
only after some pruning on the initial budget proposal), submission to
the Congress of its formal budget request is in order. Fourth, at some

---

[32] The explanation offered is framed with the ICA primarily in mind (although
a similar explanation is applicable in the case of the DLF, treated in Ch. 18). As indicated in Ch. 18 (see footnote 27), the DLF is responsible for its own budgetary request
since its incorporation as a separate legal entity. In essence, the ICA and the DLF each
initially prepares its own budgetary request, whereupon the two requests, taken together, comprise the request for the MSP.

point the Congress undertakes to consider the budget request, in the course of which many modifications may occur (including alteration of the total request, as well as a reshuffling of component amounts), and in the course of which aid-agency officials are virtually assured an invitation to appear and explain any number of matters raised, e.g., why the budget request is as it is, why particular past actions in program operations were taken, and why, indeed, there is an aid program in the first place.

In the end, an *authorization* bill is passed. This measure authorizes the aid agency to carry on operations during the following fiscal year to the extent of maximum outlays of, say, $4 billion—but it does not assure any funds. Actual funds are dependent upon the passage of a separate *appropriation* bill. This measure then provides money up to, say, $3.4 billion to carry on the general operations made permissible under the authorization measure.[33] In short, an authorization by the Congress merely sanctions continuation of the MSP at some general level, with precise substance lent only to the extent that an actual appropriation follows.

Once an appropriation is made, the aid agency can seek to tailor its specific operations in accordance with funds available. However, quite apart from considerations relating to what, specifically, is to be done in order to maximize impact in recipient countries on the basis of funds then available, the aid agency is confronted by yet another problem: What will the appropriation likely be in the next year?[34] Some persons might answer that the case for aid is a strong one, implying that the plight of potential recipients alone is enough to induce continuing appropriations by the Congress. Others, however, are inclined to believe that the stage needs to be set in order to improve prospects with the Congress for subsequent requests; specifically, a fundamental principle of bureaucracy asserts that "one must be out of funds in order to get funds." Whatever the case, the general procedure followed within the aid agency is to strive to obligate (i.e., earmark for use in connection with bilaterally-agreed-upon operations) a high proportion of the appropriated funds prior to an established deadline, thereby giving rise to a record of relatively full commitment of previously-provided funds—and hence establishing a case for additional funds.[35]

---

33 The amount of appropriation, as a general rule, is less than the amount of authorization.

34 Or in any subsequent period (e.g., were aid put on a longer-term basis).

35 The procedure associated with the obligation of funds is widely regarded as open to abuse. Because failure to obligate comes to be viewed as equivalent to "loss of funds," even slipshod exercise of the obligational authority may seem to have merit. Also, because the act of obligating funds at one date does not preclude reobligation at a later date on behalf of other uses, hasty or ill-advised exercise of the obligational authority may appear excusable on the grounds that it does not necessarily constitute final action anyway. The "rub" makes itself felt, of course, if slipshod exercise of the obligational authority is encouraged by the procedure, and is not remedied later by action to reobligate in a manner likely to yield an upgraded usage of funds.

LOANS VERSUS GRANTS

Capital assistance under the economic portion of the MSP has been provided both as grants and as loans.[36] Prior to introduction of the DLF in 1957, the great bulk of capital assistance was supplied as grants (with loans accounting for under 10% of the total obligated during 1951–57). Thereafter, however, a marked shift in emphasis toward loans became discernible.

Numerous critics of foreign economic aid were inclined to seize upon grant aid as a point of attack. Aside from giving rise to the routine charge of "giveaway," emphasis upon grants was considered conducive to wasteful operations (because common-sense business standards would allegedly be ignored), destructive of foreign morale and self-respect (implying that recipient countries were unlikely to detect implications involving the donor's own self-interest), destructive of good international relations (as poor countries came to resent handouts from a "rich uncle"), deleterious to the movement of private foreign capital (which, it was largely taken for granted, would move in much greater volume in the absence of foreign aid, and would do a superior job), and likely to "bankrupt" the US (stated as if a domestic defense outlay of more than ten-fold the amount were really non-existent), to mention but a few of the many charges made.

Unquestionably in important part because of the steady undercurrent of opposition to grants, a series of official investigating bodies (as well as several major private research groups) recommended—especially between 1953 and the time the DLF was proposed—that a greater proportion of foreign economic aid be handled on a loan basis. While some token efforts in this direction occurred within the MSP prior to the introduction of the DLF, it was not until the DLF got into operation that a marked shift toward loans became a fact.

As matters stand, economic aid under the MSP is provided in three possible forms: grants, "soft" loans (non-dollar repayable), and "hard" loans (dollar repayable). Grant aid, which exceeded 90% of total obligations during 1951–57, diminished to roughly 65% during FY's 1958–59. However, while there has been a marked shift from grants to loans, the lending during FY's 1959–60 has proven to be very largely of the "soft" variety.

PROCUREMENT

Traditionally, procurement of commodities under the MSP has been permissible in any quarter within the Free World.[37] However, in October

---

[36] Virtually all military aid has been provided on a grant basis.

[37] Exclusive of US surplus agricultural commodities supplied under Section 402 of the Mutual Security Act.

1959, following a reversal in the US balance of payments, the DLF-portion of the MSP came to be tied to the American market (Ch. 18). An attempt at the time, spearheaded by the US Treasury, to extend the tying provision also to other segments of the MSP was successfully resisted by the aid agency; consequently, with the exception of loan proceeds made available through the DLF, funds under the MSP remained usable, as before, on a non-tied basis.

Despite the traditional freedom in procurement, well over one-half of all aid goods characteristically originated in the American market. Given the tendency for a substantial portion of foreign-aid proceeds to be spent in the American market anyway, numerous persons have been prone to question the essential wisdom of resorting to a formal tying provision.[38]

VIEW ON PRIVATE ENTERPRISE

Among the world's countries, the US is a classic devotee of the cause of private enterprise. Most Americans appear convinced that an economic system heavily reliant upon the exercise of private initiative is best (measured in terms of output or in terms of some combination of output and freedom). To say the least, not all countries or peoples are similarly convinced. In numerous instances, an unfavorable reaction to past contact with private enterprise, reinforced on occasion by an attitude of desperation in the face of staggering economic problems in the present, results in distinct receptivity to public-sector emphasis (in preference to emphasis upon private enterprise).

Given this difference in views, a question arises as to standards the US should apply in the provision of its foreign economic aid. Should the US be true to its avowed principles, and accordingly limit economic aid to the promotion of private enterprise abroad? Or, should the US provide economic aid for *either* public-sector or private-sector operations, whichever recipient countries happen to prefer—in the hope that this country's basic political-military objective can thereby be advantageously served?

In practice, the US *does* provide economic aid for *both* public-sector and private-sector operations. Assistance in the realm of basic develop-

---

[38] While over one-half of the foreign-aid dollars provided as capital assistance have returned to the US on the "first round," the *full* impact exceeded this ratio (since additional amounts come to reach the US through third-country routes). Some persons, in viewing the foregoing situation, have concluded that the prop offered the American market provides the basis for an argument on behalf of foreign aid—namely, that provision of foreign aid constitutes a potent anti-recession measure. Unfortunately, if so used, a reverse argument is invited—namely, that foreign aid adds to inflationary pressure. For a survey of the impact of the foreign-aid program upon the American economy, see The National Planning Association, "The Foreign Aid Programs and the United States Economy," Study No. 9 in *Foreign Aid Program,* US Senate Document No. 52, Washington, July 1957, pp. 767–879.

ment is provided almost in its entirety for public-sector projects. Admittedly, this is to be expected, given the nature of operations in basic development. But what of those operations that can readily occur under either public or private auspices? An example is found in industrial development, in which end-items arise that are capable of sale in the marketplace. In these instances, economic aid under the MSP is available for use in either the public sector or the private sector, although the expressed preference of the US Government is for private-sector operations. A policy directive, issued in 1957 in order to clarify this country's official position on the matter, stated as follows:[39]

> The U.S. is convinced that private ownership and operation of industrial and extractive enterprises contribute more effectively than public ownership and operation to the general improvement of the economy of a country through better management, research, quality control, lower prices, increased employment and capital growth.
>
> It is therefore a basic policy of the ICA to employ U.S. assistance to aid-receiving countries in such a way as will encourage the development of the private sectors of their economies. Thus, ICA will *normally not be prepared to finance publicly owned industrial and extractive enterprises, although it is realized that there may be exceptions.*

In short, the US prefers that countries choose a private-enterprise path in the course of promoting development; however, if some countries have strong feelings to the contrary, the US—cognizant of its major objective under the Mutual Security Act—will bend on occasion in order to accommodate the needs of the situation.

The private enterprises involved in the economic growth of underdeveloped countries can be either indigenous or foreign. A widely-held view (although unquestionably not universally-held) is that achievement of the policy objective, cited above, of "[encouraging] the development of the private sectors of [the economies of underdeveloped countries]" can be best fostered by encouraging the growth of indigenous private enterprise (in preference to the entry of foreign private enterprise). Be this as it may, selective entry by foreign private enterprise is given official sanction and encouragement under the MSP, e.g., through the availability for qualifying firms of coverage under the Investment Guaranty Program. Insofar as indigenous private enterprise is to be fostered, it is widely recognized within the aid agency that an option exists as to how financial assistance is to be channeled: directly, as funds are supplied to particular private enterprises, or indirectly, as funds are supplied to central developmental institutions, e.g., government-sponsored development banks capable of making sub-loans to private enterprises.

---

[39] ICA, *Press Release* (No. 338), September 12, 1957. (Italics are mine.)

COUNTERPART FUNDS

Under terms of the governing bilateral aid-agreement, the government of any given aid-receiving country agrees to set aside an amount of its national currency equivalent to the value of particular commodity imports occurring under aid auspices. This local currency, when so set aside, constitutes a counterpart fund, the administration and utilization of which becomes a mutual affair between the US and the particular aid-receiving country.

Basically, there is a two-fold rationale behind the counterpart-fund technique. First, withdrawal from circulation of a sizable block of local currency offers a method to combat inflationary pressure within the domestic economy. In the case of some countries, this motivation has been primary. Second, some amount of local currency is needed in connection with particular foreign-aid operations within the country—e.g., some local currency is needed to cover local-currency costs incurred in the course of carrying a project through to successful conclusion. In the case of most countries, this second motivation has been fundamental.

A common use made of counterpart funds can be illustrated through reference to a hypothetical project. Assume the following circumstances in Country X. Tax revenues accruing are insufficient for sound operation of the government. The difficulty is judged to stem not from existing tax legislation, but from antiquated tax-collection procedures and poor administrative know-how. Following consultations between the appropriate officials of X and the US, a joint decision is reached that help is necessary to improve the tax-collection process. Thereupon, a project agreement is prepared to cover a new project, labeled "Revenue Development." Following mutual approval of the project agreement, the project is legally instituted.

Assume, next, the following terms under the project agreement. The US agrees to provide dollar-aid of up to $200,000 for the project during the first year (and agrees, further, to a 5-year duration for the project[40]— even though the US foreign-aid appropriation assures funds, as seen at the particular moment, for only the first year of project operations). Usage of the $200,000 is programmed as follows: $90,000 for salaries and carrying costs of three American technicians in tax administration; $90,000 for purchase abroad of needed equipment (e.g., jeeps, office equipment, and technical books); and $20,000 to cover dollar outlays involved in sending three nationals abroad as trainees. For its part, X agrees to provide in local currency the equivalent of $100,000—say, ₱100,000 (assuming an exchange rate of $1.00 = ₱1.00). Usage of the counterpart is programmed as follows: ₱20,000 to increase the salaries of present personnel (on

---

[40] Subject to "escape" provisions that make continuation conditional upon availability of funds, and upon satisfactory performance by the recipient country.

grounds that better performance may thereby result); ₱50,000 to meet the salaries of additional personnel (on grounds that understaffing had prevailed); ₱20,000 to defray the cost of a proposed district office in a remote province; and ₱10,000 to meet family allowances for the kinsfolk of the three trainees while they are abroad.

This hypothetical project, cited by way of illustration, reveals how dollar outlays and local-currency outlays come to be linked in foreign-aid operations. As is evident, the full cost of a project does not fall upon the US, and it does not do so by virtue of the existence and use of counterpart. But because some specific things get accomplished in the course of an expenditure of counterpart, an occasional person is prone to conclude that a foreign-aid program can be conducted on the basis of it *alone* (which is tantamount to holding that the US extends foreign aid when it allows a country to use some of its own currency). A conclusion in this vein appears somewhat amiss. The term *foreign aid* implies that something comes into a country that was not there before. Obviously, the act of providing assistance from external sources meets the necessary test, but the act of generating counterpart does not.

While counterpart cannot properly be regarded as foreign aid, it nevertheless can be useful in the course of the provision of foreign aid, as intimated above. Above all else, counterpart provides a ready source of local currency that, as it "pairs up" with newly-acquired external assistance, helps smooth the process of incorporation into the economy of this external assistance.

SELECTED BIBLIOGRAPHY

See the end of Chapter 21.

21

FOREIGN AID (II)

Not everyone is agreed as to how a foreign-aid program should be conducted. Indeed, there is not even agreement among firm supporters of foreign aid as to why, precisely, aid should be provided. Accordingly, the present chapter is devoted to an examination of some major issues concerning the organization and operation of a program of foreign aid.

THE RATIONALE FOR AID

Under the existing official rationale, the Mutual Security Program is held justified on the grounds that it helps promote the US interest. The test of whether or not, or how well, the US interest is served proceeds in terms of the Program's contribution toward the attainment of a central political-military objective. In efforts to attain this objective, a major implemental device is that of assistance for economic development in underdeveloped countries. Significantly, assistance for economic development is not offered for the sake simply of achieving development, but rather for the help that resulting development can give toward attainment of the central political-military objective. In short, economic assistance is regarded as the *means to an end,* and the end is not development, per se.

This is the gist of the existing rationale of the MSP, previously elaborated upon in Chapters 16 and 20. Many persons, however, are not convinced that this is as it should be. Rather, they feel that the case for economic development is strong enough to stand on its own feet, and that assistance for this purpose should not be reduced to that of an implemental device in the promotion of some political-military objective. Accordingly, the question raised here is: Should economic assistance under a US Government foreign-aid program be provided for the sake of economic development, unencumbered by other considerations?

Those who favor aid for developmental promotion, pure and simple, have two main arguments at their disposal. The first argument is that the US interest is served by development in foreign locales—in fact, that this interest is better served by aiding development directly than by doing so on the basis of some roundabout rationale. According to this argument, the peoples of underdeveloped countries want development, implying that the prestige of the US, in the eyes of these peoples, is not at its maximum when this country chooses to reduce developmental assistance to that of an implemental measure in the pursuit of another objective, non-economic in nature. Moreover, doubt comes to be expressed as to just how effective developmental impact can be when the development is regarded merely as a means of implementation.

The second argument is that the American populace would be willing to support assistance for economic development, conceivably in magnitudes far greater than currently provided, if the merits of development were only explained to them in straightforward fashion. According to this argument, public support is not taken full advantage of when the rationale is based on mutual security. It is argued that a rationale focusing simply and honestly on the needs and aspirations of underdeveloped countries would capture support in many quarters where misunderstanding, disinterest, or outright opposition currently prevail.

In opposition are those who hold that the existing rationale is both appropriate and logical. These persons have two main arguments at their disposal. The first argument proceeds in terms of what sort of rationale is needed to get the Congress to appropriate funds. According to this argument, the amount of funds likely to be gotten from the Congress is intimately dependent upon the capacity to frame a request along lines highlighting direct and prompt benefit for the US.[1] A political-military rationale, focusing upon a currently disturbed political-military situation in the world, assertedly meets the necessary test more adequately (insofar as the Congress is concerned) than does a purely economic rationale, in which impact of virtual necessity is cast in longer-range terms.

The second argument—actually a variation of the first—derives from the notion that the really important consideration is *what does happen,* not *why* it does. According to this argument, achievement of development is a worthwhile goal, but the level of aid for the associated effort is likely to be greater under a political-military rationale than under a purely

---

[1] This condition is held important, presumably, in order that individual members of the Congress might be enabled more readily or plausibly to explain their affirmative votes to their tax-conscious constituents.

economic rationale; therefore, it is concluded that the nicety of an economic rationale should be sacrificed in the interests of a larger program. In short, principle is momentarily sidetracked in the hope that recourse to a bit of subterfuge will pay off. Meanwhile, the essential point is made that regardless of the rationale relied upon, any economic development that does result is no less real.

To the two foregoing arguments a third might conceivably be added. The MSP is not the only channel through which the US undertakes to supply developmental assistance. For example, the US is the major contributor to the International Bank, which institution adheres to a rationale substantially different from that of the MSP. Therefore, it might be contended, the rationale sustaining the MSP should not be judged without cognizance also being taken of this country's concurrent activities through other channels. Perhaps appraisal should be made on the basis of the balance reflected in the country's total effort relative to the needs of underdeveloped countries.

APPROPRIATIONS: ANNUAL VERSUS MULTI-YEAR

The MSP currently operates on the basis of annual appropriations by the Congress. This procedure is criticized by some persons who feel that appropriations should be for longer periods, so that, according to them, the moneys needed for developmental undertakings capable of being launched only over a period of somewhat longer than one year can be positively assured.

The critics of annual appropriations have two main arguments. The first argument is based on a fear that adherence to a short-run view toward the provision of funds is likely to result in a preference by American foreign-aid administrators for developmental projects capable of completion during a time period coinciding roughly with the appropriation period. The unfortunate aspect of such a preference, assuming that it exists, is that action on longer-range projects tends to be inhibited, even though many of the more meaningful projects, viewed from a developmental standpoint, are as likely as not to require effort over a span of years. In short, according to this argument, American foreign-aid administrators can do a better job in promoting development if they can plan their outlays and operations over a period of years, and need not shy away from involvement in long-range undertakings simply to avoid the possible catastrophe of ending with "uncompleted monuments."

The second argument holds that it is in the US interest to fund its foreign-aid operations over a longer-run period in order to assure underdeveloped countries that this country is determined to assist in the promotion of their development beyond merely the current year. Such assurance is held vital because the manner in which aid-receiving countries are likely to commit their own resources is affected by the certainty, or lack of it, of external assistance. If recipient countries know that access to external assistance will continue to be a possibility, they can then plan, according to the argument, to launch into well-thought-out developmental programs of some duration, likely to hold greater potential for marked impact. But in the absence of a reasonable assurance of continued access to external assistance, according to the argument, there is likely to be a tendency toward laxity in what some underdeveloped countries choose to do on their own—on the grounds that the struggle is hopeless.

Contrary arguments can be advanced to support the view that annual appropriations are quite workable and do not necessarily invite the shortcomings visualized by critics. A first argument is that the programming of aid is, in fact, carried on in a manner that makes multi-year undertakings possible. Long-term projects are commenced on the assumption that future aid appropriations will enable planned outlays to occur in each of a number of succeeding years. Moreover, any doubts entertained in underdeveloped countries as to the US intention on aid-program duration are believed fundamentally needless. Not only is the multi-year method of programming employed by this country known to aid-receiving countries (since all project agreements are bilateral in nature), but the US Government is officially on record as committed to a long-term program of foreign aid.[2]

A second argument is that, over time, more funds can likely be had from the Congress if requests are made annually than if made periodically for multi-year spans. This proposition is not given to easy proof or disproof. The argument, however, is that the Congress would be inclined to be extremely cautious as to the magnitudes to which it would tie itself over a long-run period, but would feel freer to underwrite spending if close year-to-year control could be retained.

Some persons feel that a simple pro-and-con appraisal unduly complicates the issue. These persons can cite two main half-way positions. One suggestion, aimed at making possible a long-range aid commitment without forcing the Congress to put itself on the line with specific appropriations (in the face of uncertain levels of future GNP), is that the Congress approve a resolution indicating this country's willingness to provide economic assistance in an amount no less than, say, 1% of the GNP prevailing in any year.[3] The precise level of total aid is then left unstated, although a floor to the level is established. A second suggestion,

---

[2] See Ch. 16, esp. footnote 19.

[3] Given the long-run trend in this country's export surplus, capacity to render assistance—viewed in the balance-of-payments sense—exceeds the percentage cited by a considerable margin. For comment on this matter, see S. E. Harris, *Foreign Aid and Our Economy* (Washington: Public Affairs Institute, 1950), pp. 38–39.

of somewhat weaker consequence than the first, is that the Congress approve a simple resolution indicating this country's *continuing* interest in developmental progress in the underdeveloped world and its intent to provide economic assistance for this purpose to an extent consistent with current capabilities.[4]

MAGNITUDE AND DIRECTION OF AID

The total amount of economic assistance offered under the MSP is somewhat less than the aggregate of what individual recipient countries desire. Therefore, an element of competitiveness arises among recipient countries as they eye one another's aid allotments. Moreover, as recipient countries tend to scramble for a greater share of total aid, US foreign-aid administrators are forced to make decisions as to how to apportion, or reapportion, aid among various eligibles. Accordingly, what test (or tests) should be applied in determining who should receive what portion of the aid made available?

Several possible tests might be employed, the major ones being: maximization of short-run political gain; maximization of repayment prospects (i.e., minimization of risk); maximization of income generated per dollar outlay; and maximization of the catalytic effect in the mobilization for development of additional domestic resources within recipient countries. While no one of the tests, taken by itself, is likely to prove invariably infallible, the degree of merit definitely varies among them. Of the tests cited, the first three appear inferior to the last named.

Development aid should not be used as a means to gain short-run political advantage. An attempt to do so is likely to result in a jockeying and scattering of allocations in a manner yielding little developmental impact. Other segments of foreign aid (e.g., military aid) might well have merit as a means for deriving short-run political advantage, but the only political benefit which should be expected of development-aid is that likely to derive over the long-run. The process of development is time-consuming, but achievement over time of development helps create an environment from which political advantage (for the US) can spring. Development-aid should thus be directed primarily to the promotion of development, and any political gain should be viewed as a *by-product* of such development (and not as something to be had through a series of small bargains gotten in exchange for bits of economic aid).

Similarly, minimization of financial risk (relevant especially in the case of loans, involving repayment) has limitations as a test for the allocation of development-aid. After all, investment in a decidedly underdeveloped

---

4 The resolution presumably would be similar, in approach and mode of expression, to the Full Employment Act of 1946.

country may well involve far greater risk than equivalent investment in a semi-developed or developed country. Also, the process of development requires that investment occur at many points within an economy, not merely in a few select projects regarded as relatively free of risk. Therefore, if development is to be fostered, some test other than minimization of risk appears needed. Freedom from risk (i.e., creditworthiness) can represent a good supplementary test for economic aid, but should not be viewed as the basic test.

Likewise, maximization of income generated per dollar of aid has limitations as a test. If used as the test, developed countries would easily tend to outshine underdeveloped countries; in fact, the more underdeveloped a country, the poorer would tend to be its chances for aid. In decidedly underdeveloped countries, basic development is likely to get first claim to new investment. Investment in basic development yields directly only small increases in income, but without this investment other investment is handicapped. This is in contrast to semi-developed countries, in which equivalent investment—undertaken in large part for purposes beyond basic development—is virtually certain to yield far greater increases in income. Clearly, if income generation is the basic test, development-aid could well end being allocated in direct proportion to the degree of developedness, *not* in proportion to the degree of *under*developedness.

The basic aim in the allocation of development-aid should be cast in terms of the help needed to induce greater effort by recipient countries to use their own resources to good advantage in the promotion of development. While the US contribution can only be marginal (in terms of the total cost of development), the hope should be that access to it will provide underdeveloped countries with an incentive to do more on their own to foster development, and thereby speed the transition from stagnation (or near stagnation) to self-sustaining growth (when no further aid would be required). As one official study, in presenting conclusions as to what criterion should govern the allocation of economic aid, put the matter:[5]

> The general aim of [development] aid is to provide an incentive for greater national effort in each underdeveloped country so as to shorten the period after which self-sustaining growth is reached. The overall aim of aid is not to equalize incomes in different countries but to assist each country in achieving a steady, self-sustaining rate of growth.
>
> Thus the primary criterion is to *maximize additional effort*, not to maximize income created per dollar of aid. Rough commonsense rules can indicate desirable and practicable targets of national effort. . . .

---

[5] "The Objectives of United States Economic Assistance Programs," Study No. 1 in *Foreign Aid Program,* US Senate Document No. 52, Washington, July 1957, pp. 62–63. (Italics are mine.)

Capital aid should be offered . . . wherever there is reasonable assurance that it will be effectively used. The problem of how to allocate available funds "equitably" between different countries need not arise. The principle of positive incentive implies that requests which meet functional criteria of productivity should be granted. Absorptive capacity is thus the fundamental criterion of aid and the measure of its allocation between different countries.

While the total amount of aid is determined by the country's absorptive capacity, the composition of aid as between loans, "local currency loans," and grants should be determined by the country's creditworthiness. The capacity to absorb is the fundamental principle, the capacity to repay the supplementary principle of aid.

These principles must be applied with intelligence and imagination. They are not a substitute for wise administration. They can, however, provide a framework within which functional criteria of aid can be mutually agreed upon.

BILATERAL VERSUS MULTILATERAL CHANNELS

Economic aid under the MSP is offered bilaterally. Some persons believe a multilateral approach—under which numerous countries, both donor and recipient, come to have a hand—would prove superior.

Critics of bilateral aid advance three main arguments. The first argument is that bilateral aid is likely to degenerate into politically-inspired aid. According to this argument, a donor country, when able at its own discretion to extend or withhold aid from any given underdeveloped country, is likely, under the pressures of handling day-to-day international affairs, to fall back on the aid-allocation process as a means to drive political bargains. As a consequence, the effectiveness of aid as an instrument for promotion of development is held to be jeopardized, to say nothing of resentments being allegedly created in recipient countries as they come to see development-aid as a political bribe. Provision of aid through multilateral channels, on the other hand, is pictured as offering an approach in which the narrow political self interest of the donor cannot warp the economic case for aid.

The second argument is that bilateral aid, even when rendered purely for economic purposes, readily comes to have "strings" attached, i.e., some sort of *quid-pro-quo* comes to be expected as a condition of aid. Even when the conditions imposed make good economic sense (which, it is feared, is not always the case), the possibility is held out that the recipient country will consider its good faith to have been impugned, causing it to react adversely—indeed, even to the extent of causing deterioration in the immediate inter-country political relationship. Provision of aid through multilateral channels, on the other hand, is pictured either as being free of "strings," or at least as having multi-country sanction upon such "strings" as may be attached (with no need, therefore, for a recipient country to react adversely on that account toward any other single country).

X   The third argument is that the bilateral approach limits recipient countries to the amount of aid the US chooses to supply. Multilateralization of aid, it is argued, can result in more aid for development in underdeveloped countries. The view is that some countries in addition to the US (e.g., the United Kingdom, West Germany, France, Italy, Japan, and others) can be induced to contribute something through a multilateral-aid framework, so that the level of total aid can be greater—without adding to the US burden.[6]

✗   On the other hand, those who prefer a bilateral to a multilateral approach have two main counter-arguments. A first argument is that there is merit in having "strings" attached to aid, and that a bilateral approach is to be preferred because it makes "strings" possible.[7] Development-aid supplied underdeveloped countries appears small when compared with the total resources available to these countries in their developmental efforts; therefore, if major impact is to result from aid, this aid must be employed so as to achieve a leverage effect, i.e., as a basis to get the recipient countries started in a reorientation of their *own* available resources. It is too much to assume, it is argued, that recipient countries will always automatically choose to put their own available resources to better use just because some external resources are supplied; rather, recipient countries might choose to regard "string"-free external resources as a bounty that makes it possible to avoid having to make better use of their own available resources. Moreover, US foreign-aid administrators are obliged to answer to the Congress for moneys spent. These administrators, it is argued, are helped in the case they can present to the Congress if they can show what recipients did *differently* as a result of the aid provided. Specifically, if no direct (or reasonably direct) connection can be shown between aid provided and developmental progress in aid-receiving countries, what are these administrators to tell the Congress to convince it of the wisdom of further aid? And, if no funds are provided by the Congress, there is no foreign-aid program—good, bad, or indifferent!

∧   A second argument is that the amount of foreign aid likely to be had from the US may prove less, rather than more, when a multilateral approach is followed in preference to a bilateral approach. For example,

---

[6] A usual estimate is that the US might bear about 70% of the total cost of aid provided through a likely multilateral framework, while other developed countries participating might bear the remainder of the cost. For a discussion of international cost-sharing, see T. C. Schelling, *International Economics* (Boston: Allyn and Bacon, Inc., 1958), Ch. 29.

[7] It would not appear reasonable, of course, to argue for "strings" of *any* kind. Rather, the argument customarily proceeds in terms of permissibility for "strings" (leaving unanswered the question of what kind or how many are permissible).

an attitude likely to arise, it is argued, is that cooperating donor countries should carry more of the burden, and that a way to get cooperating donor countries to assume more of the burden is to reduce this country's contribution. Or, since the pooling of contributions through multilateral channels serves to make foreign aid something other than strictly an American program, the possibility arises, it is argued, that the Congress will lose interest, sympathy, and the feeling of urgency in the provision of funds—presumably because this country then has to share control, and is also no longer able to claim sole credit for the resulting benefits. Thus, while multilateralization of aid would bring together funds from a number of sources, the total magnitude of funds might nevertheless prove smaller than realizable under a bilateral approach.

Clearly, both bilateral and multilateral approaches have advantages and disadvantages. However, a third procedure, able to claim the major strengths of each while free of the major weaknesses, appears possible. This procedure involves *extension of aid bilaterally but within the framework of a consultative multi-national organization.* Under the procedure envisaged, a new international body—titled, say, the Organization for International Development—would be created to serve as a clearing house relative to certain matters of importance in the promotion of development. All donor countries and all recipient countries would be eligible for membership in the Organization, provided certain minimum tests of compliance were met; indeed, membership by the US would presumably induce numerous other countries to join. The Organization itself would have, desirably, a small but high-quality staff, recruited from various member countries.

As intimated, the major function of the Organization would be to serve as a clearinghouse, which function could be exercised in three main ways. First, the Organization could assemble information on the supply of and demand for development-aid. Thus, donor countries, while continuing to provide aid bilaterally, could be required as a condition of membership to report all aid allocations. Likewise, recipient countries could be required as a condition of membership to report all receipts of aid, along with information on current domestic developmental plans and activities. Second, the Organization could call periodic meetings (say, annually), attended by representatives of all members countries, at which meetings relevant developmental matters could be discussed.[8] Among other things, progress in development could be reviewed, information on current aid-flows could be examined, and criteria for the allocation of development-aid could be evaluated. The Organization itself would have no binding powers, only advisory powers. Third, the Organization could maintain a roster of qualified technicians of diverse

---

[8] Somewhat similar to the annual meetings of the Colombo Plan.

nationality as a service to both donor and recipient countries which, on occasion, need to locate professional talent for use in conjunction with the allocation and incorporation of development-aid, or in conjunction with the utilization of development resources generally.

The advantages of a bilateral approach seemingly would be retained, by and large, under the procedure outlined. For example, a donor country would remain free to provide aid in any amount it saw fit to any particular recipient country. Again, aid sources in the case of each program or project would remain clearly identifiable, so that a donor country could have the satisfaction of knowing precisely where funds were utilized. But, certain major disadvantages, ordinarily attributed to a bilateral approach, would seemingly be overcome or offset. For example, development-aid would be removed, for all intents and purposes, from the realm of political maneuvering. This would be accomplished by virtue of the fact that no dealings would remain above scrutiny by the staff and representatives of the multi-national Organization. Again, any resentment that might spring from "strings" attached to aid could largely be avoided. This would be accomplished by virtue of the likelihood of general acceptance of the overall criteria arrived at on a multi-national basis. Moreover, the fact that other donor and recipient countries would be involved in each aid transaction (in addition to the US and a particular recipient country) would likely help allay fears in the US, or elsewhere, that aid is in danger of being wasted by a particular country unless offered only with stringent tailor-made conditions.

The conclusion hazarded here is that provision of development-aid under the MSP on a bilateral basis is superior, on balance, to what might be expected under a straight multilateral approach (although it is recognized that a bilateral approach is not free of major drawbacks). While potent arguments can be advanced against any full shift to provision of aid through multilateral channels, a strong case can be made for organizational revisions that would permit a more effective coordination of bilateral aid with the aid arising from other countries or agencies.

ECONOMIC AND MILITARY AID

Under current procedure, economic aid and military aid are linked in the MSP. While a distinction is observed in appropriations and in subsequent accounting, the same agency and the same administrators, by and large, handle both. Some persons believe that this joint administration involves major drawbacks that might be avoided were economic aid handled completely apart from military aid.

There are two main arguments against linking administration of economic aid with that of military aid. The first argument is that the motives of the US in the extension of economic aid, alongside military aid, become vulnerable to question in recipient countries—presumably as the notion tends to arise in these countries that economic aid is really military aid in disguise. Indeed, such a questioning is considered likely even in countries receiving *only* economic aid, since it is known that Washington headquarters handles both economic and military aid. Thus, it is argued that if the US wants to assist economic development, and wants the world to recognize this as its intent, economic aid should be separated, *organizationally*, from military aid.

The second argument is that there is an important difference in the immediate criteria employed in the two cases. The immediate aim in the case of economic aid is (or should be) to stimulate greater developmental effort in recipient countries, whereas military aid is oriented directly and specifically toward political-military ends. Thus, because of this basic difference between the two, it is argued that it does not make good sense or yield good results to have the same agency and administrators handling both.

Two counter-arguments can be offered to support retention of the prevailing organizational structure. According to a first argument, economies can accrue from the union of economic and military aid, particularly because an organizational link facilitates programming operations between the two. Specifically, wide latitude then exists for shuffling dollars and local currencies between the economic and military sectors of the program, allowing the US to make a bigger "dent" than otherwise possible on the basis of whatever support is had from the Congress.[9] Admittedly, such inter-sector programming of funds is not prevented, technically, by an organizational separation of economic from military aid, but the likelihood that it will follow in practice appears lessened.

According to the second argument, divorcement of economic from military aid would invite an overall organizational realignment that would be potentially detrimental to this country's effort in the provision of economic aid. Military aid presumably would come to be handled by

---

[9] Illustrative of possible programming advantages, assume the following situation. Following an appropriation by the Congress, a military-aid allocation of, say, $10 million is made to help strengthen the military establishment of an ally, this amount to be used for the purchase of "soft goods" within that country. If military aid were handled separately, a likely procedure would be to grant dollars, which would then be converted within the recipient country—with the dollars being added to the recipient country's foreign-exchange reserves, and eligible for later use by that country in *any* way it saw fit. But, if military and economic aid were linked organizationally, a possible procedure would be for the military-aid dollars to be held within the aid agency for use as economic aid, while the military-aid allocation would be met with an equivalent amount in local currency taken from the pool of local currencies acquired by the agency in the course of its economic-aid operations (assuming, of course, that sufficient needed local currency was in the agency's possession at the time).

the Department of Defense, while the economic-aid portion of the MSP, left on its own, would then likely come to be viewed as alternative to (and hence competitive with) other domestic or international organizations supported by this country (e.g., the Export-Import Bank and the International Bank). The possible danger therein would be a resultant loss in relative strength, especially as an altered and possibly politically-weakened rationale would come to be used in backing requests of the Congress. In short, the separation of economic from military aid raises the possibility of *less* funds for economic aid, regarded by many as a high price to pay for organizational nicety.

DIVISION BETWEEN GRANTS AND LOANS

The matter of grants versus loans in the provision of economic assistance under the MSP has constituted an issue of long standing. Initially, virtually all economic aid was provided on a grant basis. A view enjoying increased acceptance, however, was that merit attached to having more economic aid move as loans. The notion was that grants are bad, generally speaking, for both the giver and the receiver: excessively burdensome for the US and demoralizing for the recipient country; besides, many types of activity were regarded perfectly capable of being financed on a loan basis. The result was a gradual shift from grants toward loans. While grant aid has continued to be highly important, economic aid through loans—encompassing both "hard" and "soft" loans—has received growing emphasis.

The form in which economic aid moves should logically be regarded as secondary to its purpose. As intimated previously, the criterion of maximum inducement of additional domestic developmental effort should take precedence over that of creditworthiness. Moreover, the form in which economic aid moves should logically prove compatible with the particular emphasis given in the aid effort. In the final analysis, the form that comes to predominate—grants, soft loans, or hard loans—should depend basically upon this country's own decision as to where and how it wishes immediate impact to be felt. For example, if emphasis in the provision of economic aid is placed upon the most underdeveloped of countries, grants should be expected to prove more important and "hard" loans less important than if emphasis is placed upon underdeveloped countries already well along in the growth process. Or, if emphasis is upon basic development, grants should be expected to prove more important and "hard" loans less important than if emphasis is upon, say, industrial development.

The desire to shift economic aid from grants to loans perhaps is understandable. Many persons feel that the traditional tests of good business, including repayment of funds provided, should be extended to cover economic aid. There are two important reasons, however, why a resort to "hard" loans is subject to distinct limitations. First, provision of economic aid in this form only would envisage an ability in recipient countries to acquire the income (and the foreign exchange) needed to effect repayment, which is not a reasonable expectation in every instance. Second, the repayment of "hard" loans involves an inflow of goods and services for the creditor country. However fine it is to expect repayment, such sometimes is difficult to accept—on both economic and political grounds. As many persons have noted, the US is a "reluctant importer," a situation attributable to more than pure whim.

Significantly, "repayment" can be achieved without a movement of goods and services—during the short-run, at least—through the expedient of "soft" loans. Indeed, the expedient of "soft" loans carries interesting economic and political implications. Technically, a "soft" loan *is* a loan; repayment is scheduled to occur, even though in local currency. But, with inconvertibility widespread in the world (and, with convertibility by no means assured in the foreseeable future for numerous countries under discussion here[10]), repayment in local currency becomes tantamount to no payment. Under the circumstances, some persons choose to refer to a "soft" loan as a disguised grant. Meanwhile, as seen by many members of the public, a "soft" loan is good (because repayment is scheduled), but a grant is bad (because it comprises a "giveaway"). It is interesting to speculate how these members of the public would react if they were to learn that what they regard as a loan is really *not* a loan, but a disguised grant. Perhaps, as an occasional individual has ventured, the "soft" loan technique helps make politically acceptable the transmission through the foreign-aid program of capital assistance in a magnitude not possible with grants.

BALANCE-OF-PAYMENTS VERSUS PROJECT ASSISTANCE

Emphasis in the provision of capital assistance under the MSP is upon project assistance, not upon balance-of-payments assistance. The logic behind project assistance is that recourse to carefully-circumscribed projects permits a pinpointing of effort in the removal or amelioration of specific shortcomings. But, in the course of rendering assistance on this basis, attention is not focused directly on the foreign-exchange impediment to development, which characteristically represents an overall shortcoming; while the balance-of-payments situations of recipient countries can be helped with project assistance, any such help is indirect.

---

[10] Even if convertibility became general, a substantial realignment in world trade would thereupon tend to follow, in turn requiring major economic readjustments for some countries.

Critics of the project approach have two main lines of argument. First, adherence to a project approach allegedly results in involvement of the US in numerous diverse and only tenuously-related efforts. Indeed, in the typical country's program, projects are found to number 50 or over. It is pretty much a case in which the pet projects of many people somehow get pressured into being—perhaps, in part, because the typical project does not cost much in itself. An awareness of this vulnerability to "scatteration" exists within the aid agency, and action has been instituted on occasion to eliminate projects covering fringe operations.

Second, the potential success of development-aid is not dependent so much upon numbers of projects in effect as it is upon the magnitude of effort made in particular well-focused connections. The fear exists that projects all too readily are aimed at the treatment of various symptoms,[11] not at the central disease. In short, flawless activity in each of, say, 50 projects needs not add up to one good aid program (when measured by what is required to stimulate developmental progress within a recipient country).

On the other hand, it can be argued that project assistance is really balance-of-payments assistance, with the following important variation: instead of providing in a lump sum an amount related to the balance-of-payments deficit likely to be experienced as a result of the initiation of certain new developmental activity, assistance is provided piecemeal to cover certain portions of the cost encountered in specific new developmental operations, e.g., portions of the direct foreign-exchange cost. Thus, development-aid supplied on this basis, while called project assistance, can be regarded as a "tied-down"-type of balance-of-payments assistance; while the aid provided may not take off the shoulders of the recipient country all of the foreign-exchange cost associated with the new developmental activity it aspires toward, aid at least covers some of the cost.

The foregoing points to a major consideration that the US finds it necessary to bear in mind. Given the amount of dollars the aid agency has at its disposal, an across-the-board balance-of-payments approach is too costly. The aid agency is obliged to spread available dollars on some other, less absorptive, basis. The project approach offers one answer.

To the extent that the projects selected for financing do yield catalytic effect, there is much to be said to recommend a project-by-project approach. In general, the tactic of fewer projects, but of high impact-potential, is to be preferred to a "scatteration" of effort among many projects, including some which are good but short of top or near-top rating as to impact-potential. Under a project approach, the idea of producing catalytic impact needs to be ever-present; in contrast, under a

---

[11] Referred to as *symptomatic sedation* by some persons within the aid agency.

straight balance-of-payments approach, the idea of across-the-board impact—involving a saturation tactic—can be entertained.

PROJECT SELECTION BY RECIPIENT COUNTRIES

A proposal, unacted upon, suggests that the US agree to finance in their entirety (without further reference to criteria of any sort) some fixed number of projects—say, 4 or 6 in number, the precise number depending upon total aid funds available—selected *by* each recipient country as rating top priority in its developmental aspirations. Advantages claimed by proponents include the following. First, the approach would make it impossible for the US to use economic aid as a device for promotion of its own narrow political self-interest. The task of selection of projects to be regarded as of highest priority would fall exclusively to individual aid-receiving countries; the US would then assume the direct cost of these projects, *whatever* their nature. Second, positive divorcement of economic aid from narrow political considerations would likely yield political gain for the US over the long-run. Recipient countries presumably would appreciate "string"-free economic aid, and hence would react favorably to the donor. Third, because the US would pick up the tab on the top-priority projects, a recipient country's own available resources, which might have gone into these top projects, would be freed for use on additional projects of its own choosing.

Appealing as the proposal may be in some respects, it has major drawbacks. First, an expression by the US of its willingness to finance some number of top projects designated by each recipient country, whatever the nature of these projects, would amount to placement of much faith in the good judgment of the planning leaders of aid-receiving countries. Such faith perhaps would not be misplaced in the case of many countries, but what of the exceptions? For example, what if some country chose to regard the erection and stocking of a zoo as of high priority?[12] To accede to requests, whatever their nature, would be to make the aid program vulnerable to some very pointed criticism by the Congress and the American public; but to refuse some requests would be to violate the spirit of the new approach, and thereby likely arouse resentment abroad.

Second, there is a presumption that if the US picks up the tab on top projects, the recipient country's own available resources freed in the process would come to be used to promote other good-caliber projects. But, what if the recipient country chooses instead to use the newly-freed resources to sustain higher consumption (in an environment of highly inequitable income distribution)? Should the US in such event simply

---

[12] Farfetched as the example may seem, it is cited here because one aid-receiving country is said to have sought assistance from the US, during a recent year, in precisely this connection.

"look the other way" and continue to finance the top projects? If this is what the US then would do, would it not be guilty of encouraging relaxation of domestic effort in the recipient country? Advocates of "aid with strings" appear to have potent questions to raise in this connection.

Third, the proposal raises serious administrative problems. For example, what portion of the cost of the top projects would the US be expected to finance: total direct cost, or only total direct foreign-exchange cost? If the answer is total direct cost, a question can be raised as to why the US should bear local-currency cost (since the recipient country can always, technically, obtain local currency on its own). Again, projects vary widely as to the financial requirements they present. What then if the financial requirements of the top projects proposed by a low-population country far exceed those of an equivalent number of projects proposed by a high-population country? Should the US simply proceed anyway, ignoring the inequity in allocations among countries? Is not each recipient country really placed under indirect pressure to "dream up" big and costly projects in order to assure itself of its "share" of available aid? And, are the costliest projects always the best ones?[13]

THE BENEFICIARIES OF AID

A criticism of economic aid under the MSP, heard both within the US and abroad, is that the benefits seem to accrue to the well-to-do in recipient underdeveloped countries, while the poor masses are left untouched. Cognizant of this criticism, aid administrators frequently venture the observation that aid should be applied so as to reach "the people."

The foregoing criticism serves to raise two closely-related questions. First, what type of aid is needed to reach people? Second, is the type of aid dictated by this test likely to be compatible with what is needed to promote development? Aid administrators, in an attempt to devise an aid program that can stand up in the light of these questions, come to be torn between two divergent approaches: a "grass-roots" approach versus a "trickle-down" approach.

A grass-roots approach tends to rate high in terms of the first question raised. Under this approach, the intent is to affect many people, and to do so promptly and in a manner clearly identifiable and readily understandable to them. A common illustration of a good grass-roots program is that of community development (Ch. 5), although perhaps a straight dole—involving, say, "handouts" in each community of food items supplied as economic aid—would offer an even better example. However,

---

[13] A possible way out of this dilemma would be for the US to offer financing for top projects up to the limit of some specified maximum sum, variable among countries. This procedure, however, would comprise a major modification in the proposal cited.

apart from the presumed merit of such programs in reaching many people, speedily and surely, how do they rate in terms of the second question raised? Are they strong in terms of promotion of development? Many persons conclude to the contrary. Support for community development, for example, is frequently advanced in terms of the "motion" it assures in the present, thereby helping to give the precious time needed for accompanying programs, from which *the* basic developmental impact is expected to stem, to come to fruition. Again, a straight dole cannot, in and of itself, assure continuously enhanced consumption for the future; impact is had while the operation is in progress, but ends when the operation ceases—as must necessarily be the case whenever production is left unaltered.

In contrast, a trickle-down approach tends to rate badly in terms of the first question raised. Under this approach, aid is injected into the economy in substantial doses at each of a relatively few points, the hope being that something "big" will come into being, and that benefits of notable magnitude will then flow to the populace at large. A common illustration is that of an industrial-development program (Ch. 7). The masses, as they observe aid allocations in such connection (assuming that they are even aware of the allocations), are likely to conclude that what is being done is "not for them." Rather, the masses may well visualize the aid flow as a further fattening of the rich, and especially so if developmental emphasis is upon the private sector. Indeed, the probable popular impression stands not to be tempered in short order in the wake of a marked outflow of benefits in the form of added employment and income, since those benefits are not likely to accrue in volume until the passage of considerable time. Thus, the trickle-down approach, in its immediate impact, tends to leave the masses basically untouched, or even alienated. However, the approach scores much better in terms of the second question raised. For example, if structural change is fundamental for initiation or acceleration of growth, there may well be no alternative but to focus on big developments of a type definitely not grass-roots in nature. In short, unless one is prepared to assess impact-potential *beyond* the initial phases, and is also prepared to attribute to aid whatever benefits accrue from it *indirectly*, the trickle-down approach stands highly vulnerable.

Clearly, aid administrators are confronted by a major dilemma in choosing between these two approaches in the allocation of aid. An expedient "way out" (although not entirely a satisfactory one), frequently followed, is to settle upon an overall country program consisting of some projects rating high by grass-roots tests and of other projects rating high by trickle-down tests. Such a country program is what some aid administrators presumably have in mind when they speak of a "balanced" program.

MATTERS OF RISK

Examination of testimony offered before the Congress by aid administrators would seem to indicate that no mistakes have been made in the
course of conduct of operations under the MSP. *Perhaps* none have been
made. Then, however, one might ask why the record has been so perfect.
Is it an indication that the program has lacked imagination and daring?
Or, *if* weak spots have shown up but are smoothed over in the telling,
why is this the case? Is it because aid administrators operate in an
environment in which a record of no mistakes seems expected? At issue,
of course, is the question of the extent to which the aid agency is willing,
or able, to "take a chance" in its operations.

Promotion of development is akin to pioneering: the outcome *may* be
very rewarding, but not always entirely predictable. One way to reduce
the chance for failure is to stick to "tried and true" paths, and to avoid
new and daring courses. But, in so reducing the chance for failure, a
record of outstanding success may also be ruled out. In short, the price
of safety can well be a humdrum program.

It is unfortunate if economic aid *has to be* allocated strictly in accordance with a philosophy that condones no error—and which, hence, precludes experimentation, the likely precursor of error. Such is not to say
that error should be invited at every turn. Rather, it is to say that some
error should be held allowable, provided the overall record of the aid
program can be judged a success (as measured in terms of high developmental-impact). A program yielding considerable success, but which
incurs a few failures in the course of achieving the overall success, is
preferable to a program free of failure, but also devoid of success. In
development, the really important consideration is the number of
"rights," and the matter of the number of "wrongs" acquires major
relevancy only as compared with the number of "rights."

The basic philosophy, therefore, should be positive, with emphasis
placed on "desire for success"; it ought not be negative, with emphasis
placed on "no failures," the effect of which would be to inhibit even
those actions likely of success. Clearly, the promotion of development
involves something more than simply making the accounting ledgers
look good.[14]

THE ROLE OF TECHNICAL ASSISTANCE

The idea of provision of technical assistance to underdeveloped countries is quite popular in American quarters. The generally lower state of

---

[14] As former President Truman expressed the central idea: ". . . don't scuttle
the ship just to stop the leaks." See Committee for International Economic Growth,
Foreign Aspects of U.S. National Security, Washington, February 1958, p. 58.

technical know-how and organization skills in underdeveloped countries is widely recognized by Americans, so that provision of specialized talent to fill important gaps appears a likely way to assist these countries in their developmental efforts. Further, provision of technical assistance holds the special appeal of being low cost. In underdeveloped countries, however, some reservations are entertained as to the merits of emphasis on technical assistance. A common criticism proceeds in terms of the need for "more money, not just more free advice." This does not mean that these critics in underdeveloped countries feel no good use can be made of technical assistance, but rather that capital assistance is needed fully as much as is technical assistance.

While it is clear, from the American standpoint, that technical assistance has an important role to play in development, it also seems clear that good advice alone rarely, if ever, is sufficient to yield markedly accelerated rates of growth. Technical assistance does not provide the additional resources needed in the total effort aimed toward this end; the best that can be claimed for technical assistance is that already-available resources will come to be utilized somewhat better. In fact, a frequent situation is that access to additional resources is a necessity to assure effective utilization of even the technical assistance being offered.

In short, technical assistance tends to yield its maximum contribution when it is part of an overall program of development-aid. Ideas are fine, but they ordinarily prove more readily translatable into action and achievement when accompanied by an injection of cooperant means. Such is the case because of physical (technical) reasons, and also because of psychological reasons. Of special significance, provision of capital assistance can serve to create a greater willingness in recipient countries to accept accompanying advice, which advice can then serve to affect the manner of utilization of all available resources, external and domestic.

POLICY FORMULATION

The broad outlines of what the MSP is and does stem from the Congress. But, subject to these broad outlines, wide latitude remains within the Executive Branch for the formulation of policies intended to govern aid operations. Where, precisely, should this power rest? Two main possibilities exist: the aid agency itself, or the Department of State.

Prior to 1955, the aid agency was organizationally distinct from the Department of State. During this period, the aid agency was able to wield considerable discretionary power, with only nominal need to "clear" with the Department of State. In 1955, however, the aid agency was brought into the Department of State as a semi-autonomous unit. During succeeding years, the aid agency progressively lost to the Department of State much of the discretionary power it previously held. As put by some persons, the aid agency has become, as a consequence, "more of an *operations* agency and less of a *policy* agency."

Not everyone is agreed that the shift in power has been advantageous. As might be expected, there are two views, each with its proponents. On the one hand, it can be argued that the shift of some policy-authority to the Department of State is entirely logical since that entity is responsible for carrying out the country's foreign policy, within the context of which foreign aid is an important implemental device.

On the other hand, it can be argued that the shift involves unfortunate consequences. Some persons, proceeding on the premise that both the outlook and concern of the Department of State are global in nature, fear that the *special* problems associated with development in underdeveloped countries all too readily get glossed over when the persons in charge have an orientation not particularly geared to the special case of the underdeveloped world.

SELECTED BIBLIOGRAPHY

Eugene W. Castle, *The Great Giveaway: The Realities of Foreign Aid.* Chicago: Henry Regnery Company, 1957.
>   Criticism of the foreign-aid program; presented in layman's language.

Harlan Cleveland, "The Convalescence of Foreign Aid," *American Economic Review Papers and Proceedings,* May 1959.
>   Views on the objectives, operations, and impact of the MSP.

Committee for Economic Development, *Economic Development Assistance,* New York, April 1957.
>   Views endorsed by a business-sponsored organization relative to what the foreign-aid program should be.

Louis De Alessi, "An Analysis of Foreign Aid Administration in Korea," *Southern Economic Journal,* July 1958.
>   Examination of one country program under the MSP.

Economic Assistance Programs and Administration (Third Interim Report by the President's Committee to Study the United States Military Assistance Program), Washington, July 13, 1959.
>   The "Draper Report," covering objectives and procedures of the foreign-aid program.

William Y. Elliott (and others), *The Political Economy of American Foreign Policy.* New York: Henry Holt and Company, 1955.
>   General survey of American foreign policy, with emphasis on objectives and strategy.

Foreign Aid Program (Compilation of Studies and Surveys, prepared under the direction of the Special Committee to Study the Foreign Aid Program, U.S. Senate), Washington, July 1957, esp. Studies No. 1, 3, and 11.

Broad survey of the foreign-aid program, covering its objectives
and operations. Presents description, analysis and appraisal, and
recommendations for future conduct.

Max F. Millikan and W. W. Rostow, *A Proposal: Key to an Effective
Foreign Policy*. New York: Harper and Brothers, 1957.
Presentation of recommendations for basic changes in the foreign-
aid program, and reasons for the proposed changes.

Gunnar Myrdal, *An International Economy*. New York: Harper and
Brothers, 1956.
Ch. IX presents the case for a multilateral approach in the pro-
vision of external assistance to underdeveloped countries.

William Reitzel, Morton A. Kaplan, and Constance G. Coblenz, *United
States Foreign Policy, 1945–1955*. Washington: The Brookings Institution, 1956.
Statement of the broad outlines of US foreign policy during the
decade 1945–1955, and examination of substantive questions
raised as a consequence; see esp. Chs. VII, XX, and XXIV.

Report to Congress on the Mutual Security Program, Washington, 1959.
Periodic official report on progress under the MSP; also see
reports covering other periods.

C. Tyler Wood, "Problems of Foreign Aid Viewed from the Inside,"
American Economic Review Papers and Proceedings, May 1959.
Observations on the MSP by an official of the agency.

22

AID THROUGH AGRICULTURAL SURPLUSES

The US has a special program for the disposal abroad of agricultural commodities regarded as surplus in the domestic market. This program, intended above all else to help rid this country of troublesome supplies of agricultural commodities, is supported by a further rationale: that transfer of surplus agricultural commodities into foreign markets can result in gains for this country in terms of its foreign-policy objectives. Of central significance, proponents of the disposal program contend that these commodities, when transferred into the domestic markets of underdeveloped countries, comprise a meaningful form of developmental assistance for the recipient countries.

The present chapter examines why agricultural surpluses arise in the US, what procedures are followed by way of disposal abroad, and what advantages (and disadvantages) allegedly accrue from receipt in foreign areas of the surpluses. The major aim is to appraise the use of surplus agricultural commodities as a form of developmental assistance.

THE ORIGIN OF SURPLUSES

Agricultural surpluses, in the form in which they currently exist in the US, are attributable to this country's particular farm program. The surpluses are the immediate result of governmental interference in the market mechanism, in the sense that some portion of supply is not absorbed by demand at prices "set" by the Government.

Traditionally, the approach followed in the US toward agriculture had been one of reliance upon free-market adjustment. The belief was that the free interplay of supply, demand, and price would result in an all-around situation best for all concerned. Unfortunately, agriculture, subject as it is to peculiar supply-and-demand conditions,[1] did not respond in the adjustment process in a manner wholly devoid of serious drawbacks. The characteristic situation in agriculture was one of many farmers with incomes at substandard levels, a widespread reluctance on the part of farmers to move out of agriculture (despite the low incomes received by many of them), and a general inability by farmers, acting singly, to pursue measures that might markedly improve prevailing incomes.

Under the weight of economic arguments (sound or unsound) and political pressures, governmental intervention in the market mechanism came to be resorted to in the hope of assuring farmers of higher incomes. The intervention was essentially two-pronged in form: an attempt to curb production and marketing of particular agricultural commodities, and an attempt to put a floor beneath unit prices of particular agricultural commodities. The attempt to curb production and marketing met with dubious success; although some acreage was removed from production, output from the remaining acreage rose. The more important form of intervention involved price supports. The aim here was to "guarantee" certain minimum prices for select categories of commodities (with corn, wheat, rice, cotton, tobacco, and peanuts comprising the six basic commodities), the hope being that assured prices would result in assured incomes—i.e., higher incomes for farmers by means of higher prices for their products. The basic method employed has been for the Government to support prices at some percentage of parity, parity being that relationship between farm income and general prices and non-farm income and general prices which would re-create in the present the same ratio as prevailed in the supposedly normal period of 1909–14. The manner in which farm prices (and hence farm income) were to be supported was through loans by the Commodity Credit Corporation. Following the negotiation of a loan, a farmer, rather than accepting a price in the commercial market below the support price (used as a base figure for loans), could simply default, thereby "selling" the commodities to the CCC at the support price. In essence, the support price became the minimum market price.

If, over a period of some duration, the support price upon each commodity is limited to the average equilibrium price, no sustained build-up of excess supplies in the hands of the control agency is to be expected.

---

[1] For a brief discussion of how industry and agriculture are affected differently by changing supply-and-demand conditions, see W. Krause, *The International Economy* (Boston: Houghton Mifflin Company, 1955), pp. 28–29.

Supply and demand then tend to equate over time, placing the control agency in the role of a stabilizer of market prices. But, if the support price for each commodity is consistently held above its equilibrium price, some current supply (output)—in each period—remains unsold in commercial markets. The control agency then in essence props up market prices at artificially-high levels, and in so doing ends, year after year, by acquiring some portion of current supply for itself. The second set of circumstances depicts the story of the CCC since the end of World War II.

In short, the policy of the US Government has been to support the prices of select agricultural commodities *above* what would have prevailed under free-market conditions. In carrying out this policy, the Government has removed some portion of the current production of select agricultural commodities from normal market channels. The commodities so removed have come to rest, in the first instance, in inventories held by the CCC.

PROCEDURES FOR DISPOSAL

Given the tendency for agricultural commodities to flow into governmentally-held inventories, the question arose as to what was to be done about the accumulations. Little enthusiasm was evident for a return to a free-market system under which agricultural surpluses might cease to accumulate. The alternative selected was to continue the price-support program, but to seek ways to dispose of the CCC inventories in foreign markets.

Disposal abroad of the surplus agricultural commodities was not to prove a simple matter. Not only had the price-support program resulted in support prices above average equilibrium prices in the domestic market, but it had resulted, additionally, in domestic prices on the supported commodities above prices prevailing in the international market. In essence, the US had priced some of its agricultural production out of foreign markets. In the absence of further intervention, the US was not in a favorable position to gain an outlet for its surpluses in foreign markets. In fact, in the absence of further intervention, the domestic market itself had become vulnerable to an influx of lower-priced competitive imports from abroad—which, if allowed to enter, would serve to undermine the price-support program on its home ground. The situation required both special aids for exportation and new barriers to importation—and this while the US Government was on record as committed, in principle, to the promotion of multilateralism.

Confronted by both a foreign-trade problem and a farm problem, the US apparently concluded that the farm problem was the more pressing. In any event, it was the country's foreign-trade practices that were adapted to accommodate the farm program, not the other way around.

Specifically, new import barriers (in the form of quotas) were introduced to prevent unwanted competition from without, and a whole series of special arrangements were devised in the hope of stimulating an exodus of surplus commodities.

The attempt to increase exportation of agricultural commodities took two main forms. The first line of attack was through surplus disposal programs, involving exportation assisted by means of grants, donations, loans, barter, and sales for inconvertible currencies—indeed, anything but outright sales calling for immediate payment in US dollars. The second line of attack was through export subsidy programs, involving direct subsidies to exporters or sales abroad for US dollars at bargain prices, i.e., below domestic (support) prices. The two lines of attack, despite the essential distinction between them, were not intended to be mutually exclusive; for example, barter transactions and sales for inconvertible currencies have generally occurred at prices below domestic market levels.

RELATION TO FOREIGN AID

Within the context of the surplus disposal programs referred to above, two programs merit attention in terms of the provision of foreign aid. The first program, known as the "Section 402" program, stems from legislation authorizing the Mutual Security Program. The second program, known as the "PL 480" program, stems from the Agricultural Trade Development and Assistance Act of 1954.

SECTION 402

Considerable exportation of agricultural commodities, in grant form, occurred under the UNRRA and Marshall Plan programs. Beginning with FY 1950, however, the annual outflow of agricultural commodities under government grant lessened from the tempo of immediately preceding years. Moreover, with FY 1953, commercial exports of agricultural commodities also declined. The result was a sharp rise in the surpluses in the hands of the CCC. Under the circumstances, the "heat was on" to find new outlets for the growing surpluses. Sentiment, in and out of the Congress, seemed to favor a closer connection between the surplus problem and foreign aid.

Specific new action intended to make the foreign-aid program more of a mechanism for the transmission of surplus agricultural commodities was reflected in the Mutual Security Act of 1953. Section 550 of this Act provided that not less than $100 million or more than $250 million of the total funds appropriated were to be earmarked for use in the purchase of surplus agricultural commodities produced in the US. Authorization was given for entry into agreements with countries receiving aid under the MSP to cover sales of these commodities for local currency. The local-currency proceeds so obtained were to be used in ways that made conversion to US dollars unnecessary, and in ways regarded as obviating the need for equivalent appropriations of US dollars. Major eligible uses included grants for military assistance (i.e., the local currency generated in a given country could be turned back to it for use in its military establishment); loans or grants for developmental purposes (i.e., the local currency generated could be made available to supplement US aid dollars, regular counterpart funds, and other sources of financing, domestic and foreign); and the means of payment for purchases by the US of commodities and services in third countries (particularly for use abroad in conjunction with this country's foreign-aid operations). The foregoing provisions, in basically the same form (but with annual amounts variable between, typically, $175 million and $350 million), were repeated in the Mutual Security Act of 1954 and in subsequent annual renewals of the legislation. The applicable section in the Mutual Security Act of 1954, and in subsequent renewals, was Section 402—hence the current label, *Section 402,* for the particular program.

An outstanding economic feature of Section 402 sales is that they occur *within* the existing balance-of-payments configuration of each recipient country. These transactions provide a recipient country with imports of a type that would likely have occurred anyway (as evidenced by the record of transactions during immediately preceding years[2]). The transactions do not represent additional agricultural imports for a recipient country; rather, they represent substitute imports, i.e., substitutes for regular commercial imports. The imports in question, if obtained through customary commercial means, require scarce foreign exchange in payment. But, when obtained under Section 402, payment occurs in local currency, so that the equivalent value in scarce foreign exchange is saved for the recipient country. The foreign exchange so saved is then available for alternate uses by the recipient country, including procurement abroad of machinery and other items needed in development (but frequently not readily obtainable in view of the prevailing shortage of foreign exchange).

Section 402 imports thus serve to free-up foreign exchange in an aid-receiving country—which, phrased differently, is to say that the transfer of surplus agricultural commodities under the Section 402 procedure is tantamount to a transfer of capital. While a direct allocation of foreign-aid funds (as an alternative to transference of agricultural commodities) can provide the equivalent amount of foreign exchange for an aid-receiving country, the added foreign exchange, when made available

---

2 In administering the Section 402 program, US aid administrators attempt to hold sales of any agricultural commodity to any country to an amount no greater than that of the recipient country's normal commercial imports of the particular commodity during immediately preceding years—say, during the three years immediately preceding.

through the Section 402 procedure, holds a potential advantage over direct allocation—at least as seen through the eyes of some aid-receiving countries. The foreign exchange freed-up by Section 402 imports, barring imposition of special conditions to the contrary, remains the aid-receiving country's own property, eligible for use entirely as the country sees fit, without even so much as a Free-World limitation upon procurement. In contrast, when foreign exchange is supplied directly under the foreign-aid program, the US holds an element of control over its usage—both because of legal requirements as to the source of procurement and because of administrative interjections encouraged under the exercise of bilateral jurisdiction. In the case of some aid-receiving countries, however, there has been a willingness to enter into a so-called "commensurate-dollar arrangement" with the US, under terms of which the recipient country agrees to earmark the foreign exchange freed-up by Section 402 imports for use along lines identical to, or similar to, those that the US might have sought had it supplied the equivalent amount in foreign exchange directly under its foreign-aid program.

From the standpoint of the US, at least three advantages can be claimed for the Section 402 procedure. First, some foreign-aid funds, which might have gone directly to aid-receiving countries for use by them within broad limits in the procurement of development-goods from anywhere within the Free World, are instead specifically earmarked to ensure the disposal of surpluses held as inventory by the CCC. As a result, the CCC is to some extent bailed out of its predicament as foreign-aid dollars accrue to it in exchange for surpluses. Second, the surpluses so disposed of can be pictured to the American public as having been sold, even while the disposal operation can be represented, both within the US and abroad, as aid for development. Third, the local currency generated through Section 402 sales serves to give the US an additional lever in its foreign-aid operations within foreign locales.

PL 480

Introduction of the Section 402 technique served in fact to whet, rather than satisfy, the appetites of those bent upon disposing this country's agricultural surpluses abroad under the guise of sales. One year following the incorporation in Mutual Security legislation of Section 550 (the predecessor of Section 402), the Congress adopted a second and more ambitious piece of legislation: the Agricultural Trade Development and Assistance Act of 1954. This Act bore the legal identification of Public Law 480 (83rd Congress)—hence the label *PL 480* for the program authorized under it.

The purposes of PL 480, according to introductory sections of the Act, were several and diverse: expansion of international trade, improvement of foreign relations, promotion of foreign-policy objectives, encouragement of foreign economic development, and procurement of strategic materials. These and similar purposes appeared definitely supplementary, however, when viewed against the full context of the Act. The main purpose was simply to step up the amount of agricultural surpluses this country might dispose of abroad.

Reflecting its origin in response to a strong "urge to export," PL 480 was established as a big-money program, and with only minimal barriers placed in the path of potential disposal operations. In one crucial connection, especially, PL 480 activities were to be less inhibited than those under Section 402: while Section 402 sales were to occur *within* the previously prevailing balance-of-payments configuration of the recipient country, PL 480 disposals were permissible—indeed, were expected to occur—*outside* and *beyond* the previously prevailing balance-of-payments configuration. Section 402 transactions were intended to provide a recipient country with substitutes for some amount of *normal* commercial imports (thereby freeing-up foreign exchange in the recipient economy), but PL 480 transactions were intended to provide additional imports *above those considered normal* (thereby ruling out any direct freeing-up of foreign exchange). In essence, the Section 402 program focused on *foreign-exchange savings* (for the recipient country), whereas the PL 480 program stressed *trade promotion* (with US agricultural surpluses intended to be the direct beneficiary).

Disposals under PL 480 were to occur along three main avenues. First, Title I (of PL 480) provided for *sales for foreign currency*. Second, Title II provided for disposals as *emergency relief*. Third, Title III provided for disposals through *voluntary relief agencies*. Of these, Title I was most important—in terms of both dollar magnitude and implications for world trade and development.

1. *Title I.* The 1954 Act provided, under Title I, for sale of surplus agricultural commodities for foreign currencies in an amount not to exceed $4 billion (valued at CCC cost) during the 4-year period ending June 30, 1958.[3] In 1958, the Act was extended through CY 1959, with a further appropriation (relative to Title I) of $2.25 billion for the period; and, in 1959, the Act was again extended, through CY 1961—with an annual appropriation to cover sales not to exceed $1.5 billion per year for CY's 1960–61.

As previously intimated, Title I sales were intended, primarily, to help develop a greater market abroad for American agricultural produce. Despite its clear-cut emphasis on magnitude of sales, the legislation laid

---

[3] The initial appropriation had been for only $700 million for a 3-year period, but three supplementary actions by the Congress occurred thereafter to accommodate the Department of Agriculture in its vigorous sales effort, bringing the final appropriation up to $4 billion for a 4-year period.

down some general provisions to which marketings were to conform. Among these provisions, reasonable precaution was to be exercised to avoid disruption of world trade and prices, and preference in marketing was to be given to private trade channels.[4]

Title I sales were to occur only after formal agreement between the governments of the US and the recipient country. Each agreement was to specify the amount and type of sales to occur, and the manner of use to which local-currency proceeds were to be put. In practice, some portion of local currency derived was to be earmarked for US use, while the remainder was eligible for mutual use as jointly agreed upon.

Retention by the US of some portion of the local-currency proceeds for its own use was supported in the light of two main purposes. First, some local currency can be used by the US for meeting obligations incurred abroad as it acts in its own behalf, with the local currency used alternatively to equivalent amounts in dollars. For example, local currency can be used to acquire local housing for American military and official personnel, or to finance local-currency costs of construction on US overseas bases. The right of decision as to how to use local currency within the US-use category remains exclusively with this country. Second, under the so-called Cooley Amendment of 1957,[5] up to 25% of local-currency proceeds can be retained by the US for subsequent use as loans, through the Export-Import Bank, to qualifying American business firms engaged in or contemplating foreign operations. Eligibility for loans is contingent upon fund use in a manner not likely to result in new competition for US agricultural commodities, and preferably in a manner likely to expand markets for this country's agricultural commodities.

The major portion of local-currency proceeds—i.e., all the local currency remaining after the prior claims for US use are satisfied—is eligible for mutual use as jointly agreed upon by the US and the recipient country. The two major mutual uses are mutual defense (e.g., construction or maintenance of military installations for use by the recipient country), and economic development in the recipient country. The local currency is treated on either a grant or loan basis. Placement for mutual defense is customarily handled as a grant, while much of the placement for development is on a loan basis. When placed as loans (through the Export-Import Bank), terms are as follows: 4% interest, whether repayment is scheduled to occur in US dollars or in local currency;[6] up to 40-year repayment, with an initial grace period of 3 years.

2. *Title II.* Under Title II, $800 million was appropriated for the

---

4 PL 480, Section 101.

5 PL 480, Section 104(e).

6 Prior to April 14, 1959, loan agreements stipulating repayment in US dollars carried a 3% interest charge, while a 4% interest charge applied when repayment was scheduled in local currency.

4-year period ending June 30, 1958, for use in the procurement of surplus agricultural commodities from the CCC for disposal, on a grant basis, in emergency situations abroad, e.g., as in famine relief. Thereafter, in 1958, legislation was approved that permitted the unexpended portions remaining to be used during the period through CY 1959; and, in 1959, an additional appropriation of $300 million per year was provided for CY's 1960–61.

3. *Title III*. Under Title III, surplus agricultural commodities from the stocks of the CCC were to be made available on a grant basis, and in indeterminate amount (subject to negotiation), to qualifying non-profit voluntary relief agencies which would undertake to distribute the commodities abroad. Voluntary agencies involved include religious groups and organized private charitable organizations.

RELATION TO DEVELOPMENT

A widely-held view is that the sale of US surplus agricultural commodities to underdeveloped countries for local currency constitutes an important form of economic-development assistance.[7] Four main lines of argument can be cited in support of the view that development is aided through the receipt of these surpluses.

FOOD TO FREE-UP WORKERS

The core argument, as suggested in Chapter 7, is that an underdeveloped country striving for development needs access to additional supplies of foodstuffs in order to assure sustenance for its population as some portion of its labor force comes to be shifted from customary pursuits to the new lines of endeavor arising in the course of development. It is argued that, in the absence of the creation of such supplies domestically, added importation is necessary. Importation through normal commercial channels requires foreign exchange, a scarce item in the typical underdeveloped country, and one readily usable in numerous alternate connections. The US surplus disposal program appears helpful in the promotion of development, therefore, because it provides needed imports without foreign-exchange cost having to be incurred by the recipient country on that account.

This argument has an element of truth in it, but it frequently is overstated (as pointed out in Ch. 7). It is obvious that as workers move into new lines of endeavor (say, into industrialization), they and their dependents continue as consumers of food supplies. It is also obvious that these new endeavors generally yield no or only small end-output during a transition period. With little or no end-output for some period, the question

---

[7] Encompassing activities under Section 402 and PL 480, Title I.

arises as to how food supplies in previous magnitudes can be assured these people (or, more accurately, can be assured the population as a whole)—either directly through domestic production, or indirectly through international exchange. The question is a very potent one when the situation in a country is that of full employment. Any movement of workers into new endeavors (say, *out* of primary production and *into* industry) then jeopardizes, at least temporarily, the physical basis for sustenance of these people, and for the population as a whole. Significantly, however, an outstanding characteristic of the typical underdeveloped country is that full employment does not prevail.

If the workers moving into new endeavors come from an overall environment of widespread unemployment or mass underemployment, food supplies for the country as a whole—obtainable either directly through domestic production or indirectly through international exchange—need not necessarily fall in the process. For example, the movement of 10% of the labor force into new endeavors need not cut available food supplies—not if the 10% are from among the unemployed or are from an environment of underemployment in which the remaining 90% can continue to produce the same total amount as was customary previously. While a distribution problem might well arise under particular circumstances (e.g., as more produce has to be transferred, physically, to the new locales of workers, accompanying a shift in population from rural areas to urban centers), the aggregative position of the economy as regards availability of a given amount of food is not necessarily adversely affected by the movement of surplus labor into new endeavors.

However, even if it is concluded—under the foregoing circumstances—that the movement of workers into new endeavors does not *reduce* the level of food supplies available, a case can be made nonetheless as to the need for *more* food supplies (as an accompaniment of the movement of workers into new endeavors). An essential fact is that workers obtaining new or upgraded employment receive wages, even during the transition period before an increase in end-output arises. To generalize, money income in the economy as a whole tends to rise as developmental operations are undertaken and come to fruition. This added income serves to create *added demand,* both for food and other items, and especially so when previous consumption levels have been low—to say nothing of possible added demand for food simply because workers, previously underfed, come to require greater food intake in view of their new work loads.[8] In the

---

[8] The Food and Agriculture Organization, following the study of an illustrative project in India, concluded that—under conditions prevailing in India—one-third to one-half of the added income resulting from a given amount of investment is likely to come into the market as a demand for *added* agricultural supplies. See FAO, *Uses of Agricultural Surpluses to Finance Economic Development in Under-Developed Areas, a Pilot Study in India,* Rome, June 1955.

absence of added food supplies, the added demand can be expected to cause a rise in prices, in turn inviting adverse balance-of-payments impact.

Given this situation, PL 480 imports (under Title I) can be supported on the grounds that supplementary food supplies are thereby provided to meet the added demand, and are provided without need to incur costly foreign-exchange outlays. A potential obstruction to smooth progress in development is thus avoided. A similar claim cannot be made for Section 402 imports, however, since these are merely substitutes for other imports that might normally have occurred (although foreign exchange freed-up in the course of the substitution might be used, conceivably, for procurement of other, additional imports).

RAW MATERIALS FOR INDUSTRY

A second argument is that the receipt of raw materials as surplus disposals can be helpful in the development of new industries. Whenever development encompasses industrialization, some import demands for industrial raw materials are likely to be generated. These raw materials, when obtained through normal commercial channels, require outlays of foreign exchange; but, if obtained under the surplus disposal program, no foreign exchange is required. The serious obstacle to development frequently presented by a general scarcity of foreign exchange is thereby overcome, or at least alleviated to some extent.

To illustrate, assume that a country seeks to develop a cotton-textile industry, but produces no cotton domestically. Importation of cotton becomes necessary, at least until domestic production of cotton gets underway—which may prove to be never. If, then, the needed cotton imports can be had under the surplus disposal program, local currency can be used to handle what would otherwise impose a foreign-exchange drain. Since the cotton imports required by the new industry are destined to occur beyond the previously prevailing balance-of-payments configuration, the applicable program is PL 480, Title I. The Section 402 program offers no help in the case at hand, since imports under it are limited to the magnitude of the country's past importation of the particular commodity (whereas the import demand at issue is a new demand).[9]

DISPOSALS TO FREE-UP FOREIGN EXCHANGE

To the extent that any imports are substitutes for normal imports, and can be had for local currency instead of foreign exchange, foreign exchange is freed-up, making it available for alternate, additional uses. Sec-

---

[9] If, in the case cited, the country already had the beginnings of a cotton-textile industry, and was currently engaged in an expansion of the industry, Section 402 would apply to cotton imports occurring within the limits of previous imports, while PL 480 (Title I) would apply to the new and additional import demands for cotton.

tion 402 imports have this merit, directly. The best that can be said for the PL 480 procedure on this score is that added importation, beyond normal imports, is made possible without *further* foreign-exchange demands being created directly.

DISPOSALS TO GENERATE LOCAL CURRENCY

The sale of surplus agricultural commodities, under either the Section 402 or the PL 480 (Title I) programs, offers a way to amass a pool of local currency. Local currency acquired under Section 402 represents a type of counterpart fund, and is ordinarily handled in a similar manner and for similar purposes. Local currency acquired under PL 480 (Title I) is used, in lesser part, to meet US obligations abroad, and, in greater part, in ways intended either to promote economic development or to bolster mutual defense.

Local currency earmarked for development is said to serve this end in either of two main ways. First, the presence of a new and sizable supply of local currency in a central pool helps remove uncertainties as to how new projects or programs are to be financed. Technically, a country has it within its capabilities to provide local-currency financing in any event. However, some underdeveloped countries lack the motivation or institutional means needed to proceed in this respect. Given this situation, a commodity-import program acquires merit in that it offers a smooth technique for bringing together in one accessible place a substantial amount of domestic money capital. Second, since claim to local currency gives claim to manpower and material resources, control over the allocation of funds amassed serves to influence what happens in the economy. Specifically, when local-currency funds, through actions taken in the provision of loans and grants, are steered into high-priority developmental efforts (in preference to forms of usage toward which funds might ordinarily have moved), the nature and tempo of economic activity tend to be altered to some extent.

Aside from the foregoing, the importation and sale for local currency of agricultural surpluses holds significant implications for those countries harassed by inflation. Surplus disposals under PL 480 (Title I), for example, both provide a country with additional imports and remove local currency from circulation, thereby exerting an anti-inflationary impact. Indeed, a general awareness exists as to the potential value of commodity-import programs as a means with which to combat inflation. But, if *the* objective of surplus disposals is to be that of combatting inflation, the local currency generated should be "frozen," not channeled back into the economy. While inactivation of local-currency proceeds is permissible (under the PL 480 program), the usual action is to pour available funds back into the economy posthaste, allegedly in support of "more economic development."[10] When inflation then continues, the situation seems to call for more commodity imports; and, as further imports occur and generate more local currency, there in turn appear to be compelling reasons for channeling the currency accumulations back into the money stream. And so the process proceeds somewhat in circular fashion: inflation, commodity imports, local-currency generation and spending, continuing inflation, more commodity imports—on and on, as though all were on a treadmill. The conclusion that appears applicable is that an early decision needs to be made as to which objective is regarded as paramount: a fight against inflation or the promotion of development. The manner in which local-currency proceeds are handled should rest on this decision, for the two basic objectives are fundamentally incompatible.

SOME LIMITATIONS

While some arguments can be advanced on behalf of surplus disposals as a form of developmental assistance, there are also some that are critical in nature. Several of the more important of these are summarized below.

COMPETITION WITH LOCAL PRODUCTION

An important obstacle to development, frequently cited, is that of limited domestic markets (Ch. 4). The logic is that there is little incentive for greater output in the absence of assured markets for the output. It is contended that if only development can in some way get started, then domestic markets will expand and thereby enable greater domestic production to find sales outlets. But, when it is found in the course of development that associated alterations in market conditions are giving rise to upward price pressures, a common conclusion is that price increases foreshadow dire consequences, that they should therefore be countered, and that importation of surpluses (say, foodstuffs under PL 480, Title I) offers an appropriate way to counter them.

Is it clear-cut that price increases of the type at issue should *always* be countered with added imports? Or, is it not likely that importation undertaken to hold the price line also serves to discourage the undertaking of added domestic production to fill the gap in domestic supply-and-demand relationships? It can be argued, of course, that rising prices in an underdeveloped country—if permitted (as in the absence of added imports)—serve to encourage added domestic production for the home market (say, in foodstuffs), the realization of which also constitutes a form of develop-

---

10 A basic motivation appears to stem from a fear that the presence of idle local-currency funds (to which the US has ownership claim) will be construed in the US, and especially in the Congress, as proof of the need for less dollar appropriations under the MSP. Rapid activation of the funds thus comes to be fostered as an attempt is made to safeguard the future level of dollar aid.

ment. In short, it can be contended that importation of surpluses in order to counter price increases—as under PL 480, Title I—undercuts *potential* domestic production.

The answer seems to lie somewhere between the two positions. Some price increases perhaps should be tolerated for their possible value in inducing stepped-up domestic productive effort. But price increases beyond a moderate amount perhaps need to be dealt with differently. In the absence of a PL 480 program for countries to draw upon, the customary way out in the event of marked price increases is greater commercial imports. With the PL 480 program open to countries, however, the added imports that ordinarily would be gotten through normal commercial channels can be had, all or in part, on a basis requiring no direct outlay of foreign exchange.

DISTORTIONS IN TRADE

The charge not only has been made that US surplus disposals on occasion have undercut domestic production in recipient countries, but also that surplus disposals have displaced and depressed the normal commercial exports of third countries. Criticism in this second form has come from a number of countries, including Argentina, Australia, Burma, Canada, Denmark, Mexico, the Netherlands, New Zealand, and Thailand.[11] The basic allegation has been either that PL 480 (Title I) sales have not always been in addition to the normal imports of the recipient country, or that Section 402 sales, even when occurring within the limits of the historic balance-of-payments configuration, have on occasion brought about a *shift* within this configuration as some export business that might normally have gone to third countries has been captured by the US. Beyond the allegation that the volume of normal commercial exports has suffered, a secondary contention has been that US surplus disposals have occurred in a magnitude and on conditions such that prices prevailing in international markets have come to be generally depressed.[12] In essence, the US has been pictured as exporting its farm problem, and doing so at least partly at the expense of other supplier countries.

Actually, criticism has been directed far more at PL 480 than at Section 402. The PL 480 (Title I) program is much the larger and is frankly

---

11 This criticism has been incorporated in formal protests, and in statements offered at various international conferences, e.g., at meetings of the GATT, the FAO, the Colombo Plan, and at UN sessions.

12 A common contention has been that the US is guilty of "dumping," in the sense that surplus agricultural commodities are sold abroad at prices *below* the domestic level. In explanation of its policy and practice, the US Government has pointed out that even though export sales under its disposal programs are "subsidized," selling prices in foreign markets are not intended to be below competitive world levels. For an elaboration of this point, see R. F. Mikesell, *Agricultural Surpluses and Export Policy* (Washington: The American Enterprise Assocation, Inc., February 1958), esp. pp. 36–37.

framed in terms of "trade promotion," so that it has been viewed as posing the greater threat to world trade. The US Government, in an attempt to allay fears, has pointed out that in negotiating bilateral agreements to cover PL 480 sales, "reasonable precautions" are taken to avoid the disruption of world market prices or the displacement of other countries from their traditional markets.[13] Policy statements on the subject have apparently calmed few skeptics, however, for the view persists in many quarters that not only are price disruption and market displacement as a consequence of past transactions a matter of record, but that the continuing urge to export on the part of the US can only eventuate in further repercussions unfavorable to competing supplier countries.[14]

BALANCE-OF-PAYMENTS IMPLICATIONS

One of the benefits claimed for surplus disposals is that of balance-of-payments assistance for the recipient country. This advantage unmistakably derives from Section 402 sales. Since these sales are substitutes for normal commercial imports, with local currency substitutable for foreign exchange in effecting payment, an equivalent value in foreign exchange is freed-up for other uses. PL 480 (Title I) sales, however, do not yield similar balance-of-payments assistance. Since these sales represent additional imports for the recipient country, no foreign exchange is freed-up. Of course, it can be argued that a form of balance-of-payments assistance derives nevertheless, in that *increased* importation is made possible without added outlays of foreign exchange being associated.

Contrary to the seemingly neutral (or even beneficial) balance-of-payments effect of PL 480 (Title I), the program is open to harsh criticism on the grounds that, in practice, it may be instrumental in bringing about *worsened* balance-of-payments conditions in recipient countries *over the longer-run*. The argument is that the increased imports made possible in the present by virtue of the program are likely to induce the evolution

---

13 See PL 480, Section 101(a).

14 Illustrative of the problem at issue, the criticism was made in Thailand (in 1960) that the US had impaired that country's rice exports and had depressed its domestic rice market (a reduction from 67¢ per bushel to 29¢ being cited) as a consequence of a sales arrangement entered into with India to supply a large amount of rice under PL 480, Title I; in fact, criticism included the charge that Thailand had not even been consulted by the US during the course of sales negotiations with India. Surface manifestations of irritation within Thailand over the arrangement were said to have included the following: resignation of the country's Foreign Minister, following charges of "failure to look after the country's interests;" a threat by other top Thai officials to undertake an "agonizing reappraisal" of the country's membership in SEATO and of her relations with the US; Cabinet action to send an "expression of dissatisfaction" to Washington; comment by the country's Premier that the US action constituted "a blow to a friend's feelings"; and appearance in the *Bangkok Post* of a statement of inquiry, attributed to "informed sources," as to "What advantages are there for Thailand to remain in the free world when countries not at all committed to the free world are getting equal benefits and, in addition to these, advantages of Communist aid?" For American press coverage, see *The New York Times,* May 13, 1960, p. 2-C.

in recipient countries of consumption patterns of a type such that a higher level of importation will continue to be expected or required in future years.[15] The fear is that present-day imports under the program will not, by and large, lead to the creation of a better basis in recipient countries for earning or saving foreign exchange later on, so that—in the absence of a continuing PL 480 program—recipient countries will some day find themselves in the position of not being able to satisfy the "heartier appetites" to which they have become accustomed.

As some persons see the matter, the PL 480 (Title I) program stands indicted on one or the other of two failings. On the assumption that larger foreign markets for US agricultural commodities come to be created over time, are these the result of greater total consumption in foreign areas, or the result of a shift in trade from other countries to the US? If they are the result of greater total consumption (with the increased consumption likely to continue), it can be alleged that the PL 480 program has added to the balance-of-payments plight of importing countries. If they are the result of a shift in trade from other countries to the US (but with total consumption relatively unchanged), it can be alleged that the PL 480 program has altered world-trade patterns to the detriment of other supplier countries. Either way the program is brought into serious question.

LOCAL-CURRENCY BACKLOGS

The sale of surplus agricultural commodities for local currency serves to give the US Government title to a pool of foreign currencies. Given the volume of surplus disposals, the magnitude of foreign currencies involved is considerable. However, far from being an unmixed blessing, claim to the currencies at issue presents special problems for the US.

First, there is a question of how and when to use the currencies. Notwithstanding numerous possibilities,[16] the matter of utilization is not a simple one. The general requirement that uses should prove mutually agreeable to the US and the recipient country serves, by itself, to raise many stumbling blocks.[17]

Second, the accumulation of currencies, held in idle form pending possible utilization, has created difficulties. Despite large-scale withdrawals for various uses, new acquisitions continue to reinforce a substantial carry-

---

[15] Indeed, the language used in PL 480 makes it clear that greater consumption and importation, over time, are expected; for example, Section 2 refers to "expansion of foreign trade in agricultural commodities," and Section 104(a) refers to "[development of] *new* markets for . . . agricultural commodities." (Italics are mine.)

[16] Eligible uses under PL 480 are itemized in Section 104 of that Act.

[17] *Mutual use* automatically applies to all local currency generated other than that specifically claimed for *US use*. The US-use portion embraces a small amount of that acquired under Section 402, usable by the US in any way it sees fit, plus that amount acquired under PL 480 to which the Cooley Amendment is applied, thereafter usable for loans mutually agreeable to the Export-Import Bank and the recipient country (see PL 480, Section 104[e]), plus any other amount acquired under PL 480 as a result of direct negotiations, then usable by the US in any way it sees fit.

forward of earlier balances, as a consequence of which uncommitted currency stocks on hand remain at a high level. As of mid-1959, the backlog of uncommitted local currencies initially acquired through disposals of surplus agricultural commodities under PL 480, Title I, alone totaled roughly the equivalent of $1.1 billion; in addition, some $0.6 billion in local currencies remained in straight counterpart.[18] The piling up of local currencies in unused form has posed a special problem because of reactions in some quarters. Particularly, some members of the Congress have been prone to ask why more dollar appropriations are necessary for foreign aid when well over a billion (even though in local currency) is still on hand. Obviously, this reaction has stemmed from a failure to distinguish between dollars, as such, and local currencies expressed in dollar terms—i.e., it is a case of confusing "apples and oranges." But, understandable as this confusion in thinking may be, the presence of idle local currencies has appeared to complicate matters for those seeking more dollar funds for foreign aid.

RELATION TO FOREIGN EXCHANGE

The local currency acquired through the sale of surpluses under PL 480 is frequently pictured as providing the financing needed for the promotion of development in a recipient country, so that need for dollar assistance (in order to supplement the recipient country's own supplies of foreign exchange) is eliminated or substantially lessened. In essence, PL 480 transactions, and the local currency generated thereby, are pictured as capable of being the core of a foreign-aid effort.

This idea is vulnerable in that local currency is viewed as being largely interchangeable with foreign exchange. Actually, local currency and foreign exchange differ widely, in terms of what can be procured through their use. Local currency can be used to procure domestic items, but access to import items customarily requires foreign exchange. Since the process of development ordinarily calls for some combination of domestic items and import items (including items beyond PL 480 imports), the local currency generated through PL 480 sales can offer, at best, no more than a partial answer. Foreign exchange is still needed to acquire the ingredients of development not readily available domestically or available under PL

---

18 ICA, *Operations Report,* Washington, FY 1959 issue No. 4, p. 20. Relative to the totals cited, the $1.1 billion amount is US-owned, whereas the $0.6 billion amount is US-owned to the extent of roughly $0.2 billion (i.e., the portion attributable to sales under Section 402) and is country-owned to the extent of roughly $0.4 billion (i.e., the portion representing counterpart other than that attributable to sales under Section 402).

Not only does that local currency currently remaining uncommitted comprise a sizable sum, but amounts placed as loans are destined to return over time, with interest, as repayments occur. Significantly, loan arrangements ordinarily provide for repayment in local currency. While repayment in dollars is permissible, few loans are negotiated on this basis.

480. This foreign exchange, if it cannot be earned by the country, has to be secured from abroad through "extraordinary" means other than PL 480.

In short, the PL 480 (Title I) program cannot be regarded as offering potential, through a stepped-up tempo in surplus disposals, as a direct substitute for all other forms of foreign aid. As long as a case can be made for access to supplementary foreign exchange, a case can also be made for a foreign-aid program going *beyond* what PL 480 (Title I) has to offer.

IMPLICATIONS FOR THE FUTURE

It is interesting to speculate as to what the future of the agricultural surplus disposal program might be. In so doing, past performance gives some clues as to possible future action.

To cite an obvious and basic fact, the surplus disposal program came into being because troublesome surpluses had come to exist. Given the surpluses, a way needed to be found to rid the country of them. The method seized upon was disposal abroad under special programs, the major one of which came to be PL 480 (Title I). Not content, however, merely with ridding the country of its accumulations of the past, the disposal technique very soon came to be viewed, and relied upon, as a means for dealing with the country's continuing overproduction in agriculture. But, despite fairly aggressive salesmanship (as reflected in stepped-up levels of foreign disposals), surpluses still on hand (as reflected in inventories held by the CCC) also showed a general tendency to rise over time.[19]

Once the decision was reached to initiate a large-scale program for foreign disposals, need was felt for a proper rationale. While a rationale along the lines of "exportation of the domestic agricultural problem" satisfied many persons, something more palatable was regarded necessary if widespread support was to be gained and held, both in the US and abroad (and especially abroad). The central rationale that came to be invoked was that of "help for economic development"—but supplemented with other, lesser rationales, generally placing emphasis upon humanitarian aspects, such as "food for hungry people." True, some surplus disposals have helped in the promotion of economic development. But by how much? *Perhaps* an equivalent dollar outlay by the American public to finance non-surplus forms of aid would have proven far more helpful in developmental promotion.

Thus, surpluses prevail and continue to accrue; and, alongside the

---

[19] The CCC's investment in price-support commodities rose from $3.6 billion at the close of 1949 to $8.2 billion in 1956, and to $8.7 billion in 1958. For data through 1956, see Department of Agriculture, *Price Programs* (Bulletin No. 135), Washington, 1957, pp. 70–72; subsequent data supplied by the Department of Agriculture per request.

surplus problem, a rationale has arisen that links surplus disposals with aid for development. Given this environmental situation, a question arises as to just how hard the US should push to export surpluses. Importantly, by way of an answer, those within the US who are kindly disposed toward subsidies for agriculture through a price-support system are not likely to favor elimination or weakening of a major outlet for the excess supplies generated under the system. A widely-held conviction is that, in the absence of some special procedure for draining off a portion of past and current output, surplus stocks acquired in the course of supporting prices would soon reach a level likely to evoke public clamor for a drastic change in the farm program itself, possibly resulting in outright termination of the price-support system. The inclination, therefore, is to "keep the heat off" the domestic situation through the expedient of continuing, or even intensifying, surplus disposals abroad— under one rationale or another (a major, and at least partially valid, rationale being aid for development).

A common argument has held that the US should put its surplus-disposal program on a long-range basis. One proposal, offered in 1959, suggested a firm commitment by the US Government to continue PL 480 for a minimum period of five additional years.[20] It was suggested, on behalf of the proposal, that a period of this duration was needed by this country to permit adjustments to be made in farm production; additionally, it was suggested that recipient countries deserved considerable advance warning so as to permit preparation for weathering attendant trade adjustments.

The proposal to continue PL 480 for five additional years raises havoc with the earlier claim that surplus disposals are geared to cope with a *temporary* maladjustment in American agriculture. Indeed, the proposal, whatever else might be said of it, carries with it no guarantee that an even longer period will not be needed. Significantly, editorial comment on the subject matter of the proposal appearing in a leading Farm Belt newspaper suggests that "five more years" is not enough, and that *greater* disposals, not a tapering off of them, may well be in order. In the words of the editorial:[21]

> It makes sense to establish the farm export programs on a long-range basis. But we doubt very much that it will be possible to taper off in five years. . . . It is more probable that the United States will have still larger surpluses of farm products in the years ahead. At any rate, a long-range plan for use of these products in foreign economic development programs *would be a good thing to have on hand.*

---

[20] J. H. Davis, *Policy Considerations Pertaining to Public Law 480* (report prepared for the Department of State; mimeographed), 1959; see esp. pp. 1, 12.
[21] "Putting Our Surpluses to Use" (editorial), *The Des Moines Sunday Register,* January 18, 1959, p. 24-G. (Italics are mine.)

This editorial comment seems to put the finger on something vital. Domestic policies result in surpluses, whereupon a long-range disposal plan (ostensibly to help foreign economic development) becomes "a good thing to have on hand!" Perhaps it is as some persons point out: the surpluses offered abroad in the name of development assistance are offered fundamentally *because they exist,* not simply because this country wants to assist in development and finds the provision of surpluses to be the best way of doing so. A danger in all this, of course, is that the foreign-aid program could become simply a convenient vehicle for unloading agricultural surpluses, with the case for other forms of aid becoming dulled as the impression is fostered at home that the country is already doing what is called for.

POSSIBLE REVISIONS

Given the difficult situation present under the prevailing price-support system, the US has open to it either of two basic courses by way of possible improvement. First, the US might seek an alternative approach to that of price supports. Second, the US, though retaining the price-support system, might seek to refine disposal operations so as to eliminate or lessen particularly obnoxious features.

ALTERNATIVES

Of the potential alternatives to the price-support system, two merit special attention. First, a system of *income payments* might be adopted to replace the system of price supports. As a substitute for higher farm income by virtue of floor prices under particular commodities, the system of income payments would offer farmers periodic lump payments to bring their total income up to desired levels, but would leave the process of price determination of commodities to the forces of a free market. Acceptance of a free-market price structure would serve to eliminate excess production and the accumulation of surpluses,[22] as a result of which subsidized exportation would cease; coincidentally, however, farmers could still be assured whatever level of individual income the Government felt they ought to have. While exportation could still occur, it would occur in response to market prices prevailing (within the US and abroad) and to related sales terms (e.g., availability of financing), not in response to special subsidization designed to shove goods into export channels. From then on, whenever agricultural commodities were provided as foreign aid, they would be provided on the same basis as had prevailed

---

[22] Even though *total* production were unaltered, excess production would cease in that *all* production would move through the free market at some level of market prices.

all along in the case of non-agricultural exports, e.g., industrial machinery.[23]

Second, a system of *production curtailment* might be adopted to replace the system of price supports. The objective here would be to lower
domestic output to that level under which all marketings might occur
through free-market channels but still yield prices, and hence incomes,
regarded as satisfactory. Because domestic commodity prices presumably
would be forced to settle at levels well above world levels (by virtue of
limitations placed upon supply), a system of restrictions upon competitive
imports (e.g., quotas) would appear essential for the success of the program. However, absence of a surplus would obviate the need for subsidized exportation. Thus, whenever agricultural commodities were provided as foreign aid, this assistance could occur on a basis similar to
non-agricultural commodities (just as would be the case under a system
of income payments).[24]

REFINEMENTS

Assuming an unwillingness to move from the price-support system to a
basically different approach, the US might, by way of less drastic action,
seek the means to make the price-support system work in a less objectionable fashion—particularly, to make it work more harmoniously within an
international context. Three major ideas appear to merit special consideration.

First, the US might, as a matter of regular practice, arrange to consult
with other exporting countries at an early date relative to pending
disposal agreements. Third countries need to have plenty of advance
warning if they are to weather readily the adjustments thrust upon them
by virtue of "extraordinary" American exports. And, in any event, third
countries should be given a chance to protest *in advance* as to US disposals, in preference to simply being reduced to registration of disap-
proval after the damage is already done.

Second, the US might take the lead in an attempt to initiate an internationalized procedure for screening transactions involving the external
disposal of surplus commodities. The intent would be to give all countries
concerned—exporter, importer, and third countries—a voice in the determination of what was or was not to be regarded as permissible; then,
once disposals were sanctioned, any damage resulting therefrom could at
least be rationalized by the exporter country as having occurred follow-

---

[23] A leading income-payments proposal in recent American history, much discussed
and highly controversial, is the so-called Brannan Plan.

[24] Various schemes might be invoked to limit production. The one that many
regard as offering greatest potential for success—and placed in operation in mild form
by the US through legislation approved in 1956—is the Soil Bank program, under
which the Government leases land to remove it from particular types of production.

ing sanction by numerous countries. Presumably, the number of protests occurring after-the-fact would be reduced by resorting to this procedure.[25]

Third, the US might assume leadership in a move to inaugurate a new international agency designed to handle surplus stocks of food and raw materials, whether arising in the US or in other member countries. The proposed agency—commonly alluded to as a *reserve* or *bank*—would concern itself with all or some of several major functions: purchase and storage of surpluses when necessary to avoid undesirable price movements; provision of middleman services in the channelization of temporary surpluses into the hands of ultimate users; maintenance of reserves for possible use in the alleviation of famine conditions; and determination of where and how currencies acquired by the reserve or bank in course of its sales might be used to finance economic development. Potential merits claimed for the agency include international control over surplus disposals, thereby lessening the danger of erratic export activity by any member country, and a stabilization-effect upon world markets and prices as applicable to food and raw materials generally. Drawbacks cited, on the other hand, include the cost of the capitalization needed to enable commencement and continuation of operations, along with a vulnerability to pressures likely to eventuate in commodity acquisitions, over time, *well in excess* of disposals.[26]

The foregoing ideas, although differing widely in form and likely direct cost, have one thing in common: concern that *unilateral* action in the handling of surpluses invites harm to other countries.

THE AGGREGATE EFFORT: SOME QUESTIONS

Part III has been concerned with a survey of the US effort relative to the problem of development in the underdeveloped world. As was seen, much has been done, and is being done.

But, is the *total* US effort adequate? Is it adequate in terms of the

---

[25] An FAO Consultative Subcommittee on Surplus Disposal was established in 1954, with a membership of 21 countries (including the US). Protests regarding US surplus disposals continued thereafter nonetheless, indicating that the consultative procedure did not work satisfactorily. A possible explanation is found in the criticism that the US, while giving notice of intent to conclude PL 480 agreements, did not always give this notice far enough in advance to allow time for full consideration of potential impact by all countries concerned.

[26] Two resolutions—one proposing the creation of an International Food and Raw Materials Reserve, and the other a World Food Bank—were introduced in the 84th Congress, but both were opposed by the Executive Branch. A basic fear in the US appears to be that this country would be expected to provide the bulk of the financing for a new agency of this type, while other member countries, or some of them, would view the agency as offering an assured market outlet for any output not otherwise exportable on advantageous terms (*and* would have the power among themselves to use the agency in this manner). In brief, there appears to be a fear that the agency could serve as a "camouflaged marketplace" in which some countries, when so minded, could "sell" their surpluses for US dollars.

needs of underdeveloped countries (given the immensity of the task there at issue—as seen in Parts I and II)? And, is it adequate in terms of this country's own self-interest?

These questions are cited here particularly because the US faces global competition from another *ism:* Communism. Attention turns, therefore, to this additional factor, and—in the light of whatever importance ought be attached to it, along with all other relevant factors—a central question of public policy then deserves consideration: *What should the US do at this juncture?* These matters provide the content of Part IV: "The Challenge."

SELECTED BIBLIOGRAPHY

Murray R. Benedict, *Farm Policies of the United States, 1790–1950.* New York: The Twentieth Century Fund, 1953.
   Survey of the origin and development of US farm policies.

——————, *Can We Solve the Farm Problem?* New York: The Twentieth Century Fund, 1955.
   Analysis of US Government aid to agriculture.

Committee for Economic Development, *Toward a Realistic Farm Program,* New York, December 1957.
   Survey of the farm problem and present-day governmental policies toward it, followed by the CED's recommendations for future action.

John H. Davis, *Policy Considerations Pertaining to Public Law 480* (report prepared for the Department of State; mimeographed), 1959.
   Overall appraisal of the PL 480 program.

Mordecai Ezekiel, "Apparent Results in Using Surplus Food for Financing Economic Development," *Journal of Farm Economics,* November 1958.
   Examination of US surplus disposals, with generally favorable conclusions.

International Wheat Surplus Utilization (*Conference Proceedings*), South Dakota State College, 1958.
   Compilation of papers presented by various persons relative to problems associated with surplus disposals in wheat.

D. Gale Johnson, *Trade and Agriculture: A Study of Inconsistent Policies.* New York: John Wiley and Sons, Inc., 1950.
   Stresses the conflict between US farm-program and foreign-trade goals.

Raymond F. Mikesell, *Agricultural Surpluses and Export Policy.* Washington: The American Enterprise Association, Inc., February 1958.
   Survey and appraisal of surplus disposal operations.

National Planning Association, "Agricultural Surplus Disposals and Foreign Aid," Study No. 5 in *Foreign Aid Program,* US Senate

Document No. 52, Washington, July 1957.
Appraisal of agricultural surpluses as a form of development assistance; recommendations for changes.

Lauren Soth, *Farm Trouble.* Princeton, N.J.: Princeton University Press, 1957.
Survey of the farm problem and possible solutions; written in easy-to-read form.

The Tenth Semiannual Report on Activities Carried on under Public Law 480, 83rd Congress, as amended, House Document No. 206, Washington, 1959.
Official report on activities under PL 480.

PART FOUR

THE
CHALLENGE

We are prepared to help you as brother helps brother, without motives. Tell us what you need and we will help you and send, according to our economic capabilities, money needed in the form of loans or aid . . . for industry, education, and hospitals. . . . We do not ask you to join any Blocs . . .; our only condition is that there will be no strings attached.

A. A. ARZUMANYAN, PRESIDENT OF THE SOVIET INSTITUTE OF INTERNATIONAL ECONOMICS, SPEAKING AT THE AFRO-ASIAN SOLIDARITY CONFERENCE, CAIRO, 1957.

We declare war upon the United States in the peaceful field of trade. . . . We will win over the United States. The threat to the United States is not the ICBM, but in the field of peaceful production. We are relentless in this and it will prove the superiority of our system.

NIKITA KHRUSHCHEV, PREMIER OF THE USSR, 1957.

Whatever the US has or has not done in the past relative to the underdeveloped world, a two-fold challenge confronts it in the present. First, the US is confronted by a global challenge in the form of Communist rivalry. Second, the US is confronted by a home-front challenge, existent in any event, in the form of the need to decide *what* to do *now*. Part Four is devoted to these matters.

23

THE COMMUNIST
ECONOMIC OFFENSIVE

For some years provision of foreign aid comprised an activity limited, for all practical purposes, to countries within the Free World. No comparable activity was supported by the Communist World. More recently, however, the Communist World pulled an about face and began to engage in substantial foreign-aid efforts of its own. The result was that the monopoly-like position of the Free World that had previously prevailed in this regard was challenged and broken.

While this new development opened the door to rivalry at yet another point between the Free World and the Communist World, whatever rivalry was in store focused particularly on two countries, the US and the USSR. True, the foreign-aid efforts of the Free World involved donor countries besides the US. Several countries other than the US (e.g., Great Britain and France) introduced independent programs of their own, and many of them cooperated with the US in an internationalized approach to the provision of aid, most importantly through support of the International Bank. The great bulk of aid arising within the Free World, however, came from the US, the one country within that alignment able to supply truly massive aid. Similarly, the projected foreign-aid efforts of the Communist World were to involve donor countries besides the USSR, e.g., Mainland (Communist) China. But, as in the case of the Free World, one country, the USSR, was destined to be the focal point.

The prize at issue in whatever rivalry was to arise was the political orientation of underdeveloped countries. In the eyes of many in underdeveloped countries, developmental progress could only be accelerated as the seemingly inevitable process of competitive wooing ushered in more generous aid. From the standpoint of the US, while the country could interpret any competitive threat as indirect proof of the potency of its own past aid efforts, the atmosphere created was one that worked against a letdown in the intensity of continuing actions.

The present chapter examines the nature and significance of the foreign-aid activity undertaken by the Communist Bloc, with attention focused particularly upon the activity of the USSR.

BACKGROUND

Historically, the USSR has been one of the world's most economically self-contained countries. Among the major countries, the USSR unquestionably has been *the* country most self-contained. In the years immediately prior to World War II, exports and imports each comprised only roughly 1% of GNP, the lowest proportion by far among the major countries. Even the US, with its reputation for high economic self-sufficiency, had a trade-income ratio at least four to five times greater.

The extreme economic self-sufficiency of the USSR was the result of two main factors. First, as a large geographic entity containing many and varied resources, the USSR did not find it necessary to cultivate economic contacts with the outside world to the same extent as did other and smaller countries. Second, the USSR, according to its own appraisal of the situation, found itself forced into economic isolation by a set of world circumstances. Following the Revolution in 1917, the new regime that came into power concluded, perhaps with justification, that survival depended upon what could be accomplished independently in spite of outright world hostility. In short, physical circumstances favored a high degree of self-sufficiency, but man-made circumstances, political in nature, seemed to rule out a course other than the deliberate pursuit of high self-sufficiency.

The two decades following the Revolution and terminating with the outbreak of World War II were years during which the USSR sought to achieve rapid economic growth, especially in the industrial sector. Marked growth was deemed essential both to enhance the country's military position relative to unfriendly external forces and to give promise of socialism's capacity to lead a population toward higher levels of living. The task was not an easy one, given the low economic base prevailing at the outset and the decision to push growth on the basis of domestic means. Stringent control measures were introduced, aimed above all to achieve higher levels of investment—and hence greater output. Notwithstanding growing output, however, consumption was retarded, by plan, so that investment might be still higher—and so on and on. Always it was a case of denial today, but with the promise of greater potential to-morrow. Clearly, the two decades constituted a period during which the USSR was oriented *inwards;* concern was with domestic growth, and thinking about foreign matters centered on the hope that nothing from the outside might come to upset domestic plans for domestic growth.

Then came World War II. The growth the economy of the USSR had undergone served it well, and in due course the country, as one of the Allied powers, was able to claim military victory. But the physical damage suffered by the country during the war was enormous. As a consequence, the immediate post-World War II period witnessed intensi-fied effort to achieve reconstruction, and to set the long-run growth process in motion again. The premium placed upon domestic growth had not lessened one iota, and in this sense the USSR was again oriented inwards. However, something new was injected in that the international aloofness characteristic of the country during prewar days was not recaptured in its former degree. Despite intense concern with domestic affairs, officials of the country exhibited unprecedented interest in the affairs of other regions. The explanation rested, presumably, upon acceptance of the idea in the USSR (impressed upon it by the events of World War II) that the country's destiny necessarily involved it in external affairs, and upon the existence of highly unsettled conditions in other regions (which con-ditions could hardly be overlooked by a country convinced as to the superiority of its particular economic order). In any event, the economic plight of Western Europe did not go unnoted within the USSR, nor did the revolution of rising expectations in the underdeveloped world. Sig-nificantly, however, the interest of the USSR in these matters external to it served, during the early postwar period, to bring forth an abundance of colorful words, but no bona fide physical contributions.[1]

In 1953, the USSR decided to go a full step further and commence actions that might buttress words with deeds. The year witnessed the beginnings of what later came to be known as the Soviet *trade-and-aid offensive.* Important occurrences during the transitional year included the following. In a speech before the UN, during which Western aid and private investment in respect to underdeveloped countries were criticized, the Soviet delegate announced that the USSR would undertake to con-tribute financially to the support of the technical-assistance program (and stated an amount offered as the country's initial contribution). Shortly thereafter, Soviet trade delegations began visits to various underdeveloped countries, prepared to negotiate agreements for expanded trade with the

---

[1] The USSR, although invited to do so (in 1948), refused to join with the countries of Western Europe in plans relative to the Marshall Plan. Likewise, the USSR, vocal in its support of technical assistance for underdeveloped countries, refrained from participation when a program was inaugurated under auspices of the UN (in 1948), citing as grounds the allegation that the program was really a Western imperialist plot to undermine the sovereignties of recipient countries.

USSR. Parallel to the trade effort, a program of loans for economic development was announced, and the prompt formalization of seemingly attractive arrangements with particular countries invited the conclusion that the USSR was no longer just talking about the plight of underdeveloped countries, but was now prepared to do something tangible about it. Strong evidence of the importance attributed to the trade-and-aid offensive within Soviet circles was found in the bureaucratic prominence given the attendant activities and in the assignment of some top-strata governmental personnel to the activities.

In retrospect, it appears doubtful whether the USSR's official concept of right and wrong in international relationships underwent any basic change as a prelude to the initiation of the trade-and-aid offensive; what appears to have changed was simply the USSR's willingness to throw its economic weight around in international affairs in a new fashion. But why, it might be asked, did the USSR choose to initiate the trade-and-aid offensive when it did, and not earlier or later? Four factors appear to have figured importantly in the decision. First, Stalin died in early 1953 and was succeeded by Malenkov. While Stalin had been isolationist in his outlook,[2] Malenkov showed receptivity to the notion of a growing international role for the USSR. Second, the revolution of rising expectations in the underdeveloped world gave promise of fertile ground for the propagation of the socialist philosophy. The USSR, of course, had long sought to convey its message through words, but it became clear in due course that underdeveloped countries had come to expect much more than words. Third, the US had earlier instituted a large-scale program of foreign aid, one apparent effect of which was to check further Communist inroads. As matters stood, the USSR seemed to have become less effective in its attempts to "reach" people in underdeveloped countries. Fourth, the capacity of the USSR to counter US activities relative to underdeveloped countries had increased enormously. Recovery from wartime devastation was largely completed in the USSR by 1948, and marked growth was experienced during succeeding years. For the first time the USSR could generate the surplus needed to support substantial peacetime activities outside its own borders. In short, in 1953 the international setting was right, the capacity to branch out existed, and the attitude was favorable for "getting going." It was no accident, therefore, that the trade-and-aid offensive should have come into being at this particular time.

In the years after 1953, the trade-and-aid offensive gradually gained strength and stature. On the one hand, the USSR came to devote added energies to the offensive. On the other hand, additional countries within

---

2 As a possible indication of his basic attitude, Stalin is said to have shown extreme reluctance to accept even occasional foreign travel.

the Communist World (e.g., Mainland China) undertook foreign activities supplementary to those of the USSR, so that the offensive really became a Bloc effort. Numerous underdeveloped countries came to regard the Communist effort as a boon, offering them a potential "add-on" to whatever help might be had from within the Free World, or a potential lever for use in eliciting help from within the Free World, or even an outright substitute for help proffered by the Free World. Indeed, support from within the Communist World and the receptivity in quarters without were such that, within five years of its inception, little room remained for anyone in the Free World to toss off the Communist effort as merely peripheral. Rather, whether or not the Free World (and particularly the US) wanted to recognize it as such, a competitive threat of the first magnitude had evolved.

MOTIVES

The motives of the USSR in the day-to-day operations under its economic offensive appear to be primarily political, and only secondarily economic. Political gain is expected to derive in four main, and somewhat related, ways.

First, the USSR is interested in giving tangible support to its propaganda objectives. A central Soviet contention is that the major industrial countries of the West wish to retain, insofar as reasonably possible, the same basic economic and political relationships between themselves and underdeveloped countries as have prevailed in the past, and that they wish this situation because of the particular benefits they stand to reap as a consequence. Thus, the presumed interest of major industrial countries of the West in the promotion of "balanced" development in underdeveloped countries is pictured as a thinly veiled attempt to distract these countries from making any concerted effort to shift away from primary production, as their inclinations might otherwise lead them to do. Again, major countries of the West are pictured as fearful of genuine nationalist movements in underdeveloped countries, and as willing to use economic and other means to delay or divert the growth of nationalism—allegedly because its spread might in due course alienate these countries from the West. In contrast, the USSR pictures itself as a proponent of industrial development, regarded in many underdeveloped countries as virtually synonymous with economic development. Similarly, the USSR tries to align itself with the growing forces of nationalism by playing on the popular notion that only if there is economic independence (implying need for industrial growth) can there be political independence. In short, the USSR pursues a propaganda line that takes its cue from various "gripes" underdeveloped countries have relative to their dealings with the major powers of the West, and then reinforces its propaganda with tangible actions intended to make the Soviet Union appear as the champion of these countries in their struggle with the "imperialist West."[3]

Second, the economic offensive, while in support of propaganda objectives, is expected to pay off, in part, through its influence upon the foreign policies of recipient underdeveloped countries. Given no alternative, these countries might simply be inclined to string along with the West, notwithstanding occasional misgivings. Indeed, while absence of choice may result in close economic linkage with the West, the economic association may serve, additionally, as a prelude to military linkage. Significantly, most countries receiving economic assistance from the US (under the MSP) also receive military assistance, with the military assistance provided subsequent to negotiation of a military commitment. But, entry of the USSR into the field gives recipient countries an element of choice formerly non-existent. Given greater capacity to exercise choice, countries are enabled to vent particular feelings and even turn anti-West (e.g., as did Egypt and Syria in 1957); certainly the course of neutrality is thereby made much more attractive. In short, potential benefits under the Soviet economic offensive serve, in the opinion of some recipients, to cancel out reasons for close alignment with the West.

Third, the economic offensive is also expected to pay off through its influence upon the domestic policies of underdeveloped countries. In its economic offensive, the USSR in essence offers living proof that rapid economic development is possible, and implies to present-day underdeveloped countries that they can make similar gains if only they are prepared to imitate the USSR as to method.[4] Because countries desiring marked development during the near-term future can hardly be other than impressed by the distinctive developmental history of the USSR, advice the USSR may choose to offer as an accompaniment of transactions may even be welcomed—even while parallel advice emanating from, say, the US may be resented as an attempt to interfere.

Fourth, there is an intelligence angle. In the course of conduct of the economic offensive, some Soviet nationals come to visit and reside in recipient countries. Because of their usually good linguistic training and their seemingly extraordinary willingness to integrate with the local populace, there is an inclination in some circles within the West to think of these persons as comprising a force engaged, actually or potentially, in

---

[3] Department of State, *The Sino-Soviet Economic Offensive in the Less Developed Countries,* Washington, May 1958, Part II, esp. pp. 10–13.

[4] The view of the USSR, as intimated in an earlier day by one Soviet writer, is that ". . . the experience of *socialist* industrialization of the USSR serves as the classical model. . . ." See I. Dudinskii, "Uspekhi sotsialisticheskoi industrializatsii evropeiskikh stran narodnoi demokratii," *Bol'shevik,* 1950, No. 19, p. 33. (Italics are mine.)

espionage or conspiratorial activities. In short, the economic offensive comes to be pictured as a cover-up for undercover work. Suspicions in this vein are ordinarily difficult either to prove or disprove. However, if it is assumed that *the* major objective of the USSR is to influence the foreign policies of recipient countries (presumably a reasonable assumption), it would seem that the Soviet Union would strive to be very cautious not to jeopardize its basic objective by risking possible exposure of involvement in clandestine activities.[5]

The view that the USSR's economic offensive is intended primarily to serve political ends, rather than economic ends, is given added strength by the fact that no great economic benefits are potentially derivable in any direct sense by the Soviet Union as a consequence of its efforts. First, the USSR is not very dependent upon imports of raw materials such as might arise in the course of development abroad or in the process of repayment of loans. In fact, evidence exists that some raw materials that the Soviet Union has felt compelled to accept have already posed a problem, with the country seeking an "out" through resale in third-country markets, presumably at a loss.[6] Second, the USSR is not so rich or highly developed but that any assistance provided under its economic offensive could, alternatively, have been used to good advantage at home. The weight of the economic offensive, at least at this juncture in the country's history, still causes a pinch in the domestic economy. The indisputable conclusion seems to be that the USSR sees political advantage as a product of its economic offensive, and that it regards the associated economic cost as a bearable price for potential political gains.

As intimated earlier, the USSR's economic offensive is reinforced by activities undertaken by other countries within the Communist World, specifically Mainland China and the satellite countries of Eastern Europe. The motivation of Mainland China, like that of the USSR, is heavily political and only secondarily economic. The political gains that Mainland China seeks to derive are basically two-fold. First, Mainland China desires to obtain diplomatic recognition internationally, and sees the offer of advantageous economic relationships as the bait that might lure other countries to grant recognition.[7] Second, Mainland China is striving for recognition as the leader in Asia (with India regarded as its chief rival), and therefore wishes to give other Asian countries the impression that its economic progress since "liberation from Western influence" has

---

[5] For an elaboration of this point, see J. S. Berliner, *Soviet Economic Aid* (New York: Council on Foreign Relations, 1958), pp. 26–29.

[6] This is said to have been the case with Egyptian cotton and Burmese rice. See Department of State, *The Sino-Soviet Economic Offensive in the Less Developed Countries,* Washington, May 1958, p. 43.

[7] Of the four countries which recognized Mainland China during the years between termination of the Korean conflict and 1958, three—Nepal, Egypt, and Yemen—were "rewarded" with allocations of economic aid.

been very great—so great, in fact, that an external economic offensive is possible! Evidence that the motivation of Mainland China in its economic offensive is *not* primarily economic is found in the fact that the country is not particularly dependent at its present stage of development upon the types of imports potentially obtainable from the countries toward which its offensive is geared, and in the fact that the energies directed toward external activities are extremely costly in terms of the need for them in conjunction with the intense domestic effort.

The case of the satellites of Eastern Europe appears to be somewhat different from that of Mainland China, offering a "mixed" picture. For the greater part, the primary interest of these countries in participation in an economic offensive, alongside the USSR, is economic. The countries find it advantageous to play the various angles that can provide them with essential raw materials from abroad and with needed foreign markets for their manufactures. A political motivation is not absent however. For example, East Germany has much to gain, politically, from participation in an economic offensive; for it, trade and loan activities represent a possible means to respectability and representation abroad, and even to diplomatic recognition in non-Bloc countries.

ACTIVITIES

From the outset, there was much speculation within the Free World (and especially within the US) as to the nature, magnitude, and effectiveness of the Communist economic offensive. However, information that reached the public during the early years was piecemeal and incomplete. Information released by both donor countries and recipient countries invariably dealt with specific deals, leaving the overall picture open to conjecture. With the passage of time, however, a considerable amount of information was amassed, so that a good basis for description and appraisal was available.[8]

The most basic overall feature of the Communist economic offensive is that it has two main, but closely related, facets: aid *and* trade—hence its designation as a "trade-and-aid offensive." The following brief description of activities under the Communist offensive, accordingly, is grouped under these two main headings.

---

[8] Early American impressions of the Communist offensive ranged from small-scale and ineffectual to large-scale and potent. Over time, however, there appeared to be a tendency for reports on the Communist effort to become less belittling.

In 1958, two major publications appeared relative to this area of subject matter. The first was a private study: J. S. Berliner, *Soviet Economic Aid* (New York: Council on Foreign Relations, 1958). The second was an official US Government release: Department of State, *The Sino-Soviet Economic Offensive in the Less Developed Countries*, Washington, May 1958.

THE ASSISTANCE PROGRAM

1. *Forms of assistance.* The Communist Bloc has provided aid both as economic assistance (including technical assistance) and as military assistance.

2. *Magnitude of assistance.* Between 1955 and the close of 1959, Bloc countries concluded agreements to provide assistance in excess of $3.2 billion to 19 underdeveloped countries (Fig. 14).[9] Of this amount, some $2.5 billion involved economic assistance, while the remainder, or roughly $0.8 billion, covered military assistance. Virtually all assistance was extended on a credit (loan) basis.[10] Amounts actually "drawn upon," through 1959, totaled roughly one-half of the total assistance "extended."[11]

In addition to material assistance, technical assistance has been provided. By late 1959, some 6,500 Bloc technicians were being utilized in recipient countries, roughly two-thirds of them engaged in economic-development work and the remainder in connection with military programs.[12] Concurrently, some 2,000 technicians and students from underdeveloped countries were engaged in training and study in Bloc countries.

Beyond the foregoing Bloc efforts, the USSR has contributed a nominal amount, since 1953, in support of technical assistance by the UN.

3. *Donors.* Of the total assistance extended, roughly 70% was attributable to the USSR, and the remainder was provided almost entirely by Eastern European satellites. Mainland China's contribution was relatively small, but growing.

In the allocation of economic assistance, the practice of the USSR was to concentrate on a relatively few major deals. To illustrate, over $1 billion was involved in only 8 distinct agreements, no one of which claimed less than $100 million. In contrast, economic assistance extended by the satellites involved, as a rule, amounts of only a few million dollars each.

Military assistance, like economic assistance, stemmed mostly from the

---

9 The 19 countries include Yugoslavia and Iceland (with $116 million in economic assistance between them), classed as "less developed" in the composition of Fig. 14. For comment, see Department of State (and others), *The Mutual Security Program,* Washington, March 1960, p. 5.

10 In contrast to the general pattern, Mainland China emphasized grants in its contributions. Through February 1958, grants by Mainland China totaled $55 million, and involved Cambodia, Ceylon, Nepal, and Egypt.

11 Utilization by late 1958 was placed at roughly one-half of assistance extended; see A. Nove, "Soviet Trade and Soviet Aid," *Lloyds Bank Review,* January 1959, Table D, p. 17. During 1959, utilization was said to have "reached a new high" (in absolute magnitude, although the ratio of utilization to total assistance extended appeared to have remained much as before); see Department of State (and others), *The Mutual Security Program,* Washington, March 1960, p. 5.

12 As of late 1959, the technicians were located chiefly in the United Arab Republic, Yemen, Afghanistan, India, Iraq, Cambodia, and Indonesia; see *Ibid.,* p. 7. The cited number of 6,500 represents an increase from 2,800, a number cited one year previously.

Fig. 14. Sino-Soviet Bloc Assistance Agreements, 1955–1959
(Amounts in millions of US dollars)

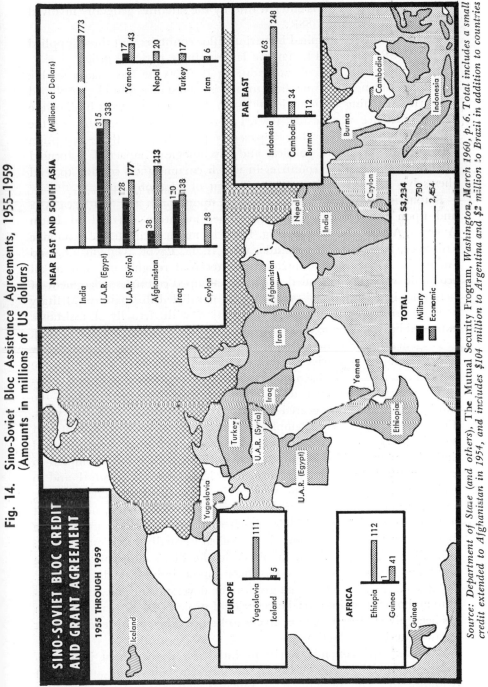

Source: Department of State (and others), The Mutual Security Program, Washington, March 1960, p. 6. Total includes a small credit extended to Afghanistan in 1954, and includes $104 million to Argentina and $2 million to Brazil in addition to countries shown.

479

USSR. In fact, arms deals entered into by the satellites generally involved participation with the USSR.

Technicians were supplied by various Bloc countries, but those supplied by the USSR comprised by far the largest single national group.

4. *Beneficiaries.* As indicated, during 1955–59 the Bloc had a sizable number of arrangements in effect to provide assistance to underdeveloped countries (reaching 19 countries by 1959). However, the great bulk of the Bloc's assistance was geared toward a relatively small number of the countries covered. The Bloc apparently proceeded on the assumption that it could maximize political and psychological impact if it focused attention on a few key countries in which circumstances seemed to lend themselves to exploitation for attainment of Bloc objectives.

Emphasis in the Bloc's effort has been upon South and Southeast Asia and upon the Middle East, with lesser attention devoted to Latin America, Africa, and Europe (Fig. 14). The major recipients of economic assistance, in order of magnitude, were India, Egypt, Afghanistan, and Indonesia. These four countries alone received roughly one-half of all economic assistance extended to underdeveloped countries. Placement of personnel in technical assistance roughly paralleled this pattern. Military assistance showed even further concentration, with virtually all assistance extended having gone to four countries: Egypt, Indonesia, Syria, and Iraq.

To generalize, the Bloc's effort has been heavily geared toward a few underdeveloped countries in Asia and the Middle East. Typically, the favored countries have been neutrals—or were neutrals at the time assistance commenced, but turned pro-Bloc thereafter. To a lesser extent, the Bloc's effort has been geared toward countries allied with the West. Turkey and Iceland are examples of countries allied with the West that have been targets of continuing Bloc offers, and that have accepted limited economic aid. The implication is that the Bloc has attempted to induce neutrals to become pro-Bloc, or at least to remain neutral, and to entice pro-West countries to weaken in their leanings. The growing attention allegedly given Latin America and Africa during more recent years, especially during 1958–59, is cited in some quarters as evidence that a major aim in Bloc efforts is to weaken normally pro-West leanings.

5. *Developmental biases.* Emphasis in the Bloc's economic assistance to underdeveloped countries has been upon industrial development. While some assistance has been given basic development (e.g., transportation) and other non-industrial categories of projects, literally no attention has been directed in a manner likely to be construed as an endorsement of raw-materials production.

Whatever the economic merits of industrial development in the recipient countries might be (as compared with equivalent amounts of assistance for, say, promotion of raw-materials production), the Bloc apparently has felt that its own cause is best served when it caters to the widespread and largely unmet desire for industrial growth. By so doing, the Communist World (and, presumably, the USSR especially) has hoped to lend support to its propaganda contention that its intentions toward underdeveloped countries are more noble than those of the large industrial powers of the West, which countries are pictured as interested in freezing underdeveloped countries in their lowly status as poorly-rewarded suppliers of raw materials. And, by so doing, the USSR and Mainland China, especially, have been aided in their efforts to impress underdeveloped countries of their own rapid progress in industrialization, and in driving home the point that a planned economy of their type has merit for countries interested in accelerated development.

6. *Intra-Bloc relationships.* Despite the dominant position of the USSR within its total context, the Communist aid effort is a Bloc effort in a very special sense. A considerable amount of the assistance offered to non-Bloc countries occurs as a joint venture, with one or more satellite countries participating with the USSR. Concurrently, the USSR provides assistance to some of its satellites, even while the satellites provide some assistance to the USSR.[13] The result is a complex intermingling of *two-way* assistance within the Bloc and of *net* assistance by the Bloc to non-Bloc countries.

THE TRADE DRIVE

Historically, the foreign trade of the Soviet Union has been small, relative to GNP. Such trade as did occur was largely with industrial countries of the West. Trade with underdeveloped countries was limited almost entirely to occasional imports of raw materials not available within the Soviet orbit, with payment being made through the use of proceeds acquired in sales to industrial countries of the West.

This historic picture underwent two basic changes during the post-World War II period, both of which served to increase the Soviet Union's importance as a trading country. First, the Soviet Union undertook to expand its trade with other countries in Europe. As for the newly-oriented satellite countries of Eastern Europe, the Soviet Union presumably hoped to tie these countries more closely to itself by inducing them to trade with it in preference to the West. As for the industrial countries of Western Europe (and especially Great Britain), the Soviet Union presumably hoped to capitalize on these countries' persistent balance-of-payments

---

13 According to an estimate of the West German Finance Ministry, the Soviet Union loaned or gave $7 billion to other Bloc countries between 1945 and mid-1958, in addition to having committed itself for $1 billion in aid to underdeveloped non-Bloc countries. Concurrently, reverse aid, frequently in the form of requisitioned items, was gotten by the Soviet Union from other Bloc countries. For example, forced deliveries of industrial goods and occupation costs exacted from East Germany alone were estimated to total several billions of dollars. See *The New York Times,* October 3, 1958, p. 2-L.

difficulties, offering them particular foodstuffs and raw materials in exchange for manufactures (for which the Soviet Union continued to have a great need during the course of its own industrial reconstruction and build-up).

Second, the Soviet Union undertook to expand its trade with underdeveloped countries. Beginning in 1953, and increasingly thereafter, trade offers—both as to exports and imports—were held out to underdeveloped countries. As in the case of foreign aid, the Soviet Union was soon joined in its trade drive by other Bloc countries, making it a Bloc effort also. Among them, the Bloc countries became active in sending out trade missions, in pressing for bilateral trade agreements, in participation in trade fairs and exhibitions, and in stressing opportunities for expanded trade in their propaganda media.

1. *Importance of the trade drive.* Publicity within the Free World given to the Communist economic offensive relative to underdeveloped countries has emphasized foreign-aid activities. Significantly, however, the USSR's own evaluation has assigned first importance to the trade aspects of the offensive. For example, a leading Soviet economist has stated: "The most important form of economic cooperation of the U.S.S.R. with other powers, including the countries which are poorly developed in regard to economic relationships, is foreign trade. . . ."[14]

In turn, the basic objective in the trade drive has been political, not economic. In the words of one who later became Premier of the USSR: "We value trade least for economic reasons and most for political purposes."[15] It would be erroneous, however, to conclude that *everything* that has occurred in reference to trade has been motivated *solely* by political considerations. On the contrary, while the political motivation appears to have been paramount, an economic motivation has not been absent. For example, some strategic imports were needed, e.g., copper and rubber; and, in general terms, the country's program of forced growth led to uneven growth, creating a situation in which foreign trade could logically be viewed as a means to alleviate both acute shortages and temporary surpluses. But even when an economic motivation has appeared clearly evident, the trade action invoked has commonly been one intended to yield political benefit to the USSR, quite apart from whatever economic benefit was expected.[16]

2. *Magnitude, direction, and composition of trade.* While the USSR's overall volume of foreign trade remained small (relative to GNP), it showed a marked tendency for growth in the years after 1950. The in-

---

[14] V. Alkhimov, "Cooperation between the U.S.S.R. and Economically Underdeveloped Countries," *Voprosi Ekonomiki*, No. 6, June 1957.

[15] Nikita Khrushchev, speaking in 1955; see Department of State, *The Sino-Soviet Economic Offensive in the Less Developed Countries*, Washington, May 1958, p. 6.

[16] For an elaboration of this point, see A. Nove, "Soviet Trade and Soviet Aid," *Lloyds Bank Review*, January 1959, esp. pp. 5–15.

crease between 1950 and 1957 was roughly 150%—from 13 to 33 billion rubles.[17] Also, while most trade throughout continued to be with other Bloc countries (roughly 80% in 1950 and 70% in 1957), a growing proportion of added trade was with underdeveloped non-Bloc countries, reflecting an important shift for the USSR in trade direction and composition.

Bloc efforts at trade promotion, while geographically widespread, had particular impact in a few underdeveloped non-Bloc countries. While trade between the Bloc and these underdeveloped countries, as a group, more than doubled between 1954 and 1957, individual countries whose trade with the Bloc rose especially sharply included Egypt, Syria, India, Burma, Indonesia, and Malaya. By 1956, exports to the Bloc accounted for 10% or more of the total exports of several countries: Egypt (34%), Iran (17%), Burma (14%), and Ceylon (11%); imports from the Bloc were 10% or more of the total in the case of two of these countries: Burma (19%) and Egypt (14%); and, in the case of Afghanistan, some 35% of total foreign trade was with the USSR alone.

The USSR's exports to underdeveloped countries during roughly the mid-1950's consisted chiefly of rolled steel, petroleum products, lumber, cement, cotton cloth, sugar, and wheat; imports from these countries consisted mainly of foodstuffs and raw materials—e.g., cotton, wool, raw hides, rubber, nonferrous metal ores, oilseeds, rice, tea, and coffee. According to Soviet statistics, little machinery and equipment were supplied to underdeveloped countries. Interpretation of this in the West has been either that the USSR is failing to fulfill its propaganda claim of supplying the means of production, or that these categories of exports are destined to occur in volume *later* as assistance agreements come to be implemented. Despite the cited paucity of machinery and equipment, however, Soviet trade has generally been considered highly important to its trading partners in the underdeveloped world. Particular trade items have accounted for a large fraction of individual trading countries' total foreign trade in these items; for example, 75% of Afghanistan's imports of petroleum products and 15% of India's imports of rolled steel came from the USSR in 1956, while the USSR was a major buyer of Egyptian cotton and Burmese rice.

In contrast, the trade of the European satellites with underdeveloped countries during the same period was characterized by considerable exportation of manufactures (including machinery and equipment) in exchange for raw materials and foodstuffs. And, in contrast to both the USSR and its European satellites, the case of Mainland China reflected an economy in transition. While the overall pattern of its trade with underdeveloped countries was one of raw materials and foodstuffs being exchanged for other raw materials and foodstuffs, manufactured goods

---

[17] The official exchange rate is 4 rubles per US dollar.

(e.g., cotton textiles, cement, chemicals, and steel products) came to be exported in small but growing volume during later years as the country's own industrialization program began to bear fruit.

3. *Trade agreements.* The Bloc's trade drive in underdeveloped non-Bloc countries has been spearheaded by a campaign to conclude bilateral trade agreements. By 1958, some 150 trade agreements were in existence between Bloc countries and underdeveloped non-Bloc countries, triple the number existent in 1953.[18]

In form, these agreements express a willingness by both parties to engage in trade, establish the types of commodities to be exchanged, sometimes set target quotas for these items (but leave individual transactions to be worked out within the general framework), and establish procedures for payment (frequently through reference to clearing accounts). The agreements resemble hunting licenses; they are important as an indication of intentions, not as firm contracts. While no prior assurance exists as to just how much trade actually will occur, significant increases in trade generally do follow from the agreements.

Since the agreements specify a regimen of commodities to be offered by each trading partner, and then also concern themselves with procedures to be followed to secure a balance in accounts as between the pair, the end result that tends to be achieved is akin to outright barter. While specific goods may not be exchanged directly for other specific goods, an equality of aggregate import and export values comes to be the norm in each bilateral trading relationship. It is a case of one package of goods being exchanged for another package of goods, but with the component transactions occurring over time and with resort to the monetary mechanism.

The agreements readily lend themselves for propaganda purposes. Bloc countries, in announcing the signing of agreements, are able to call attention to themselves simply on the basis of intentions (in advance of any performance whatsoever), and are able to call attention to themselves again later, if or when actual performance does occur—occurring, as it ordinarily does, in a series of transactions, each negotiated individually.

4. *Relation of trade to aid.* In the Communist economic offensive, trade and aid are viewed not as alternatives, one for the other, but as being complementary. It is a "trade-*and*-aid offensive." Complementarity between trade and aid is held to rest on two main bases. First, trade can serve as aid—e.g., exports can give a country access to the means needed to acquire desired imports, including essential ingredients of the developmental process. Second, the concomitant of aid is trade. In the short-run, aid is transmitted as goods and services, while repayment—under loan

---

18 Among Bloc countries, Czechoslovakia led with 26 agreements signed; the USSR had 20 agreements. Among non-Bloc countries, India, with 10 agreements, led as a signatory.

arrangements—proceeds in terms of a reverse flow; hence, trade figures directly in the aid process. Over the longer-run, the successful use of aid leads to heightened output, which then, indirectly, facilitates greater trade.

Significantly, commitment to the principle of "trade *and* aid" appears to recommend itself in terms of the Bloc's own position and interests. Beyond being able to cater to the desire of underdeveloped countries for aid, acceptance of subsequent aid-repayments (in the wake of heavy reliance upon loans) enables the Bloc to depict itself as willing to provide underdeveloped countries with added markets—thereby presumably accentuating a contrast with the US, which country is frequently criticized on the grounds of being a reluctant importer.

TERMS OF AID

It is widely accepted as fact that the Bloc extends assistance on terms highly favorable to recipient countries. A description of the terms applied follows.

EMPHASIS ON LOANS

The Bloc has consistently emphasized loans, not grants. Not only capital assistance for economic development, but also technical assistance and military assistance have been offered in great measure on a loan basis.[19] Assistance typically has been made available for specific projects or purposes, somewhat as a package in each instance—with the assistance encompassed being covered by an agreement, in the case of loans, which details the amount and form of repayment of principal, plus the amount of interest chargeable.

Rather than to regard its preference of loans over grants as an admission of weakness, the Bloc apparently proceeds on the assumption that adherence to loan arrangements holds major advantages for it. Potential advantages include the following. First, the practice of extending assistance on a loan basis can help Bloc countries to create the impression that they are interested only in business-like deals—capitalizing, as it were, on the presumed inclination of recipient countries to regard grants as the price paid them for passive acceptance of accompanying "strings."

Second, reliance upon loan arrangements helps make the assistance effort less costly for the Bloc. Not only is repayment, with interest, then had over time, but knowledge that repayment *is* expected likely serves to restrain the volume of requests for assistance.

---

[19] Unlike the USSR and its European satellites, which extended little as grants, assistance extended by Mainland China was heavily biased toward grants (but comprised only a small part of the total Bloc effort). See earlier comment in footnote 10.

Third, the use of loans, rather than grants, can give rise to several important political advantages. The repayment requirement, acting as it presumably does to restrain the volume of requests for assistance, helps to hold down the overall scope of the aid effort—and does so with a minimum need to risk the adverse political effects that ordinarily accompany outright denials of aid requests. Further, the process of repayment, as seen by many producers and exporters in aid-receiving countries, is a case of more markets, frequently providing a welcome outlet for surplus commodities not readily disposable elsewhere. Moreover, insofar as exports of aid-receiving countries come to be diverted from traditional markets in the West to the Bloc during the process of repayment, a new or strengthened economic tie tends to be cultivated, with the possibility that the tie (along with any concomitant political ties) will endure even after repayment is completed. Finally, liability for the repayment of principal with interest, should such prove especially burdensome upon aid-receiving countries, gives opportunity within the Bloc to offer concessions (e.g., a moratorium, or renegotiation of terms), a tactic to which the response might well be one of gratitude and respect.

LOAN PROVISIONS

1. *Few "strings."* The Bloc has maintained that its assistance is free of "strings." It has tried to foster the notion that it gives countries what they want (e.g., emphasis on new industry), and with minimum interference.

With potential political advantage foremost in Bloc calculations, concern as to how to assure economically-sound utilization of resources, which concern readily invites attachment of "strings," has presumably merited only little emphasis in the scheme of things. Actually, however, "strings" of a sort have come into being—if not directly, then certainly indirectly. An objective of assistance has been closer ties, economically and politically, between the Bloc and aid-receiving countries. When aid is deliberately designed and consciously placed to yield the expected ties, it may well be stretching a point to maintain that it has been free of "strings," even though the outward appearance of individual transactions seems to indicate their absence. And, with negotiation of trade agreements a common accompaniment of assistance, even some of the appearance as to the absence of "strings" comes readily to be dulled.

2. *Procurement.* While aid-receiving countries are said to be eligible to use credits extended to them in the procurement of goods anywhere within the Bloc, the usual situation is that the covering agreement describes the assistance in terms such that the country or countries extending the credits end, in practice, as the sources of supply.

3. *Duration.* Loans are of relatively long duration—generally from 10

to 30 years, with a short grace period preceding commencement of repayment.

Drawings upon credits generally occur over several years—e.g., one block of credit extended to Syria provided for drawings over a 7-year period. In some instances, the initial grace period is timed so that repayment commences only after completion of all scheduled deliveries.

4. *Interest charges.* Loans carry relatively low rates of interest—typically $2\frac{1}{2}\%$, but sometimes as low as 1%.

The fact that an interest charge is attached, even though a relatively low rate, tends to lend the impression within the Bloc that the assistance extended is mutually profitable; and, since the charge is below rates prevalent in the West, the further impression tends to be lent, both within the Bloc and within aid-receiving countries, that the West's rates are designed to yield capitalist profit.

5. *Repayment.* Repayment is scheduled to occur in goods or local currency. Loan agreements typically specify the general categories of goods held acceptable in repayment (but allow flexibility for subsequent annual negotiation as to what, specifically, is to figure in repayment). When local currency is accepted in repayment, actual movement of goods tends to be delayed somewhat, but also the door is opened to some degree of multilateral trading.

Goods accepted by way of repayment are said to be valued at world market prices. Special merit can be claimed for this method of valuation. Debt burden upon debtors is eased if prices rise; and, while debt burden becomes greater in the event of price declines, a market is nevertheless assured. Either way the Bloc's position relative to debtors is made to look good. Further, acceptance of this method of valuation makes unnecessary any direct reference, in the course of negotiations, to the touchy matter of maintenance-of-value clauses.

IMPLEMENTATION

The Bloc's approach is basically a project approach. The preferred procedure is to help get a specific project underway, and to bow out as soon as possible thereafter. To illustrate, assistance is rendered to establish an industrial plant, but no direct contact is ordinarily continued beyond the point at which end-output begins to flow from the plant. Through this approach, the Bloc is able to concentrate on relatively few impact projects, avoiding involvement in vague programs of long duration in which contribution is not easy to identify; is able to claim credit for establishment of specific facilities, without inviting blame toward itself for difficulties that might show up subsequently in actual operation; and is able to minimize the frictions inherent in close contact—and, particularly, is able to undermine the basis for the possible charge of foreign domination.

Arrangements for individual projects are the product, typically, of negotiations following the conclusion of *general* assistance agreements, which ordinarily specify only overall magnitudes and normative terms. The record of Bloc countries in complying with project arrangements is reasonably good as to the timing of deliveries, although the quality of goods supplied is sometimes questioned.[20] Technical-assistance commitments are typically met very promptly.

Administration of assistance efforts typically has been of good caliber. In its attempt to get "most bounce per ounce," the Bloc apparently has gone out of its way to put able people in charge. Beyond this, the Bloc effort has been of a type capable of high-type administration. Assistance has been concentrated upon specific projects, offering identifiable limits as to scope and duration—not upon broad, nebulous, or long-run programs; and, the fact that the assistance effort has been relatively small-scale has favored a perfectionist attitude toward its administration. Additionally, socialist organization in the Bloc countries has provided government with a high degree of control over the various ingredients embodied in foreign efforts.[21]

SOME COMPARISONS

How does the Bloc's aid effort compare with the US effort under the MSP? Direct comparison on some major scores is undertaken in the following paragraphs.

The basic forms of assistance employed by the Bloc and the US are similar; each extends economic assistance (including technical assistance) and military assistance. But, while the basic forms parallel, the programs differ widely in particulars involving emphasis, terms, and practices.

The magnitude of the Bloc's effort, thus far, is much smaller than that of the US, measured either aggregatively or in terms of economic assistance alone. The Bloc's assistance commitments total $3.2 billion for the period 1955–59, as compared with $15.8 billion in appropriations by the US during roughly the same period; for economic assistance alone, the relevant totals are $2.5 billion and $8.6 billion, respectively. However, among countries receiving assistance from both the Bloc and the US, particular countries receive far more assistance from the Bloc than from the US. A dramatic case in point is Afghanistan, to which country the Bloc extended $213 million in assistance during 1955–59, as compared with $86 million by the US. The essential point is that the US assistance effort, while much larger than that of the Bloc, is also spread over many

---

20 Department of State, *The Sino-Soviet Economic Offensive in the Less Developed Countries,* Washington, May 1958, p. 43.
21 See J. S. Berliner, *Soviet Economic Aid* (New York: Council on Foreign Relations, 1958), esp. pp. 167–176.

more countries than that of the Bloc. The Bloc's effort is concentrated—for reasons of intended impact—on a relatively few countries, regarded by the Bloc as key countries.

A greater proportion of the Bloc's assistance is classified as economic, and a smaller proportion as military, than is the case with American assistance. Examination of aggregates during the period 1955–59 reveals roughly a 3:1 economic-military ratio for the Bloc and a 1:1 ratio for the US (compare Fig. 14 with Fig. 11 in Ch. 20).

The Bloc's assistance is geared much more to loans than is that of the US. For all practical purposes, the Bloc's effort is that of a loan program; grant assistance, while it exists, is relatively small. In contrast, US assistance is heavily grant, even the purely economic portions of it (Table 22 in Ch. 20). However, as indicated in Chapter 20, the trend in American assistance is for more emphasis upon loans.

Some observers regard the Bloc's terms on assistance as easier than those offered by the US. Approached from the standpoint of all assistance offered, there is a question—considering the prevalence of grants in American aid—whether the Bloc's assistance is really more liberal. However, approached solely from the standpoint of the terms applicable to loans, the Bloc's competitive position appears strong. For example, the typical interest charge on loans from the Bloc is $2\frac{1}{2}\%$, as compared with roughly double this figure in the case of US dollar loans. Even loans made by the US from its acquisitions of local currencies bear rates above the usual Bloc rates. Again, the problems of loan repayment are eased for debtor countries through the willingness of the Bloc countries to accept installments in the form of direct imports of foodstuffs and raw materials. The US, of course, is widely regarded as a reluctant importer.

The Bloc plays up industrial development in its economic assistance, and gives little attention to agricultural development and only moderate attention to basic development. In so doing, the Bloc apparently considers that it is providing assistance of *the type recipients prefer*. In contrast, American assistance reflects greater "balance" in that agricultural development, basic development, and industrial development are all end objects of aid—although aid for industrial development, in some country programs, is relatively small or entirely non-existent. The US apparently considers that it is providing assistance for purposes from which *maximum benefit for recipients* can accrue.

By way of summarization, the Bloc's statements of sympathy for the aspiration of industrial development in underdeveloped countries appear to gain reinforcement through an appealing pattern of support: relatively heavy emphasis in the assistance effort is upon the needs of industrial development, and surplus primary goods are accepted over time in payment for the assistance rendered. The US, in contrast, is made to appear as interested to a relatively lesser extent in the promotion of industrial development in underdeveloped countries, and as relatively more interested in the disposal in underdeveloped countries of its own excess supplies of particular commodities, e.g., agricultural surpluses.

Few people bother to inquire why the Bloc can afford to be so generous in its expressions of willingness to accept imports of foodstuffs and raw materials, when the US seemingly is unable to come forth with similar expressions. Two basic factors favor the Bloc on this score. First, the Bloc countries (including the USSR) are still basically deficit countries, in the sense that real incomes are at levels low enough to make imports appear as a very welcome supplement. Second, the Bloc countries have tightly controlled economies, so that imports can be integrated into the economies with relative ease—with, among other things, no vocal group of private entrepreneurs around ready to raise the issue of unfair competition.

FUTURE CAPABILITIES

Viewed some 5 years after its inception, the Bloc's program of economic assistance remained small, compared with that of the US. However, the program was growing, both in magnitude and scope. In the light of this growth, an important question arises: What might the Bloc's assistance effort become in the future?

The answer to this question rests, in the main, upon two central considerations: the Bloc's foreign-policy attitudes and the Bloc's economic capabilities. Entry into the assistance field, followed by growing activity within it, lends support to the conclusion that the Bloc is concerned about its relationships with underdeveloped non-Bloc countries, and that it is willing to use assistance as a means for the possible enhancement of its position relative to these countries. On the assumption that the foregoing conclusion is a valid one, the basic consideration left for discussion concerns the capacity to perform.

CAPACITY: 1960

At the center of the Bloc stands the USSR, just as the US stands at the center of the Free World. In any all-out race in the assistance field, the two main contestants are certain to be these two countries. But, in terms of GNP, the US leads the USSR roughly $2\frac{1}{2}$ to 1. It would appear, on the surface at least, that the USSR is in a poor competitive position. However, a direct comparison of GNP data, without benefit of qualification, is likely to invite a slanted conclusion. The essential point is that additional factors are present and have a direct and important bearing on the capacity of the USSR to engage in assistance.

The USSR is subject to two major disadvantages, each of which serves to make a lesser portion of GNP available for assistance to underdeveloped non-Bloc countries than would otherwise prove possible. First, the USSR has heavy requirements at home. The country wishes to foster its own rapid growth and improved well-being, and whatever is made available externally cannot be used domestically, either for investment or as consumption. Second, the USSR has responsibilities toward other Bloc countries. Some of these countries are much in need of particular types of assistance from the USSR, and are even inclined to view their membership in the Bloc as a basis for preferred treatment in the allocation of whatever surplus the USSR feels it has available. Whatever assistance the USSR feels obliged to extend to other Bloc countries cannot be extended by it to underdeveloped non-Bloc countries.

On the other hand, a number of factors are present that appear to have a favorable bearing on the amount of assistance the USSR might hope to extend, given its prevailing GNP. First, the magnitude of assistance extended by the USSR, relative to its GNP, is low. Judged on the basis of its early record, the USSR's effort would have to be increased roughly four-fold in order to reach a proportion of GNP equivalent to that existent in the American case. While the implication is that some latitude exists within which the country could act to expand assistance, recognition needs to be given the fact that the same percentage-amount of assistance (i.e., assistance measured as a percentage of GNP) weighs more heavily upon a country of low per-capita income than upon one blessed with high per-capita income.

Second, the goods-composition of the USSR's own output is conducive to provision of the particular form of assistance it chooses to emphasize. The USSR places stress in its assistance program upon provision of producers goods usable in industrial development. It happens that the production of the USSR is relatively strong in producers goods. Some 70% of the USSR's industrial output is in producers goods, roughly *twice* the US percentage.

Third, while the USSR extends assistance to other members of the Bloc, these countries in turn assist the USSR—either directly through trade and other avenues, or indirectly through activities undertaken within the overall outlines of the Bloc's trade-and-aid offensive toward non-Bloc countries. Because it is a Bloc effort, the contributions of these countries, actual and potential, need to be reckoned with in any attempt to determine Soviet strength.[22]

Fourth, the forced growth of the USSR is prone to result in uneven growth, in the sense that surpluses in some lines come to parallel shortages in others. Items in temporary excess supply have little immediate value within the domestic economy, and frequently there is little point to hold them over. Consequently, to the extent that items in temporary surplus

---

[22] The European satellites have a combined GNP of roughly 40% that of the USSR, while the GNP of Mainland China appears to be roughly 25% that of the USSR.

can be used for purposes of assistance abroad, the task of providing foreign assistance is less a burden than might otherwise appear.

Fifth, the USSR is well situated to supply technical assistance. Quite apart from the size of its GNP, the end product of the country's considerable emphasis upon education, especially in scientific fields, is a steady increase in the number of technical personnel available. The services of relatively many of these persons can be supplied underdeveloped countries, with no particular strain upon the Soviet economy being induced thereby.

Sixth, given its particular economic and governmental organization, the USSR tends to have extraordinary success in any efforts seriously undertaken to shift goods and people into assistance channels. Physical commodities can be routed within the framework of the country's overall economic plan, the components of which are subject to almost constant manipulation. Further, the recruitment of technicians ordinarily occurs with dispatch; personnel frequently arrive on the scene in underdeveloped countries only days following a request.

A general conclusion that appears warranted in the light of the foregoing considerations is that the USSR has the means available to it to allow support of a somewhat greater assistance effort, but that any really substantial increase in assistance during the near future would likely pinch the domestic economy in severe fashion.

PROSPECTS

There is good reason to believe that the assistance potential of the USSR over the longer-run is relatively bright. Three factors especially lend credence to this view.

First, the growth rate of the USSR is high. Estimates point to an annual growth rate in GNP of 7% during 1950–55, as compared with 4% for the US.[23] Moreover, goals under the USSR's Seven-Year Plan (1959–65) envisage a continuation of rapid growth.[24] The income goal is attainment by 1965 of a level 62% to 65% above that of 1958. The cited Seven-Year Plan, according to announcements, is to lead into a second Seven-Year Plan, at the end of which (in 1972) the output of the USSR is expected to be double to triple the 1958 volume. Obviously, given a sufficiently high growth rate, the capacity of the USSR to extend assistance is destined to increase substantially; indeed, a growth rate in excess of that of the US is destined to bring the capacities of the two countries closer together for rendering assistance.[25]

---

[23] For summary data covering 20 countries, see CED, *Economic Growth in the United States,* New York, February 1958, p. 57.

[24] For a summary of the contents of the projected Seven-Year Plan, see *The New York Times,* November 15, 1958, p. 1-L.

[25] Other Bloc countries are also experiencing growth, and are planning for further growth, even at accelerated rates (e.g., Mainland China). In a Bloc effort, their production gains also need to be taken into account.

Second, the composition of output, as planned under the Seven-Year Plan, is further weighted toward producers goods. Output goals, by 1965, are for an increase over 1958 of from 85% to 88% in heavy industry, an increase of from 62% to 65% in consumers goods, and an increase of about 70% in agriculture. The fact that the relatively greatest increase in output is scheduled for producers goods creates a situation likely to add further strength to the position of the USSR in its assistance dealings with underdeveloped countries.

Third, loan repayments, as they occur, will provide the USSR with an inflow of goods, offsetting to some extent the outflow associated with any new assistance being extended.

In the light of the preceding analysis, two major conclusions appear reasonable. First, as matters currently stand, the Bloc could do more in the assistance field, if it so chose. Second, with the passage of time, the likelihood is that the Bloc will be able to do much more in the assistance field. Attendant implications, viewed from the standpoint of the US, are far-reaching and profound.

SELECTED BIBLIOGRAPHY

Robert L. Allen, "Economic Motives in Soviet Foreign Trade Policy," *Southern Economic Journal*, October 1958.
> Examination of the role economic factors play in the USSR's foreign-trade policy.

Abram Bergson (ed.), *Soviet Economic Growth*. Evanston: Row, Peterson and Company, 1953.
> Ch. 11, Examination of the USSR's economic relationships with other Bloc countries.

Joseph S. Berliner, *Soviet Economic Aid*. New York: Council on Foreign Relations, 1958.
> Comprehensive treatment of the Soviet trade and aid offensive.

Council for Economic and Industry Research, Inc., "Foreign Assistance Activities of the Communist Bloc and Their Implications for the United States," Study No. 8 in *Foreign Aid Program*, U.S. Senate Document No. 52, Washington, July 1957.
> Examination of the Bloc's objectives, capacity, strengths, and weaknesses relative to its economic offensive.

Department of State, *The Sino-Soviet Economic Offensive in the Less Developed Countries*, Washington, May 1958.
> An official report on the Soviet economic offensive.

Calvin B. Hoover, *The Economy, Liberty and the State*. New York: The Twentieth Century Fund, 1959.
> General treatise on the world's political and economic *isms*.

Joint Economic Committee, *Comparison of the United States and Soviet Economies*, Washington, 1959, Part I.

Papers submitted by panelists, treating the relative strengths of the US and USSR economies.

Choh-Ming Li, *Economic Development of Communist China*. Berkeley: University of California Press, 1959.
Case study of development in China, with emphasis upon 1953–57.

Raymond F. Mikesell and Jack N. Behrman, *Financing Free World Trade with the Sino-Soviet Bloc* (Princeton Studies in International Finance, No. 8, Princeton University), 1958.
Description and analysis of how East-West trade is handled by the Bloc.

Alec Nove, "Soviet Trade and Soviet Aid," *Lloyds Bank Review*, January 1959.
Concise survey of the Soviet trade-and-aid offensive; focuses on the economic-political relationship in the offensive.

Harry Schwartz, *Russia's Soviet Economy*. Englewood Cliffs, N.J.: Prentice-Hall, Inc. (2nd ed.), 1954.
Ch. XIV, Concise survey of the USSR's foreign economic relations.

Henry H. Villard, *Economic Development*. New York: Rinehart & Company, Inc., 1959.
Contrasts developmental methods employed by the US and the USSR.

24

WHAT TO DO?[1]

It is clear that the US is interested in assisting underdeveloped countries in their own efforts to promote development. However, it is not always clear as to what
concrete steps the US should take. The central question
to be explored in this chapter is the very practical one
of: "What should the US do next?"

RECAPITULATION

A logical starting point for this question is the situation in the underdeveloped world itself. Therefore, a
brief résumé of materials presented in Parts One and
Two may prove helpful.

Many people in underdeveloped countries want economic development. Indeed, it is their dissatisfaction
with the attributes of underdevelopedness that, in important measure, creates the problem under discussion.
Economic development, in turn, is possible everywhere—
to greater or lesser extent, but at least to some extent in
every country. If marked progress is to be made in development, however, intensified effort along reoriented
lines becomes essential. Accordingly, it follows that underdeveloped countries need to employ their available means
in special ways. Frequently, however, the actions of these
countries are hesitant, poorly conceived, and even more
poorly administered. Technically, the underdeveloped
world could do better than it is doing with the means
it has at its disposal. While its failure to do better may
be regrettable, and while upgraded effort is ever to be

---

[1] Material included in this chapter derives, in part, from a
paper titled "The U.S. Foreign-Aid Program: Appraisal and Proposal," presented at Southern Methodist University under auspices
of the Jno. E. Owens Memorial Foundation, April 1960.

desired, it nevertheless remains far from clear that individual countries at present possess both the resources and the skill to do what it takes to achieve marked acceleration in development, and especially to do so without resort to the measures and mechanics of an extreme totalitarian-type approach. In short, underdeveloped countries can do more in their own behalf than they have been doing, and it is not amiss—within reason— to expect that they strive to do better; however, even if absolute perfection itself governed in everything they do or could now do, the likelihood would remain that they would be unable to achieve truly sizable gains in development solely on the basis of what they, unassisted, can bring to bear on the situation—not if resort to outright totalitarian-type methods is to be avoided. This is the essence of the "message" offered in Part Two.

Concurrently, the US finds itself in a position of affluence and is looked to for assistance. By the very nature of things, given the role of the American economy in the world economy, whatever the US does or fails to do cannot help but be of relevance for the poorer countries. The US is cognizant of this relationship, of course, and takes it into account in the shaping of its foreign economic policy. Specifically, it comes to have a bearing upon decisions made in regard to the essential triad: trade, investment, and aid. As for decisions in the area of aid, the US gives precise recognition to the matter of development in underdeveloped countries by its contributions through both multilateral and bilateral channels. Especially important within this context is its own foreign-aid program, the Mutual Security Program. In short, the US Government and the American populace are aware of the problem in underdeveloped countries, and much has been done, and is being done, in the light of this awareness. All this appears clear from Part Three.

But, is the US doing a good job through its current efforts? Or, is something more or different in order? These questions obviously merit consideration—indeed, they merit *continuing* reconsideration. Involved is the subject matter of the second challenge alluded to earlier: determination of what the US should try to do relative to underdeveloped countries, given the overall situation currently prevailing.

APPRAISAL

Approximately a decade has elapsed since the US first chose to place special emphasis upon underdeveloped countries in its foreign-aid program (i.e., via the MSP). As a consequence of what has occurred during this interval, is it now quite evident that the rate of growth in aid-receiving countries has been markedly accelerated, and that therefore these countries are much nearer the point of self-sustained growth today than they were several years ago? (And, if the US effort has not resulted in meaningful acceleration in the rate of growth, does not the foreign-aid program then stand vulnerable to serious indictment?)

Much conjecture prevails as to the rate of growth in individual underdeveloped countries, both currently and in earlier years. Data on the subject leave much to be desired; data for individual countries for particular periods frequently seem not to depict what meets the eye, and comparability in data over time and among countries seems poor indeed. Moreover, unsatisfactory as income data may be in this connection, nothing vastly better is had from an attempt to fall back on production data, or employment data, or other selective data; in each case, many shortcomings rise quickly to the surface to unnerve one as one attempts to be "scientific." At best, one is treading on soft terrain, and it is well to recognize this as fact. Unfortunately, the alternative to reliance upon statistics in this matter is simply that of on-the-scene observation. This approach admittedly also has its limitations; however, when all is said and done, it may not comprise so unscientific an approach as might seem at first glance, provided the observation process has behind it a goodly measure of perspective and insight.

In whatever way approached (and no method seems entirely satisfactory), a conclusion to which many persons—including this author—are drawn is that, *with rare exception, the overall rate of growth in underdeveloped countries within the orbit of the US assistance program has not increased to a truly marked extent during recent years.* In some few underdeveloped countries, a substantial increase in the rate of growth may well have been the case—e.g., Israel and possibly Mexico.[2] In most underdeveloped countries, however, any increase in the rate of growth appears to have been strictly moderate. Indeed, taking population increases into account, the status of the average person, including his prospects for the near-term future, seems to have been left pretty much unaltered. And, in some underdeveloped countries, next to nothing seems to have occurred to get things out of their customary rut, so that the situation of the average person, viewed within the context of growing numbers, may actually have worsened.

Thus, *if* the underdeveloped world is somewhat better off today than it was several years ago, it is really *not much* better off, and it is certainly *still quite badly off*. With matters having this complexion, it can only be

---

[2] Significantly, external assistance had by these two countries, while an important factor in their growth, accrued in major proportion from sources other than the official US foreign-aid effort. The influx of tourist dollars loomed far more importantly as a factor for Mexico, while contributions by world Jewry were of crucial importance in the case of Israel.

Some question exists as to whether or not Brazil should be included in this category, along with Israel and Mexico. The country is excluded here because its gains, although notable on many scores, appear tempered when viewed against the overall economy, characterized by a relatively large and rapidly growing population.

concluded that if the thought in the US a decade ago was to help underdeveloped countries achieve *marked* improvement in reasonably short
order, the results are hard to become ecstatic about. In defense of the
American effort, it can be argued that many factors were involved
throughout, so that this country at no time had full control over or full
responsibility for the shaping of the economic destinies of the aid-
receiving countries. This point can readily be granted, but the fact remains that the US assistance effort under the MSP proceeds on the
assumption that economic development will be helped—indeed, that
progress in economic development in aid-receiving underdeveloped countries is necessary in terms of promotion of the American interest (Ch. 16).
Perhaps, then, the US assistance effort has failed in terms of this country's
own rationale, quite apart from what the failure to achieve a higher
overall rate of developmental progress may mean within the underdeveloped world itself. Perhaps the US assistance effort helped prevent
outright deterioration, but what is to be said of appreciable developmental progress?

A dilemma of sorts exists. The underdeveloped world wants economic
development, and the US says it wants underdeveloped countries to
undergo development; indeed, for reasons of its own, the US regards it
in its own interest that the countries experience development. But
achievements of the past decade leave much to be desired. If development
is expected, and little proves forthcoming, will hope in the subject countries not at some point come to be dulled? Is there not danger that people
will come to ask why the improvement they have been led to believe
might reasonably be theirs has failed to take place? And, is not the US
position relative to the underdeveloped world damaged in that event?
Specifically, what might then be said of the American foreign-aid program, considering the nature of the intentions and expectations that
figured in this country's decision to offer assistance in the first place?

Given the foregoing, the US seemingly has good reason to ask itself
now: What should be done next?

REDEDICATION

Many persons find it easy to criticize the American foreign-assistance
effort on one score or another, but these critics very often appear to have
remarkably little of a constructive nature to offer as a follow-up. Actually,
of course, three basic positions might be held relative to the foreign-aid
program: (1) liquidate the formal foreign-aid program, (2) accept the
program in its present outlines, but strive to handle customary operations
in better fashion, or (3) revamp or reorient the program in some basic
manner. The first position cited is ruled out here, on the assumption that

economic development is desirable, and that this country is justified in its concern about the matter. This leaves two basic positions, to each of which attention is directed in the following paragraphs.

Those who find the foreign-aid program fundamentally all right in its present form and approach can nevertheless still argue that somewhat better results might be had if the program were more adequately complemented within the context of overall US policy and if various refinements were introduced in respect to customary operations. Two main categories of possibilities quickly rise to the surface: those based on general principles, and those based on pinpointed measures. Thus, the US could reaffirm its dedication to certain overall *principles*, in the hope that operations under the MSP and within recipient countries themselves might thereby be encouraged to proceed full-force in pro-development fashion, with minimum inhibition or doubt. To cite examples of what the US might strive to do along these lines:

1. Reaffirm, in word and action, its determination to assure *peace,* without which prospect for developmental progress is undercut.
2. Reaffirm its determination to maintain high-level *prosperity* at home, thereby to assure underdeveloped countries of sizable market outlets and reasonable access to private capital supplies.
3. Reaffirm its *genuine desire for development* in underdeveloped countries—buttressed, possibly, with a policy statement by the Congress to the effect that this country sees itself as committed to the long-range provision of assistance.

Beyond the foregoing reaffirmation of principles, the US could seek to adopt *measures* on its own account in the hope of giving underdeveloped countries a better chance to reap developmental impact. To cite examples of what the US might do along these lines:

1. Lessen some of its own *barriers to trade,* thereby facilitating foreign access to dollars.
2. Adopt specific measures that carry high likelihood for a greater flow of *private investment* to underdeveloped countries.
3. Loosen up the rules and regulations to which aid operations are subject, so that aid administrators will be encouraged to exercise greater *imagination.*

Unfortunately, virtually all of the above sounds very familiar. One can well wonder what would be different were one to proceed on this basis, and on this basis alone—especially in view of the fate of past efforts in these various connections. Importantly, would it not likely in the end be a case of basically the same aid program within basically the same environment, the only notable addition being simply a new flow of words? Of course, were the total aid-allotment materially augmented as an accompaniment of whatever else was done or attempted, one could creditably argue that something was really different. But this comprises yet another matter.

This, then, brings us to the final position cited: basic alteration of the aid program.

REVISION

If the foreign-aid program stands vulnerable to criticism, it is fundamentally because developmental progress in underdeveloped countries has remained at a low ebb. The real issue, then, becomes one of: *How is foreign aid to be handled so as to yield substantially greater developmental impact in the underdeveloped world?*

First, however, why has the foreign-aid program not yielded greater developmental impact in underdeveloped countries heretofore? Whatever else might be said on the subject, the seemingly central reason has been that *the US approach has called for a fairly moderate amount of aid to be spread over a very wide area.* Essentially, the US notion has been that development is possible in some amount in all countries—in greater or lesser amount, but at least in *some* amount in *every* country—and that available aid should therefore be applied widely among countries in the hope that as much developmental impact as possible might derive in each. Unfortunately, an across-the-board approach has meant that available aid, itself distinctly limited, has had to be applied thinly. The result, as suggested, has been pretty much a case of "token aid for all, but no big developmental impact anywhere"—indeed, with aid handled in this manner, there is no concrete proof that the capacity even exists to push an underdeveloped country over the threshold to self-sustained growth.

One quick remedy to which thought turns is the application of more funds. Obviously, if considerably augmented funds could be brought to bear everywhere, the situation would be far different. Unfortunately, the prospect for more funds for the MSP does not appear good—or, at least this is what many persons tend to conclude. No assurance exists that the Congress is disposed to become much more generous in the foreseeable future.[3] Nor does replacement of the bilateral approach with an outright multilateral approach necessarily offer hope on this score; the foreign contribution gained could as readily as not be paralleled by a lessened effort by the US as existing motivations come to be undermined (Ch. 21). Nor does a satisfactory answer derive from resorting to the argument that the MSP is only *part* of the US effort, and therefore should

---

[3] Each year the foreign-aid program seems forced to fight to hold its own, let alone gain access to substantially greater funds. Presumably, the Congress and the American public feel that the aid effort is already getting what it merits, given this country's total scheme of things. Typically (during recent years), this means an appropriation for the MSP (economic and military) of something less than 5% of the total federal budget, and *less than 10% of the amount allotted for defense outlays.*

somehow be absolved of special responsibility when judgment is passed; after all, the MSP operates on the basis of a rationale, and judgment needs of necessity to be passed in terms of this rationale (Chs. 16 and 21).

If more funds are not likely to prove forthcoming, attention logically seems directed to the basic alternative: *a different use of existing funds.* Therefore, the question raised here is: Is there a different way to use existing funds that might yield results preferable to those now occurring? (Indeed, even in the event of some augmentation of funds, the question still seems much to the point.)

ALTERNATIVE

In reference to the matter of utilization of aid, this author—upon reflection as to what might comprise a logical course in the light of the analysis offered in preceding paragraphs—is attracted to a particular approach, the broad outlines of which are presented below. Involved is a framework for the dispensation of economic aid under the MSP that links three ingredients (one major and two subsidiary): (1) special aid emphasis for particular countries, (2) special effort to use aid funds so as to attract other funds, and (3) willingness to sanction particular regional arrangements.

The core idea of this approach is to channel more of the available aid to a relatively few select countries. The motivating thought is that it is *better to concentrate a goodly portion of total available aid upon a relatively few countries in which developmental potential appears particularly good, and thereby assure major developmental impact in at least these countries, than it is to spread the same aid with roughly equal thinness over a wide area on an across-the-board approach, and thereby risk having no major developmental impact anywhere.*

Under this approach, the US would attempt to ascertain for itself which of the aid-receiving underdeveloped countries offer the best prospect for marked developmental progress during, say, the following decade, provided stepped-up external assistance were made available to them. All the while, the US would continue to recognize that some developmental progress is technically possible in every country, and would continue to hope that circumstances might somehow prove conducive for development everywhere; but, for purposes of action under its own assistance effort, the US would be especially interested in singling out a few countries that it could regard as having far-above-average developmental potential during the near-term future. These few countries would then represent primary countries for the US in its thinking as to what it might do to assure developmental progress in the underdeveloped world. Upon selection of the particular countries, the US would officially approach responsible authorities in each country in order to feel out the extent to which willingness exists in each to support an all-out developmental effort. If the countries gave evidence of truly serious intent, the US would suggest backing them with considerably augmented assistance. Assuming that adequate understanding was reached thereafter on all relevant scores (which would entail "strings"), the US would then proceed to allot to these countries a substantially larger portion of the economic assistance available under the MSP. Further, insofar as practicable, the US would attempt to use this assistance in various ways—indeed, in rather direct ways—as a lever with which to enlist the support of accompanying funds derived from other sources, e.g., the International Bank, the Export-Import Bank, private American capital, public and private capital from particular other developed countries, etc. Thus, the countries given primary emphasis would become the recipients of enlarged capital inflows—in part because of assured access to a larger portion of economic assistance under the MSP, and in part because some of this assistance would consciously be used to entice external assistance from other sources (e.g., as through various cooperative-financing schemes).

A question arises as to what countries might be regarded as primary in this context. Reasonable tests seemingly might include the following. First, eligible countries could be limited to those whose potential for marked development during the near-term future is relatively great and who genuinely want development, but who are stymied only because, basically, they lack enough capital (and possibly some accompanying technical assistance). Second, eligible countries could be limited to major countries—i.e., they would be countries of sizable populations, and desirably would loom already as major powers within the regions in which they are situated. Given these particular tests, cases that seem to stand out include India and Brazil (and conceivably also Turkey, despite its somewhat smaller population).

While some few countries would be given preferential recognition, other aid-receiving countries would not be ignored. Economic assistance under the MSP would still be allotted to them, but they would henceforth have positive assurance of a *smaller portion* of the total allocation. Developmental progress would still be prized in their case, should it occur, but attention to this goal through assured fund allotment under the MSP would frankly be limited to whatever gains might still prove possible within the framework of an altered pattern of aid distribution; rather, the minimum position to be taken in their case during the near-term future would be the simple one of avoidance of outright economic and political deterioration. Significantly, a holding action tends to be relatively low-cost (and this in itself would help to free-up funds for use in primary countries, in which development is considered to be an early goal); indeed, much of the holding action, at least for some period, could be viewed as a responsibility of the military portion of the MSP, involving a body of funds quite apart from those at issue in the shift envisaged in economic assistance. Of course, if the secondary countries (i.e., those downgraded in the aid-distribution process) desired more economic assistance, as would prove likely, the US would need to be prepared to deal with them in constructive fashion, but hopefully not in terms of suddenly augmented advance-allotments, under pressure, through the MSP. One tactic would be to steer these countries to other capital sources—in fact, the US might use some portion of that economic assistance still being assured these countries under the MSP as a means to draw in capital from other sources, and might take positive steps, as with technical assistance, to help them document their cases as they approach alternate capital sources. A second tactic would be to urge the countries to contemplate regional economic arrangements that might enable them to tie in more closely with the particular country (or countries) within their area that is being given primary-country emphasis under the MSP. In the final analysis, possible resentment in countries downgraded in the aid-distribution process might be countered somewhat by honest advancement of the argument that concentration of aid is necessary at this juncture in order to assure marked development within the underdeveloped world, and that "once things are moving" in some locales, other locales, in turn, can be dealt with more generously; in short, the matter becomes one of *timing,* not one of outright denial, or neglect, or disinterest.

To sum up to this point, the approach outlined embraces the following major procedural ingredients:

1. The distribution of that economic assistance under the MSP treated on an advance-allotment basis would be altered so as to assure a larger portion of available assistance to some few countries having exceptional developmental potential—hence a program of *aid concentration.*

2. All economic assistance[4] would be used, insofar as practicable (and, desirably, much more so than heretofore), as a *lever*—(a) to induce more serious effort within recipient countries, and (b) to attract capital from various other sources (including particular third countries within the developed category).

3. The *regional approach* would be fostered; especially, countries downgraded in the aid-distribution process would be encouraged, insofar as practicable, to seek closer economic ties with other countries within their particular region (one or more of which might be treated as primary)—in the hope that some gain, lesser or greater, might accrue to them through this course.

4. The overall objective would be to use the limited aid available under the MSP in a way so as to *positively assure marked developmental progress in fairly short order in at least some countries.* Once real developmental progress could be pointed to in some instances, it would be time to look further. This would be the guiding philosophy.

---

[4] Meaning particularly capital assistance, rather than technical assistance.

To offer an overall characterization of the approach outlined, the task of aid-allocation among countries would be viewed as one of how to produce *catalytic impact within the underdeveloped world,* much as particular projects long have been viewed as potential catalysts within the confines of individual countries.

POINTS OF STRENGTH

The approach outlined appears to embody a number of features that serve to recommend it. Several of these merit specific examination.

1. *Conducive to development.* The basic objective of the approach is to assure development. Three elements tend especially to work in this direction. First, in order to receive preferential recognition, a country would need—among other things—to demonstrate a high degree of willingness to use its own available means in better fashion to foster accelerated development. The idealistic notion that a recipient country will automatically tend to put its own means to better use whenever it receives external assistance would largely be discarded as aid-allotments were contemplated (at least insofar as decisions affecting primary countries were concerned).

Second, countries accorded preferential recognition would receive substantially augmented assistance, so that bigger developmental impact in these locales would become possible on this account alone. In a sense, the US would shift toward balance-of-payments assistance in its aid approach relative to these countries.

Third, the US hopefully would strive harder to use its aid as a means to draw in capital from other outside sources. Specifically, the US could seek to use some substantial portion of its aid in direct conjunction with capital from other outside sources. Especially important is what might be done to attract capital from other developed countries, e.g., from Western Europe and Japan. While the US would retain the bilateral approach for itself, other countries, proceeding similarly, could also be encouraged to make capital available. One possible method that might attract such capital would be willingness by the US to "talk business" with other countries in terms of *consortium-type arrangements,* an approach already well known to the international banking community. A multilateral-type approach could thus result from the parallel actions of several countries, each proceeding bilaterally. The expected end result, of course, would be more capital for the selected underdeveloped countries, which could serve as a powerful force to underwrite their own developmental efforts.

2. *Offsets the Communist Bloc.* Viewed in terms of potency as America's answer to a growing Bloc economic offensive, the approach also seems to have some merit. It would seem advantageous, from the US standpoint,

that at least some underdeveloped countries be pushed over the threshold to self-sustained growth in the reasonably near future—thereby giving proof to the underdeveloped world that major developmental progress is possible in this day and age, and that *it is possible without wholesale resort to totalitarian-type methods*. A solid demonstration along these lines seemingly would do much to enhance this country's status as it conducts its global dealings.

Thus, some few countries would be given the "big-push" treatment under the approach, but others would likely be able to do little more than hold their own, at least for some period. Actually, this situation would not be new for the second group. Importantly, however, the approach would envisage economic assistance in their case in an amount at least sufficient to prevent outright economic and political deterioration, while military assistance presumably would be available much as before. In short, the shift in special emphasis to a few countries, as envisaged, would not force other countries to fall victim to Bloc inroads, although pronounced development in them would frankly not be regarded as of first priority during the near-term future (as far as the MSP is directly concerned).[5]

3. *Fits the tempo of the times*. The approach seems in line with other major policy positions toward which the US Government appears to be moving. Three major policy areas can be cited to demonstrate this point. First, the stress placed upon balanced budgets and fiscal conservatism in Administration policy during recent years has not sparked hope for vastly augmented appropriations for the MSP.[6] Assuming that aid-dollars will continue to be hard to get, the premium is on how to get more mileage out of the aid funds that are made available. The latter, of course, is one of the objectives of the alternative outlined.

Second, the notion has taken hold in particular US Government quarters that other developed countries (i.e., Western Europe and Japan)

---

5 Additionally, one can always speculate as to the composition of the "Big Five" a generation or so hence, and as to how the US might shape up within the context. Assume, however, that the future "Big Five" consists of the following countries: US, USSR, Mainland China, India, and Great Britain. Assume, further, that the US at that point has only moderate rapport with the USSR and Mainland China. An assured 3–2 vote for the US then requires it to have sympathetic relationships with *both* Great Britain and India. The outlined situation seems to give India a balance-of-power position. To recall an earlier observation (Ch. 10), India and Mainland China are currently undergoing the trials of growth, with India seemingly lagging in the race. Given this developmental situation, plus the *possible* future global political situation, can the US afford *not to help* India on a grand basis? If the US feels so obliged, what aid framework would most readily accommodate placement of special emphasis upon India (as one of a few countries)? Obviously, the approach to aid-distribution outlined could provide the basis, even if introduced for reasons other than or going far beyond those associated with "Big Five" considerations.

6 Comments by Treasury officials during 1959, especially, could readily be interpreted as somewhat critical of prevailing aid costs; as a minimum, opposition appeared present in Treasury quarters to *more* aid by the US.

have recovered from their postwar miseries, and are thus in a position to take some of the aid-load off this country's shoulders. This view received great impetus especially during 1958–59, during which period the American economy experienced sudden adverse balance-of-payments repercussions, losing some gold in the process.[7] The alternative outlined, of course, envisages action by the US to encourage other developed countries to complement the US assistance effort, ideally by means of a consortium-type approach.[8] Indeed, the US Government gave an indication in early 1960 of its intent to proceed with international discussions that were expected to lead to working arrangements in this realm.[9]

Third, the late 1950's may well be remembered as the period when regional approaches came into their own.[10] A number of regional arrangements have come into being, and others are in the discussion stage. The US Government, after some apparent indecision, has lent a measure of support to this form of approach. Significantly, the alternative outlined, by virtue of its stress upon special aid emphasis for countries that loom large within their respective regions, appears entirely compatible with the new willingness to tackle some problems along regional lines.[11]

POSSIBLE WEAKNESSES

Whatever points of strength might be cited, one factor especially is likely to be raised as comprising a weakness: possible resentment by countries downgraded in the course of a shift in aid-allotments. What is to be said to offset this possible criticism?

The central reply that might be offered is evident in earlier paragraphs. Briefly, support for a revamped pattern of aid distribution is premised on the belief that more development can thereby be had in the under-

---

[7] For earlier comment on these matters, see Ch. 20 (in which references to sample news coverage and editorial appraisal are cited).

[8] Should all other means for eliciting cooperative action from other developed countries fail, the point could be driven home that non-cooperation might force the US to reduce its own bilateral effort or to invoke added trade barriers in order thereby to protect its own balance-of-payments position.

[9] See "U.S. Urges Europe Join World Plan for Economic Aid," *The New York Times,* January 13, 1960, p. 1-C; "Talks on Sharing Aid Load Expected Soon in Capital," *The New York Times,* January 17, 1960, p. 1-L.

[10] For background material, see again Ch. 11, the section on "Regional Development."

[11] In addition to the foregoing factors, cited as samples of the tempo of the times, it is significant that the proposed FY 61 MSP made reference to the concept of concentrated development aid in relation to the current policy of the Development Loan Fund. It was stated that special emphasis was being given in DLF loan policy to placement of economic assistance in ". . . those less developed countries which meet three principal tests: first, a major United States foreign policy interest in a high rate of economic development; second, a capacity to mobilize domestic resources and to use foreign assistance effectively in furthering their economic development; third, a need for foreign resources which cannot be financed by other public and private institutions." Of interest, a further statement read as follows: "The Taiwan program . . . is an example of this promising approach." See Department of State (and others), *The Mutual Security Program,* Washington, March 1960, p. 18.

developed world than otherwise likely, and that *all* countries will become beneficiaries—if not immediately, then at least at some point. Even if a reply in these terms is entirely reasonable, however, there is no assurance that every country will necessarily see matters in this vein. Therefore, some means doubtless need to be "on tap" to placate particular countries. One course would be to help these countries obtain assistance from other acceptable quarters, in ways suggested above. If no added assistance proved forthcoming, blame would then at least be shared with others. Another course would be to urge countries to seek gain through regional arrangements. It may well be that, actually, only moderate gain could be had in this way during the near-term future (although the creation of a *basis* for added economic effort along regional lines may prove highly meritorious as a prelude for longer-run progress).

When all is said and done, the possibility exists that the foregoing courses may not satisfy some countries, and particularly not during early phases of an attempt to revamp aid distribution. The situation would then doubtless compel the US simply to play things by ear, a tactic not exactly new in the conduct of international affairs. Hopefully, special concessions could be held to a minimum—but, when found necessary, a first line of defense against retrenchment from initial intent could be sought in reliance upon local-currency loan funds in possession of the US, in offers of PL 480 goods, and to some extent in limited allocations from the MSP's contingency-category of funds.

A QUESTION

It is all well and good to observe that economic development is possible to greater or lesser extent in every underdeveloped country; that the record of developmental progress, while generally bleak, is not equally bleak in all locales; that the US is interested in helping underdeveloped countries in pro-development efforts; and that the US might possibly improve its means of assistance on behalf of underdeveloped countries. Thereafter, the question *still* remains: Is major and widespread developmental progress likely to be experienced within the underdeveloped world "during our time" (even while basically democratic institutions are fostered)?

Even if population in the underdeveloped world remained stationary, the task would not be a simple one. But population is growing—indeed, at a rapid pace virtually everywhere. The result is that the task assumes simply formidable proportions. Meanwhile, no guarantee exists that the required action in the economic field will be forthcoming, soon enough and in the right amount and form. One cannot help but wonder what the future holds.

Authors often like to end their books by posing a challenge and holding out a hope. In this volume, the author poses a challenge, but he is not sure whether he should be an optimist or whether he should lean toward "gloom and doom." He does feel, however, that the situation calls for *action*, and much of the material presented has been aimed in this direction.

One thing is certain: action or inaction, success or failure, a significant chapter in history will stem from *the problem of the underdeveloped world* now at hand.

GLOSSARY OF ABBREVIATIONS

AOFC	American Overseas Finance Corporation
CCC	Commodity Credit Corporation
CED	Committee for Economic Development
CY	Calendar Year
DLF	Development Loan Fund
ECA	Economic Cooperation Administration
EPU	European Payments Union
ERIOA	Economic Rehabilitation in Occupied Areas
FAO	Food and Agriculture Organization (of the United Nations)
FOA	Foreign Operations Administration
FY	Fiscal Year
GARIOA	Government and Relief in Occupied Areas
GATT	General Agreement on Tariffs and Trade
GNP	Gross National Product
IBRD	International Bank for Reconstruction and Development
ICA	International Cooperation Administration
ICBM	Intercontinental Ballistics Missile
ICICI	Industrial Credit and Investment Corporation of India
ICOR	Incremental capital—output ratio
IDA	International Development Association
IDC	Industrial Development Center
IFC	International Finance Corporation
IMF	International Monetary Fund
MSA	Mutual Security Agency
MSP	Mutual Security Program
NATO	North Atlantic Treaty Organization
OAS	Organization of American States
OEEC	Organization for European Economic Cooperation
PL 480	Public Law 480
SEATO	Southeast Asia Treaty Organization
SUNFED	Special United Nations Fund for Economic Development
UN	United Nations

UNICEF   United Nations International Children's Emergency Fund
UNRRA   United Nations Relief and Rehabilitation Administration
USSR   Union of Socialist Soviet Republics
WHTC   Western Hemisphere Trade Corporation

AUTHOR INDEX

SUBJECT INDEX